GREEN GUIDE

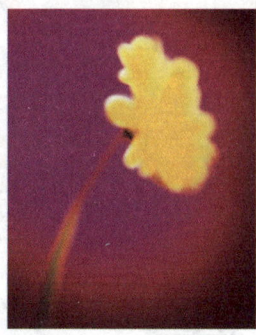

Contents

Welcome	3
How to use the Guide	5
Pure Modern Lifestyle	6
Organics – what's it all about?	9
Food & Drink	13

▶ Organic Home Delivery ▶ Shops
▶ Wholesalers & Distributors
▶ Brands & Manufacturers
▶ Restaurants & Cafés ▶ Catering Services
▶ Cookery Courses ▶ Organisations

Clothing & Cosmetics	45

▶ Clothing ▶ Cosmetics & Toiletries
▶ Sanitary Protection

Home & Garden	57

▶ Building & Design ▶ Furniture & Decoration
▶ Cleaning & Laundry ▶ Water ▶ Gardening

Energy & Recycling	77

▶ Energy Efficiency ▶ Renewable Energy
▶ Recycling

Health	90

▶ Products ▶ Centres ▶ Retreats
▶ Courses & Colleges ▶ Organisations

Family & Children	123

▶ Babies & Children ▶ Education
▶ Friends & Partners ▶ Vets & Pets
▶ Communities ▶ Natural Death ▶ Organisations

Transport	137

▶ Transport ▶ Cycling
▶ Water Transport ▶ Sustainable Vehicles

Travel & Leisure	145

▶ North West ▶ National ▶ Abroad

Business & Finance	159

▶ Business & Office ▶ Ethical Investment
▶ New Economics

Government & Organisations	175

▶ Local Government ▶ National Government
▶ Campaigns & Organisations

Media	203

▶ Bookshops & Books by Mail Order
▶ Publications ▶ Publishers
▶ Internet ▶ Organisations

Information & Education	215

▶ Environment Centres
▶ Information Services ▶ Courses & Colleges

Indexes	224

▶ Alphabetical index of entries
▶ Categories & Sections ▶ Advertisers

Listings entry form	238
Reader's questionnaire	239

GET A FREE Divine CHOCOLATE BAR
See page 237

GREEN GUIDE

Editor & Publisher
Gavin Markham

Assistant Editor
Avni Trivedi

Research
Zoë Sanders, Lauren Pett,
Jennifer Paganelli, Tara Karasch,
Brooke Starkoff, David Robinson

Art Direction
Omaid Hiwaizi

Cover Photography
Jean-Paul Froget

Advertising Sales
Elaine Kennedy
Sherry Nichols

Thanks to
Hubbard Hiwaizi McCann
and to all the contributors

Editorial office
271 Upper Street, London N1 2UQ
Tel: 020 7354 2709
Fax: 020 7226 1311
Email: info@greenguide.co.uk
Web: www.greenguideonline.com

Printed By
Cambrian Printers, Aberystwyth
Tel: 01970 613 037

The views expressed in this publication are not necessarily those of the publishers.

No part of this publication may be reproduced, stored or transmitted in any form without the prior written consent of the publishers

**Published By
Green Guide Publishing Ltd**

© 2001 Green Guide Publishing Ltd

**To purchase copies of the Green Guide, call us on
020 7354 2709**

Welcome

Not a day goes by without some reference in the media to concerns about the food we eat or to the damage we inflict upon our environment. Some of the stories are negative, but, increasingly, more are positive. Whether it is about organic food or renewable energy, many of the consumer choices we now face are about how we can act more sustainably. The growth in the Green Guides reflects this. Each year the number of listings and the coverage of the Guides has increased until now there really is a sustainable choice for every aspect of modern living.

Acting sustainably – which in its widest sense means acting responsibly towards each other and our resources, whether at home or far away – is something we can all attempt. By being discerning consumers, we can have an impact at many different levels. Being green is no longer about giving things up. In fact, it's the opposite. Being green means being sustainable and being positive in our choices, purchasing products which are better for us, our families and our planet. Just read through the hundreds of products, services and organisations contained in the twelve chapters of this Guide to get a feel for how things have changed. Businesses are being more responsive to their customer requirements and there probably hasn't been a better time to use your consumer power than now.

Choice is at the heart of the Green Guides. Our aim is not to be prescriptive but to show you what is available. You don't have to change your entire way of life in one jump. Small individual steps are enough to start making a difference and get onto the path of a more sustainable lifestyle. Go at your own pace and make changes you are comfortable with. Once you start acting more sustainably you'll be surprised how quickly it becomes second nature and spreads into all areas of life.

As well as changing our purchasing habits, we have to make our political institutions work for us: whether through local councils, Members of Parliament at Westminster or even the European Parliament. To effect change on a wider scale, it's vital for us to act collectively, to behave as a community. The Green Guide tells you how you can make your voice heard, whether through politics or through some of the many hundreds of organisations campaigning for a better and safer world.

Whatever your point of view, you can make a difference. And the best way to start is with the Green Guide.

ORGANiCO
www.organico.co.uk

future perfect

A comprehensive range of authentic and natural organic foods including Babynat baby foods, Vitalia pure pressed juices, Bio Planète virgin oil, Organico pasta olive oil and tomato sauces, Biosun ready meals, Choconat swiss chocolate, Le Piagge Tuscan specialities, Soto Tofu and Moulin de Valdonne cordials.

natural food produced naturally

63 High Street, London N8 7QB • Tel: 0281 340 0401, Fax: 0402 Web: www.organico.co.uk

Nad's
NATURAL HAIR REMOVAL GEL

NO MESS
NO FUSS
NO HEAT
NO HAIR

THE FASTEST SELLING PERSONAL CARE PRODUCT IN AUSTRALIA

Nad's Gel 100% natural substance is a breakthrough requiring no heat as it melts with your own body heat. Nad's is so effective that regrowth is reduced considerably and hair is softer each time.

The water soluble base of the product makes cleaning up easy no mess - no fuss. Simple and easy to use. Nad's Gel effectively removes unwanted body and facial hair from all areas instantly - Legs, Arms, Armpits, Bikini Line, Chest & Back. You will find that Nad's unique applicator is perfect for treating sensitive lip and eyebrow areas.

Nad's
Total Hair Removal Solution for all parts of the body.

FOR FURTHER INFORMATION CALL 020 7453 0575

CENTRE FOR ALTERNATIVE TECHNOLOGY

Europe's leading eco-centre

✺ visitor complex for all the family
✺ residential courses throughout the year
✺ CAT publications: definitive 'how to' guides
✺ mail order catalogue: buy green by mail
✺ Alternative Technology Association - join us!

CAT, Machynlleth, Powys, SY20 9AZ
main office tel: 01654 702400
mail order tel/fax: 01654 703409
courses tel: 01654 703743
www.cat.org.uk

How to use the guide

Listings

The directory includes products, services and organisations that help promote and encourage a sustainable lifestyle. Also included are ethical and fair trade businesses. The listings are intended to be inclusive and are free of charge. We make every effort to keep the entries accurate and up-to-date. However, we cannot be held responsible for any inaccuracies

Most of the organisations listed in the guide will have completed a listings questionnaire form or given us their details over the phone. Some entrants we visit, but there are simply too many for all to receive a personal visit. For a few we gather information from other sources, but we will always endeavour to verify details with the organisation before we publish.

Very few organisations refuse to supply information and fewer still request not to be listed. We try hard to contact organisations but we assume that if we find it impossible to get information – because forms and faxes are not sent back, phones ring unanswered and answerphone messages are not returned – then readers will not have much luck either.

If you find the inclusion of any organisation unreasonable or unjustifiable, please inform us. We will attempt to explain our reasoning, or if we fail to do so, remove the listing.

If you want an organisation's green claims verified, consult one of the larger bodies. They will be able to give you advice or refer you on.

Opening hours and costs

While every effort has been made to ensure that the listings are correct at the time of going to press, details such as opening times and costs do change. If you're making a special trip to a shop or an organisation, do call first. Smaller businesses, in particular, appreciate advance warning of intended visits. *The Green Guide* cannot be held responsible for any inconveniences caused by your failure to check if someone is at home.

Reviews

Restaurant reviews in the guide were usually conducted with the full knowledge of the restaurant visited. Shop reviews tend to be the results of impromptu drop-ins. If you want to contribute or have views on the goods and services, please let us know. Your input is valuable.

Things to do

The Impact Boxes contain easy-to-follow, accessible tips on how to make a difference to your life now. Some of these take a little more effort, but many are common sense. The suggestions are not designed to make you feel guilty if you don't complete all or any of them. Impact boxes are suggestive, not prescriptive and we recognise that for many people some of the ideas are not practicable. Aim to do as little or as much as you are comfortable with.

Mail order

The Green Guide covers local resources as well as mail order suppliers which distribute throughout the UK. We urge you to check order details with your chosen supplier when you make an order – some suppliers have set times for delivery which require the customer to be present. This is especially important when dealing with food items. Find out where you stand with returns and damaged goods and check to see if your supplier offers a money-back guarantee.

Being included

We have tried to be as comprehensive as possible but we know we've not got everyone! If you know a business or organisation that needs to be included, use the listings form at the back of the guide to send us its details. Alternatively, tell the organisation about us. All listings are published free of charge and our listing address is freepost so you don't even have to pay for a stamp.

www.greenguideonline.com

The Green Guide database is now available to search online. This is a totally free service and can be used as often as you like. The online database is updated once a month and users have access to all the regional data – useful for friends or when you're travelling. Other services on our website include news, editorial, e-commerce, competitions and useful links

Get a FREE bar of Divine chocolate

We want to make the next editions of the guide even better as well as more comprehensive. Fill out the reader response form at the back of this guide and send it back to us using our Freepost address and you could get a FREE bar of chocolate (details on page 239). The information you provide helps us to make improvements to our publications and services. We look forward to hearing from you. ∎

Pure Modern Lifestye

The magazine for people who want more from life, naturally

In October 2000, Green Guide Publishing launched a new magazine called *Pure Modern Lifestyle*. The magazine is aimed at the rapidly growing number of people in the UK who are looking for a more natural and sustainable lifestyle. Packed with exclusive interviews, feature articles, regular columns, news, reviews and loads of reader give-aways and offers, *Pure Modern Lifestyle* covers the whole spectrum of living in the 21st Century.

Recent issues have included a special feature on organic food, including a look at the supermarkets' policy towards organic foods and farming, and an exclusive interview with the president of the Soil Association, Jonathan Dimbleby. Other interviews have included TV chef Hugh Fearnley-Whittingstall; natural interior designer Kelly Hoppen; organic retail pioneer Renée Elliott; and Geetie Singh and Esther Boulton who together opened the first organic pub in the UK.

Regular columns cover food and recipes, wine and drink, the home and furnishings, kids and parenting, finance and investment, health and beauty, travel and weekends away, the pick of *Green Guide* listings, product tests on items such as organic cotton towels and taste tests on food and drink like organic chocolate or vodka. Other regulars include *My Perfect World* where we invite a celebrity to describe their ideal life and *Twentyfour-Seven* where we focus on the day in the life of someone working in a sustainable occupation. The magazine is also packed with news and reviews of all sorts of consumer products and each issue is full of reader offers. ∎

To subscribe, call on **020 7354 2709**.
Green Guide readers can subscribe for
20% off – 12 issues for £28.30.

You can also subscribe online at
www.greenguideonline.com

The magazine is on sale nationwide
at newsagents, book shops and
health food stores, price £2.95.

www.greenguideonline.com

SHOPPING for clothes, furnishings, household items, food books and magazines

NEWS updated daily

COMPETITIONS new prizes every month and great giveaways

1,000s of products & services

The easiest and most comprehesive online source of organic, natural and ethical goods and services – everything you need for a planet-friendly lifestyle

---

ORGANIC Pertwood FARM

Wake up to Organic Cereals

A range of five organic cereals:

Pertwood Muesli with Delicious Fruits – contains oats, barley and rye with sultanas, dates, apricot, orange, pineapple and apple

Pertwood Muesli with Fruit and Seeds – blended from oats, barley and rye with sultanas, apricots, sunflower, pumpkin, sesame seeds and linseed

Pertwood Crunchy with Raisin and Almond – wheat and dairy-free and made with unrefined organic cane sugar

Pertwood Crunchy with Mixed Nuts – wheat and dairy-free and made with unrefined organic cane sugar

Pertwood Organic Porridge Oats – won a Gold Award in the West Country Food Awards in May 2000.

Available nationwide from health food shops and independent grocers, or call the farm direct.

Pertwood Organic Cereal Co Ltd, Lower Pertwood Farm, Hindon, Salisbury, Wiltshire SP3 6TA
Tel: 01747 820 720

No more itchy heads!

DELACET™

Organic herbal formula which puts parents in control

Children & adults have been using it in Europe for over 40 years (!) and it is now available in the UK.

DELACET
✽ 100% natural ingredients – **no toxic chemicals**
✽ effective, simple and safe to use
✽ excellent scalp disinfectant and hair conditioner
✽ head lice and nit repellent
✽ suitable for Afro hair and dreadlocks (no more prolonged combing)
✽ safe for nursing mothers and children over 1 year

DELACET is available from some chemists and health food shops or by mail order from
HEALTHPOL Tel: 020 8360 0386

Traidcraft

For a Whole World of Fair Trade

Honey producers from Chile.

GEOBAR - The first Fair Trade snack bar of its kind.

Fairly Traded Organic Swiss Made Chocolate

Raisin producers from South Africa.

Join the Fair Trade revolution!

Find more information on Traidcraft and Fair Trade by visiting our website www.traidcraft.co.uk or contact us at Traidcraft, Kingsway, Gateshead, Tyne & Wear NE11 0NE. Telephone: 0191 491 0591

Organics – what's it all about?

More and more people are putting their forks down and thinking twice. We find ourselves trapped in a time when our concerns about the food industry are multiplying but solutions are hard to find. The jargon is endless and it is difficult to understand all the terms the media throws our way. Phrases like genetic engineering, food labelling, sustainable agriculture bombard us, but what does it all mean and what do we do with this information? **Jennifer Paganelli** *provides some answers.*

First things first – what is organic food? Simply put, organic food is produced from safe, sustainable farming systems which produce healthy crops and livestock. Organic production does not damage the environment. Chiefly, it avoids the unnecessary use of harmful chemical fertilisers and pesticides on the land and instead focuses on developing the soil and growing a variety of crops. This means the farm land can remain biologically balanced and sustainable. The law clearly defines the term organic and all production and processing is held to a strict set of rules. Food that is intended for sale as organic must be inspected annually and by an authorised body such as the Soil Association.

So, why is this idea of organic so important? The multitude of benefits to the earth, producers, and consumers are hard to ignore. The rules of conventional agriculture are thrown out the door and a renewed focus is placed on animal welfare, the environment, resources, and basic health. When food is not organic, animals in massive farming systems are often reared in cramped quarters without open space. Often they lack exposure to light and fresh air and are fed a drug-rich diet to make them grow larger and more quickly. Organic farming does not follow these unnatural practices. Instead, animals have access to open fields, are allowed to behave in natural patterns, and are provided with comfortable bedding. If livestock becomes sick, homeopathic and herbal remedies are often used. However, if an animal with an acute illness is thought to be suffering, a conventional drug treatment would be available and allowed.

Organic production works wonders for our declining environmental quality. Research has shown that organic farming can be more beneficial to the environment than conventional methods of agriculture. Studies by the Ministry of Agriculture and the British Trust for Ornithology have both shown a positive impact of organic farming on wildlife, and for good reason. Because no pesticides are used, organic farming doesn't kill natural soil organisms, insects and other larger species. Plants considered to be weeds by pesticides are left untouched. The result is an increase in food sources available for other animals and the maintenance of habitats and biodiversity.

By utilising organic methods of farming, the earth's resources flourish instead of disappear. Organic farmers can minimise their own health and pollution problems because they stay away from chemicals. Organic farming relies on a modern scientific understanding of ecology and soil science coupled with traditional methods of crop rotation to ensure fertility and the control of weeds and pests.

Perhaps one of the most striking impacts of organic foods is on our health. It has been shown that organic foods have more vitamins and trace elements than conventionally grown foods, without the harmful chemical residues. It is no secret ▶

WHAT LEGACY ARE YOU LEAVING?

To find out more about a sustainable future in your financial planning
Contact:
The Ethical Investment Co-operative Ltd
Vincent House
5 Victoria Road
Darlington
Co Durham
DL1 5SF
Tel: 01325 267228
Fax: 01325 267200
e-mail: greeninvest@gn.apc.org

Specialists in Investments that will not cost the Earth

Regulated by The Personal Investment Authority

ALOE VERA

Juice and Skin Care

**Purest Therapeutic Grade
Organically grown in Australia**

For further information please call us on
01666 504718
The Aloe Care Centre
Tetbury, GL8 8EB

For Good Health and Radiant Skin

The Empty Homes Agency

Highlighting the scandal of England's 770,000 empty homes and other wasted buildings.

Working with councils, housing associations, private developers, owners and community groups to devise solutions and help deliver real achievements.

For more information see out web site at:
www.emptyhomes.com
Tel: 020 7828 6288 email: eha@globalnet.co.uk

€nergetix

The world's leading therapeutic magnetic jeweller

The use of magnetic products offers a source of natural benefits and has been shown to have a positive effect on both humans and animals. The Chinese and Egyptians have been using magnets to help the healing process for centuries.

Many users swear that wearing magnetic jewellery has helped to relieve pain and discomfort caused by a wide range of ailments. They have also reported a general increase in energy levels and a sense of wellbeing.

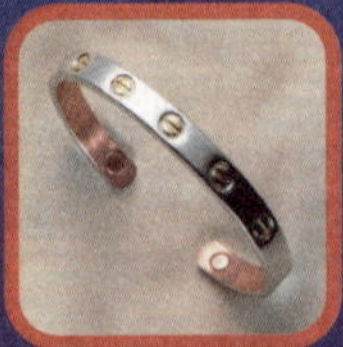

Men and women of all ages will want to wear products from the Energetix range both for their fashionable elegance and their therapeutic properties. They make ideal gifts and come in a gift box.

Energetix (UK) Limited, The Boat Yard, 105 Straight Road, Old Windsor, Windsor, Berks SL4 2SE
Tel: 01753 831 111 Fax: 01753 831 122

PEN Y COED CONSTRUCTION & INSULATION

Specialists in timber frame building and design

Pen y coed is a family business specializing in all aspects of green construction

- Green oak framing
- Modern timber frame techniques
- Installation of solar panels
- Sewage Systems incorporating reed beds and composting toilets
- BBA registered installers of Warmcel 500 Insulation

PEN Y LAN, MEIFOD, POWYS, SY22 6DA
Tel/Fax : 01938 500643
E-mail : penycoed.construction@btinternet.com

that a vast array of pesticides are used in conventional agriculture production. While 'acceptable levels' are calculated by the powers that be, surveys repeatedly indicate higher residues in a proportion of food samples than government regulations permit. The obvious question arises 'what are the long term effects on our bodies from this chemical use?' For now, there is little knowledge of the effects of these compounds and their toxicity. With organic production, the food is contaminant-free, resulting in safe, nutritious and unadulterated food.

So, as a consumer, how can you be certain that the foods you buy are organic? Currently, law prohibits using the term 'organic' on products that fail to meet a strict set of standards. All products must be certified by a government approved body which is registered with the United Kingdom Register of Organic Food Standards (UKROFS). This governing body sets the basic ground rules and standards to which the different organic producers must adhere to in order to call their products 'organic'. UKROFS standards conform to the European Community guidelines for organic production.

Each of these approved certification bodies has its own symbol and EU code number. The Soil Association symbol accounts for 70% of all certified organic products in the UK. When you spot this symbol and others, you are assured that the food producers met a wide host of standards including: maintaining adequate records, annual monitoring and inspection, and strict labelling requirements for the use of additives and processing aids. This certification is not something farmers can receive overnight. On the contrary, there is a two year 'conversion period' for farmers before full organic status is achieved.

Imported organic foods must be produced and inspected to an equivalent standard in order to earn the same mark for quality. Just like the UK, each EU country has its own national organic certification authority which conforms to EU standards. With food imported from outside Europe into the EU, the situation becomes a little more complicated, but is still subjected to identical inspections and guarantees. To avoid confusion or doubt, always check for the symbol or number of the certification bodies like the Soil Association. Consumers can rest assured that all organic manufacturers must be registered with a certification body and some shops even pay a certification fee to register as organic. Any infringement can result in the suspension of licence and withdrawal of products from the market.

It is important to examine an issue considered the antithesis of the organic food industry – GM foods. Genetically modified (GM) foods involve genetic engineering, or the artificial insertion of a gene from one species into the genetic material of another. The problem is that the interactions of these genes are not well understood, and this unpredictability is of constant concern. Some impacts are already being felt.

The release of untested genetically engineered organisms (GMOs) into the environment has unknown consequences for the future, with unpredictable effects on ecological systems at stake. Plants that are genetically engineered to ward off pests can kill 'good' insects at the same time. Similarly, genetic engineering for the development of insect resistant crops is likely to encourage even quicker development of resistance in insect populations to pest control.

Genetically engineered foods also impact upon human health. Biotechnology companies have failed to conduct long-term studies on the effects on animals and humans from ingesting GM organisms. Some concerns include antibiotic resistance in humans, the creation of new toxins and unsuspected allergic reactions.

Wildlife also faces harsh effects from the use of genetic engineering. Farming methods that are based on chemicals have already created loss of farmland and birds. Some GM crops are resistant to certain herbicides, which, when used in pest control, kill a wide range of plants, insects, birds, and other animals that rely on these plants for survival.

Labelling questions are also raised. Under the current system of food labelling, the majority of foods containing ingredients

from genetically engineered sources are not made visible to consumers.

The sad reality is that many agricultural companies are bottom-line oriented, and the environment and consumers pay the price. The approach these companies use to boost their profitability is by using gene technologies that disregard the irreversible global consequences. Combining genetic material from plants and animals throws the safety and quality of food into jeopardy because the genes have unknown effects when moved from one species to another.

Another, often silent, consequence of the modern farming industry is the ignorance of human welfare. It is believed that nearly one quarter of Britain's farmers are living at or below the poverty line. With low wages and low social standing, they continue to play the role of victim by a system more concerned with mass-production than with quality food. Rural areas continue their downward spiral due to the practice of replacing people with machines. It can be argued that organic farming methods, with a focus on people rather than machines, can create more jobs while still fulfilling the needs of the land. ∎

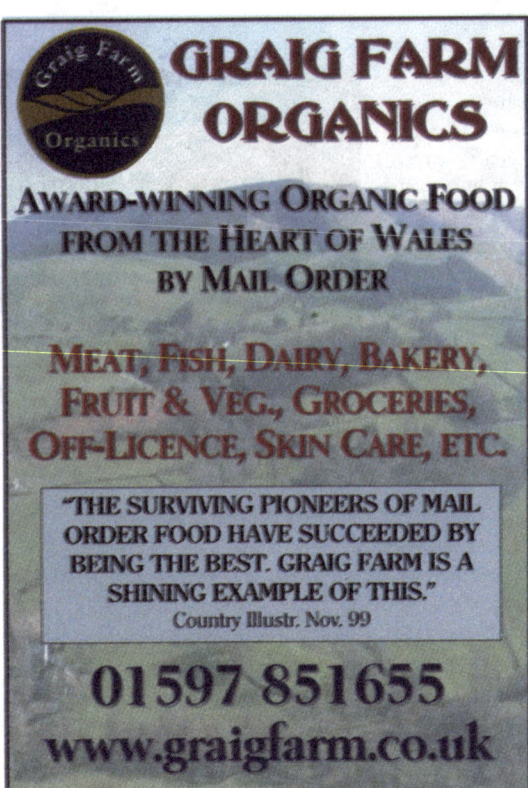

The Highland Organic Food Centre

Be Safe – Organic produce does not contain GMOs. Highlander offers a wide range of Organic & additive free meat, Organic cheeses, butter, milk, tinned goods, Organic bread fresh daily and organic vegetables

Free delivery within 5 miles • 5-10 miles £2.50
• Nationwide £10 next day delivery

Tel: 020 8346 1055

14 Bittacy Hill, Mill Hill, London NW7 1LB
www.highlandorganics.co.uk

Stewart Distribution

A family owned company based in Brighton distributing a unique range of natural products that truly make a difference to health and well-being

- the original Nutritional Wall Chart
- Crystal Spring Natural Deodorant
- all natural Gallunac soap
- potent immune-boosting mushroom products of MRL

44 Park Crescent Terrace, Brighton BN2 3HE
Tel: 01273 625 988 Fax: 0870 120 8566
info@lemonburst.net www.lemonburst.net

Park Attwood Clinic.......

Anthroposophical Medicine

Integrating orthodox and complementary treatment

Look for our listing under 'Centres'

Park Attwood Clinic, Trimpley, Bewdley, Worcs DY12 1RE
Tel 01299 861 444   Fax 01299 861375
E-mail park.attwood@btinternet.com   Site HTTP://www.park attwood.com/

THE GREEN STATIONERY COMPANY
COMMUNICATING

The Green Stationery Company is the complete green office supplier. We stock laser, inkjet and copier papers, fax and listing papers, labels, envelopes, pads, packaging, files and desk accessories, all made to the highest quality recycled specification. We print letterheads, remanufacture guaranteed laser and inkjet cartridges and many machine consumables including green disks. We also hold a complete range of original printer cartridges and magnetic media.

CALL US FOR A FREE COPY OF OUR CATALOGUE
TEL: 01225 480556
FAX: 01225 481221
Nationwide free delivery on orders over £80
All major credit cards accepted for telephone orders

STUDIO ONE
114 WALCOT STREET
BATH BA1 5BG
TEL: 01225 480556
FAX: 01225 481211
E-MAIL jay@greenstat.co.uk
http://www.greenstat.co.uk
CONSERVATION

Fad or future – is organic here to stay?

Around 60% of households buy some organic items with demand rocketing over the last few years. The market has recently passed £1bn in annual sales as a result of new consumer concerns and awareness over the food we buy. However, does current growth represent a long term trend or a passing phase? And how can we be sure about the quality of food and where is the best place to buy organic? The Soil Association provides some of the answers.

Formed in 1946 the Soil Association has always been at the forefront of organic farming. Champions in the drive to increase public awareness about the benefits of organic food, the Soil Association ensures integrity and high standards by stamping approved products with their symbol.

A crucial part of the the Association's work is campaigning for the increased use of organic and natural farming methods. Key campaigns include the prevention of Genetically Modified Organisms entering the food chain, the issue of antibiotics in food and the promotion of organic farming as a means to reverse the loss of biodiversity.

With the help of the Soil Association, farmers all over the UK are enthusiastically spreading the organic ethos by inviting members of the public onto their land to see the organic revolution taking place. The Organic Farms Network consists of 25 working farms, each with its own special feature to explore and admire – whether a wildflower meadow or a wildlife trail – and the opportunity to buy organic produce direct from the farm shop.

A major part of the Soil Association's work has been the promotion of local food for local people. The connection between the type of food you eat and the impact upon the countryside where it is grown goes to the heart of the organic movement. For example, the Soil Association was instrumental in setting up the National Association of Farmers Markets and there are now more than 300 farmers' markets across the UK, all providing locally grown food.

Another notable success story has been the rise of the organic box scheme. Delivered to your home straight from the farm, boxes provide a great way to try fresh and seasonally grown local vegetables. Many schemes include newsletters about the local farm, and seasonal recipes to get the best from fresh produce. Currently, there are approximately 300 box schemes in the UK. Your nearest scheme can be found by using the *Green Guide* listings or by looking at the Organic Directory on-line, available on the Soil Association website.

In keeping with the forward thinking reputation of the Soil Association, orders for food and other organic produce can be made on-line. Websites are becoming an increasingly popular way to shop and find information about local services and have the advantage of offering home delivery. Many Internet companies can now deliver a huge range of products from fresh food to wines and groceries.

So, the Soil Association is beginning to realise its raison d'être by making organic food accessible to everyone. It is no longer difficult to find local farm shops, supermarkets and independent shops all stocking an increasing range of organic produce, from fruit and vegetables to organic wine and beer. They provide a great opportunity to shop locally, supporting local farms and independent food shops.

The Soil Association is a charity that depends on donations and the support of its members to carry on its work. If you are passionate about the environment, local food issues and want to see more humane and natural farming then join the Soil Association and add your voice to its call for 30% of farmland to be under organic production by 2010. For £24 a year you will receive four copies of the award winning magazine *Living Earth* and a free copy of the video *Organic Farming: food for life* narrated by Soil Association president Jonathan Dimbleby. For a membership pack call 0117 912 2447 or send an email to pbrown@soilassociation.uk ■

For more information about organic issues, the Soil Association can be contacted at Bristol House, 40-56 Victoria Street, Bristol, BS1 6BY.
Tel: **0117 929 0661** Fax: **0117 925 2504**
Email: **info@soil association.org**
Web: **www.soil association.org**

Evening up the playing field

Not many consumers think about international trade when choosing products. However, it's an issue of mounting importance. When the price of a commodity falls, the impact on small-scale producers in Third World countries is devastating. The Fairtrade Foundation looks to solve this crippling problem.

The Fairtrade Foundation was set up by a host of companies including CAFOD, Christian Aid, Oxfam, the World Development Movement and others. The Foundation exists to solve the problems faced by poorer farmers. It awards a consumer label called the Fairtrade Mark on internationally approved commodities. No matter how low market prices may fall, this mark ensures the small-scale farmers are guaranteed better prices that cover their production costs.

This sense of security encourages poorer farmers to take an active role in the rehabilitation of their land and improving social and environmental policies. They are not worried about losing their land or homes due to even the slightest fall in prices, an event that would otherwise bury them in debt. Essentially, fair trade protects international, small-scale farmers by ensuring them a fair deal for their products – a guarantee that protects them from circumstances beyond their control that would otherwise have devastating impacts on their businesses and lives.

Most importantly, fair trade brings hope for Third World workers, new opportunities for children's education, and basic social improvements. The Foundation has worked to ensure a better deal for over 120,000 Third World producers.

The Fairtrade Mark plays many important roles. It guarantees that the producers are getting a fair deal. It protects small and disadvantaged Third World producers, shielding them from the effects of falling commodity prices while encouraging them to invest in their land. The symbol also promises consumers that those products meet internationally recognised standards of fair trade.

The Fairtrade Foundation understands that problems faced by poor producers and workers in developing countries vary greatly from product to product. Therefore, it takes different approaches to different products, but still applies a core set of production conditions.

The first criteria encourages small-scale farmers to get involved in a democratic organisation. Also, plantation and factory workers can take part in trade union activities for decent wages, housing, and health and safety. Two other vital principals are that no use of child or forced labour is allowed and that programmes for environmental sustainability must be put in place.

The Foundation also follows set terms of trading which includes: a price that covers the cost of production; a social premium that can be used by producers to improve their living and working conditions; advance payment to help smaller producers from falling into debt; and contracts that allow planning and sustainable production practices.

Constant monitoring by the Fairtrade Foundation and its partners ensures that products are checked and meet these criteria. This means consumers can also feel confident about the products they purchase and the farmers who produce them.

There are many ways to take action to support fair trade. Purchasing products such as tea, coffee, bananas and others with the Fairtrade Mark guarantees the Third World producers are getting a fair deal. Only products that carry the Fairtrade Mark are independently guaranteed to meet internationally recognised fair trade standards.

Currently, more than 70 varieties of coffee, tea, bananas, chocolate, cocoa, sugar and honey products carry the Fairtrade Mark, but if you have trouble finding products with this label, voice your concerns. If supermarkets see consumers requesting these products, they will be more inclined to carry them.

Staying updated and informed about Third World producers and the Fairtrade Foundation is easy. Simply log on to their user-friendly website for information on upcoming events, news, and subscriptions to their newsletter, *Fair Comment*.

By challenging the traditional model of trade and offering a modern alternative for a sustainable future, the impact of the Fairtrade Foundation is being felt around the world. Fairtrade is not about charity, but giving a fair deal to small Third World producers. It is the purchasing power of informed consumers that helps the Fairtrade Foundation make such a world-wide impact. ■

---

*For more information about fair trade and the Fairtrade Foundation, call **020 7404 5942** or visit the website at **www.fairtrade.org.uk***

Food & Drink

CASE STUDY: Support your local farmer

Farmers' Markets offer a chance to return to a traditional way of buying and selling food, that is to say 'Local Produce for Local People', with all the health, economic and social advantages that accompany low tech production and marketing methods.

Customers and producers have the opportunity to discuss the goods on sale, the method of production, whether pesticides or growth hormones have been used, or how long it has been in transit from the farm. The producer also benefits from first-hand feedback from the customers whilst instilling customer confidence in the food they are buying. Many of the farmers use low intensity farming methods while some are in transition to organic status.

A return to localised production and selling has breathed new life into villages and town centres that had otherwise suffered in the move to out-of-town retail parks. By cutting out the middleman, Farmers' Markets enable producers to retain the profit on their goods whilst keeping the money within the local economy.

Selling locally enables farmers to minimise transport distances and thereby reduce the pollution created. It reduces the need for additional packaging and helps to maintain the diversity and beauty of the countryside.

Shoppers are encouraged to ask the market organisers what criteria they set for producers attending their market. Each will have a definition of 'local' – often a 30 mile radius from the site of the market.

The seasonality of food production has been forgotten with supermarkets offering a range of produce from around the world. The very nature of Farmers' Markets means that some produce will be seasonal, with many of the markets offering imaginative recipes to stimulate people's desire for fresh, local food. ■

For further information and where to find Farmers' Markets visit the website at
www.farmersmarkets.net

For a printed list, send an SAE to the National Association of Farmers' Markets, South Vaults, Green Park Station, Bath BA1 1JB.

CASE STUDY: The Food Commission – uncovering the facts

Eating a healthy diet can be harder than you think. Reduced fat foods can legally be 40% fat, sausages can contain 33% water and foods that are described as 'strawberry flavour' usually don't contain any strawberries! Foods that are marketed and labelled as 'healthy' don't have to be healthy at all. For example, foods with 'no added sugar' are often sweetened with apple juice, syrup or honey and can be just as bad for your teeth as products made with normal sugar.

Additives such as colourings and flavourings are used to disguise low quality ingredients, encouraging people to buy food with little nutritional value (despite all the 'added vitamins'). Other additives are even more devious, such as polyphosphates which are added to meat and fish products to make them soak up extra water, which the shopper ends up paying for.

The Food Commission is an independent watchdog which campaigns on food issues like these. Working from a small office in North London its award-winning researchers are able to expose the facts about modern food production and the secrets which the food industry prefers to keep hidden. It is funded solely by public subscriptions and donations. It doesn't take any money from the government and won't accept commercial sponsorship. Its newsletter *The Food Magazine* is free of commercial advertising – but packed with brand name product investigations and the latest news on food and health. This independence from the government and food companies means that it can provide unbiased, accurate research which really does help people to eat a healthier diet.

A subscription to *The Food Magazine* (four issues a year) costs £19.50. Mention the *Green Guide* when ordering and you will also be sent three free poster guides which explain food labelling, children's food and genetically modified foods. ■

Written by Ian Tokelove of the Food Commission, 94 White Lion Street, London N1 9PF.
Tel: **020 7837 2250** *Fax:* **020 7837 1141**
Email: **foodcomm@compuserve.com**
Web: **www.foodcomm.org.uk**

Four seasons

Seasonal eating simply means eating what local produce is at its best at that particular time of year. **Sally Cuningham** *sings its praises*

Why eat seasonally? Well, first of all, it's cheaper. Vegetables which mature naturally need far less chemical manipulation and heat than if they're forced to develop in an inappropriate season so not only do you save on shopping bills, it's cheaper for the farmer to produce them and better for the environment. They have extra flavour, for the same reason. Compare the difference between the scrunchy, day-neutral strawberries airfreighted from California in January with the succulent sweetness of a sun-ripened English July strawberry. No contest as to which I'd sooner eat!

As a child, I looked forward to the new peas ('Reckon they be ready the first Sunday after Derby Day', said our neighbour, Mr Clayton, who had been a Head Gardener before he retired), not simply because of their taste but the sensuous pleasure of unzipping them from their smooth skinned pods and splatting them, rattling machine gun-fashion, into the waiting saucepan. Different areas of the country found their own specialities, from the first Evesham asparagus through the Ormskirk cauliflowers and spring cabbage to Pembrokeshire early potatoes. Then the supermarkets came and everybody turned to frozen peas and, later on, mangetout or sugar snaps all year round. Who will remember the pleasures of opening a plastic packet of frozen green ball bearings?

Third World growers struggle to continuously crop for export on their best land and, as a result, grow less food for their own populations. Many feel they must use large doses of chemicals in order to meet ever higher specifications, and sprays long banned in Europe are often used with little or no protection for the workers. Meanwhile, in Britain, growers often cannot sell their produce, while lorries laden with imported foodstuff which we could easily grow ourselves clog the roads.

You can help both our own countryside and overseas in the way you shop for food. Whenever you can, eat what's in season and produced locally. It will be fresher, because it hasn't travelled as far and the vitamin content will be higher. It will (usually) cost less. Local growers will be able to continue farming in more environmentally aware methods. You will be in touch with the cycle of the changing year again – and perhaps your children too will have memories of munching sweet young peas from the pod. ∎

Sally Cuningham writes for the HDRA (Henry Doubleday Research Association).
Tel: **024 7630 3517**

IMPACT — How you shop for food can make a huge difference to what and how food is produced

- Reduce your food miles – walk or cycle to shops and buy local and regional foods.
- Ask your food supplier where food comes from if it is not clear on the shelf or labels.
- Reduce pesticide pollution by supporting organic farmers and try to buy organic foods in season (Use the *Green Guide* listings or contact the Soil Association for organic suppliers. The Henry Doubleday Research Association can provide a wallchart of seasonal foods).
- Encourage and enjoy biodiversity. Check out what varieties of fresh fruit and vegetables are available in your local stores and buy direct from farms, farm shops, farmers' markets and vegetable box schemes.
- Think global. Buy produce with the Fairtrade Mark – tea, coffee and even bananas are available from suppliers who ensure the farmers and workers get a fair deal.
- Support welfare-friendly farming. Purchase free range dairy, eggs and meat produce and, if you can't find any, ask your store to stock some.
- Make no food miles with DIY food. Grow your own organically – in window boxes, allotments or gardens – and ask your council what it is doing to encourage food growing.

Food Facts leaflets and briefings are available from Sustain: the alliance for better food and farming,
94 White Lion Street, London N1 9PF.
Tel: **020 7837 1228** *Fax:* **020 7837 1141**

GM foods explained

What is genetic engineering? Genes are the inherited blueprints of life. Breeding between closely related forms of life exchanges variations of the same genes in their natural groupings. This brings out traits that have evolved to work harmoniously together over millions of years. Genetic engineering (GE) involves the artificial insertion of a gene from one species into another. For the last 15 years, since scientists identified the effects that specific genes have on an organism (for example, which gene in a plant makes it resistant to a particular insect pest), the technology has been applied to an increasing range of food crops.

So what's the fuss about? GE allows the isolation and transfer of selected genes between totally unrelated organisms and brings about combinations of genes that would never occur naturally. But it is not its artificial nature that makes GE dangerous. It is the imprecise way in which genes are combined and the unpredictability of how foreign genes behave. They could affect the beneficial processes in an organism and/or produce new toxins and allergens.

How does it affect the environment? Traditional pollution incidents such as oil spills usually have a limited environmental impact. In most cases, nature recovers the polluted areas. The release of genetically modified organisms (GMOs) is entirely different. New gene combinations could be transferred to other crops and weeds with unpredictable effects and, once released, are impossible to 'clean up'.

What about wildlife? GE plants which have been designed to kill pests can also kill beneficial insects. Rapeseed engineered to produce a natural insecticide, for example, has been shown to kill not only caterpillars and beetles but also bees. Monsanto's Round-up Ready crops, which are resistant to the herbicide Glyphosate, allow crops to be sprayed with impunity. However, Glyphosate is a broad spectrum herbicide which kills a wide range of wild plants as well as the insects, birds and animals that depend on these plants for food and shelter.

Insect populations may develop resistance to the very crops designed to kill them. A number of commercial GE crops contain a gene taken from soil bacteria which causes plants to produce a natural toxin lethal to many caterpillars and grubs. However, according to the US Environment Protection Agency, due to constant exposure to high levels, these pests become resistant to the toxin within three to four years. The only answer then for farmers will be to use new, more powerful brands of pesticide.

The detrimental effect of GE crops on wildlife is sometimes more direct. For example, the death rate of lacewings, a food source for birds, doubled when they were fed on plant-eating larvae raised on GE maize.

So we just won't buy GMOs. Most of the time, you won't know whether a food contains GMOs or not. Under current labelling directives, about 90% of products containing GE ingredients or derivatives do not need to be labelled.

Well, it won't kill us. There's been very little research done to assess the health and safety implications to humans from ingesting GMOs. Health risks of GE foods are only assessed biochemically and in short-term feeding trials with animals. No tests with human volunteers are required.

There are some obvious dangers. Unexpected allergic reactions can be triggered (a brazil nut gene inserted into soya resulted in a reaction in people allergic to nuts) and there are concerns that genetically engineered soya may contain higher oestrogen levels. There is also a risk of increasing the incidence of antibiotic resistance in humans. GMOs often carry antibiotic resistant 'marker genes' to help scientists identify where modified genes rest in the plant. When a GE food containing the 'marker gene' is ingested by humans or animals, this could also make the consumer resistant to that particular antibiotic.

The inherent, unpredictable component to GE appears to be more fully appreciated in medical applications than in food production. A new drug or therapy produced using GE undergoes extensive preclinical and clinical trials to assess efficacy and to detect unexpected, undesirable side effects.

OK, so we'll go organic. Even organic foods, which expressly prohibit the use of GE, may not be able to claim their GE-free status in the future if commercial planting of such crops is allowed to happen in the UK. This is due to the process of 'genetic pollution' – the spread of genes through cross-fertilisation.

What can we do? The Soil Association is campaigning against the introduction of the untested and unnecessary technology. It is calling for a ban on the use of GE ingredients in human and animal foods and on the commercial planting of GE crops in the UK, as well as for stringent regulations for clear and informative labelling. Join the Association or make a donation.

Write to your Member of Parliament. Politicians take a lot of notice of their postbags. Boycott GM food. The best way to do this is to eat organic. Organic food is produced without the use of pesticides, fertilisers or GMOs. Finally, if you do use a supermarket regularly, write to the head office and demand that they recognise your right to avoid GM foods. ∎

*With thanks to the Soil Association. Call **0117 929 0661** for more information*

Food & Drink

Organic Home Delivery

Organic & Wholefoods

North West

Abbots Vegetable and Herb Garden
45 Glenavon Road, Prenton,
Birkenhead, Wirral L43 0RB
Tel: 0151 608 4566
▶ Vegetable box scheme delivering local produce.

Chorlton Wholefoods
64 Beech Road,
Chorlton-cum-Hardy,
Manchester M21 9EG
Tel: 0161 881 6399
Fax: 0161 881 6399
Email: georgereynolds@yahoo.com
Web: www.chorltonwholefoods.com
Open: Mon-Sat 9am-6pm;
Sun 10.30am-4.30pm
▶ Wholefood shop running an organic fruit and veg delivery service throughout the Greater Manchester area (see listing in the Wholefood Shops section).

Foodlife
68 Buckingham Road,
Cheadle, Hulme,
Stockport SK8 5NA
Tel: 0161 486 1173
Fax: 0161 486 1173
▶ Established in 1995 with support from the Princes Youth Business Trust, this box scheme company delivers organic and free range produce including fruit and veg, dairy items, herbs, breads, fruit juices, eggs and meat direct to customers on a weekly basis. Welcomes customer comment and input, and publishes a newsletter with local food news and recipes.

Growing with Nature
Bradshaw Lane Nursery,
Pilling near Preston PR3 6AX
Tel: 01253 790 046
Fax: 01253 790 046
▶ Localised home delivery service of own grown seasonal organic vegetables and salads. Operative in Lancashire only.

Home Farm Deliveries
Studio 19, Imex Business Park,
Hamilton Road,
Manchester M13 0PD
Tel: 0161 224 8884
Fax: 0161 224 8826
Email: home.farm@tvc.org.uk
Web: www.homefarm.co.uk
Open: Mon-Fri 9.30am-5.30pm
▶ Organic box delivery scheme with a wide selection of fresh fruit, veg and meat, serving Greater Manchester and Stockport. There are three organic veg packs increasing in size and a standard fruit pack. Also supplies a wide selection of organic breads, fruit juices, milks, cheeses, eggs and yoghurts.

Howbarrow Organic Farm
Howbarrow Farm, Cartmel,
Grange-over-Sands LA11 7SS
Tel: 015395 36330
Fax: 015395 36300
Email: Enquiries@howbarroworganic.demon.co.uk
Web: www.howbarroworganic.demon.co.uk
▶ A small mixed holding licenced with the Soil Association and part of the demonstration farm network, with a farm shop, box scheme and mail order. Extensive range of own grown produce and meat. Highly commended in the 1999 *Mail on Sunday* 'You' food awards for its eggs and chickens.

Limited Resources
53 Old Birley Street, Hulme,
Manchester M15 5RF
Tel: 0161 226 4777
Fax: 0161 226 3777
Email: office@limitedresources.co.uk
Web: www.limitedresources.co.uk
Open: Mon-Fri 9am-5pm
▶ Promotes the ethos of a sustainable society by delivering organic foods and green household products to homes in Central and South Manchester. Most deliveries are made by bicycle and trailer and all products are sourced from companies with a clean ethical record (ie not involved in the arms trade, animal testing, oppressive regimes, etc). Over 400 products are available in a free catalogue, including fruit and veg, wine, beer and cider, dairy products, tea and coffee, beans and pulses, grains and cereals, cleaning products and cosmetics.

Organic Direct
22 Grosvenor Street,
Liverpool L3 3BB
Tel: 0151 298 2468
Fax: 0151 298 2468
Email: organic.direct@lineone.net
Open: Wed 11.30am-5.30pm; Thurs 9.30am-5.30pm; Fri 11am-1pm
▶ Over 30 varieties of organic fruit and vegetables, organic bread and a wide range of organic wholefoods. Free local delivery. Soil Association registered.

Organic Shop, The
3 Sett Close, Market Street,
New Mills, High Peak SK22 4DW
Tel: 01663 747 550
Fax: 01663 7410411
Open: Mon-Fri 9am-5.30pm (Wed half day)
▶ Provides free home delivery of a wide range of organic produce including fruit, vegetables, bread, milk, cheese, eggs, meat and fish, wine, wholefoods, garden supplies, cosmetics, clothing, an Ecover Refill service to South Manchester, High Peak and Cheshire.

Organic Way, The
Unit 6a, Britannia Mills,
Cobden Street, Bury BL9 6AW
Tel: 01204 592 222
Fax: 01204 592 222
Open: Mon 9am-1pm; Tues-Sat 9am-6pm (Thurs to 7pm)
▶ Originally a delivery service, The Organic Way now has shop premises from where it supplies fresh organic fruit and veg, household products and natural toiletries. Deliveries to the North West Manchester areas include Prestwich, Bolton, Rochdale and Bury. Won a highly commended award from the Princes Youth Business Trust in 1998.

Sunflower Wholefoods
34 Beech Road,
Chorlton-cum-Hardy
Tel: 0161 881 6399
Fax: 0161 881 6399
▶ Organic food home delivery-box scheme.

Zedz Foods
Unit 4, Arena Court, Mirabel Street,
Manchester M3 1PJ
Tel: 0161 835 1442
Fax: 0161 835 1541
Email: zarenaallan@appleonline.net
Web: www.zedzfoods.co.uk
▶ Manufacturers of vegetarian, vegan and special dietary foods, especially gluten-free foods. Sells to local outlets and to individuals by mail order. Foods are freshly made on the premises, using organic ingredients whenever feasible.

National

AAA Greenthings
58 Kingly Close,
Wickford SS12 0EN
Tel: 01268 450 024
Email: info@pathcom.co.uk
Web: www.green4u.co.uk
▶ Website supplying food and drink.

Organic fruit & vegetables free-range meat

No pesticides
No growth hormones
No antibiotics
No genetically engineered foods

Quality local & national growers, friendly personal service.

For information about our weekly home delivery services in the South Manchester / North Cheshire area and all our other delicious dairy / bread / juice etc.. products, call 0161 - 446 - 1123.

Food for life as nature intended.

Food & Drink

Allergyfree Direct Ltd
5 Centremead, Osney Mead, Oxford OX2 0ES
Tel: 01865 722003
Fax: 01865 244 134
Email: info@allergyfreedirect.co.uk
Web: www.allergyfreedirect.co.uk
▶ Offers UK home delivery of a wide range of foods suitable for people suffering from food allergies and/or intolerances. Specialises in supplying foods which are dairy free and gluten free. Most foods are organic and does not knowingly supply any containing genetically modified organisms.

Baldwin's Health Food Centre
171-173 Walworth Road, London SE17 1RW
Tel: 020 7703 5550
Fax: 020 7252 6264
Email: sales@baldwins.co.uk
Web: www.baldwins.co.uk
Open: Mon-Sat 9am-5.30pm
▶ Supplies herbs, essential oils, base oils, supplements and natural foods (both organic and non-organic) by mail order available. Call for free catalogue.

Fresh Food Company
326 Portobello Road, London W10 5RU
Tel: 020 8969 0351
Fax: 020 8964 8050
Email: organics@freshfood.co.uk
Web: www.freshfood.co.uk
▶ The UK's original and biggest nationwide online organic food home delivery service. Think of FFC as the Virtual Organic Farmers' Market. 4,000 lines, in six categories and 450 sub-categories, including fruit & veg; meat, fish & dairy; bakery; wines, beers & spirits; groceries; low toxicity cleaning products; more. And the list of green products is still growing. Check out the website for the full list, or phone for a print catalogue.

Green Gourmet
PO Box 25, Congleton CW12 4FG
Tel: 01477 500 703
Fax: 01477 500 703
Web: www.greengourmet.com
▶ Tailor-made vegetarian, vegan and organic hampers and gift boxes available all year round.

Highland Organic Foods
4 Bittacy Hill, Mill Hill, London NW7 1LB
Tel: 020 8346 1055
Fax: 020 8349 4623
Email: sales@highlandorganics.co.uk
Web: www.highlandorganics.co.uk
Open: Mon-Sat 8am-6pm
▶ Organic food centre stocking fresh meat, dairy produce, tinned goods and dried products. Delivery all over the UK. GM free. Call for a price list.

Neal's Yard Dairy
6 Park Street, London SE1 9AB
Tel: 020 7645 3552
Fax: 020 7378 0400
Open: Mon-Fri 10am-6pm; Sat 10am-5pm
▶ Wholesale, mail order and export branch of the Neal's Yard Dairy stocking the same range as is available over the counter in the Covent Garden store.

Organic Pudding Company, The
Howbarrow Farm, Cartmel, Grange-over-Sands LA11 7SS
Tel: 015395 36330
Fax: 015395 36330
Email: sales@wildpuddings.com
Web: www.wildpuddings.com
▶ A range of traditional puddings including sticky toffee, chocolate fudge sauce, using vegetarian and vegan recipes. Registered with the Soil Association. Available from independent retailers or via mail order.

OrganicOxygen.com
89a Manor Road, Banbury
Tel: 0800 195 7844
Fax: 0870 121 7520
Email: alec@organicoxygen.com
Web: www.organic-oxygen.co.uk
▶ An on-line organic, GM-free, gluten-free and fair trade shop, selling everything from hampers to vegan shoes. Free delivery for vegetable, fruit and dairy boxes.

Simply Organic Food Co
Units A62-64, New Covent Garden, London SW8 5EE
Tel: 0845 100 0444
Fax: 020 7622 4447
Email: info@simplyorganic.net
Web: www.simplyorganic.net

▶ One of the UK's largest organic home delivery supermarkets with nationwide delivery of over 1,000 organic products, including fruit & vegetables, meat & fish, dairy, groceries, wines & beer and infantcare. Customers select the delivery day of their choice and SimplyOrganic guarantee delivery before midday. Order via phone, fax or email using full colour catalogue or via the company's fully interactive home shopping website.

Take It From Here Limited
Unit 04 BetaWay, Thorpe Industrial Estate, Egham TW20 8RX
Tel: 01784 477 812
(Freephone: 0800 137 064)
Fax: 01784 477 813
Email: lara@danmar.demon.co.uk
Web: www.danmar.demon.co.uk
▶ Authentic and Artisan Italian products delievered to your door. The range includes a number of organic products, pasta, pasta sauces, extra virgin olive oil and 24 month old Parmiggiano Reaggiano.

Other Foods

Halzephron Herb Farm
Gunwallow, Helston TR12 7QD
Tel: 01326 240 652
Fax: 01326 241 125
Web: www.halzherb.com
▶ Cornish farm growing herbs free from pesticides and artificial growing agents. The herbs are sold dried or processed as marinades, sauces, dips and dressings. Also produces herb honey, a wonderfully aromatic mixture of Cornish honey and rosemary, and a range of herbal remedies. The products are available by mail order but, if you are in the area, the farm shop is well worth a visit.

Organic Herb Trading Company
Court Farm, Milverton TA4 1NF
Tel: 01823 401 205
Email: info@organicherbtrading.com
Web: www.organicherbtrading.com
▶ Organic herb specialists supplying over 550 different herbs and spices to the food and herbal medicine trade. Reliable and respected source of bulk or small quantities of herbs spices, essential oils, tinctures, and plant derived products. Will undertake processing to customer specification. Fast reliable delivery, friendly efficient staff. Producers and distributors of the award winning Hambleden Herbs range of 130 herbs, spices, herbal teas, tinctures and vinegards. Certified by the Soil Association.

Hemp Collective Ltd
Silverdale, Clyde Road, Didsbury, Manchester M20 2NJ
Tel: 0161 445 5227
Fax: 0161 445 2556
Email: talk2us@thehempcollective.com
Web: www.thehempcollective.com
Open: Mon-Fri 9am-9pm
▶ Provides a diverse range of hemp products encompassing body care, clothing, foodstuffs, paper and sundries. Mail order and wholesale facilities for people looking to make a positive difference to themselves and the planet. Write or call for a catalogue or visit the website.

G. BALDWIN & Co
Est. 1844

WE ARE SPECIALIST SUPPLIERS OF COMPLEMENTARY MEDICINES AND OFFER AN EXTENSIVE RANGE OF:

- Aromatherapy Oils
- Herbal Tinctures
- Health Foods & Drinks
- Bach Flower Remedies
- Homoeopathy
- Vitamin, Mineral & Herbal Supplements
- Herbs & Roots
- Carrier Oils
- Books
- Herbal Medicine
- Natural Cosmetics

All Products Are Available From Our Shop or by Mail Order.
For a FREE Mail Order Catalogue Call Now.

FOR FRIENDLY & HELPFUL ADVICE PHONE 020 7703 5550

Fax: 020 7252 6264   Email: sales@baldwins.co.uk   Website: www.baldwins.co.uk
171/173 Walworth Road, London, SE17 1RW

Hemp Union Foods
Lower Pertwood Farm,
Hindon SP3 6TA
Tel: 01747 820 889
Fax: 01747 820 889
▶ Highest quality cold-pressed organic hemp seed table oil, hemp seed, hemp seed flour, hemp 'burger' mix, hemp oil soap and body-care range, hemp seed grinders and burger presses, hemp accessories, stationary etc. Also second grade hemp seed oil for soap and candle-making, wood and leather preservative, etc. Mail order, trade and wholesale supplier. Call for more information.

Hempseed Organics
FREEPOST, PO Box 11797,
London N22 8NE
Tel: 020 8888 9277
Fax: 020 8888 9277
Email: hempseed@gn.apc.org
▶ Wholesale suppliers of a variety of hemp seed food products from baked goods to hemp butter. Available by mail order or at selected health food shops. Call for details of your nearest stockist.

Little Salkeld Watermill
Little Salkeld, Penrith CA10 1NN
Tel: 01768 881 523
Fax: 01768 895 920
Email: organicflour@aol.com
Web: www.cumbria.com/watermill
Open: Mon-Fri 10.30am-5pm (shop only in Dec & Jan)
▶ Working traditional watermill producing organic and biodynamic stoneground flours. Mill shop sells a wide range of organic food – pulses, pasta, nuts, seeds, dried fruit, juices, teas, coffee, etc. Mail order service available. Also runs baking courses. Tea-room serves homemade wholefood lunches and teas.

Peppers by Post
Sea Spring Farm, West Bexington,
Dorchester DT2 9DD
Tel: 01308 897 892
Fax: 01308 897 735
▶ Wide range of organic peppers by post, all grown in a market garden in West Dorset. Each order is posted by first class post on the same day as the chillies are picked.

Phytofoods
Middle Travelly, Beguildy,
Knighton LD7 1UW
Tel: 01547 510 242
Fax: 01547 510 317
Email: polly@micropix.demon.co.uk
Web: www.micropix.demon.co.uk/tempeh
▶ Markets complete kits for the home production of Tempeh, a fermented soy food which is a highly nutritious protein food. Cruelty-free and organic, if organic and GM-free soy beans are used, it is a cheap, easy and quick food to make in the home. Tempeh is rich in vitamin B12, making it an especially important food for vegetarians and vegans. It contains no cholesterol and it is consumed daily in Indonesia, usually with rice as part of the main meal or sometimes alone as a snack. As it is made with whole beans it is a fibre-rich food. Tempeh is an extremely versatile food and can be used in thousands of recipes. Call for more information.

Meat & Fish

Eastbrook Farm Organic Meats
Bishopstone, Swindon SN6 8PW
Tel: 01793 790 460 (orders)
01793 782 211 (shop)
Fax: 01793 791 239
Email: eastbrookfarm@demon.co.uk
▶ Integrated fresh meat business operating to strict Soil Association organic standards. Pork, lamb, beef, sausages, pies, cured meats and eggs available from the shop in Shrivenham (call for details), by mail order or overnight courier service. The 1350 acre farm is open to schools and groups by prior arrangement and the farm trail is open all year round.

Graig Farm Organics
Dolau, Llandrindod Wells LD1 5TL
Tel: 01597 851 655
Fax: 01597 851 991
Email: sales@graigfarm.co.uk
Web: www.graigfarm.co.uk
Open: Mon-Sat 9am-5.30pm
▶ From the heart of mid-Wales, Graig Farm, winners or finalists of Organic Food Awards every year since 1993, offers probably the widest range of organic meats and other produce by mail order. The range includes all the usual meats, as well as sepcilities such as Welsh Mountain mutton & lamb, wild and farmed fish and quality handmade pies. The mail order range also includes groceries, alcohol, books and skin care. Also available from farm shop and selected retail outlets, as well as on-line ordering.

Jamesfield Organic Meats
Endrigg, Jamesfield Farm,
Newburgh KY14 6EW
Tel: 01738 850 498
Fax: 01738 850 741
▶ Free range and organic meat. Delivers anywhere in mainland UK.

Longwood Farm
Tuddenham St Mary, Bury St Edmunds IP28 6TB
Tel: 01638 717 120
Fax: 01638 717 120
Open: Wed & Fri 8.30am-4.30pm;
Sat 8.30am-2pm (farm and shop)

▶ Nationwide mail order delivery service of a wide range of Soil Association-approved organic meat and poultry products including sausages, burgers and cured and cooked meats.

Meadowland Meats
Model Farm, Hildersley,
Ross-on-Wye HR9 7NN
Tel: 01989 562 208
(24 hour answer machine)
Fax: 01989 769 724
Open: Mon-Fri 10am-5pm
▶ Farm shop run selling a wide range of products at 'prices real people can afford'. The group of farmers who run the shop aim to give their customers assurances of quality, purity and traceability. Delivers organic vegetables and herbs (all fresh and grown by the farmers themselves) to London, the Home Counties, Birmingham and Bristol. Sells organic cheeses as well as organic and additive-free meat (please talk to the farmers about the difference between the two) including beef, lamb, pork, chicken, wild venison and game. Mail order available.

Meat Matters
2 Blandys Farm Cottages,
Bassett Road,
Letcombe Regis OX12 9LJ
Tel: 01235 762 461;
Freephone 0808 006 7426
Fax: 01235 772 526
Email: www.meatmatters.uk.com
Web: diane@meatmatters.uk.com
Open: Mon-Fri 8.30am-7pm,
Sat 8.30am-6pm
▶ Delivers fresh organic meat, poultry, eggs, fish, dairy products, vegetables, fruit and groceries to over 3,000 families in the UK. Deliveries are free of charge in the M25 area, Oxfordshire, Berkshire, South Herts and South Bucks, with a small charge elsewhere, and are made to pre-agreed times using their own refrigerated vans and chilled, insulated packaging for health and safety. The produce comes from a small selection of carefully chosen organic farms and the butchers are happy to prepare any cuts of meat. Produces

---

Little Salkeld Watermill

Little Salkeld Watermill, 6 miles from Penrith (M6 J40) in Cumbria produces a fine range of breadmaking & baking flours plus a special range for adventurous bakers who want to try something different – like **Miller's Magic**, or **Special Blend**, or **Flour Grain Blend**! All our flours are milled the traditional way – water-powered overshot waterwheels turning French Burr millstones. We *only* mill **ORGANIC** and **BIODYNAMIC** British grain. Stone-grinding is cool, slow, and retains the flavour and goodness of the wheat germ oil. We do **Mail Order**. **Mill** and **Tearoom** open Mondays to Fridays (Feb-Nov). **Millshop** weekdays (all year). **Baking Courses**.

**Tel: 01768 881523   e-mail: organicflour@aol.com
Web: www.cumbria.com/watermill**

Food & Drink 21

home made sausages, made to traditional recipes, dry cured bacon and pies, with chipolatas and burgers for kids. Has special barbecue products for the summer and a full range of seasonal Christmas fayre. For further information and a catalogue, call on the freephone number.

Pure Organic Foods Ltd
Unit 5, Eastlands Industrial Estate,
Leiston IP16 4LL
Tel: 01728 830 575
Fax: 01728 833 660
Email:
enquiries@pureorganicfoods.co.uk
Web: www.pureorganicfoods.co.uk
▶ Certified organic meat – beef, lamb and pork, poultry and smoked salmon, prepared in organically-dedicated processing and packing plant in Suffolk. Products tray-sealed within a protective environment. Suitable for home freezing. Available through various stockists or by home delivery box scheme. Orders by fax, email or on Internet shopping basket, to be received by 10am for next day delivery.

Saxonbury Wood
2 Sham Farm Cottage, Eridge Green,
Tunbridge Wells TN3 9JA
Tel: 020 7227 0937
Fax: 020 7359 6351
Email: geo@saxonbury-wood.co.uk
Web: www.saxonbury-wood.co.uk
▶ Saxonbury Wood, 120 acres of ancient woodland on the Kent/Sussex border is home to free range organic pigs. Bred and spending their entire lives in the woods (their natural habitat), the pigs consume a natural diet, free from additives, antiboitics and growth promoters. The pigs are not subject to tail docking, castration or tusk cutting. Aims to produce the country's best-tasting organic pork, in a humane way that is beneficial to the environment.

Somerset Organics
Manor Farm, Rodney Stoke,
Cheddar BS27 3UN
Tel: 01749 870 919
Email:
somersetorganics@hotmail.com

▶ The UK's largest supplier of rare breed organic meats offering a 24 hour delivery service. All the animals are from farms on the Somerset Levels and include: Gloucester Old Spot Pork, Aberdeen Angus/longhorn cattle, Welsh Black and Galloway beef. Nationwide delivery of just £5.00 per order.

Westcountry Organics Ltd
Natson Farm, Tedburn St Mary,
Exeter EX6 6ET
Tel: 0164 724 724
Fax: 0164 724 031
Email:
Wbb@westcountryorganics.co.uk
Web:
www.westcountryorganics.co.uk
▶ Freshly packed organic meats including beef, lamb, pork, poultry, dry cured bacon, speciality sausages, gammon, ham, organic cheese, tofu burgers and a range of vegetarian pies. Nationwide delivery service offered.

Organic Alcohol

Bramley and Gage
Unit 2B Long Meadow,
South Brent TQ10 9YT
Tel: 01364 737 22
Fax: 01364 737 22
Email: bramleygage@fsbdial.co.uk
Web: www.speciality-foods.com
Open: Mon-Fri 9am-5pm
▶ Makers of sloe gin and fruit liqueurs available via the website, by mail order and through local stockists in the West Country.

Broughton Pastures Organic Wine
The Old Brewery, 24 High Street,
Tring HP23 5AH
Tel: 01442 823 993
▶ The country's foremost producer of organic fruit wines and mead. Its mead was highly commended in the 1997 and 1998 Organic Food & Drink Awards. Call for nearest stockist.

Brown Forman Wines International
Cavendish House, 51-55 Mortimer Street, London W1N 8JE
Tel: 020 7462 3349
Fax: 020 7323 5316

Email: lucy_whetman@b-f.com
Web: www.bonterra.com
▶ Fetzer Vineyards embarked on its misssion to farm grapes organically in the late eighties as a result of experiments in their five acre Bonterra Organic Garden. As with organic fruits and vegetables believes that organically farmed grapes 'simply taste better'. The Bonterra wine range includes examples of familiar Chardonnay and Cabernet, as well as more unusual Roussanne and Sangiovese. They are excellent, distinctive wines and easy matches with food.

Crone's
Fairview, Fersfield Road,
Kenninghall, Norfolk NR16 2DP
Tel: 01379 687 687
Fax: 01379 688 323
Email: robert@crones.co.uk
Web: www.crones.co.uk
Open: Mon-Fri 8.30am-6pm
▶ Makers of an extensive range of award-winning organic ciders and apple juices. Also supplies organic Pear and Apple juice, Apple and Cherry, and now a Cider and Perry vinegar. For the full range of available juices and details of your nearest stockist, visit the website, or contact by fax or phone.

Disos Pure Wine
PO Box 23, Cheadle SK8 4FF
Tel: 0161 428 7666
▶ Supplier of two pure vegetarian wines (Vin de Pay d'Oc from Southern France) available direct by the case or through 200 independent stockists. Call for details of your nearest stockist.

Grapevine Organics
39 Carlyle Street, Brighton BN2 2XU
Tel: 01273 819 055
Fax: 01273 705 028
Email:
sales@grapevine-organics.co.uk
Web: www.grapevine-organics.co.uk
Open: Mon-Fri 8am-9pm
(24 hour website/email access)
▶ Small, family-run business based in Brighton selling organic beverages by mail order (both trade and retail).

MEAT MATTERS
organic food • delivered to your door

- Soil Association certified organic food.
- Organic meat, poultry, fish and eggs.
- Organic fruit, vegetables and groceries.
- Delivery throughout the UK.
- Call for information and a catalogue.

FREEPHONE: 08080 067426

CRONE'S

Makers of a range of award-winning organic apple juices and ciders. Also pear & apple, apple & cherry, and cider vinegar. Please contact us for our full range of products.

FAIRVIEW, KENNINGHALL, NORFOLK, NR16 2DP.
TEL: 01379 687687 www.crones.co.uk

Has a growing range of wines, beers, ciders and juices which are all vegetarian (some are also vegan). Also offers a number of biodynamic wines. Wines are sold by the case, but will mix and match up to 12 diferent bottles. Delivery throughout the UK is available.

H Weston & Sons Ltd
The Bounds, Much Marcle,
Ledbury HR8 2NQ
Tel: *01531 660 233*
Fax: *01531 660 619*
Email: *tradition@westons-cider.co.uk*
Web: *www.westons-cider.co.uk*
▶ Winner of the Organic Food Awards 1998 for Best Alcoholic Product with Westons Organic Cider. This traditionally produced cider comes from locally grown organic cider apples. Fermented in old oak vats, it has a ripe apple aroma and well balanced taste. Organic Spritzer is made from a sparkling blend of natural spring water, organic cider, and organic apple juice, selected to create a highly refreshing drink. On site has The Scrumpy House Restaurant and Bar set in a converted 17th century cattle shed. The shop provides the venue for free tastings.

Organic Spirits Company Ltd, The
Meadow View House,
Tannery Lane, Bramley GU5 0AB
Tel: *01483 894 650*
Fax: *01483 894 651*
Email: *office@londonandscottish.co.uk*
Web: *www.uk5.org or*
www.junipergreen.org
▶ Supplies organic vodka and gin. Juniper Green is the world's first Organic London Dry Gin. It is distilled and bottled in the heart of London. All the ingredients are 100% organic and Juniper Green was declared best gin in the Year 2000 International Wine & Spirit Challenge. The judges stated that it had 'all the hallmarks of a classic gin, with delicately balanced botanicals and a refreshing finish'. UK5 Organic Vodka is deliciously smooth and clean with a hint of fruit esters. It was awarded a gold medal in The International Wine & Spirit Competition. For more information, visit the websites.

Organic Wine Company
PO Box 81, High Wycombe HP13 5QN
Tel: *01494 446 557*
Fax: *01494 446 557*
Email: *afm@lineone.net*
Web: *www.organicwinecompany.com*
▶ Mail order suppliers of over 200 lines in organic wine, beer, cider, brandy, olive oil, vinegar and juices. Free quarterly newsletter available. Also has two organic olive oils.

Pure Wine Company, The
Unit 18 Woods-Browning Industrial Estate, Respryn Road,
Bodmin PL31 1DQ
Tel: *01208 79300*
Fax: *01208 79393*
Email: *service@purewine.co.uk*
Web: *www.purewine.co.uk*
Open: *Mon-Fri 9am-6pm*

▶ Launched in 1999, the company supplies organic, vegetarian, vegan and biodynamic wines via mail order to the trade and general public. Aims to combine affordable prices with a high quality of customer care and a friendly, helpful service. The website and the trade and retail catalogues detail the current range of over 170 wines and there are quarterly newsletters with special offers, free gifts and discounts. Runs a Cellar Club which offers free half bottles for every case purchased, £5 vouchers for customer referrals and a free wedding advisory service. Currently offers the largest range of Italian organic wines in the UK along with a number of Australian organic varieties.

Ravensbourne Wine Company
6-0-2 Bell House, 49 Greenwich High Road, London SE10 8JL
Tel: *020 8692 9655*
Fax: *020 8692 9655*
Open: *Mon-Fri 9am-5pm*

Organic & Vegetarian Wines

Also juices, beers and ciders

Rapid nationwide delivery

Free list from Vinceremos
19 New Street, Leeds LS18 4BH
email info@vinceremos.co.uk
www.vinceremos.co.uk
0113 205 4545

the organic wine specialists

Organic wines
worldwide range (many vegetarian/ vegan), beers, ciders, spirits, juices, oils and chocolates.

Fast nationwide delivery service.

Phone now for a free wine list

TEL **0800 980 4992**

▶ Retail, wholesale, delivery and mail order of a small range of organic wines. Free delivery of mixed cases to London addresses.

Rose Blanc Rouge
8 Union Drive, London E1 4PE
Tel/Fax: 020 7690 0437
Email: contact@rose-blanc-rouge.com
Web: www.rose-blanc-rouge.com
▶ Offers selection of organic wines, beers and juices from a St. Emilion Grand CRV 1993 to Belgium beer and original juice mixes. Mail order and on-line order available.

St. Peter's Brewery Company Ltd
St. Peter, South Elmham, Bungay NR35 1NQ
Tel: 01986 782 322
Fax: 01986 782 505
Email: beers@stpetersbrewery.co.uk
Web: www.stpetersbrewery.co.uk
Open: Fri, Sat 11am-11pm; Sun & Bank Hols 11am-7pm
▶ Produces a range of traditional and speciality beers against backdrop of St. Peter's Hall, a medieval former monastry. Based there because of water that comes up from its own deep-water base hole. Licensed by the Soil Association for production of organic beer and produces St. Peter's Organic Ale and Organic Best Bitter. Both won medals at 2000 International Beer and Cider Competition. For more information, see website as listed above.

Sedlescombe Vineyard
Cripps Corner, Robertsbridge TN32 55A
Tel: 01580 830 715
Fax: 01580 830 122
Email: rcook91137@aol.com
Web: www.tor.co.uk/sedlescombe/
Open: April-Dec Mon-Fri 10am-5.30pm; Jan-Mar Sat-Sun, Noon-5pm
▶ Planted in 1979, the Sedlescombe Vineyard produces organic wines, ciders and fruit juices, all fully certified by the Soil Association and approved by the Vegan Society. Trade and retail price lists are available. Wine, cider, juice and wholefoods are sold in the vineyard shop with wine tasting available. Group tours and educational visits by appointment.

Vinceremos Organic Wines
19 New Street, Leeds LS18 4BH
Tel: 0113 205 4545
Fax: 0113 205 4546
Email: info@vinceremos.co.uk
Web: www.vinceremos.co.uk
Open: Mon-Fri 9am-5.30pm
▶ Organic and vegetarian wines, many suitable for vegans, delivered to your door. Its catalogue features a wide range of award-winning organic wines from around the world as well as organic beers, ciders, spirits and grape juice. Write or call for a free catalogue.

Vintage Roots
Farley Farms, Bridge Farm, Reading Road, Arborfield RG2 9HT
Tel: 0118 976 1999
Fax: 0118 976 1998
Email: info@vintageroots.co.uk
Web: www.vintageroots.co.uk
▶ With over 300 wines from 14 different countries around the world, Vintage Roots offers the most comprehensive range of organic/vegetarian and vegan drinks in the country. Also stocks organic beers, ciders and assorted spirits, juices, oils and chocolates. Mail order direct to your door using a fast and efficient delivery service. Trade enquiries welcome. France, Spain and Italian specialists.

SHOPS

For more shops that sell wholefoods, see Health Product Shops in Chapter Five: Health.

Wholefood, Organic & Fair Trade

Appleseeds
59 Market Street, Ulverston LA12 7LT
Tel: 01229 583 394
Fax: 01229 583 394
▶ Newly enlarged store stocking fresh organic fruit and vegetables, organic chocolates, sweets, crisps, wines and beer, frozen ready meals and more. Also aromatherapy treatment and products. Large selection of herbal remedies, vitamins, minerals and homeopathic remedies.

Ashfield Organic Farm
Chester High Road, Neston CH64 3RY
Tel: 0151 336 8788
Email: enquiries.ashfieldfarm.co.uk
Web: www.ashfieldfarm.co.uk
▶ Farm shop selling organic produce.

Body Health Products
Unit 91 Market Hall, Market Street, Ashton-under-Lyme OL6 7JU
Tel: 0161 343 3287
Open: Mon, Weds-Sat 9am-5.30pm; Tues 9am-4.30pm
▶ Wholefoods and health products including vitamins, supplements and body building products.

Bury Nutrition Centre
6 The Mall, Bury BL9 0QQ
Tel: 0161 761 6445
Open: Mon-Sat 9am-5.30pm
▶ Wholefood and organic foods.

Chester Fair Trading
St Peter's Church, The Cross, Chester CH1 2LA
Tel: 01244 313 920/ 01829 770847
Open: Mon-Sat 10am-3.30pm
▶ Fair trade organisation which works with groups in Africa, Asia and Latin America to supply a wide selection of beautiful handmade crafts and fairly traded foods and beverages. Includes products from the Traidcraft catalogue, as well as special promotional items. Can provide talks to community groups.

Chorlton Wholefoods
64 Beech Road, Chorlton-cum-Hardy, Manchester M21 9EG
Tel: 0161 881 6399
Fax: 0161 881 6399
Email: georgereynolds@yahoo.co.uk
Web: www.chorltonwholefoods.com
Open: Mon-Sat 9am-6pm; Sun 10.30am-4.30pm
▶ Established in 1982, this small family business has always sold organic fruit and vegetables via the shop and a delivery service throughout Greater Manchester. Also stocks organic dairy produce, dried wholefoods, homeopathic and Bach flower remedies, fair trade and household cleaning products. Will recycle egg boxes and (clean) carrier bags.

Church Farm Organics
Church Lane, Thurstaston, Wirral CH61 0HW
Tel: 0151 648 7838
Fax: 0151 648 9644
Email: sales@churchfarm.org.uk
Open: Wed-Sun 10am-5pm
▶ Family-run organic farm and shop with over 300 organic lines; organic refreshments; caravaning and camping; bed and organic breakfast; educational visits.

Country Bumpkin
40 Cross Street, Altrincham WA14 1EQ
Tel: 0161 941 4663
Open: Mon-Sat 9am-5pm
▶ Wholefood and organic food shop.

Country Living
96-98 Park Lane, Poynton SK12 1RE
Tel: 01625 876 115
Open: Mon-Tues, Thurs-Sat 9am-5.30pm; Weds 9am-1pm
▶ Extensive range of wholefoods and health products including homeopathic and herbal remedies, vitamins, aromatherapy oils, etc. Mail order service available.

Demeter Wholefoods
12 Welles Street, Sandbach CW11 1GT
Tel: 01270 760 445
Email: phillipdemeter@cs.com
▶ Large and centrally located wholefood shop with a special commitment to organic produce. Plenty of curiosi-

ties such as asfoetida and nigari. Over 140 different varieties of herbal teas and 100 medicinal herbs. Information sheets about basic foods freely available. Fine food and health lines include Whole Earth, Meridian, Suma, Provomel and Aspalls. Encourages preventative medicine through dietary advice and supplementation. Also supplies toothpaste, cosmetics, eco-friendly cleaners and books. Run a permanent stall at Nantwich Indoor Market (Tues and Fri mornings, Thurs and Sat all day).

Duttons Health Foods
Godstall Lane, St Werburgh Street,
Chester, CH1 1NL
Tel: *01244 316 255*
Fax: *01244 403 523*
Email: *wendy@duttons88.freeserve.co.uk*
Open: *Mon-Sat 9am-5.30pm*
▶ Established for over 35 years, stocks a comprehensive range of organic foods, health foods, supplements, fresh breads and chilled takeaway items.

Farmhouse Kitchens
39 London Road,
Alderley Edge SK9 7JT
Tel: *01625 584 395*
Fax: *01625 583 728*
Open: *Mon-Fri 9.15am-5.30pm;*
Sat 9.15am-5pm
▶ Stocks organic produce including vegetables, food for special diets including dairy-free, a range of vitamins and supplements and alternative and complementary remedies. Organic veg boxes can be ordered for collection at the shop.

Fit As A Fiddle
108 Mill Street,
Macclesfield SK11 6NR
Tel: *01625 612 555*
▶ First opened 10 years ago, this is an old fashioned wholefood shop with wide range of vitamins and supplements, alternative therapy products, pulses and grains, herbs and spices, herbals teas, jams and honeys, dried products and eco-friendly household products. The shop also has a small lending library with books on health issues. Informal health advice given on premises.

Full of Beans
93 Witton Street,
Northwich CW9 5DR
Tel: *01606 41778*
Open: *Mon-Sat 9am-5.30pm*
▶ Stocks dried wholefoods, organic and gluten-free products, vitamins and minerals, and Beauty Without Cruelty cosmetics and toiletries.

Glossop Whole Food Co-Op Ltd
8 Henry Street, Glossop SK13 8BW
Tel: *01457 865 678*
▶ Mainly organic wholefood shop with lots of organic fruit and veg, pulses and grains, herbs and spices, herbal teas and coffees, jams and honeys, dried products, vitamins and supplements, alternative therapy products, a selection of alternative and local magazines and publications and eco-friendly household products. A large range of fresh organic bread includes a gluten-free loaf. Mail order service available on request.

Good Health
13 Armentieres Square,
Stalybridge SK15 2BR
Tel: *0161 338 8385*
Email: *healthal@aol.com*
Open: *Mon-Sat 9.30am-5pm;*
Tues early closing at 1pm
▶ Stocks wholefoods (many organic) vitamin and mineral supplements, herbal and homeopathic remedies, sports nutrition and aromatherapy oils. A food allergy testing service is available. Qualified nutritionist Yvonne Sharratt DN. This also available by appintment. Send for her self-help questionnaire. 'Prevention rather than Cure' is the store's aim.

Great Bear Trading Co Ltd
29 Rochdale Road,
Todmorden OL14 7LA
Tel: *01706 813 737*
Fax: *01706 819 492*
Open: *Mon, Weds-Fri 9.30am-5.30pm; Tues 9.30am-3.30pm;*
Sat 9am-5pm. Café closes 30 min earlier each day
▶ Workers co-operative established for over 20 years. Stocks a wide range of wholefoods, deli products, chilled and frozen vegetarian foods, and increasing amounts of fair trade produce. Also stocks alternative medicines, herbal and homeopathic remedies and vitamins and supplements. Cruelty-free bodycare and household cleaning products. There is a vegetarian café on the first floor and on the top floor alternative therapies are provided with a herbalist, counsellor and hypnotherapist.

Half Moon Wholefoods
14 Front Street,
Brampton CA8 1NG
Tel: *016977 3775*
▶ Sell a vast wholefood range including tahini, mollases, muesli, rice and pulses. Organic food wherever possible, such as porridge oats, tea, cereals and fruitbars.

Hazel Grove Nutrition Centre
307 London Road, Hazel Grove,
Stockport SK7 4PS
Tel: *0161 483 1576*
Open: *Mon, Tues, Thur, Fri*
9.30am-5pm

▶ Stocks herbal teas and fair trade coffees, dried products including herbs and cereals, jams and honeys, eco-friendly household products including a full range of Ecover products, vitamins and supplements, and essential oils. Small selection of books. Also a health centre on site.

Health Food Centre
113 Yorkshire Street,
Rochdale OL16 1DR
Tel: *01706 648 141*
▶ Stockists of dried organic foods, dried products including herbs, teas and coffees, vitamins and supplements, herbal medicine, aromatherapy oils and Ecover household products. Also a small selection of free magazines.

Health Food Centre
152 Deansgate,
Bolton BL1 1BB
Tel: *01204 525 084*
Open: *Mon-Fri 9am-5pm*
▶ Open for over 25 years, the Health Food Centre stocks one of the area's widest selections of vitamins and supplements – as well as a range of wholefoods, tea and coffee, cereals, frozen products, books and magazines. All staff hold certificates from the National Association of Health Stores. Mail order available.

Health Rack
92 Deansgate, Bolton BL1 2BD
Tel: *01204 380 660*
▶ Health products such as vitamins and supplements, alternative therapy remedies and aromatherapy oils and a selection of dried wholefood products. Mail order available.

Health & Vegetarian Store
33 Old Church Street,
Newton Heath, Manchester M40 2JN
Tel: *0161 683 4456*
Open: *Mon-Fri 10am-5pm;*
Sat 10am-4pm; closed Tue
▶ Organic vegetarian food, fruit and vegetables, homoeopathic and herbal remedies, Aloe Vera and collagen pills. A friendly atmosphere with on-hand advice for health problems. Also stocks Solgar and Bioforce products, chilled and frozen foods and special dietary foods. Operates a non-GM policy.

Great Bear Trading Co Ltd

29 Rochdale Road, Todmorden OL14 7LA
Tel: 01706 813 737   Fax: 01706 819 492

A workers' co-operative established for over 20 years, stocking a wide range of:

- wholefoods
- deli products
- chilled and frozen vegetarian foods
- fair trade produce
- alternative medicines
- herbal and homeopathic remedies
- vitamins and supplements.
- Cruelty-free bodycare and household cleaning products
- vegetarian café
- alternative therapies with a herbalist, counsellor and hypnotherapist.

Mon, Weds-Fri 9.30am-5.30pm; Tues 9.30am-3.30pm;
Sat 9am-5pm. Café closes 30 min earlier each day

Food & Drink

Healthy Herbs
11 Tatton Street, Knutsford WA16 6AB
Tel: 01565 755 022
Fax: 01565 822 502
▶ Although this shop stocks a wide range of wholefoods, its speciality is herbal remedies for which it manufactures its own herb-based skin care products. Also sells vitamins, supplements and homeopathic remedies.

High Street Wholefoods
8 High Street, New Mills,
High Peak SK22 4AL
Tel: 01663 743 669
▶ Stocks organic produce including vegetables, jams, honeys, pulses, beans, lentils, as well as some Traidcraft items. All products are vegetarian. Home delivery service available. Cookery evenings are occasionally held on the premises and a monthly newsletter is produced.

Holland & Barrett
Head Office, Samuel Rider House,
Townsend Drive, Attleborough,
Nuneaton CV11 6XW
Tel: 024 7624 4400
Fax: 024 7632 0135
▶ Europe's largest health food retailer, Holland and Barrett has been going for over 75 years. Offers a range of products including food supplements, dried wholefoods, beverages, natural remedies and beauty care products. Call the above number for details of your local branch.

Honeysuckle Health Foods
4 Hawthorn Lane, Wilmslow SK9 1AA
Tel: 01625 526 144
Fax: 01625 526 144
Open: Mon-Sat 9.30am-5.30pm
▶ Health food shop stocking vitamins, herbal products and homeopathic products. Also sells aromatherapy oils, a large range of toiletries, eco-friendly household products, teas and coffee, pulses and dried goods, and frozen foods. Some organic produce now on the shelves. Free magazines given to customers and the staff are always willing to give advice. Appointments necessary for the allergy specialist who visits once a month.

Jeans Health Foods
Market Hall, The Mall, Bury BL9 OBD
Tel: 0161 761 2145
Email: martin@jeanshf.fset.co.uk
Open: Mon-Sat 9am-5pm;
closed Tues
▶ Stockists of natural wholefoods including some organic items, and a range of quality vitamins and nutritional supplements.

Jeans Health Foods
Unit 2, Bolton Market, Ashburner Street, Bolton BL1 1TQ
Tel: 01204 366 287
Open: Mon-Sat 8.30am-5.30pm
▶ Stockists of natural wholefoods including some organic items, and a range of quality vitamins and nutritional supplements.

Just Sharing
30 Mersey Square,
Stockport SK1 1RA
Tel: 0161 480 0522
Open: Mon-Sat 9.30am-5.30pm
▶ Company based on the ethos of fair and equitable trading and is a member of BAFTS. Sells a wide range of crafts, clothing, handmade paper and food from commmunity businesses and co-ops in the Third World. Also stocks recycled, handmade paper products, aromatherapy oils and some crafts from co-ops in the UK.

Kan Foods
9 New Shambles, Kendal LA9 4TS
Tel: 01539 721 190
Fax: 01539 738 116
▶ Wholefood store selling a large range of organic foods including porridge oats, dried fruits and brown rice. Also vitamins and supplements, health books and Healing Herbs flower remedies (which are made using organic brandy). Runs an organic vegetable box scheme with a weekly pick-up arrangement.

Marple Health
72a Stockport Road, Marple,
Stockport SK6 6AB
Tel: 0161 427 5662
▶ Speciality breads, vegetarian cheeses and milks, a range of alternative remedies, own label vitamins and handsome selection of books.

Mawson's
16 Rochdale Road, Royton,
Oldham OL2 6QJ
Tel: 0161 626 0341
▶ Herbalist and health food store. Particular rare gem is the sasparilla cordial, originally produced to celebrate the 65th anniversary of the shop, but has remained a main product in-store.

Mossley Fine and Organic Foods
11-13 Arundel Street, Mossley,
Manchester OL5 0NY
Tel: 01457 837 743
Fax: 01457 837 743
Email: organics@
mossleyfoods.freeserve.co.uk
Open: Mon-Fri 9am-5.30pm;
Sat 9am-5pm
▶ Large wholefood shop with extensive range of fresh, dry and frozen foods and specialty foods. Large organic fruit and vegetable section, deli counter with organic cheeses, olives, etc. Organic wine range and an interesting choice of beers. Health supplements, books and refills for the Ecover range.

Natural Choice
24 St John Street,
Ashbourne DE6 1GH
Tel: 01335 346 096
Fax: 01335 346 096
Email: naturalchoice@lineone.net
Web:
www.naturalchoicehealth.co.uk
Open: Mon-Sat 9am-5pm
▶ Sells health foods, supplements, wide range of herbs and spices, New World music, recycled glassware, recycled paper, cosmetics, books. Caters for special diets, such as gluten-free and diabetic.

Natural Delivery
The Old Kings, Buxton Road,
Bakewell DE45 1DA
Tel: 01629 814 507
Fax: 01629 814 507
Open: Tues-Fri 9am-5pm;
Sat 9am-1pm
▶ Wholefood shop selling all the staples as well as herbs, etc. Organic box scheme on a weekly basis in Derbyshire and North Yorkshire.

Natures Best
74A Bryn Street, Ashton in Makerfield,
Wigan WN4 9AU
Tel: 01942 204 038
Open: Mon-Tues, Thurs-Sat 9am-5pm; Weds 9am-1pm
▶ Healthfood store selling vitamins, supplements, health foods, Bach remedies, essential oils and more.

Natures Grace
37 Barlow Moor Road, Didsbury,
Manchester M20 6TW
Tel: 0161 434 6784
Open: Mon-Fri 9am-5.45pm;
Sat 9am-5pm
▶ Small range of breads, pulses, cereals, tinned veg, tea and coffee, frozen products, Beauty Without Cruelty make up, household products and a range of vitamins and supplements and alternative remedies.

Oakcroft Organic Gardens
Cross O' Th' Hill, Malpas SY14 8DH
Tel: 01948 860 213
Open: Mon-Sun 8am-4.30pm
▶ Grows and sells organic vegetables and fruit and is registered with the Soil Association. Has been growing organically since 1962. Outlet to public at the garden, local farmers markets, Chester market, with boxes delivered to Chester, Nantwich, Northwich, Knutsford and places in between. Aims to work with nature and produce food to promote good health and vitality. Also stocks bought in organic fruit, veg, eggs, cheese, breads and other foods.

On The Eighth Day
107-111 Oxford Road, All Saints,
Manchester M1 7DU
Tel: 0161 273 4878
Fax: 0161 273 4878
Email: 8th-Day@eighthy.demon.co.uk
Web: www.eighthy.demon.co.uk
Open: Mon-Sat 9.30am-5.30pm
▶ Long-established workers co-operative (since 1976) running a vegetarian café and wholefood shop. Stocks an enormous range of vegetarian food from strictly wholefood products to the organic and exotic, arts and crafts, books and magazines, cruelty-free cosmetics and homeopathic and herbal medicines.

Food & Drink

Organix Healthfoods
Unit 6, Sevendale House,
7 Dale Street, Manchester M1 1JA
Tel: 0161 228 0220
Fax: 0161 228 0220
Open: Mon-Sat 9.30am-5.30pm
▶ One stop natural food shop stocking organic fruit and veg, bread, dairy produce, eco-friendly household products, wines and beer, and herbal remedies and flower essences. Also offers a wholesome veggie takeaway.

Queenswood Natural Foods
2 Robins Drive, Apple Business Park,
Bridgwater TA6 4DL
Tel: 01278 423 440
Fax: 01278 424 084
Email: sales@queenswoodfoods.co.uk
Web: www.queenswoodfoods.co.uk
Open: Mon-Sat 8am-5pm
▶ Supplies a wide range of organic wholefoods.

Ray Cornmell Organic Foods
459 Halliwell Road, Bolton BL1 8DE
Tel: 01204 846 844
Open: Organic Market if not open
▶ Farm shop offering a full range of organic produce including meat (dry-cured bacon and ham, sausages, beef burgers), dairy products, bread, and wholefoods. The produce can also be brought from the Organic Market at Altrincham on Thursdays (9am-4pm).

St Annes Wine Stores
3 St Annes Road,
Chorlton-Cum-Hardy, M21 8TA
Tel: 0161 881 3901
▶ Off licence selling wide range of organic wine and beer.

Stalybridge Health & Food Store
39 Market Hall, Albion Street,
Oldham OL1 3BG
Tel: 0161 624 3045
Fax: 0161 624 3045
Open: Mon-Sat 9am-5pm
▶ Established for 25 years, this health food shop stocks herbal and homeopathic remedies, dietary supplements, aromatherapy oils, Bach Flower remedies, body building products, in addition to a range of wholefoods and herbs.

Stalybridge Health & Food Store
Unit 107 Indoor Market Hall,
Ashton-under-Lyne OL6 6BZ
Tel: 0161 330 4447
Fax: 0161 330 4447
Open: Mon-Sat 9am-5pm
▶ Established for 25 years, this health food shop stocks herbal and homeopathic remedies, dietary supplements, aromatherapy oils, Bach Flower remedies, body building products, in addition to a range of wholefoods and herbs.

Stalybridge Health & Food Store
Unit 17 Indoor Market Hall,
Hyde SK14 2QT
Tel/Fax: 0161 366 6909
Open: Mon-Sat 9am-5pm
▶ Established for 25 years, this health food shop stocks herbal and homeopathic remedies, dietary supplements, aromatherapy oils, Bach Flower remedies, body building products, in addition to a range of wholefoods and herbs.

Sundance Wholefoods
33 Main Street, Keswick CA12 5BL
Tel: 017687 74712
▶ Wholefood store with an increasing range of organic food.

Swinton Health Foods
177 Moorside Road, Swinton,
Manchester M27 9LD
Tel: 0161 793 0091
Fax: 0161 728 6087
Open: Mon-Tues, Thurs-Sat 9am-5pm
▶ General health food store selling food items, essential oils, cosmetics, books, supplements and Homeopathy.

Taste Connection
76 Bridge Street,
Ramsbottom,
Bury BL0 9AG
Tel: 01706 822 175
Fax: 0176 821941 821 941
Email: tasteconnection@aol.com
Web: www.tasteconnection.com
▶ Organic and fine food specialists. Products include organic fresh fruit and vegetables, dairy, breads, grocery and household items. Specialities include an extensive range of only the highest quality olive oils and Balsamics (such as Nunez de Prado, Ravida, Colonna, etc). Also a Neal's Yard stockist carrying a full complement of their exclusive range. Also cheese, paté, meat and fish, chocolates (Green and Blacks, Michel Cruizel, Chocca Mocha), tea, coffee. Home delivery, mail order, gift hampers and corporate orders.

The Good Food Shop
2 Melbourne Street,
Stalybridge SK15 2JE
Tel: 0161 304 9225
Open: Mon-Sat 9.30am-5.30pm
▶ Stocks dried wholefoods, a range of organic products, and health products including homeopathic and herbal remedies and essential oils.

The Granary
108 Northgate Street,
Chester CH1 2HT
Tel: 01244 318 553
Fax: 01244 378 960
Email: cmq@clara.net
Web: www.granaryhealth.co.uk
Open: Mon-Sat 9am-5pm

▶ Part of a chain of six health food shops selling organic food, vegetarian diets, herbal remedies, vitamins, organic cleaners and more. Also supplies by mail order.

The Granary
20b Market Hall, Chester CH1 2HH
Tel: 01244 349 892
Fax: 01244 378 960
Email: cmq@clara.net
Web: www.granaryhealth.co.uk
Open: Mon-Sat 9am-5pm
▶ Part of a chain of six health food shops selling organic food, vegetarian diets, herbal remedies, vitamins, organic cleaners and more. Also supplies by mail order.

The Granary
11 Grange Road,
West Kirby CH48 4DY
Tel: 0151 625 0581
Fax: 01244 378 960
Email: cmq@clara.net
Web: www.granaryhealth.co.uk
Open: Mon-Sat 9am-5pm
▶ Part of a chain of six health food shops selling organic food, vegetarian diets, herbal remedies, vitamins, organic cleaners and more. Also supplies by mail order.

The Granary
2 Parkgate Road, Neston CH64 9XE
Tel: 0151 353 1331
Fax: 01244 375 960
Email: cmq@clara.net
Web: www.granaryhealth.co.uk
Open: Mon-Sat 9am-5pm
▶ Part of a chain of six health food shops selling organic food, vegetarian diets, herbal remedies, vitamins, organic cleaners and more. Also supplies by mail order.

The Granary
17 Pensby Road, Heswall CH6 07RA
Tel: 0151 342 7428
Fax: 01244 378960
Email: cmq@clara.net
Web: www.granaryhealth.co.uk
Open: Mon-Sat 9am-5pm
▶ Part of a chain of six health food shops selling organic food, vegetarian diets, herbal remedies, vitamins, organic cleaners and more. Also supplies by mail order.

Taste Connection

76 Bridge Street, Ramsbottom, Bury BL0 9AG
Tel: 01706 822 175   Fax: 0176 821941 821 941
tasteconnection@aol.com   www.tasteconnection.com

Organic and fine food specialists. Products include organic fresh fruit and vegetables, dairy, breads, grocery and household items. Specialities include an extensive range of only the highest quality olive oils and Balsamics (such as Nunez de Prado, Ravida, Colonna, etc). Also a Neal's Yard stockist carrying a full complement of their exclusive range. Also cheese, paté, meat and fish, chocolates (Green and Blacks, Michel Cruizel, Chocca Mocha), tea, coffee. Home delivery, mail order, gift hampers and corporate orders.

Food & Drink

The Granary
Kwiksave Mall, Woodchurch Road,
Prenton, Birkenhead CH42 8PG
Tel: 0151 608 0411
Fax: 01244 378 960
Email: cmq@clara.net
Web: www.granaryhealth.co.uk
Open: Mon-Sat 8.30am-6pm,
late opening Thurs, Fri until 8pm
▶ Part of a chain of six health food shops selling organic food, vegetarian diets, herbal remedies, vitamins, organic cleaners and more. Also supplies by mail order.

The Greenhouse
41 Oxford Road,
Altrincham WA14 2ED
Tel: 0161 928 4399
Open: Mon-Sat 9am-5pm
▶ Stockists of dried products including herbs, beans and pulses, jams and honey, teas and coffees, vitamins and supplements, herbal remedies, aromatherapy oils, and Ecover household products. Also a small selection of magazines.

The Laughing Lentil
10 King Edwards Buildings,
Bury Old Road, Salford M7 4QJ
Tel: 0161 740 5766
Open: Mon-Sat 10am-5.30pm;
Wed 10am-1.30pm
▶ Classic wholefood shop stocking dried and frozen foods, soya and dairy products, vegetarian/vegan foods, a wide range of vitamins and supplements, essential oils, biochemic tissue salts, and Bach flower remedies.

Unicorn Grocery
89 Albany Road, Chorlton-cum-Hardy, Manchester M21 0BN
Tel: 0161 861 0010
Fax: 0161 861 7675
Email: office@unicorn-grocery.co.uk
Web: www.unicorn-grocery.co.uk
Open: Tues-Weds, Sat 9.30am-6pm;
Thurs-Fri 9.30am-7pm;
Sun 11am-5pm
As retailers of organic food which has undergone a minimum amount of processing and household goods of non-animal origin, Unicorn is committed to fair trade and to a sustainable world environment and economy. Also aims to provide secure employment for members, to offer equal opportunities to all and to reserve employment for people with learning disabilities. Unicorn supports like-minded projects and has set up a community fund to which it commits 1% of wage costs.

Village Health Food Store
47 Church Street, Eccles,
Manchester M30 0BJ
Tel: 0161 788 9745
Open: Mon-Tues, Thurs-Sat
9am-5pm; Weds 9am-3pm
▶ Stockists of a wide range of vegetarian, vegan and gluten-free products, and food for diabetics.

Wild Carrot
Bridge Street Workers Co-op,
5 Bridge Street, Buxton
Tel: 01298 22843
Email: wildcarr@globalnet.co.uk
Web:
www.users.globalnet.co.uk/~wildcarr
▶ Wholefood shop run by a workers co-operative.

Windmill Wholefoods
337 Smithdown Road, Wavertree,
Liverpool Ll5 3JJ
Tel: 0151 734 1919
Email:
windmill@windmill.abelgratis.co.uk
Web:
www.merseyworld.com/windmill
Open: Mon, Weds, Fri 9:30am-6pm;
Tues 9:30am-1:30pm; Thurs 9:30am-7:30pm; Sat 9:30am-5:30pm
▶ A workers co-operative that provides a local source of vegetarian and vegan organic wholefoods, and aims to ensure that all its products are GM-free. Sells a wide range of wholefoods, organic and non-organic, household products, organic fruit and vegetables, organic wines and beer (guaranteed vegan) and fair trade products such as coffee, tea and chocolate. Also a recycling point for shoes and aluminium cans.

Withington Healthfoods
486-488 Wilmslow Road,
Withington, Manchester M20 3BG
Tel: 0161 445 6696
Email: vitaminuk@aol.com
Open: Mon-Sat 9am-6pm
▶ Good selection of health foods, vitamins, aromatherapy oils, herbal and homeopathic remedies. Special ordering service for obtaining obscure products if required. Resident qualified herbalist, acupuncturist and reflexologist on hand to advise. Mail order service available.

Organic Meat

Bank House Farm
Silverdale, Carnforth LA5 0RE
Tel: 01524 701 280
Email: cath@
bankhousefarm.freeserve.co.uk
▶ Sells organic beef and lamb, wool and rugs.

Lodge Farm
Kirk Langley, Asbourne DE6 4NX
Tel: 01332 824 815/ 207
Email: organic@
meynell-langley.co.uk
Open: Fri 1pm-6.30pm; Sat 10am-2pm; or by arrangement
▶ Produces organic meat, beef, lamb, chicken, vegetables, and eggs. Sold in farm shop direct to the public. Call for a leaflet.

Markets

Colne Farmer's Market
The Adapt Growing Business Project,
Pendle Business Centre,
Commercial Road, Nelson BB9 9BT
Tel: 01282 661 676
Web: www.growbusiness.cjb.net
▶ Operates within the National Association of Farmers Markets criteria.

Knutsford Farmers Market
c/o Cheshire County Council, Room 251, County Hall, Chester CH1 1SF
Tel: 01244 603 373
Fax: 01244 603 003
Email: bowenjonesg@cheshire.gov.uk
▶ Knutsford Farmers Market, based in Silk Mill Street, helps to provide local small scale producers and processors with a forum in which to sell direct to the consumer. It is held on the first Saturday of every month and consumers can buy many things from ostrich meat and local pork, to wine and cheese. It provides a way for consumers to help ensure the sustainability of their local farming community whilst buying fresh and local produce.

Nantwich Farmers Market
Nantwich Town Square, Nantwich
Tel: 01270 537 424
Fax: 01270 537 758
Email: env.health@
crewe-nantwich.gov.uk
Web: www.crewe-nanatwich.gov.uk
Open: Last Saturday of every month from 9am
▶ Contact the Environmental Health Administration Section of Crewe and Nantwich Borough Council for more information.

WI Country Markets Ltd.
183a Oxford Road, Reading RG1 7XA
Tel: 0118 939 4646
Fax: 0118 939 4747
Email: info@wimarkets.co.uk
Web: www.wimarkets.co.uk
▶ A network of market stalls held in over 500 towns throughout England, Wales and Chanel Islands selling locally produced baked goods, hand crafted and home grown produce. WI markets are truly co-operative and

---

UNICORN GROCERY
MANCHESTER'S WHOLESOME FOODSTORE

THE FRESH, FAIR AND ORGANIC
ALTERNATIVE TO THE SUPERMARKET

Fast Food Idea no. 106: Bored with jam & toast? Try spreading margarine & yeast extract on your toast then spread a little tahini on top and pop back under the grill for a few seconds, scrummy!

Runners up of Natural Products Large Retailer Of
The Year 2000, we specialise in good food & drink at
decent prices, simple!

Visit us at 89 Albany Road, Chorlton, Manchester, M21 0BN.
T. 0161 861 0010 www.unicorn-grocery.co.uk
Unicorn is a workers co-operative.

welcome producers over the age of 16. Visit the website to find out where your local WI market is held. You can also send a parcel of home made produce through the WI Markets Parcel Scheme – call 0118 939 4646.

Organic Supermarkets

Out of this World
Head Office, 106 High Street, Gosforth, Newcastle NE3 1HB
Tel: 0191 213 5377
Fax: 0191 213 5378
Email: info@ootw.co.uk
Web: www.ootw.co.uk
▶ National consumer co-op with 18,000 members which launched the first National high street chain of ethical supermarkets. Shops currently in Cheltenham, Nottingham and Newcastle. The 4,000 products on offer are chosen for their contribution to healthy eating, fair trade, environmental sustainablity, animal welfare and community development. Members receive a magazine three times per year, and can buy shares in the company Call for more information and mail order catalogue.

Supermarkets

Asda Stores Ltd
Asda House, Southbank, Great Wilson Street, Leeds OS11 5AD
Tel:
Customer Careline: 0500 100 055
Fax: 0113 241 8666
Web: www.asda.co.uk
▶ Stocks a range of 400 organic items, including fruit and vegetables and some dried products which include some of the eco-friendly food names usually found in health food shops. Meridian Spanish extra virgin olive oil is available, as is Cranks wholemeal bread, Doves Farm flapjacks, Ridgeways teabags, Percol & Clipper organic coffee, Hipp baby foods and Green & Blacks Maya Gold milk chocolate. Uses British suppliers wherever possible.

Booths Supermarkets
4 Fishergate, Preston PR1 3LJ
Tel: 01772 251 701
Fax: 01772 255 669

Email:
mlough@booths-supermarkets.co.uk
Web:
www.booths-supermarkets.co.uk
▶ Offers a complete range of Organic foods throughout its stores in the North West of England. The largest supporter of real food and drink with an emphasis on regional suppliers Booths quality is recognised throughout the country.

Co-operative Stores
Sandbrook Park, Sandbrook Way, Rochdale OS11 1Sa
Tel: 0161 834 1212
▶ Commited to making organics more affordable and accessible, by increasing availability of organic products in all its 1100 stores- at superstore prices. The range features over 200 branded and own label products. In addition, Co-op are price matching on selected organic lines with the equivalent standard product. This is an attempt to offer customers the choice to buy organic, without the issues of price and availability.

J Sainsbury plc
Stamford House, Stamford Street, London SE1 9LL
Tel:
Customer Careline: 0800 636 262
Fax: 020 7695 0156
▶ Sainsbury's supports the development of the organic industry through the Sainsbury's Organic Resourcing Club (SOuRCe) which aims to develop the organic trade, especially through new products that appeal to consumers who might not otherwise consider buying organic. Sainsbury's Transitional supports the process of converting to fully-certified organic production and labels products from transitional suppliers as such. Works closely with suppliers and organisations like the Soil Association. It was the first to sell in-store organic baked bread, bananas, ready meals, sandwiches and own-label chocolate ice cream; its organic range is comprehensive and growing all the time – though sometimes short on the shelf at the end of the day. Look for bread, meat, dairy produce, fruit and veg as well as baby food, biscuits, breakfast cereals, chocolate, dried fruit and pulses, fresh soups, frozen vegetables, herbs and spices and drinks.

Marks & Spencer
Michael House, Baker Street, London W1A 1DN
Tel: 020 7268 1234
(Food Customer Services)
Fax: 020 7487 2675
Web: www.marksandspencer.co.uk
▶ Currently launching a major expansion of its organic foods with an exclusive range of organic ready meals. Includes organic shepherd's pie and macaroni cheese, as well as soups, pizzas and chicken dishes. After withdrawing their organic ranges of fruit and vegetables in 1993 due to lack of customer demand, Marks & Spencer re-entered the organic market in 1998. The organic range is available in 150 stores nationwide, and all ingredients in these ranges are naturally produced using farming methods developed to protect and enhance the environment, and all dairy products are sourced from suppliers that adhere to Marks & Spencer's strict standards of animal welfare. To qualify for organic accreditation, producers must undergo a two-three year monitoring process, which is carried out by the Soil Association to ensure that the land meets organic standards and contains no chemicals and pesticides.

Safeway
6 Millington Road, Hayes UB3 4AY
Tel:
Customer enquiries: 01622 712 000
▶ In 1981 Safeway were the first major UK supermarket to offer organic foods to its customers. Since then, they have been supportive of organic agriculture and now offer a growing range of organic food and drink which meets demand and offers all customers a choice. All organic products sold at its stores are accredited with the Soil Association or another regulatory body. At the end of 1999, Safeway completed a process of removing all GM ingredients and derivatives from its own brand products. This process included items that did not require labelling under EU regulations.

Somerfield Stores Ltd
Somerfield House, Whitchurch Lane, Bristol BS14 1TJ
Tel: 0117 935 6669
Fax: 0117 935 6566
Web: www.somerfield.co.uk
▶ Somerfield has expanded its range of organics to include almost 350 food and drink products including dog and cat food. Aims to offer shoppers a choice of organic alternatives to conventional foods. Size of range varies from store to store depending on local demand. In some stores large portions of the range is locally sourced, thereby satisfying the need for both organic and local products. Constantly reviewing the range to try to exapnd the organic option to as many products as possible. Customer suggestions welcome instore, or via website.

Tesco Stores Ltd
Tesco House, P O Box 18, Delamare Road, Cheshunt EN8 9SL
Tel: 0800 505 555
▶ By April 1999, Tesco had expanded its organic range to include over 350 products – fruit, vegetables, meat and bread, baby foods, groceries, beer, wine and desserts. These products are available in 200 stores throughout the UK. All other stores will feature a core range of 50 lines including fruit and vegetables, dairy and eggs, meat and poultry, grocery and store cupboard products, beers and wines.

Waitrose
Customer Services,
Waitrose Limited, Doncaster Road, Bracknell RG12 8YA
Tel:
Customer Service: 0800 188 884
Web: www.waitrose.co.uk
▶ Waitrose won the Organic Supermarket of the Year Award in 1998 and again in 1999. Organic products include groceries, breads and cakes, beers, wine, ciders and cordials, dairy products, meat, frozen foods, baby foods and delicatessen. Some products are only available in larger branches. All items are subject to availability. Waitrose took on Charlotte Mitchell, ex-Chair of the

Soil Association, as its organic consultant to ensure that their range is as comprehensive as possible, to seek out the best organic suppliers and to be a source of advice for those considering converting to organic production. With regards to GMOs, Waitrose do not sell any genetically modified foods as such and its own label foods do not contain any genetically modified ingredients. Additives which may contain traces of GMO will be labelled.

WHOLESALERS & DISTRUBUTORS

Some of the companies listed in this section will also supply directly to the public via mail order.

Bewley's Tea & Coffee
9/10 Raynham Road,
Bishop's Stortford CM23 5PB
Tel: 01279 466 100
Fax: 01279 657 707
Email: tea&coffee@bewley's.co.uk
Open: Mon-Fri 9am-5.30pm
▶ Offers national Distribution. By holding stocks in over 60 locations throughout the UK, Bewley's provide a local service to the catering trade. Supply pour & serve machines and branded flasks. Phone for closest supplier.

Big Oz Industries Ltd
Unit 30, Rainbow Industrial Estate,
Trent Road, West Drayton UB9 7XT
Tel: 01895 445 896
Fax: 01895 434 845
Email: enquiries@bigoz.co.uk
Web: www.bigoz.co.uk
Open: Mon-Fri 9am-5.30pm
▶ Specialises in organic produce from Australia, currently importing seven different kinds of organic puffed breakfast cereals which are all 100% natural, with nothing added to them. Four are suitable for gluten free diets. Also imports Australiana, an organic soft fruit drink available in four flavours – wild lime, wild lemon, wild berry and wild fruit. Sells wholesale and retail.

Brilliant Bread Company, The
Unit 3, Hope Enterprise Centre,
Scot Lane,
Wigan WN5 OPN
Tel: 01942 768 803
Fax: 01942 208 801
▶ Wholesaler of additive-free, preservative-free, wholly organic bread and bread-based products including baps, pizza bases, herb loaves, mini baguettes, and cheese wheels. Wholemeal, white, rye and soda (both wheat-free) and granary breads available. Bread can be made to order for next day collection.

Cedar Health Ltd
Pepper Road, Bramhall Moor Lane,
Hazel Grove, Stockport SK7 5BW
Tel: 0161 483 1235
Fax: 0161 456 4321
Email: cedarhealth@compuserve.com
▶ Supplies organic fruit and vegetable juices from Switzerland.

Choice Organics
Unit 2, Bridges Wharf, Bridges Court
(off York Road), London SW11 3QS
Tel: 020 7924 1700
Fax: 020 7924 1330
▶ Wholesaler of organic fruit and veg and UK and imported products. Certified as organic traders under the Organic Farmers and Growers Certification Scheme.

Crazy Jack
Community Foods, Micross,
Brent Terrace, London NW2 1LT
Tel: 020 8450 9411
Fax: 020 8208 1803
Email: enquiries@communityfoods.co.uk
Web: www.communityfoods.co.uk

▶ Crazy Jack (from Community Foods) is becoming one of the established brands for organic staple foods. This quality range of organic dried fruit, nuts, seeds, grains, pulses and flakes, with its distinctive packaging, highlights the 'new' world of organic foods. Although the name is new, the team behind the brand has decades of experience. Community Foods has pioneered natural and organic wholefoods since the early 1970's and is a leading supplier to health stores and supermarkets. A sophisticated trading operation sources and supplies a large range of organic foods worldwide and the company has acquired a reputation for commercial integrity and marketing of high quality goods. As part of the Good Food Foundation, an environment-friendly organisation dedicated to the advancement of organic agriculture, they help small producers to convert or set-up organic projects and also guarantee markets. An in-house Quality Assurance Department with a fully-equipped analytical laboratory

facility monitors incoming consignments, which enables Community to set standards and to identify and quickly resolve quality problems. Community also handles other brands, including Sanchi Japanese foods, Orgran gluten-free foods and Nature's Path organic breakfast cereals, amongst others. Email or call for more information.

Essential Trading Co-operative
Unit 3, Lodge Causeway Trading Estate, Fishponds, Bristol BS16 3JB
Tel: 0117 958 3550
Fax: 0117 958 3551
Email: soles@essential-trading.co.uk
Web: www.essential-trading.co.uk
Open: Mon-Fri 9am-5.30pm
▶ The largest workers' co-operative in south Britain and a natural foods wholesaler supplying the independent retail sector with over 1,000 vegetarian and vegan foods. As well as being national leaders in sourcing and supplying organic foods from both the UK and abroad, Essential is part of the lobby group Genetic Food Alert, campaigning against the reckless introduction of GMOs into the food chain. The Essential brand is guaranteed free of GMOs and suppliers are continually vetted to ensure that everything supplied is also GMO-free. Free trade catalogue available.

Infinity Foods Co-operative Ltd
67 Norway Street, Portslade, Brighton BN41 1AE
Tel: 01273 424 060
Fax: 01273 417 739

Email: petercowl@virgin.net
Open: Mon-Fri 9am-5pm
▶ Began as small wholefood shop in Brighton in 1970. Now a major supplier of organic and whole foods with over 4,000 lines and an efficient national delivery service. Carries one of the most extensive selection of organically grown foods available, especially dried foods. All have the Soil Association symbol. Their shop has expanded and includes a wholegrain bakery and cash-and-carry.

Nature's Own
Unit 8, Hanley Workshops, Hanley Road, Hanley Swan WR8 ODX
Tel: 01684 310 022
Fax: 01684 312 022
▶ Supplier of the unique range of food store supplements. Available directly or from shops and wholesalers.

Nordex Foods UK Ltd
Wynchfield House, Kingscote, Near Tetbury GL8 8YN
Tel: 01666 890 500
Fax: 01666 890 522
Email: dairyland@nordex-food.co.uk
Web: www.nordex-food.co.uk
▶ Major supplier of continental organic cheeses and dairy products sourced fron their land of origin to capture the true authenticity and flavour. Supplies over 50 types of organic cheeses from Europe to the UK via retailers, manufacturers and wholesalers. Includes the renowned and recommended Dairyland Organic Range. Cheeses include cheddar, Edam, Feta, Mozarella and Parmesan. Other products include butter, children's yoghurts, quark desserts and more. Winners of the Best Large Stand Award 2000 at the Natural Products Exhibition. Eye-catching range with attractive, simple packaging.

Organic Food Company, The
Unit 2 Blacknest Industrial Estate, Nr Alton GU34 4PX
Tel: 01420 520 530
Fax: 01420 23985
Email: sarah@tofc.co.uk
Web: www.tofc.co.uk
Open: Wed-Fri 10am-4pm
▶ Supplies organic foods (wholesale and retail) including vegetable juices, baby food, nappies, baby cosmetics, cold-pressed oils (culinary and cosmetic) biscuits, fruit bars, sauces, spreads. Mail order available.

Organic Warehouse Ltd
Bank Farm, Seland Road, Chester CH1 6BS
Tel: 01244 390 945
Fax: 01244 370 717
Email: www.kwikfruit.co.uk
▶ Wholesale and distributor of organic products.

Organico
SDF Limited, 63 High Street, London N8 7QB
Tel: 020 8340 0401
Fax: 020 8340 0402
Email: info@organico.co.uk
Web: www.organico.co.uk
Open: Mon-Fri 9am-6pm
▶ Committed to importing only high quality organic products and brands which do not contain cheap and unnecessary ingredients or additives, even if allowed under organic regulations. Works with dedicated organic suppliers and retailers. Brands include Babynat, Vitalia, Biosun, Naté, Sucanat, Moulin de Valdonne. Soto Tofu and Terra Verde. Visit the website for latest developments and further information.

Rainbow Wholefoods
21 White Lodge Estate, Hall Road, Norwich NR4 6DG
Tel: 01603 630 484
Fax: 01603 664 066
Email: info@rainbowwholefoods.co.uk
Web: www.rainbowwholefoods.co.uk
▶ Offers entire range of wholefoods, mainly organic and all GMO free. Includes Hipp and Baby Organix, as well as the formula products Nanny, Babynat and the Kingfisher range of natural toothpastes.

Ridgway's Fairtrade Teas
75 Wilton Road, Victoria, London SW1V 1DE
Tel: 020 7233 8400
Fax: 020 7233 8422
▶ Wholesaler of fair trade tea (some of which is organic) with the Fairtrade Foundation mark of approval. On sale in major supermarkets.

Thames Organic Produce
Sheerness Produce Terminal, Spade Lane, Sittingbourne ME9 7TT
Tel: 01634 269 202
Fax: 01634 269 269
Email: S.Bilecki@thamesfruit.co.uk
Web: www.teresagroup.com
Open: Mon-Fri 7.30am-6.30pm; Sun 8am-1pm
▶ Growers, importers and packers of a wide range of high quality fresh produce. Suppliers to wholesalers, retailers, processors and box schemes.

Tropical Wholefoods
Unit 9, Hamilton Road Industrial Estate, West Norwood, London SE27 9SF
Tel: 020 8670 1114
Fax: 020 8670 1117
Email: tropicalwf@aol.com
Web: www.wholefood.co.uk/tropical.htm
▶ Small wholesale company importing and processing 100% fairly traded, sun-dried fruit and vegetables, produced with absolutely no additives. Heavily involved in the establishment and running of solar fruit-drying projects in Uganda, Burkina Faso, Pakistan and Tanzania. Winners of the 1998 World Vision Award for individual development initiative, and the 2000 National Westminster/ Directory of Social Change Enterprising Solutions Award.

Wholebake Ltd
Tyn Y Llidiart Industrial Estate, Corwen LL21 9RR
Tel: 01490 412 297
Fax: 01490 412 053

INFINITY FOODS

- Over 4,000 lines – many organic
- Full range of commodities and branded goods – gluten-free, Fair Trade, etc
- Full range of Infinity Label pre-packed commodities
- Efficient national delivery service
- Ring for a catalogue today!

Tel: 01273 424060 • Fax: 01273 417739
67 Norway Street Portslade East Sussex BN4 1AE

Food & Drink 31

Email: wholebake@aol.com
Web: www.wholebake.co.uk
▶ Manufacturers of flapjacks, cereal bars and hempseed snack bars, using all natural ingredients. All are suitable for vegetarians and vegans and eight varieties are organic. Deals only with the wholesale trade.

Yerba Mate
Swan House, 69-71 Windmill Road, Sunbury on Thames TW16 7DT
Tel: 01932 710 888
Fax: 01932 710 889
Email: alex@storacall.co.uk
▶ Distributes the Taragui brand of Mexican herbal drinks and is the sole importer for UK and Ireland.

BRANDS & MANUFACTURERS

Aspall
The Cyder House, Aspall Hall, Stowmarket IP14 6PD
Tel: 01728 860 510
Fax: 01728 861 031
Email: info@aspall.co.uk
Web: www.aspall.co.uk
▶ Established in 1728. Since 1947 Aspall's orchards have been grown and managed to organic standards. Certified by the Soil Association, produces organic apple juice, cider vinegar, balsamic vinegar, white and red wine vinegar. All products are made using the juice of whole fruit to ensure that maximum flavour and aroma can be found in the bottle. To maintain this quality their products are free from concentrates and artificial flavourings. Their Cyder Vinegar was an award-winner at the 1998 Mail on Sunday 'You' Organic Food Awards. Eight generations of the family have been making cider for 272 years without compromising quality for price. Available in local health food stores and supermarkets.

Authentic Bread Company, The
Strawberry Hill Farm, Strawberry Hill, Newent GL18 1LR
Tel: 01531 890 348
Fax: 01531 890 348
▶ Formed in 1995 by a keen, self-taught baker with the aim to return the taste, texture and variety to bread, which has diminished in the last 30 years. After only a year in business, they won their category at the Soil Association Good Food Awards with their Olive Bread. Subsequently, they have gone on to achieve a Highly Commended Award at the 1998 Good Food Awards for their mixed Seed Bread. Natural fermentation techniques are used instead of improvers which, combined with an unerring commitment to use only organic ingredients of the highest standard, creates a flavour which is second to none. Presently has a range of 30 types of bakery products, suitable for a variety of special dietry needs, with new products being produced on a regular basis. All products are registered with the Soil Association.

Booja Booja Company, The
Hall Farm, Bungay Road, Hempnall NR15 2LJ
Tel: 01508 499 049
Fax: 01508 498 770
▶ Manufacturer of delicious organic and dairy-free chocolates. Winner of Soil Association 'Best organic snack and confectionary product'. Certified with the Soil Association and Vegan Society. Also gluten and wheat free. Available in most fine food stores and wholefood shops throughout the UK.

Billington Food Group
Cunard Building, Liverpool L3 1EL
Tel: 0151 236 2265
Fax: 0151 236 2493
Email: billmail@billingtons.cybase.co.uk
Web: www.billingtons.co.uk
▶ Produces unrefined organic sugar cane.

Brewhurst Health Food Supplies Ltd
Abbot Close,
Oyster Lane,
Byfleet KT14 7JP
Tel: 01932 334 501
Fax: 01932 336 235
Email: info@brewhurst.com
Web: www.brewhurst.com
▶ Supplies the Evernat range of organic produce and the Ephytem herbal hayfever remedy. Also supplies the Healthrite range of foods.

Cafédirect Ltd
66 Clifton Street,
London EC2A 4HB
Tel: 020 7422 0730
Fax: 020 7422 0731
▶ Cafédirect is one of the few fair trade coffee producers supplying supermarkets as well as independent retailers. It now supplies a range of fair trade teas in addition to its roast, ground and freeze dried instant coffees.

the Authentic Bread Company

Strawberry Hill, Newent, Glos, GL18 1LH
Proprietors: A.K. & J.T. Davis
Tel 01531 828181
Fax 01531 828151

Bakers of Award Winning Speciality Organic Bread and Cakes

*Mail Order Available
Wholesale Enquiries Welcome*

Clearspring Ltd
19A Acton Park Estate,
London W3 7QE
Tel: 020 8749 1781
Fax: 020 8811 8893
Email: info@clearspring.co.uk
Open: Mon-Fri 8.30am-5.30pm
▶ The company's chairman, Christopher Dawson, has searched the world for 20 years for foods that meet the highest standards of taste and quality. Offers the most extensive certified organic Japanese products available in the UK as well as a comprehensive range of products including food ingredients, ready-made meals, savoury and sweet snacks, beverages and more. Clearspring is committed to supplying foods without the use of GMOs, chemical fertilisers, animal manure, pesticides or herbicides.

Clipper Teas Ltd
Beaminster Business Park,
Broadwindsor Road,
Beaminster DT8 3PR
Tel: 01308 863 344
Fax: 01308 863 847
Email: enquiries@clipper-teas.com
Web: www.clipper-teas.com
Open: Mon-Fri 9am-5pm
▶ A family owned, specialist tea company with a passion for fine teas and coffees. Having achieved 12 Food Awards, Clipper stretches the boundaries of tea innovation to provide delicious, natural teas and coffees that not only taste great but care for the environment, the people who produce it and the customer's health. Is an ethical company and by taking a fresh approach to tea, has achieved a world-wide reputation for supplying natural, great tasting products. The only tea company in the last 30 years to break into the mainstream market in the UK and the first tea company in the world to be awarded The Fairtrade Mark. Clipper guarantees high quality teas and coffees sourced from producers who implement comprehensive welfare and environmental policies, with particular emphasis on better trading relations.

Dove's Farm Foods
Salisbury Road, Hungerford RG17 0RF
Tel: 01488 684 880
Fax: 01488 685 235
Email: mail@dovesfarm.co.uk
▶ Supplier of organic flours including Spelt flour which is milled from an ancient variety of wheat that is low in gluten and has a nutty flavour. Available from most wholefood shops and major supermarkets.

Duchy Originals
Ambassadors Court,
St James's Palace,
London SW1A 1BS
Tel: 020 7930 4516
Fax: 020 7930 4645
Email: office@duchyoriginals.com
▶ Established by HRH The Prince of Wales to promote organic food and farming and raise funds for The Prince of Wales' Charitable Foundation. Produces a range of organic foods under licence including biscuits, preserves, chocolates, bread, bacon, and a soft drink called Lemon Refresher.

Eco-Zone Ltd
12 Snarsgate Street,
London W10 6QP
Tel: 020 8962 6399
Fax: 020 8962 6399
Email: vagniez@btinternet.com
Web: www.ecozseaweed.co.uk
▶ Sells both fresh and dry seaweed and a range of innovative seaweed based products. Seaweed is a natural condiment, it's very easy to use and will bring flavour and health to many dishes. Works in close partnership with seaweed producers, with regular testing on site and in the laboratory. Supplies distributors, delicatessens, and restaurants. Also available by mail order.

Equal Exchange Trading Ltd
10a Queensferry Street,
Edinburgh EH2 4PG
Tel: 0131 220 3484
Fax: 0131 220 3565
Email: judith@equalexchange.co.uk
▶ Fair trade company supplying high quality food and beverages sourced from small-scale farmers who receive a fair return for their labour. Communities benefit from the greater economic security and improved health and education that long term fair trading relationships bring. Range of organic and fair trade produce includes coffee, tea, cocoa, sugar, honey, nut butters, tahini and confectionery. Available in wholefood stores or by mail order. Call for more info.

Everfresh Natural Foods
Gatehouse Close,
Aylesbury HP19 8DE
Tel: 01296 425 333
Fax: 01296 422 545
Email: sunnyvaleo@aol.com
▶ Organic bread and cakes.

Fir Tree Farm Food Processing Ltd
1 Chapel Street, Wigan WN3 4EG
Tel: 01942 826 618
Fax: 01942 700 188
Open: Mon-Sat 8am-4pm
▶ Organic and non-organic vegetable processing company. Registered with the Soil Association.

First Quality Foods
Unit 29 The Beeches, Yate,
Bristol BS37 5QX
Tel: 01454 880 044
Fax: 01454 853 355
▶ Manufacturers and distributors of organic fine foods. Brands include Sammy's range of flavoured couscous and polenta in retail and food service sizes, the popular range of Ma Baker Giant Bars available in 16 different fruit and nut flavours which are wheat free, vegetarian and vegan and the new organic bars in apple, apricot and orange flavours. All products are vegetarian, mainly vegan and the polenta is also gluten free. All organic products certified by The Organic Food Federation. Stockists include Asda, Safeway, all good health food shops and for mail order, call on 0700 9000 222.

FZ Organic Food
7 Church Street, Kenton,
Exeter EX6 8LU
Tel: 01626 890 635
Fax: 01626 891 683
Email: kwhidden@fzorganicfood.com
▶ A Dutch-based manufacturer and distributor of organic products, founded in the early 1980s. As well as producing and packing many own label products for major players in the European natural food market, FZ also produce a wide range of branded goods including the Bionova range of dressings, jams, squashes and soups; the Tra'fo range of crisps, tortilla chips and snacks; the Yakso range of Japanese products; and Frans Andringa cheese. Available only to the natural food market, and guaranteed organic, GM-free and vegetarian, with much of the range being vegan.

Gala Coffee & Tea Ltd
Mill House, Riverside Way,
Dartford DA1 5BS
Tel: 01322 272 411
Fax: 01322 278 600
Email: gala@gala-coffee-tea.co.uk
▶ A mixed blend of organically grown fresh ground coffee widely stocked in supermarkets.

George Skoulikas Ltd
Unit 5, 998 North Circular Road,
Coles Green Road, London NW2 7JR
Tel: 020 8452 8465
Fax: 020 8452 8273
Open: Mon-Fri 8.30am-4.30pm
▶ Imports a premium range of organic foods from the Mediterranean under the 'Sunita' brand, including extra-virgin olive oil from Greece and Spain, succulent olives available either whole, pitted or stuffed, lemon and orange juice squeezed from fresh Sicilian fruits, sundried tomatoes in halves or dice, capers in salt, halva and sesame bars sweetened only with honey, tahini paste for spreads, dips and dressings, and ready to eat polenta.

Get Real Organic Foods
Shotton Farm, Harmer Hill,
Shrewsbury SY4 3DN
Tel: 01939 290 925
Fax: 01939 210 925
Email: info@get-real.co.uk
Web: www.get-real.co.uk
Open: Tues-Thurs 9am-5pm
▶ With the slogan 'Bringing the Pie into the 21st Century', produces organic meat and vegetable pies which are available from the freezer

Food & Drink

compartment in Waitrose and health food stores.

Gluten Free Foods Ltd
Unit 270, Centennial Park,
Centennial Avenue,
Elstree WD6 355
Tel: 020 8953 4444
Fax: 020 8953 8285
Email: info@glutenfree-foods.co.uk
▶ Offers a range of wheat-free, gluten free, milk-free, egg-free, soya-free and GMO-free pasta. For children has animal shaped pasta.

Goodlife Foods Ltd
35 Tatton Court,
Warrington WA1 4FF
Tel: 01925 837 810
Fax: 01925 838 648
Email: enquiry@goodlife.co.uk
Web: www.goodlife.co.uk
Open: Mon-Sat 9am-5pm
▶ Specialist manufacturer of vegetarian frozen foods in the UK. Aim to make wholesome, natural, tasty products for discerning customers. Range includes nut cutlets, nut burgers, falafel, and cauliflower cheese grills. Range of organic frozen foods has been recently introduced. All foods are free from genetically modified ingredients.

Gordon's Fine Foods
Gordon House,
Littlemead Industrial Estate,
Alfold Road, Cranleigh GU6 8ND
Tel: 01483 267 707
Fax: 01483 267 783
Email: gordonspot@aol.com
▶ Producers of organic and natural mustards, chutney, sauces, and jellies. All products are licensed by the Soil Association and are produced to the highest production standards.

Granose Foods
Howard Way,
Newport Pagnell MR16 9PY
Tel: 01908 211 311
Fax: 01908 613 242
Email: rowntree@haldanefoods.co.uk
▶ One of the UK's oldest food brands, suitable for vegetarian and/or vegan diets or those looking for an alternative to dairy products.

Green & Black's
c/o Whole EarthFoods Ltd,
2 Valentine Place, London SE1 8QH
Tel: 020 7633 5900
Fax: 020 7633 5901
Email: clunyb@wholeearthfoods.co.uk
Web: www.wholeearthfoods.com
▶ Award-winning, quality organic chocolate combining the highest environmental and ethical standards. Their delicious range of organic chocolate products include chocolate bars, hot chocolate, cocoa, ice cream, chocolate-covered almonds and chocolate hazelnut spread. All products are certified by the Soil Association.

Hampstead Tea & Coffee Company Ltd
PO Box 2448, London NW11 7DR
Tel: 020 8731 9833
Fax: 020 8458 3547
▶ Organic and fair trade tea

Heath & Heather
Premier Brands, PO Box 8,
Moreton, Wirral L46 8XF
Tel: 0151 522 4000
Fax: 0151 522 4020
▶ Fruit and herb teas made with only the finest ingredients each bursting with the pure taste and goodness of nature. All teas in the Heath and Heather range are 100% natural and contain no added sugars, flavours and preservatives and are caffeine free. Enjoy classic fruit and herb combinations like Blackcurrant & Fennel or mouthwatering fruit or herb teas such as Wild Raspberry or Rosehip. Alternatively try the new speciality teas – Green Tea and Rooibos Tea. Believes in maintaining and promoting a better environment. This belief is reflected not only in its use of natural ingredients but also in its packaging, which is sourced from sustainable forestry. Available from all good health stores.

Hemp Food Corporation, The
Healthcross House, Cross Street,
Syston, Leicester Le7 2JG
Tel: 0116 260 2992
Fax: 0116 269 3106
Email: david.revitt@talk21.com
Web: www.hemp-food.co.uk

▶ Taken over by Shepherdboy Ltd in 1999. The range includes: the 'Hempower' Fruit and Nut Bar, a blend of fruit and nuts with crushed hemp seed; Hempower capsules, one of natures most balanced oils containing both Omega 3 and Omega 6 and GLA essential fatty acids; and Hemp Muesli, a delicious bend of fruit and nuts with crushed hemp seed. Stocked by many health food shops or available online at www.shepherdboy.co.uk or the website above.

Jack in a Bottle
Dinglewood House, Bospin Lane,
Woodchester, Stroud GL5 5EH
Tel: 01453 873 455
Fax: 01453 873 455
Email: jackinabottle@tinyworld.co.uk
▶ Importer and distributor of a range of gourmet and organic foods and natural soft drinks. Products include fruit purées, preserves, coulis, vegetable and fish soups, Guerande sea salt and fruit juices. All products have a long shelf life, require only ambient temperature storage and contain no genetically modified ingredients, artificial colourings, flavourings or other additives. Supplies to trade, retail and mail order customers.

James White Apple Juices
Whites Fruit Farm, Ashbocking,
Ipswich IP6 9JS
Tel: 01473 890 111
Fax: 01473 890 001
Email: info@jameswhite.co.uk
Web: www.jameswhite.co.uk
Open: Mon-Fri 9am-5.30pm
▶ Bottles a wide range of freshly pressed apple juices at Whites Farm in Suffolk. A Soil Association registered organic range includes Apple, Pear, Cranberry & Apple and Carrot & Apple. Also produces single variety apple juices of Bramley, Cox and Russet and combinations of Apple & Elderflower, Apple & Blackberry and Apple & Cinnamon. All of these, together with Big Tom spicy tomato juice, non-alcoholic aperitif, Great

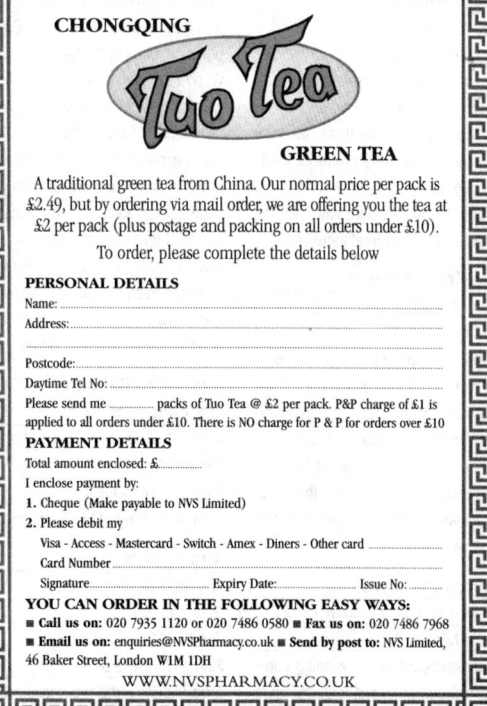

Uncle Cornelius' Finest Spiced Ginger, and a range of fruit coulis are available on a trade basis and for home delivery throughout the UK. Call or order via the internet.

London Herb & Spice
Premier Brands, PO Box 8,
Moreton, Wirral L46 8XF
Tel: 0151 522 4000
Fax: 0151 522 4020
▶ Wild range of delicious fruit and herb teas of outstanding taste and quality. Made naturally with a mix of fruit, flowers, herbs and spices which are harvested and dried, fruit and herbal infusions contain no caffeine, artificial colours or preservatives. So you can enjoy them to your heart's content. Try flavours such as fruity Blackcurrant Bracer, calming Camomile and Honey or refreshing Elderflower & lemon. Each tea is carefully blended to create a flavour that is every bit as good as it smells. Available from all major supermarkets nationwide.

Loseley Chilled Products Ltd
The Dairy, Loseley Park,
Guildford GU3 1HS
Tel: 01483 417 006
Fax: 01483 417 015
Email: enquiries@loseley.com
Web: www.loseley.com
▶ Leading manufacturer of high quality organic dairy products. Made on the farm using milk from their accredited Jersey herd with only the most pure and natural ingredients.

Lye Cross Farm
Redhill BS40 5RH
▶ Began making organic Cheddar in 1993. Strict organic standards cover all aspects of milk production, farming methods, transport of milk to the dairy and the whole cheesemaking process. Has a range of organic cheeses, certified by the Soil Association, including Cheshire and Double Gloucester.

Martin Pitt Eggs
Great House, Gwehelog NP15 1RJ
Tel: 01672 512 035
▶ Independent award winning commercial egg producer, with 35 years experience. Not registered organic, but the hens graze on organic land. Animal welfare is seen as vital.

Meridian Foods Ltd
Corwen LL21 9RJ
Tel: 01490 413 151
Fax: 01490 412 032
Email: meridianfoods@enta.net
Open: Mon-Fri 9am-5pm
▶ As a top five supplier of natural foods to the health food trade, Meridian has 82 products ranging from organic wholewheat spaghetti and organic tomato and herb pasta sauce, to organic extra virgin olive oil. All Meridian products are made with minimal processing, are free from artificial additives and are suitable for vegetarians. Exports to all over Europe and is committed to achieving major growth into the millenium.

Miniscoff
219a Stephendale Road,
London SW6 2PR
Tel: 020 7731 1605
Fax: 020 7731 1605
Email: goodfood@miniscoff.co.uk
Web: www.miniscoff.co.uk
▶ A new range of fresh, tasty organic meals for children and currently one of a kind in the marketplace. Choose between Old MacDonald's Pie, Curly Wurly Pasta (with chicken meatballs) and Fruity Lamb with Apricots, with a changeable Munch of the Month, usually vegetarian. To cook, just put them in the oven or microwave. Each meal comes complete with vegetables and can feed up to two children (under 5) and is suitable from 12 months. Available fresh but can also be home-frozen. Recommended by *BBC Good Food Magazine* and *The Times*.

Mornflake Oats Ltd/ Morning Foods Ltd
North Western Mills, Crewe CW2 6HP
Tel: 01270 213 261
Fax: 01270 500 291
▶ Manufacturer of breakfast cereals.

Mrs Moon's
Walton farm, Kilmersdon,
Bath BA3 5SX
Tel: 01761 432 383
Fax: 01761 439 645
Email: anthonyd@mrsmoons.com
Web: www.mrsmoons.com

▶ A small family business producing a range of organic home baking mixes, enabling busy people to bake delicous organic cookies and muffins. Range include Heavenly Chocolate Chip Cookies and Apple Sultana Muffin Mixes. The products are packaged in paper sacks.

Muncaster Water Mill
Ravenglass CA18 1ST
Tel: 01229 717 232
Fax: 01229 717 232
Email: mill@muncaster.co.uk
Web: www.muncaster.co.uk
▶ Organic mill producing 12 types of flour, such as cracked wheat, semolina, fine brown and more.

Nature's Way
9 Crowndale Road, London NW1 1TU
Tel: 020 7388 8882
Fax: 020 7387 7700
Open: Mon-Fri 9.30am-6.30pm
▶ Producer and wholesaler of organic food and drink. Uses an air-drying method for its products that ensures that all the original goodness and taste is preserved. The air-drying system has been registered with the Patent Office.

Old Plawhatch Farm
Sharpthorne RH19 4JL
Tel: 01342 810 201
Fax: 01342 810 478
Open: Mon-Sat 9-6.30pm;
Sun 10am-4pm
▶ Project which aims to foster the responsible stewardship of farm land and to demonstrate that agriculture can be ecologically and economically sound. It is a mixed bio-dynamic farm of 210 acres which supports a herd of horned dairy cattle, pigs, chickens, cereals and a vegetable enterprise. The farm does not apply any chemicals or artificial fertilisers on the land and using crop rotation, composted manure and natural homeopathic preparations, can sustain itself from its own resources.

Organic-Haldane Foods
Howard Way,
Newport Pagnell MK16 9PY
Tel: 01908 211 311
Fax: 01908 613 242
Email: rowntree@haldanefoods.co.uk

▶ An organic range aimed at vegetarians and vegans or people wanting an alternative to dairy products and includes Organic Nut Roast, Sosmix, Burgamix, Ice Delight, Yoga and Snackmeals.

Pertwood Organic Cereal Co
Lower Pertwood Farm, Hindon,
Salisbury SP3 6TA
Tel: 01747 820 720
Fax: 01747 820 499
▶ Lower Pertwood Farm is a Soil Association registered mixed farm on the west Wiltshire downs producing a range of 100% organic cereals from its grains. There are five cereals in the range. Pertwood Muesli with Delicious Fruits contains oats, barley and rye with sultanas, dates, apricot, orange, pineapple and apple. Pertwood Muesli with Fruit and Seeds is blended from oats, barley and rye with sultanas, apricots, sunflower, pumpkin, sesame seeds and linseed. Both of these are free of wheat, added sugar and dairy products. Pertwood Crunchy with Raison and Almond and Pertwood Crunchy with Mixed Nuts are both free of wheat and dairy products and made with unrefined organic cane sugar. The range is completed by Pertwood Organic Porridge Oats which won a Gold Award in the West Country Food Awards in May 2000. All of these varieties are packed in 750g cartons. The range is available nationwide from health food shops and independent grocers. In case of difficulty of abtaining supply, call the farm direct.

PJ Onions
Shelton Lodge, near Newark,
Nottingham NG23 5JJ
Tel: 01949 850 268
Fax: 01949 850 714
Open: Tues 3-5pm
▶ Sells organic poultry including chickens all year and turkeys for Christmas. Produce is available at Shelton Lodge and at London branches of Sainsburys, G Sparkes (Old Rover Road, Blackheath) and all branches of Out of This World.

Food & Drink

Plamil Foods Ltd
Plamil House, Bowles Well Gardens,
Folkestone CT19 6PQ
Tel: 01303 850 588
Fax: 01303 850 015
Email: contact-us@plamilfoods.co.uk
Web: www.plamilfoods.co.uk
Open: Mon-Fri 9am-5pm
▶ Produces a range of vegan foods, all GMO free, including five alternatives to milk (three based on soya and two on pea protein); egg-free mayonnaises in table and catering sizes; non-dairy chocolate bars, carob bars and drops and organic chocolate bars and drops; three new organic sandwich spreads; and a new organic and egg-free mayonnaise. Available from health food stores throughout the UK and exported to a number of countries.

Provamel
Ashley House, 86-94 High Street,
Hounslow TW3 1NH
Tel: 020 8577 2727
Fax: 020 8570 9364
▶ Manufacturer of soya alternatives to milk, desserts, cream, yoghurts and ice cream. Variety of organic and products with added calcium available. Stockists include supermarkets, Holland and Barrett shops and independent health food stores.

Pure Organic Foods Ltd
Unit 5, Eastlands Industrial Estate,
Leiston IP16 4LL
Tel: 01728 830 575
Fax: 01728 833 660
Email: enquiries@pureorganicfoods.co.uk
Web: www.pureorganicfoods.co.uk
▶ Certified wholesaler of organic meat and poultry, prepared in organically-dedicated processing and packing plant in Suffolk. Sells domestic portions tray-sealed within a protective environment. Products are labelled, bar-coded and can be priced to retailer's required mark-up. Daily deliveries to small supermarkets, delicatessens and butchers in London and weekly to Home Counties. Also operates a home delivery scheme nationwide.

Quiet Revolution
6 Duncan Street, London N1 8BW
Tel: 020 7278 1958
Fax: 020 7278 2121
Email: info@quietrevolution.co.uk
Web: www.quietrevolution.co.uk
Open: Mon-Fri 9am-5pm
▶ Fresh organic soup company selling vegetarian and vegan soups, all completely naturally made with filtered water and free of gluten, sugar, additives and preservatives. Soil Association certified and a winner of the Organic Food Awards in 1996-7 and 1997-8. Also manufactures organic sauces.

Rachel's Organic Dairy
Unit 63, Glanyrafon Industrial Estate,
Aberystwyth SY23 3JQ
Tel: 01970 625 805
Fax: 01970 626 591
Email: enqs@rachelsdairy.co.uk
Web: www.rachelsdairy.co.uk
Open: Mon-Fri 9am-5pm
▶ Produces and distributes organic dairy products of the highest quality nationwide. Committed to making organic food widely available to all consumers. Its customer base ranges from local people who call at the door through to independent health stores/retailers and supermarkets. Delivers from Scotland to Cornwall. Product lines include wholemilk live yogurt, very low fat live yogurt, both natural and real fruit flavours, Greek style yogurt, crème fraîche and cream.

Releat Foods
Howard Way,
Newport Pagnell MK16 9PY
Tel: 01908 211 311
Fax: 01908 613 242
Email: rowntree@haldanefoods.co.uk
▶ A range of products to replace meat in your diet, with products such as VegeMince, VegeRoast, VegeBurger and VegeBanger.

Rocks Organic Cordials
Loddon Park Farm, Twyford,
Reading RG10 9RY
Tel: 01189 344 342
Fax: 01189 344 539
Email: hugh.rock@tesco.net
Web: www.rocksorganiccordials.com

▶ Produces organic squash and cordials using 100% organic ingredients with the aim of providing a healthy alternative to regular soft drinks. A leaflet is available on request about the products, or visit the website for more information.

Rocombe Farm Fresh Ice Cream Ltd
Old Newton Road, Heathfield,
Newton Abbot TQ12 6RA
Tel: 01626 834 545
(01626 872 291 for mail order)
Fax: 01626 835 777
Email: peter@rocombefarm.co.uk
Web: www.rocombefarm.co.uk
▶ Innovative Devon company with a passion for making superbly delicious organic ice creams, high fruit sorbets and frozen yogurts (with Yeo Valley organic yogurt). The company began making ice cream in a shop in Torquay in 1987, using rich organic Jersey milk from the farm. Now produced in a modern purpose-built factory, to the highest hygiene standards, Rocombe's award-winning organic products are available in a wide range of independent stores and supermarkets, via home delivery services and even by mail order direct from Devon.

Seagreens Ltd
21 Ivor Place, Marylebone,
London NW1 6EU
Tel: 020 7723 5968
Fax: 020 7723 6131
Email: post@seagreens.com
Web: www.seagreens.com
▶ Providers of organic wild seaweed food products on sale in health and natural food stores, food halls, delicatessens and Waitrose supermarkets. A pure wild seaweed table condiment, cooking ingredient, and food capsules. All organic, vegetarian, vegan. Harvesting is environmentally benign.

Seeds of Change
Freeby Lane,
Waltham-on-the-Wolds, LE14 4RS
Tel: 0800 952 0000
▶ Started in 1989 and offering a range of organic pasta and pasta sauces. All ingredients are 100%

certified organic and grown according to the most traditional farming practices. Free of genetic modification and all the processes used in their production are as natural as possible.

Shepherdboy Ltd
Healthcross House,
Cross Street, Syston,
Leicester Le7 2JG
Tel: 0116 260 2992
Fax: 0116 269 3106
Email: david.revitt@talk21.com
Web: www.shepherdboy.co.uk
▶ The Shepherdboy range includes seven natural fruit and nut bars and one organic sunflower bar, all made from the finest ingredients and without sugar, preservatives, colourings or artificial flavourings, dairy products. They are also gluten-free, suitable for diabetics, vegetarians and coeliacs. The bars are stocked by all good health food shops. New in 2000 was a complete range of Organic Muesli – Fruit & Nut, Tropical, Original and Hemp.

Simmers of Edinburgh Ltd
90 Peffermill Road,
Edinburgh EH16 5UU
Tel: 0131 620 7000
Fax: 0131 620 7750
Email: mail@simmersofedinburgh.co.uk
Web: www.simmers-nairns.com
▶ The leading producer of oatcakes. The Traditional and Organic Rough recipes are full of natural flavour and the wholesome goodness of oats. Both are wheat and sugar free. Other recipes include Fine and Cheese Oatcakes and an Organic Wholemeal Cracker. No genetically modified ingredients are used.

Soya Health Foods Ltd
Unit 4, Guinness Road,
Trafford Park,
Manchester M17 1SD
Tel: 0161 872 0549
Fax: 0161 872 6776
Email: info@soya-group.com
Web: www.soya-group.com
▶ Has a range of flavoured soya milks and non dairy ice creams, under the Sunrise brand. Non-GMO and the majority of ingredients are organic.

Stamp Collection, The
Buxton Foods Limited,
12 Harley Street, London W1G 9PG
Tel: 020 7637 5505
Fax: 020 7436 0979
Email: k.towers@stamp-collection.co.uk
Web: www.stamp-collection.co.uk

▶ Actor & writer Terence Stamp launched the Stamp Collection range of products in 1994 in order to bring wheat-free and dairy-free products to the millions of people who, like himself, have an intolerance to wheat and dairy products made from cow's milk. Now produces a variety of award-winning organic products which are suitable for vegetarians and free from GMOs. For more information see the website, and for stockist details send an email.

Sussex High Weald Dairy Products
Putlands Farm, Duddleswell,
Uckfield TN22 3BJ
Tel: 01825 712 647
Fax: 01825 712 474
Email: mhardy@agnet.co.uk
Web: www.sussexhighwealddairy.co.uk

▶ Produces a wide range of cheese from organic sheep milk and organic cows' milk, including Duddleswell hard sheep cheese (plain and smoked), Sussex Slipcote soft cheese in 3 varieties, Halloumi, Feta and Ricotta cheese. Ashdown Foresters Hard Cheese and Moonlight soft cheeses are made from cows milk. The Dairy supplies outlets throughout London and the South East. Available via mail order and also online. Call for further details.

Taylors of Harrogate
Pagoda House, Plumpton Park,
Harrogate HG2 7LD
Tel: 01423 814 000
Fax: 01423 814 001
Web: www.feelgoodcoffee.co.uk

▶ Tea and coffee merchants established in 1886, producing Crystal Mountain, Mountains of the Moon and Wild Mountain organic green teas available from major supermarkets, fine food shops and independent delicatessans. In 1990 they launched their 'Trees for Life' project to plant a million trees by the Millenium — which they surpassed — and they are still planting and supporting community and environmental projects world wide through Oxfam and through one of their brands, Feel Good Coffee. This organic, Soil Association registered coffee is grown on small family farms and co-operatives where the farmers enjoy the benefit of a long term trading partnership and guaranteed premium prices.

TopQualiTea
3 Braytoft Close,
Holbrooks, Coventry CV6 4ED
Tel: 024 7668 7353
Fax: 024 7666 2340

▶ Small tea company supplying organic and fair trade teas.

Traidcraft plc
Kingsway North,
Gateshead NE11 0NE
Tel: 0191 491 0591
Fax: 0191 482 2690
Email: comm@traidcraft.co.uk
Web: www.traidcraft.co.uk

▶ Manufacturer and distributor of fairly traded fine foods from around the world. Increasingly healthy and organic in orientation, Traidcraft's products include muesli, nuts, dried fruits, teas, coffees, snack bars, organic chocolate, organic honey and organic coffee beans. Call for stockists.

Twinings Speciality Teas
Tel: 01264 334 477

▶ Twinings, the speciality tea experts, have recently launched a brand of organic tea. Twinings Organic is a mix of quality teas from South Africa and Sri Lanka, grown without the use of artificial fertilisers or pesticides and carefully blended. The tea is available in most major supermarkets and retails from £2.49 for 80 tea bags.

Vegetarian Express
Unit 28, WENTA Business Centre,
Cole Way, Watford WD2 4NP
Tel: 01923 249 714
Email: vegexp@globalnet.co.uk

▶ Sells wholefood and organic products as well as a wide range of international cuisine, ready prepared meals.

Village Bakery
Melmerby, Penrith CA10 1HE
Tel: 01768 881 515
Fax: 01768 881 848
Email: admin@village-bakery.com
Web: www.village-bakery.com
Open: Mon-Sat 8.30am-5pm;
Sun 9.30am-5pm

▶ Bakes handmade organic speciality breads and confectionary in wood-fired brick ovens. Produces a gluten-free bread; wheat-free ryes and sourdoughs; flavoured breads such as Wild Mushroom & Garlic; foccacias; spelt bread; sunflower bread; wholemeals and whites. The confectionary range includes sugar-free cakes; a gluten-free chocolate cake; flapjacks; apricot & date slices; Hazelnutters, oatcakes, blue cheese and savoury seed biscuits; cereal bars; and a full range of Christmas goods. All products are vegetarian and many fall into special diet categories such as sugar-free, wheat-free, vegan, etc. Supplies retail outlets nationwide by overnight carrier and has a mail order service for deliveries direct to the customer's door. Guarantees that all products are free of GMOs. At Melmerby their restaurant serves freshly made meals using organic ingredients and the Bakery Shop stocks the full range of organic bakery goods. Call for further information and mail order.

Whole Earth Foods Ltd
2 Valentine Place,
London SE1 8QH
Tel: 020 7633 5900
Fax: 020 7633 5901
Email: clunyb@wholeearthfoods.co.uk
Web: www.earthfoods.co.uk

▶ Pioneering organic food company dedicated to healthy eating since 1967. Delicious range of organic foods including breakfast cereals, peanut butter, soft drinks (including Organic Cola), baked beans, jams, and coffee substitutes. All products certified by the Soil Association.

The Village Bakery
MELMERBY

- Organic bakery goods
- Mail Order
- Nationwide retail outlets
- Special diet products
- Bread making courses
- Licensed Restaurant

Penrith
Cumbria
CA10 1HE

Tel: 01768 881251
Fax: 01768 881848
admin@village-bakery.com
www.village-bakery.com

RESTAURANTS & CAFÉS

Organic

Blacksmith's Arms
Ricknall Lane, Preston-le-Skerne
Tel: 01325 314 873
▶ Buys vegetables from organic suppliers and meat from a local butcher. Good vegetarian dishes and children's menu. Food is available at lunchtimes and in the evenings (not Sundays). Supports small craft breweries. The beers change every week, options available are Castle Eden Nimmos XXXX and Hambleton Nightmare and White Boar. Organic wines, with free wine and ale tastings on Friday nights, including rare bottled beers.

Ramsons
18 Market Place, Ramsbottom,
Greater Manchester, BL0 9HT
Tel: 01706 825 070
Fax: 01706 822 005
▶ The meaning of the name of the establishment, 'wild garlic', reflects the link with Italian cuisine. This is a mainly organic restaurant with a wide Anglo-Italian a la carte menu listing dishes as vegetables, meat, fish, cheese and sweets without the formality of starters and main courses. Portion size is variable to suit the appetite. Sources fresh produce from home and abroad, and uses no salt in the cooking. Inexpensive.

Vegetarian

60-40 Vegetarian Café Bar
448 Wilmslow Road, Withington,
Manchester M20 3BW
Tel: 0161 374 1746
Fax: 0161 448 2351
Email: café6040@yahoo.com
Open: Mon-Sun 10am-12.30 midnight
▶ 100% vegetarian restaurant with Vegetarian Society approval serving a variety of panini, burritos, chimichangas with chunky Belgian waffles, muffins and pastries for dessert. Speciality teas, ten varieties of ground coffee, cappuccino, latte, mocha and espresso. Room available for hire. Internet access.

Bear Café
29 Rochdale Road,
Todmorden OL14 7LA
Tel: 01706 819 690
▶ Vegetarian Café.

Cachumba Café
220 Burton Road, West Didsbury,
Manchester M20 2LW
Tel: 0161 445 2479
Open: Mon-Sat 6-10pm
▶ Almost veggie restaurant serving a variety of home-cooked food from around the world including Vietnamese, South Indian, Thai and Gujarati. There is a good selection of vegetarian and vegan options. Prices are reasonable ranging from £1.95-£7.95. Unlicensed but bring your own.

Café Lusid
60 Nelson Street, Chorlton-on-Medlock, Manchester M13 9WP
Tel: 0161 274 3425
Open: Mon-Fri 10am-3pm
▶ Situated in a museum dedicated to the suffragette movement (once the home of arch-suffragette Sylvia Pankhurst) and surrounded by women's resource centre groups, this bright, cheery daytime café features a 90% vegan menu. Specials include the daily combo – homemade vegan soup, ciabatta bread and beverage. A bargain at £2.75. Prices go up to £3.90 for main meals. Desserts include banana and apple crumble, continental biscuit cake and cheesecakes. Takeaways and party bookings available. Unlicensed.

Café Pop
34-36 Oldham Street,
Manchester M1 1JN
Tel: 0161 237 9688
Open: Mon-Sat 9.30am-5.30pm;
Sun open seasonally
▶ Northern quarter-based, daytime only vegetarian café offering huge veggie breakfasts (£3.50) and vegan options. Prices range from £1.50 for eggs on toast to £3.50 for main meals. Milkshakes and cakes for dessert. Access for the disabled. Unlicensed.

Café Vienna
204 Wigan Road, Deane,
Bolton BL3 5QE
Tel: 01204 627 738
Open: Tues-Fri 9.30am-7pm;
Sat-Sun 10am-6.30pm
▶ Small café with about third of its menu comprising vegetarian options. Prices are reasonable starting at £1.50 for a veggie burger.

Cornerhouse
70 Oxford Street,
Manchester M1 5NH
Tel: 0161 228 7621
Fax: 0161 200 1506
Email: comments@cornerhouse.org.uk
Web: www.cornerhouse.org.uk
Open: Every day 11am-9pm
▶ With three galleries, three cinemas and a media and education space, the Cornerhouse buzzes with activity. The café is situated on the first floor and looks out over Oxford Road through huge ceiling to floor glass windows. Licensed, its public bar has its own snack menu. Meals priced around £5, or choose from make-your-own-sandwich bar, homemade soups or tempting pastries.

Earth
16-20 Turner Street,
Northern Quarter,
Manchester M4 1D2
Tel: 0121 834 1996
Open: 12-7pm Monday-Saturday
▶ A vegetarian and vegan café serving quality food by a trained chef, from a wide range of organic and fair trade produce. Tries to operate according to Buddhist values. Uses organic fruit and vegetables as much as possible in a smoke-free environment.

Egg Café, The
Newington Buildings,
16-18 Newington (Top Floor),
Liverpool L1 4ED
Tel: 0151 707 2755
▶ Vegetarian café.

Food Parcel, The
Stockton International Family Centre,
66 Dovecot Street,
Stockton on Tees TS18 1LL
Tel: 01642 612 400
Fax: 01642 608 432

▶ Vegetarian café run by and serving food prepared by NVQ students. Offers three course meals for £3.50.

Frog & Bucket Comedy Club
102 Oldham Street,
Manchester M4 4LJ
Tel: 0161 236 9805
Fax: 0161 288 1652
Web: www.frogandbucket.com
▶ Alternative comedy club serving vegetarian meals.

Gaylord's Indian Restaurant
Amethyst House,
Spring Gardens,
Manchester M2 1EA
Tel: 0161 832 4866
Fax: 0161 832 6037
Open: Mon-Sun 12noon-3pm & 6-11pm
▶ Much recommended North Indian restaurant specialising in Punjabi cuisine, with between 25 and 30 vegetarian options. The chef comes from a five star hotel in India. The vegetarian thali costs £12.95, and other veggie dishes range in price from £4.75 to £5.75. Catering for functions. Is listed in the Good Curry Guide.

Good Life, The
6 Victoria Station Approach,
Manchester M3 1NY
Tel: 0161 834 5224
Open: Mon-Fri 7am-6pm;
Sat 8.30am-5.30pm
▶ Health foods and vegetarian and vegan takeaways including hot and cold snacks and sandwiches.

Great Bear Trading Co Ltd
29 Rochdale Road,
Todmorden OL14 7LA
Tel: 01706 813 737
Fax: 01706 919 492
Open: Mon, Weds-Fri 9.30am-5pm;
Tues 9.30am-3pm; Sat 9am-4.30pm.
Café closes 30 min earlier each day
▶ Vegetarian café on the first floor of workers co-operative run wholefood shop.

Green Fish Café
11 Upper Newington,
Liverpool L1 2SR
Tel: 0151 707 8592
Web: www.greenfishcafe.co.uk
Open: Mon-Sat 11am-6pm

► City centre café serving vegetarian and vegan food. The food is freshly prepared on the premises.

Greenbank Restaurant
332-338 Smithdown Road,
Liverpool L15 3AM
Tel: 0151 734 4498
► Serves a range of vegetarian options.

Greenhouse, The
331 Great Western Street,
Rusholme, Manchester M14 4AN
Tel: 0161 224 0730
Fax: 0161 256 0943
Email: greenhouse@euphony.net
Web: www.greenhouserest.freeuk.com
Open: Mon-Sat 12 noon-12 midnight; Sun 12 noon-11pm
► The biggest vegetarian restaurant in the city offering a huge menu with vegetarian and vegan options.

Greenhouse, The
41-43 Oxford Road,
Altrincham WA14 2ED

Tel: 0161 929 4141
Open: Mon-Weds 8.30am-5.30pm; Thurs-Sat 8.30am-5.30pm & 6pm-late
► Fully vegetarian restaurant which serving all home-cooked food. French flans, salads, soups and hot dishes by day, and more sophisticated food from an à la carte menu in the evenings. A take-away menu and a full outside catering service are offered, and the owners also run a busy health food centre (see separate listing).

Greens Restaurant
43 Lapwing Lane, West Didsbury,
Manchester M20 2NT
Tel: 0161 434 4259
Fax: 0161 448 2098
Open: Tues-Fri 12 noon-2pm; Everyday 5.30-10.30pm
► Vegetarian restaurant with modern cuisine. Unlicensed, no corkage charge.

Jigsaw Pantry, The
Trinity Youth & Community Centre,
Weslyan Row, Clitheroe BB7 2JY

EXCELLENT HOME-COOKED FOOD
OUTSIDE CATERING OUR SPECIALITY
MEGA SUNDAY LUNCH   LARGE VEGAN CHOICE
CHILDREN WELCOME

MISTY'S VEGETARIAN CAFE

Opening Hours
Mon-Sat 9-6, Sun 11-5
UNIT 3 LONGSIGHT SHOPPING CENTRE,
(NEAR ASDA). 531 STOCKPORT ROAD,
LONGSIGHT, MANCHESTER M12 4JH
Tel 0161 256 3355

Red Triangle Café

Intimate and co-operatively-run daytime café and evening restaurant with a wholly vegetarian menu, which changes daily.

Prices range from 80p for a piece of cake to £1 for a bowl of soup to £2.95 for a main meal such as Provençal Bean Stew with garlic bread

- Vegan options always available
- a selection of organic vegetarian wines and beers.
- Bookings for parties
- outside catering is also offered –
'healthy buffets made to order'
160 St James Street, Burnley BB11 1NR Tel: 01282 832 319
Open: Tue-Thu 10.30am-7pm; Fri-Sat 8am-10pm

Tel: 01200 27886
► Vegetarian café.

Jim's Caff
19-21 New Market Street,
Pendle BB8 9BJ
Tel: 01282 868 828
► Vegetarian restaurant.

Lakeland Pedlar Wholefood Café & Bicycle Centre, The
Bell Close, Keswick CA12 5JD
Tel: 017687 74492
Fax: 017687 75202
Email: lakeland.pedlar@btclick.com
Open: Daily 9am-5pm; plus evenings during main hiliday periods
► Keswick's only true vegetarian café-restaurant is an ideal meeting place for a day out in the hills, a cycle ride, shopping or simply a chat. During the day, the menu includes a selection of home-baked breads, cakes, pizzas, spicy chillis and other sweet and savoury eats. On selected evenings throughout the year offers a feast of imaginative vegetarian cuisine from around the world. With a relaxed non-smoking atmosphere, good music, fine views with outside tables and a take-away service, worth a visit.

Misty's Vegetarian Café
Unit 3, Longsight Shopping Centre,
531 Stockport Road, Longsight,
Manchester M12 4JH
Tel: 0161 256 3355
Open: Mon-Thurs, Sat 9am-6pm; Fri 9am-10pm; Sun 11am-5pm
► Friendly café offering a good choice of vegan and vegetarian food, all made in their kitchen with a large amount of organic ingredients. All day breakfasts, hot meals, snacks, milk shakes, vegan shakes, coffee and tea, and Manchester's biggest selection of vegan cakes and desserts. Special meals on Thursday and Friday evenings and Sunday lunch. Full disabled access and very child friendly. Catering service offered.

Neal's Yard Remedies
29 John Dalton Street,
Manchester M2 6DS
Tel: 0161 835 1713
Open: Mon-Sat 10am-5.30pm; Sun 12 noon-4pm

► Bright and spacious shop featuring a herbal tea bar where exhausted shoppers can sit with a cup of chamomile, rosehip or hibiscus (to name just a few). All herbal teas reflect Neal's Yard's care and concern for the environment and are grown without the use of pesticides and fertilisers and are certified by the Soil Association. The paper used for tea bags is non-chlorine bleached. Mail order 0161 831 7875.

On The Eighth Day
101-111 Oxford Road, All Saints,
Manchester M1 7DU
Tel: 0161 273 4878
Fax: 0161 273 4878
Email: 8th-Day@eighthy.demon.co.uk
Web: www.eighthy.demon.co.uk
Open: Mon-Fri 9am-7pm;
Sat 10am-4.30pm
► Co-operative-run vegetarian café, on the same site as the wholefood shop, serving a wide selection of freshly-prepared vegetarian and vegan foods. Hot veggie breakfasts, snacks, soups, lunches, cakes and early evening meals at reasonable prices. Licensed. A catering service is also offered.

Patagonia Café
116 Bradshawgate, Bolton BL2 1AY
Tel: 01204 528 533
Open: Mon-Sat 9am-5pm
► Spanish American café with lots of veggie options including soups, salads, hot dishes and desserts.

Punjb Tandoori Indian Restaurant
177 Wilmslow Road, Rusholme,
Manchester M14 5AP
Tel: 0161 225 2960
Open: Every day 12 noon-12 midnight
► Vegetarian and non-veg restaurant specialising in Punjabi and Southern Indian cuisine.

Quince and Medlar Fine Food Vegetarian Restaurant
13 Castlegate,
Cockermouth CA13 9EU
Tel: 01900 823 579
Open: Tues-Sat 7pm-late (last orders 9.30pm); Open bank holiday Sundays

Food & Drink

▶ A fine food vegetarian restaurant, licensed and non-smoking. The menu changes bi-monthly. Twice winner of the 'National Vegetarian Restaurant of the Year' and three times runner-up. Colin and Louisa Le Voi have run the restaurant for twelve years. The restaurant has been listed in the Which Good Food Guide every year.

Red Triangle Café
160 St James Street,
Burnley BB11 1NR
Tel: *01282 832 319*
Open: *Tue-Thur 10.30am-7pm;*
Fri-Sat 8am-10pm
▶ Small, intimate, co-operatively-run daytime café and evening restaurant with a wholly vegetarian menu, which changes daily. Prices range from 80p for a piece of cake to £1 for a bowl of soup to £2.95 for a main meal (such as provencal bean stew with garlic bread). Vegan options are always available as are a selection of organic vegetarian wines and beers. Takes bookings for parties and outside catering is also offered ('healthy buffets made to order'). Regularly updated noticeboard displays local events – arts, entertainment, politics – generated at the subsidised and grassroots level, and which produces an address book and diary for green and left campaigns in the area.

Rowan Tree, The
Church Bridge, Grassmere LA22 9SN
Tel: *01539 435 528*
▶ Vegetarian café and tea-rooms by day and vegetarian restaurant by night. Situated overlooking the river, and opposite a church. Covered patio and indoor seating. Specialities include homity pie, pancakes, home-made cakes and mediterranean pie.

Waiting Room Vegetarian Restaurant, The
9 Station Road,
Eaglescliffe TS16 0BU
Tel: *01642 780 465*
Email: *jenny.harding@virgin.net*
Open: *Mon-Sun 11am-2pm,*
7pm onwards (except Sun)
▶ Vegetarian restaurant.

Watermill Restaurant, The
Priests Mill, Caldbeck,
Wigton CA7 8DR
Tel: *016974 78267*
Fax: *016974 78267*
Email: *joeshort@*
watermillrestaurant.sagehost.co.uk
Web:
www.watermillrestaurant.
sagehost.co.uk
Open: *Tues-Sun 10am-5pm;*
Mon 11am-4pm
▶ Specialises in vegetarian cuisine with the food made daily on the premises from the best quality produce. The choice ranges from light refreshments to full meals. Some tables overlook the river, or you may sit outside on the grassy terrace next to the village cricket pitch. During the winter months the restaurant is warm and inviting with a cosy log stove and candles on the talbles. Evening dinner parties and outside catering by arrangement. Exhibition space available

Waterside Wholefoods
Kent View, Off Lowther Street,
Waterside, Kendal LA9 4DZ
Tel: *01539 729 743*
Fax: *01539 733 011*
Web: *www.lakelandnatural.co.uk*
Open: *Mon-Sat 8.30am-4pm,*
closed Sunday
▶ Vegetarian café and shop selling vegetarian produce. Waterside walkway, picnic tables by River Kent.

Wesley Community Café
The Russell Club, Royce Road,
Hulme, Manchester M15 5EA
Tel: *0161 226 9051*
Fax: *0161 226 9051*
▶ Cheap, wholesome food with many vegetarian and vegan options. Unlicensed.

Whale Tail, The
78a Penny Street,
Lancaster LA1 1XN
Tel: *01524 845 133*
Open: *Mon-Fri 9am-4pm;*
Sat 9am-5pm; Sun 10.30am-3pm
▶ Vegetarian and vegan café serving meals and light snacks. GM free and licensed with a patio-garden. Children are warmly welcomed.

Woody's Vegetarian Restaurant
5 King Street, Delph, Saddleworth,
Oldham OL3 5DL
Tel: *01457 871 197*
Fax: *01457 678 8389*
Open: *Thurs-Sat 7.30-11pm.*
Last booking at 9pm
▶ Established for 10 years, Woody's is found in picturesque Pennine Saddleworth, just off the A62. Serves award-winning vegetarian cuisine including such dishes as cranberry terrine and blue cheese nut parcels. Call to book a table.

Yellow Brick Café
47 Old Birley Street, Hulme,
Manchester M15 5RF
Tel: *0161 227 9008*
Email: *YBC@limitedresources.co.uk*
Open: *Mon-Weds, Fri 10am-5pm;*
Thurs 9am-9.30pm;
Sat-Sun 11am-4pm
▶ Vegetarian and vegan café selling an imaginative selection of good quality café food including breakfasts, sandwiches, stews, soups, salads and dips. Some dishes are organic. Specials of the day include spinach and feta parcels served with tangy tomato sauce or mixed veg in a loaf with cheese sauce. Salads, dips, savoury pancakes, omelettes, baked potatoes. Trading under the umbrella of Limited Resources (see Food Delivery), this is has the same friendly atmosphere with a modern design and is a forum for local art. Takeaway and business delivery available within Hulme area. Outside catering. Restaurant for hire for parties. Unlicensed. Call for music events and poetry evenings, and film showing.

Zeffirellis
Compston Road,
Ambleside LA22 9AD
Tel: *015394 33845*
Fax: *015394 32986*
Web: *www.zeffirellis.co.uk*
Open: *5pm-10pm*
▶ Stylish Italian vegetarian pizzeria with 2 cinemas in the heart of the Lake District.

CATERING SERVICES

Misty's
Unit 3, Longsight Shopping Centre,
531 Stockport Road, Longsight,
Manchester M12 4JH
Tel: *0161 256 3355*
Open: *Mon-Thurs, Sat 9am-6pm;*
Fri 9am-10pm; Sun 11am-5pm
▶ Catering service offered to meetings, conferences and parties by this popular vegetarian and vegan café. Particularly well known for their large selection of vegan cakes and desserts.

On The Eighth Day
101-111 Oxford Road, All Saints,
Manchester M1 7DU
Tel: *0161 273 4878*
Fax: *0161 273 4878*
Email: *8th-*
Day@eighthy.demon.co.uk
Web: *www.eighthy.demon.co.uk*
Open: *Mon-Fri 9am-7pm;*
Sat 10am-4.30pm
▶ Catering service offered by co-operative-run vegetarian café, serving a wide selection of freshly-prepared vegetarian and vegan foods. Hot veggie breakfasts, snacks, soups, lunches, cakes and early evening meals at reasonable prices. Licensed.

Party Organic
The Kensington Provision Company,
Unit 15D Farm Lane, Farm Lane
Trading Estate, London SW6 1QJ
Tel: *020 7386 7778*
Fax: *020 7610 1972*
Email:
anglocontracts.kpc@virgin.net
▶ Certified organic catering for children's parties. Supplies party food bursting with organic goodness and fun, sourced and created especially with the smaller variety of party-animals in mind. Seeks out organic party food, that is otherwise not widely available and also ensures it is tasty and appealing (all the party food is taste-tested by little people). Caters for children with dietary requirements too, and although small people are their speciality, will happily cater for adults.

Food & Drink

Yellow Brick Café Catering
47 Old Birley Street, Hulme, Manchester M15 5RF
Tel: *0161 227 9008*
Open: *Mon-Weds, Fri 10am-5pm; Thurs 9am-9.30pm; Sat-Sun 11am-4pm*
▶ Workers' co-operative run vegetarian restaurant that also offers an outside catering service. Call for further details.

COOKERY COURSES

Ashburton Centre, The
79 East Street, Ashburton TQ13 7AL
Tel: *01364 652 784*
Fax: *01364 653 825*
Web: *www.ashburtoncentre.co.uk*
▶ Practical, hands on, vegetarian cooking courses, from introductory weekends (£215) to professional training. All courses include full board. Call for course details and availability.

Cordon Vert Cookery School
Parkdale, Dunham Road, Altringham WA14 4QG
Tel: *0161 925 2000/2014*
Fax: *0161 926 9182*
Email: *lyn@vegsoc.org*
▶ Cookery school which teaches students how to prepare imaginative vegetarian food. Diploma, weekend and day courses available. Organised by the Vegetarian Society (see Organisations).

Green Cuisine Limited
Penrhos Court, Kington HR5 3LH
Tel: *01544 230 720*
Fax: *01544 230 754*
Email: *daphne@greencuisine.org*
Web: *www.greencuisine.org*
▶ Chef and nutritionist Daphne Lambert runs her Food and Health Cookery courses at Penrhos Court. There are four courses: Basic Food & Health; Women's Health; Pregnancy & Child Foods; and Sports Nutrition. The courses are based on holistic nutrition and teach the benefits of organic and vegetarian diets in order to optimise health. Also runs special events and seminars, and a small shop online for organic health supplies. Call for further information, consultancy or advice.

Natural Cookery School, The
Greenfields, Lovington, Castle Cary BA7 7PX
Tel: *01963 240 641*
Fax: *01963 240 229*
Web: *www.montsebradford.com*
▶ Montse Bradford is the creator of the Natural Cookery School in Bath. She has also been successfully offering training at her Natural Cookery School in her home town of Barcelona, Spain for the past 10 years. The uniqueness of the training lies in its holistic approach, which consists of a comprehensive experience and study of the human being as an energetic entitiy, travelling through unique individual needs in the Physical Body, Mind and Emotions. Through practical experiences in cooking and other practices you embark on a journey of self-discovery, empowerment and fun, to achieve a greater understanding of your energy, needs and connection with yourself. In-depth Teacher's Training also available.

Old Court House, The
Trefin, Near St Davids, Haverfordwest SA62 5AX
Tel: *01438 837 095*
▶ An exclusively vegetarian guesthouse situated on the stunning North Pembrokeshire Coast. Relax and unwind in the 200 year -old cosy cottage with ensuite accomodation and an open fire. The manager Lynne is a Cordon Vert cook and uses local produce to produce delicious vegetarian and vegan food each day. Trefin is an ideal base to walk the coastal path, visit sandy beaches, off-shore islands and the city of St Davids. Lynne also runs vegetarian cookery courses and demonstrations.

ORGANISATIONS

The organisations in this section look at the wider issues around food, the people that produce it and the environment. Animal rights groups are listed in Chapter Ten: Government & Organisations.

Organic

Organic Farmers and Growers Ltd
Church House, 50 High Street, Soham, Ely CB7 5HF
Tel: *01353 720 250*
Fax: *01353 46720 289*
▶ One of several national organic sector bodies recognised by the UK Register of Organic Food Standards. The aim of the organisation is to promote the concept and principles of organic food production while protecting the interests of its members. It exists to help both current and would-be organic farmers. For those considering becoming organic food producers, it offers advice and practical guidance on conversion and compliance procedures – taking would-be producers through to official registered organic status. A regular newsletter is mailed to all members to keep them informed about the latest developments within the organisation and the organic sector as a whole.

Applied Rural Alternatives
10 Highfield Close, Wokingham RG40 1DG
Tel: *0118 962 7797*
▶ Promotes the understanding of organic farming.

Biodynamic Agricultural Association (BDAA)
Painswick Inn Project, Gloucester Street, Stroud, GL5 1Q9
Tel: *01453 759 501*
Fax: *01453 759 501*
Email: *bdaa@biodynamic.freeserve.co.uk*
▶ National organisation promoting a unique organic approach to farming and gardening following the philosophy of Rudolf Steiner and anthroposophy. Operates the inter-

nationally recognised Demeter symbol guaranteeing strict biodynamic growing standards. Contact the BDAA for books, leaflets and a copy of the *Star and Furrow* newsletter. Their logo is *Demeter* which certifies around ninety-five companies in the UK. Operates in thirty-eight countries, and is an international trademark.

Centre for Organic Husbandry and Agroecology
Welsh Institute of Rural Studies,
University of Wales,
Aberystwyth SY23 3AL
Tel: *01970 622 248*
Fax: *01970 622 238*
▶ Research and development of organic farming systems.

Elm Farm Research Centre
Hamstead Marshall,
Newbury RG20 0HR
Tel: *01488 658 298*
Fax: *01488 658 503*
Email: *elmfarm@efrc.com*
Web: *www.efrc.com*
Open: *Mon-Fri 9am-5pm*
▶ International research, advisory and educational organisation based in UK aiming to change agricultural policy to bring about a greater uptake of organic farming as a way of contributing towards sustainability in farming and land use in the UK and internationally. Produces a range of publications, information and a regular bulletin. Delivers MAFF-funded conversion visits to those considering conversion to organic farming. See also the following listing for the Organic Advisory Service.

IFOAM (International Federation of Organic Agricultural Movements)
Oekozentrum, Imsbach,
D-66636 Tholey-Theley, Germany
Tel: *6853 6190*
Fax: *49 6853 30844*
Email: *info@ifoam.org*
Web: *www.ifoam.org*
▶ World umbrella organisation of the organic agriculture movement with 670 memebers in 102 countries. Publishes a magazine called *Ecology & Farming*.

Land Heritage
Pound Corner, Whitestone,
Exeter EX4 2HP
Tel: *01647 61099*
Fax: *01647 61134*
Email:
101500.2204@compuserve.com
Open: *Mon-Fri 9am-5pm*
▶ Protects small family farms, wildlife and rural communities. It aquires farms to secure their organic status, establishing tenancies for young families and new entrants. It explores new ways of linking people with the land through the formation of Community Supported Agriculture initiatives, encouraging Farmers Markets and promoting the advantages of local organic food through educational programmes for both children and adults. Believes that small farms are a national asset, contributing to the long term security of sustainable food production. By becoming a supporter (minimum subscription of £15), you can help to preserve a heritage which is constantly under threat.

Organic Advisory Service
Elm Farm Research Centre,
Hamstead Marshall,
near Newbury RG20 0HR
Tel: *01488 658 279*
Fax: *01488 658 503*
Email: *oas@efrc.com*
▶ Operating as part of the Elm Farm Research Centre, offers advice and information for organic producers. Provides free advisory visits as part of the MAFF-supported Organic Conversion Information Service; feasibility studies; conversion planning; consultancy services; telephone services; full financial services; specialist services' producer groups and soil analysis as well as an *Organic Farm Management Handbook*. The flexible, confidential service is tailored to meet the needs of each client.

Organic Food Federation
1 Mowles Manor Enterprise Centre,
Elting Green,
East Dereham NR20 3EZ
Tel: *01362 637 314*
Fax: *01362 637 980*
Email: *organicfood@freenet.co.uk*

▶ Originally established in 1986, the Federation is an inspection, certification and registration body for organic foods. Members include importers, farmers, horticulturalists and retailers. The Federation's aim is to ensure that members maintain high standards in all aspects of organic production and to offer information accordingly. Also represents members' interests in communicating with government and European institutions as appropriate.

Organic Livestock Marketing Co-operative
Welcome Hill, Shebbear,
Beaworthy EX21 5SN
Tel: *01409 281 365*
Email: *ralph.human@virgin.net*
▶ Largest organic livestock selling organisation in England with over 40% of UK sales in organic lamb and beef. Provides an effective link between producers and the expanding market for organic meat, by means of advice, support and marketing information to potential, converting and existing organic producers. Aims to grow the organic market for livestock in a sustainable way and works to ensure that producers get best possible returns.

Organic Living Association
St Mary's Villa, Hanley Swan WR8 0EA
▶ Aims to inform the public on sustainable measures necessary to improve health in humans and livestock, organic farming and gardening; also advises on alternatives to allapathic medicine; and promotes the creation of ecological, self-sufficient villages. Produces a newsletter (six issues per annum). SAE required for enquiries.

Soil Association
Bristol House, 40-56 Victoria Street,
Bristol BS1 4BY
Tel: *0117 929 0661*
Fax: *0117 925 2504*
Email: *info@soilassociation.org*
Web: *www.soilassociation.org*
▶ The UK's leading organisation working to promote the benefits of organic food, farming and sustainable forestry to human health, animal welfare and the environment. Its symbol can be found on numerous food products as a sign of quality and high standards. Organic is a term defined by law and all organic food production and processing is governed by a strict set of rules. The main campaign is currently the promotion of organic farming as a means to increase the level of wildlife in the countryside: this follows the publication of the *Biodiversity Report* in May 2000. The Soil Association is a membership organisation with more than 14,000 members, with benefits including the quarterly magazine, *Living Earth*. Books and guides on a wide variety of organic subjects can be purchased through a mail order service and the website has a comprehensive library with information on all aspects of organic food and farming.

Soil Association – Liverpool Organic Gardeners
70 Herrondale Road,
Liverpool L18 1LB
Tel: *0151 280 5065*
▶ Local branch of the Soil Association.

Soil Association – Staffordshire Group
35 Dartmouth Street,
Stafford ST16 3TU
Tel: *01785 248 394*
▶ Local branch of the Soil Association.

Soil Association – Treowweard Organic Conservation Land Army
109 Gorsedale Road, Poulton,
Wallasey, Wirrel L44 4AN
Tel: *0151 639 9840*
▶ Local branch of the Soil Association.

Soil Association – West Yorkshire & Kirklees Group
34 St Andrews Crescent,
Oakenshaw, Bradford BD12 7EL
Tel: *01274 678 007*
▶ Local branch of the Soil Association.

Soil Association – Wirral Organic Group
3 Oakfield Road, Childer Thornton,
Ellesmere Port CH66 7NY
Tel: *0151 339 7315*
▶ Local branch of the Soil Association.

United Kingdom Register of Organic Food Standards (UKROFS)
Room 118, Nobel House, 17 Smith Square, London SW1P 3JR
Tel: 020 7238 5915
Fax: 020 7238 6148
Email: alex.dasi-sutton@maff.grfi.gov.uk
▶ Organisation setting the standards for a certification system for organically produced food. UKROFS has compiled a register of organic producers – but not products themselves (£27.50) – and a register of organic standards (£20).

Non-GMOs

Genetic Engineering Network
PO Box 9656, London N4 4JY
Tel: 020 7690 0626
Email: info@genetix.freeserve.co.uk
Web: www.dmac.co.uk/gen.html
▶ Networking organisation for individuals, groups and organisations who work on all aspects of genetic engineering. Runs an email information list, which is free, and can put readers in touch with local campaigns. Publishes Genetix Update, a free newsletter. Order a copy either by email or subscription.

Genetic Food Alert
c/o Greencity, 23 Fleming Street, Glasgow G31 1PQ
Tel: 0141 554 6099
▶ Trade association representing members of the health food trade. Aims to have the health food trade GM-free. Politically, the association lobbies for a five year freeze on imports and commercial growing of GM crops. Produces a quarterly newsletter for the members of the public and can also give out information over the phone. Send an SAE for a list of suppliers of non-GM goods around the country.

GM Free
c/o KMI Publications, Beacon House, Woodley Park, Skelmersdale WN8 6UR
Tel: 01695 50504
Fax: 01695 559556
Email: clairejr@btinternet.com
Web: www.btinternet.com/~clairejr
▶ Website which aims to inform the public of the risks to health and the environment posed by genetically modified foods and crops. Includes scientific research, articles and news updates. Information is the most effective weapon in the fight against enforced contamination of food and the environment. Also holds back issues of a useful magazine, published in 1999, GM-Free.

Nationwide Food Survey
Beacon House, Skelmersdale N8 6UR
▶ Small group which has published a booklet on How to Avoid Genetic Foods, available for £2.50. Cheques should be made payable to Nationwide Publications.

Fair Trade

British Association of Fair Trade Shops (BAFTS)
c/o Gateway World Shop, Market Place, Durham DH1 3NJ
Tel: 0191 384 7173
Fax: 0191 375 0729
▶ A network of Fair Trade shops promoting fair trade retailing and organising campaigns to promote awareness of unfair practices. Works with European partners. Most major cities have a shop member. Send an SAE for information and a list of members.

Fairtrade Foundation
Suite 204, 16 Baldwin's Gardens, London EC1N 7RJ
Tel: 020 7405 5942
Fax: 020 7405 5943
Email: mail@fairtrade.org.uk
Web: www.fairtrade.org.uk
▶ The Fairtrade Foundation awards the Fairtrade Mark, the independent consumer label which guarantees that third world producers get a better deal. The Mark appears on coffee, tea, cocoa, chocolate, bananas, sugar and honey sold in supermarkets, health food shops and One World Shops. Visit the web site for more information.

Traidcraft Exchange
Kingsway North, Gateshead NE11 0NE
Tel: 0191 491 0591
Fax: 0191 482 2690
Email: fionat@traidcraft.co.uk
Web: www.traidcraft.co.uk
▶ Leading international development organisation working to fight poverty through fair trade. It does this by supporting business in the developing world, raising awareness amongst consumers in the UK and promoting ethical business practices. Call for further information.

Vegetarian & Vegan

Contact Centre
BCM Cuddle, London WC1N 6XX
Tel: 01706 227 632
Fax: 01706 227 632
▶ The only agency in Britain catering exclusively for vegetarians and vegans offering a low-fee support organisation both in Britain and abroad for any purposes. Approach is non-judgemental, with personal attention, care and discretion, a listening ear and 20 years' experience. Write stating your gender and enclosing an SAE.

Jewish Vegetarian Society
855 Finchley Road, Golders Green, London NW11 8LX
Tel: 020 8455 0692
Fax: 020 8455 1465
Email: ijvs@yahoo.com
Open: Mon-Fri 10am-4pm
▶ The Society has been in existence since 1966 and is open to non-vegetarians who are sympathetic to its aims. Membership is open to all and the Society is an international movement.

Manchester Vegan Information
11 Upper Moss Lane, Hulme, Manchester M15 5JG
Tel: 0161 232 1294
▶ Anne Barr, the local contact of The Vegan Society, is available to answer enquiries on all aspects of veganism. Information sheets, cookery books, diet and nutrition publications, travel guides and animal-free shoppers are available through the Head Office or through Anne. An SAE is appreciated for all enquiries.

National Vegetarian Week
c/o The Vegetarian Society, Parkdale, Dunham Road, Altrincham WA14 4QG
Tel: 0161 925 2000
Fax: 0161 926 9182
Email: info@vegsoc.org
Web: www.vegsoc.org
Open: Mon-Fri 9am-5pm
▶ Nationwide promotion of the vegetarian diet, encouraging everyone to go veggie for the week. Free publicity material available. Local events.

North Manchester Vegetarian Information Centre
12 Gwendor Avenue, Crumpsall, Manchester M8 4LE
Tel: 0161 740 5917
Fax: 0161 740 4747
Email: harfleet@easynet.co.uk
Web: www.harfleetnutrition.com
Open: Mon-Fri 9am-5pm
▶ Nutritional therapy uses combination of diet, naturopathic techniques and appropriate supplements to help the body repair and maintain itself. Treatment of wide range of physical and mental disorders. Long distance consultation available.

North West Veggie Guide
31 Alexandria Drive, Westhoughton, Bolton BL5 3HF
Tel: 01942 817 533
▶ Annual publication full of essential information for all those wishing to avoid meat. It contains details of restaurants, cafés, hotels and guest houses. Some are exclusively vegetarian or vegan whilst others serve meat and a good selection of veggie dishes. The Guide covers all of Greater Manchester and adjoining counties of Lancashire, Cheshire and Merseyside and is available at health food shops, bookshops and information centres at a cost of £2 or by mail order.

Vegan Organic Network (VOHAN)
58 High Lane, Chorlton, Manchester M21 9DZ
Tel: 0161 860 4869
Fax: 0161 860 4869

Food & Drink

Email: vohan@net-work.co.uk
Web: www.veganvillage.co.uk
▶ Agricultural and horticultural network organisation with contacts across the UK and abroad, encouraging the practical application of vegan organic methods of food production. Produces *VOHAN News International Magazine* and a more informal newsletter. Also organises a volunteer network working on organic farms.

Vegan Society
Donald Watson House,
7 Battle Road,
St Leonards-on-Sea TN37 7AA
Tel: 01424 427 393
Fax: 01424 717 064
Email: info@vegansociety.com
Web: www.vegansociety.com
Open: Mon 9.30am-5pm;
Tues-Fri 9am-5pm
(visitors by appointment only)
▶ Education charity providing information on all aspects of veganism to schools, health care professionals, the media, food manufacturers and individuals. Promotes ways of living which avoid the use of animal products – for food, clothing or any other purpose – for the benefit of people, animals and the environment. Publishes a quarterly magazine (*The Vegan*), a shopping guide (*The Animal Free Shopper*), the *Vegan Travel Guide* and around 60 information sheets and booklets. Has a network of local contacts around the UK and abroad. Use the website or contact the office for information.

Vegetarian Charity
14 Winters Lane,
Ottery St Mary EX11 1AR
▶ Charity providing financial assistance to young vegetarians for specific courses and projects in cases of individual need. Write for grant information.

Vegetarian Society UK Ltd
Parkdale, Dunham Road,
Altringham WA14 4QG
Tel: 0161 925 2000
Fax: 0161 926 9182
Email: info@vegsoc.org
Web: www.vegsoc.org
Open: Mon-Fri 9am-5pm

▶ Registered educational charity which promoting knowledge of vegetarianism nationwide. The Cordon Vert Cookery Society trains amateur and professional chefs as well as undertaking consultancy work. V-symbol approval scheme is used for over 2000 products. Provides free information packs on becoming a vegetarian to adults and children and produces specific literature for teachers, pupils, school caterers, parents of vegetarian children and people concerned with healthy eating, as well as recipe booklets. Promotes National Vegetarian Week (see separate listing) runs an informative website, a membership scheme and publishes *The Vegetarian* magazine quarterly.

Vegfam
The Sanctuary, Near Lydford,
Okehampton EX20 4AL
Tel: 01822 820 203
Fax: 01822 820 203
Email: vegfam@veganvillage.co.uk
Web: www.veganvillage.co.uk/vegfam
Open: All days 10am-10pm
▶ For over 30 years has provided short and long term relief to victims of drought, flood, cyclone or war and believes that the fragile environments of developing countries cannot support the two populations of humans and food animals. Projects include water boreholes, vegetable gardens, fruit and nut tree planting and are carried out by UK charities working closely with indigenous community-based groups. Argues for non-GM plant-based foods grown from local varieties and is against mono-culture farming and the chemical inputs required to sustain it. Also provides self-catering holiday accommodation for vegans and vegetarians at its riverside nature reserve HQ. Supporters can control how their donations are used as Vegfam operates separate accounts for Projects, Administration and Premises. Call for more information.

General

Federation of City Farms and Community Gardens
The Green House, Hereford Street,
Bedminster, Bristol BS3 4NA
Tel: 0117 923 1800
Fax: 0117 923 1900
Email: admin@farmgarden.org.uk
Web: www.farmgarden.org
▶ Promotes and supports sustainable regeneration through community-managed farming and gardening. Each city farm is unique, varying in size, services and facilities offered to the public for recreation and education. To find out more about City Farms in your area and their activities, send an SAE for a free list of UK City Farms (see also individual City Farm listings in Chapter 8).

Food and Farming Education Service
National Agricultural Centre,
Stoneleigh Park, Stoneleigh CV8 2LZ
Tel: 024 7685 8261
Fax: 024 7669 6388

Email: foodandfarming@ruralnet.org
Web: www.foodandfarming.org
▶ A one stop shop for educational materials and enquiries on all aspects of food and farming.

Food Commission
94 White Lion Street,
London N1 9PF
Tel: 020 7837 2250
Fax: 020 7837 1141
Email: foodcomm@compuserve.com
Web: www.foodcomm.org.uk
▶ National, non-profit making organisation which acts as a consumer watchdog campaigning for the right to safer, healthier food in the UK. Publishes a quarterly journal *The Food Magazine*. Send an SAE for publications list and membership details.

Food Ethics Council
Minster Chambers, Church Street,
Southwell ng25 0HD
Tel/Fax: 01636 812 622
Email: foodeth@globalnet.co.uk
Web: www.users.globalnet.co.uk/~foodeth

---

fresh network
Are you looking for Vibrant Health?

Why not join in the raw food revolution and revolutionise your own health with the power of natural living foods?

The *fresh network* is here to help

Advice • support • information

Plus wide range of books • juicers dehydrators • sprouting kits and much more

Extensive events programme throughout the year
featuring leading health promoters from all over the world

**To learn more
call or write for our free enquiry pack
and get *fresh* for life**

fresh network • PO Box 71 • Ely • Cambs • CB7 4GU
Tel: 0870 800 7070 • Fax: 0870 800 7071
e-mail: info@fresh-network.com • website: www.fresh-network.com

▶ Established as a result of widespread public concern over recent developments in the agricultural and food industries, some of which may offend generally accepted ethical principles. Much present day agribusiness often appears to pay insufficient attention to adverse effects on the health and safety of consumers, farm animal welfare, the livelihood of many farmers, preservation of the natural environment and, not least, the well-being of the less privileged in developing countries. The Council's aims are to: raise public awareness of the erosion of ethical standards which may accompany the pursuit of short-term profit; alert the public to ethical concerns over new biotechnologies; and influence governments, food producers and food retailers to operate within an appropriate, publicly acceptable ethical framework.

fresh network
PO Box 71, Ely CB7 4GU
Tel: 0870 800 7071
Fax: 0870 800 7070
Email: info@fresh-network.com
Web: www.fresh-network.com
▶ The fresh network is the UK's national organisation for the promotion of the raw/living food diet. Its aim is to inform and educate on the benefits of a diet consisting of 100% or a high percentage of natural raw plant foods, and to support and help those already following a living foods lifestyle. Fresh offers a wide range of products and services including: membership (5 issues of *Get fresh!* magazine per year plus special offers); an extensive mail order catalogue of books, videos, juicers, sprouters, dehydrators and other useful equipment; a regular and varied events programme and ongoing support and help via a comprehensive website and internet linked e-groups. Write or call for a free enquiry pack.

LEAF – Linking Environment And Farming
The National Agricultural Centre,
Stoneleigh, Warwickshire, CV8 2LZ
Tel: 024 7641 3911
Fax: 024 7641 3636
Email: leaf@farmline.com
Web: www.leafuk.org
▶ LEAF's aims are to develop and promote farm practices which combine care and concern for the environment with the responsible and economic use of modern methods to produce safe and wholesome food. This is achieved through the setting up of demonstration farms throughout the country and through practical guidelines and environmental audits. To arrange a free visit to a LEAF Demonstration Farm, please contact the LEAF Office.

National Farmers' Union
Agriculture House,
164 Shaftesbury Avenue,
London WC2H 8HL
Tel: 020 7331 7200
Fax: 020 7331 7313
Web: www.nfu.org.uk
▶ Lobbying organisations that represents more than 130,000 farmers and growers in England and Wales. Its main objective is to promote the interests of those farming businesses that produce high quality food and drink products for customers and markets at home and abroad. Central to this objective is the NFU's encouragement of environmentally friendly and welfare-conscious farming practices and a desire to ensure the longterm survival of viable rural communities.

National Association of Farmers Markets
c/o Envolve, Green Park Station,
Green Park Road,
Bath BA1 1JB
Tel: 01225 787 914
Fax: 01225 460840
Email:
charlotte@farmersmarkets.net
Web: www.farmersmarket.net
▶ Non-profit organisation set up in 1999 to promote the formation of new farmers markets and to support existing ones with advice and an accreditation scheme. Information packs and list of existing farmers markets available, send large SAE.

Sustain: The alliance for better food and farming
94 White Lion Street,
London N1 9PF
Tel: 020 7837 1228
Fax: 020 7837 1141
Email: sustain@sustainweb.org
Web: www.sustainweb.org
▶ Advocates food and agriculture policies and practices that enhance the health and welfare of people and animals, improve the living and working environment, enrich society and culture and promote equity. Represents over 100 national public interest organisations working at international, national, regional and local level. Current activities include agriculture, trade and rural policy reform, engaging with the Food Standards Agency, tackling food poverty, promoting urban agriculture, and challenging misleading advertising and labelling.

What the label says about you

There is much more to labels than the designer logo and today it's not just food which comes with an eco-friendly guarantee. Textile experts BTTG are at the forefront of developing a standard, Oeko-Tex 100, for textiles that means clothes are healthier for you and for the planet.

The Oeko-Tex 100 standard was developed by a European group of textile institutes as a testing programme to screen for the presence of certain hazardous elements and compounds within consumer textiles. The response to this was so positive that this group has now expanded to 14 institutes, including BTTG, representing the premier collection of textile ecological expertise within Europe.

Textiles are the result of a complex series of manufacturing processes, in the course of which an extremely diverse range of chemicals may be used. Oeko-Tex 100 specifies the allowable levels in textiles of defined substances, known to be a health risk to humans. The permissible limits are based on scientific research and, as this is an ongoing process, are kept constantly under review. The scheme is unique in offering the opportunity to label textile products indicating their ecological acceptability for consumer use.

Application for an Oeko-Tex certificate is straightforward. Following simple guidelines, applicants complete an application form and then are requested to submit a selection of samples, along with details of manufacture, to BTTG. Once an Oeko-Tex 100 certificate has been awarded to a company, it should maintain an effective quality system to ensure that its products reach the correct standards when tested (usually twice yearly).

The Oeko-Tex certificate authorises the products concerned to be labelled with the internationally recognised Oeko-Tex signet. This is a declaration that the product totally satisfies the condition of the Oeko-Tex standard 100 and that the manufacturer is under constant evaluation and guidance by BTTG. A company or manufacturer then has complete use of the official Oeko-Tex logo, or 'signet', to endorse its products. The Oeko-Tex tests cover:

- acidity/alkalinity (pH level)
- pesticides
- dyestuffs
  (banned azo dyes, allergenic dyes)
- formaldehyde
- chlorinated phenols
  (eg pentachlorophenol)
- phthalates
- biocides
- flame retardants
- extractable heavy metals
- dibutyl and tributyl tin
  (DBT and TBT)
- dye-carriers
  (chloro-organic compounds)
- volatile compounds (eg solvents)
- loose dye/colour
- odours.

The Oeko-Tex label is divided into classes according to utilisation. In the different product classes not only the ready to sell articles may be certified, but also their preliminary products at all levels of manufacturing (fibres, yarns, fabrics) and accessories. Classes are:

- products for babies (under 2 years)
- products with direct contact to skin
  (blouses, shirts, underwear, etc)
- products without skin contact
  (eg outer fabrics, linings, stuffings)
- household (decorative) products
  (tablecloths, floor coverings, mattresses, etc).

Since its establishment, the Oeko-Tex scheme has continued to gain acceptance from a range of textile producers as awareness on human ecological issues increases. The Oeko-Tex scheme is the dominant player in the textile eco-labelling field and the Oeko-Tex Association is committed to a continuing process of improvement. BTTG works with the other Institutes to carefully monitor developments in order to maintain its leading technical status. The label has grown to be such a well-known brand that manufacturers willingly approach BTTG for Oeko-Tex endorsement, often as a response prompted by customer request. Voluntary certification has given accredited firms advantages at well below the expected cost.

BTTG is the United Kingdom's exclusive certifying body and has enjoyed working with a range of international market leaders on this human ecology label since joining the Oeko-Tex Association in 1994. In addition to providing a full testing and monitoring service, BTTG offers comprehensive guidance and advice to prospective and current holders of Oeko-Tex certificates. ■

*For more information of Oeko-Tex and BTTG, visit **www.bttg.org.uk***

From personal to commercial

So many of the products and services listed in the Green Guide originate from the desire of ordinary people to replace processed and synthetic products with something natural and safe for their own or their family's use. **Merri Mayers** *describes how she started her own cosmetics company as a direct response to a personal need.*

How many of you are happy with the way your skin looks and performs? Really, really happy? If there are more than three of you holding up your hands, I'll be surprised. But if you are unhappy with the way your skin looks and you haven't got a clinically diagnosed problem, then you should stand up, stamp your size fives and ask why and what you can do about it. If your skin is happy and in a balanced state it will look great and so will you, I promise.

I had dreadful skin – spots galore, sensitive and reactive to travel and hormonal shifts. So did my mother. I tried everything, you name a brand, I tried it. I spent a fortune over the years. Then, I came down with pneumonia and was told to do nothing. So, with necessity as the mother of my invention and time to devote, I threw out everything in my bathroom cupboard except deodorant and toothpaste and resolved to make my own. It couldn't, I reasoned, have a worse effect than the products I had been using – and at least I'd understand what the ingredients were!

My skin altered dramatically with what became my first product – in minutes – and my friends started bringing sterilised baby food jars over for me to fill with gloop; thus Comfort and Joy was born. Well, actually Comfort and Joy was born over a bar of chocolate in the bath as I realised what we were about – we have never been about making loads of money. If we don't help, then we don't exist, and that's a promise from my heart – life is too short to add to the piles and piles of products that pay only lip service to this concept!

My central premise was to achieve 'gentle'. Plant based and natural, after loads of research (on my face and the face of my toddler), seemed the best way to achieve 'gentle'. Vegetable oils and butters, more and more often organic (happily!), form the basis of what we do. I formulate without preservatives when I can. Nothing we make which you use on your face as a cleanser or moisturiser, absolute necessities for your face's well-being, will include synthetic preservatives. The products shouldn't have to irritate in order to do their jobs.

That is not to say that we won't use synthetics – we will and do. The stuff we use to get a shampoo to bubble, for example, is a gentler alternative to soapwort. The mixture is synthetic, but virtuous, so I use it quite happily. Don't get so hung up on the concept of natural that you disdain anything synthetic because sometimes synthetic can be useful too. What you need to know is which ones are healthy – for both you and the environment – and the concentrations that are involved. All of our bubbling mixtures are made with very low concentrations of detergents (not a nice word, but that's what they are). So don't expect a hugely foaming bubble bath from us; bubbles can be irritants for both you and the ecosystem. You'll get some bubbles, but more important you'll get both smooth, moisturised skin due to the high levels of vegetable oils and a problem sorted (hopefully) as we make nothing without a therapeutic intent.

To do this we use essential oils judiciously – they are powerful, potent and very effective. Essential oils smell great and, at Comfort and Joy, they have important jobs to do as well. Our bath preparations address issues from hangovers to bereavement, from achy muscles to crisis management. We don't use fragrances ('parfum' on an ingredients list) – why waste bottle space on an ingredient which has no hope of helping you out? Also, synthetic perfumes are a very common source of irritation.

From my start at the kitchen table, I've not looked back. My skin has improved beyond belief, and my children are reaping the benefit of what we do. We became a business almost in spite of ourselves, and run it as a family because when you take someone's face in your hands, you take their lives as well. If you believe that you are what you eat and therefore eat healthily and well, and your skin is not reflecting that, then take a second look at the labels of the products you are using. Ask for explanations about those ingredients you don't understand. You should know not just what they are, but why they are there. If the answer isn't forthcoming, then you have a very potent response: you can vote with your feet, and you should. Good luck, happy hunting, and remember, it can be sorted. ∎

Contact Merri Mayers at Baytree Cottage, Eastleach, Nr. Cirencester GL7 3NL.
Tel: **01367 850 278**
Email: **merri@ comfortandjoy.co.uk**

Clothing & Cosmetics 47

INFO — Green pros and cons of common fabrics

Viscose	**Pros** ● Biodegradable ● Sheds dirt so needs minimal care ● Fairly strong **Cons** ● Human-made so involves the use of chemicals in production
Rayon	**Pros** ● Biodegradable and recyclable, manufactured from processed wood pulp from farmed trees ● Low energy upkeep **Cons** ● Cellulose is extracted from the trees and chemically reacted with highly toxic compounds to form a spinning solution ● Energy intensive production
Silk	**Pros** ● Biodegradable and recyclable ● Natural fibre ● Soft and unrestricting **Cons** ● Vast consumption of water needed to clean silk ● Toxic dyes and finishing treatments are used ● Silk moths are killed by suffocation ● For 1kg of silk, 200kg of mulberry leaves are eaten by larvae
Linen	**Pros** ● Biodegradable and recyclable ● Natural fibre ● Less quantities of pesticides and fertilisers required than cotton ● Shorter growing cycle **Cons** ● Printing and colouring use synthetic dyes leading to water contamination ● Treated with formaldehyde ● Bleaching processes required to fix dye
Wool	**Pros** ● Biodegradable and recyclable ● Natural fibre ● Long-lasting ● Waterproof **Cons** ● Sheep dips (mainly used for cleaning) are highly toxic ● Moth-proofing processes are toxic to fish and marine life ● Metallic dyes are required which accumulate underground and eventually spread to water supplies
Tencel	**Pros** ● Biodegradable ● Derived from managed forests grown on poor agricultural land ● Environmentally favourable process ● Doesn't need to be dry cleaned ● Ideal for blending with other fibres for very strong yarns, enhancing performance without diminishing look or feel ● Its high tenacity allows the yarn to be spun to very fine counts, enabling the production of lighter fabrics with exceptional strengths **Cons** ● Issues around farming on poor agricultural land

IMPACT — Caring for the planet through your appearance

Clothing

- Demand and buy well-made, quality clothes that last.
- Ask for clothing which uses recycled fibres and for unbleached and organic cotton.
- Mend and make your own clothes.
- Use natural, animal-friendly products.
- Avoid harmful dry cleaning.
- Keep washing and the use of dryers to a minimum to save energy and money. Choose a lower temperature or economy cycle on your machine. Iron only when necessary.
- Avoid silk if possible and oppose the fur trade.
- Recycle clothes. Charities such as Oxfam and Scope run textile banks for unwanted clothing. Even damaged or unwearable clothing can be converted into items such as cleaning cloths.
- Dry clothes outside instead of using fabric softeners. Use alternatives to bleach such as boiling white cotton, using lemon juice or drying clothes in sunlight.

Cosmetics

- Use you consumer power to buy make-up products which are as simply formulated and ecologically sound as possible.
- Beware of the pressures of glossy adverts and exploitative media images.
- Avoid excessively packaged goods and write to manufacturers to complain if goods are over-packaged.
- Write to Beauty Without Cruelty for a list of companies which produce cosmetics without cruelty to animals.
- Support companies with recycling policies for packaging.

CLOTHING

Natural & Recycled

The following section includes shops, manufacturers and mail order companies which sell fair trade or natural clothing.

Amano
16 Chalk Farm Road, Camden, London, NW1 8AG
Tel: 020 7267 6918
Fax: 020 7267 6918
▶ Company started in 1988 at a stall in Camden Market, now supplies shops around the country. Fabrics are sourced for ethical and environmental values. A lot of its knitwear is hand-spun and dyed in Bolivia. Recycled knitwear is made from wool, hemp, denim and plastic bottles.

Bishopston Trading Company
193 Gloucester Road, Bishopston, Bristol BS7 8BG
Tel: 0117 924 5598
Fax: 0117 975 3590
Email: bishopston.trading@btinternet.com
Open: Mon-Sat 9.30am-5.30pm
▶ A workers' co-operative set up in 1985 to create employment in the South Indian village of K V Kuppam which has been linked to Bishopton since 1978. Sells clothing for adults and children made exclusively to their design from cotton and silk by a team of 410 tailors, weavers, embroiderers, batik workers and hand finishers. Has five shops located in Bristol, Bradford-on-Avon, Glastonbury, Totnes and Stroud. Also produces four mail order catalogues a year and sells wholesale.

Conscious Earthwear
6A Iliffe Yard, Crampton Street, London SE17 3QA
Tel: 020 7252 4802
Fax: 020 7252 5460
Email: productaura_conscious@btinternet.com
▶ Started in 1993, produces fashionable clothes from environmentally friendly fabrics. Uses materials that bear the Ecotex logo, a European standard that indicates that textile manufacturing processes are ecologically sound. They used hemp linen and jersey in their spring/summer 1999 collection.

Eco Clothworks
PO Box 16109, London SE23 3WA
Tel: 020 8299 1619
Fax: 020 8299 6997
▶ Organic 'eco-textile' clothes and bed linen including a range for kids under five years, hemp, silk and organic linen shirt collections.

Greenfibres Eco Goods & Garments
99 High Street, Totnes TQ9 5PF
Tel: 01803 868 001
Fax: 01803 868 002
Email: mail@greenfibres.com
Web: www.greenfibres.com
Open: Mon-Fri 9.30am-5.30pm
▶ Sells high quality clothes for women, men and children made from environmentally responsible materials (organic cotton, linen, wool and untreated hemp and silk) under fair and safe working conditions. Products include organic cotton oxford shirts, wool baby blankets, cotton underwear and fabrics by the metre. Call for a free catalogue. Have just opened a new shop at 99 High Street, Totnes, for those who want to visit.

Hemp Collective, The
Silverdale, Clyde Road, Didsbury, Manchester M20 2NJ
Tel: 0161 445 5227
Fax: 0161 445 2556
Email: talk2us@thehempcollective.com
Web: www.thehempcollective.com
Open: Mon-Fri 9am-9pm
▶ Provides a diverse range of hemp products encompassing bodycare, clothing, foodstuffs, paper and sundries. Mail order and wholesale facilities for people looking to make a positive difference to themselves and the planet. Write or call for a catalogue or visit the website.

Hemp Trading Company, The
The Barn, Elliots Court, Biddestone, Chippenham, Bath SN14 7DG
Tel: 01249 701 588
Fax: 01249 701 566
Email: dan@thehempcollective.com
Web: www.thehempcollective.com
▶ Recently started urban eco fashion label targeted at the 18-35 year olds. Functional designs with streetwear in mind. Combines the direct action and subversive nature of today's youth with the wisdom and spiritual eco-friendly awareness of yesterday.

Hemp Union
24 Anlaby Road, Hull HU1 2PA
Tel: 01482 225 328
Fax: 01482 225 328
Email: sales@hemp-union.karoo.co.uk
Web: www.hemp-union.karoo.net
▶ The original hemp company in the UK, established in 1993, and now producing a wide range of hemp products from foods, oil and toiletries to textiles, paper and accessories. Profits are invested back into hemp

---

GREENFIBRES
eco-goods and garments

- organic cotton
- organic linen
- organic wool
- natural hemp

for adults, babies, and children

FREE CATALOGUE
FREEPOST LON7805 (GG)
TOTNES, DEVON, TQ9 5PF

SHOWROOM
99 HIGH ST., TOTNES

TEL 01803.868.001/FAX 002
WWW.GREENFIBRES.COM

HEMP UNION
Specialists in CLOTHING, T-SHIRTS, ACCESSORIES STATIONERY, FOOD PRODUCTS, COSMETICS...
Ethically produced, eco-friendly products made from CANNABIS HEMP, the world's most valuable natural resource.

NEW INFO. PACK   NOW AVAILABLE:
inc. catalogue, hemp info/history, paper + fabric samples, & a selection of 'trial size' products,
just £ 5.00 (inc. P+P)
MAILORDER CATALOGUE AVAILABLE:
Please send a large s.a.e. + 2 x 1st class stamps
(QUOTE 'GREEN GUIDE' FOR YOUR FREE DISCOUNT VOUCHER !)
Vegan
HEMP UNION LTD, 24 ANLABY ROAD, HULL, HU12PA

Clothing & Cosmetics

as a sustainable crop for the environment. The systems being developed are designed to produce locally added value from the growing of the crop for production of food, fibre, fuel, composites and building materials.

House of Hemp
PO Box 12108, London N5 2WA
Tel: *020 7274 1131*
Fax: *020 7274 1131*
Email: *matt@houseofhemp.co.uk*
Web: *www.houseofhemp.co.uk*
▶ Supplier of a basic range of hemp fabrics. Send an A5 SAE for more info. For a fabric swatch sample, send £3.50.

J P Textiles
13 Maltkiln Row, Cawthorne,
Barnsley S75 4HH
Tel: *01226 791 358*
Fax: *01226 791 358*
Email: *john.parkinson@virgin.net*
Web: *www.ever-green.co.uk*
Open: *24hr answerphone*
▶ Recycles post and pre-consumer textiles with a product range now limited to fabrics and yarns. Provides a consultancy service and is also available for lectures and teaching.

Katherine Hamnett Ltd.
202 New North Road,
London N1 7BJ
Tel: *020 7354 4400*
Fax: *020 7354 5246*
▶ Supplies some organic cotton garments.

Komodo
50-56 Wharf Road, London N1 7SE
Tel: *020 7490 8101*
Fax: *020 7490 8098*
Email: *joekomodo@aol.com*
Web: *www.komodo.co.uk*
▶ Fabrics are sourced for ethical and environmental qualities. Some items are made in Nepal using traditional techniques and organic dyes, and fabrics such as hemp-mix jersey and banana leaves.

Liverpool World Shop
64 Bold Street, Liverpool L1 4EA
Tel: *0151 708 7328*
Open: *Mon-Fri 10am-5.30pm*
▶ Ethical business providing a market for Southern Hemisphere producers, avoiding, as far as possible, middle men and speculators. Aims to pay a fair price for these goods to cover costs of production, basic needs and leaving a margin for investment while building a long-term relationship with producers. Sells a wide range of crafts, clothing and musical instruments as well as fairly traded beverages, snacks and foods. Currently involved in launching the Liverpool World Group, an association of organisations and individuals committed to a more sustainable world, with the aim of establishing a world development and education centre in Merseyside to increase understanding between people locally and globally.

Motherhemp Ltd
Tilton Barns, Near Firle,
Lewes BN8 6LL
Tel: *01323 811 909*
Fax: *020 7691 7475*
Email: *info@motherhemp.com*
Web: *www.motherhemp.com*
Open: *Mon-Fri 8.30am-6.30pm*
▶ Created to re-establish the hemp market for farming, processing and distribution of hemp products in the UK. Environmental and ethical values are central to its agenda. MotherHemp manufacturers and supplies a range of superior hemp-derived products to the retail and wholesale markets including a range of organic hemp foods, health and beauty products, and exlusive range of hemp clothing, fabrics, bags, and accessories. MotherHemp has recently opened its first retail outlet in The Lanes, Brighton.

Natural Collection
19a Monmouth Place,
Bath BA1 2DQ
Tel: *0870 331 3333*
Fax: *01225 469 673*
web: *www.naturalcollection.com*
▶ The UK's most extensive green mail order catalogue containing a range of organic cotton clothing, underwear, babywear, bed linen, stationery, cleaning products, toiletries, food, wine and much more.

Natural Selection
17 Sheep Street,
Petersfield GU32 3JX
Tel: *01730 267171*
Fax: *01730 267171*
Email: *naturalselection@supanet.com*
Open: *Mon-Sat 9.30am-5.30pm;*
1st Sun of each month 10am-2pm
▶ An alternative giftshop that sells much more than just gifts; hemp clothing, foods & accessories, organic cotton clothes, bath time wear, kid's clothes, *Permaculture* and *Kindred Spirit* magazines and related books. Gifts include local crafts, eco-friendly toys and games, incense and aromatherapy. New World music, recycled cards and other items. The body care range consists predominately of Green People and NHR, with other essentials such as Natracare and Toms of Maine. Aims to supply a green alternative for people buying a special gift for someone else, or just for themselves.

Oasis Training and Trading
23 New Mount Street,
Manchester M4 4DE
Tel: *0161 953 4039*
Fax: *0161 953 4001*
Email: *oasistrainingandtrade@compuserve.com*
▶ Supplier of a fair trade catalogue which includes products from Jacobs Well, Just Prospects and The Paperworks, and their bi-annual newsletter. Some of the new items shown in the catalogue include men's and women's pyjamas, and an extended range of children's wear from Jacob's Well; a range of screen printed cards from Just Prospects, and mirrors and mantlepiece clocks from The Paperworks. To avoid disappointment place your order at your earliest convenience. Every purchase made ensures that more vulnerable individuals in Bombay and Bangalore are able to receive training and decent employment. Offers mail order, call for more information.

Organicwool Company
Pwll-y-Broga, Pontfaen,
Fishguard SA65 9TY
Tel: *01239 821 171*
Email: *douglaswhitelaw@organicwool.freeserve.co.uk*
Web: *www.organicwool.co.uk*
▶ Makes baby blankets, rugs, throws, scarves and shawls using organic wool and wool from pesticide free farms. Does not use bleach or chemical finishes such as moth proofing in the manufacturing process. Call for mail order.

Patagonia
Unit 705, 50 Westminster Bridge Road, London SE1 7QY
Tel: *020 7721 8717*
Fax: *020 7721 8714*
Web: *www.patagonia.com*
▶ Environmentally responsible company which makes durable, outdoors clothing. Patagonia is the only company still making fleece from recycled plastic bottles and now only uses organic cotton for its clothing. The company has ongoing commitment to the environment – 10% of profits or 1% of turnover, whichever is greater, goes into environmental campaigns. Its stated purpose is to use business to inspire and implement solutions to the environmental crisis. Call or write for a mail order catalogue and stockists.

Quest Organic Clothing
Cow Pasture Farm, Hainton,
Near Market Rasen LN8 6LX
Tel: *01507 313 401*
Fax: *01507 313 609*
▶ Offers the environmentally conscious traveller a hard wearing range of practical garments that are 100% organic.

RE-VIV
16 Alma Road, Retford DN22 6LW
Tel: *01777 705 557*
Email: *Revivl@yahoo.co.uk*
Open: *24 answerphone*
▶ Makes a range of clothing and some accessories entirely from salvaged textiles. Free mail order brochure twice a year – summer and winter. English hand-knitted jumpers and velvet duffle coats are two of its popular winter lines. The summer range includes trousers and dresses made from vintage sarees. Call for a free brochure.

Clothing & Cosmetics

ROM UK
Walhampton Lodge,
Lymington SO41 5SB
Tel: 01590 674 117
Fax: 01590 676 364
Email: brook@walhampton.demon.co.uk
▶ Importers of hemp cloth and clothing, natural unbleached or dyed using Swiss, certified ecological dyes. A range of cloth weights from 200gsm. Yarn, string, rope and seed also available.

Schmidt Natural Clothing
21 Post Horn Close,
Forest Row RH18 5DE
Tel/Fax: 01342 822 169
Email: glenn@naturalclothing.co.uk
▶ Sells a wide range of organic and chemical-free clothing including underwear, pyjamas, socks, baby wear and children's wear. Also sells a wide range of reusable organic cotton nappies. Mail order only. Call for a catalogue. Offers a six month interest free credit plan.

Spirit of Nature Ltd
Burrhart House, Cradock Road,
Luton LU4 0JF
Tel: 01582 847 370
Fax: 01582 847 371
Email: oliver@spiritofnature.co.uk
Web: www.spiritofnature.co.uk
Open: Mon-Fri 9am-5.30pm
▶ Family-run business selling a comprehensive range of natural clothing, underwear and sleepwear for women and men made from 100% natural materials. All products are certified free from harmful residues and are manufactured under fair and safe working conditions. Also available: eco-household cleaning products, natural bodycare products, bedlinen, plus an extensive range of clothing and accessories for babies and toddlers, including organic washable nappy systems, eco-disposables and more. Call for free catalogue.

Traidcraft plc
Kingsway North,
Gateshead NE11 0NE
Tel: 0191 491 0591/0191 491 1001 mail order; 0191 491 3388 wholesale
Fax: 0191 482 2690
Email: comm@traidcraft.co.uk
Web: www.traidcraft.co.uk
▶ Sells a range of fairly traded, natural and organic cotton clothing for women, men and children plus a range of jewellery and many kinds of bags. Available by mail order catalogue.

Tucano
Pound House, Pound Road,
West Wittering PO20 8AJ
Tel: 01243 513 757/ 673 380
Fax: 01243 671 884
Email: mail@tucagua.com
Web: www.tucanobeach.com
▶ Clothing range is mostly handmade using natural cotton and hemp from Nepal. Also stocks organic cotton from Peru. Simple and natural.

Woollibacks
43 Blenheim Road, Cheadle,
Hulme SK8 7BD
Tel: 0161 485 2551
Fax: 0161 482 8212
▶ Small knitwear company using un-dyed, un-bleached and cruelty free wools.

Charity & Secondhand

Charity shops take old clothes and other goods so, whether you're shopping or donating, you'll be supporting a good cause.

Oxfam Head Office
Tel: 01865 311 311
▶ Oxfam shops around the country sell secondhand clothing, original crafts, clothes and foods from the developing world, which are available in their shops and catalogue. All are fairly traded and always have been. Balls of knitting wool are also accepted for making into blankets. Call the above number for details of your local branch or 01392 429 428 for a free copy of the Oxfam mail order catalogue.

Oxfam Shops
778 Wilmslow Road, Didsbury,
Manchester M20
Tel: 0161 434 5380
Open: Mon-Sat 9am-5pm

45 Blackburn Street, Radcliffe,
Manchester M26
Tel: 0161 724 5726
12 Middleton Gardens, Middleton,
Manchester M24
Tel: 0161 653 2002
31 Yorkshire Street, Oldham OL1
Tel: 0161 652 4697
449a Bury New Road, Prestwich,
Bury M25
Tel: 0161 798 0602
302 Oxford Road, Manchester M13
Tel: 0161 273 2019
11 Piccadilly Plaza, Manchester M1
Tel: 0161 228 6273
10 Station Bridge, Urmston,
Trafford M41
Tel: 0161 755 3013
17 The Parade, Sinton,
Manchester M27
Tel: 0161 794 3829
494 Wilbraham Road, Chorlton-cum-Hardy, Manchester M21
Tel: 0161 861 0108
86 George street,
Altrincham WA14 1RF
Tel: 0161 928 1877
Open: Mon-Sat 9.30am-4.30pm
323 Hale Road, Halebarns,
Wakefield WA15
Tel: 0161 904 9907
204 London Road, Hazel Grove,
Stockport SK7
Tel: 0161 487 1614
132 Market Street, Hyde,
Tameside SK4
Tel: 0161 368 2618
32 School Road, Sale M33
Tel: 0161 962 7784
23 The Precinct, Cheadle Hulme,
Stockport SK8
Tel: 0161 485 3009

Scope
6 Market Road, London N7 9PW
Tel: 0808 800 3333
Email: cphelpline@scope.org.uk
Web: www.scope.org.uk
▶ A national disability organisation focusing on people with cerebral palsy. The aim is to see disabled people achieve equality in a society in which they are as valued, and have the same human and civil rights as others. Provides housing, education and employment services. Also has 300 secondhand shops around the

Spirit Of Nature Ltd
Burrhart House, Cradock Road, Luton LU4 0JF
Website: www.spiritofnature.co.uk

For a Catalogue call 01582 847370

Natural Clothing,
Eco Household Products and more ...
by mail order. The textiles is made from organically grown raw materials like cotton, linen, silk and wool. All certified free from toxic residues.
Call or send for a free catalogue.
Organic Baby catalogue also available.

Clothing & Cosmetics

UK and runs a toner cartridge recycling scheme through the shops or through office box collection schemes. Manages a large number of textile recycling bins from which clothes and textiles are taken for reuse, resale or recycling. Call for details of your nearest shop.

Footwear

Charles MacWatt Handmade Boots & Shoes
7 Christmas Steps, Bristol BS1 5BS
Tel: 0117 921 4247
Fax: 0117 921 4247
▶ Handmade leather shoes in a large selection of styles and colours for children and adults. Leather and non-leather shoes with recycled rubber 'Vibram Ecostep' soles available. Free mail order catalogue.

Conker Shoe Co
High Street, Totnes TQ9 5PB
Tel: 01803 862 490
Web: www.conkershoes.co.uk
▶ Low impact Devon based business which makes shoes specifically to fit your feet. Working with a wide range of durable natural materials, it offers an incredible selection of colours and designs, including 100% rubber crepe soles, a sustainable resource.

Ethical Wares
Caegwyn, Temple Bar,
Felinfach SA48 7SA
Tel: 01570 471 155
Fax: 01570 471 166
Email: vegans@ethicalwares
Web: www.ethicalwares.com
▶ Vegan company selling breathable non-leather footwear and accessories and seeking to trade in a way which does not exploit animals, humans or the wider environment. Will not trade with countries which have repressive regimes or which allow exploitative practices. By selling vegan products, it hopes to play its part in the promotion of a cruelty-free lifestyle.

Green Shoes
69 High Street, Totnes TQ9 5PB
Tel: 01803 864 997
Fax: 01803 864 997
Email: info@greenshoes.co.uk
Web: www.greenshoes.co.uk

▶ Handmade shoes for men, women and children in leather and non-leather. From traditional walking boots to slip-on clog-like and trainer inspired styles with chunky soles. Off the shelf, made to order or mail order available.

Made to Last
8 The Crescent, Hyde Park,
Leeds LS6 2NW
Tel: 0113 230 4983
Fax: 0113 230 4983
Email: madetolast@ukf.net
Web: www.madetolast.org.uk
Open: Tues-Fri 10am-6pm;
Sat 11am-5pm
▶ Workers' co-operative producing high quality handmade leather and non-leather footwear in an exciting range of styles and colours for children and adults. Caters for all foot widths. Send an SAE for a catalogue or visit the website.

Veganline
Freepost LON10506,
London SW14 1YY
Tel: 0800 458 4442
Fax: 020 8878 3006
Email: veg@animal.nu
Web: www.animal.nu
Open: 24hr answerphone
▶ Animal-free shoes with very bouncy soles and post-free from this vegan mail order company that enables you to order catalogues or pay by credit card over the phone. Current stock includes hikers, goodyear-welted boots and shoes, and a platform range. Also supplies Global Warning hemp wallets and t-shirts, backpacks, hemp shoes, bags, and some macho non-leather belts. Does not buy trainers manufactured in the Far-East, but has its stock made to order in UK and European factories, and sells at high street prices. Currently looking for stockists.

Vegetarian Shoes
12 Gardner Street,
Brighton BN1 1UP
Tel: 01273 691 913
Fax: 01273 679 379
Email: information@
vegetarian-shoes.co.uk

Web: www.vegetarianshoes.co.uk
Open: Mon-Sat 10am-5.30pm
▶ Sells a wide range of vegetarian and vegan shoes which look and feel like supple leather but are in fact 100% manmade. Uppers made from Vegetan, a revolutionary, cruelty-free synthetic fibre that is water-resistant, lightweight and breathable. Specialises in Doc Martens of many styles and colours. Mail order available. Call for a free colour brochure.

Textile Recycling

Oxfam Shops
Head Office, Oxford
Tel: 01865 311 311
▶ Oxfam shops around the country sell secondhand clothing as well as original crafts, clothes and foods from the developing world. These are available in their shops and catalogue, are fairly traded and always have been. All branches accept aluminium foil for recycling and used postage stamps. Balls of knitting wool are also accepted for making into blankets. Call for details of your local branch or 01392 429 428 for a free copy of the mail order catalogue.

Textile Recycling
5 High Street, Boxworth,
Cambridge CB3 8LY
Tel: 01954 268 000
Fax: 01954 268 001
Email: tra@pwatterson.freeserve.co.uk
▶ Trade association for the textile recycling industry.

Organisations

BTTG
Shirley House, Towers Business Park,
856 Wilmslow Road, Didsbury,
Manchester M20 2RB
Tel: 0161 445 8141
Fax: 0161 434 9957
Email: info@bttg.co.uk
Web: www.bttg.co.uk
▶ International textile eco-labels. EC standard for eco-wear. Exclusive certifying body for the United Kingdom,

SCOPE — FOR PEOPLE WITH CEREBRAL PALSY

Recycle your printer toner and/or inkjet cartridges and help people with cerebral palsy and related disabilities.

It's easy and it's free!

To obtain a starter pack or further information about the 'Toner Donor' recycling scheme, call **020 7619 7239** and quote: **GG**.

Scope, 6 Market Road, London N7 9PW
Web: www.scope.org.uk
Registered charity No. 208231

Clothing & Cosmetics

accredited to undertake assesment testing in strict accordance with Oko-Tex specifications.

Textile Environmental Network
c/o National Centre for Business Ecology, The Peel Building, University of Salford, Manchester M5 4WT
Tel: 0161 295 5271
Fax: 0161 295 5041
Email: Ten@mailbase.ac.uk; mailbase@mailbase.ac.uk
▶ Network providing and exchanging information, knowledge and ideas relating to the environmental performance of clothing and textiles, through a programme of seminars and conferences, exhibitions and a newsletter. Aims to foster co-operation and understanding between design centres, the textile and clothing industries and small-scale producers to raise awareness and promote better environmental practice. The network communicates mainly through email.

COSMETICS & TOILETRIES

Many wholefood shops and shops selling complementary health products will stock small ranges of cosmetics and toiletries. See Chapter One: Food & Drink and Chapter Five: Health for more stockists.

Shops

Body Shop, The
Head Office, Watersmead, Littlehampton
Tel: 01903 731 500
▶ The best known high street chain of natural hair and body care products. Fundamental to The Body Shop's ethos are the core values of concern for human and civil rights, care for the environment and opposition to animal exploitation. It is committed to building up fair trade networks with people around the world. Through the shop's refill bar and minimal packaging, The Body Shop conserves resources, reduces waste and saves customers money. Contact the head office for details of your nearest retail outlet or look them up in the following listings.

Body Shops
28 Barbirolli Mall,
Arndale Shopping Centre,
Manchester M4 3AA
Tel: 0161 832 5378
Fax: 0161 839 3005
Open: Mon-Weds, Fri 9.30am-5.45pm; Thurs 9.30am-7pm; Sat 9.30am-5.45pm; Sun 11am-5pm
Royal Exchange Shopping Centre, Cross Street, Manchester M2 7DB
Tel: 0161 832 9148
Open: Mon-Fri 9am-5.30pm;
Sat 9am-6pm
26 George Street, Altrincham, Cheshire WA14 1RH
Tel: 0161 926 9284
Fax: 0161 929 8930
Open: Mon-Sat 9am-5.30pm
8-10 Merseyway, Stockport SK1 1PJ
Tel: 0161 429 6912
Fax: 0161 429 6503
Open: Mon-Sat 9am-5.30pm;
Sun 11am-4pm

Culpeper Herbalists
Head Office, Hadstock Road, Linton, Cambridge CB1 6NJ
Tel: 01223 891 196
Fax: 01223 893 104
Email: info@culpeper.co.uk
Web: www.culpeper.co.uk
▶ Culpeper products take their name from seventeenth century Nicholas Culpeper, who believed strongly in the healing powers of herbs, pure food and exercise. Founded in 1927 by Mrs C.F Leyel, the Culpeper's aim was, and still is today, to provide the public with simple herbal remedies, pure cosmetics and natural perfumes. No animal testing, artificial colours or enhancers in Culpeper foods. Culpeper – the original green scene, 20 shops nationwide.

Culpeper Herbalists
1 Cavern Walks, Mathew Street, Liverpool L2 6RE
Tel: 0151 236 5780
Fax: 0151 236 5780
Open: Mon-Sat 9.30am-5.30pm

Shared Earth
51 Piccadilly, Manchester M1 2AP
Tel: 0161 236 1014
Fax: 0161 237 1206
Web: www.sharedearth.co.uk
Open: Mon-Sat 9am-6pm;
Sun 10am-4pm
▶ Wide range of fair trade items, such as stationery, picture frames, soaps and bath blasters.

Mail Order & Manufacturers

Aloe Care – Grace Cosmetics
The Piece, Cutwell, Tetbury GL8 8EB
Tel: 01666 504 718
Fax: 01666 505 310
Email: woeac@msn.com
▶ Launched 35 years ago by Lucille Flint in Australia, the range has established a reputation for purity, quality and performance. From the outset – and before regulations required – the ingredients were listed on each container. Preparations consist of an abundance of pure, processed, biologically active and therapeutic grade Australian-grown Aloe Vera, complimented and enhanced by pure plant and herbal extracts and essential oils, with skin vitamins, all in a natural form. None of the preparations contain any beeswax, lanolin, collagen, or any other animal or placenta extracts, alcohol or petro-chemical derivatives and are not tested on animals or subject to genetic modification. Suitable for all skin types and possessing anti-ageing properties, the range can be of benefit to many types of skin disorder.

Annemarie Börlind
Old Factory Buildings, Battenhurst Road, Stonegate TN5 7DU
Tel: 01580 201 687
Fax: 01580 201 697
Email: info@simply-nature.co.uk
Open: Mon-Fri 8.30am-5.30pm;
Sat 9am-12noon
▶ Pure, natural beauty products which are carefully created using GM free botanical ingredients derived from controlled organic sources, which support the natural regeneration process and involve no animal testing. With 40 years manufacturing experience, the company is dedicated to the continued development of natural beauty. Distributed by Simply Nature and available by mail order with a full brochure and trial sizes available on request. Other healthy lifestyle products are also available from Simply Nature.

Ascent
Long Barn, Felindre,
Brecon LD3 0TE
Tel: 01497 847 788
Fax: 01497 847 788
Email: morrisj@gonegardening.com
▶ A smal, natural perfumery blending the purest essential oils and absolutes to create scent in its indigenous form. Aims to bring the true fragrance that comes from the plant and not from the laboratory bench. Will not use any flower, seed or spice which cannot be extracted from the original plant. Has now applied the same philosophy to soaps, with the colouring made from natural roots and spices. Using this gentle process creates scented soaps, naturally coloured with fra-

Clothing & Cosmetics

grant themes. All soaps are hand-cut and come in a simple box set. Call for a brochure.

Aveda Cosmetics Ltd
7 Munton Road,
London SE17 1NR
Tel: 020 7410 1600
Fax: 020 7410 1899
Web: www.aveda.com
▶ BUAV-approved environmentally friendly beauty and non-petrochemical based products, made entirely of natural ingredients. Over 700 products including haircare, skincare, makeup and perfumes, etc. Available at selected stores and hairdressing salons nationwide. Call for stockist details.

Barry M Cosmetics Ltd
1 Bittacy Business Centre,
Bittacy Hill, London NW7 1BA
Tel: 020 8349 2992
Fax: 020 8346 7773
Email: info@barrym.co.uk
Web: www.barrym.co.uk
▶ BUAV-approved toiletries and huge range of cosmetics.

Beauty Without Cruelty
Devonshire Road Industrial Estate,
Millom LA18 4JS
Tel: 020 8979 8156
Fax: 020 8979 6602
Email: sarah_edgell@englishbrands.com
Open: Mon-Fri 9am-5pm
▶ Manufacturer of cruelty-free, quality make-up and skin care products All our products are not tested on animals, there are no animal-derived ingredients, they are suitable for vegetarians, fragrance and lanolin free. Call for mail order details.

Benrené Health International
18 Chatsmore House, Goring By Sea, Worthing BN12 5AH
Tel: 01903 505 180
Fax: 01903 245 718
Email: chris@kf-g.com
Web: www.nawt.net
▶ Collection of pure natural hair and skin care products also on offer from a company that started out selling eco-friendly household products (see Chapter Three: Home). Call for a mail order catalogue.

Bio-D Company Ltd
64 St Nicholas Gate, Hedon,
Kingston-upon-Hull HU12 8HS
Tel: 01482 229 950
Fax: 01482 229 921
Email: bio-d@ecodet.karoo.co.uk
▶ In addition to household cleaning products, Bio-D also sells hemp oil body and hair care products, hand-made vegetable oil soaps and fruit shampoos (see Chapter Three: Home).

biOrganic Hair Therapy
Unit 2, Caxton Park, Wright Street,
Old Trafford, Manchester M16 9EW
Tel: 0161 872 9813
Fax: 0161 872 9848
Email: sales@biorganics.co.uk
Web: www.biorganics.co.uk
▶ Supplier of Vegetarian Society, RSPCA and BUAV-approved organic hair treatments made using essential oils, vitamins and minerals and vegetable proteins. All products are highly concentrated so a small quantity goes a long way. Mostly supplied to hairdressing salons but also to individuals. Call for a mail order catalogue.

Blackmores Ltd
Willow Tree Marina, West Quay Drive,
Yeading UB4 5TA
Tel: 020 8842 3956
Fax: 020 8841 7557
Email: sales@nhb-company.co.uk
Web: www.blackmores.com
Open: Mon-Fri 9am-5pm
▶ Australian natural, cruelty-free skin and haircare products, herbal remedies and nutritional supplements. Available at selected health shops and by mail order.

Cameo Essential Oils
522 Manchester Road, Rixton,
Warrington WA3 6JT
Tel/Fax: 0161 775 4535
▶ Supplier of 100% pure essential oils and associated aromatherapy products. Wholesale and retail. Call for mail order catalogue.

Clearly Natural
PO Box 4, Camberley G15 2YY
Tel/Fax: 01276 675 609
Web: www.clearly-natural.co.uk
▶ Supplies a range of over 200 natural and organic toiletries and cosmetics, available by mail order or direct from the website. Products include face creams and cleansers, toothpastes, shampoos, body care, soaps, ranges for men, babies and children, organic cotton towels and bedding, feminine hygiene products and aromatherapy essential oils. Over 80% of products are organic and three-quarters are suitable for vegans. Also available are luxury gift boxes for men, women, children, new mothers and special occasions, containing organic cotton face cloths, conditioning shampoos, aromatherapy moisture lotions, organic creams and scented soaps. Boxes can be personalised and gift vouchers can be purchased. Call for a brochure.

Cosmetics To Go
PO Box 2150, Hastings TN35 5ZX
Tel: 01424 201 202
Fax: 01424 715 793
Email: costogo@hastings16.fsnet.co.uk
Web: www.cosmetics.to.go.uk.com
Open: 24hr answer phone

▶ Sells highly original, quirky, cruelty-free toiletries and cosmetics for all the family. All products are tested on humans. Were the first company to not use animals and started the Asissi Test (using human volunteers). A mail order company with a shop in Hastings. Most products are natural and vegan and all are delivered fully wrapped.

Creightons Naturally Plc
Water Lane, Storrington RH20 3DP
Tel: 01903 745 611
Fax: 01903 745 986
Email: sales@creightons.com
Web: www.creightons.com
▶ BUAV-approved makers of skin and haircare products available by mail order.

Daniel Field – Organic and Mineral Hairdressing
8 Broadwick Street, London W1
Tel: 020 7439 8223
Fax: 020 7287 4954
Email: sueblake@blakes0.demon.co.uk

Animal-friendly cosmetics which won't hurt your purse

Beauty without cruelty

- No testing on animals
- No animal-derived ingredients
- Gentle, fragrance-free formulations

All products cost less than £5

Available from pharmacies & health food stores.
Call 01229 775185 for stockists and mail order.

Clothing & Cosmetics

▶ Daniel Field is a pioneer of organic and mineral hairdressing, and a natural hairdresser. Supplies an extensive range of organic shampoos, conditioners, treatments and hair colourants available by mail order. To receive a brochure send an SAE to: Daniel Field, Freepost, Nottingham.

Dead Sea Magik
Finders International Ltd,
Orchard House,
Winchet Hill,
Gourdhurst TN17 1JY
Tel: 01580 211 055
Fax: 01580 212 062
Email: findersinternational@compuserve.co.uk
▶ BUAV-approved toiletries formulated with minerals from the Dead Sea including moisturisers, mud masks, bath salts, shampoo, etc. Available by mail order and stocked in Holland & Barrett and independent health food shops and chemists.

Deodorant Stone (UK) Ltd, The
2 Lime Tree Cottage, Forley,
Malmesbury SN16 0JJ
Tel: 01666 826 515
Fax: 01666 823186
Email: info@deodorant-stone.co.uk
Open: Mon-Fri 9am-5pm
▶ Sells a unique range of aluminium chlorohydrate free body deodorants, based on the food grade mineral salt potassium alum (which is also used for preserving pickles). The products stop the bacteria which causes body odour from growing on the skin. The original deodorant stones are available in two sizes: 60g which lasts for approximately 6 months; and 120g which will last well over a year. To use, simply wet the strone and rub it on. A fine layer of salt is left on the skin which prevents bacteria but allows the body to sweat and function naturally. For those who prefer a more conventional type of deodorant the company also have a roll-on and a spray-on stone, which are available in unscented different fragrances. A peppermint foot spray is also avaliable.

Diana Drummond Ltd
Arichastlich, Glen Orchy, near
Dalmally PA33 1BD
Tel: 01838 200 450
Email: sales@dianadrummond.com
▶ Specialist natural seaweed skin care company blending local seaweeds and plants to formulate creams, lotions and soaps. Edible seaweed also on offer. All harvesting is done by hand, using techniques that ensure regeneration of the plant communities.

Dolma
19 Royce Avenue, Hucknall,
Nottingham NG15 6FU
Tel: 0115 963 4237
Fax: 0115 963 4237
Email: dolma@veganvillage.co.uk
Web: www.veganvillage.co.uk/dolma
Open: Mon-Fri 9am-5pm
▶ Entirely vegan, BUAV-approved company producing an exclusive range of vegan perfumes, skin care and toiletries based on pure essential oils, herbal extracts and floral waters. Does not use any animal-derived materials and neither the products nor the materials from which they are made are tested on animals. A fixed cut-off date of 1976 applies. Send SAE (1st class stamp) for free mail order catalogue. The boxed set of ten, trial sized perfumes at £14.95 makes an ideal gift.

Elysia Natural Skin Care
19/20 Stockwood Business Park,
Redditch B96 6SX
Tel: 01386 792 622
Fax: 01386 792 623
Email: elysia@ava.compulink.co.uk
▶ Supplies Dr Hauschka skin care – a holistic range using biodynamically grown and hand-harvested plants and herbs. Wherever possible hand labour replaces machines. Sells by mail order and through some retail outlets, and also accredited Estheticians who can advise on a suitable skincare programme.

Toiletries and cosmetics with organic and natural ingredients to care for all the family

Face and Body Care
Men's Toiletries
Children's and Babies' Ranges
Hair Care
Soap & Toothpaste
Aromatherapy
Feminine Hygiene
Gift Boxes
Sun Tan Creams
Organic Cotton Textiles

Because being beautiful needn't cost the earth!

Clearly Natural
Toiletries From Natural & Organic Sources

www.clearly-natural.co.uk
(01276) 675609 for more information

Clothing & Cosmetics

Escential Botanicals Ltd
Unit 25 Mountbatten Road,
Kennedy Way,
Tiverton EX16 6SW
Tel: 01884 257 612
Fax: 01884 258 928
Email: archie@escential.com
Web: www.escential.com
▶ Escential Botanicals is a carefully designed 100% natural face, hair and body care product range that uses only the best flower, fruit and herb extracts and essential oils available.

Faith in Nature
5 Kay Street,
Bury BL9 6BU
Tel: 0161 764 2555
Fax: 0161 762 9129
Email: sales@safeproducts.com
Web: www.safeproducts.com
▶ Produces BUAV-approved skin and hair care products as well as the Clear Spring range of eco-friendly household cleaning products. Stocked in health food shops and available by mail order.

Farrow & Humphreys Ltd
Meadow Park Industrial Estate,
Bourne Road, Essendine,
Near Stamford PE9 4LT
Tel: 01780 482200
Fax: 01780 482112
Email: paul@fpisales.com
Web: www.fpisales.com
Open: Mon-Fri 9am-5pm
▶ The therapeutic properties of essential oils, herbs and flowers, combined with a continuing resistance to the use of any animal ingredients or animal derivatives, have led to 20 years of a great range of hand and body balms, soaps and bath products. Call for a free brochure and mail order or a list of local stockists.

Green People Company
Brighton Road, Handcross RH17 6BZ
Tel: 01444 401 444
Fax: 01444 401 011
▶ Supplies herbal tonics, dietary supplements, 100% natural cosmetics for hair, body and skin care and home cleaning products. Also available is a range of toothpaste and mouthwashes certified by the Soil Association.

Green Things
PO Box 59, Tunbridge Wells TN3 9PT
Tel: 01892 861 132
Web: www.green-things.com
▶ Manufactures an extensive range of BUAV-approved beauty care products using natural organic ingredients and without causing suffering to animals.

Hemp Pot, The
Space Base. The Hemp Pot,
5 Imperial Way, Croydon,
Surrey CR0 4RR
Tel: 020 8760 0800
Open: Mon-Fri 10am-4pm
▶ Sells a large selection of hemp products. Toiletries include handmade soaps, shampoo, conditioner, bubble bath, bath salt's, moisturising face oil etc. and a hair oil made with 100% natural ingredients for the treatment of Alopcia. Call for a catologue.

Honesty Cosmetics
Lumford Mill, Bakewell DE45 1GS
Tel: 01629 814 888
Fax: 01629 814 111
Email: honesty.cosmetics@virgin.net
Web: freespace.virgin.net/honesty.cosmetics
▶ Vegan skin and haircare products from the founder members of the cosmetics industry's coalition for animal welfare which campaigns for a fixed cut off date for use of ingredients tested on animals and for meaningful product labelling. Full mail order service available for both their products and those of other, like-minded companies.

Kinetic Enterprises Ltd
48 Harvard Court, Honeybourne Road,
London NW6 1HN
Tel: 020 7435 5911
Fax: 020 7431 5935
Email: kinetic@globalnet.co.uk
▶ Natural, cruelty free cosmetics from US and Europe. Specialises in skin, body and haircare.

Maxim Marketing
169 Empire Road, Perivale, UB6 7HA
Tel: 020 8998 2357
Fax: 020 8998 2357
▶ Supplies vegan and BUAV-approved Amber toothpaste, moisturising cream soap and Weikfield Jelly Crystals soap and toothpaste. Available in many Hindu and Moslem-owned shops and in cash and carrys such as Bestways and TRS. The company allows charities to sell its products at cost and keep the profits. Send an SAE for a mail order catalogue.

Montagne Jeunesse
Eco Factory, Off Valley Way,
Swansea Enterprise Park,
Cllansamlet, Swansea SA6 8QP
Tel: 01792 310 306
Fax: 01792 795 422
Email: katen@montagnejeunesse.co.uk
▶ A leading toiletries company based in the UK marketing and supplying a full range of natural ingredient, non animal tested and award winning bath and skin care products. A unique range includes the highly successful anti-stress face treatment masks, together with a range of foot care, bath treatment and depilatory sachets. Also offers a range of facial care and real fruit soaps.

Nad's Natural Hair Removal Gel
31 Maryan Mews,
Off South End Road,
London NW3 2PU
Tel: 020 7433 0373
Fax: 020 7813 7130
▶ A 100% natural substance that is a breakthrough in natural hair removal. It requires no heating as it melts with your own body heat. So effective that regrowth is reduced considerably and hair is softer each time. The water soluble base of the product makes cleaning up easy with no mess and no fuss. It is simple and easy to use. Effectively removes unwanted body and facial hair from all areas instantly – legs, arms, armpits, bikini line, chest and back. Ideal for treating sensitive lip and eyebrow areas.

Nature's Treasures Ltd
Bridge Industrial Estate,
New Portreath Road, Bridge,
Cornwall TR16 4QL
Tel: 01209 843 881
Fax: 01209 843 882
Email: naturestreasures@ndirect.co.uk
Web: www.aromatherapy.ndirect.co.uk
Open: Mon-Fri 9am-5pm
▶ 'Simply pure, simply priced and simply packaged' is Nature's Treasures motto backed by a friendly and fast mail order service. Stocks 120 essential oils suitable for therapists as well as a wide range of vegetables oils including unusual and organic herb oils. This list of products may seem endless but the company aims to be able to provide users with a complete range of basic ingredients in small to large sizes so that a product can be made or blended for each individual. No minimum order.

Neal's Yard Remedies Mail Order
29 John Dalton Street,
Manchester M2 6DS
Tel: 0161 831 7875
Fax: 0161 835 9322
▶ Supplier of products on sale at Neal's Yard Remedies shops.

Network Health
41 Invincible Road,
Farnborough GU14 7QU
Tel: 01252 533 333
Fax: 01252 533 344
Email: enquiries@networkhealth-beauty.co.uk
▶ Owner and distributor of BUAV-approved brands of toiletries, cosmetics and perfumes including Christy, Keromask, Leichner, Innoxa, Zero Sun, Linden Voss, Cachet and Noir. Call for local stockists.

Nirvana Natural
Gardners House, Parmoor,
Near Henley-on-Thames RG9 6NN
Tel: 01494 880 885
Fax: 01494 880 886
Email: info@NirvanaNatural.com
Web: www.NirvanaNatural.co.uk
▶ Haircare company specialising in selling natural and creulty free products. Available in top West End salons and also stores such as Selfridges, Fortnum & Mason, John Lewis and House of Frasier. Aims to produce a high quality product that actually produces visable results.

Clothing & Cosmetics

Organic Botanics
PO Box 2140, Hove BN3 5BX
Tel: 01273 773 182
Fax: 01273 773 182
▶ Range of skin care made from organically grown ingredients – organically grown cold-pressed oils and fresh organic plant extracts. All products are suitable for vegans and are not tested on animals.

Potions & Possibilities
The Aromatherapy Practice,
Stable Court, Martlesham Heath,
Ipswich IP5 3UQ
Tel: 01394 386 161
Fax: 01473 631 774
Email: julie.foster@btinternet.com
▶ Herbal cosmetics and medicinal body care made by aromatherapist Julie Foster for everyday use and for treatment of common ailments such as eczema, cuts and grazes, headaches, dry and cracked skin. Soothing, aromatherapy bath oils for specific ailments such as arthritis, exhaustion, etc. Call for mail order catalogue.

Simply Soaps
Brillig, Rackheath Park, Rackheath,
Norwich NR13 6LP
Tel: 07775 564 802
Email: soapdeli@aol.com
Web: www.simplysoaps.com
▶ A range of 10 soaps, shampoos, shaving bars, moisturising creams, massage oils and sea-sponges. The products are handmade using natural exotic oils and organic herbs and spices. Free from petrochemicals and preservatives. Mail order or wholesale available on request.

Stargazer Products
1 Knightshill Square,
London SE27 0HP
Tel: 020 8655 7005
Fax: 020 8655 7007
Web: www.stargazer/products.com
▶ Maker of an entirely vegan, BUAV-approved range of cosmetics and hair colourants. Make-up and hair dyes come in every colour you can imagine.

Stewart Distribution
44 Park Crescent Terrace,
Brighton BN2 3HE
Tel: 01273 625 988
Fax: 0870 120 8566
Email: info@lemonburst.net
Web: www.lemonburst.net
▶ A family owned company based in Brighton that distributes unique natural products. Products that truly make a difference to one's health and well being – from the original Nutritional Wall Chart, to the very effective Crystal Spring Natural Deodorant, to the all natural Gallunac soap (think 'great gift') to the potent immune-boosting mushroom products of MRL.

Weleda (UK) Ltd
Heanor Road,
Ilkeston DE7 8DR
Tel: 0115 944 8200
Fax: 0115 944 8210
Email: weledauk@compuserve.com
Web: www.weleda.co.uk
▶ BUAV-approved skin and hair care products, toothpaste, sun protection and aftershave sold through health food stores and chemists. Call for details of your local stockists.

Woodspirits
Unit 42 New Lydenburg Industrial Estate, New Lydenburg Street,
London SE7 8NE
Tel: 020 8293 4949
Fax: 020 8293 4949
▶ Bodycare products made from biodegradable, natural ingredients formulated by a medical herbalist with skills in aromatherapy. Products include shampoo bars for no-bottle hair washing, ginger soap for tired muscles, seaweed scrub soap, 12 different non-soap body scrub, exfoliants and more. Call for a mail order catalogue.

Your Body Limited
Units 52-54, Milmead Industrial Estate, Mill Mead Road,
Tottenham, London N17 9QU
Tel: 020 8808 2662
Fax: 020 8801 8498
▶ Offers an exclusive range of beauty products for hair, face and body which are based on ingredients taken from herbs, plants and fruit extracts. Every product is animal free and does not contain lanolin or any ingredients derived from slaughtered animals. Does not use GM ingredients. Call for a free mail order catalogue.

Sanitary Protection

Look for unbleached or reusable sanitary products which are made of biodegradable materials such as cardboard and cotton.

Bodywise (UK) Ltd
Unit 23 Marsh Lane Industrial Estate,
Marsh Lane, Portbury,
Bristol BS20 0NH
Tel: 01275 371 764
Fax: 01275 371 765
Email: info@natracare.com
Web: www.natracare.com
▶ Supplies Natracare certified organic 100% cotton tampons. GMO free. Non-chlorine bleached, no additives. Degradable sanitary pads with wings made from natural materials. Breathable panty shields, and nighttime/maternity sanitary pads are also available.

Earthwise Baby
PO Box 1708, Aspley Guise,
Milton Keynes MK17 8YA
Tel: 01908 585 769
Fax: 01908 585 771
Email: sales@earthwisebaby.com
Web: www.earthwisebaby.com
▶ Unbleached cotton sanitary protection products. Mail order only. Call for a free catalogue.

Ecofemme UK
15 Holmesdale Road,
Bristol BS3 4QL
Tel: 0117 904 9726
Email: dompahud@hotmail.com
▶ Ecofemme are 100% cotton reusable menstrual pads., made in lots of different colours. Each one will last about five years so they make sense economically as well as environmentally. Each pack contains an outer case and two liners costing £4.50. More products and services in development. Call for more information.

Natural Collection
19a Monmouth Place, Bath BA1 2AY
Tel: 0870 331 3333
Fax: 01225 469 673
Web: www.naturalcollection.com
▶ Mail order catalogue selling some sanitary protection items including unbleached organic products. Also available bed linen, cleaning products, stationery and low-energy lighting.

Nature's Alternative
P O Box 194, Leeds LS6 2ZX
Tel: 0113 2818
Email: naturesalternative@hotmail.com
Open: Mon-Fri 9am-5.30pm
▶ Certified organic fabric washable menstrual pads in undyed and vibrant block and tie-dyed colours, handmade in the UK. Call for more information, mail order or list of stockists

Spirit of Nature Ltd
Burrhart House, Cradock Road,
Luton LU4 0JF
Tel: 01582 847 370
Fax: 01582 847 371
Email: oliver@spiritofnature.co.uk
Web: www.spiritofnature.co.uk
Open: Mon-Fri 9am-5.30pm
▶ Mail order catalogue selling unbleached cotton sanitary protection products. Also available: natural clothing collection for women and men, eco-household products, bed linen, natural bodycare products and an extensive range of clothing and accessories for babies and toddlers. Call for a free catalogue.

Helping us to save the forests

***Gill Harrison** of The Forest Stewardship Council writes about the work of the organisation which helps consumers identify sustainable and eco-friendly wood products.*

We continually hear bad news about the loss of the earth's natural forests and it is a sad fact that nearly two thirds have been destroyed forever – nearly 50% of them during the last thirty years. And the devastation goes on: 26 hectares, the equivalent of 37 football pitches, are being lost every minute. We might feel helpless in the face of this, but forests are often lost to meet our needs for timber and timber products and so, as consumers, there is something we can do to help. Buying products made with wood from responsibly managed forests is a good start, and the Forest Stewardship Council (FSC) logo provides the assurance that your purchase is helping to safeguard the future of the world's forests.

The future of the forests, and their sustainability, depends on responsible management which meets the needs of all concerned. Responsible management includes everything from limiting the amount of pesticides used and the methods used to move timber around, through to respecting the rights of local people and maintaining the biodiversity of a forest. The FSC promotes and supports responsible management through its certification and labelling system.

The FSC is an independent, non-profit making, international organisation which grew out of consumer concerns in the early 1990s about deforestation. The resulting profusion of differing 'green' labels that suddenly appeared on everything from furniture to disposable nappies only led to confusion. The claims made by these labels were often dubious. A survey carried out by WWF in 1993 revealed that only 3 out of every 80 users of such labels were able to back up their claims with any evidence. The FSC aims to clear up that confusion with a guarantee that the products really do meet the claims made about them.

The distinctive logo seen on any piece of timber, or timber product, shows that it comes from a well-managed forest – a forest that is being looked after in a responsible way, benefiting not only the trees and other wildlife, but also the communities who live and work there. There are now over 20 million hectares of FSC endorsed forests around the world, made up of over 200 forests in 32 countries, from small-scale community forests in the Solomon Islands to large state-owned forests in the USA.

FSC certification ensures forest owners take environmental, social and economic factors into account when managing their forests. There are two phases to the certification process. The first stage is the assessment of the forest of origin by an independent Certification Body. This inspection evaluates the forest's ecological health, the social impact of the operation and its economic viability against a set of internationally agreed standards for responsible forest management. The second stage is a monitoring and tracking system to ensure that only products made from genuinely certified timber can carry the FSC seal of approval. This 'chain of custody' is a vital part of the system's credibility and prevents false claims on products.

The FSC logo can now be seen on more 10,000 products, everything from chopping boards, pepper mills and wallpaper to garden furniture, bird boxes and charcoal. Every day more and more FSC certified items are appearing on shelves in high street stores such as B&Q, Sainsbury's and Woolworth's. The FSC is also supported by many environmental organisations such as WWF, Friends of the Earth, Greenpeace and the Woodland Trust as well as businesses including Railtrack and Bovis Lend Lease.

So look for the FSC logo to put a better future for the world's forests within reach. ■

For further information on the work of the FSC, and how you can help, visit the website at
www.fsc-uk.demon.co.uk
or write to the Forest Stewardship Council UK Working Group, Unit D, Station Building, Llanidloes, Powys, SY18 6EB
Tel: **01686 413916** *Fax:* **01686 412176**
Email: **fsc-uk@fsc-uk.demon.co.uk**

Gardening for a future

HDRA (the Henry Doubleday Research Association) is Europe's largest organic organisation with an international membership. **Sally Furness** *describes its aims and activities.*

HDRA was founded in 1958 by horticulturalist, Lawrence D Hills, who named the organisation after a Quaker smallholder of the last century who was interested in natural growing. HDRA is a registered charity of which the Prince of Wales became patron in 1989. It researches and promotes organic gardening, farming and food both in the UK and abroad – it is a fascinating organisation involved in many diverse projects.

The organisation is based in the Warwickshire countryside at Ryton Organic Gardens where there are 10 acres of delightful display gardens open to the public throughout the year. There are regular events, lots for the children to do and guided tours of the gardens on offer. Ryton also has an organic restaurant, conference facilities and a shop with the biggest range of organic food and wine to be found in the Midlands. Entry to the gardens is free of charge for children as HDRA are very keen to encourage the gardeners of the future. For adults the cost is £3 per head.

There are also display gardens at Yalding in Kent which are beautifully designed in such a way as to tell the history of gardening. Entrance costs are the same as for Ryton. They have been highly acclaimed since opening to the public in 1995 and are open throughout the summer months offering guided tours, an organic cafe and a well stocked shop.

HDRA are working with English Heritage to restore their Walled Kitchen Garden at Audley End in Saffron Walden. It was officially opened in July 2000 by the Prince of Wales and offers a superb opportunity to see such restoration in progress – all on organic principles and including many of the Heritage Seed Library vegetables held by HDRA.

Behind the scenes at Ryton is the scientific research department, carrying out valuable work both here and overseas. This includes reforestation and agroforestry projects in developing countries, helping to relieve poverty and improve livelihoods. The Information and Education Department looks after the organisation's 28,000 members providing them with a quarterly magazine, *The Organic Way*, and answering their gardening enquiries. HDRA members enjoy other benefits including free entry to Ryton, Yalding and Audley End plus another eight gardens. The Department also produces a wide range of publications and runs courses throughout the year.

HDRA has a mail order catalogue (*The Organic Gardening Catalogue*) which supplies a vast range of organic products. Plus there is a network of 80 gardening groups affiliated to HDRA and covering the length and breadth of Britain. During the summer months HDRA runs the 'Organic Gardens Open' scheme when organic gardeners open their gardens to display organic methods and hopefully inspire others.

The Heritage Seed Library (HSL) saves rare and endangered vegetables. It does so by giving HSL members seeds of vegetable varieties which, due to European legislation, are no longer commercially available and are therefore threatened with extinction.

HDRA Consultants Ltd is the consultancy wing of the organisation. It runs an Organic Gardening and Landscape Design Service and also researches and provides advice on composting as a sustainable solution to organic waste management. It is the largest such consultancy in the UK. The Consultancy accepts a variety of assignments, ranging from short tailor-made projects to extensive ongoing contracts and partnerships. Furthermore, HDRA has staff dedicated to working with schools throughout the country encouraging them to go organic in their school grounds and assisting with project work. ■

To learn more about HDRA and its wide range of activities contact them at HDRA, Ryton Organic Gardens, Coventry CV8 3LG. Tel: **024 7630 3517** *Fax:* **024 7663 9229** *Email:* **enquiry@hdra.org.uk** *Web:* **www.hdra.org.uk**

CASE STUDY: Construction with less destruction

The Association for Environment Conscious Building (AECB) was established in 1989 as an independent, non profit-making, trade association. Its objective is to facilitate environmentally responsible practices within building. Specifically the AECB aims: to promote the use of products and materials which are safe, healthy and sustainable; to encourage projects that respect, protect and enhance the environment; to make available comprehensive information and guidance about products, methods and projects; and to support the interests and endeavours of its members in achieving these aims

Its membership consists of architects, builders, surveyors, local authorities, housing associations, suppliers and manufacturers and is open to any individual or organisation that is involved with or interested in the building industry. Being 'green' is something that requires constant attention and there is rarely an easy answer. Every action has some sort of impact upon the environment. The AECB exists to try to reduce that impact and recognises that 'green' awareness can only be brought about through education and information.

The AECB publishes a quarterly magazine, *Building for a Future*, full of information and articles about environmentally conscious design and building. It also publishes a product and services directory, *Greener Building*, and a CD version called *GreenPro*, which guides the user through building issues and provides lists of the healthiest and least environmentally-damaging materials and products.

The AECB can also provide displays and participates in exhibitions all over the UK. It has a range of speakers available to deliver talks on subjects relating to 'green' buildings and 'construction with less destruction'. Each year the AECB produces the *Real Green Building Book*, which is full of information on how to build and renovate in a 'green' way. It also includes a list of AECB members by trade and county. To obtain a free copy of the latest edition, send an A5 SAE for 60p. ■

For more information, contact the AECB at PO Box 32, Llandysul, SA44 5ZA or visit the website at **www.aecb.net**

CASE STUDY: Taking control with the Walter Segal Self Build Trust

Taking control of a basic need – for shelter – is the idea behind 'self build'. It is a way to provide housing for ownership or rent, for people who are in housing need or on low incomes (or both), through using empty or poorly-used land in cities, towns, and even in villages. Self build is a great way for people to take control and responsibility for providing buildings which meet the specific needs of their own community, whether for housing or other uses. It is a process which can be undertaken as an individual or in groups – working on a community self build project. Individuals usually undertake house building work while groups form to build houses or community buildings together.

The Trust is a small national charity which aims to help people to build their own homes and community buildings. Its services are available to everyone, especially those in housing need or on low incomes, as well as local authorities, housing associations and anyone else interested in building. There is no such thing as a typical self builder – and the Segal approach aims to assist people to choose the most appropriate construction method to suit their specific circumstances – it has a broad experience of the many variations of environmentally-friendly timber frame construction available, and encourages self builders to get involved from the earliest stages of design.

With over twenty years experience in self build the Trust knows of many successes as well as some failures. Experience has shown that being steered around pitfalls and difficulties is just as important as being encouraged to proceed. So, although the Trust knows you can do it, it also knows that the more help you can get, the better. ■

For more information, visit the website at **www.segalselfbuild.co.uk**

or contact The Walter Segal Self Build Trust, 15 High St, Belford, Northumberland NE70 7NG. Tel: **01668 213 544** *Fax:* **01668 219 247**

Home & Garden

IMPACT — Make your home more sustainable

Household and electrical goods

- There are very few facilities for recycling household electrical or electronic waste. BT telephones can be returned and there is a scheme for recycling certain types of mobile phone. There are a number of schemes for repairing and recycling goods, such as washing machines, that can then be passed onto low income households. Some charity shops may take old electrical equipment that is still working. Check to see if your council has facilities for household appliances, electronic equipment or CFC extraction for old refrigerators. You can arrange for the council to remove bulky household items for disposal.

- Look for the Energy Star rating if you buy a new computer. This scheme is run by the US Government but it covers many products sold in the UK.

- A Savaplug, available from DIY shops, saves energy by matching the energy the fridge consumes with the amount it actually needs in its cooling cycle.

Furniture

- A network of small scale furniture projects takes old household furniture and passes it onto low income families and other groups in need. Contact your council to dispose of broken bulky household waste

Cleaning and Laundry

- Launderettes are the greenest option as the shared machines save on resources and are far more energy-efficient than domestic machines because the water is centrally heated. If you need to buy a new machine, look for the EU energy ratings.

- Buy proper cotton dishcloths, wire wool scourers, string mops, and wooden handled brushes with natural fibre bristles. They tend to last longer than the cheaper, synthetic options.

- Wash vegetables in a bowl of water, cleanest ones first, rather than under a running tap.

Gardening

- Next time you're at the garden centre, consider plants that will tolerate dry conditions better than others.

- A deep mulch of organic material after planting up will keep moisture in and weeds down.

- Terracotta pots and hanging baskets look attractive but lose moisture easily. Line them with polythene but remember to make a few drainage holes.

- Give your plants an occasional soaking and always water in the evening. Frequent watering only encourages roots to stay near the surface.

CASE STUDY — How pure is the water you drink?

At The Pure H20 Company, it's our mission to help people take a positive step to improve the quality of the water they drink and cook with. We believe that having access to an abundant supply of healthy, pure and affordable water means you will drink more often and feel the natural benefits of regular hydration.

Most of us are concerned about the quality of the water we drink, and rightly so. UK tap water contains pesticides, herbicides, chemicals, metals, oestrogens, and bacteria. How to rid water of these impurities has become an increasing challenge. Our unique water purification technology combines reverse osmosis with deionisation to produce the purest freshly squeezed water available.

When choosing your water purification system, the key factor to look for is it's effectiveness in reducing the Total Dissolved Solids (TDS) in the water being purified. Tap water ranges from 500ppm to 300ppm. The medical definition of pure water is 'water that contains less than 10mg/ltr Total Dissolved Solids and is free of disease-causing micro-organisms.' Pure H20 is the only water that meets the definition of pure water with an average TDS of 2 ppm. Our patented Aquathin® purifiers are proven to be the most efficient and technologically advanced systems in the world and completely eliminate all contaminants and pollutants found in tap water. Nutritionists and doctors recommend our systems throughout the UK. ∎

*The Pure H20 Company. Tel: **01252 860111**
Website: **www.pureh2o.co.uk***

BUILDING & DESIGN

For more organisations involved in urban and community regeneration, see Built Environment in Chapter Ten: Government & Organisations. For products for increased energy efficiency, see Chapter Four: Energy & Recycling.

Architects, Designers & Builders

Acanthus Lowe Rae Architects
Three Crowns Yard,
Penrith CA11 7PH
Tel: 01768 863 812
Fax: 01768 890 067
Email:
mail@LoweRaeArchitects.co.uk
▶ Architects with experience of sustainable construction and development. Current projects include commercial, retail, housing, leisure and conservation projects. Has particular expertise in rural areas and existing buildings. Members of the Association of Environment Conscious Building as well as founders of Action for Sustainable Rural Communities – a network of agencies and organisations involved with sustainable and/or rural development. Welcomes the challenge to develop integrated sustainable design solutions with individual or community-based clients.

Amazon Nails
Hollinroyd Farm, Butts Lane,
Todmorden OL14 8RJ
Tel: 01706 814 696
Fax: 01706 812 190
Email: jbarbara@gn.apc.org
Web: www.zen.co.uk/home/
page/deaftdesign
▶ An all-women team, experienced in strawbale building, mud and lime plastering, and all aspects of construction. Aims to empower people to be involved in the building process and to make it more accessible. Offers advice and help to self-builders and professionals; runs hands-on teaching workshops in straw bale building, plastering and construction crafts; gives lectures and slideshows; and can make site visits to consult on building projects.

Build For Change Ltd
Unit 19, 41 Old Birley Street, Hulme,
Manchester M15 5RF
Tel: 0161 232 1588
Fax: 0161 232 1582
Email: build-for-change@urbed.co.uk
Web:
www.rectangle.demon.co.uk/build
▶ Design and fabrication co-operative specialising in sustainability from architectural design to furniture. The company combines designers, metalworkers and woodworkers to create innovative solutions of quality to a wide range of design problems. Recent projects include a 40ft high lighthouse for firework performances, office furniture using recycled timber, shop fitting for an organic shop and café and decorative fencing for a community centre.

Community Regeneration Ltd
Giants Basin, Potato Wharf,
Castlefield, Manchester M3 4LA
Tel: 0161 834 2214
Fax: 0161 834 9909
▶ Non-profit community architecture practice which evolved out of the growing need for assistance from community groups who wanted to get involved in the renewal of their own areas. As well as providing a full architectural service, Community Regeneration discusses ideas and problems and can provide advice on the constitution and management of groups, assessment of community needs, help with the production of promotional literature and the development of scheme design with the preparation of grant applications. Call the information officer on the above number for more information.

Constructive Individuals
Trinity Buoy Wharf, 64 Orchard Place,
London E1 4 0JW
Tel: 020 7515 9299
Fax: 020 7515 9737
Email: design@
constructive-i.freeserve.co.uk
Web:
www.constructiveindividuals.com
▶ Environmentally-aware architects, eco-designers and self-build consultants offering design and building services to a wide range of businesses, community groups and individual clients. Supplies and installs Warmcel cellulose fibre insulation (recycled newspaper) for lofts, floors and timber buildings. Also offers courses in practical building, including one where an eco-house is built in three weeks.

Downs & Variava
The Towers, The Towers Business Parks, Wilmslow Road,
Manchester M20 2DD
Tel: 0161 434 4414
Fax: 0161 446 2206
▶ Environmentally-conscious interior architects.

Gale & Snowden
18 Market Place, Bideford EX39 2DR
Tel: 01237 474 952
Fax: 01237 425 669
Email: galesnow@ecodesign.co.uk
Web: www.ecodesign.co.uk
▶ Offers full architectural services specialising in energy-efficient, ecological design for domestic, commercial and community projects including landscaping and interiors. Holds regular monthly surgeries at the Ecological Building Centre (16 Great Guildford Street, London SE1 4HR, 020 7450 2211) for discussion and advice. Call for a newsletter or further info.

GreenMarque Art and Landscape
c/o Docklands Garden Centre,
244-246 Ratcliffe Lane,
London E14 7JE
Tel: 020 7923 9622
Fax: 020 7790 5025
Email: info@flowforms.com
Web: www.flowforms.com
Open: Mon-Fri 9am-9pm
▶ Unique water features incorporating holistic pattern principals. Flowforms and sculptures for inside and art, large or small. Full colour gallery at the website and enquiries welcome for any environmental landscape project especially for schools and community. Solar powered options available.

Pen y Coed Construction
Pen y Lan, Meifod SY22 6DA
Tel: 01938 500 643
▶ Specialists in timber framed building and design, from traditional green oak framing and random slate roofs to softwood and masonite beam construction. Incorportaing ecological specifications to all building elements, from installation of solar panels to insulation. Approved specialist installers of Warmcel cellulose fibre insulation offering a consultancy service for all aspects of breathing wall and roof insulation. Thermal and condensation calculations undertaken.

Shelters Unlimited
The Old Station Yard, Heol-y-Doll,
Machynlleth SY20 8BL
Tel: 01654 702 086
Fax: 01654 702 086
Email:
shelters@tentdesign.demon.co.uk
Open: Mon-Fri 10am-6pm
▶ Tent design company specialising in the production of authentic Native American tipis and other tribal tents. Tipi made in a range of sizes from 10 feet children's lodges up to very large ceremonial lodges which are 28 feet in diameter. Offers a hire service and can provide furnished tipis for holidays in mid-Wales. Also creates a world music party environment involving tipis and a lightshow called Touching the Earth.

The Picturehouse
8 Brighton Street,
Todmorden OL14 8LA
Tel/Fax: 01706 816 615
Email: info@thepicturehouse.net
Web: www.thepicturehouse.net/
Open: Always
▶ Professional mural painters create original images for any environment, inside or out, schools, homes, shops, etc. Visit website or send off for information.

Wimtec Environmental Ltd
St Peter's House, 6-8 High Street,
Iver SL0 9NG
Tel: 01753 737 744
Fax: 01753 792 321
Email: wimtecenvironmental1@
compuserve.com

Home & Garden

Web:
www.oneworld.compuserve.com/homepages/wimtecenvironmental1
▶ Specialists in the built environment providing advice on building technology, asbestos, air quality, water quality, occupational hygiene, health and safety, noise and vibration and a comprehensive range of environmental audits. Can also provide site investigations with surveys and advice for dealing with contaminated land.

Flooring

Crucial Trading Ltd
79 Westbourne Park Road,
London W2 5QH
Tel: 020 7221 9000
Fax: 020 7727 3634
Email: crucial@dial.pipex.com
▶ Supplier and installer of a wide range of natural floor coverings including sisal, seagrass, coir, jute, wool and etc – the natural alternative to carpets. Fittings can be arranged throughout the UK. Call for free samples and a catalogue on 01562 835 656 (Head Office).

Natural Flooring Company
13 Gordon Avenue,
Twickenham TW1 1NH
Tel: 020 8892 8535
Fax: 020 8892 8535
▶ Supplier and installer of natural floor coverings such as sisal and seagrass. Call for samples and more information.

Rosewood Flooring
The Woodland Centre,
Whitesmith, near Lewes BN8 6JB
Tel: 01825 872 025
Fax: 01825 872 971
▶ English, European and American hardwood and softwood flooring from sustainable sources certified by the Soil Association and the Forest Stewardship Council. The tropical timbers are produced by small and medium scale community-based projects, mainly in West Africa.

Windows & Joinery

Environmental Construction Products Ltd
11 Huddersfield Road, Meltham,
Huddersfield HD7 3NJ
Tel: 01484 854 898
Fax: 01484 854 899
Email: sales@ecoproducts.co.uk
Web: www.ecoproducts.co.uk
▶ Specialist company offering a range of environmentally sensitive building products. Ecoplus System windows, doors and conservatories are manufactured in the UK to exacting environmental specifications. Ultra-efficient glazing, boron timber treatment, plant oil based finishes and advanced design make Ecoplus System energy-efficient, durable, safe and non-toxic. Ecoplus System are available throughout the UK. The company's Green Building Store by Mail sells environmentally friendly paints, insulation etc by mail order.

Prontapanel Ltd
57 Sladefield Road, Ward End,
Birmingham B8 3PF
Tel: 0121 247 0619
Fax: 0121 247 0974
Email: steve@pronta.softnet.co.uk
▶ Window frames and double-glazing made of pultruded glass fibre, a strong, weather-resistant material with lower environmental impact than most other frame materials.

Swedish Window Company
Earls Colne Industrial Park,
The Airfield, Earls Colne,
Colchester CO6 2NS
Tel: 01787 223 931
Fax: 01787 220 525
Email: info@swedishwindows.com
Web: www.swedishwindows.com
▶ Importers of laminated timber windows and doors from Scandinavia, sourced from sustainable forests and used for replacement and new build projects. Involved in a number of projects ranging from the self-builder to large developments. Call or go to the website for further information.

Merewood Joinery
Unit 2, Service Street, Cheadle Heath, Stockport SK3 0HU
Tel: 0161 480 0363
Fax: 0161 480 0363
▶ Manufacturers of purpose-made joinery including windows, doors, doorsets, patio doors, conservatories, stairs and other ecologically-sound building products. Committed to using timber that comes only from sustainable sources and is certified by the Soil Association's Woodmark Scheme. The majority of the timber has travelled less than 300 miles from its source and includes indigenous species such as oak, douglas fir and larch.

Materials

Bollards Ltd
Twinlakes Industrial Park,
Croston, Prseton PR5 7RF
Tel: 01772 601 070
Fax: 01772 600 490
Email: sales@bollards.co.uk
Web: www.bollards.co.uk
▶ Distriubutors of recycled plastic profiles and finished products such as benches, seating, litter bins, parking bollards, fencing and posts. Available in three standard colours, the products require minimal maintenance.

Ecomerchant
The Old Filling Station,
Head Hill Road, Goodnestone,
Faversham ME13 9BY
Tel: 01795 530 130
Fax: 01795 530 430
Email: joe@ecomerchant.demon.co.uk
Open: Mon-Fri 8am-5pm;
Sat 9am-5pm;
Sun & Bank Holidays 10am-4pm
▶ Suppliers of sustainable building and interior products and materials to the trade and general public, promoting products which create a healthy and natural environment in which to live and work. Aims to make eco-friendly products more accessible to the general public and trade at affordable prices, whilst linking reclaimed and new products to promote reuse with minimal waste. Product range includes natural paints from Livos, NBT, OS and Auro; earth plasters and plaster boards; lime putty; lime mortars and washes; solar panels and

---

ECOMERCHANT

PLANET CONSCIOUS BUILDING MATERIALS

Organic & Natural Paints
Extensive range of clay plasters & coloured finishes, emulsions, casien, natural oils, preservatives, stains & waxes

Eco Materials
Natural insulations, solar panels, wind generators, water conservation, reed boards & sunpipes

Natural Flooring - Reclaimed & New
Floorboards, woodstrip & block, stone & lino

Architectural Reclamation
Roll top baths, basins, fireplaces, stoves, stone, bricks, architectural features & railway sleepers

Conservation Materials
Lime Putty, ready mix lime mortars, hair, laths, hydraulic lime, coloured lime washes, skylights

Wooden Furniture
Kitchen units, tables, shelving, chairs and all forms of bespoke furniture made from sustainable and reclaimed timber using natural finishes and glues

Head Hill Road, Goodnestone, Nr Faversham, Kent ME13 9BY
01795 530 130   www.ecomerchant.demon.co.uk

PV's; wind generators; sunpipes; water saving products; natural insulations including wool and cellulose; eco and conservation books and magazines; an extensive range of conservation products including hydraulic lime and skylights; reclaimed building materials including timber joists, oak beams and stone for the garden and flooring; new and reclaimed floorboards; marmoleum; handmade kitchen units; all forms of furniture using reclaimed and locally sourced hardwoods with natural finishes and glues; unique sculptural furniture items; rustic hazel and chestnut garden furniture; woodland garden products, including fencing and furniture; and green oak and reclaimed pine decking.

Envest
Building Research Establishment,
Garston, Watford WD1 2RB
Tel: 01923 664 308
Fax: 01923 664 984
Email: envest@bre.co.uk
Web: www.bre.co.uk/envest
▶ Envest is the first UK software for estimating the lifecycle environmental impacts of a building from the early design stage. This version is designed for office buildings, and considers the environmental impacts of both materials used during construction and resources consumed over the building's life. Using minimal input data Envest allows designers to instantly identify those aspects of the building which have the greatest influence on the overall impact. The designers would also be able to compare two or more alternative schemes for a given project.

Harvest Forestry
1 New England Street,
Brighton BN1 4GT
Tel: 01273 689 725
Fax: 01273 622 727
Email: harvestforestry@fastnet.co.uk
Web: www.harvestforestry.co.uk
▶ Offers a wide range of services and products based on the principles of sustainability, including: tree surgery work; woodland management contracting; English hardwood sales; wooden furniture and artifacts; and organic food and drinks. The forestry operations are based on environmental improvement, ecology and the use of all forestry bi-products. Large timber is planked and sold in the timber yard or used to produce a range of unique furniture and accessories to sell in the shop or make to order. Smaller timber is cut for firewood or converted into soil improving compost and woodchip mulch.

Klober Limited UK
Pear Tree Industrial Estate,
Upper Langford BS40 7DW
Tel: 01934 853 224/5
Fax: 01934 853 221
Email: support@klober.co.uk
Web: www.klober.co.uk
▶ Commercial trader of products for ecological and energy efficient building, including Tyvek (recyclable, fully waterproof, vapour permeable, roof and wall breather membrane) used in place of traditional underlays, copper rainwater systems, double glazed roof windows, sheep's wool building insulation from New Zealand flocks.

Timber Intent
32 Belton Road, Bristol BS5 0JS
Tel: 0117 939 6948
Fax: 0117 993 6948
Email: timberintent@compuserve.com
▶ Specialist company designing and manufacturing high quality timber and fabric structures. Offers a green appproach to design and manufacture and incorporates the latest in modern technology to arrive at appropriate, innovative and stimulating solutions. Creates versatile structures which lift the spirit through the use of natural materials and good design and uses timber grown and harvested on a planned basis, and fabrics such as cottons, canvas, hemp and recycled textiles.

Organisations

Action for Sustainable Rural Communities (ASRC)
c/o Lowe Rae Architects, Three Crowns Yard, Penrith CA11 7PH
Tel: 01768 863 812
Fax: 01768 890 067
Email: rod@loweraearchitects.co.uk
▶ Aims to form a national network of individuals, agencies, organisations and Local Authorities with a commitment to sustainable rural development and conservation. ASRC's two core activities are, firstly, to be an information network which will act as a clearing house for technical, policy and funding, information and, secondly, to be) a project group which will provide access to consultants and advisers providing appropriate local development skills.

Association for Environment Conscious Building (AECB)
PO Box 32, Llandysul SA44 52A
Tel: 01559 370 908
Email: admin@aecb.net
Web: www.aecb.net
▶ The objective of the AECB is to facilitate environmentally responsible practices within building. Promotes the use of products and materials which are safe, healthy and sustainable; encourages projects that respect, protect and enhance the environment; makes available comprehensive information and guidance about products, methods and projects; and supports the interests and endeavours of its members in achieving these aims.

Association of Self Builders
Room 23, The Rufus Centre,
Steppingley, Flitwick MK45 1AN
Tel: 0704 154 4126
Fax: 0704 154 4126
Web: www.self-builder.org.uk
▶ Voluntary association offering advice and information and support for self-builders – those planning or actually building, renovating or converting their own properties. Services include free information sheets, free video hire, members discounts and a quaterly magazine *The Self-Builder*.

British Straw Bale Building Association
5 Chataway Road, Crumpsall,
Manchester M8 5UU
Tel: 0161 202 3566
Email: straw@globalnet.co.uk
Web: www.global.users.uk/straw
▶ Set up in January 1998 to act as a forum for exchanging information and experiences relevant to this country about straw bale building. Aims to be a first point of call for people seeking information on bale building and promotes and campaigns for the wider use of this sustainable building technique. Runs regular courses for all levels and will give demonstrations. Members receive a magazine published three times year and all the help and information the Association can give.

Building Advisory Service & Information Network
The Schumacher Centre for Technology and Development,
Bourton Hall, Bourton-on-Dusmore,
Rugby CV23 9QZ
Tel: 01788 661 100
Fax: 01788 661 101
Email: itdg@itdg.org.uk
Web: www.oneworld.org/itdg or www.gtz.de/basin
▶ Network of organisations working on various aspects of eco-friendly building techniques around the World. One of its members, Intermediate Technology, is primarily concerned with these issues in the context of the developing world.

Centre for Sustainable Construction
Building Research Establishment,
Garston, Watford,
Hertfordshire WD2 7JR
Tel: 01923 664 664
Email: enquiries@bre.co.uk
Web: www.bre.co.uk
Open: Mon-Fri 8.30am-5pm
▶ BRE provides advice and guidance on buildings and how to run and build them in an environmentally sustainable manner – often with clear financial benefits. This information is available through books and easy-to-use tools, as well as consultancy services.

Community Technical Aid Centre
2nd Floor, 3 Stevenson Square,
Manchester M1 1DN
Tel: 0161 236 5195
Fax: 0161 236 5836
Email: info@ctac.co.uk
Web: www.ctac.co.uk

Home & Garden

▶ Provides project development advice to community groups and voluntary organisations. Architectural and landscape design services, advice on funding and methods of community participation throughout the process. CTAC is the home of the Green Architecture Project (GAP), under which community and local groups are advised on energy efficiency, environmental policy development and the use of renewable energy. Initial development and design advice is free of charge to groups within Greater Manchester.

Construction Industry Enviromental Forum

6 Storey's Gate, Westminster, London SW1P 3AU
Tel: 020 7222 8891
Fax: 020 7222 1708
Email: enquiries@cief.org.uk
Web: www.ciria.org.uk
Open: Mon-Fri 9am-5.30pm

▶ The CIEF is a forum working to improve the environmental and sustainability performance of all involved in construction. Organises regular meetings including executive seminars, discussion workshops, best practice seminars, site visits and conferences in Scotland, the North of England, Wales and South East England. Activities include: improving industry awareness of environmental and sustainability issues; identifying problems and their solutions; producing appropriate guidance information; promoting enviornmental and sustainability research; and indentifying opportunities for innovation. It addresses a wide range of issues, which are: sustainable construction; environmental management; resources, waste minimisation and recycling; pollution and hazardous substances; internal environment; planning, land use and conservation; and energy use, global warming and climate change.

Construction Industry Research & Information Association (CIRIA)

6 Storey's Gate, Westminster, London SW1P 3AU
Tel: 020 7222 8891
Fax: 020 7222 1708
Email: enquiries@ciria.org.uk
Web: www.ciria.org.uk
Open: Mon-Fri 9am-5.30pm

▶ CIRIA is a UK-based research association that works to improve the performance of all involved with construction and the environment by developing and implementing best practice. CIRIA's independence and wide membership base make it uniquely placed to bring together all parties with an interest in improving corporate and site performance, contractors, clients, designers, regulators, financiers and government are all regularly involved in CIRIA's activities. The Environment Group helps improve environmental performance on a wide range of environmental topics, including: waste minimisation; sustainable development; contaminated land; environmental management; and the Construction Industry Environmental Forum.

Ecological Design Association

The British School, Slad Road, Stroud GL5 1QW
Tel: 01453 765 575
Fax: 01453 759 211
Email: ecological@designassociation.freeserve.co.uk
Web: www.eclaweb.org
Open: Tue-Fri 10am-5pm

▶ Promotes awareness and practice of the design of products, systems and environments for healthy and sustainable living. Encourages interdisciplinary contact between all designers – from architects to planners. Publishes the journal *EcoDesign* (three issues per annum), fact sheets and a mail order book service. Also publishes a directory of members from which they can supply names of local green designers and architects.

Green Savings... Green Mortgages

The Ecology is
a mutual building society dedicated to improving the environment by promoting sustainable housing and communities. Your investment in the Ecology funds mortgages for:

> renovation of derelict and redundant properties
> green self-build houses
> housing co-operatives and ecological enterprises
> back-to-back houses, which are energy efficient by nature

For more information on our range of mortgages or savings accounts telephone our local rate number:

Tel: 0845 674 5566

Ecology Building Society
Ref GG20, FREEPOST
18 Station Rd, Cross Hills
Keighley BD20 5BR

the Ecology Building Society

YOUR HOME IS AT RISK IF YOU DO NOT KEEP UP REPAYMENTS ON A MORTGAGE OR OTHER LOAN SECURED ON IT
Further details and written quotations on request. All mortgages subject to status, first charge on the property and satisfactory valuation.

ECOLOGICAL DESIGN ASSOCIATION

The Ecological Design Association aims to enhance awareness of environmental issues amongst members of the public and design professionals, whatever your area of interest.

The charity promotes awareness of ecologically sustainable design at all levels, working with children in schools, students, designers, and anyone who wants to live in a more sustainable way.

Join the EDA today, and you will be joining a network of people who care about the environment and the impact we make upon it. The EDA acts as an information and networking service, organises events, exhibitions and gatherings; provides a bi-monthly newsletter keeping you up to date with latest Eco Events and publishes a Directory of fellow members. Local groups meet regularly to organise their own events and campaigns.

You will also receive EcoDesign, the EDA's exciting journal, produced three or four times a year. This is the forum for design information, with eco-news, features, projects and plenty of facts. It is a valuable resource with all the latest on sustainable materials, techniques and systems.

I AM INTERESTED IN BECOMING A MEMBER OF THE EDA. PLEASE SEND MORE INFORMATION
NAME:
ADDRESS:
TEL:
E-MAIL:

Simply complete the coupon and send it to the EDA at

The British School,
Slad Road, Stroud,
Glos GL5 1QW

or call the central office for further information.

tel **01453 765575**

fax **01453 759211**

Home & Garden

Environment Conscious Design Group
c/o 7a Elm Walk,
Aylesford ME20 7LR
Tel: 01622 792 366;
01732 358 890
▶ Concerned with the active promotion of designs in the professional and public sphere that reduce pollution, remove hazards from our everyday environment, cut down the material and energy demands we make and promotes practices that encompass sustainability, energy efficiency, regeneration, healthier lifestyles and sensitivity to our surroundings. The group meets regularly in the southeast and publishes a quarterly newsletter. It supports the aims and ideals of the AECB and the EDA and is currently initiating a CPD programme for architects, planners, surveyors, etc. All new members welcome.

Feng Shui Network International
8 Kings Court, Pateley Bridge,
Harrogate HG3 5JW
Tel: 01423 712 868
Fax: 01423 712 869
Email: Feng1@aol.com
Web: www.FengShuiNet.com
▶ Call for consultations.

Feng Shui Society
377 Edgware Road, London W2 1BT
Tel: 07050 289 200
Fax: 020 8566 0898
Email: karenayers@fengshui.cor.uk
Web: www.fengshuisociety.org.uk
▶ Established in the UK in 1993 as an unincoporated non-profit organisation formed to advance Feng Shui principles and concepts as a contribution to the creation of harmonious environments. For individuals and society in general. The Feng Shui Society is the registry for professional Feng Shui consultants in the UK.

Forest Stewardship Council (FSC)
Working Group, Unit D, Station Building, Llanidloes SY18 6EB
Tel: 01686 412 176
Fax: 01686 412 176
▶ The FSC trademark is found only on wood certified as coming from a forest that is managed according to agreed social, economic and enviromental principles and criteria. Certified stick timber is easy to find and Homebase are amongst 85 companies belonging to WWF's 95 Plus Group which is committed to sourcing wood from sustainably-managed forests.

Royal Institute of British Architects (RIBA) Bookshop
113-115 Portland Place,
Manchester M1 6FB
Tel: 0161 236 7691
Fax: 0161 236 1153
Email: riba.bookshop@virgin.net
Open: Mon-Fri 9.30am-5.30pm; Sat 12pm-4pm
▶ Local outlet for RIBA, stocking architectural and building books including a range of eco-design and self-build titles. Mail order service available. Attached to CUBE (Centre for Understanding Built Environment) Gallery.

Straw Bale Building Association for Wales, Ireland, Scotland and England
PO Box 17, Todmorden OL14 8FD
Tel: 01706 818126
▶ Publishes *Baling Out* newletter for self- and community-built buildings, homes, extensions, community centres, cottages, animal shelters, structures, sculptures and spaces.

Town & Country Planning Association
17 Carlton House Terrace,
London SW1Y 5AS
Tel: 020 7930 8903
Fax: 020 7930 3280
Email: tcpa@tcpa.org.uk
Web: www.tcpa.org.uk
▶ Promotes planning with a human face.

Walter Segal Self Build Trust
15 High St, Belford NE70 7NG
Tel: 01668 213 544
Fax: 01668 219 247
Email: info@segalselfbuild.co.uk
Web: www.segalselfbuild.co.uk
▶ A small national charity which helps people to build their own homes and community buildings. Services are available to everyone, especially those in housing need or on low incomes, including local authorities, housing associations and any other body interested in building. Provides advice and information in the following areas: building methods; land acquisition; finance and funding; professional services; contract management; and training arrangements.

FURNITURE & DECORATION

Paints

AURO Organic Paint Supplies Ltd
Unit 2 Pamphillions Farm, Purton End, Debden, Saffron Walden CB11 3JT
Tel: 01799 543 077
Fax: 01799 542 187
Email: sales@auroorganic.co.uk
Web: www.auroorganic.co.uk
▶ Supplies a complete range of environmentally benign decorating finishes – interior and exterior – for wood, cork and plaster surfaces. A large part of production takes place within growing plants. These are then converted, using simple procedures and a low energy input, into a wide range of products without creating any hazardous waste. Auro is distinguished by its uncompromising exclusion of petrochemicals from its formulations.

AURO ORGANIC PAINTS

GOING WITH THE GRAIN OF NATURE SAFE AND PLEASANT TO USE

Auro paints represent a return to the tradition of using natural, self-regenerating materials that breathe and move with changes in temperature and humidity – a characteristic which contributes to their toughness and durability. Information on the full range of Auro materials (including a number of interesting new products) is available on request.

Mail order deliveries normally within 7 days.

Tel: (01799) 584 888 Fax: (01799) 584 041
Auro Organic Paints Supplies Ltd
Unit 1, Goldstones Farm, Ashdon,
Safron Walden, Essex CB10 2LZ

Clearwell Caves
near Coleford,
Royal Forest of Dean GL16 8JR
Tel: *01594 832 535*
Fax: *01594 833 362*
▶ Producer of natural iron-based ochre paints: yellow, brown, red and violet, mined on a small scale by freeminers. Natural paint courses are run for artists and home decorators where you can learn how to make limewashes, distempers, washes from natural raw materials, stamps and stencils.

Eco Solutions
Summerleaze House, Church Road,
Winscombe BS25 1BH
Tel: *01934 844 484*
Fax: *01934 844 119*
Email:
avt.eco.solutions@btinternet.com
Web: *www.ecosolutions.co.uk*
▶ Award-winning, eco-friendly, cost-effective and efficient, water-based, solvent-free paint strippers and coatings removal products. The product range includes application strippers, immersion strippers, a brush restorer and a graffiti-remover, which will remove any graffiti from any wall. The products are free from hazardous substances, 'nasty smells' and other dangers normally associated with paint removal, containing no dangerous solvents or hazardous chemicals and emitting 0.0004% volatile organic compounds. Conventional solvent-based equivalents can contain carcinogens and other substances hazardous to health and emit over 70% VOC's, more than seventeen thousand five hundred times as much as these products.

ECOS Organic Paints
c/o Lakeland Paints, Unit 19,
Lake District Business Park,
Kendal LA9 6NH
Tel: *01539 732 866*
Fax: *01539 734 400*
▶ Award-winning Environment Conscious Odourless Solvent-free (ECOS) paints and varnishes.

ECOS Organic Paints

■ Environment Conscious ■ **Odourless** ■ Solvent Free

WINNER OF 4 NATIONAL AWARDS

Conventional gloss paints and emulsion paints contain solvents which are the major cause of sick building syndrome, asthma, allergies and chemical sensitivities, etc. ECOS paints are made entirely without VOCs, solvents, formaldehyde, lead, glycols, etc, so that your rooms are safe to live in, play in and sleep in (US EPA & Swedish tests – 0.0% VOC).
85 co-ordinated colours. A Millennium Product

- **Free technical advice** • **Low-cost delivery in 2 working days**
- **Phone for free brochure**

LAKELAND PAINTS
Tel: 01539 732866 Fax: 01539 734400

Reportedly the only solvent-free range in the world. Available in a range of 85 colours, these paints have excellent durability and finish and their odourless, solvent-free nature makes them suitable for all household purposes and particularly suitable for asthmatics and allergy sufferers. Mail order only, so call for a free catalogue. Deliveries are made by UPS and normally within two days of ordering.

Green Paints
Lock Farm, Lock Road,
Alvingham, Louth LN11 7EU
Tel: *01507 327 362*
▶ Small family firm specialising in the development and manufacture of water borne paints for domestic and industrial use, operating from converted farm premises in Lincolnshire. They are happy to consider developing special products for customers who require a benign replacement for conventional harmful paints but have a number of standard products, unique to their own manufacture, that fulfil most requirements. One of their most recent developments, Novocoat, is probably one of the most environmentally benign performance paint available anywhere in the world.

Lizzy Induni Traditional Paints
11 Park Road, Swanage BH19 2AA
Tel: *01929 423 776*
Email: *induni@valhalla.net*
Open: *Mon-Fri 9.30am-9.30pm*
▶ Specialises in the manufacture of traditional lime-based paint. Aims to provide a first class product and to support it with impartial education. Limewash can create unique decorative effects, but more importantly, has relatively low energy inputs, contains no toxic materials, does not release VOCs, is non-combustible and does not give off gas when heated.

Nature Maid Company
Unit 7, Maws Croft Centre,
Jackfield, Ironbridge TF8 7LS
Tel: *01952 883 288*
Fax: *01952 883 200*
Email: *paint@livos.demon.co.uk*
Open: *Mon-Sun 10am-5pm*
▶ Supplies Livos Natural Paints and Pigments. Available at the shop or via mail order (£8 flat rate). Livos is the original and world-leader in the production of natural paints. All products are carefully selected and chosen to avoid any adverse effects on the body, home or environment. Natural oils like organic linseed oil are used and contain no pesticides or herbicides.

Nutshell Natural Paints
PO Box 72, South Brent TQ10 9YR
Tel: *01364 738 01*
Fax: *01364 730 68*
Email: *info@nutshellpaints.com*
Web: *www.nutshellpaints.com*
Open: *Mon-Fri 9am-5pm*
▶ Products are derived from natural raw materials, working from traditional recipes. Through modern research the company has identified which ingredients can be safely reintegrated into the cycle of nature. Products are not tested on animals and Nutshell aims to promote health in humans, the environment and the continuity of life on the planet. The range has a pleasant fresh smell and many people experiencing sensitivity or allergies to conventional paints will no longer suffer from symptoms when using Nutshell. Products have been widely used on conservation properties and modern buildings.

OSMO
Ostermann & Scheiwe UK Ltd,
Unit 2 Pembroke Road,
Stocklake Industrial Estate,
Aylesbury HT20 1DB
Tel: *01296 481 220*
Fax: *01296 424 090*
Email: *osmo@btconnect.com*
Web: *www.ostermann.scheiwe.com*
Open: *Mon-Fri 9am-5pm*
▶ Manufacturer and supplier of OS colour biocide and preservative-free, natural, oil-based timber finishes. Also hardwax oil finishes for wood or cork flooring, stain-resistant against wine, beer, cola, coffee and tea. Safe for children's furniture and toys.

New Furniture

Comfort Chair Company
3C Wilson Street, London N21 1BP
Tel: *0705 003 1021*

Home & Garden

▶ Mail order suppliers of the Comfort Chair which is built to a curvaceous, modern design, is relaxing to sit in and gives ideal postural support.

Full Moon Futons
20 Bulmershe Road,
Reading RG1 5RJ
Tel: 0118 926 5648
Email: fullmoonfutons@talk21.com
▶ Futons, cribs and cot mattresses in 100% pure cotton with unbleached cotton covers. Mattresses can be made to order, using other natural fibres as requested. Call for mail order catalogue.

Jason Griffiths Furniture
Higher Tideford, Cornworthy,
Totnes TQ9 7HL
Tel: 01803 712 387
Fax: 01803 712 388
▶ Wooden furniture made from native trees such as oak, hazel and ash grown and managed using sustainable traditional techniques by the carpenter himself.

Scan-Sit Ltd
Third Cross Road,
Twickenham TW2 5EB
Tel: 020 8893 3100
Fax: 020 8893 3985
Email: sac@scan-sit.com
Web: www.scan-sit.com
▶ Importer of furniture from various countries in Europe providing chairs and desks that are good for your back and your posture. A wide range of designs suitable for adults and kids from office chairs to rocking chairs and high chairs to recumbent chairs.

Treske Ltd
Station Works, Thirsk YO7 4NY
Tel: 01845 522 770
Fax: 01845 522 692
Email: treske@btinternet.com
▶ Manufacturer of a wide range of eco-friendly furniture for the stylish home using British hardwoods grown under sustainable woodland husbandry and processed using only natural means for timber drying and curing, rejecting all laquers, polishes and foams which damage the ozone layer and adopting energy conservation measures wherever possible. Hypo-allergenic finishes available.

Call for a free catalogue or visit our workshops in Thirsk.

Wildwood Designs
Unit 5, Aberuchaf, Lon Garmon,
Abersoch, Pwuheli LL53 7UG
Tel/Fax: 01758 712161
Open: Mon-Sat 9am-5pm
▶ Contemporary handcrafted furniture utilising Welsh hardwoods. Wildwood tree services fells, converts and seasons diseased or dangerous trees. Brings alive the magic of the Welsh timbers used in the designs with an emphasis on design and quality.

Salvage & Secondhand

Old furniture is rarely unusable. Some of the charitable organisations below welcome donations, even if it needs some repair, and may come to 'uplift' them from your home.

Architectural Salvage Register
Hutton & Rostron, Netley House,
Gormshall GU5 9QA
Tel: 01483 203 221
Fax: 01483 202 911
Email: admin@handr.co.uk
▶ Good source of architectural antiques and materials around the country. A small fee gives you access to the register.

Furniture Recycling Network
Unit 3A, Pilot House,
41 King Street, Leicester LE1 6RN
Tel: 0116 254 4189
Fax: 0116 254 4189
▶ Network of groups which collect and renovate furniture and domestic goods to sell to low income families. Call for details of local groups.

Grand Illusions
2-4 Crown Road, St Margarets,
Twickenham TW1 3EE
Tel: 020 8744 1046
Fax: 020 8744 2017
Open: Mon-Sat 10am-6pm
▶ Mail order supplier of a wide range of design items for the home, including 'aged' furniture (most of which is made from 100-year-old recycled timber) and natural, water-based paints manufactured from earth pigments. Also runs courses on painting furniture, walls and floors and fabric painting.

Pendlewood
The Old Officers' Mess,
Barton Aerodrome, Eccles,
Salford M30 7SA
Tel: 0161 789 4441
Fax: 0161 787 7400
Email: Alan@pendlewood.co.uk
Web: www.pendlewood.co.uk
▶ A sustainable recycling company that focuses on the reuse of quality timber for custom-made furniture for the home, office or community. Showroom and workshop open seven days a week. Located close to the Trafford centre. From the M60 take Junction 11.

Senior & Carmichael
Whitehouse Workshops,
Church Street, Betchworth RH3 7DN
Tel: 01737 844 316
Fax: 01737 844 464
Open: Mon-Fri 9am-6pm
▶ Designers and makers of one-off and limited edition handmade furniture sold direct from the workshop. In particular manufactures the hurricane and lilliput chairs, adult and children's chairs made from locally grown timbers salvaged from the hurricane of 1987 and finished in a natural oil finish.

Tumble Home Furniture
5a High Street, Totnes TQ9 5NN
Tel: 01803 863 024
Fax: 01803 867 052
Open: Mon-Fri 10am-4pm;
Sat 10am-5pm
▶ Handmade contemporary furniture using reclaimed timber sourced from local redundant industrial and agricultural sites. Hand finished using non-toxic products – natural earth pigment paints, water based lacquers and natural waxes. Designed in a simple country style, very robust but with a warm and mellow rustic feel. Can mix timbers with steel and glass or mirror to create individual pieces with more of an urban feel. Commissions large or small undertaken.

Wesley Community Project
The Russell Club, Royce Road,
Hulme, Manchester M15 5EA
Tel: 0161 226 9051
Fax: 0161 226 9051
▶ Collects donated furniture which is then passed on people coming out of hostels and people referred to the project by organisations such as the probation services, social services and the Citizens Advice Bureaus. Call the above number for collections.

Furnishings

This combination of shops and mail order companies sell a range of eco-friendly and ethical items for the home.

Fired Earth
Head Office, Twyford Mill,
Oxford Road, Adderbury OX17 3HP
Tel: 01295 812 088
Fax: 01295 812 189
Open: Mon-Fri 8.30am-5.30pm
▶ Has 44 UK retail outlets. Supplies wall and floor tiles including handmade and hand-decorated and slate, stone and terracota floors, decorative paints (historic, art nouveau and Kelly Hoppen ranges), fabrics, natural

---

FULL MOON FUTONS Have a healthy night's sleep on **the natural mattress**

Helps maintain normal body temperature during sleep

- Unbleached 100% cotton cover filled with layers of pure cotton for comfort and support
- Cots, cribs, and all larger bed sizes from **£69** inc. p+p
- Delivery arranged within 14 working days
- Cheques payable to:
  E Colios, 20 Bulmershe Road, Reading, RG1 5RJ

To order or for more information: tel/fax 0118 926 5648
Email: fullmoonfutons@colios-terry.demon.co.uk

flooring (seagrass, jute, sisal, and coir), authentic tribal rugs, wood flooring, and bathroom accessories.

Fired Earth Shop
2 Church Street,
Wilmslow SK9 1AU
Tel: 01625 548 048
Fax: 01625 548054
Email: wilmslow@firedearth.com
▶ Traditional, natural paints and natural flooring coverings made of coir, jute and sisal. Classic tiles and authentic 'tribal' rugs. Visit the shop or call for a new catalogue.

Hamacas Mexicanas: The Mexican Hammock Co
42 Hill Avenue, Victoria Park,
Bristol BS3 4SR
Tel: 0117 972 4234
Fax: 0117 972 4234
Email: hammocks@clara.co.uk
Web: www.hammocks.co.uk
▶ Producer of classic Mexican handwoven hammocks, hammock chairs, baby hammocks, etc. Follows a fair trade ethic working directly with Mexican villages at a grass roots level so as to maintain a steady, small-scale trade.

Latitude Imports
Unit M, Station Buildings,
Llanidlogs S718 6Eb
Tel: 01686 411 132
Fax: 01686 411 132
Email: richard@latitudeimports.com
Web: www.latitudeimports.com
Open: Mon-Fri 9am-5.30pm
▶ Native American products, minerals and jewellery importers from North America. Free wholesale and retail catalogues available. Available by mail order or visit the showroom. Range includes smudge sticks, incense, rattes, pipes, dream catchers, Iroquois jewellery, Navajo silver jewellery, crafts supplies and crystals.

Lawrence T Bridgeman Ltd
No 1 Church Road,
Robertown WF15 7LS
Tel: 01924 413 813
Fax: 01924 413 801
Open: Mon-Fri 9am-5.30pm
▶ Mail order supplier of the Homestead Collection, including American homespun fabrics handwoven using traditional techniques. Call for mail order catalogue and a list of stockists.

Natural Collection
19 Monmouth Place, Bath BA1 2AY
Tel: 0870 331 3333
Fax: 01225 469 673
Web: www.naturalcollection.com
▶ Catalogue selling over 1500 environmentally-friendly products from all over the world including a selection of bed linens, towelling products and home furnishings.

One Village
Direct (Mail Order),
Charlbury OX7 3SQ
Tel: 01608 811 811
Fax: 01608 811 911
Email: progress@onevillage.co.uk
▶ Sells a range of fairly traded home furnishings including throws, curtain fabrics, bedcovers, tablecloths, cushions, rugs, etc. Works directly with craftspeople in Asia, Africa and South America encouraging community-based enterprises and co-operatives and a community surcharge included in prices helps finance social progress. Call for mail order catalogue.

Rush Matters
Struttle End Farm, Oldways Road,
Ravensden, Bedford MK44 2RH
Tel: 01234 771 980
Fax: 01234 771 980
▶ Furniture, mats, screens, bags and more handmade to traditional techniques from bulrushes along the River Ouse in Bedfordshire. Call for mail order catalogue.

Shared Earth
51 Piccadilly, Manchester M60
Tel: 0161 236 1014
Open: Every day 9am-6pm
▶ Sells a good range of mostly fairly traded, all animal-friendly gift products such as chimes, cards and stationery, diaries, candles, mobiles, mugs, picture frames, and more. Also a range of clothes and vegetarian shoes and jewellery, as well as the Opal range of vegan cosmetics and toiletries. Some African products like soap stone sculpture and drums.

Smile Plastics Ltd
The Mansion House, Ford,
Shrewsbury SY5 9LZ
Tel: 01743 850 267
Fax: 01743 851 067
Email: smileplas@aol.com
▶ Small company supplyng innovative, distinctive sheets made from recycled plastics. Sheets are supplied from 2mm to 25mm thick and are used for furniture, work surfaces, floors, panelling, etc. Delivery anywhere in the UK.

Texture
84 Stoke Newington Church Street,
London N16 0AP
Tel: 020 7241 0990
Fax: 020 7241 1991
Email: texture@jag.u-net.com
Web: www.textilesfromnature.com
Open: Tues-Sat 10am-5.30pm
▶ Retail, wholesale and mail order suppliers of a range of organic and eco-friendly products for the home. These include: organic fabric by the metre; a curtain and blind making service; organic paints; organic bedding and clothes; gifts; aromatherapy pillows and cushions; and sisal and coconut carpeting.

The Healthy House
Cold Harbour,
Ruscombe,
Stroud GL6 6DA
Tel: 01453 752 216
Fax: 01453 753 533
Email: info@healthy-house.co.uk
Web: www.healthy-house.co.uk
▶ A mail order company specialising in products for people with allergies, asthma, skin disorders and environmental illness. Call for a free catalogue which includes untreated cotton bedding, dust mite proof bedding cases, air purifiers, water purifiers, products for electromagnetic pollution, non toxic paints, vacuum cleaners, steam cleaners, masks, light boxes and much more. Offers a wide range of products for the home including pure organic cotton bedding, environmentally friendly paints and varnishes, dust mite-proof bedding and products fro allergy suffers.

The Natural Home Shop
387 Manchester Road,
Heaton Chapel, Stockport SK4 5BY
Tel: 0161 442 1400
Fax: 0161 442 9242
Email: k.large@mcc.ac.uk
▶ Stocks hardwood floors, natural fibre flooring and rugs, linoleum, and other furnishings.

Traidcraft plc
Kingsway North, Gateshead NE11 0NE
Tel: 0191 491 0591
Fax: 0191 482 2690
Email: comm@traidcraft.co.uk
Web: www.traidcraft.co.uk
▶ New range of soft furnishings, small furniture and decorative objects for the home, available by mail order catalogue from 0191 491 1001.

Fridges, Freezers & Washing Machines

Bosch
Grand Union House,
Old Wolverton Road,
Wolverton MK12 5PT
Tel: 01908 328 200
Fax: 01908 328 299
Web: www.boschappliances.co.uk
▶ Excellent brochures and website detailing how appliance energy efficiency labelling relates to the company itself, the environment, and the consumer. In production, energy saving methods such as heat recovery and energy supplied on demand are employed. Uses recyclable plastics as far as possible, and avoids harmful emissions and effluent by means of effective filtering and purification systems. The finished products are extremely low on energy consumption. 88% of washing machines are 'A' rated, and uses 'Fuzzy Logic', a precise monitoring system to ensure that as little electricity and water as possible is used. Bosch was one of the first companies to reduce the CFC content in their refrigeration appliances by 50% in 1989. Now, in 2000, all but one model are CFC and HFC free. 42% and 58% of their fridge/freezers are 'A' and 'B' graded respectively. Dishwashers use energy saving technology such as hydrosensors and heat recycling systems.

Home & Garden

Creda
c/o General Domestic Appliances Ltd,
Morley Way, Peterborough PE2 9JB
Tel: 08701 546 474
Fax: 01733 341 783
Web: www.creda.co.uk
▶ Eco Sensor Control features automatically reduces the heat when clothes are dry, thereby saving electricity. Of the home laundry appliances, 82% were at least 'C' rated on the Energy Efficiency Scale. Accessories are often available for people who have a disability, impaired vision or arthritis.

Gaggenau
Grand Union House,
Old Wolverton Road, Wolverton,
Milton Keynes MK12 5PT
Tel: 01780 722 144
Fax: 01908 328 370
Web: www.gaggenau.com
▶ German company whose range includes fridge/freezers and dishwashers. All fridge/freezers are CFC and HFC free. 50% were 'A' rated, and 38% were 'B' rated. The dishwashers use technology to recover heat from used water to save energy, as well as an 'eco-dispenser' to measure the required amount of detergent. 75% of dishwashers were 'A' or 'B' rated.

Hotpoint
c/o General Domestic Appliances Ltd,
Morley Way, Peterborough PE2 9JB
Tel: 01733 568 989
Fax: 01733 341 783
Web: www.hotpoint.co.uk
▶ All refrigeration appliances are fitted with compressors, which incorporate high quality motors and are therefore more efficient. The models featured in the brochure are at least 'C' rated, and nearly a quarter of these are 'A' rated. All dishwashers have low water and energy consumption. A heat exchanger uses heat from the previous wash cycle to heat up the cold water for the next stage of the programme. Washing machines are designed to use less water, energy and detergent. Information line 08701 50 60 70

Iceland Frozen Foods Plc
Second Avenue,
Deeside Industrial Park,
Deeside CH5 2NW
Tel: 01244 830 100
Fax: 01244 814 531
▶ Has launched a range of Greenpeace backed, environmentally friendly fridges, freezers and fridge freezers. Named after the Kyoto protocol signed in 1997, a pledge to cut the amount of climate changing gases being pumped in to the skies, their 'Kyoto' range is designed with the environment in mind and uses a refrigerant gas that is not only harmless to the ozone layer, but is also climate friendly.

Liebherr
Express Way, Whitwood,
Near Wakefield WF10 5QJ
Tel: 01977 665 665
Fax: 01977 665 669
Web: www.lhg.liebherr.de
▶ Fridge and freezer specialists. In 1993, they were the first company to produce 100% CFC free appliances, and products are now almost all HFC free as well and have non-polluting coatings, and include the utilisation of some recyclable materials in manufacture.

Miele
Fairacres, Marcham Road,
Abingdon OX14 1TW
Tel: 01235 554 477
Fax: 01235 554 477
Web: www.miele.co.uk
▶ Domestic appliances designed to meet the following environmental criteria; energy saving, minimum pollution of waste water, reductions in detergents needed, elimination of CFCs and HFCs wherever possible, sound insulation, and clean air. Runs an easy to understand website detailing the companies' environmental focus and publishes a comprehensive and glossy environmental report. At production stage, the heat generated is used to heat offices, and the volume of waste is reduced by recycling. Ethos on packaging is to use 'as much as necessary – as little as possible', and recycled packaging as far as possible. Appliances are made from recyclable materials. 100% of washing machines in brochure are 'A' rated, and 93% of the fridge/freezers featured were 'A' or 'B' rated.

Neff
Grand Union House,
Old Wolverton Road, Wolverton,
Milton Keynes MK12 5PT
Tel: 01908 328 300
Fax: 01908 328 399
Web: www.neff.co.uk
▶ German company which includes ranges of fridge/freezers, dishwashers, and home laundry appliances. 'Appliance Care' after sales service ensures any problems will usually be solved within 2 working days. Free demonstration sessions at showroom and training centre in Milton Keynes. Neff appliances are used in the Vegetarian Cookery School. Their dishwashers are especially renowned for their energy efficiency, including their first triple 'A' rated model. All washing appliances are recyclable; from the packing materials to the products themselves.

Siemens
Grand Union House,
Old Wolverton Road,
Wolverton MK12 5PT
Tel: 01908 328 400
Fax: 01908 328 499
▶ Of the 60 appliances in the brochure, over 50% were 'A' graded, and a third were 'B' graded. In particular, an 'A' rated dishwasher is featured, a grading which is rarer to obtain than for other appliances. Energy saving features in the fridge/freezers include halogen lighting, which consume less energy and emit less heat than standard lighting; improved insulation; and energy efficient internal ventialtor fans. All models are CFC and HFC free and all synthetic materials and plastics used are recyclable. Washing machines feature a rinse system that ensures all detergent is removed to save water and energy. The energy efficient sensor dryer is used in washer/dryers and dishwashers. A heat exchanger for dishwashers saves water and electricity.

Zanussi
55-77 High Street, Slough,
Berkshire SL1 1DZ
Tel: 08705 727 727
Web: www.zanussi.co.uk
▶ 'Aqua-save' wash system cleans and recycles water during the wash, reducing water consumption to a minimum. 78% of appliances rated 'C' or above.

Miscellaneous Suppliers

Candle Makers Supplies
Candle Workshop, Gelligroes Mill,
Gelligroes, Pontllanfraith,
Blackwood Np12 2HY
Tel: 01495 222 322
Fax: 01495 222 053
Email: candles@candlemakers.co.uk
Open: Mon-Sat 9am-5pm
▶ Supplies handcrafted candles, ready-made and made to order. Also runs candlemaking courses and supplies candlemaking materials. The 400 year old watermill has played an integral part in the local history – it was here that Islwyn, the bard, poet and minister first learned the traditional metre, and where the radio pioneer Artie Moore picked up the Titanic's SOS.

Candle Makers Supplies
28 Blythe Road, London W14 0HA
Tel: 020 7602 4031
Fax: 020 7602 2796
Email: candles@candlemakers.co.uk
Web: www.candlemakers.co.uk
Open: Mon-Fri 10.30am-6pm;
Sat 10.30am-5pm
▶ Offers a mail order service of all the essential materials needed for candlemaking including beaded paraffin wax specially blended for cabdlemaking, beeswax, stearin, appliqué wax, wicks, dyes, pigments, perfumes and glass and metal candle moulds. Also stocks books and videos and publishes a newsletter.

County Loos
Hill Croft, Bradeley Green,
Whitchurch SY13 4HE
Tel: 01948 666 396
▶ Environmentally friendly toilet hire. Serviced daily or weekly as required, no mains needed. Loos also available for those with physical disabilities.

Home & Garden

Earth Friendly Supplies Ltd
PO Box 22, Leeds LS17 0XF
Tel: 01423 734 849
Email: reg@earthfriendly.co.uk
Web: www.earthfriendly.co.uk
▶ Supplies information and products via the internet to help people to live a more earth-friendly lifestyle.

Full Spectrum Lighting Ltd
19 Lincoln Road, Cressex Business Park, High Wyocmbe HP12 3FX
Tel: 01494 526 051
Fax: 01494 527 005
Email: info@sad.uk.com
▶ Brings the benefits of natural outdoor light indoors. FSL fluorescent tubes are available in all sizes and wattages and will fit existing fittings. Daylight long life energy saving bulbs are also available.

Green Shop, The
Bisley, near Stroud GL6 7BX
Tel: 01452 770 629
Fax: 01452 770 204
Email: jane@greenshop.co.uk
Web: www.greenshop.co.uk
▶ Mail order products for a sustainable future: paints and finishes; household cleaners; fair trade and cruelty free products; books, rainwater harvesting systems; sunpipes; wormeries and lots more.

Hemp Collective Ltd
Silverdale, Clyde Road, Didsbury, Manchester M20 2NJ
Tel: 0161 445 5227
Fax: 0161 445 2556
Email: talk2us@thehempcollective.com
Web: www.thehempcollective.com
Open: Mon-Fri 9am-9pm
▶ Provides a diverse range of hemp products encompassing body care, clothing foodstuffs, paper and sundries. Mail order and wholesale facilities for people looking to make a positive difference to themselves and the planet. Write or call for a catalogue or visit the website.

Mr Collier's Emporium
Manchester Methodist Central Hall, Oldham Street, Manchester M1
Tel: 0161 236 2462/5141
Fax: 0161 237 1585
▶ Collier's is part of the Manchester and Salford Methodist Mission and runs a restaurant/tea shop and a shop selling arts and crafts and fair trade products.

Oxfam Fairtrade Company
Salestrack, 3 Manor Court, Dix's Field EX1 1ST
Tel: 01392 429 428
▶ The Oxfam mail order catalogue sells a range of fairly-traded crafts, stationery, toys, kitchen and gardening items and foods. Call for a copy.

Papeterie
Tel: 020 8546 0313
▶ Wholesaler and distributor of decorative artist paper and eco-friendly stationery products. Ring for more information.

Traider Pete
St Peter's House, University Precinct, Oxford Road, Manchester M13
Tel: 0161 273 1465
Open: Mon-Fri 12pm-2pm
▶ Traidcraft fairly-traded products on sale during University term times.

Willey Winkle
Offa House, Offa Street, Hereford HR1 2LH
Tel: 01432 268 018
Fax: 01432 268 018
Open: Mon-Fri 9am-6pm; Sat 9am-2pm
▶ For over 40 years Jeff Wilkes has handmade a full range of traditional mattresses for cots, cribs, Moses baskets and for children's and adult's beds. Recently, an organic range has been introduced. The organic wool is shorn from sheep raised under an organic regime on Highgrove Estate in Gloucestershire, on land certified as organic by the Soill Association. Grading, storage and handling by the British Wool Marketing Board ensures there is no accidental contamination of the pure fleeces. The wool is then stuffed into mattress casings made from organically grown and unbleached cotton. Duvets and bedding are also available. Call for a mail order catalogue.

CLEANING & LAUNDRY

Some wholefood shops (see Chapter One: Food & Drink) stock eco-friendly cleaning products. We've listed manufacturers and mail order suppliers only below.

Products

21st Century Health
3 Water Gardens, Stanmore HA7 3QA
Tel: 020 7935 5440
Fax: 020 7487 3710
Email: 21st.Century@easynet.co.uk
Web: www.21stCenturyhealth.co.uk
Open: Mon-Fri 10am-6pm
▶ Supplies products for a chemical-free home, body and spirit. Dedicated to finding the best natural alternatives from around the world with a simple philosophy – no harsh chemicals and no animal testing. Call for a catalogue or buy online.

Benrené Health International
18 Chatsmore House, Goring By Sea, Worthing BN12 5AH
Tel: 01903 505 180
Fax: 01903 245 718
Email: chris@kf-g.com
Web: www.nawt.net
▶ Collection of pure, effective, economically priced household cleaning products, skincare, haircare, nailcare, dentalcare and nutritional and mineral health products all of which meet the stringent OECD tests which require that all ingredients must biodegrade five to seven days after use. Natural hair and skincare products also on offer. Call for a mail order catalogue.

Bio-D Company Ltd
64 St Nicholas Gate, Hedon, Kingston upon Hull HU12 8HS
Tel: 01482 229 950
Fax: 01482 229 921
Email: bio-d@ecodet.karoo.co.uk
▶ Vegan Society-approved household products made from renewable resources, containing totally biodegradable detergents, no phosphates and no chlorine bleaches. The

Sleep soundly on nature's own materials.

Mattresses and Bedding in Organic and Luxury Wool for Adults and Children

Willey Winkle
Offa House, Offa Street,
Hereford HR1 2LH
Tel: 01432 268018 Fax: 01432 340880

Home & Garden

range includes dishwasher liquid, cleaners, spray polish, washing up liquid and more.

Down to Earth
Reckitt Benckiser Ltd,
PO Box 118, Clevedon BS21 7ZH
Tel: 01482 326 151
Fax: 01482 582 532
Open: Mon-Fri 9am-5.30pm
▶ Phosphate-free, bio-degradable washing products including washing up liquid, washing powder and fabric conditioner. Stocked in most supermarkets.

Eco-Co Products
Birchwood House, Briar Lane,
Croydon, Surrey CR0 5AD
Tel: 020 8777 3121
Fax: 020 8777 3393
Email: info@ecozone.co.uk
Web: www.ecozone.co.uk
▶ Sells 'eco-balls', chemical-free refillable laundry balls. Eco-zyme chemical-free cleaning cleaning.

Ecover UK Ltd
165 Main Street,
New Greenham Park RG19 6HN
Tel: 01635 528 240
Fax: 01635 528 271
Email: 106252.2565@compuserve.com
▶ Makes products using only natural botanical and mineral ingredients. Range includes wool wash, fabric conditioner and stain remover. They are available in most health shops (some of which offer Ecover Refill service), Sainsburys, Asda and in the Natural Collection catalogue.

Hakawerk Neutralseife
Sailcote, Old Yarmouth Road,
Sutton, Norwich NR12 9QZ
Tel: 01692 580 933
Fax: 01692 580 933
Open: Mon-Fri 9am-5pm
▶ Importer and distributor of Hakawerk range of environmentally correct cleaning and laundering products and a series of skin care toiletries and skin lotions. Hakawerk has been in business for over 50 years and is the first holder of the German Government's Eco-Diploma. Distribution is to end users and agents.

Little Green Shop
PO Box 2892, Brighton BN1 5QZ
Tel: 01273 508 126
Fax: 01273 506 723
Open: Mon-Sat 9am-5.30pm
▶ Produces household cleaning products, toiletries and cosmetics that are kind to the environment and effective to use. Safe for children and animals, the products contain no harmful chemicals, no animal derivatives and have never been tested on animals. BUAV and Vegetarian Society-approved. Call for mail order.

Natural Collection
19 Monmouth Place, Bath BA1 2AY
Tel: 0870 331 3333
Fax: 01225 469 673
Email: naturalcollection@ecotrade.co.uk
▶ Catalogue selling a whole range of household cleaners, cleansers and polishes including products by Ark, Ecover, Q2 and Bio-D. Also low energy lamps, solar battery chargers, rechargeable batteries, savaplugs and a recycled vacuum cleaner called Recyclone (£229.99).

Planit Earth
80 Mayall Road,
London SE24 OPJ
Tel: 020 7274 8554
Fax: 020 7274 0244
▶ Supplies washing disks which launder clothes by ionising the water with naturally negatively charged pellets which weaken the surface tension of the water enabling smaller droplets to penetrate the fabric more deeply. The dirt sticks to the water and is washed away. Particularly useful for eczema sufferers.

Spirit of Nature Ltd
Burrhart House,
Cradock Road,
Luton LU4 OJF
Tel: 01582 847 370
Fax: 01582 847 371
Email: oliver@spiritofnature.co.uk
Web: www.spiritofnature.co.uk
Open: Mon-Fri 9am-5.30pm
▶ Mail order catalogue selling eco-household products. Also available: natural clothing collection for adults and babies/toddlers, bedlinen, natural bodycare products, organic washable nappy systems and more. Call for a free catalogue.

Super Globe
LightNet, PO Box 9640,
London E11 2XY
Tel: 020 8518 8633
Fax: 020 8518 8633
Email: i.am@lightnet.co.uk
Web: www.lightnet.co.uk
▶ Network for personal and planetary empowerment. Covers interests such as free energy, alternative technology and environmental issues. Publishes a quarterly newsletter. Send an SAE for copy.

WATER

Filters

Aquasaver Ltd
Unit 10, Efford Farm Business Park,
Vicarage Road,
Bude EX23 8LT
Tel: 01288 354 425
Fax: 01288 354 447
Email: aquasaver@aquasaver.demon.co.uk
Open: Mon-Fri 9am-5pm
▶ Supplier and installer of a system to collect and treat 'grey water' (eg used bath water) for reuse for toilet flushing, washing machines and other domestic water uses.

Culligan International UK Ltd
Blenheim Road,
Cressex Business Park,
High Wycombe HP12 3RS
Tel: 01494 436 484
Fax: 01494 523 833
Open: Mon-Fri 9am-5pm
▶ Supplier and installer of water treatment systems for the commercial, industrial and domestic markets.

Earthly Goods
8 Fields Close,
Grafham,
Huntingdon PE28 0AY
Tel: 01480 812 004
Fax: 01480 812 004
▶ Supplier of water filtration and purification systems. Cover homes and businesses throughout the UK.

NEVER BUY LAUNDRY DETERGENT AGAIN!

NEW

AQUA BALL

CLEANER, BRIGHTER, SOFTER WASHES WITHOUT THE USE OF HARSH CHEMICAL DETERGENTS OR SOFTENERS

For further details of AQUA BALL, & our MONEY BACK GUARANTEE, RING FREEPHONE 0800 026 0220

Fresh Water Filter Company
Gem House, 895 High Road,
Chadwell Heath RM6 4HL
Tel: 020 8597 3223
Fax: 020 8590 3229
Email: dw@freshwaterfilter.com
Web: www.freshwaterfilter.com
▶ Strives to provide high quality products and services that produce safe and healthy water as efficiently and profitably as possible for all. The units ensure an ever ready flow of purified water for drinking and cooking and come fully guaranteed and with a comprehensive backup service network. The Fresh Water 1000 system is for the provision of natural safe fresh healthy drinking water. and removing all unwanted contaminates including bacteria, chemicals, organophosphates, metals, unsavoury odours and tastes. Supplies water treatment units (purifiers, filters, coolers, softeners) which remove many of the harmful pollutants in tap water for domestic and industrial use. Call for free advice.

Pure H2O Company
The Business Village, Blackbushe
Business Park, Yateley GU46 6GA
Tel: 01252 860 111
Fax: 01252 860 811
Email: aquathin@pureh2o.co.uk
Web: www.pureh20.co.uk
Open: Mon to Fri 9am to 5.30pm
▶ For patented Aquathin purifiers producing medically approved water, with systems able to produce up to 18 megaohm purity. Provides world-class domestic and industrial Reverse Osmosis/De-ionisation systems. Full year on year site guarantee. Water delivery and home water softening systems. Free water testing and site surveys. Full quality assurance guarantee and swift customer service response. Provides seminars on the hydration cycle, and unique energy products that turn Pure H2O into true glacial water.

The Healthy House
Cold Harbour, Ruscombe,
Stroud GL6 6DA
Tel: 01453 752 216
Fax: 01453 753 533
Email: info@healthy-house.co.uk
Web: www.healthy-house.co.uk
▶ The Healthy House is a mail order company specialising in products for people with allergies, asthma, skin disorders and environmental illness. Please send for our free catalogue which includes untreated cotton bedding, dust mite proof bedding cases, air purifiers, water purifiers, products for electromagnetic pollution, non toxic paints, vacuum cleaners, steam cleaners, masks, light boxes and much more. Offers a complete range of water filters; counter top units and stainless steel under sinkunits for drinking and cooking; wholehouse units to filter all the water in the home; shower filters to remove chlorine in the shower; and distillers and reverse osmosis units for pure water. Please phone for advice.

UVO(UK) Limited
P.O. Box 160,
Hay-on-Wye HR3 6ES
Tel: 01497 831 029
Fax: 01497 831 420
Email: uvo.uk@virgin.net
Web: www.grander.com
▶ Distributes several devices to revitalise water – whether single glasses or the complete house water supply, based on the principles of the Austrian naturalist Johann Grander, whose prime interest is to return drinking water to what it once was: the wellspring of all life.

Organisations

DWI (Drinking Water Inspectorate)
Floor 2/C1 Ashdown House, 123 Victoria Street, London SW1E 6DE
Tel: 020 7944 5956
Fax: 020 7944 5969
Email: dwi_enquiries@detr.gov.uk
Web: www.dwi.detr.gov.uk
▶ Set up in 1990, its main task is to check that water companies in England and Wales supply wholesome, safe-to-drink water and comply with the requirements of the Water Quality Regulations. If you are experiencing a problem with your drinking water quality, contact your water company. If a quality problem is not rectified you should contact OFWAT or DWI for further assistance.

International Society for the Prevention of Water Pollution
Little Orchard, Bentworth,
Alton GU34 5RB
Tel: 01420 562 225
▶ Worldwide charity engaged in the fight against water pollution in streams, lakes, rivers and the seas, anywhere in the world, with several branches in Europe and the USA. Will take up any case of pollution from concerned individuals. All requests for help and information should be in writing accompanied by a large SAE.

National Pure Water Association
12 Dennington Lane, Crigglestone,
Wakefield WF4 3ET
Tel: 01924 254 433
Fax: 01924 242 380
▶ Campaigning for safe drinking water since 1960. Networks scientific advisers internationally and is a major opponent to water fluoridation. Produces a newsletter and leaflets. Funded only by members subscriptions.

Water UK
1 Queen Annes Gate,
London SW1H 9BT
Tel: 020 7344 1844
Web: www.water.org.uk
▶ Trade organisation for all the water suppliers in the UK. Runs the Bag It and Bin It campaign which works towards cleaner beaches and riverbanks in Britain by encouraging people not to dispose of waste down the toilet. Visit the website for more information.

Pure H2O now on tap

Drinking water is the first step to optimum health.
Now you can have the purest water right from your own tap.

pure H2O®

TEL 01252 860111
WWW.PUREH2O.CO.UK

THE PURE H2O COMPANY, THE BUSINESS VILLAGE,
BLACKBUSHE BUSINESS PARK, YATELEY GU46 6GA

Home & Garden 73

GARDENING

Nurseries & Garden Centres

Buckingham Nurseries and Garden Centre
20 Tingewick Road,
Buckingham MK18 4AE
Tel: 01280 813 556
Fax: 01280 815 491
Email: enquiries@bucknur.com
Web: www.buckingham-nurseries.co.uk
Open: Mon-Fri 8.30am-6pm,
Thurs 8pm; Sun 10am-4pm
▶ Family business with 50 years experience producing and retailing a wide range of good quality, well priced plants. Specialising in bare rooted hedging plants, young forest and ornamental trees including many native varieties. 28 page A4 catalogue available free of charge listing hedging plants, young forest trees, ornamental trees, shrubs, climbers, ground cover plants, fruit trees, soft fruit and gardening sundries. All plants and sundries are available for collection or by mail order.

Cool Temperate
5 Colville Villas, Nottingham NG1 4HN
Tel: 0115 947 4977
Email: philcorbett53@hotmail.com
▶ Offers a plant nursery, a permaculture design consultancy and a teaching service. The nursery specialises in practical plants – fruit trees and bushes, nuts, hedging, nitrogen fixers, perennnial herbaceous. Supply is by mail order only in the autumn and winter or by collection from the nursery. Send two first class stamps for a price list. Cool Temperate uses its profits for researching new sustainable systems and techniques, particularly the Coppice Orchard, using fruit trees on their own roots.

Composting & Growing Mediums

Blackwall Ltd
Seacroft Estate, Coal Road,
Leeds LS14 2AQ
Tel: 0113 201 8000
Fax: 0113 201 8001
Email: info@blackwall-ltd.com
Web: www.blackwall-ltd.com
Open: Mon-Fri 8.30am-5.30pm
▶ Specialists in environmental product promotions and provide an all inclusive marketing, customer service and distribution package for councils and water authorities wishing to promote home composting or water conservation. Also offers many other gardening products direct to customers. Wherever possible manufactures or supplies products made with recycled materials.

Fertile Fibre
Knighton-on-Teme, Tenbury Wells,
Worcester WR15 8LT
Tel: 01584 781 575
Fax: 01584 781 483
▶ Mail order supplier of coir blocks, coir compost, cocoshell mulch and eco-friendly fertilizers. The latter include Fertile Fibre Multipurpose, suitable for seeds, cuttings, potting and containers; 5F's fertilizer, a pelleted, all year round organic feed; and Nu-Gro, a new product, an excellent liquid fertilizer based on fish derivatives. Cocoshells are chocolate bean husks that provide the perfect mulch. Also sells bark peelings and high quality composted bark. All products carry the Soil Association symbol and special mixes are available. Call for free information and a sample pack.

Humus Wyse Ltd
Gallants Bower, Dartmouth TQ6 0JN
Tel: 01803 834 687
Fax: 01803 834 687
Email: humuswyse.swic@farmline.com
Open: Mon-Fri 9am-5pm
▶ Specialises in finding viable solutions for local recycling of organic waste. A priority is to return compost to farmland, thus closing the organic loop. Launching a project this summer in Devon which will demonstrate a new approach to local composting. The system can be replicated so call if you have a need for composting in your area.

Organa
12 Bedehouse Bank,
Bourne PE10 9JX
Tel: 01778 421 052
Fax: 01778 421 052
Email: george@gail63.freeserve.co.uk
Web: www.organa.cc
▶ Supplier of organic fertiliser.

Super Natural Ltd
Bore Place, Chiddingstone,
Edenbridge TN8 7AR
Tel: 01732 463 255
Fax: 01732 740 264
Email: info@commonwork.org
Open: Mon-Fri 9am-5.30pm
▶ Rural enterprise on 500 acre organic dairy farm producing range of organic composts, mulch and soil conditioner, liquid plant food from own cow manure. Soil Association approved and available also for amateur gardeners and growers. Availability: for growers, direct from company; and for amateur gardeners, from garden centres, branches of Homebase and Robert Dyas. Company has been trading since 1985 and is linked to the Educational Trust. Profits are used to help to fund educational school visits for over 3,000 children each year. Colour leaflets and Growers Information available.

Wiggly Wigglers
Lower Blakemere Farm,
Blakemere HR2 9PX
Tel: 01981 500 391/
0800 216 990 (helpline)
Fax: 01981 500 108
Email: wiggly@wigglywigglers.co.uk
Web: www.wigglywigglers.co.uk
Open: Mon-Fri 9am-5pm
▶ Practical mail order company promoting worms and worm composting for organic home waste. Offers a range of wormeries for kitchen waste including the innovative 'Can-O-Worms', and other worm kits for garden waste and soil improvement. Offers free advice and information including a free *Home Guide – Worms at Work* and produces a quarterly newsletter. Also runs the country's only freephone worm composting helpdesk on 0800 216 990.

Plants & Seeds

Brogdale Orchards Ltd
Brogdale Road, Faversham ME13 8XZ
Tel: 01795 535 286/01795 535 462
Fax: 01795 531 710
Web: www.brogdale.co.uk
Open: Mon-Sun 9.30am-5pm
▶ The home of the National Fruit Collections, with a wide range of distinct apple, pear, plum, cherry and nut varieties. Also offers grafting services and a series of events throughout the year.

Chiltern Seeds
Bortree Stile, Ulverston LA12 7PB
Tel: 01229 581 137
Fax: 01229 584 549
Email: info@chilternseeds.co.uk
Web: www.chilternseeds.co.uk
▶ A mail order seed company exporting to over 90 countries and importing rare seeds from all over the world. The catalogue is the largest of its kind, listing over 4,600 items. Aims to introduce into general cultivation unusual, rare and even endangered species, and to introduce gardeners to the fascination of growing from seed. Specialises in non-specialisation – an item is only selected for inclusion in the catalogue if it thought to be of interest to the general grower of seeds. As well as the unusual, virtually every plant commonly grown from seed is represented.

Edwin Tucker and Sons Ltd
Brewery Meadow,
Stonepark, Ashburton TQ13 7DG
Tel: 01364 652 403
Fax: 01364 654 300
Open: Mon-Fri 8am-5pm;
Sat 8am-4pm
▶ Provides a vegetarian seed catalogue which is Soil Association approved.

Postcode Plants Database
Flora-for-Fauna Database,
Biogeography and Conservation Lab,
The Natural History Museum,
Cromwell Road, South Kensington,
London SW7 5BD
Email: fff@nhm.ac.uk
Web: www.nhm.ac.uk/science/projects/fff/

Home & Garden

▶ It is often difficult for people to find out which plants are local to their area. The Database locates the names of flowers, trees, butterflies and birds for each home address in Scotland. Simply by typing in the first four characters of their postcode, householders, schools, garden centres and councils can obtain tailor-made lists of local plants which are both hospitable and gardenworthy. By selecting the right plants from the Database, people can help the environment.

Suffolk Herbs
Monks Farm, Pantlings Lane, Kelvedon CO5 9PG
Tel: *01376 572 456*
Fax: *01376 571 189*
Email: *suffolkherbs@btinternet.com*
Web: *www.suffolkherbs.com*
▶ Seed company with a beautiful mail order catalogue and wide selection of seeds (herbs, unusual vegetables, wild flowers), organic products and books.

Terre De Semences
Ripple Farm, Crundale, Canterbury CT4 7EB
Tel: *0966 448 379*
▶ Supplies a huge range of organic or bio-dynamic vegetable, grain and flower seeds. The seeds are from France and are certified by Ecocert (the French equivalent of the Soil Association). The seed packets are made of kraft paper and are printed in English with the species and varietal names, including some gardening advice. They also carry the year of production and the viable life of the seed. Packets contain the kind of quantity required by a large family – some a lot more. Catalogue is available for £4 including posting and packaging.

Supplies

Agralan Ltd
The Old Brickyard, Ashton Keynes SN6 6QR
Tel: *01285 860 015*
Fax: *01285 860 056*
Email: *agralan@cybermail.uk.com*
▶ Gardening supplies for the fully organic gardener, including products such as fine mesh netting for crop protection, soaker hoses for water conservation, moth traps for reducing damage to fruit crops and hanging basket liners made from 100% natural fibres.

Chase Organics Ltd
River Dene Estate, Molesey Road, Hersham KT12 4RG
Tel: *01932 253 666*
Fax: *01932 252 707*
Email: *chaseorg@aol.com*
▶ Publishes the *Organic Gardening Catalogue*, the official mail order catalogue of the Henry Doubleday Research Association, which offers organic and untreated vegetable, herb and flower seeds and a wide range of fertilizers, peat-free growing media, pest controls and equipment. Good source of leaflets on topics such as making compost and leafmould and many other aspects of organic gardening.

Earthworks Trading
Foresthill Cottage (GG), Broughton, Biggar ML12 6QH
Email: *anna@clan.com*
▶ The KIRPI hand-weeding tool is made in India and half of the profit from sales support an organic farming project in Gujarat, India. The KIRPI is a sickle-shaped tool with a serrated cutting edge on the inside and a hoeing blade on the outside. Once you strart using it you will wonder how you managed without it! It makes a good present for fellow gardeners too. To order, send a cheque for £9.80 (inc. p&p), made payable to Earthworks Trading.

English Hurdle
Curload, Stoke St Gregory, Taunton TA3 6JD
Tel: *01823 698 418*
Fax: *01823 698 859*
Email: *hurdle@enterprise.net*
Web: *www.hurdle.co.uk*
Open: *Mon-Fri 8am-5pm; Sat 9am-1pm*
▶ Supplies wattle fencing panels traditionally made from woven wil-low. Also plant climbing poles, garden furniture, living willow trellises, arbours and summerhouses. Call for a mail order catalogue.

Green Ways Environmental Care
Dept GG, Southend Farm, Long Reach, Ockham, Woking GU23 6PF
Tel: *01483 281 391*
Fax: *01483 281 392*
Email: *green.ways@btinternet.com*
Web: *www.btinternet.com/~green.ways*
Open: *Mon-Fri 9am-5pm*
▶ Supplies Pond Pads, a safe, effective and fully biodegradable barley straw treatment which gives protection against algae in ponds using a method supported by research at the Open University and the Royal Horticultural Society. One pack of three Pads gives a year's protection to ponds of up to 700 gallons. Available from aquatics and water garden centres or mail order.

Organic Gardening Catalogue
River Dene Estate, Molesey Road, Hersham KT12 4RG
Tel: *01932 253 666*
Fax: *01932 252 707*
Open: *Mon-Fri 9.30am-4.30pm*
▶ Published by Chase Organics, this is the official mail order catalogue of the Henry Doubleday Research Association, offering organic and untreated vegetable, herb and flower seeds, fertilizers, peat-free growing media, pest controls and equipment. Good source of leaflets on many other aspects of organic gardening.

Original Organics Ltd
Unit 9, Langlands Business Park, Cullompton EX15 3DA
Tel: *01884 841 515*
Fax: *01884 841 717*
Email: *sales@originalorganics.co.uk*
Open: *Mail Order*
▶ Garden supply company specialising in equipment for organic gardening. Supplies the Original Wormery and the Junior Wormery composting bins, peat-free composts, a range of organic plant foods and more.

RAIN SAVA

Stop Rainwater going down the drain

Forget water shortages and the hosepipe ban this summer... FIT a versatile RainSava to your house downpipe and FILL storage tanks anywhere you want in the garden!

- SAVE WATER – SAVE MONEY
- AUTOMATIC OVERFLOW (Option 1)
- EASY TO FIT – IN MINUTES
- STORE WATER WHERE YOU WANT IT
- FITS ROUND OR SQUARE DOWN PIPES
- LEAVES & DEBRIS REMOVED IN SECONDS

£15.99

• AS SEEN ON TV •

To place your order or request further information, either phone or write with a cheque to: Raindrain Ltd, Albert Mills, Mill Street West, Dewsbury, W.Yorks. WF12 9AE
Telephone: 01924 468341   Fax: 01924 465925

Please send me........Rainsavas to the following:
Name..
Address...
....
....
Cheques payable to Raindrain Ltd

Raindrain Ltd
Albert Mills, Mill Street West,
Dewsbury WF12 9AE
Tel: 01924 468 564
Fax: 01924 465 925
Open: Mon-Fri 9am-5pm
▶ Manufacturers of the ingenious 'Rain-Sava', an effective rainwater diverting unit which easily fits into standard (63/68mm round, 65mm square) and European (82mm) downpipes to enable environmentally conscious gardeners to collect and store rainwater. The unique sliding collar attachment enables the Rain-Sava to be inserted into the downpipe simply and easily. It is manaufactured to high standards with British Standard Kitemark BS4576 from moulded thermoplastic and can be fitted in minutes with the help of a template to take the guessing out of cutting. As water conservation is an increasingly important issue and hose pipe bans are becoming commonplace – not to mention the high cost of metered water – the Rain-Sava is ideal for any house. Comes complete with fitting kit and full instructions. Available by mail order. Call to order or for more information

Scarletts Plant Care
Nayland Road, West Bergholt,
Colchester CO6 3DH
Tel: 01206 242 533
Fax: 01206 242 530
Email: bio@scarletts.co.uk
Open: Mon-Fri 8am-5pm
▶ Mail order supplier of biological controls for the following pests: slugs, vine weevil, aphid/greenfly, red spider mite, thrips, meelybug, caterpillar etc. Advice over the phone or via email, particularly on identifying pests. Order direct online.

Organisations & Services

Brogdale Horticultural Trust
Brogdale Road,
Faversham ME13 8XZ
Tel: 01795 535 286/ 535462
Fax: 01795 531 710
Web: www.info@brogdale.org.uk
▶ Independent non profit making charitable organisation which aims to promote research in use and appreciation of fruits and other horticultural products. Formed in 1990 to safeguard the long term future of the National Fruit Collections.

English Gardening School, The
at the Chelsea Physic Garden,
66 Royal Hospital Road,
London SW3 4HS
Tel: 020 7352 4347
Fax: 020 7376 3936
Email: egs@dircon.co.uk
Web: www.englishgardeningschool.co.uk
▶ Founded in 1983 by Rosemary Alexander, the school offers a wide range of courses from within the historic Chelsea Physic Garden, central London. Affiliated to the RHS, the school offer Diploma courses in Garden Design, Practical Horticulture, Plants and Plantsmanship and Botanical painting. Part-time study over a year. Also courses via distance learning and a seasonal programme of short courses covering a range of subjects. Highlights include Planning and Planting, The New Kitchen Garden, Down to Earth Gardening, Botanical Painting and Photography.

Fauna & Flora International
Great Eastern House, Tenison Road,
Cambridge CB1 2DT
Tel: 01223 571 000
Fax: 01223 461 481
Email: info@fauna-flora.org
Web: www.ffi.org.uk
Open: Mon-Fri 9am-5.30pm
▶ Conservation charity working to protect wildlife worldwide from Asian elephants to mountain gorillas, through a range of campaigns including one to make the lucrative garden bulb trade more eco-friendly. Send an A5 SAE for a copy of The Good Bulb Guide to make sure you only buy bulbs from horticultural, rather than wild, origins.

Green Gardeners
PO Box 206,
Worcester WR1 1YS
▶ A sustainable gardening group which campaigns, provides information and offers an advisory service. Also works with, and through, other voluntary organisations to promote sustainable, and especially urban, gardening concepts.

Hardy Plant Society
Little Orchard, Great Comberton,
Nr Pershore, Worcester WR10 3DP
Tel: 01386 710317
Fax: 01386 710 117
Email: admin@hardy-plant.org.uk
Web: www.hardy-plant.org.uk
Open: Mon-Fri 9am-5pm
▶ Explores, encourages and conserves all that is best in gardens.

HDRA – the organic organisation
Ryton Organic Gardens,
Ryton-on-Rushmore,
Coventry CV8 3LG
Tel: 024 7630 3517
Fax: 024 7663 9229
Email: enquiry@hdra.org.uk
Web: www.hdra.org.uk
Open: Mon-Fri 9am-5pm
▶ HDRA – the organic organisation is Europe's largest organic organisation. Based at Ryton Organic Gardens in Warwickshire, HDRA also runs Yalding Organic Gardens in Kent and an organic walled garden at Audley End in Essex. All three gardens are open to visitors and have shops and restaurants. At Ryton there are also conference facilities. HDRA members enjoy an organic gardening telephone advice line, a quarterly magazine, free entry to many gardens plus other benefits. HDRA runs the Heritage Seed Library which saves rare and endangered varieties of vegetables. There is also an organic gardening catalogue, organic garden and landscape design consultancy, a wide range of books, various schools projects and a network of local groups.

Herb Society
Deddington Hill Farm, Warmington,
Banbury OX17 1XB
Tel: 01295 692 000
Fax: 01295 692 004
Email: email@herbsociety.co.uk
Web: www.herbsociety.co.uk

Europe's largest organic organisation

HDRA – the organic organisation

We offer
- Expert organic gardening advice
- Delightful display gardens at Ryton, Yalding and Audley End with free entry for children
- Organic gardening catalogue, a range of books and member's magazine, 'The Organic Way'
- Organic garden design consultancy
- Events and courses galore

Plus much more. Do contact us...

HDRA – the organic organisation
Ryton Organic Gardens
Coventry
CV8 3LG
Tel: (024) 7630 3517

Visit our website at www.hdra.org.uk

▶ Society bringing together all those who are interested in herbs, from growers to enthusiasts, providing a quarterly magazine and library. Areas of interest include the history, development, culinary, medicinal and cosmetic uses of herbs. Call for details of membership.

Institute of Horticulture
14/15 Belgrave Square,
London SW1X 8PS
Tel: 020 7245 6943
Fax: 020 7245 6943
Email: ioh@horticulture.org.uk
Web: www.horticulture.demon.co.uk
Open: Mon-Fri 9.30am-5pm
▶ The IoH is the single voice for the whole of horticulture, dedicated to promoting the profession and providing recognition of status for its members engaged in every aspect of the industry. The various grades of membership each require specific entry qualifications and experience, thus catering for professional horticulturists at all levels. Actively encourages career progression. Visit the website for further information on the work and meetings, to join and to discover the wide range of benefits available to members. Provides advice and information to those wishing to consider horticulture as a career.

National Society of Allotment & Leisure Gardeners Ltd
O'Dell House, Hunters Road,
Corby NN17 5JE
Tel: 01536 266 576
Fax: 01536 264 509
Email: natsoc@nsalg.demon.co.uk
Open: Mon-Fri 9am-5pm
▶ Representative body for the allotment movement. Aims to ensure that facilities are available to all who would like to garden, to protect allotments for future generations and to promote the fact that gardening is a recreation for the mind and body as well as a source of economic wealth. Free advice is given to members on all matters relating to allotment gardening. Also runs a discounted seed scheme for members in addition to allotment insurance.

Plants for a Future
The Field, Penpol,
Lostwithiel PL22 0NG
Tel: 01208 872 963
Web: www.scs.leeds.ac.uk/pfaf/
▶ Registered charity, researching and providing information on edible and otherwise useful plants. Promoting perennials, woodland gardening and wildlife habitats. Provides many services and publications. Plants are available by mail order. In the process of moving to a new site in Devon, 14 acres of which will be open to visitors, volunteers and course attendents.

Royal Horticultural Society
PO Box 313, 80 Vincent Square,
London SW1P 2PE
Tel: 020 7834 4333
Fax: 020 7630 6060
Web: www.rhs.org.uk
Open: Mon-Fri 9.30am-5.30pm
▶ Examines areas where gardening has an impact on environmental and conservation concerns and produces regular leaflets publicising important issues and providing gardeners with practical guidelines on a variety of topics including: potentially harmful garden plants, water supplies (conservation and pollution), energy conservation in greenhouses and wild and endangered plants in cultivation.

Women's Farm & Garden Association
175 Gloucester Street,
Cirencester GL7 2DP
Tel: 01285 658 839
Fax: 01285 642 356
▶ A charity working since 1899 for women who earn their living in agriculture and horticulture. The current training programme 'Women Returners to Amenity Gardening' teaches women in private gardens throughout England on a part-time basis within their home location. Membership offers a full programme of workshops on specialist subjects, garden tours and visits, career advice, regional groups, newsletters, special offers on tools, books, entrance fees to shows and exhibitions, grants, etc. An annual travel bursary is awarded for projects both at home and overseas. Membership is open to both men and women for £15 per year, with students and retired members paying £7.50.

What we can recycle

We produce around 28 million tonnes of household waste in the UK every year. In just one hour we produce enough waste to fill the Albert Hall! Waste Watch suggests how consumers can lead the way in the battle to reduce, re-use and recycle

The most effective way of dealing with our waste is not to create so much in the first place. However, this is also very difficult as almost all purchases are packaged, and a great deal of what we buy is designed to be used once and then disposed of. Instead of worrying about how to recycle plastic bags for instance, why not take your own bags to the supermarket? Use rechargeable batteries which will not only reduce your waste but also save you money. Try to cut down on the amount of packaging you take home with you. Store food in resealable containers rather than using cling film or foil. Milk delivery in returnable bottles is a great example of waste reduction in action!

Although household waste represents only 5% of the total amount of waste produced in the UK, it is a highly significant portion as it contains large quantities of organic waste which can cause pollution problems, as well as materials such as glass and plastics which do not easily break down.

Material for recycling needs to be clean and uncontaminated, which means that problems are caused when the wrong materials are put into the wrong recycling banks. Don't deposit mixed material or material that is dirty. Make sure that you wash bottles and cans in left-over washing up water (running the hot water specially is a waste of water and energy!). Always put the correct materials in the correct recycling bank.

Technology is developing that will be able to deal with more mixed and contaminated material. However, at present, we need to take care in order to for recycling to be efficient.

Glass

Bottle banks are found in many local council areas and are divided into those accepting clear, green and brown glass. Blue glass can be put into the green bank, and clear glass with coloured coatings can be put into the clear bank as the coating will burn off. The labels on bottles and jars will be removed during the recycling process, however remove as many plastic or metal rings and tops as possible. Only recycle bottles and jars – never lightbulbs, sheet glass or Pyrex type dishes as these are made from a different type of glass.

Paper

Most local authorities have recycling banks for newspapers and magazines, as this is the most abundant type of paper in household waste. Make sure that you don't put other types of paper in, such as cardboard or junk mail, as this will contaminate the load and the reprocessors will not accept it. Some local authorities may have separate banks for these. Packaging such as milk and juice cartons cannot be recycled as paper as they have a plastic lining which would contaminate the process.

Aluminium and steel cans

Many local authorities have mixed can banks accepting both aluminium and steel cans, although some have aluminium only banks as uncontaminated aluminium has a higher value. Aluminium can be recognised by the fact that it does not stick to a magnet, has a very shiny silver base and is very light in weight. Steel cans are also called 'tins' as they contain a very thin layer of tin. Try to crush drink cans before recycling, either with a can crusher or by squashing them underfoot. Aerosol cans made from steel or aluminium can be recycled in Save-a-can banks (check the front of the banks for guidance), but they must be empty and should not be crushed.

Textiles

Charities such as Oxfam and Scope run textiles banks for unwanted clothing, which are then sold in charity shops, given to the homeless or sent abroad. Even damaged or unwearable clothing can be converted into items such as wiping cloths, shredded for use as filling for items such as furniture or car insulation, or rewoven into new yarn or fabric. If you deposit shoes, tie them together as they tend to go astray!

Plastic

Plastic is a difficult material to recycle as there are many different types of plastic (often indicated by a number, or letters such as PP, PET or PVC). The variation in plastic means that different reprocessing techniques are required. The different types of plastic therefore need to be collected separately, or sorted after collection, as reprocessors will specify which type of plastic they will accept. Plastic in household waste is often food packaging and therefore too contaminated to be recycled effectively.

Plastic is a light, bulky part of household waste, and therefore it is difficult for councils to store and transport sufficient quantities of plastic to make recycling economically viable. Many councils have found it to be too expensive and do not have facilities for plastic at all, while others recycle only plastic bottles which are worth more money. If your council does not recycle plastic, you could try putting pressure on them to start one, but meanwhile try to reduce and re-use as much plastic as possible. If your council does ▶

▶ recycle plastic, make sure that you are recycling the right type of plastic, and always remove the tops of plastic containers so that they can be crushed.

Organic waste

Organic household waste is food and garden waste. Organic waste is a problem if sent to landfill, because it is impossible to separate out from other waste once mingled, and will rot, producing methane, a greenhouse gas responsible for global warming. The best use of organic waste is to either compost it through a centralised composting scheme run by your council, or to compost it at home. Find out if your council has facilities for taking garden waste for composting, or you may be able to separate kitchen waste for a kerbside collection scheme if one exists in your area. Alternatively, build or invest in a home composter for the garden, or try a worm bin for indoor use! Check to see if your council supplies reduced cost recycling bins.

Electrical and electronic equipment

There are very few facilities for recycling household electrical or electronic waste. British Telecom telephones can be returned and there is a scheme for recycling certain types of mobile phone. There are a number of schemes for repairing and recycling goods such as refrigerators and washing machines which can then be passed on to low income households. Call the Waste Watch Wasteline on 0870 243 0136 for details of schemes in your area. Check with your council to see if they have facilities for household appliances, electronic equipment, or CFC extraction for old refrigerators. You can arrange for the council to remove bulky household items for disposal.

Batteries

There is currently one facility for collecting ordinary household batteries in the UK – in Lancashire. Batteries are varied and complex, come in different shapes and types, and are consequently very difficult to sort and recycle. The toxic materials have now been removed from ordinary batteries and they are safe to dispose of with your normal household waste. Rechargeable batteries, or nickel cadmium batteries, do still contain hazardous metals and should be returned to the manufacturer where possible. A few local authorities provide facilities for recycling these, as well as lead acid car batteries, which may also be returned to garages. If you use rechargeable batteries, look out for the new versions containing no mercury or cadmium.

Furniture

A network of furniture projects exists across the UK consisting of small scale local projects that take unwanted household furniture and items, and pass it onto community groups, low income families and other groups in need. Call the Wasteline for further details. Contact your council to dispose of broken bulky household waste.

Hazardous waste

Household hazardous waste such as paint, solvents and garden chemicals comes under the jurisdiction of your local council. Take them to a civic amenity site if facilities exist, or contact your council. Some councils also provide facilities for de-gassing fridges and for recycling fluorescent tubes.

Mixed packaging

Packaging is often made up of a mixture of materials, such as 'tetra paks' which can be made up of paper, plastic and metal, making recycling difficult. There is a lack of facilities and technology for recycling mixed packaging, meaning that the materials are difficult to separate out without contamination. Packaging is a very visible form of waste, making up around one third of the average household dustbin. Packaging is often necessary to protect the product, to prolong its lifespan and to provide essential information. However, over-packaging does occur, especially for marketing purposes. Basic foods such as bread and rice are rarely overpackaged, while convenience foods often have two or three layers of packaging. Try to avoid overpackaging where possible, and when choosing a product, pick the packaging material which is easiest for you to recycle locally.

The recycling symbol

Products and packaging often have some kind of recycling symbol on them. The most common is the mobius loop which can mean that a product is either recyclable or has some recycled content. Unless the product states the percentage of recycled content, the symbol usually means that the product can be recycled. However, this does not mean that it will be recycled, or that such facilities exist. Many products can be recycled in theory, but the technology may not be available to provide collections schemes for householders. ∎

For more information, contact Waste Watch at Ground Floor, Europa House, 13-17 Ironmonger Row, London EC1V 3QG.
*Tel: **0870 243 0136***
*Web: **www.wastewatch.org.uk***

Using renewable energy

Did you know that the amount of energy the earth receives from our own solar system in 30 minutes is the equivalent of the power used by the entire population of the earth in one year! Do you care? Well, someone has to because energy derived from fossil fuels is rising in price; OPEC is seeking to reduce the amount of oil it produces; governments are introducing taxes on the way people use energy; and our disregard for the earth's natural resources, and how we use and abuse them, is causing climate change.

Scientists tell us that the Earth has some five billion years left to live and so the majority of people and businesses think it will be someone else's problem and they're right – it will be their children's. What we forget is that the industrial revolution only began around 150 years ago, when the earth was already five billion years old. In a century and a half, we've done more damage to the environment because of our dependency on fossil fuels, the increase in CO_2 emissions, the devastation of forests and the failure to build energy efficient homes and working environments, than in all that time previously. What chance another five billion years now?

So what can we do? We can capture the free energy that hits the planet every day. This can be done in a number of ways. We can use solar panels that will collect the energy from solar radiation and convert that into heat for hot water. Heating systems can be designed to meet the most demanding of needs. Turbines can create electricity by capturing the power of the wind and can be built in varying sizes. Photovoltaic (PV) panels that capture solar radiation and convert this into electricity can be designed for the domestic and industrial markets. Closer to home and for larger applications, Biomass systems can convert the burning of waste matter into energy with combined heat and power systems that can provide energy for the largest of needs. Geo Thermal is a system which uses the energy from below the ground to create heating and cooling for buildings. We don't have to look too far to make ourselves more energy self-sufficient. ■

*By Keith Hutson of Solarsaver, an energy and environmental management group. For help and advice call on **01529 304 027** or visit the website at **www.solarsaver.co.uk***

CASE STUDY: Local sustainability in action

BioRegional is an independent environmental organisation bringing local sustainability into the mainstream. It aims to encourage the use of local resources from sustainable farming, forestry, recycling and re-use of materials. Current projects include:

Local paper for London – a sustainable office paper cycle for London and the South-East. Organisations sign up to recycle their office paper to a local mill, buy back the top quality 100% recycled paper, and reduce paper consumption.

Beddington Zero Energy Development – an 82 home and workspace development in south London, in partnership with Bill Dunster Architects and the Peabody Trust. BedZED will be the UK's largest carbon-neutral development, highly energy efficient and using local renewable energy, making sustainable living easy, attractive and affordable.

Urban Forestry – pioneering the processing and distributing of local wood products made from sustainably managed woodlands and from London's urban tree surgery waste.

Local Lavender – reviving south London's historic lavender industry, showing how urban waste land can be used in a productive way.

MiniMills – development of small scale clean technology to pulp hemp, flax and straw fibres for use in papermaking.

BioRegional has also set up a trading subsidiary: **BioRegional Charcoal Company** – a national network of local charcoal and firewood makers, supplying on a local basis to retailers such as B&Q. The products are all certified to the international standards of the Forest Stewardship Council, supporting environmentally friendly practices such as coppicing which provide habitats for wildlife. Local charcoal production and supply within the UK reduces the pressure on forests in the developing world, while reducing CO_2 emissions from transport by 85% compared with imported charcoal. ■

For more information about BioRegional, contact Emily Hurst at the Sutton Ecology Centre, Honeywood Walk, Carshalton, Surrey SM5 3NX.
*Tel: **020 8773 2322***
*Email: **info@ bioregional.com***
*Web: **www.bioregional.com***

How green is your electricity?

Since 30% of the UK's energy use is in the home, this is the time to get electricity companies switched on to providing green and efficient energy.

Do you want to find out how 'green' your electricity company is? Or if you don't want to increase the cost of your electric bill, then consider switching your supplier to one of the top three companies on Friends of the Earth's (FoE) green energy league table, rated according to companies' policies on renewable investment and energy efficiency. The following table is based on a summary of the research findings by FoE and is accurate up to January 2001. Companies are placed in order of rank according to FoE mainstream electricity suppliers chart. ■

*For more detailed information on the judging criteria, league tables for each category, methodology and sources are available from FoE on **020 7490 1555** or visit the website at **www.foe.co.uk***

FoE can also provide contact details for the companies listed above and information on schemes which have been recently introduced.

	Green Tariff?	Renewable Energy	Energy Efficient
Scottish Power inc. Manweb	yes	average	v. good
TXU/NORWEB	yes	good	v. good
Scottish & Southern/SWALEC	yes	good	good
Northern Ireland Electricity	yes	average	v. good
PowerGen	yes	average	v. good
London Electricity/SWEB	yes	good	v. good
Innogy	-	good	good
SEEBOARD	no	average	good
Northern Electric and Gas	no	poor	good
Yorkshire Electric	yes	poor	good

CASE STUDY: Affecting climate change

Over the last decade we have witnessed a great change in the climate in Britain. Last year it was brought home with the disastrous floods; this year it's gales and a scientific warning that malaria will return to Britain's mainland after a 300 year absence.

In fact, our weather is changing much more rapidly than previously predicted and environmental experts believe that the main cause of this is our increasing use of energy. When power stations burn oil, gas or coal, they pump dangerous gasses into the atmosphere. These waste gasses heat up the earth like a greenhouse and lead to 'global warming'. The increasing temperatures, melting ice caps and rising sea levels result, in turn, in climate change.

The Energy Saving Trust (EST) was set up after the Earth Summit in Rio de Janeiro to help reduce carbon dioxide (CO_2) emissions in the UK – the greenhouse gas most responsible for climate change. The main job of the EST is to promote the social, environmental and economic benefits of saving energy. By being more energy efficient, we can reduce the need for energy production. And by cutting the production, we reduce the emissions pumped into the environment.

The truth is, we can all play our part in the bigger picture. Households in the UK are responsible for a quarter of the total CO_2 emitted into the environment every year – that's enough to fill 35 double-decker busses. The bonus is that by saving energy we can cut our annual bills too – by up to £250 per household.

There are many ways you can save energy in the home. Some things cost nothing, like turning the lights off when we leave a room. Other things cost a little more, such as buying energy saving light bulbs. Replacing old electrical appliances and boiler systems will also help – when buying an appliance, look out for the Energy Efficiency Recommended logo. ■

Contact the Energy Efficiency Hotline
0845 727 7200
or visit the EST's website at
www.saveenergy.co.uk

The Energy Efficiency Hotline can also put homeowners in touch with a local Energy Efficiency Advice centre (EEAC), which can give personal energy efficiency evaluations, as well as details of Government grants.

Energy & Recycling 81

ENERGY EFFICIENCY

Products

BioSave
37 Rocks Park Road,
Uckfield TN22 2AT
Tel: 01825 767 616
Fax: 01825 767 616
Email: john@mifflin.fsbusiness.co.uk
▶ Manufacturers of the Endocube, a millenium product producing energy savings of 20%-50% in running refrigeration equipment. It consists of a gel incorporating a thermistor and can be quickly and easily retrofitted into the existing electrical circuits of the appliance without any additional modifications. It operates by shadowing the temperature of the food. Unlike other products it is not persuaded to cycle the motor just on changes in ambient air temperature which occur each time the door is opened or closed. Savings on running costs, the life of the appliance and premature disposal of CFC's are just some of the immediate benefits to be obtained.

Dunsley Heat Ltd
Fearnought, Huddersfield Road,
Holmfirth, Huddersfield HD7 2TU
Tel: 01484 682 635
Fax: 01484 688 428
Email: sales@dunsleyheat.co.uk
Open: Mon-Fri 9am-5pm
▶ Manufacturers, suppliers of the Yorkshire multi fuel stove, which is superior in cleanburning technology, over 70% efficient, granted Parliamentary approval for use in Smoke Control areas and other areas for burning a full range of fuels, including wood, signite, briguettes, petroleum copes and many others. Coal can also be burnt on the Yorkshire with smoke emission considerably reduced. On official tests the Yorkshire has proved to be the cleanest burning stove.

Energyways
Lordship Cottage, Barwick Road,
Standon SG11 1PR
Tel: 01920 821 069
Fax: 01920 821 069

Email: warmcel@free.uk.com
Open: Mon-Fri 9am-5pm
▶ Cellulose fibre insulation made from 100% recycled newsprint paper which would otherwise go to landfill. Manufactured to a British standard, Warmcel is ideal insulation for walls, roofs, lofts and floors of timber-frame houses and forms the heart of the 'breathing wall', an ecologically-sound building system which achieves high levels of energy efficiency and a healthy indoor environment. Treated against vermin attack. Call for details of your nearest stockist.

Filsol Solar Ltd
15 Ponthenri Industrial Estate,
Ponthenri SA15 5RA
Tel: 01629 860 229
Fax: 01629 860 979
Email: info@filsol.co.uk
Web: users.tinyonline.co.uk/filsol
Open: Mon-Fri 9am-5pm
▶ UK manufacturers, suppliers and installers of high quality, high performance solar panels for domestic, commercial and swimming pool applications. Manufacturers of PV modules for OEM manufacturers. Project managers of 'SHINE 21' A project supported by the DTI and The European Social Fund to train plumbers and system designers in the requirements of solar system design and installation.

Services

Atlantic Energy
1 Riverside House, Heron Way,
Newham, Cornwall TR1 2XN
Tel: 01872 260 423
Fax: 01872 222 424
Email: atlanticen@aol.com
▶ Experienced in renewable energy and energy efficiency. Operates ethically using sustainable technologies in harmony with their surrounding environments. Presently working in a consortium with TXU Europe Power and BLS, Truro in building a 10mW power plant in Falmouth docks to burn recovered marine oils to supply electricity to the locality. Working with rural communities to convert municipal solid wastes and locally grown willow into heat and electricity for local businesses.

Energy Services Ltd
The Greenhouse Energy Centre,
35 Mill Street,
St Peter Port GY1 1HG
Tel: 01481 722 299
Fax: 01481 723 200
Email: energyservices@begin666.com
Web: www.begin666.com
▶ Europe's leading energy services consultancy for domestic and small commercial clients dedicated to the design, supply and installation of integrated personally tailored energy solutions.

MVM Starpoint
MVM House, 2 Oakfield Road,
Clifton, Bristol BS8 2AL
Tel: 0117 974 4477
Fax: 0117 970 6897
Email: starpoint@mvm.co.uk
Web: www.mvm.co.uk/starpoint.html
▶ Offers software, consultancy, surveying & training services designed to meet all the domestic energy efficiency needs of the public and private organisations, large and small. Of particular note is their work with local authorities, helping these to meet their requirements under the Home Energy Conservation Act, and with mortgage lenders, supplying software and services to enable them to offer home energy advice to homebuyers, as required by the Sellers Information Pack legislation.

Solar Housing Design & Build
Tir Gaia Solar Village, East Street,
Rhayader LD6 5DY
Tel: 01597 810 929
▶ Tir Gaia is an environmentally friendly housing development in the small town of Rhyader in Mid Wales. Plots are available to clients who then build their own energy-efficient house to the design of their choice. Several different types of house are expected to be built: traditional, passive solar, earth-sheltered, Swedish timber frame, etc. Technical advice on design and energy efficiency issues is available. Call for more information.

Advice & Organisations

Association for the Conservation of Energy
Westgate House, Prebend Street,
London N1 8PT
Tel: 020 7359 8000
Fax: 020 7359 0863
Email: info@ukace.org
Web: www.ukace.org
▶ Lobby group of major UK-based companies which carries out policy research on energy conservation. Formed in 1981, its remit is to encourage a positive national awareness of the need for and the benefits of using energy conservation in buildings. Copies of The Fifth Fuel, a free newsletter, are available on request, as is a publications list.

Council for Energy Efficiency Development
PO Box 12, Haslemere GU27 3AH
Tel: 01428 654 011
Fax: 01428 651 401
Email: theceed@compuserve.com
Web: www.nationline.co.uk/ceed
Open: Mon-Fri 9am-5.30pm
▶ The Council for Energy Efficiency Development is established to expand this market for installers and manufacturers offering quality products and services, for the immediate and long term benefit of the specifiers, the property owner, the householder or tenant, the country and the environment. Specifiers and customers of CEED products and processes may be confident that they are of durable quality and that CEED installers are vetted for their experience and quality of workmanship.

Design Advice Scheme
The Bartlett Graduate School,
Philips House, UCL, Gower Street,
London WC1E 6BT
Tel: 01923 664 258
Email: edas.s@ucl.ac.uk
▶ Covers energy and environmental issues associated with building design, both for refurbishment and new build. Regional Centre staff can give up to one day's free advice on projects greater than 500m^2. Informal and confidential meetings can be arranged over the telephone.

Energy & Recycling

Energy and Environmental Programme
Royal Institute of International Affairs, Chatham House,
10 St James's Square,
London SW1Y 4LE
Tel: 020 7314 3639
Fax: 020 7957 5710
Email: eep-admin@riia.org
Web: www.riia.org
▶ The Energy & Research Programme is the largest of the research programmes at the Royal Institute of International affairs. The programme works with business, government, academic and NGO experts to carry out and publish research and to stimulate debate on key energy and environmental issues with international implications, particularly those just emerging into the consciousness of policy makers.

Energy Club
Northern Electric, Carliol House,
Market Street,
Newcastle-upon-Tyne NE1 6NE
Tel: 0191 210 2000
Fax: 0191 210 2898
Email: margaret.grundy@northern-electric.co.uk
Web: www.northern-electric.co.uk
Open: Mon-Fri 9am-5pm
▶ Supported by the Department of the Environment and the Centre for Sustainable Energy, the Energy Club gives information on how to cut bills by improving energy efficiency and offers discounts on installation of energy-saving features.

Energy Conservation & Solar
Unit 327, 30 Great Guildford Street,
London SE1 0HS
Tel: 020 7922 1660
Fax: 020 7771 2344
Email: john.thorp@ecsc.org.uk
Open: Mon-Fri 9am-5pm
▶ National educational charity working to improve awareness of energy efficiency issues through targeted advice and development programmes, volunteer networks, developing skills, energy advice and information materials, publications (including the *Heating Advice Handbook*) and promotion of good practice.

Energy Efficiency Advice Centres
Tel: 0800 512 012
Web: www.est.org.uk
▶ Supported by the Government's Energy Saving Trust (see following listing) and local sponsors, these advice centres throughout the UK provide free expert advice to householders and small businesses on ways to save energy and reduce fuel bills. Using specially designed software, they can recommend energy saving improvements for the home and workplace. Call for information on grants, special offers and local advice centres.

Energy Efficiency Best Practice Programme
Building Research Establishment,
Garston, Watford WD2 7JR
Tel: 01923 664 258
Fax: 01923 664 787
Email: enquiries@bre.co.uk
Web: www.bre.co.uk
▶ Government initiative providing a range of free publications on energy management and efficiency for the commercial and domestic sectors. Subjects cover technical issues ranging from building your own energy efficient house to energy efficiency in offices and schools or in refurbishment.

Energy Saving Trust
21 Dartmouth Street,
London SW1H 9BP
Tel: Energy Efficiency Hotline 0345 277 200
Fax: 020 7654 2444
Email: chrisb@est.co.uk
Web: www.est.co.uk
▶ Energy Centre Advice centres are situated all over the country. They offer free independent advice to all householders and small businesses on energy conservation – how to reduce fuel bills, grants available to help cover costs, how to get the best from your appliances, etc. Call the Hotline for a free information pack.

GREENTIE
Bld 156, Harwell, Didcot OX11 0RA
Tel: 01235 433 564
Email: mike.morrell@aeat.co.uk
Web: www.etsu.com/greentie
▶ GREENTIE is a worldwide scheme initiated by the IEA and the OECD to identify and transfer information on greenhouse gas reduction technologies. To register or to browse the database visit the website or call Adele Currant on 01235 433235.

Home Energy Efficiency Scheme
EAGA, FREEPOST, PO Box 130,
Newcastle-upon-Tyne NE99 2RP
Tel: 0800 072 0150
▶ Call for information on grants and assistance available for draught-proofing, loft insulation, cavity wall insulation and heating controls for those over 60 years old, on a low income or on certain types of benefit.

Institute of Energy, The
18 Devonshire Street,
London W1G 7AU
Tel: 020 7580 7124
Fax: 020 7580 4420
Email: madams@instenergy.org.uk
Web: www.instenergy.org.uk
▶ A professional body nominated by the Engineering Council, providing a variety of services for individual and company members. Free energy management training consultation and staff awareness programmes are available for companies in membership.

International Institute for Energy Conservation (IIEC)
21 Tavern Quay, London SE16 7TX
Tel: 020 7237 6523
Fax: 020 7237 2462
Email: iiec.europe@dial.pipex.com
Open: Mon-Fri 10am-6pm
▶ Works to bring the power of sustainable energy solutions to developing countries and economies in transition since 1984. Through its offices in Africa, Europe and North America, IIEC builds in-country capacity for comprehensive, practical, energy efficient, sustainable energy solutions in the buildings, industrial, power and transport sectors. Solutions include energy efficiency, renewable energy and integrated transport planning. A non-profit organisation, it specialises in the technical and financial dimensions of energy policy and sustainable energy projects. Seeks to accelerate the adoption of sustainable energy policies, technologies and practices – energy solutions that foster environmentally and economically sound development around the world.

National Energy Services
1st Floor, The National Energy Centre,
Davy Avenue, Knowlhill,
Milton Keynes MK5 8NA
Tel: 01908 672 787
Fax: 01908 662 296
Email: enquiry@nesltd.demon.co.uk
▶ National Energy Services Ltd (NES) is the trading subsidiary of the National Energy Foundation. It provides integrated energy software products and related research and consultancy services. The main activities of NES are: the development, administration and regulation of the National Home Energy Rating Scheme (NHER); the development, production and distribution of software for evaluating energy use in domestic and non-domestic properties, promoting energy efficient measures; consultancy and research into energy use, particularly in buildings; and energy performance monitoring services.

RENEWABLE ENERGY

Suppliers

AES Ltd
AES Building, Lea Road,
Forres IV36 1AU
Tel: 01309 676 911
Fax: 01309 671 086
Email: info@AESsolar.co.uk
Open: Mon-Fri 8am-6pm;
Sat 9am-1pm
▶ Manufacturers of high efficiency solar water heating systems since 1979. Fully installed and commissioned systems for around £1,800 plus only 5% VAT including new dual coil cylinder. Optional drainback operation and roof integrated collectors. Over 25,000 systems installed. Simple to install DIY kits available with full instructions. Applications range from small domestic to large-scale housing projects and commercial systems up to 2,400 square metres. Comprehensive in-house system design service and installation teams available to assist with clients' requirements.

Baywind Energy Co-op
Unit 29, Trinity Enterprise Centre,
Furness Business Park,
Barrow-in-Furness LA14 2PN
Tel: 01229 821 028
Fax: 01229 821 104
Email: user@windco.furness.co.uk
Open: Mon-Fri 9am-5pm
▶ The UK's first windpower co-operative supplying electricity to the National Grid. Call for further info.

Biodesign
15 Sandyhurst Lane,
Ashford TN25 4NS
Tel: 01233 626 677
Fax: 01233 626 677
Email: biodes@bigfoot.com
Web: www.web.onetel.net.uk/~bio
▶ Not-for-profit company involved with a solar PV project supplying materials and instructions to people in rural areas of developing countries, ie those who are without mains electricity and currently have no alternative to dry cells and wick lamps. Solar panels are far cheaper than dry cells. To minimise costs, solar plates are assembled locally and thus cost under $2 per watt. Projects are underway in Africa and South America. DIY Solar training has been carried out in Madagascar and further training will be funded by UK DFID wherever a suitable organisation is found.

Ecotricity
Axiom House, Station Road,
Stroud GL5 3AP
Tel: 01453 756 111
Fax: 01453 756 222
Email: info@ecotricity.co.uk
▶ Founded the UK's 'green' electricity market in 1996. Ecotricity is electricity derived from sources which are significantly less polluting and more sustainable than conventional fuel sources. Aim to help sustain the environment for current and future generations by stimulating a mass market for Ecotricity.

Freeplay Energy Ltd
Cirencester Business Park,
Love Lane, Cirencester GL7 1xd
Tel: 01285 659 559
Fax: 01285 659 550
Email: info@freeplay.co.uk
Web: www.freeplay.net
Open: Mon-Fri 8.30am-5pm
▶ Manufacturers of self powered energy products including radios and flashlights. All products are powered by a patented spring generator and do not require either electricity or replacement batteries. Freeplay radios are also fitted with solar panels which will provide power for continuous play in direct sunlight.

Keysolar Systems
4 Glanmor Crescent,
Newport NP19 8AX
Tel: 01633 280 958
Fax: 01633 280 958
Open: Mon-Fri 9am-9pm
▶ Supplier of small scale solar and wind power products such as garden fountains, pond pumps, battery chargers. Systems made to order for any location no matter how remote. Send SAE with four 1st class stamps for catalogue.

Natural Energy Systems
2 Arderon Court, Adelaide Street,
Norwich NR2 4ER
Tel: 01603 661 863
Fax: 01603 618 145
Email: solar@naten.freeserve.co.uk
Open: Mon-Fri 9am-6pm
▶ Designs, supplies and installs domestic and commercial solar hot water systems and energy efficient central heating systems. Also supplies woodburning and multi-fuel stoves.

Proven Engineering
Moorfield Industrial Estate,
Kilmarnock KA2 0BA
Tel: 01563 543 020
Fax: 01563 539 119
Email: gproven@provenenergy.com
Web: www.provenenergy.com
▶ Specialists in power that 'does not cost the earth', providing small renewable energy systems to supply clean, economical power wherever it is needed. Experienced with wind, solar and hydro systems and have exported to 20 countries around the world. Systems offered include a patented wind turbine design (600, 2,500 and 6,000W), custom built hydro turbines (300W to 20 kW) and solar photovoltaics (BP Solar and Siemens panels).

Solar Sense
Tree Tops, Sandy Lane,
Pennard, Swansea SA3 2EN
Tel: 01792 371 690
Fax: 01792 371 690
Email: solarsense.force9.co.uk
Open: Mon-Fri 9am-5.30pm
▶ Consultancy, design and supply service of renewable energy systems to trade and domestic DIY market. Full and wide range of renewable energy and solar hot water systems on offer including SOLUX roof-integrated water heating collectors.

SunDog (Renewable Energy & Environmental Services)
Fell Cottage, Matterdale End,
Penrith CA11 0LF
Tel: 017684 82282
Fax: 017684 82600
Email: info@sundog-energy.co.uk
Web: www.sundog-energy.co.uk
Open: Mon-Fri 9am-5pm
▶ Renewable energy consultants supplying, designing, advising and installing renewable wind, solar and water energy systems. Anything from wind or water turbines and photo-voltaic panels to batteries and inverters. Designs, supplies and installs renewable energy systems including stand-alone wind and photovoltaic (PV) systems, grid connected and building integrated PV, and hybrid schemes. DIY kits also available.

Wavegen
50 Seafield Road,
Longman Industrial Estate,
Inverness IV1 1LZ
Tel: 01463 238 094
Fax: 01463 238 096
Email: enquiries@wavegen.co.uk
Web: www.wavegen.co.uk
▶ Produces commercial wave powered electrical generation technology. Has pioneered the research, development and manufacture of several innovative marine power systems. Generates power which is inflation free and emission free. Capable of generating electricity at a price that is competitive with fossil-fuelled power stations and other renewables.

Utilities

Eastern Group Plc
Wherstead Park, PO Box 40,
Wherstead, Ipswich IP9 2AQ
Tel: 01473 688 688
Web: www.eastern.co.uk
▶ Has set up the EcoPower Trust, a fund that encourages renewable power initiatives. Its first projects are the installation of a wind-generator at a vineyard and the positioning of solar panels on a school library roof. Money for the projects comes from their EcoPower and EcoPower Plus pricing scheme. It gives customers the opportunity to contribute to renewable energy projects through their fuel bills. They can choose to pay a 5% or 10% supplement respectively on their annual electricity bill, so if a customer's bill is £240 they would pay an additional £12 or £24 a year. This amount is being matched up to £1 million over the

next year. The funds are placed in an independent trust to support projects powered by renewables, such as wind, wave or solar energy.

Manweb (Scottish Power)
Manweb House,
Chester Business Park,
Wrexham Road,
Chester CH4 9RF
Tel: 0845 272 1212

▶ Has a Green Energy tariff which promotes renewable energy. Has the support of the respected environmental research organisation, the Centre for Alternative Technology. Also has official accreditation from the Government's 'Future Energy' scheme, launched by the Energy Savings Trust. Households and businesses can become Green Energy customers for about 4p a day (around £15 a year) more. The money will be invested in a trust and will be managed by an independent environmental committee that will decide how the money is spent. Funds raised via Green Energy will help finance new projects to produce more environmentally friendly renewable energy, such as small scale hydro schemes and wind farms. The companies chosen to build the renewable energy projects will be expected to match the funds raised by Green Energy customers.

Midlands Electricity Board (National Power)
Whittington, Worcester WR5 2RB
Tel: 01905 613 191

▶ Has launched an environmental package for customers who want to support new alternative sources of energy. The package, called MEB Evergreen will be managed by Marches Energy Agency, a registered charity which aims to fund the development of new sustainable and renewable generation schemes. Has gained accreditation from the Energy Savings Trust and approval from Ofgem (Office of gas and electricity markets). Customers are invited to contribute a £5 annual donation by cheque or pay a subscription of £1.25 a quarter, which is added to their MEB electricity bill. All donations then go to Marches Energy Agency which will research and develop energy schemes such as solar, wind, hydropower and biomass.

Northern Electric
Carilio House, Market Street,
Newcastle-Upon-Tyne NE1 7NE
Tel: 0191 210 2000

▶ Researching a domestic 'Renewable Resources' tariff which is still at the planning stage.

Npower
PO Box 8007, Oldbury B69 2AL
Tel: 0800 389 2388
Fax: 0121 544 2987
Web: www.npower.com
Open: Mon-Fri 8am-8pm; Sat 9am-1pm

▶ Evergreen gives the customer the opportunity to help develop new sustainable and renewable forms of electricity generation. For just £5 a year you can increase the amount of electricity produced from 'green' sources, making the supplier less reliant on fossil fuels. All donations go directly to a fund manged by Marches Energy Agency, a registered charity, who then use the money to help fund green energy generation projects. These will include hydro, wind or landfill schemes.

PowerGen
Westwood Way,
Westwood Business Park,
Coventry CV4 8LG
Tel: 024 7642 4000
Fax: 024 7642 5226
Web: www.pgen.com

▶ Integrated electricity and gas business. Their energy efficiency programme is geared towards helping disadvantaged customers who will benefit most from the electricity savings, namely the fuel poor, older customers, people with disabilities and schools. They have gained corporate certification to ISO 14001, the international standard for environmental management. They are supporting the Government's target to achieve 10% of generation from renewable energy resources by 2010 and have developed the second largest renewable energy business and the largest hydro generation business in England and Wales. A leading purchaser of renewable energy from small generators. Offers total energy advice, management and monitoring services to customers and are developing new products to help them reduce energy consumption. Offers 'green energy' contracts for industrial and commercial customers.

Scottish Power
1 Atlantic Quay, Glasgow, G2 8SP
Tel: 0845 272 7111
Web: www.scottishpower.plc.uk

▶ Has introduced a Green Energy Tariff. There are plans to extend this offer to customers in other areas. Has helped set up an education initiative, whereby a specially-trained teacher, funded by the company, will visit 1,300 primary classes, over two years, to teach youngsters how electricity is produced, how it is used in their homes and why we need to save energy to reduce the risk of global warming. As part of its merger with the US utility PacifiCorp, made a number of environmental commitments, based on its approach to the environment in the UK.

Seeboard plc
Brighton Road, Forest Gate,
Crawley RH11 9BH
Tel: 0800 056 8888
Open: Mon-Fri 8am-8pm; Sat 8am-1pm

▶ Seeboard, the only regional utility company to win regional, national and international awards for customer service, offers gas and electricity to customers throughout the UK. Among its tariffs is a Green Fund Tariff which encourages the development of renewable energy schemes.

Southern Electric
Southern Electric House,
Westacott Way, Littlewick Green,
Maidenhead SL6 3QB
Tel: 01628 822 166 (0345 776 633 – Acorn Tariff)

▶ Has a green 'Acorn' tariff, whereby more of your electricity can be supplied from renewable energy generators. Renewable energy will cost 5% on top of your exisitng rate. Quarterly standing charge remains the same. Only available to customers on General Domestic or Economy 7 tariffs. The additional income that the company receives will ensure the continued supply and generation of renewable energy. Guarantee to purchase enough renewable energy to meet the needs of customers joining the tariff.

Yorkshire Electricity Group
Scarcroft, Wetherby Road,
Leeds LS14 3HS
Tel: 0800 073 3000
Email: customer.services@yeg.co.uk
Web: www.yeg.co.uk
Open: Mon-Fri 8am-8pm; Sat 8am-5pm for domestic enquiry line

▶ Supplies electricity produced from renewable sources and accredited by the Energy Savings Trust. Assisted by Worldwide Fund for Nature and the Open University. Provides energy efficiency advice for domestic and business customers. Energy efficiency advice for domestic customers on 0800 591 748 and for business customers on 0845 722 7733 (opening times for the business helpline are Mon-Fri 8am-8pm; Sat-Sun 10am-4pm).

Organisations

Association of Electricity Producers
1st Floor, 17 Waterloo Place,
London SW1Y 4AR
Tel: 020 7930 9390
Fax: 020 7930 9391
Email: enquiries@aepuk.com
Open: Mon-Fri 9am-5pm

▶ Trade association representing some 100 companies involved in electricity production. The members range from family businesses to major PLCs. Between them, they represent virtually all the generating technologies used commercially in the UK, from coal, oil, gas and nuclear power to wind, wave, hydro and different forms of energy from waste. The Association has a target of 10% of UK electricity producedfrom renewable energy by 2010, proposed in its report *Renewable Energy: Building on Success* (1997).

Energy & Recycling

British Wind Energy Association
26 Spring Street,
London W2 1JA
Tel: *020 7402 7102*
Fax: *020 7402 7107*
Email: *info@bwea.com*
Web: *www.bwea.com*
Open: *Mon-Fri 9am-5pm*
▶ The Association is at the heart of the wind energy industry in the UK. Members range from the largest international corporations to ordinary members of the public, united in a commitment to seeing the UK's vast wind resource better harnessed in the production of electricity. As the largest of the renewable energy trade associations, BWEA is uniquely placed to promote the use of wind energy in and around the UK.

Centre for Alternative Technology (CAT)
Machynlleth SY20 9AZ
Tel: *01654 702 400*
Fax: *01654 702 782*
Email: *steven.jones@cat.org.uk*
Web: *www.cat.org.uk*
▶ Concerned with the search for globally sustainable technologies and ways of life. CAT aims to inspire people to use resources wisely and live in harmony with nature. Its display and education centre, researcher and information provider offers practical ideas and information on environmentally sound technologies. Its eight acre visitor centre has working displays of wind, water and solar power, low energy building, organic growing and natural sewage systems. Also offers residential courses, facilities for school groups, a 'green' shop and mail order service, free information and a professional consultancy service. Also runs the Alternative Technology Association which publishes Clean Slate magazine, a practical journal of sustainable living.

Ecotechnica
The Create Environment Centre,
Smeaton Road, Bristol BS1 6XN
Tel: *0117 903 1080*
Fax: *0117 903 1081*
Open: *Mon-Fri 9am-5pm*
▶ Environmental consultancy specialising in renewable energy and green building projects. Links with the Centre for Alternative Technology in Wales, the Centre for Sustainable Energy in Bristol and the Schumacher Society. Act as 'Environmental GP's' for a wide range of institutions and individuals.

Energy from Waste Association
26 Spring Street,
London W2 1JA
Tel: *020 7402 7110*
Fax: *020 7402 7115*
Email: *info@efw.bdx.co.uk*
Web: *www.efw.org.uk*
▶ Non-profit making business association independent of one company or technology. Its mission is to build awareness of the environmental benefits of energy from waste (EfW) – that is, the combustion of household and suitable commercial waste for energy recovery – and to facilitate the construction of modern EfW plants in the UK. Aims to be a centre for information exchange on all aspects of EfW.

Energy Solutions
79 Pitcairn House,
St Thomas Square, London E9 6PU
Tel: *020 8533 5880*
Fax: *020 8985 1379*
Email: *energy@gold.globalcafé.co.uk*
Web: *www.backspace.org/energysolutions*
▶ Non-profit making organisation promoting new energy technologies and ethical and environmental solutions to energy problems. Acts as a reliable source of information on a wide range of energy-related issues from water-powered cars to cold fusion and radioactive remediation kits to energy devices.

European Wind Energy Association (EWEA)
Rue du Trone, 26,
Brussels B-1000
Tel: *+32 2 546 1940*
Fax: *+32 2 546 1944*
Email: *ewea@eawa.org*
Web: *www.ewea.org*
▶ Non-profit, non-governmental association with a membership of national associations, companies and organisations involved in wind energy. EWEA's main objective is to ensure that the general public, decision makers and media are made aware of the reality of wind power and understand the rapid progress in the sector which will give wind energy an increasing role in clean power for generations to come.

Gazelle Wind Turbines Ltd
Stargate Industrial Estate,
Stargate, Ryton NE40 3EX
Tel: *01670 516 949*
Fax: *01670 510 300*
Email: *gazelle@northenergy.co.uk*
Open: *Mon-Fri 9am-5pm*
▶ The Gazelle 20kW wind turbine has been developed to provide clean, green energy to schools, small businesses and farms. Power from the turbine at 3 phase, 400 volts, substiututes for bought-in electricity when the wind is blowing. Connection is in to the normal electricity supply. The turbine is 10 metres in diameter and 15 metres to the hub. It costs about the same as an upmarket 4WD vehicle.

RENUE (Renewable Energy in the Urban Environment)
95 East Hill, Wandsworth,
London SW18 2QD
Tel: *020 8871 4647*
Fax: *020 8871 4647*
Email: *cleanpower@renue.freeserve.co.uk*
▶ Community-based charity working to develop and promote clean energy in our cities, based around the five themes of renewable energy, energy efficiency, education, ecology and the arts. By creating practical examples of renewable energy in South-West London, RENUE provides a working vision of sustainable energy use. Currently creating a sustainable building which will be the focus for a programme of education and arts events, conferences/seminars and renewable energy advice services, which opened in Autumn 2000.

Solar Century
Unit 5 Sandycombe Centre,
1-9 Sandycombe Road,
Richmond TW9 2EP
Tel: *0870 735 8100*
Fax: *0870 735 8101*
Email: *enquiries@solarcentury.co.uk*
Web: *www.solarcentury.co.uk*
Open: *Mon-Fri 9am-6pm*
▶ Independent suppliers of the world's leading solar electric technologies. Designs tailor made solar solutions to best suit client needs; installs solar systems for residential and commerical projects and supplies small-scale products from solar torches to mobile power units. Socially responsible company committed to reducing global warming by promoting solar electricity as a viable and responsible option for modern living; and a way to meet growing global energy needs sustainably.

Solar Energy Society
c/o School of Engineering,
Oxford Brookes University,
Gipsy Lane, Headington,
Oxford OX3 0BP
Tel: *01865 484 367*
Fax: *01865 484 263*
Email: *uk-ises@brookes.ac.uk*
Web: *www.brookes.ac.uk/uk-ises*
▶ UK section of the International Solar Energy Society which works closely with other renewable energy organisations and government bodies in the UK and overseas to promote all forms of solar energy. Communicates information, news and ideas through publications and conferences. Membership open to professionals and lay people.

RECYCLING

For business recycling (toner cartridges, computers and paper, etc) see listings in Chapter Nine: Business & Finance.

Councils

Bolsover District Council
Sherwood Lodge, Bolsover,
Chesterfield S44 6NF
Tel: 01246 240 000
Fax: 01246 242 424
Web: www.bolsover.gov.uk
Open: Mon-Fri 9am-5pm
▶ There are a number of recycling sites over the county for the public to deliver their cans, glasses, textiles and paper. Call for your closest site. Every Saturday, the public can bring their non-useable household items to the Civic Community site.

Bolton Metropolitan Borough Council
The Environment Team, Milton House, Wellington Street, Bolton BL3 5DG
Tel: 01204 336 653
Fax: 01204 336 695
Email: j.cuncliffe@bolton.gov.uk
Web: www.bolton.gov.uk
Open: Mon-Fri 9am-5pm
▶ Promotion of recycling and sustainanble waste management of household and municipal waste. For further information, contact Jim Cunliffe.

Bury Metropolitan Borough Council
Department of Competitive Services, Craig House, Bank Street,
Bury BL9 0DN
Tel: 0161 253 5000
Fax: 0161 253 6605
Web: www.bury.gov.uk
Open: Mon-Fri 9am-5pm
▶ Bury has recycling facilities at supermarket and car park sites throughout the borough and is running a waste management campaign to reduce the amount of waste thrown away by householders. A leaflet advising on waste reduction, composting and recycling has been circulated to all residents and is available from the above address.

Cut price compost bins are also available to residents.

Carlisle City Council
Environmental Services Department, Carlisle City Council, Civic Council, Carlisle CA3 8QG
Tel: 01228 817 000
Fax: 01228 817 346
Email: mike.b@carlisle-city.gov.uk
▶ Call Mike Battesby for further information.

City of Salford Metropolitan Council
Environmental Services Directorate, Turnpike House, 631 Eccles New Road, Salford M6 2SH
Tel: 0161 925 1028
Fax: 0161 925 1024
Email: clare.taylor@salford.gov.uk
Web: www.salford.gov.uk
Open: Mon-Fri 9am-4.30pm
▶ Salford Pride is Salford Council's Anti-Litter & Recycling action team covering the whole Salford area, providing support and information to both community groups and schools by the provision of recycling facilities, clean-up equipment, a graffiti removal service, and an environmental education programme.

Eden District Council
Mansion House, Penrith CA11 7YG
Tel: 01768 212 472
Fax: 01768 890 732
Web: www.eden.gov.uk
Open: Mon-Fri 9am-5pm
▶ Has a recycling scheme for household waste and also assists third party recyclers. Also actively involved in the development of Local Agenda 21 and is represented on the Eden LA21 Executive Committee.

Kirklees Metropolitan Borough Council
Department of Environmental Waste, Civic Centre, Vine Street, Huddersfield HD1 6NT
Tel: 01484 221 000
Fax: 01484 223 155
Web: www.kirklees.gov.uk
Open: Mon-Fri 9am-5pm
▶ The council offers many recycling sites across the borough for clothing, shoes, cans, bottles and paper. Call the above number for more information.

Knowsley Metropolitan Borough Council
Department of Planning and Development, PO Box 26, Archway Road, Huyton L36 9FB
Tel: 0151 443 2371
Fax: 0151 443 2210
Email: tina.deegan.dpd@knowsley.gov.uk
Web: www.knowsley.gov.uk
Open: Mon-Fri 9am-5pm
▶ Promotes the development of sustainable recycling and waste minimisation initiatives for household waste.

Lancashire County Council
Waste Management Group, Guild House, Cross Street, Preston PR1 8RD
Tel: 01772 264 432
Fax: 01772 263 732
Email: g.harding@lancashire.gov.uk
Web: www.lancashire.gov.uk
Open: Mon-Fri 9am-5pm
▶ Provides 23 household waste recycling/disposal centres, collecting paper, glass, metals, oil, bric-a-brac, batteries, clothes and shoes for recycling and green waste for composting. Has also developed a Waste Awareness campaign featuring 'Molennium', the waste awareness mole who spreads the message to turn Lancashire's waste mountain into a molehill. For further information contact the Recycling Officer on 01772 264 432.

Liverpool City Council
Municipal Buildings, Department of Environment, Dale Street, Liverpool L69 2DH
Tel: 0151 233 5227
Fax: 0151 225 5229
Email: j.liddle@liverpool.gov.uk
Web: www.liverpool.gov.uk
Open: Mon-Fri 9am-5pm
▶ Call for specific enquiries about recycling sites and doorstep collection.

Manchester City Council
Environment and Development Department, PO Box 463, Town Hall, Manchester M60 3NY
Tel: 0161 234 4629
Fax: 0161 234 4679
Web: www.manchester.gov.uk
Open: 24 hr answer phone

▶ Supports full range of recycling sites. The Council obtained funding to begin doorstep waste recycling in 2000. The service will use electrically powered vehicles and aims to reach 20,000 households in two years. Subsidised home composters are available from the Council.

Oldham Metropolitan Borough Council
Policy, Performance and Regeneration, Metropolitan House (3rd Floor), Hobson Street, Oldham OL1 1QD
Tel: 0161 911 4479
Fax: 0161 911 4162
Email: ppr.stratpol@oldham.gov.uk
Web: www.oldham.gov.uk
Open: Mon-Fri 9am-5pm
▶ The Council has launched a successful environmental campaign which details some of the hopes and aspiriatons of local people who are interested in shaping the Borough of Oldham. The Environment Forum and the council are currently working with a wide range of people and organisations to help implement the plan in the areas such as waste and transport. Projects to date include a community repaint scheme, a 'real' nappy trial and a Council employee car sharing scheme.

Rochdale Metropolitan Borough Council
Department of Environmental Development & Health, Telegraph House, Baillie Street, Rochdale OL16 1JH
Tel: 01706 647 474
Fax: 01706 864 185
Email: a.howard@rochdale.gov.uk
Web: www.rochdale.gov.uk
Open: Mon-Fri 9am-5pm
▶ The Council has several refuse sites througout the borough for paper, clothes, textiles etc. Call for further information.

Rossendale Borough Council
Department of Waste Management, Henrietta Street, Backup OL13 0AR
Tel: 01706 878 660
Fax: 01706 873 556
Web: www.rossendale.gov.uk
Open: Mon-Fri 9am-5pm

Energy & Recycling | 87

▶ The Council offers doorstep collection for household paper, and many recycling sites across the borough for clothing, shoes, cans, bottles and paper. Contact the above number for more information.

Rotherham Metropolitan Borough Council
Department of Environment,
Elm Bank, 77 Alma Road,
Rotheram S60 2BU
Tel: 01709 382 121
Fax: 01709 882 183
Web: www.rotheram.gov.uk
Open: Mon-Fri 9am-5pm
▶ The Council ha s numerous collection points around the borough for textiles, books, glasses, paper, etc. For further information, call the above number.

Sefton Metropolitan Borough Council
Department of Environmental Services, 3rd Floor, Balliol House, Balliol Road, Bootle, Merseyside L20 3AH
Tel: 0151 934 4294
Fax: 0151 934 4290
Email: cleansing.sefton@ukgateway.net
Web: www.sefton.gov.uk
Open: Mon-Fri 9am-5pm
▶ Sefton Council is a Merseyside authority running from Bootle to Southport and inland to Maghull. The Environmental Protection Depart-ment provides quality services that improve our built, natural and living environment. The officers of environmental protection include those working to develop Local Agenda 21 and environmental and waste management initiatives, including 'Make Sefton Sparkle', an anti-litter and waste focused campaign, that helps promote general good environmental practice.

South Derbyshire District Council
Civic Offices, Department of Environmental Health, Civic Way, Swadlincote DE11 0AH
Tel: 01283 221 000
Fax: 01283 595 858
Web: www.s.derbyshire.gov.uk
Open: Mon-Fri 9am-5pm

▶ Call for further information about recycling textiles, cans and bottles.

South Lakeland District Council
South Lakeland House,
Lowther Street, Kendal LA 9 4UQ
Tel: 01539 733 333
Fax: 01539 740 300
Email: sldc@compuserve.com
Open: Mon-Fri 9am-5pm
▶ The Council has over 62 centres for bin collection for textiles, paper etc, and has introduced approximately 12,500 home composting bins. The farm firm collection has been introduced to recycle wood into park benches. Also offers a service for small businesses to recycle their paper.

St Helens Metropolitan Borough Council
Environmental Protection Department, Wesley House, Corporation Street, St Helens WA10 4ND
Tel: 01744 456 725
Fax: 01744 24055
Open: Mon-Fri 9am-5.15pm
▶ The Council is very active in publicising how to care for the environment in terms of recycling. It has been involving charities and small enterprises. Kerbside collection of waste paper is being extended.

Staffordshire Moorlands District Council
Moorlands, Stockwell Street,
Stafford ST18 0DN
Tel: 01538 483 483
Fax: 01538 388 393
Web: www.staffordshire.gov.uk
Open: Mon-Fri 9am-5pm
▶ Various sites throughout the area for recycling of newspapers, textiles, cans, shoes, etc. Kerbside recycling in some southern areas including books, junk mail and soil. Call on freephone 0800 169 3159. Also sells home composting bins.

Stockport Metropolitan Borough Council
Waste and Environmental Services, EEDD Stockford House, Piccadilly, Stockport SK1 3XE
Tel: 0161 474 4889
Fax: 0161 474 4888
Email: g.cassem@stockport.co.uk

Web: www.stockport.gov.uk
Open: Mon-Fri 9am-5pm
▶ Kerbside collection scheme for paper and numerous recycling sites for a variety of materials around the borough in civic amenity sites, social clubs and supermarkets.

Stockton-on-Tees Borough Council
Energy Advice Centre,
Blue Post Yard,
Stockton on Tees TS18 1DA
Tel: 01642 391 186
Fax: 01642 391 190
Email: bsimpson@stockton.gov.uk
Web: www.stockton.gov.co.uk
Open: Mon Fri9am-4pm
▶ Focal point for Local Agenda 21 and range of environmental projects in Stockton-on-Tees. Advice on energy efficiency, recycling, composting and home security. Training facility also available. Available for businesses and the community.

Tameside Metropolitan Borough Council
Council Offices, Wellington Road, Ashton-under-Lyne OL6 6DL
Tel: 0161 342 3757
Fax: 0161 342 2266
Email: sarah.schofield@mail.tameside.gov.uk
Web: www.tameside.gov.uk
Open: Mon-Fri 9am-5pm
▶ Provides a comprehensive recycling service for households, businesses and schools. Current projects include: kerbside collection of paper; Schools Take Action Recycling Trash (START); trial kerbside collection of glass; compost bins delivered to the door; meals on wheels; and foil recycling. To find out more, contact the Recycling Officer.

Trafford Metropolitan Borough Council
Dept of Housing and Environmental Services, PO Box 14 Trafford Town Hall, Talbot Road, Stretford, Manchester M32 0YZ
Tel: 0161 912 4912
Fax: 0161 912 4917
Email: glenn.stuart@trafford.gov.uk
Web: www.trafford.gov.uk
Open: Mon-Fri 9am-5pm
▶ Local authority offering recycling services and advice to Trafford residents and businesses.

Wigan Metropolitan Borough Council
Bury Engineers Department Services, PO Box 86, Civic Buildings,
New Market Street,
Wigan WN1 1RP
Tel: 01942 404 380
Fax: 01942 404 210
Email: d.bullock.wigan.uk
Web: www.wigan.gov.uk
Open: Mon-Fri 9am-5pm
▶ Operates 37 sites for paper, 38 for glass, approximately 27 for cans, and 40 charity book, bric-a-brac, shoe and textile banks from organisations such as Oxfam, Humana, Salvation Army, and SCOPE. Also 4 oil banks and 1 oil filter bank, 1 site for fluorescent tubes and 5 sites for car batteries. The Cheshire recycling banks also take the BT white page phone books and the recycling of the Yellow Pages can be arranged.

POVERTY:RECYCLING:AIR POLLUTION:
TRANSPORT: EQUITY:BIODIVERSITY:
DEMOCRACY:HEALTH:LITTER:RACISM:
DOGMESS:GREENHOUSE EFFECT:ENERGY

IF YOU WANT TO MAKE A DIFFERENCE

Come along to the Oldham Borough Environment Forum

For a full programme of meetings and events visit
www.oldhamagenda21.demon.co.uk
or contact
Michele Carr 0161 911 4475.
Email: ppr.stratpol@oldham.gov.uk.

Energy & Recycling

Wirral Metropolitan Borough Council
Environmental & Housing Department,
Westminster House, Hamilton Street,
Birkenhead, Wirral CH4 5FN
Tel: 0151 647 7000
Fax: 0151 666 5122
Email: p.jones@wirral.com
Web: www.wirral.gov.uk
Open: Mon-Fri 9am-5pm
▶ Offers doorstep collection for household paper only plus further sites for clothing, shoes, bottles and cans. Call for futher information.

Services

ACRE Recycling
Civic Amenity Site, Bridge Street,
Middleton, Manchester M24 1TP
Tel: 0161 653 5377
Fax: 0161 655 4446
Email: info@acrenet.force9.co.uk
Web: www.acrenet.force9.co.uk
Open: Mon-Fri 8.30am-5pm
▶ Community recycling organisation offering a collection service to members who include both commercial organisations and community enterprises and provides kerb-side recycling for domestic households. Can also advise on any area of recycling and provides speakers at conferences and seminars at schools and communities.

Aluminium Packaging Recycling Organisation (ALUPRO)
5 Gatsby Court, 176 Holliday Street,
Birmingham B1 1TJ
Tel: 0121 633 4656
Fax: 0121 633 4698
Email: recycling@alucan.org.uk
Web: www.alucan.org.uk
▶ Alupro is a 'one-stop shop' for all matters relating to aluminium packaging. It has targeted a 50% recycling rate in the UK by 2002 and has consistently called for much more attention to the collection of all aluminium packaging materials arising in the domestic waste stream in order to achieve this figure. Promotes the collection of aluminium packaging through all routes: local authority bring and kerb-side systems and 'cash for cans' recycling centres, including non-ferrous metal merchants. Collection is driven by the value of the metal, with many schemes benefiting charities and community projects. Over £30 million worth of aluminium packaging is available for recycling every year.

BPB Recycling UK
Folds Road, Bolton BL1 2SW
Tel: 01204 372 700
▶ Waste paper merchants.

Bytes Twice
Save Waste & Prosper,
74 Kirkgate, Leeds LS2 7DJ
Tel: 0113 243 8777
Fax: 0113 234 4222
Email: swap@geo2.poptel.org.uk
▶ Recycles office IT equipment, putting people in contact with their nearest computer reuse scheme.

Cheshire Recycling
Hooton Road, Hooton,
South Wirral L66 7NA
Tel: 0151 327 4241
▶ Waste paper merchants.

Cleanworld UK
Birches Brow, Formby Lane,
Ormskirk L39 7HG
Tel: 01695 422 759
▶ Waste paper merchants.

Derby & Laurel Co Ltd
Unit 3-6, Derby Workshop Centre,
Bedford Place,
Bootle L20 8NQ
Tel: 0151 922 4044
▶ Waste paper merchants.

EMERGE Recycling
The Old Iron Duke,
Stretford Road,
Manchester
Tel: 0161 232 8014
Fax: 0161 226 1946
Email: and@emergemanchester.co.uk
Web: www.emergemanchester.co.uk
▶ A Manchester-based community recycling business. Currently operates a free door to door paper recycling scheme for 30,000 Manchester households, a multi material box recycling scheme as well as a service for business recycling and an Arts and Education department. Through voluntary and paid posts, provides training and work experience for a wide variety of people ranging from those working for the New Deal scheme to graduate students.

Pearson Waste Paper Services
21 Hillbrook Road, Offerton,
Stockport SK1 4JW
Tel: 0161 477 2716
▶ Waste paper merchants.

Rishton Waste Paper
Unit 12, Riverside Industrial Estate,
St Rishton, Blackburn BB1 4NF
Tel: 01254 885 606
▶ Waste paper merchants.

Smurfit Recycling
Isabella Road,
Workington CA14 2JS
Tel: 01900 605 556
▶ Waste paper merchants.

UK Waste Paper Ltd
Venture House, Cross Street,
Macclesfield SK11 7PG
Tel: 01625 616 700
▶ Waste paper merchants.

Walker Paper Recycling Ltd
Ledbury Road, Failsworth,
Manchester M35 0PB
Tel: 0161 688 5391
▶ Waste paper merchants.

Wastepaper Services
Unit 3, Tame Street Business Park,
Tame Street,
Stalybridge SK15 1ST
Tel: 0161 343 6543
▶ Waste paper merchants.

Wiggly Wigglers
Lower Blakemere Farm,
Blakemere HR2 9PX
Tel: 01981 500 391
Fax: 01981 500 108
Email: wiggly@wigglywigglers.co.uk
Web: www.wigglywigglers.co.uk
Open: Mon-Fri 9am-5pm
▶ Practical mail order company promoting worms and worm composting for organic home waste. Offers a range of wormeries for kitchen waste including the innovative 'Can-O-Worms' and other worm kits for garden waste and soil improvement. Offers free advice and information, including a free Home Guide – Worms at Work, and produces a quarterly newsletter. Also runs the country's only freephone worm composting helpdesk on 0800 216 990.

Organisations

Automotive Comsortium on Recycling & Disposal
Society of Motor Manufacturers and Traders, Forbes House,
Halkin Street, London SW1X 7DS
Tel: 020 7235 7000
Fax: 020 7235 7112
Email: smmt@dial.pipex.com
▶ Industry association providing information on the recycling and the disposal of cars.

British Glass Manufacturers Confederation
Northumberland Road,
Sheffield S10 2UA
Tel: 0114 268 6201
Fax: 0114 268 1073
Email: recycling@britglass.co.uk
Web: www.britglass.co.uk
Open: Mon-Fri 8.30am-5.30pm

ACRE Recycling

- Office paper collections.
- Advice on waste minimisation.
- Education service.
- Domestic recycling.

Civic Amenity Site, Bridge St, Middleton, M24 1TP
Tel: 0161 653 5377
e-mail: info@acrenet.force9.co.uk

Energy & Recycling

▶ Confederation for all sectors of the UK glass industry, representing it in dealings with governments, both in the UK and Europe. Provides information and advice on glass recycling, collates bottle bank statistics. Also provides educational material, including Key Stage I and II approved CD-Rom with website and teachers notes.

British Oil Spill Control Association
4th Floor, 30 Great Guildford Street,
London SE1 0HS
Tel: 020 7928 9199
Fax: 020 7928 6599
Email: bosca@bmec.org.uk
Web:
www.bmec.org.uk/bosintro.htm
▶ BOSCA represents the UK spill response industry. Its membership includes equipment manufacturers, service contractors and consultants, covering every aspect of pollution prevention, control and clean-up at sea, along coastlines and inland. Has service contracts with both the Government's Maritime and Coastguard Agency (MCA) and the Environment Agency, under the terms of which it maintains the National Equipment Database for use in spill incidents, and, through its members, plays an active role in clean-up operations undertaken by these organisations. Members of the Association also produce round-the-clock spill response services for commercial organisations and the general public.

British Recovered Paper Association
Papermaker's House,
Rivenhall Road, Westlea,
Swindon SN5 7BD
Tel: 01793 889 600
Fax: 01793 886 182
Email: fedn@paper.org.uk
Web: www.paper.org.uk
Open: Mon-Fri 9am-5pm
▶ This trade association is the successor of the British Waste Paper Association (1921-1996) and acts to represent its members who include both paper manufacturers and those collecting and recycling paper.

Can Makers Information Service
1 Chelsea Manor Gardens,
London SW3 5PN
Tel: 020 7351 2400
Fax: 020 7352 6244
▶ Represents the UK manufacturers of beer and soft drinks cans, together with their suppliers of aluminium and steel. Is dedicated to conserving energy and raw materials and developments into reducing the material content of the can.

Community Recycling Network (CRN)
10-12 Picton Street, Montpelier,
Bristol BS6 5QA
Tel: 0117 942 0142
Fax: 0117 942 0164
Email: info@crn.org.uk
Web: www.crn.org.uk
Open: Mon-Fri 9am-5pm
▶ National voluntary organisation established in 1990 by Friends of the Earth. Aims to promote community recycling as a practical way of tackling the UK's waste problem. In many instances, community-based recycling has proved to be the most effective way of encouraging individuals to reduce, reuse and recycle. Provides advice, training, information and practical initiatives for over one hundred local projects around the UK. Membership costs £25 per year and includes advice and support from staff and other members, a regular bulletin, links into national trading opportunities, conferences and training days and a directory of members.

Entrust
Acre House, 2 Town Square,
Sale M33 7WZ
Tel: 0161 972 0044
Fax: 0161 972 0055
Email: information@entrust.org.uk
Web: www.entrust.org.uk
▶ The regulator for the Landfill Tax Credit Scheme, a private company that is self-financing but not-for-profit. Enrols environmental bodies who then receive money for environmental projects from Landfill Operators through the scheme. A tax on landfill waste was introduced to promote a shift to more sustainable methods of waste management and provides a financial incentive to reduce waste pollution, to dispose of less waste at landfill, and to recover more value from waste that is produced. The scheme creates a partnership for LOs and environmental bodies to work in partnership to create greater significant environmental benefits, jobs and sustainable waste management.

Environet 2000
c/o National Centre for Business Sustainability (NCBS),
The Peel Building, University of Salford, Manchester M5 4WT
Tel: 0161 295 5276
Fax: 0161 295 5041
Email: thencbs@thencbs.co.uk
Web: www.thencbs.co.uk
▶ Innovative waste minimisation project aimed at industry sectors in the North West. The NCBS was project manager for the Textiles Sector of the project. Free case history material is available on request. Other details on SME projects (generally free-of-charge) are also available.

Industry Council for Electronic and Electrical Equipment Recycling
6 Bath Place, Rivington Street,
London EC2A 3JE
Tel: 020 7729 4766
Web: www.icer.org.uk
▶ Cross-industry association with over 50 members from the UK and other European countries. Pulls together the whole spectrum of interests concerned with recycling electronic and electrical equipment – materials suppliers, manufacturers, retailers, waste managements, recyclers and more.

Institute of Wastes Management
9 Saxon Court,
St Peter's Gardens,
Northampton NN1 1SX
Tel: 01604 620 426
Fax: 01604 621 339
Email: paul.frith@iwm.co.uk
Web: www.iwm.co.uk
Open: Mon-Fri 9am-5pm
▶ Professional body representing and regulating over 4,000 waste management professionals, mainly in the UK. Sets the standards for individuals working in the waste management industry and aims to advance the scientific, technical and practical aspects of waste management for the safeguarding of the environment.

National Recycling Forum
Europa House, Ground Floor,
13-17 Ironmonger Row,
London EC1V 3QG
Tel: 020 7253 6266
Fax: 020 7253 5962
Web: www.wastewatch.org.uk
Open: Mon-Fri 9am-5pm
▶ Independent organisation bringing together industry, retailers, local authorities and businesses relating to waste, to promote waste reduction, reuse and recycling. Produced the *Recycled Products Guide*.

Pulp & Paper Information Centre
1 Rivenhall Road, Westlea,
Swindon SN5 7BD
Tel: 0906 680 0035
(calls cost 25p per min)
Fax: 01793 886 182
Email: ppic@paper.org.uk
Web: www.ppic.org.uk
Open: Mon-Fri 8.45am-5pm
▶ Provider of information on the responsible production, use and disposal of paper and board products to government departments, legislators, media, retailers, the general public and those involved in education and industry. Promotes understanding of the industry and the issues it faces.

Residual Ltd
Heath House, 133 High Street,
Tonbridge TN9 1DH
Tel: 01732 368 333
Fax: 01732 368 337
Email: library@wrf.org.uk
Web: www.wrf.org.uk
▶ Provides a worldwide information service on the sustainable management and recovery of resources from post-consumer waste. Publishes a free bi-monthly journal, *Warmer Bulletin*. Subscription is for six issues – £20 individual and £60 corporate.

Energy & Recycling

Waste Management Information Bureau
AEA Technology Environment,
F6 Culham, Abingdon OX14 3ED
Tel: *01235 463 162*
Fax: *01235 463 004*
Email: *wmib@aeat.co.uk*
▶ National information centre with government support, providing information on the full range of waste management issues via a library and database (on-line via an international database host). Produces reading lists for a large number of waste topics such as recycling, energy from waste and landfill.

Wastewatch
Europa House, Ground Floor,
13-17 Ironmonger Row,
London EC1V 3QG
Tel: *0870 243 0136*
Fax: *020 7253 6266*
Email: *info@wastewatch.org.uk*
Web: *www.wastewatch.org.uk*
Open: *Wasteline Mon-Fri 10am-5pm*
▶ National charity promoting waste reduction and recycling. Call the Wasteline for general information.

Changing approaches to health

Wendy Miller, Executive Director of the British Holistic Medical Association (BHMA) looks at why more and more people are turning towards complementary therapies and a more holistic approach to health.

If you feel ill, do you go to your local chemist or doctor – or do you perhaps go to a healthfood shop to buy a supplement or seek out a complementary therapist? If so, you are not alone.

Although you can get free treatment from the NHS, many people are more and more dissatisfied with the way the medical profession works. If you break a bone, then you would want to go to the Emergency Department in your local hospital. To deal with common infections, you might just want a prescription of antibiotics. But, very often, many people are looking for something they don't get from a short consultation with their GP.

Alongside the dissatisfaction with mainstream medicine, there has been a phenomenal rise in the number of people now seeking treatment for health problems from complementary therapists – around 40% of the population according to latest estimates. People are also spending a lot of money on these treatments, and on various supplements and remedies sold in healthfood stores – estimated to total £1.6bn every year.

But how do you know which supplement to take or which therapist to go to? Which therapist is properly qualified to deal with your particular problem? And will they really sort out any underlying chronic illnesses? Rather than one specific therapy or medication (pharmaceutical or 'natural'), what is important is to take a holistic approach – to consider body, mind and spirit, and to recognise the vital role of psychological, social and environmental factors in health creation and maintenance.

The British Holistic Medical Association (BHMA) was founded in 1983 by a group of doctors and medical students to address these kinds of problems. Its mission is to provide education in the principles and practice of holistic medicine, and its members include doctors, consultants, complementary therapists and the public.

A main part of the Association's work is to help doctors and medical students realise that treating the body alone may well not be the whole answer. The BHMA holds meetings and conferences and publishes a quarterly news journal, *Holistic Health*, for its members. The Association also provides an information service to its members on all aspects of holistic medicine – for example, on appropriate therapies and therapists, and on research which is proving the interaction of mind and body.

BHMA Basics: the whole is greater than the sum of the parts

Medical science has developed its knowledge and power using the underlying idea that the proper way to comprehend human life and illness is to take the person apart. Then, by identifying the components and how they operate or fail, we can know what the human being is, why people become ill and how to cure them. This reductionist approach has paid off in so many ways, allowing science to master and even overcome many diseases, that there can be no denying its usefulness.

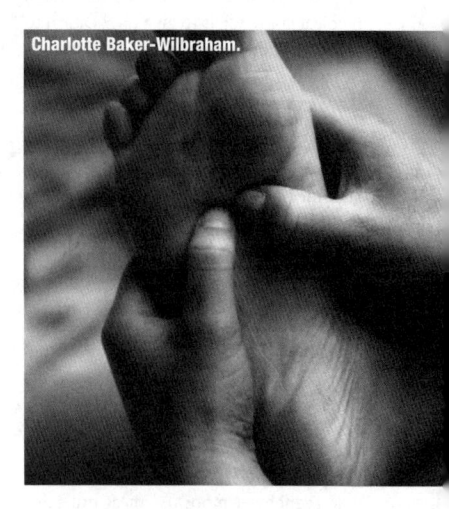

Charlotte Baker-Wilbraham.

Yet the main concern now is no longer how to stop so many people dying of infectious diseases. With the advent of antibiotics (themselves now a cause of problems) the major causes of death have instead become chronic or 'lifestyle' diseases such as heart disease and cancer. As well as this, people are beginning to recognise that the 'placebo effect', so long dismissed as an inconvenience in medical research, is actually strong evidence of the ability of our thoughts, feelings and experiences to affect our bodies.

In fact, the whole person is a hierarchy of natural systems, each level being simultaneously a component in higher systems. The central theme of holistic medicine is that all these systems influence each other – change one and potentially you change them all. So the balance between health and illness can be maintained or ▶

disturbed at any level. In these terms, diagnosis involves identifying the most appropriate level at which to make an effective intervention.

The other axis of holistic medicine is developmental, for we live in time, continually adapting. How we relate, consciously and unconsciously to our past, and how we imagine the future will influence how we live in, and cope with, the present moment.

What does holistic medicine mean in practice?

Take heart disease. The conventional medical approach is to give medication to reduce blood pressure or cholesterol. Advice is given to stop smoking and take more exercise.

An holistic approach would also take into account factors such as social status and income, ability to take control in daily working life, and relationships with others – most especially levels of hostility. It might involve complementary therapies such as herbal medicines, or stress management and visualisation techniques.

You get different diagnoses according to the lens you look through, or the level at which the problem is approached. The so-called French paradox also illustrates this. French eat more red meat but have lower levels of heart disease than people in the UK. This has been attributed to their consumption of red wine, and research has shown that certain chemicals in red grapes do indeed have the potential to lower cholesterol. And now research is also showing that beer can have the same effect. But it could equally be that the amount of red wine drunk in France is part of a wider social picture – or that the benefits in fact come from getting together with friends and family and having a good laugh.

To keep on the same theme, cancer is treated with chemo- and radiotherapy. Yet, if environmental pollution or psychological factors are responsible, this approach will never provide all the answers. Many complementary therapists view cancer as a disease which partly results from pollution or toxicity, and lack of necessary nutrients to enable the body to clear this. Cancer is an emotive disease and there are strict rules governing its treatment. Anyone offering an alternative approach – such as Linus Pauling who suggested that Vitamin C could help – has been harangued and criticised by the mainstream. There has been great controversy in the UK over the approach of the Bristol Cancer Help Centre which helps cancer patients using nutritional therapies, art therapy and visualisation – and whose workers cite research supporting the fact that a 'fighting spirit' aids quality of life and even survival.

Nevertheless these therapies and approaches increasingly are accepted as being able to help at least in reducing pain and negative side effects of conventional treatments. Many hospices and a growing number of hospitals are using reflexology, acupuncture and aromatherapy.

How can I get holistic treatment on the NHS?

As with mainstream treatments it is still a postcode lottery whether you can get complementary therapy treatments or be seen by a GP who takes an holistic approach on the NHS in the area where you live.

In the main, people want to be sure that a therapist is qualified and will do no harm. The recent House of Lords *Science & Technology Report* made many recommendations on regulation, education and training for complementary therapies and this has helped raise the issue enormously.

Even so, wider acceptance of these approaches by those responsible for spending NHS budgets – Primary Care Groups – will depend on there being enough evidence that these treatments and approaches work, and that they don't cost too much. While the main academic researcher into complementary therapies in the UK, Professor Ernst at Exeter University, has dismissed aromatherapy as a diversion for the better off, those who can afford it are voting with their feet and with their purses. Yet, according to Andrew Weil, a major proponent of integrated medicine in the USA, we do not need more evidence that mind-body linkages exist, or that a placebo effect exists, or that the body has self-healing processes. He cites Max Planck who says that science progresses funeral by funeral.

Ultimately, the holistic approach contends that, if we are healthy, then we move within a sea of pathogens without becoming ill. Much of complementay and alternative medicine is directed towards helping this – so research needs not only to show that therapies work, but that their self-help techniques also help avoid visits to the doctor.

Interesting results have come out from studies at Glastonbury, where locals are lucky enough to have access to an NHS practice which employs several different therapists in an integrated team. In Maidstone, the Blackthorn Medical Centre is run by GPs who prescribe clowning. In London, the University of Westminster runs a polyclinic for those who cannot afford complementary therapies, and at Archway, there is a herbal medicine clinic.

In the meantime there are hundreds of different organisations for the different therapies, and several different national practitioner associations. There is no one central register yet where people can turn to find out this information. The BHMA tries to help here. It provides lists of its members and organisations throughout the country to enquirers, along with information on which approaches might be helpful for different problems. When people phone to find out where their nearest holistic GP is, we point them in the right directions for their area. ∎

For more information about holistic health, contact the BHMA at 59 Lansdowne Place, Hove, East Sussex BN3 1FL
*Tel: **01237 725 951** Fax: **01273 725 951***
*Email: **bhma@bhma.org***
*Web: **www.bhma.org***

Training as a therapist

For the would-be therapist drawn to a career in complementary medicine, finding a suitable training programme may not be easy. Courses in complementary therapy are included in the curriculum of a number of Further Education colleges, but sometimes they do not employ qualified practitioners in the subject being taught. Often the qualifications achieved are well below the existing qualifications of individual member associations of the British Complementary Medicine Association (BCMA) and less than A-level attainment, which puts their credibility in doubt.

Tutors require at least three years accredited practice experience in the therapy they teach, yet some have no experience to draw on at all. Courses offered by such colleges usually have a short duration of 10 to 20 weeks, with no more than 20 to 40 hours tuition. The result is that poorly trained and unqualified therapists are unleashed to practice on an unsuspecting public.

For most therapies the minimum period of practical training is two years or more. This goes beyond the theoretical study course and covers patients problems, practice management, administration and supervision of clinic and therapy centres, records, report systems, assessments and customer care.

The national training organisation for complementary medicine is Healthwork UK and its objective is that all qualifications should eventually meet National Occupational Standards, in contrast to education and training standards. National Occupation Standards focus on the outcomes which individuals have to achieve when they are delivering services to users, whereas education and training standards are centred on learning, either by specifying the input or detailing the outcomes of learning.

Before enrolling on a specific training course in complementary medicine check the length and detail of the training; the full cost involved; the credibility of the qualifications offered; accreditation for acceptance on a particular register; insurance cover needed; and how much supervised experience is included in the course.

Practising therapists who are members of the BCMA have regulatory bodies which ensure high quality standards among their practitioners and will regulate standards, ethics, education and training within their particular profession.

Every practitioner of complementary or alternative therapy must be covered by the appropriate insurance for themselves and third party liability, including malpractice, public liability and product liability. There are several companies who will insure you if you are qualified to practice.

It is a normal requirement for members to abide by a code of conduct as laid down by the association. Practitioners will receive a valid certificate of insurance which should be displayed in the clinic or workplace. ∎

*For further information contact the British Complementary Medicine Association on **0845 345 5977***

IMPACT Staying healthy

- Eat a wide variety of fresh, nutritious whole food. Many experts recommend one raw meal of salad, vegetables or fruit each day.

- Just as important is how you eat. Take your meals in a calm, quiet environment.

- Cut down, or eliminate if you can, things that you know are unhealthy, such as smoking, too much alcohol and processed foods.

- Vitamins and minerals should supplement a healthy diet and should not be used as replacements for certain food groups.

- Regular exercise helps the lungs and heart work more efficiently, increases stamina, firms muscles and eliminates fat. It also boosts the immune system. Choose an activity you enjoy – such as dancing, swimming or walking.

- Counter-act stress by using simple relaxation and mediation techniques to help you switch off. Regular exercise also helps discharge stress hormones.

- Get a good night's sleep. Check your exercise routine and diet to make sure you are getting grid of stress hormones.

- Resolve emotional difficulties by sharing your problems with your partner, a friend or counsellor and, before you go to bed, spend time winding down.

- Become aware of the spiritual aspects of life. Practise meditation, contemplate beautiful surroundings, use alternative therapies or listen to music.

PRODUCTS

Many wholefood shops (see Chapter One: Food & Drink) also stock alternative and complementary health products. The shops in this section tend to specialise in health products. Some of the Centres in the following pages also stock health products.

Shops

Alpha Health & Beauty
30a The Precinct, Cheadle Hulme,
Stockport SK8 5BB
Tel: 0161 482 8153
Open: Mon-Fri 9am-5pm
▶ Stockists of mainly vitamins and supplements including an extensive homeopathic range. Also stocks flower remedies, aromatherapy oils and a small range of health food products.

Body Health Products
Unit 91 Market Hall, Market Street,
Ashton-under-Lyme OL6 7JU
Tel: 0161 343 3287

Napiers Herbal Dispensary & Clinics

Creams & Oils
Essential Oils
Organic Tinctures
Organic Teas
Bach Flower Remedies

Advice
Qualified Practitioners
Herbal Remedies
Massage
Reflexology

Established 1860

Visit our unique dispensaries in
Edinburgh: (0131) 315 2130
& (0131) 225 5542
and Glasgow: (0141) 339 5859

Or shop from home with
Napiers Direct
Tel: 0131 553 3500
www.napierstheherbalists.com

Open: Mon, Weds-Sat 9am-5.30pm;
Tues 9am-4.30pm
▶ Wholefoods and health products including vitamins, supplements and body building products.

Complete Remedy
2 Market Hall, Cheadle Hulme,
Stockport SK1
Tel: 0161 477 9869
Fax: 0151 486 1187
Open: Mon, Wed 9am-2.30pm;
Tues, Fri, Sat 9am-4pm
▶ Stocks vitamins and supplements, alternative therapies and body building products in Stockport Market.

Country World
12 Sundial Shopping Mall,
Common Lane,
Culcheth WA3 4EH
Tel: 01925 765 448
Open: Mon-Fri 9am-5.30pm;
Sat 9am-5pm
▶ Stocks a range of health foods, vitamins and supplements, aromatherapy oils and crystals.

Fragrant Pharmacy
16 Whittle Street, off Tib Street,
Manchester M4 1LT
Tel: 0161 835 1658
Fax: 0161 835 1658
▶ Stocks 100% pure essential oils, absolute oils and dilutions, hand-blended fragrances, associated aromatherapy products and a large range of candles, oil burners, fountains, chimes, candlesticks, wall sconces, etc. Aromatherapy massage and other beauty treatments available. Call for price list.

General Nutrition Centre
155 Marsden Way, Arndale Centre,
Manchester M4 2EB
Tel: 0161 819 2201
Open: Mon-Sat 9am-5.30pm;
Sun 11.30am-4.30pm
▶ Stocks a wide range of homeopathic and herbal supplements, vitamins and essential oils as well as nuts and seeds, dried fruits, herbal teas, gluten-free and dairy-free products. Also stocks sports nutrition and diabetic alternatives.

Great Bear Trading Co Ltd
29 Rochdale Road,
Todmorden OL14 7LA
Tel: 01706 813 737
Fax: 01706 819 492
Open: Mon, Weds-Fri 9.30am-5.30pm; Tues 9.30am-3.30pm;
Sat 9am-5pm
▶ Workers co-operative established for over 20 years. Stocks a wide range of wholefoods as well as alternative medicines, herbal and homeopathic remedies and vitamins and supplements. Cruelty-free bodycare and household cleaning products. There is a vegetarian café on the first floor and on the top floor alternative therapies are provided with a herbalist, counsellor and hypnotherapist.

Hazel Grove Nutrition Centre
307 London Road, Hazel Grove,
Stockport SK7 4PS
Tel: 0161 483 1576
▶ Sells vitamins, supplements, dietary foods and more.

Health Rack
92 Deansgate, Bolton BL1 2BD
Tel: 01204 380 660

▶ Range of vitamins and supplements, alternative therapy products such as aromatherapy oils and a selection of dried wholefood products. Mail order available.

Healthy Herbs
11 Tatton Street,
Knutsford WA16 6AB
Tel: 01565 755 022
Open: Mon-Fri 10am-5.30pm
▶ Specialists in herbal remedies from which it manufactures its own herb-based, own-brand skin care products. Also, range of wholefoods, vitamins and supplements and homeopathic remedies.

Napiers Herbalists
3 Queen Charlotte Lane,
Edinburgh EH6 6AY
Tel: 0131 315 2130
Open: Mon 10am-5.30pm;
Tues-Sat 9am-5.30pm
▶ Established as a Herbal House in 1860, Napiers has been making up and prescribing Herbal Medicines ever since. All the assistants have qualified from a five-year training course in Medical Herbalism. Also stocks homoeopathic remedies, essential oils, Bach Flower remedies, and a wide range of cough syrups, tonics and creams. Mail order service available throughout the UK.

Natures Remedies
10 Time Square,
Warrington WA1 2AR
Tel: 01925 444 885
Fax: 01925 444 885
Email: higgyfamily@cwctv.net
Open: Mon-Sat 9am-5.30pm
▶ Offer excellent nutritional advice and customer service. Wide range of nutritional supplements and sports nutrition products. Wholefoods, organic foods and more. Free mail order service as well.

Neal's Yard Remedies
29 John Dalton Street,
Manchester M2 6DS
Tel: 0161 835 1713
Fax: 0161 831 7875
Open: Mon-Sat 10am-5.30pm;
Sun 12 noon-4pm
▶ Stockists of an extensive range of herbs, essential oils and homeopath-

ic remedies, plus a selection of natural skin and haircare products. Utilising the finest ingredients, including pure (and often organic) essential oils and packed in signature blue glass bottles. All toiletries are suitable for vegetarians.

Norford Health Foods
Unit 1, Indoor Market,
Hunters Lane, Rochdale OL16 1EA
Tel: 01706 355 387
Fax: 01706 355 387
Open: Mon, Weds-Sat 8.30am-5pm; closed Tues
▶ Stockists of vitamins, herbal remedies, homeopathic medicines and chemist sundries. Provides a vast range, which is backed up with expert advice and a pricing policy worth going out of your way for.

Stalybridge Health & Food Store
39 Market Hall, Albion Street,
Oldham OL1 3BG
Tel: 0161 624 3045
Fax: 0161 624 3045
Open: Mon-Sat 9am-5pm
▶ Established for 25 years, this health food shop stocks herbal and homeopathic remedies, dietary supplements, aromatherapy oils, Bach Flower remedies, body building products, in addition to a range of wholefoods and herbs.

Stalybridge Health Food Store
Unit 107 Indoor Market Hall,
Ashton-under-Lyne OL6 6BZ
Tel: 0161 330 4447
Fax: 0161 330 4447
Open: Mon-Sat 9am-5pm
▶ Established for 25 years, this health food shop stocks herbal and homeopathic remedies, dietary supplements, aromatherapy oils, Bach Flower remedies, body building products, in addition to a range of wholefoods and herbs.

Stalybridge Health & Food Store
Unit17 Indoor Market Hall,
Hyde SK14 2QT
Tel: 0161 366 6909
Fax: 0161 366 6909
Open: Mon-Sat 9am-5pm

▶ Established for 25 years, this health food shop stocks herbal and homeopathic remedies, dietary supplements, aromatherapy oils, Bach Flower remedies, body building products, in addition to a range of wholefoods and herbs.

The Aromatherapy Centre
77 School Lane, Didsbury,
Manchester M20 6WN
Tel: 0161 445 4445
▶ Stocks of a range of aromatherapy products including the Centre's own brand products. Aromatherapy treatments available (see listing in Health Centres).

The Health Shop
22 Queens Walk, Droylsden,
Tameside M43 7AD
Tel: 0161 301 5287
Open: Mon-Fri 9am-5pm; Wed until 1pm
▶ Stocks mainly essential oils, homeopathic remedies and food supplements including a range of own brand products. Some foods including tea and coffee and an extensive selection of honey and sugar-free jams, but no fresh produce.

The Healthy Option
Food Hall, Market Way,
Salford M6 5JT
Tel: 0161 736 9663
▶ Stocks mainly vitamins and supplements, such as garlic, oil of evening primrose and cod liver oil, as well as a small range of soya foods. The shop has an efficient refill bag scheme that has proved particularly popular with customers.

The Medicine Shop and Clinic
48b London Road,
Alderley Edge SK9 7DZ
Tel: 01625 582 900/01625 599 777
Fax: 01625 599 333
▶ Alternative therapy shop with comprehensive range of nutritional supplements, essential oils, Bach Flower remedies, herbal tinctures, crystals, chakra healing sets, Feng Shui cards, books on related subjects from diet to self healing, and much more. The clinic offers a range of therapies (see separate listing).

Mail Order

Absolute Aromas
2 Grove Park, Mill Lane,
Alton GU34 2QG
Tel: 01420 549 991
Fax: 01420 549 992
Email: relax@absolute-aromas.com
Web: www.absolute-aromas.com
Open: Mon-Fri 9am-5pm
▶ Stocks 96 essential oils, 22 carrier oils and a wide range of Aromatherapy accessories such as diffusers, books, blending bottles, etc. Products available through health food shops, pharmacies and by mail order. Please state if you are a qualified practitioner or diploma student. The aim of the company is to offer exceptional quality products, professionally packaged, at a reasonable price. The essential oils and other products are continually monitored and tested for purity and quality.

Aromatherapy Associates
PO Box 14891, London SW6 2WH
Tel: 020 7371 9878
Fax: 020 7371 9894
Email: info@aromatherapyassociates.com
Web: www.aromatherapy.com
Open: Mon-Fri 9am-5pm
▶ Range of essential oils, bath and shower oils, body and facial oils and a mother and baby range produced by an association of practising aromatherapists. Call for a price list.

Bennett Natural Products
Dept P2, 209 Blackburn Road,
Wheelton, Chorley PR6 8EP
Tel: 01254 831 520
Fax: 01254 831 988
Email: jmb@bennett.sagehost.co.uk
Web: www.healthremedies.co.uk
▶ Import and distribution agents for 'Obbekjaers' Peppermint Products, a comprehensive range of the finest oil of peppermint supplements available. Range comprises oil tablets, capsules (including one-a-day and Enteric coated capsules), Pure Japanese Peppermint Oil and Peppermint Powder. Peppermint oil is a traditional herbal treatment for a variety of health problems including Irritable Bowel Syndrome, indiges-

tion and poor circulation. Supplies both wholesalers and retailers and provides an efficient mail order service to consumers.

Best Care Products Ltd
73 Gardenwood Road, East Grinstead
Tel: 01342 410 303
Fax: 01342 410 909
Email: info@bestcare-uk.com
Web: www.naturopathy-uk.com
Open: Mon-Fri 9-5pm
▶ Offers the Robert Gray Intestinal Cleansing Programme, herbal detox tea, organic minerals and water distiller. All products are designed to care for the bowel. The company is also available to give free seminars on how to detox and keep your body clear.

Bioflow
5 North Road, Huntley GL19 3DU
Tel: 01452 831 518
Fax: 01452 511111
Email: paul.drinkwater@ukgateway.net
Open: Mon-Fri 9am-5pm
▶ Distributor of magnotherapy products for people and animals. No pills, no drugs, no medication and no repeat charges. Magnotherapy is used by some doctors, physiotherapists and chiropractors.

Bruce Copen Laboratories
Lindfield Enterprise Park,
Lindfield RH16 2LX
Tel: 01444 487 900
Email: hrauer@copen.com
Web: www.copen.co.uk
Open: Mon-Fri 8am-11.30am & 1.30pm-5pm
▶ Radionics and Homeopathy products.

Energetix
The Boatyard, 105 Straight Road,
Old Windsor SL4 2SE
Tel: 01753 831 111
Fax: 01753 831 122
▶ Good health, vitality and general well-being are essential for everyone in today's modern society. The worldwide growth in the health food market with its emphasis on vitamins, minerals and herbal supplements bears witness to this. The use of magnetic products can offer an additional source of natural benefits and

has been shown to have a positive effect on both humans and animals. The Chinese and Egyptians have been using magnets to help the healing process for centuries. Many users claim that wearing magnetic jewellery has helped to relieve pain and discomfort caused by a wide range of ailments. They have also reported a general increase in energy levels and a sense of wellbeing. Energetix sells its products in over 20 countries including the USA and Japan. The products are on sale in Harrods, Selfridges and Fenwicks and are also available by mail order. The range combine fashionable elegance and therapeutic properties. They make ideal gifts and come in a gift box.

Erevna
26 The Hill, Caterham CR3 6SD
Tel: *01883 330 828*
Email: *info@erevna.co.uk*
Web: *www.erevna.co.uk*
▶ Supplies pure essential oils, base oils, flower waters, macerated herb oils and tinctures all from organically grown plants. Also offering herb creams and a range of natural bodycare products not tested on animals and made with natural ingredients. Call free for the catalogue on 0800 0749645.

Essential Organics
Unit 42, 10-20 Castle Street,
Luton LU1 3AT
Tel: *01908 511 799*
Fax: *01908 566 988*
▶ Mail order suppliers to trade or individuals of essential oils made from organically grown plants, vegetables oils and infused oils, hypoallergenic base creams, lotions, and various shampoo and bath products. Call for a price list.

Forever Living Products
16 Treverbyn Road, Truro TR1 1RG
Tel: *01872 276398*
Fax: *01872 276 398*
Email: *greg.walker@virgin.net*
Web: *www.aloevera.co.uk*
Open: *Mon-Fri 9am-5pm*

IBIS International Corporation
is dedicated to promoting a total physical, spiritual and mental strength through Ayurveda – the ancient science of healthy living.

Ayurvedic treatments work on the energy levels of the organic systems by way of balancing the life forces within (the Three Doshas). All living bodies – humans and pets alike – can benefit from the gentle action of pure herbs.

All our products are based on 2500 year old Ayurvedic scriptures and do not contain synthetic chemicals of any description, animal derivatives or preparations that have been, at any time in history, tested on animals. They are suitable for vegetarians and vegans.

IBIS ranges include: herbal teas and tonics, massage oils, herbal skin cream, balms, hair care, immune system enhancing remedies, soap (70% pure Aloe Vera) and herbal toothpaste (lauryl sulphate-free) and many others.

IBIS supports the foundation of complete health through our own Ayurvedic Health Resort when authentic treatments (Panchakarma) include many genuine traditional approaches to total wellness. Meditation and yoga help to achieve "Samma Samadhi" – the Right Concentration.

Learn Ayurveda, visit ancient monuments and spiritually important sites and benefit from full Detoxification and Rejuvenation.

Please ring us on 01442 242 866
or email us on
sales@ibis-ayurveda.com
www.ibis-ayurveda.com

▶ Aloe Vera contains 75 known natural ingredients and its inner gel can be taken internally for nutritional benefits and combined with other ingredients to produce tropical creams and lotions to nourish and improve skin quality. Aloe Vera has been found to be beneficial for arthritus, asthma, athletes foot, burns, Irritable Bowel Syndrome, ulcers, Crohn's disease, colitus, the immune system, Eczema, Psoriasis and Dermatitus. It is also beneficial for animals. FLP are the world's largest growers of Aloe Vera, known to be beneficial for thousands of years.

Green People Company
Brighton Road,
Handcross RH17 6BZ
Tel: *01444 401 444*
Fax: *01444 401 011*
Email: *organic@greenpeople.co.uk*
Web: *www.greenpeople.co.uk*
Open: *Mon-Fri 9am-5pm*
▶ Supplies a range of herbal tonics and personal care products for healthy skin, teeth and hair. All are based on 100% natural and organic ingredients. The products contain no synthetic preservatives, no perfumes and no petrochemicals and are approved by the Vegan Society. The company is in the process of getting Soil Association certification for its products. It aims to offer you a chemical-free lifestyle. For and further information or a free catalogue, call the Careline on the above number.

Halzephron Herb Farm
Gunwallow, Helston TR12 7QD
Tel: *01326 240 652*
Fax: *01326 241 125*
Web: *www.hazelherb.com*
Open: *Mon-Fri 9am-5pm,
shop open 11am-4pm*
▶ Supplier of herbal remedies, available in capsule form, from this Cornish herb farm, where herbs are grown without pesticides or artificial growing agents. Culinary herbs also on sale.

Helios Homœopathic Pharmacy
97 Camden Road,
Tunbridge Wells TN1 2QR
Tel: *01892 537 254*
Fax: *01892 546 850*
Email: *pharmacy@helios.co.uk*
Web: *www.helios.co.uk*
Open: *Mon-Fri 9.45am-5.30pm;
Sat 10am-2pm*
▶ Homeopathic pharmacy supplying homeopathic remedies and herbal tinctures by post. Supplies a range of vitamins and suppliments, Bach Flower Remedies and Weleda products.

Holden's Herbal Health
The Bield, Lewes Road,
Forest Row RH18 5AF
Tel: *01342 826 896*
Fax: *01342 826 896*
Email: *info@holherbs.com*
Web: *www.holherbs.com*
Open: *Mon-Fri 9am-5.30pm*
▶ Supplies the Coleanse Herbal Detox Programme, the foundation of 15 years successful practice at the Holden Natural Health Clinic and available by mail order. Also supplies Nature's Superfood, a 100% organic vitamin and mineral food concentrate (all ingredients are from the richest whole food sources on the planet, as opposed to man made synthetic vitamins) and an extensive range of herbal tinctures for use in easy to follow 'self heal' programmes. Call us or visit the website for literature on how to review your lifestyle and diet, restore and support natural health and to rediscover vibrant energy using herbal formulas.

IBIS International Corporation
Suite 3, 32 Chilworth Street,
London W2 6DT
Tel: *01442 242 866*
Fax: *01442 242 866*
Email: *sales@ibis-ayurveda.com*
Web: *www.ibis-ayurveda.com*
▶ IBIS International Corporation is dedicated to the promotion of total physical, mental and spiritual strength through Ayurveda – the ancient science of healthy living. Ayurvedic treatments work on the energy levels of organic systems by way of balancing the life forces within (the Three Doshas). All their products are based on 2500 year old Ayurvedic scriptures

and do not contain synthetic chemicals of any description, animal derivitives or preparations that have been at any time in history tested on animals. They are suitable for vegetarians and vegans. The IBIS range includes: herbal teas and tonics, massage oils, skin and hair care, balms, soap and toothpaste (lauryl sulphate-free), immune system enhancing remedies and many others. Supplied via mail order and through retail outlets. Ayurvedic life-style consultations are also available. IBIS supports the foundations of complete health though its own Ayurvedic Health Resort where authentic treatments (Panchakarma) are employed including full detoxification, rejuvination, weight control and kidney, liver and skin cleansing. Nutritional advice, many other genuine traditional approaches to total wellness as well as Meditation and Yoga can all help to achieve 'Samma Samadhi' – the Right Concentration.

Manchester Cushion Company, The
120 Grosvenor Street,
Manchester M1 7HL
Tel: 0161 272 7991
Fax: 0161 272 7991
Email: cushionco@zen.co.uk
Web: www.cushion.org.uk
▶ Suppliers of quality handmade cushions and floor mats for meditation, yoga, massage and shiatsu. Available in a range of sizes and colours, using 100% cotton for covers and fillings. Call, write, or email for a brochure request, or place your order online.

Materia Aromatica
148 Mallinson Road,
London SW11 1BJ
Tel: 020 7207 3461
Fax: 020 7771 1486
Email: sales@
materiaaromatica.demon.co.uk
Web:
www.materiaaromatica.demon.co.uk
Open: Mon-Fri 9am-5pm
▶ Pure and blended essential oils, vegetable oils and flower waters made from certified organically-grown plants. Call for a price list.

Meadows Aromatherapy
Unit 2, Stour Valley Business Park,
Chartham, Canterbury, CT1 2DY
Tel: 01227 731 489
Fax: 01227 731 810
Email: enquiries@
meadowsaromatherapy.com
Web:
www.meadowsaromatherapy.com
Open: Mon-Fri 9am-5pm
▶ Wide range of essential oils (labelled with country of source), massage and carrier oils, creams, lotions, and body products, natural perfumes, head-lice treatment and after-sun lotion. For each pot of their Elephant Balm (made of essential oils and natural beeswax and used for minor ailments from headaches to insect bites and cold sores) 10p is donated to animal conservation. Also sell oil burners. Call to find your nearest stockist or for a mail order catalogue.

Natural Health Care
89 Lonsdale Avenue,
Wembley HA9 7EW
Tel: 020 8903 1931
Fax: 020 8903 1931
Open: By appointment only
▶ Independent supplier of New Way International products. Also supplies high quality sub-colloidal minerals and very high spectrum anti-oxidants. Call for details.

Natural Health Remedies
10 Bamborough Gardens,
London W12 8QN
Tel: 020 8746 0890;
Freephone 0800 074 7744
Fax: 020 8743 9485
Email: organica@NHR.kz
Web: www.NHR.kz
Open: 24hr answer phone
▶ Aromatherapy products including organic or pure grade essential oils and floral waters, massage base and blended oils, hair and body products, aromatherapy kits and even aromatherapy chocolates in lavender, bergamont, orange, rose, gold and fankinsence flavours in both plain and white chocolate. Good range of natural health books also available. Mail order only.

Natures Cocoons
Galamar, 17 Rooborough Avenue,
Stroud GL5 3RR
Tel: 01453 767 973
Email: info@naturescocoons
▶ Offers hampers for children that bring together Homeopathy, Aromatherapy, Flower Remedies, natural healthcare and organic food. There is a hamper for each stage of a child's development – all at less than High Street prices. Aims to help the parent help the child and so help the Earth.

NHR Organic Oils
10 Bamborough Gardens,
London W12 8QN
Tel: 020 746 0890
Fax: 0845 310 8068
Email: organic@nhr.kz
Web: www.nhr.kz
▶ Supplies pure organic essential oils at affordable prices. Certified by Ecocert. Sold in clear glass bottles to appreciate the vibrant colours of the oils. Also supplies aromatherapy, organic chocolates, kit boxes, organic shampoo, and much more. Buy direct from the website and get a free aromatherapy book.

Nutri Centre, The
7 Park Crescent, London W1N 3HE
Tel: 020 7436 5122
Fax: 020 7436 5171
Email: enq@nutricentre.com
Web: www.nutricentre.com
Open: Mon-Fri 9am-7pm;
Sat 10am-5pm
▶ The Centre is located on the lower ground floor of the world renowned Hale Clinic. Opened by Prince Charles in 1988, the Clinic has become one of Europe's leading centres for complementary medicine, housing some of the UK's most eminent practitioners, Europe's leading natural medicines dispensary and an extensive library and bookshop covering the whole range of complementary medicine. The dispensary is the UK's leading supplier of nutritional products, from those found in health food shops and practitioner products to exclusive lines and even the occasional batch made up for specific requirements. There are over 22,000 products on offer. The Centre goes to great lengths to source and research new products that become available. The Complementary Medicine Education Resource Centre incorporates a book shop and library with a range of books and journals on health and nutrition and a wider range of topics for the mind, body and soul. Requests for books not in stock are welcome and hard-to-find US titles will be tracked down.

Oralgum
Ecolabs Ltd, 3 Adam & Eve Mews,
London W8 6UG
Tel: 020 7460 8101
Fax: 020 7565 8779
Email: robin@ecolabs.co.uk
Web: www.ecolabs.co.uk
Open: Mon-Fri 10am-6pm
▶ Specialises in marketing a range of products designed to enable people to make positive changes to their health and lifestyle, naturally. Sells the Oralgum Toothbrush made from natural rubber. Order by phone or see website.

Outside In (Cambridge) Ltd
21 Scotland Rd Estate, Dry Drayton,
Cambridge CB3 8AT
Tel: 01954 211 955
Fax: 01954 211 956
Email: info@outsidein.co.uk
Web: www.outsidein.co.uk
Open: Mon-Fri 9am-5pm
▶ Commercial company supplying lights for treating Seasonal Affective Disorder (SAD), winter blues and other bodyclock problems, including shiftwork, jetlag, and sleep pattern disorders.

Phyto Pharmaceuticals
Park Works, Park Road,
Mansfield NG10 8EF
Tel: 01623 644 334
Fax: 01623 657 232
Email: info@phyto.co.uk
Open: Mon-Fri 9am-5pm
▶ Manufacturer and stockist of Herbal Medicines: tinctures, extracts, herbs and spices, creams, oils, syrups, tablets and the full range of Schoenenberger pure fresh plant juices (organically grown). Mail order service promises goods despatched within 24 hours.

Phytobotanica
Molyneux, Medicinal and Aromatic Plant Farm and Research Centre, Mill House Farm, Lydiate L31 4HS
Tel: 0151 526 0139
Fax: 0151 526 0139
Email: drcollins@madasafish.com
Web: www.phytobotanica.com

▶ Retailers and wholesalers of organic essential oils produced on the farm. Includes lavender, Roman chamomile and peppermint. All oils are analysed using gas chromatography and mass spectroscopy. The land is registered with the Soil Association. Offer 'on-farm' days to demonstrate the UK production of essential oils, as well as farm-based tutor support days and a tutor support pack. The company evolved and developed from a unique partnership between university research scientists, major professional UK farmers, academics, the essential oil industry and end-users including the Aromatherapy industry.

Really Healthy Company Ltd
PO Box 4390, London SW15 6YQ
Tel: 020 8780 5200
Fax: 020 8780 5199
Email: sales@healthy.co.uk
Web: www.healthy.co.uk
Open: Mon-Fri 9am-5pm

▶ The Really Healthy Company Ltd has built a reputation for introducing leading edge health supplements to Europe, including organic blue/green algea and other organic green food. Call, write or email for more information or visit the website. Credit card orders received before 2pm are usually sent out the same day.

Spice Direct
10 Three Crowns Road, Colchester CO4 5AD
Tel: 01206 751660
Fax: 01206 751084
Email: Sarah@spicedirect.co.uk
Web: www.spicedirect.co.uk

▶ Contributing money to Amnesty International, Spice Direct supplies complementary health, aromatherapy & herbal products to the public and the trade. Also supplying hers, spices, herbal teas and natural beauty products and not forgetting discounted health books.

The Healthy House
Cold Harbour, Ruscombe, Stroud GL6 6DA
Tel: 01453 752 216
Fax: 01453 753 533
Email: info@healthy-house.co.uk
Web: www.healthy-house.co.uk

▶ Mail order company specialising in products for people with allergies, asthma, skin disorders and environmental illness. Call for a free catalogue. Dust allergy is caused by dust mites and their faeces. The dust mite thrives in warm humid conditions and feeds on human skin scales. Products include dust mite proof bedding cases, vacuum cleaners, steam cleaners, dust mite sprays and air purifiers. Asthma and other respiratory problems can be triggered by food sensitivities, mould, the house dust mite, animals and chemicals. Air purifiers, ionisers, vacuum cleaners and natural bedding all help to reduce irritation. Eczema and skin conditions can be affected by a food allergy and house dust mites, pollens, moulds, furry pets and chlorine in tap water. An undersink water purifier installed for drinking and cooking and a whole-house unit for filtering the water for baths, showers and washing will greatly reduce the irritation for eczema sufferers. Natural bedding and dust mite protection is also recommended. Electromagnetic pollution is also on the increase and they can supply a range of products to counter the effects. Call for more information and advice.

Think Natural Ltd
Unit 7, Riverpark, Billet Lane, Berkhamsted HP4 1DP
Tel: 01442 299200
Fax: 01442 866977
Email: info@thinknatural.com
Web: www.thinknatural.com
Open: Mon-Fri 10am-5pm

▶ An online health and beauty site selling natural health and bodycare products with vitamins and minerals homeopathic and medicinal plants, as well as information and features on specific conditions. Has its own warehouse with 5,000 products – a range that is continually growing – and can turn around stock items in 24 hours. Encourages feedback from the public and is very interested in setting up more communication and chat as it grows.

Vegetarian & Vegan Bodybuilding
17 Inglewood Road, Rainford, St Helens WA10 4PB
Tel: 07050 396 611
Fax: 07050 005 180
Email: david.fairclough5@virgin.net

▶ Free to join group supporting animal free bodybuilding and sport. Personal diet plans, contacts with other members and product information. The main aim is to prove that plant protein is adequate for full muscle growth. Send an SAE for an information pack.

Wellbeing
Wellbeing Freepost BM4601, Birmingham B14 4BR
Tel: 0121 444 6585
(24 hr ordering line)
Fax: 0121 444 3339
Email: wellbeing@dial.pipex.com
Web: www.wellbeing-uk.com
Open: Mon-Fri 9am-5pm

▶ Sells Wellbeing vitamins and minerals, ESI optima Aloe Vera products and Thursday Plantation Tea-Tree oil. Mail order only.

Wholistic Research Company
The Old Forge, Mill Green, Hatfield AL9 5NZ
Tel: 01707 262 686
Fax: 01707 258 828

▶ Supplier of health products including allergy control products and natural health books. Agent and trade enquiries welcome.

Yoga Mats Express
12 Roseneath Place, Edinburgh EH9 1JB
Tel: 0131 221 9977
Fax: 0131 221 9697
Email: yme@ednet.co.uk
Web: www.yoga.co.uk
Open: Mon-Fri 9am-5pm

A HARMONY OF SCIENCE & NATURE

Stop! Before You Buy

JUICERS ★ WATER PURIFIERS ★ AIR IONISERS
REBOUNDERS ★ ENEMA KITS ★ GRAIN MILLS
SPROUTERS ★ DEHYDRATORS ★ BIO-MAGNETS
BACKSWINGS ★ SLANT-BOARDS ★ IRIDOLOGY &
NATURAL FERTILITY AWARENESS EQUIPMENT
HERBAL TABLET MAKERS ★ DOWSING RODS
HUMANE MOUSE TRAPS, REFLEX FOOT ROLLERS
ALOE VERA PLANTS, S/S STEAMERS, SUNBOXES
DAYLIGHT LIGHTING ★ PULSORS ★ VDU FILTERS
ALLERGY CONTROL PRODUCTS & MANY BOOKS
ON THESE & OTHER NATURAL HEALTH TOPICS

Get ALL the Facts – Free!
from our famous 72 page book:

A HARMONY OF SCIENCE & NATURE
Ways of Staying Healthy in a Modern World
by John & Lucie Davidson

FREE! – FOR A LIMITED PERIOD ONLY – FREE!
Sold in bookshops for £3.95
It's essential reading – everyone should have a copy!

Over 300 Selected Products & Books

WHOLISTIC RESEARCH COMPANY LIMITED
Dept GG, The Old Forge, Mill Green
Hatfield, Herts AL9 5NZ

FREE BOOK! **Call 01707 - 262686 (24 hrs)** FREE BOOK!
Agent & Trade Enquiries Welcome

Health

▶ Visit the secure online shopping page on www.yoga.co.uk for Yoga mats and other useful Yoga items.

Manufacturers

Aloe Care – Pro-Ma International
The Piece, Cutwell, Tetbury GL8 8EB
Tel: 01666 504 718
Fax: 01666 505 301
Email: woeac@msn.com
▶ PRO-MA of Australia have been associated with the growing and processing of Aloe Vera to the highest possible consistent therapeutic standards for over 25 years. Properly processed therapeutic grade Aloe Vera possesses the following properties: it is a natural anti-inflammatory and anti-histamine; it relieves pain and is an anti-pruritic; and it normalises and balances the body's system; and has been shown scientifically to generate healthy tissue at the cellular level by up to 8.83 times the norm. It is non-toxic, has no known side effects, and it is therefore very safe to use. It is grown organically in nutrient rich soil and cold processed to retain optimum potency. The Aloin is carefully removed. No added thickeners, artificial sweeteners, flavourings or colours are used in the manufacturing process. It is not supplied in tablet form, but is available in 500ml, 1 litre, 2 litre and 5 litre containers.

Bioforce (UK) Ltd
2 Brewster Place,
Irvine KA11 5DD
Tel: 01294 277 344
Fax: 01294 277 922
Web: www.bioforce.co.uk
Open: Mon-Fri 9am-5pm
▶ Leading producer of fresh herb tinctures. These holistically-standardised tinctures are made using fresh herbs organically grown in Switzerland. Brand leader Echinaforce is a licensed herbal medicine for colds and flu. Other popular tinctures include Aesculus, Hypericum and Gingko. In addition, Bioforce boasts a large range of health foods including award-winning Bambu Coffee substitute.

Chirali Old Remedies
163 Upton Road,
Bexleyheath DA6 8LY
Tel: 020 8306 6736
Email: ilkaychirali@compuserve.com
▶ Manufacturer of herbal skin and hair care, including muscle and joint soothing cream, dry skin cream, itching skin cream and hair tonic. Retail and wholesale enquiries welcomed.

Ephytem
Abbot Close, Oyster Lane,
Byfleet KT14 7JP
Tel: 01932 334 501
Fax: 01932 336 235
Email: info@brewhurst.com
Web: www.brewhurst.com
▶ A revolutionary range of supplements, Ephytem has been created by alternative health practitioners and university researchers – each category includes only natural ingredients with unique combinations the efficacy of which has always been independently tested. The range includes Microspheres (22 herbals), Frutex (a laxative bar), Biopura (probiotic and prebiotic) and a 10-day detox programme.

Forever Living Products (UK) Ltd
Longbridge Manor,
Longbridge, Warwick CV34 6RB
Tel: 01926 408 800
Fax: 01926 408 833
Email: CliveNorton@compuserve.com
▶ Health, beauty and nutrition products. Forever Living is the world's largest producer of aloe vera and beehive products.

G and G Vitamins
Vitality House, 2-3 Imberhorne Lane,
East Grinstead RH19 1RL
Tel: 01342 312 811
Fax: 01342 315 938
Email: exec@gandgvitamins.com
Web: www.gandgvitamins.com
Open: Mon-Fri 9am-5.30pm
▶ Manufacturers of vitamins and minerals and organic herbs. Range includes products especially for children, such as 'Crunchy Creatures'- chewable animal shaped, fruit flavoured tablets. 24 hour mail order around the world. Over 200 high quality, high-tech, high strength supplements at low prices.

Health and Diet Company Ltd
Europa Park, Stonelough Road,
Radcliffe, Manchester M26 1GG
Tel: 01204 707 420
Fax: 01204 792 238
Email: info@fsc-vitamins.com
Web: www.fsc-vitamins.com
Open: Mon-Sat 9am-5.30pm
▶ Offers a wide range of vitamin, mineral and herbal supplements for all the family. The supplements are formulated by leading nutritionists and are based on widely recognised scientific evidence (largely human studies rather than test tube). Provides a variety of information tools allowing the consumer to make better informed choices including their HealthNotes Online database available in a growing number of health food stores. FSC is the main brand. For nearest stockist call 020 8477 5358.

Korean Red Ginseng Company Ltd
PO Box 16018, London SW11 3WH
Tel: 020 7585 0312
Fax: 020 7738 0775
Email: info@redginseng.co.uk
Open: 24 hours
▶ Sole importer and distributor in the UK of all red ginseng products as produced by the Korean Government. Red ginseng is a major ingredient in Chinese Medicine and is used to combat stress, fatigue and general tiredness. Available in capsules, tablets, tea and the root form. Call for information and orders.

Naturally Nova Scotia
c/o Bodywise (UK) Ltd., Unit 23,
Marsh Lane Industrial Estate,
Marsh Lane, Portbury,
Bristol BS20 0NH
Tel: 01275 371 764
Email: info@natracare.com
Web: www.natracare.com
▶ Herbal tinctures made from the freshest organic herbs, picked on a certified organic herb farm in Nova Scotia and processed within two hours of leaving the earth they grow in. Soil Association certified.

Nature's Plus UK
12 Harley Street, London W1N 1AA
Tel: 020 7637 4849
Fax: 020 7681 2040
Email: uksales@naturesplus.com
Web: www.naturesplus.com
▶ The largest independent manufacturer of quality nutritional supplements in the United States. The same selection and product availability is now available in the UK. For almost 30 years the product range has been distributed exclusively through independent health food shops, and this tradition will continue in the UK. Call for a free catalogue and product samples and for details of your nearest stockist.

S.A.D. Lightbox Co Ltd
19 Lincoln Road, Cressex Business Park, High Wycombe HP12 3fx
Tel: 01494 448 727
Fax: 01494 527 005
Email: info@sad.uk.com
Web: www.sad.uk.com
▶ The longest established manufacturer of lightboxes for Seasonal Affective Disorder (Winter Blues) in the UK. This light therapy equipment can also help with imbalances of circadian rhythms such as sleep disorders, jet lag and ME. Free information pack is available.

Solgar Vitamins
Aldbury, Tring HP23 5PT
Tel: 01442 890 355
Fax: 01442 890 366
Web: www.solgar.com
▶ Manufacturers of the Gold Label range of over 400 vitamins, minerals, herbs and amino acids. Solgar vitamins are available wherever fine health foods are sold. Call for a list of stockists.

Vitabiotics Ltd
1 Beresford Avenue,
Wembley HA0 1NU
Tel: 020 8902 4455
Fax: 020 8902 4466
Email: tmaxwell@vitabiotics.com
Web: www.vitabiotics.com
▶ A British-based healthcare company with over 28 years experience in research-based nutrition supplements, offering an alternative solution for health in specific health areas

or for different stages of life. Formulated by highly qualified medical consultants, prodcts are produced to the highest pharmaceutical standards of quality control, are 100% free of drugs, hormones, artificial colours, gluten, fat or yeast and are developed without animal testing. The formulations are sold in over 60 countries world-wide.

Yunnan Tuocha
Abbot Close, Oyster Lane, Byfleet KT14 7JP
Tel: *01932 334 501*
Fax: *01932 336 235*
Email: *info@brewhurst.com*
Web: *www.brewhurst.com*
▶ The positive virtues of Yunnan Tuocha tea have long been recognised by traditional Chinese medicine. Preliminary studies now indicate that this unique tea may play a role in the metabolism of fats and cholesterol, and aid digestion. Its low caffeine content makes it a perfect beverage for any time of the day. It is available as original, with ginseng and with lotus.

CENTRES

Most of the centres listed in this section are located in the North West. We have included some outside the region because they offer a nationwide service.

Aromatherapy Centre
77 School Lane, Didsbury, Manchester M20 6WN
Tel: *0161 445 4445*
▶ Centre with four aromatherapy practitioners (all qualified nurses) and two therapy rooms. Their shop stocks a range of aromatherapy products including the Centre's own brand products. Call to book an appointment.

Atlow Mill Centre
Hognaston, Ashbourne DE6 1PX
Tel: *01335 370 494*
Fax: *01335 370 279*
Email: *centre@atlowmill.ndo.co.uk*
Web: *www.atlowmill.ndo.co.uk*
▶ A registered charity specialising in delivering courses in Emotional Education to the general public and disadvantaged groups. Public courses include Healing the Wound of Childhood, Creative Anger, Emergence, Initmate Connections and Men's groups. Charitable projects include Preventing School Exclusion, Bullying and Preventing the cycle of Domestic Violence. Committed to creating a society where people live as a 'community' which includes the development of the potential of each human being and the peaceful resolution of conflict.

Bodywise Natural Health Centre
2nd Floor Manchester Buddhist Centre, 16-20 Turner Street, Northern Quarter, Manchester M4 1DZ
Tel: *0161 833 2528*
Email: *bodywise@altavista.net*
▶ A natural health centre offering holistic treatments and running courses in Massage, Aromatherapy, Acupuncture, Yoga, Shiatsu, and Reiki. Concessionary rates offered. Call for a brochure. Managed and treated by a team of Buddhist women.

Bolton Clinic of Traditional Acupuncture
557 Chorley Old Road, Bolton BL1 6AE
Tel: *01204 841 060*
▶ Offers Acupuncture and Osteopathy treatments.

Bolton Therapy Centre
13 Chorley Old Road, Bolton BL1 3AD
Tel: *01204 386 170*
Fax: *01204 386 170*
Open: *Mon-Sat 9.30am-7pm*
▶ Located close to Bolton town centre, this centre was established in 1992 and offers wide range of treatments including Physiotherapy, Massage, Acupuncture, Homeopathy, Aromatherapy, Reiki, Hypnotherapy, Counselling, Reflexology and Alexander Technique from fully qualified and experienced therapists.

Bristol Cancer Help Centre
Grove House, Cornwallis Grove, Clifton, Bristol BS8 4PG
Tel: *0117 980 9500*
Helpline: *0117 980 9505*
Fax: *0117 923 9184*
Email: *info@bristolcancerhelp.org*
Web: *www.bristolcancerhelp.org*
Open: *Mon-Fri 9am-5.30pm*
▶ Offers an holistic and complementary approach to cancer care for those with cancer and their supporters. The Centre runs a carefully devised therapy programme in Bristol. All the therapies offered are entirely natural and non-invasive, and can be used in unison with medical treatment. The therapy team at the Centre will explore each person's needs, both in groups and individually. Some people come with supporters, others alone. Advice will be given on nutrition, and how to introduce dietary change based on the latest research, as well as on vitamins and supplements. Self-help methods of relaxation, meditation and visualisation are taught to reduce fear and stress, offering ways on managing pain and replacing negative attitudes and beliefs. Through individual counselling sessions each person can reassess and express their own needs to highly trained therapists and holistic doctors; and healing, art therapy, massage and shiatsu are also offered on courses. It is an all embracing approach, and through assessment the therapies that best suit each individual will be discovered. Research shows that those who become hopeless and helpless following a diagnosis of cancer have less chance of survival than those who have a more positive attitude. The approach, therefore, is to help people to develop and use a positive approach to their illness, releasing their own potential to help themselves. Most importantly the approach can be used away from the Centre, so the benefits can contnue at home, or while undergoing treatment. The Centre does, of course, offer follow-up visits and services and can always be contacted.

Bury Complementary Health Centre
12 Tenterden Street, Bury BL9 0EG
Tel/Fax: *0161 763 1660*
▶ Offers allergy and food intolerance testing and treatment, Acupuncture, Homeopathy, clinical Hypnotherapy, Psychotherapy, personal counselling, Alexander Technique, clinical Aromatherapy, Reflexology, Reiki, Bowen Technique and therapeutic Swedish and sports massage. The Centre is registered with the Department of Health and all treatments are conducted by qualified practitioners.

Centre for Advanced Reflexology
204 Mauldeth Road, Burnage, Manchester M19 1AJ
Tel: *0161 443 1582*
Fax: *0161 286 2336*
Web: *www.reflexologycentre.co.uk*
Open: *Mon-Fri 9am-9pm; Sat 9am-5pm*
▶ Specialists in the teaching, training and practice of Reflexology and Aromatherapy. Also offer body massage. Call for course info or to book an appointment.

China Traditional Therapy Clinic
407 Palatine Road, Manchester M22 4JS
Tel: *0161 902 0201*
Open: *Mon-Sun 10am-6pm*

Health 101

▶ Offers massage, Acupuncture, Acupressure, moxibustion and other traditional Chinese treatments.

Chris & Kate Quartermaine
23 Upton Park, Chester CH2 1DF
Tel: 01244 378 787
Fax: 01244 378 960
Email: cmq@clara.net
▶ Complementary Therapists, specialising in the Bowen Technique. Kate Quartermaine is also qualified in Clinical Kinesiology, Reflexology and Reiki.

Creative Living Centre
(Behind TGI Friday's), Bury New Road, Prestwich, Manchester M25 3BL
Tel: 0161 772 3524
Fax: 0161 772 3797
Open: Mon-Fri 10am-4pm
▶ Centre providing support and resources for people experiencing mental or emotional distress and encouraging active participation towards health and well-being through the development of inner resources and self-awareness. The centre offers complementary therapies, creative arts, social space, volunteer opportunities and a garden project.

Detoxify Naturally
9 Stocks Avenue, Boughton, Chester CH3 5TJ
Tel: 01244 322 927
▶ Offers natural, holistic detoxification physically by means of lymphatic drainage techniques and biochemically by nutritional advice. Used especially for clients with ME, MS, or those who have a history of long-term antibiotics.

European Ayur Veda
Hoar Cross Hall, Yoxall DE138QS
Tel: 01283 575 040
Fax: 01283 575 030
Email: info@europeanayurveda.com
Web: www.europeanayurveda.com
▶ Therapies designed to help you get more energy, eliminate stress, find your ideal weight, achieve an extraordinarily deep relaxation and make you look and feel years younger. The fusion of the residence of Hoar Cross Hall, modern spa luxury and ancient knowledge of Ayurveda is unique in the United Kingdom

Heswall Holistic Centre
4 Milner Road, Heswall, Wirral CH60 5RZ
Tel: 0151 342 7272
▶ Offers Hypnotherapy, hypnosis, holistic massage, Swedish Massage, Osteopathy, Reflexology, Acupuncture and Chiropody.

Independent Dental Practice
216 Washway Road, Sale M33 4RA
Tel: 0161 973 3594
Fax: 0161 976 3415
Open: lMon-Fri 9am-5pm
▶ Holistic dentist who takes the whole body into account, working alongside homeopaths and chiropractors. Patients are asked about past dental history, expectations and general health. Personal and painless care. Dental hygienist available. Mercury free.

Ji Chun Chinese Medical Centre
54 Arderne Road, Timperley, Altrincham WA15 6HL
Tel: 0161 973 2107
▶ Offers Acupuncture, herbal remedies, traditional Chinese medicine and Chinese massage.

Manchester Buddhist Centre
16-20 Turner Street, Northern Quarter, Manchester M4 1DZ
Tel: 0161 834 9232
Fax: 0161 839 4815
Email: info@manchesterbuddhistcentre.org.uk
Web: www.manchesterbuddhistcentre.org.uk
Open: Mon-Thurs 11am-7pm; Fri & Sat 11am-5pm
▶ Offers meditation, yoga and other natural health therapies. Meditation and Buddhist courses. There is a bookshop on the premises. Earth café in basement serving vegetarian meals and snacks.

Manchester Homeopathic Clinic
Brunswick Street, Manchester M13 9ST
Tel: 0161 273 2446
Fax: 0161 273 2446
Web: www.manchesterhomeopathic.co.uk
▶ Registered charity established in 1860 offering homeopathic treatments and remedies. Practitioners are medical doctors as well as qualified homeopaths. Treatments available on the NHS.

MAVMC Ltd
Oak Hall, 9 Wizfred Road, Boscombe Manor, Bournemouth BH5 1ND
Tel: 01283 576 515
Fax: 01283 575 224
Open: Availability Times: Mon-Sun 10am-5pm (office)
▶ Maharishi Ayurveda at Oak Hall is the first and only residential Ayurveda Centre in the UK. With over ten years experience of giving Mav therapies to the public. All its therapists have successfuly graduated from the Maharishi Vedic University in Valkenburg, Holland. Specialises in Panchakarma (PK) rejuvenation and revitalisation programme for perfect health. With programmes designed from one day to six weeks, the centre also offers Mav educational courses, Pulse diagnosis, lifestyle evaluation, doctor consultations and a range of products.

Monkton Wyld Court
Charmouth, Bridport DT6 6DQ
Tel: 01297 560 342
Fax: 01297 560 395
Email: monktonwyldcourt@btinternet.com
▶ Holistic education centre run by a resident community, three miles from the sea at Lyme Regis. Offers a varied programme of courses including retreats, arts and crafts, music and dance, shamanic studies and family events. All meals are vegetarian using homegrown, organic produce when possible. Call for details of current workshop programme.

Natural Choice Therapy Centre
24 St John Street, Ashbourne DE6 1GH
Tel: 01335 346 096
Fax: 01335 346 096
Email: naturalchoice@lineone.net
Open: Mon-Wed 9am-5pm; Thurs to Sat 9am-5.30pm
▶ Therapies cover a vast range, including; Acupuncture, Reiki, Reflexology, Shiatsu, Aromatherapy Massage, Therapeutic Massage, Kinesiology, Feng Shui, Homeopathy, Hypnotherapy, Counselling, Nutrition Therapy, Neuro-Lnguistic Programming, and food sensitivity testing.

Natural Health Clinic, The
133 Gatley Road, Gatley, Cheadle SK8 4PD
Tel: 0161 428 4980
Fax: 0161 491 4190
Open: Mon-Weds 8.30am-1pm
▶ Alternative therapy treatments in Osteopathy, Acupuncture, Applied Kinesiology, Herbal Medicine, Nutrition and Homeopathy. Call for further details.

Natural Health Network
Chardstock House, Chard TA20 2TL
Tel: 01460 63229
Fax: 01460 63809
Open: Mon-Fri 10am-2pm
▶ Formed in 1981 as an association for natural health centres/clinics. In 1986, the Network set up the Natural Health Week. Readers wishing to give their time to these two important elements of natural health care should contact the address above. Volunteers urgently required to run this association

North West Complementary Therapy Centre
Subud House, 28 Dudley Road (off Withington Road), Manchester M16 8DE
Tel: 0161 226 0953
Fax: 0161 226 0953
Open: Mon-Fri 9.45am-5pm
▶ Offers tuition leading to the Professional Practitioner Diploma in Clinical Aromatherapy which is accredited by the International Society of Professional Aroma-therapists (ISPA). The school is member of the AOC foru. Training comprises part-time weekend/weekday courses over a 10 month period in aromatherapy and all related subjects – anatomy and physiology, Counselling, Swedish Massage, Shiatsu, reflex indications and business management skills. Tuition is given by a team of specialist professional teachers. Courses usually begin in spring and autumn.

Health

Northern Acupuncture & Osteopath Medical Centre
Carne House, Parsons Lane,
Bury BL9
Tel: *0161 797 3607*
▶ Centre offering Acupuncture and Osteopathy treatments. Call for more info.

Park Attwood Clinic
Trimpley, Bewdley DY12 1RE
Tel: *01299 861 444*
Fax: *01299 861 375*
Email: *park.attwood@btinternet.com*
Web: *www.park_attwood.com*
Open: *Office Mon-Fri 9am-5pm with residential treatment available 365 days a year*
▶ A 14 bed treatment centre offering a unique approach to health care. The clinic is staffed by fully-qualified doctors, nurses and therapists who work as a team to find the most effective combination of conventional and complementary medicine to meet the needs of each individual patient. It is one of an increasing number of hospitals and medical practices working with Anthroposophical medicine which aims to address the whole person and not just the illness or symptoms. A wide range of conditions are treated, including cancer, cardiovascular diseases, muscular and skeletal disorders, neurological problems, immune system disorders, life crisis and associated medical complaints. The usual length of stay is 2-4 weeks with follow-up consultations when appropriate. Care can also be delivered on an out-patient basis.

Rossendale Natural Health Clinic
227 Bury Road,
Rawtenstall BB4 6DJ
Tel: *01706 213 671*
Open: *Tues & Thurs; 4.30pm-8.30pm, Wed 1.30pm-5.30pm, Fri 11am-4pm, or by appointment*
▶ Offers laser Acupuncture, Remedial Massage, Homeopathy, Hypnotherapy, Crystal Therapy, Aromatherapy Massage, Reflexology, Reiki healing and dousing from qualified practitioners. The Centre is accessible to the disabled.

Shanghai Acupuncture Clinic
74 Portland Street,
Manchester M1 4GU
Tel: *0161 236 1319*
Fax: *0161 236 1319*
▶ Chinese medicine clinic offering Acupuncture and herbal treatments.

Shanghai Acupuncture & Herbal Medicine Clinic
74 Portland Street,
Manchester M1 4GU
Tel: *0161 236 1319*
Open: *Mon-Tues 12pm-6pm; Sat-Sun 12pm-5pm*
▶ Offers Acupuncture and Chinese herbal medicine.

Shizhen Clinic of Acupuncture & Chinese Herbs
50 Sandy Lane Chorton,
Manchester M21 8TN
Tel: *0161 881 8576*
▶ Offers Acupuncture, Chinese Herbal Remedies and Chinese Massage.

Sino-European Clinics
2 St John Street,
Manchester M3 4BD
Tel: *0161 839 9283*
Fax: *0161 831 7956*
Email: *enquiry@secbath.demon.co.uk*
Web: *www.acumedic.com*
Open: *Mon-Fri 9.30am-1.30pm, 2pm-6pm, Thurs 10.30am-2.30pm, 3pm-7pm*
▶ Chinese medical centre offering Acupuncture, Chinese Herbal Therapy and Massage. Both on-site practitioners are qualified doctors in Chinese and Western medicine. Specialises in skin, digestive and gynaecological problems but also deals with a wide range of other conditions. The company has a branch in Bath, and both are members of the Acumedic group.

StressBusters UK
Tel: *020 8450 7999*
Email: *info@stressbusters.demon.co.uk*
Web: *www.stressbusters.co.uk*
▶ Established in 1991 and is the first company to offer on-site chair massage throughout the UK. Offers specially structured 'Vitality Breaks' of 10-30 minutes of fully clothed seated massage which are designed to relax yet revitalise clients. These make the health giving benefits of massage easily accesible and suitable for the workplace and public forums. Call for more information.

Traditional Acupuncture Clinic
6 Station Road, White Hart Fold,
Todmorden OL14 7BD
Tel: *01706 813 527*
Open: *Tues-Sat by appt.*
▶ Acupuncture treatments from qualified and experienced practitioners Alison West and Stella King. Initial consultation fee is £46 and treatment is £23, with reductions for the unemployed. Call for further details and to make an appointment.

Traditional Acupuncture Clinic
259 Wigan Road, Bolton BL3 5QP
Tel: *01204 658 532*
Email: *vivien.onslow@euphony.net*
▶ Traditional Chinese Acupuncture treatment of a wide range of acute, chronic and painful conditions as well as for emotional problems, stress and long-established illness, through its power in stimulating the body's own healing response. Suitable for people of all ages.

Warrington Acupuncture Clinic
7 Bold Street, Warrington WA1 1DN
Tel: *01925 231 200*
▶ Offers Acupuncture and Remedial Massage.

Wybunbury Acupuncture Clinic
1 Moorlands Drive, Wybunbury,
Nantwich CW5 7PA
Tel: *01270 842 276*
▶ Offers traditional Acupuncture.

RETREATS

Most retreats offer an opportunity for serenity, contemplation and escape from the fast pace of modern life. Some retreats hold regular workshops and lectures on subjects such as meditation or yoga; others pretty much allow visitors to relax and move at their own pace. Costs vary widely. Write to the community or centre you're interested in. For more information contact the Retreat Association (see listing).

Brahma Kumaris World Spiritual University
Global Co-operation House, 65
Pound Lane, London NW10 2HH
Tel: *020 8459 1400*
▶ The Brahama Kumaris University was founded in 1937; an administrative office was opened in London in the Seventies. Both the office in London and the retreat centre near Oxford offer courses, workshops, seminars and conferences on subjects such as self-development and meditation. The centre has residential facilities.

Canon Frome Court
Near Ledbury HR8 2TD
Tel: *01531 670 417*
▶ Organic farming community in a Georgian house surrounded by 35 acres of park and farmland in beautiful countryside. New community members and short-stay visitors welcome. There are also rooms available for workshops.

Middle Piccadilly Natural Healing Centre
Middle Piccadilly, Holwell,
Sherborne DT9 5LW
Tel: *01963 23468*
Fax: *01963 23764*
Email: *info@middlepiccadilly.com*
Web: *www.middlepiccadilly.com*
Open: *Mon-Sun 9am-9pm*
▶ Residential alternative health centre set in a 17th century thatched property in the beautiful Dorset countryside. An oasis of peace and tranquility, offering a range of wholistic packages which include alternative therapies, beauty treatments and

Health

mud/marine baths. Vegetarian cuisine. Costs start from £225.50 for a basic 2 day package.

Minton House
Findhorn Bay,
Findhorn IV36 3YY
Tel: 01309 690 819
Fax: 01309 691 583
Email: minton@findhorn.org
Web: www.mintonhouse.co.uk
Open: All year
▶ Retreat/workshop centre and guest house accommodation in a beautiful pink mansion on the shores of Findhorn Bay. A place of peace with a unique atmosphere of warmth and healing. The food is vegetarian and the vegetables are mainly organic and locally grown.

Nutcombe Farm
Nutcombe Hil,
Coombe Martin EX34 0PQ
Tel: 01271 883 689
Fax: 01271 883 689
Email: nutcombe2000@onetel.net.uk
Open: Open by appointment
▶ In the rolling hills of Exmoor's western edges lies a farmhouse high in a sheltered valley. Nutcombe is a haven of peace and tranquility and a source of natural spring water and energy, with a little help from a generator. A unique retreat offering art therapy and a healing room. Accomodation is of a high standard and there is an extensive library of books and music.

Osho Leela
Thorngrove House,
Common Mead Lane,
Gillingham SP8 4RE
Tel: 01747 821 221
Fax: 01747 826 386
Email: info@oshleela.co.uk
▶ Residential community, therapist training centre and meditation centre with caravan and camping facilities set in beautiful Dorset countryside with easy access to main line railway station. Aim to develop friendship in a loving, caring and relaxed atmosphere. Venue available for hire for workshops from 10-65 people, for parties and weddings.

Practice, The
The Manor House,
Kings Norton LE7 9BA
Tel: 0116 259 6633
Fax: 0116 259 6633
Email: psmjo@thepractice.demon.co.uk
Open: Mon-Fri 9.30am-5pm
▶ Centre for 'transformation'. Specialises in offering Ayurvedic Massage and Panchakarma Rejuvenation Treatments, classes in Meditation, Yoga and Healthy Living. Also offers Homeopathy, Reflexology, and healing. One to one tailor-made programmes available. Deepak Chopra course in meditation.

Quiraing Lodge Retreat Centre
Staffin IVS1 9JS
Tel: 01470 562330
Open: All year except Christmas
▶ Open retreat centre offering both structured retreats and quiet space just to 'be' and to enjoy the beauty of Skye. Wide variety of walks, seaviews, open fires, library and meditation room. All catering is home-cooked and vegetarian.

Retreat Association
Central Hall, 256 Bermondsey Street, London SE1 3UJ
Tel: 020 7357 7736
Email: info@retreats.org.uk
Web: www.retreats.org.uk
Open: Mon-Fri 9am-5pm
▶ Christian umbrella body representing, amongst others, Anglican and Catholic retreats. Publishes an annual journal, *Retreats*, listing over 200 retreats and their programmes around the country. The journal costs £4.20 from the bookshop, £5.00 mail order.

Retreat Company, The
The Manor House,
Kings Norton, LE7 9BA
Tel: 0116 259 9211
Fax: 0166 259 6633
Email: timeout@retreat_co.co.uk
Web: www.retreat_co.co.uk
▶ Complete service for 'taking time out' to enhance personal growth and well being. Free publication three times a year which is informative and educational, offering a range of retreat ideas and holidays, as well as services, products and ideas to create your own sacred space at home. See the website for more details.

Trigonos Centre
Plas Baladeulyn, Nantlle,
Caernarfon LL54 6BW
Tel: 01286 882 388
Fax: 01286 882 424
▶ Conference, workshop and retreat centre in Snowdonia National Park offering relaxed surroundings and catering for a range of needs and interests. Accommodation is available for up to 30 visitors and facilities include a meeting room, gallery, library, photographic darkroom and studio/study centre.

Yoga for Health Foundation
Ickwell Bury,
Biggleswade SG18 9EF
Tel: 01767 627 271
Fax: 01767 627 266
Open: Mon-Sun 9am-5pm
▶ Residential centre of an international Yoga organisation, noted for using Yoga both to maintain health and to overcome chronic illness and disabilities. Courses are held for those with cancer, arthritis, breathing problems, MS, ME, Parkinson's and other problems.

COURSES & COLLEGES

Academy of On-Site Massage
Avon Road, Charfield,
Wotton-Under-Edge GL12 8TT
Tel: 01454 261900
Fax: 01454 261900
Email: all@onsitemassage.softnet.co.uk
Web: www.mbs.org.uk/on-site-massage
Open: Mon-Fri 9am-5.30pm
▶ The original training school for qualified therapists wishing to add seated chair massage to their repertoire. The course is held over three non-consecutive weekends in London and nine other venues throughout the UK. Also has showrooms in Gloucestershire & Bow Wharf in London with displays of massage tables and chairs form Oakworks, Darley, New Concept, VATstar & Plynth 2000, together with Biotone oile and creams. Stocks tapes, CDs and a range of books and aromatherapy oils and Bach Flower Remedies.

Alternative Therapies
16 Dukes Wood Drive,
Gerrards Cross SL9 7LR
Tel: 01753 890 202
Fax: 01753 884 069
Email: patrick@therapies.com
Web: www.therapies.com
Open: Mon-Fri 9am-9pm
▶ Training courses in Reiki, Reflexology, Aromatherapy, Massage, Anatomy & Physiology, Karuna healing, On-site massage, Indian Head Massage, Acupressure, Macrobiotics, Oriental diagnosis, etc. Also supplies charts, health supplements, magnets, crystals, essential oils and books.

Angelgate Foundation
6 Combermere Road,
St. Leonards on Sea TW38 0RR
Tel: 01424 430 001
▶ A foundation for complementary therapies established in 1990 offering professional standard training in Reflexology, Aromatherapy, Therapeutic Massage and Spinal Touch Treatment. It is registered with the

British Complementary Medicine Association and diploma courses are accredited by the International Examination Board, International Federation of Reflexologists, Aromatherapy Organisations Council and the Association of Light Touch Therapists.

Aromatherapy Associates Training
68 Maltings Place, Bagleys Lane, London SW6 2BY
Tel: 020 7371 9878
Fax: 020 7371 9894
Email: info@aromatherapyassociation.com
Web: www.aromatherapyassociation.com
Open: Mon-Fri 9am-5.30pm
▶ An association of three practising aromatherapists offering training courses recognised by the International Federation of Aromatherapists. Established in 1985 to provide the best personal treatments to a discerning and international clientele, to train therapists and to produce oils, creams and essences of a professional standard for use at home. Every oil is made from quality plants, fruit, flowers, herbs and spcices. The preparations are designed to encourage natural good health, lift the spirits and help alleviate specific problems caused by stress. The range includes: body, mind, spirit and skin preparations.

B.K. Heather Reflexology Practitioner Course
Villas Road, Plumstead, Woolich, London SE18 7PN
Tel: 020 8488 4800
Fax: 020 8488 4899
Web: www.woolich@c.uk
Open: Mon-Fri 9am-5pm
▶ Practitioner training courses accredited by the Association of Reflexologists. Courses start in September of each year and comprise 30 sessions.

Bayley School of Reflexology
Monks Orchard, Whitbourne, Worcester WR6 5RB
Tel: 01886 821 207
Fax: 01886 822 017
Email: bayley@britreflex.co.uk
Web: www.britreflex.co.uk
Open: Mon-Fri 9am-4.30pm
▶ Founded in 1978 by Doreen Bayley, the School is the official teaching body of the British Reflexology association. Part-time courses leading to a practitioner's certificate are held regularly in London, Birmingham, Edinburgh, Leeds and Liverpool with branches of the School overseas. Involves attendance at five weekends spread over a period of about one year with case work and home study in between the courses. On completion of the course, a written and practical examination is taken by students.

Biodanza UK/Rolando Toro School of Biodanza
48 Clifford Avenue, London SW14 7BP
Tel: 020 8392 1433
Email: biodanza@biodanza.demon.co.uk
Open: Mon-Fri 9.30am-9.30pm
▶ The training course of the Biodanza system consists of a deep development, evolution and understanding of movement, music and expression of emotions which are channelled through the Five Lines of Vivencia: Vitality, Sexuality, Creativity, Affectivity and Transcendence. Patricia Martello introduced this technique into the UK in order to restore psychological, motor, emotional and organic balance in our daily life, through dance, music and exercises of human communication suitable for everybody.

Bowen Technique (Courses)
3 Peony Gardens, Shepherds Bush, London W12 0RX
Tel: 020 8749 6952
Email: bowen@bizonline.co.uk
Web: www.therapy-training.com
Open: Mon-Fri 10am-6pm
▶ Divided into four modules, these practitioner courses are suitable both for those already working in, and those with little or no experience in, the healthcare field. The four-day introductory course gives a basic working knowledge for those wishing only to work on family and friends. Modules two and three refine the technique to a greater depth and include examinations. Module four covers additional procedures, accreditation and certification with Ossie and Elaine Rentsch, who learnt from Tom Bowen himself. Review workshops for practitioners also available.

British College of Naturopathy and Osteopathy
Lief House, 3 Sumpter Close, 120-122 Finchley Road, London NW3 5HR
Tel: 020 7435 6464
Fax: 020 7431 3630
Email: njwbcd@bcno.org.uk
Web: www.bcn.org.uk
Open: Mon-Fri 9am-5pm
▶ Offers a four-year full-time BSc Hons OSTMED course. A four-year BSc Hons NATMED course and also a one year MSc OSTMED course.

British Institute of Homœopathy
Cygnet House, Market Square, Staines TW18 4RH
Tel: 01784 440 467
Fax: 01784 449 887
Email: britinsthom@compuserve.com
Web: www.britishhom.com
Open: Mon-Fri 8.30am-6pm
▶ Established in 1987, the institute is now one of the largest and most respected bodies in distance learning courses in Homeopathy in the world with over 6,000 students in 67 countries. Diploma and post-graduate courses available by home study with expert personal tutors.

British School of Complementary Therapies
140 Harley Street, London W1N 1AH
Tel: 020 7224 2394
Fax: 020 7486 2513
Email: selfcentre@ukonline.co.uk
Web: www.bsct.co.uk
Open: Mon-Fri 9am-5.30pm
▶ The BSCT is accredited by the Institute of Complementary Medicine and The Association of Reflexology. Training courses offered leading to professional diplomas in Reflexology, Swedish massage and aromatherapy. A certificate course (2 days) in Indian head massage is also offered. Call for further information or a prospectus.

British School of Homeopathy
Homelands Cottage, Burrington EX37 9HF
Tel: 01769 520 462
Email: learnhomoeopathy@aol.com
Web: www.homoeopathy.co.uk
Open: 24hr answerphone
▶ Provides professional and self help training in Homeopathy. Runs part time and open learning courses. Part time courses are based in Bath or Birmingham. The courses are recognised by all the registering bodies for professional homeopaths.

British School of Reflex Zone Therapy (RZT) of The Feet
23 Marsh Hall, Talisman Way, Wembley Park, London HA9 8JJ
Tel: 020 8904 4825
Fax: 020 8904 4825
Open: Mon-Fri 9am-5pm
▶ Training courses for qualified midwives, nurses, physiotherapists and comparable health professions. Training lays equal emphasis on theory and practice, ensuring safe practice in a variety of settings, hospitals, clinics and private clininics. Syllabus comprises RZT of the back, hands and feet in health, acute sickness, chronic illness, midwifery, children. Courses validated at University Diploma level.

British School of Reflexology
Holistic Healing Centre, 92 Sheering Road, Harlow CM17 0JW
Tel: 01279 429 060
Fax: 01279 445 234
Email: reflexology.bsr@tesco.net
Web: www.footreflexlology.com
Open: Mon-Fri 9am-6pm
▶ Opened in 1988 after Ann Gillanders had spent several years as Director of the International Institute of Reflexology which brought modern Reflexology to the UK from America. An ongoing process of development has been followed to produce excellent courses for the professional therapist requiring recognition by the medical profession. Graduates are encouraged to join the Holistic

Association of Reflexologists, a member Association of the BCMA. Mail order books, charts and equipment from the above address.

Burton Manor College
Burton, Neston ch64 5sj
Tel: 0151 336 5172
Fax: 0151 336 6586
Email: info@burtonmanor.com
Web: www.burtonmanor.com
▶ Residential college set in beautiful grounds and gardens, surrounded by its own meadow in a village overlooking the Dee estuary and Welsh hills. The college is housed in a distinguished listed building. There are 49 bedrooms, 8 seminar rooms, 6 study rooms, a bar, lounge, dining rooms, art centre and day nursery. Aims to encourage and enable individuals to develop their full potential by providing a high quality and stimulating learning environment. Offers day, midweek and weekend courses including Aromatherapy, Reiki, Alexander Technique and Shiatsu, as well as Textiles, Photography, Art and Creative Studies.

Central School of Reflexology
15 King Street, Covent Garden,
London WC2E 8HN
Tel: 020 7240 1438
Fax: 020 7240 1438
Email: clsr@clara-net
Web: www.clsr.clara.net
Open: Mon-Fri 9am-5.30pm
▶ Reflexoloy practitioner course accredited by the Association of Reflexologists. The courses have been specially designed for individuals wishing to study for a new career and for those already in a caring profession. Courses start monthly from August to December, and in February, April and June, and comprise monthly weekend sessions over a nine month period. The school gives its graduates useful help in setting up a practice and is committed to helping them find work. Call for a prospectus.

College of Cranio-Sacral Therapy
9 St George's Mews,
Primrose Hill, London NW1 8XE
Tel: 0207 586 0148
Fax: 0207 586 9550
Email: info@cranio.co.uk
Web: www.cranio.co.uk
Open: Mon-Fri 9am-6pm
▶ Professional level training course in Cranio-Sacral Therapy, accredited by the Cranio-Sacral Therapy Association (UK). One or two year diploma courses are offered, taught over 6 six day stages or 18 weekends respectively. Short introductory courses are also offered at several locations around the country. Call for a course brochure and application form.

College of Healing
Runnings Park, Croft Bank,
West Malvern WR14 4DU
Tel: 01684 566 450
Fax: 01684 892 047
Email: info@collegeofhealing.freeserve.co.uk
Open: Mon-Fri 9am-5pm
▶ The first UK organisation to be established specifically to teach healing to individuals. It has continued at the leading edge of Healing tuition within this country from its early roots in 1983, offering a diverse programme of Healing tuition from Foundation to Post Graduate level. It is also the first organisation to have its courses accredited by the Open College Network, the first to offer a Tutor Training programme, the first to offer a Diploma in Healing for those wishing to take their study to a professional level and the first to shortly have this Diploma accredited by BTEC to level 4.

College of Homeopathy
Regent's College, Inner Circle,
Regent's Park, London NW1 4NS
Tel: 020 7487 4322
Fax: 020 7487 7675
Email: coh@homoepathic-education.com
Web: www.lcch.com
Open: Mon-Fri 9am-5pm
▶ Courses in homeopathy leading to a professional standard Licentiate award recognised by The Society of Homeopaths. The full-time course is run over 3 years comprising 3 days' attendance per week for 3 weeks per month. The part-time course is run on 11 weekend sessions per year over 4 years. Other courses offered include a MCH postgraduate award, and courses in anatomy and physiology. Contact Amber Harwood-Payne for admissions details.

College of Integrated Chinese Medicine
19 Castle Street, Reading RG1 7SB
Tel: 0118 950 8880
Fax: 0118 950 8890
Email: info@cicm.org.uk
Web: www.cicm.org.uk
Open: Mon-Sun 9am-6pm
▶ The largest college for Acupuncture in the UK. It trains practitioners in an integrated style. This style uses the strengths of Yin and Yang theory and five element constitutional diagnosis in one integrated whole. Its aim is to produce the highest quality practitioners who can diagnose both the person and the complaint using the concepts of Traditional Chinese Medicine. Courses start in October and April.

College of Natural Nutrition
1 Halthaies, Bradninch,
near Exeter EX5 4LQ
Tel: 01392 881 091
Fax: 01392 881 122
Email: cnn@globalnet.co.uk
Web: www.natnut.co.uk
Open: Mon-Fri 9.30am-5pm
▶ One of the leading alternative nutritional colleges in the UK. Offers the opportunity to explore a unique holistic therapy, based upon a naturopathic philosophy that treats the physical, mental and emotional self as a whole being. Practitioner, one-year intensive course (100 hours in-class tuition) available as well as practitioner correspondence course. Call or write for a prospectus.

College of Natural Therapy
133 Gatley Road, Gatley,
Cheadle SK8 4PD
Tel: 0161 491 4313
Fax: 0161 491 4190
Email: info@colnat.co.uk
Web: www.colnat.co.uk
Open: Mon-Thurs 8.30am-3.30pm
▶ Diploma correspondence courses are offered in Herbal Medicine, Homeopathy, Naturopathy and Nutrition. Founded in 1979, the college enjoys an excellent reputation for its high standards of training which is reflected in the content and quality of the courses.

College of Naturopathic and Complementary Medicine
73 Gardenwood Road, East Grinstead RH19 1RX
Tel: 01342 410 505
Fax: 01342 410 909
Email: info@bestcare-uk.com
Web: www.naturopathy-uk.com
Open: Mon-Fri 8am-8pm
▶ The term 'naturopath' describes the professional who applies natural therapy in practice. Its spectrum comprises fasting, detoxification, nutrition and water treatments as well as Homeopathy, Acupuncture, Herbal Medicine and Reflexology, etc. The CNM runs courses in Central London and Manchester. After successful full or part-time study, students get a Diploma which is fully recognised.

College of Osteopaths Educational Trust
13 Furzehill Road,
Borehamwood WD6 2DG
Tel: 020 8905 1937
Fax: 020 8953 0320
Email: Rachelives@aol.com
Open: Mon-Fri 9am-5.30pm
▶ Offers a five-year 'Extended Pathway Course' leading to a BSc (Hons) Osteopathy in collaboration with Middlesex University. Lecture/Seminar attendance in years one to five is supplemented by required clinical practice throughout the course. Entry requirements are two 'A' levels (preferably in the sciences). A Science Access course is available for entry into other areas. Call for a prospectus.

College of Psychic Studies
16 Queensberry Place,
London SW7 2EB
Tel: 020 7589 3292
Fax: 020 7589 2824
Email: cpstudies@aol.com
Web: www.psychic-studies.org.uk
Open: Mon-Thurs 10am-7.30pm;
Fri 10am-4.30pm
▶ Founded in 1884, the College is an educational charity which seeks to

promote spiritual values and a greater understanding of the wider areas of human consciousness, welcoming the truths of all spiritual traditions and, equally, each and every individual. All lectures, workshops and courses are devoted to encouraging awareness and understanding of these values. For a programme of courses, contact the above number.

Combined Colleges of Homœopathy
Hanemann House,
32 Welbeck Street, London W1M 7PG
Tel: 020 7487 4322
Fax: 020 7487 4299
Email: coh@homoeopathic-education.com
Web: www.lcch.com
Open: Mon-Fri 9am-5pm
▶ Central admissions and administration for a group of homoeopathic colleges, with branches throughout the UK. All full-time and part-time Licentiate, Membership and BSc Degree courses are recognised or conditionally recognised by Society of Homoeopaths and Homœopathic Medical Association. Introduction to Homœopathy, Anatomy & Physiology, home study and short courses are also available. Call for a prospectuses.

Craniosacral Therapy Trust
77 Cranwich Road,
Stamford Hill, London N16 5JA
Tel: 020 7502 1126
Fax: 020 7502 1126
Email: gedsumner@compuserve.com
Web: www.craniosacral.co.uk
Open: Mon-Fri 9am-5.30pm
▶ Provides professional training courses that integrate work within the field over the past 80 years. Comprehensive training over a period of one to two years leads to accreditation with the Craniosacral Therapy Association of the UK.

Devon School of Shiatsu
The Coach House, Buckyette Farm,
Littlehempston, Totnes TQ9 6ND
Tel/Fax: 01803 762 593
Email: info@devonshiatsu.co.uk
Web: www.devonshiatsu.co.uk
Open: Mon-Wed 1.30pm-4.30pm; Thur 12pm-3pm

▶ Runs weekend courses and a three-year Practitioner Training Course leading to a professional qualification. All courses are on weekends, with some additional home study. Has been running courses for over 15 years and has well trained, experienced teachers. The school has its own purpose-built premises in the beautiful Devonshire countryside three miles from Totnes. Small class sizes allow plenty of individual guidance and a supportive, friendly and fun learning environment.

East West College of Herbalism
Hartswood, Marsh Green,
Hartfield TN7 4ET
Tel: 01342 822 312
Fax: 01342 826 347
Email: ewcolherb@aol.com
▶ Offers an introductory professional Diploma in Herbalism. Herbal seminars with Dr Michael Tierra and Lesley Tierra. Ayurvedic studies course by Dr David Frawley. Feng Shui consultations. Call for a prospectus.

European College of Bowen Studies
38 Portway, Frome BA11 1QU
Tel: 01373 461 873
Fax: 01373 461 873
Email: bowen@globalnet.co.uk
Web: www.TheBowenTechnique.com
Open: Mon-Fri 9am-5.30pm
▶ Since 1994, the College has offered full tuition and certification in the Bowen Technique in Europe. With years of experience, Julian Baker and his company offer comprehensive training in this powerful, effective therapy. ECBS teachers are all experienced Bowen therapists and have undergone over 300 hours of specialised teacher training. Full training comprises five levels of instruction; courses are offered in venues around the UK throughout the year. Technical and practical support are available to therapists and their clients at all times. Office staff are available to answer any queries five days a week.

European Shiatsu School
High Banks, Lockeridge,
Marlborough SN8 4EQ

Tel: 01672 513 444
Fax: 01672 861 459
Email: info@shiatsu.org.uk
Web: www.shiatsu.org.uk
Open: Mon-Fri 10.30am-5.30pm
▶ Has schools throughout the UK and Europe offering courses from beginner to Diploma level and which range from one weekend to three years in length, including residential intensive options. Classes are taught by leading Shiatsu Society registered teachers. Established in 1985, the School has the most flexible and extensive range of Shiatsu study options in Europe.

Faculty of Homœopathy
15 Clerkenwell Close,
London EC1R 0AA
Tel: 020 7566 7810
Fax: 020 7566 7815
Email: info@trusthomoeopathy.com
Web: www.trusthomoeopathy.org
Open: Mon-Fri 9am-5pm
▶ The Faculty of Homœopathy was incorporated by an Act of Parliament in 1950 to regulate the education, training and practice of Homeopathy by doctors, vets, dentists and other healthcare professionals. The Faculty's internationally recognised qualifications are LFHom (licenced Associate), MFHom (Member of the Faculty of Homœopathy) and FFHom (Fellow of the Faculty of Homœopathy) and are obtained following postgraduate study at one of four teaching centres in the UK leading to the Faculty's Primary Health Care and Membership Examinations. A free list of doctors qualified in Homeopathy, who practise on the NHS and privately, is available on request.

Feng Shui Network International
8 Kings Court, Pateley Bridge,
Harrogate HG3 5JW
Tel: 0700 033 6474
Fax: 01423 712 869
Email: Feng1@aol.com
Web: www.FengShuiNet.com
Open: Mon-Fri 9am-5.30pm
▶ The world's leading school of Feng Shui launches a new and exciting education programme for 1999. This highly respected professional training programme offers the widest selection of teaching with some of the world's most renowned Feng Shui practitioners and authors. Three new ways to train include for the first time a flexible home study course, a fast-track intensive option and the original two year study programme. Courses are part-time and cover all aspects of Feng Shui. Call for more information.

Flower Essence Fellowship
Northbreach, Ashton Hill,
Corston, Nr Bath BA2 9EY
Tel: 01225 872663
Fax: 01225 874988
▶ One of the Fellowship's most important aims is to share teachings and research with individuals who are interested in Flower Essence Therapy. The FEF has developed a Professional Course of Training and a series of weekend workshops in Flower Essence Therapy. Being a member of the FEF entitles you to 10% off all FEF courses and Essences, a quarterly newsletter which informs you about what has been happening in the area of Flower Therapy both in the UK and Europe. Call for more information.

Foundation for Emotional Therapy
20 Coldicott Gardens, Cheltenham Road, Evesham WR11 6JW
Tel: 01202 477 858
Fax: 01202 477 858
Open: Mon-Fri 9am-5pm
▶ Aims to provide trained Emotional Therapists to help people who are suffering emotional turmoil, persistant unhappiness, depression, difficult relationships. Seeks to promote healing of original emotional wounds through the feelings. Training consists of a 10-day Foundation course (5 weekends over 5 months), 10 one-day workshops and an assessment weekend.

Gestalt Centre
First Floor, 62 Paul Street,
London ECZA 4NA
Tel: 020 7613 4480
Fax: 020 7613 4737
Email: gestaltcentre@dial.pipex.com
Open: Mon-Fri 8am-5pm
▶ Offers a part-time MA in Gestalt Psychotherapy from the University of

Health

North London. Graduates are eligible for inclusion on the UK Council for Psychotherapy (UKCP) register. Also offers a two-year Diploma in Counselling accredited by the BAC. In addition, the centre provides a client referral service including low cost therapy for individuals and groups, a short course programme and consultation rooms for hire. The Gestalt Centre is located in a newly refurbished premises in the heart of London.

Hahnemann College of Homeopathy
164 Ballards Road,
Dagenham RM10 9AB
Tel/Fax: *020 8984 9240*
Open: *Mon-Fri 9am-5pm*
▶ Provides three or four year part-time Diploma courses and one year post-graduate courses in Homoeopathy. Ideal for health care practitioners or others looking for a potentially worthwhile career in natural medicine. This powerful but gentle system of medicine offers remedies which have no known side effects and are non-addictive. Successful students may use the designated letters DHom(med), and PG Hom for post-graduates. The courses lead to prospective membership of the Homeopathic Medical Association (HMA). For further details and a free college prospectus, contact the secretary on the number above.

Healing Tao Centre and Zen School of Shiatsu
East West Centre, 188 Old Street,
London EC1V 9BP
Tel: *0700 078 1195*
Email: *enquiries@healing-tao.co.uk*
Web: *www.healing-tao.co.uk (and)*
www.learn-shiatsu.co.uk
▶ Zen Shiatsu, Taoist Healing including Taoist Massage and Taoist Colour Therapy, Tai Chi, Qi Gong, Taoist Tantra, Meditation and self-development are on the menu at the Centre which offers training and treatments based on the teachings of Taoist Master Mantak Chia by his personal student and authorised instructor, Kris Larthe. Training offered to qualification standards as recognised by the ICM, The Shiatsu Society of Great Britain, and the Guild of Complementary Practitioners.

Herm College
Wayland Farm, Stockland,
near Bridgewater TA5 2PY
Tel/Fax: *01278 653 808*
Open: *24hour answer phone*
▶ Small, independent college offering specialist, weekend residential, self-development and Yoga workshops; and professional training courses in therapeutic counselling. Situated in a Somerset farmhouse close to the sea and a three hour journey from London, it offers supportive, rigorous and thorough, small group trainings in a relaxed, beautiful setting. Hermes was the Greek god for guiding souls through times of change. For a free, illustrated brochure, call or write to the address above.

Holistic Health Consultancy and College
94 Grosvenor Road,
London SW1V 3LF
Tel: *020 7834 3578*
Fax: *020 7834 3579*
Web:
www.natural-healing.co.uk/iridology
Open: *Mon & Tues 8am-6pm;*
Wed & Thurs 10am-6pm
▶ Established in 1993, the College provides Diploma courses in Iridology. There is a six to eight month Intensive Iridology course for practitioners only. There are also courses for beginners, for those wishing to complement Iridology with therapeutics such as Naturopathy, Western Herbal Medicine, Nutrition and a basic grounding in Homeopathy, along with Anatomy and Physiology. The 18-module Naturopathic Iridology Course takes 18-24 months. These courses are affiliated to the Euorpean Herbal practitioners Association Guild of Naturopathy and Iridology Institute.

Hygeia College of Colour Therapy
Brook House, Avening,
Tetbury GL8 8NS
Tel: *01453 832 150*
Fax: *01453 835 757*
Open: *Mon-Fri 9am-5pm*
▶ Trains health practitioners or any applicants who wish to seriously learn the techniques and application of colour to improve the health status of their clients. Students are required to attend all the weekend courses and complete the homework. Practicals are part of the training. At the end of the Advanced Course, students sit an exam and enter a full year of probation. At the end of this year, they receive their Diploma, provided they have attained a pass mark at all stages. Students who have been successful practitioners for two or more years may submit a thesis and earn the Hygeia Fellowship document. The College is registered with the ICM and IACT.

Indian Champissage Head Massage Course
136 Holloway Road, London N7 8DD
Tel: *020 7609 3590*
Fax: *020 7607 4228*
Email:
Meth@indianchampissage.com
Web: *www.indianchampissage.com*
▶ Short intensive courses in Indian head massage (Champi is an Indian word for head massage) which is based on traditional massage techniques used on head, neck, shoulder and face for healing and relaxation in India for over a thousand years. The course is structured over 5 days (including 2 weekends) and includes written study, case-work and an exam. Call for further details. Also has a clinic offering a range of body and head massage, Reiki, natural face lift and Osteopathy.

Institute of Psychosynthesis
65a Watford Way, Hendon,
London NW4 3AQ
Tel: *020 8202 4525*
Fax: *020 8202 6166*
Email: *institute@psychosynthesis.org*
Web: *www.psychosynthesis.org/uk*
Open: *Mon-Fri 9am-6pm*
▶ Established in 1973 with the encouragement and support of Roberto Assagiolo, founder of psychosynthesis, to actualise its principals and practice. This is carried out through training professionals, through research, publishing and offering educational, counselling and Psychotherapy services to the general public. Offers in-depth professional training programmes in both psychosynthesis counselling and Psychotherapy, advanced post-graduate programmes for supervisors, trainers and teachers, as well as the application of psychosynthesis to other fields of service.

Institute of Traditional Herbal Medicine and Aromatherapy
Oaklands, Postman's Lane,
Little Baddow, Chelmsford CM3 4SF
Tel: *01245 223187*
Fax: *01245 222152*
Email:
info@aromatherapy-studies.com
Web: *www.aromtherapy.com*
Open: *Mon-Fri 9am-6pm*
▶ The Institute has offered professional Aromatherapy training since 1987 and currently holds all its courses at Regent's College in central London's Regent's Park. Offers a one-year Diploma course in Aromatherapy and Therapeutic Massage, accredited by the Register of Qualified Aromatherapists (RQA), a member of the AOC. Also offers training courses in Aromatic Indian Head Massage and Acupressure Massage Therapy.

International Kinesiology College
143a Iffley Road, Oxford, OX4 1EJ
Tel: *01865 798 885*
Fax: *01865 798 885*
Email: *natkin@globalnet.uk*
▶ Formed in 1990 to oversee the Touch for Health training worldwide, the College is represented by Faculty members in more than 20 countries.

Linda Harness School of Holistic Massage
Swanfleet Centre, 93 Fortis Road,
London NW5 1AG
Tel: *020 7419 1325*
Open: *Mon-Fri 9.30am-6pm*
▶ A well-established School – teaching since 1986 and with a 97% pass rate – which offers an introduction to holistic massage, holistic massage practitioner training (ITEC

Diploma) and on-site massage certificate training. Emphasis is holistic, professional and friendly, with courses in: Anatomy; Physiology and Pathology; a wide range of massage skills; practitioner development (breath, posture, energy work, grounding) and a team of experienced, skilled and qualified tutors. Practitioner training last five months.

Liverpool John Moores University, School of Pharmacy and Chemistry
Byrom Street, Liverpool, L3 3AF
Tel: 0151 231 2258
Fax: 0151 231 2170
Email: recruitment@livjm.ac.uk & j.hughes@livjm.ac.uk
Web: www.livjm.ac.uk
Open: Mon-Fri 9am-5pm (24 hour answerphone)
▶ Offers a Certificate/Diploma of Higher Education in Aromatherapy. The part-time course commences in January each year. Attendance for one weekend per month, plus a one week intensive in July each year. The course combines practical learning (massage) with academic expertise dedicated to the development of Aromatherapy as a healthcare profession in its own right.

London College of Massage
5 Newman Passage, London W1P 3PF
Tel: 020 7323 3574
Fax: 020 7367 7125
Email: admin@massagelondon.com
Web: www.massagelondon.com
Open: Mon-Fri 11am-7pm
▶ Situated in the heart of London, the College, established in 1987, teaches massage vocationally and professionally. As well as courses and workshops there is a professional complementary therapy clinic. Also provides a range of products and corporate services for professional and public alike. Call for more information.

London College of Traditional Acupuncture & Oriental Medicine
1st Floor, HR House, 447 High Road, North Finchley, London N12 0AZ
Tel: 020 8371 0820
Fax: 020 8371 0830
Email: lcta@bogo.co.uk
Web: www.ltca.com\lcta
Open: Mon-Fri 9am-5.30pm
▶ Full or part-time professional training courses in traditional Acupuncture and a part-time course in Oriental Herbal Medicine taught by staff from the UK, China and Vietnam. Runs presentation days over the summer for prospective trainees to learn more about the college. The Teaching Clinics offer students supervised practise in diagnosing and treating patients.

London School of Eclectic Therapies Ltd
808A High Road, North Finchley, London N12 9QU
Tel: 020 8446 2210
Fax: 020 8446 2210
Email: Info@icet.net
Web: www.icet.net
Open: Mon-Fri 10am-9.30pm
▶ Umbrella organisation for the Association of Stress Management Counsellors, the Association of GOLD Counsellors and the London School of Eclectic Hypnotherapy and Psychotherapy. Offers training in Hypnotherapy and Psychotherapy, NLP, Gold Counselling and Stress Management Counselling. The School has developed a unique training program with an eclectic approach. Courses are approved by UKCHO and other organisations. An option of in-house and correspondence courses are offered.

Manchester School of Massage
77 Russell Road, Manchester M16 8AR
Tel: 0161 862 9752
Fax: 0161 881 3863
Email: bev@schoolof massage.com
Web: www.schoolofmssage.co.uk
Open: Mon-Sun 9am-9pm
▶ Certificate and diploma courses in massage, aromatherapy massage and Reflexology and Indian Head Massage. Call for course details.

McTimoney Chiropractic College (Oxford) Limited
22-26 Ock Street, Abingdon OX14 5SH
Tel: 01235 523 336
Fax: 01235 523 576
Email: chiropractic@mctimoney-college.ac.uk
Open: 9am-5pm 7 days a week
▶ McTimoney Chiropractic College is the largest independent college in the UK offering distance learning courses in chiropractic. Founded nearly 30 years ago, the College has graduated 400 practitioners, which represents over a third of the chiropractors in the UK today. The College offers a four-year honours degree (validated by the University of Wales) in human chiropractic with emphasis on the McTimoney method of chiropractic. The mixed mode study includes distance learning of academic modules, together with College based lectures, tutorials, practicals, sessions and placements. In addition, the College offers a full-time chiropractic degree course in conjunction with Westminster University, London. Applicants should usually possess two A-levels in Science subjects, although other qualifications and experience are taken into account. An Access course is available for those without the necessary Science background. For more information on how to become a chiropractor, or a for a McTimoney chirpractor in your area, contact the College via email or call on the above number.

Metanoia Institute – Counselling and Psychotherapy
13 North Common Road, Ealing, London W5 2QB
Tel: 020 8579 2505
Fax: 020 8566 4349
Email: kate@metanoia.ac.uk
Web: www.the.met.demon.co.uk
Open: Mon-Fri 9am-5pm
▶ Metanoia offers nationally and internationally accredited Masters/Doctorate, MSc, post-graduate, BA (hons) and diploma courses in a number of counselling and Psychotherapy approaches. Degree courses are validated by Middlesex University. Graduation from the Gestalt, Integrative and Transactional Analysis Psychotherapy courses leads to UKCP Registration, with the option of taking an MSc degree. Counselling courses are offered at diploma and degree level. Attendance at an introductory workshop is a prerequisite of all courses.

National College of Hypnosis and Psychotherapy
12 Cross Street, Nelson BB9 7EN
Tel: 01282 699 378
Fax: 01282 698 633
Email: Hypnosis_NCHP@CompuServe.com
Web: www.nchp.clarets.co.uk
Open: Mon-Fri 9.30am-12.30pm; 1.30pm-5.30pm
▶ Provides a thorough, integrated training in hypno-psychotherapy, with comprehensive coverage of hypnotherapeutic techniques and various schools of psychological thought. The College has training venues in London, Edinburgh and Cheshire. Formal assessment is by written assignments, written and practical examinations and submission of a research-based dissertation (all externally marked and moderated). The performance and suitability of students is also continually informally assessed by course tutors. The National College is accredited by the British Accreditation Council for Independent Further and Higher Education.

National School of Hypnosis and Psychotherapy
28 Finsbury Park Road, London N4 2JX
Tel: 020 7359 6991
Web: www.users.globalnet.co.uk/~enneauk
Open: Contact by letter in first instance (interviews by arrangement)
▶ Hypnotherapy training at the N-SHAP School of Ericksonian Hypnosis (established in 1980). Offers part-time training courses which are recognised nationally. Call, or use website, to obtain a free 22-page guide, which explains syllabus, training, clinical supervision, professional registration and legislation concerning the practice of hypnotherapy.

Natural Therapeutic Research Trust
The Old Rectory, Gislingham, near Eye IP23 8JD
Tel: *01379 783 527*
Fax: *01379 783 653*
Open: *10am-1pm and 2pm-5pm*
▶ Now offers mainly weekend workshops for different subjects helpful to health including Dietetic Nutrition, Osteopathy, Acupuncture and Homeopathy. Has the only Pyramid Tank in the UK.

Northern College of Acupuncture
61 Mickelgate, York YO1 6LJ
Tel: *01904 343305*
Fax: *01904 330370*
Email: *info@chinese-medicine.co.uk*
Web: *www.chinese-medicine-co.uk*
Open: *Mon-Fri 9am-5pm*
▶ The college strongly believes in Chinese medicine's potential for healing and transformation at all levels. Has been educating acupuncturists since 1988, and has taken a leading role in the development of the profession in the UK. Their Acupuncture course was the first to be validated at degree level in the UK. The college prides itself on pioneering high standards in professional education, as well as providing comprehensive training in Chinese medicine. They are currently recruiting for the October 2001 intake of a part-time Diploma in Acupuncture, with the option to gain an MSc validated by the University of Wales. For qualified acupuncturists, there is a range of options offered, including a Diploma in Chinese Herbal medicine; a Post-registration MSc and a varied programme of seminars and short courses.

Oriental Therapy International
2 Lime Tree Terrace, Highfields, Burwash TN19 7HE
Tel: *01435 883 077*
Fax: *01435 883 707*
Email: *wrio@orientaltherapy.co.uk*
Web: *www.orientaltherapy.co.uk*
Open: *Mon-Fri 9am-6pm*
▶ The purpose of OTI is to provide courses and classes in a range of the Oriental Qi-based health and healing arts. The teaching is of the highest standard and most of the courses are run in London and East Sussex. The programme includes Thai Yoga Massage, Accupuncture seminars, Reiki, Anatomy and Physiology (accelerated learning), Qi Gong, Learn Power Seminars, Feng Shui, Indian Head Massage and Thai Yoga Massage holiday courses in Thailand.

Osteopathic Information Service
General Osteopathic Council (GOsC), Osteopathy House, 176 Tower Bridge Road, London SE1 3LU
Tel: *020 7357 6655*
Fax: *020 7357 0011*
Email: *margaretv@osteopathy.org.uk*
Web: *www.osteopathy.org.uk*
Open: *9am-5pm telephone information service*
▶ Information service run by the GOsC, the organisation charged with implementing the Osteopathic Act 1993 and bringing in statutory regulation for the profession. The new register opened on May 1998 and practising osetopaths have had two years in which to apply to become registered.

Oxford College of Chiropractic
The Old Post Office, Cherry Street, Stratton Audley, near Bicester OX6 9BA
Tel/Fax: *01869 277 111*
Email: *OCC.Admin@btinternet.com*
Open: *Mon-Fri 9am-5pm*
▶ The course starts each September, and is designed to enable people to study Chiropractic whilst continuing in their existing employment. Course duration is currently four years and the primary method taught is McTimoney-Corley technique. The course of the study is mixed-mode, with students studying much of the academic work at home based on set assignments and notes supplied by the college, which includes lectures, tests, examinations and closely supervised training in palpation, adjustment and manipulative techniques. The educational programme is evolving rapidly to meet the requirements for UK National Registration. The College now has secured BSc honours degree validation with Oxford Brookes University.

Plaskett Nutritional Medicine College
14 Southgate Chambers, Launceston PL15 9DY
Tel: *01566 86118*
Fax: *01566 86301*
Email: *lgplaskett@aol.com*
Web: *www.pnmcollege.com*
Open: *Mon-Fri 9.30am-5.30pm*
▶ Offers professional Diploma courses by distance learning, with optional central London attendance weekends. Its teaching can be accredited by the University of Exeter at postgraduate level. Courses are delivered by the principal, Dr Lawrence Plaskett, and his team of practitioner tutors, based upon years of clinical experience and scientific validation. Once qualified, students usually establish themselves in their own private practice or make arrangements to join an Alternative Therapy Clinic on a self-employed basis.

Practitioners School of Reflexology
Administrative Office, 47 Leyborne Park, Kew, Richmond TW9 3HB
Tel: *020 8948 2380*
Fax: *020 8255 0963*
Open: *Mon-Fri 9.30am-5pm*
▶ Foundation and practitioner training courses in Reflexology accredited by the Association of Reflexologists, held monthly over 12 Sundays at St Mary's University in Twickenham. Call for a prospectus.

Premier Training and Development Ltd
Parade House, 70 Fore Street, Trowbridge BA14 8HQ
Tel: *01225 353 555*
Fax: *01225 353 556*
Email: *enquiries@premiertd.co.uk*
Open: *Mon-Thur 8.30am-5.30pm; Fri 8.30am-4.30pm*
▶ Provides vocational training courses for the health & fitness industry. Premier's qualifiactions are respect-

---

Northern College of Acupuncture

Are you looking for a new direction?

Studying acupuncture can offer you positive life and career change.

Embark on a journey of personal and professional discovery as you explore Chinese medicine and its profound insights into the understanding of health and disease.

Part-time Diploma in Acupuncture

with an option to gain an MSc validated by the University of Wales

Contact us for the prospectus
Northern College of Acupuncture
61 Micklegate, York YO1 6LJ
Telephone: (01904) 343305
e-mail: info@chinese-medicine.co.uk
website: www.chinese-medicine.co.uk

ed throughout the industry and are accepted by major health club operators such as David Lloyd, Fitness First and Holmes Place. The courses are specifically designed for anyone wishing to pursue a career as a personal trainer, sports therapist or nutritionist. Call for further deatils.

Rainbow Bridge Studio
7 Hastings Road, Crawley RH10 7AL
Tel: 01293 408 554
Email: smith9157@yahoo.com
Web: www.uktaro.co.uk
Open: Mon-Fri 9am-4pm
By appointment at any other time
▶ Reiki and Seichem attunements and treatments. There are five-day Diploma Tarot courses available as well as correspondance courses. Taped telephone readings and postal readings.

Reiki Experience
6 Croftersvale Park,
Main Street Barlestone,
Nuneaton CV13 0ED
Tel: 01455 292 083;
Mobile 07961 344 185
▶ Teaches Tera Mai Reiki and Seichem. For those who have already done traditional Reiki, re-attuning to the Tera Mai system of Reiki and Seichem is well worth thinking about. Certificates are given as well as full backup and help at any time that it is needed. Also runs regular healing evenings for all to enjoy. Courses are kept small to ensure that all students get full, intensive teaching. For more information, call the above number.

Rowan School of Healing and Personal Development
126 Chase Way, Southgate,
London N14 5DH
Tel: 0208 368 9868
Fax: 015395 52047
Email: rowan-school@virgin.net
Open: Mon-Fri 9am-5.30pm
▶ Provides beginners' courses and professional training. The approach combines the ancient art of laying on hands with modern humanistic and transpersonal psychology. Adheres to the Confederation of Healing Organisation's Code of Ethics and Practice, and courses are recognised by the ATH and the HF. Experience the satisfaction of learning to use energy awareness in everyday life.

Ruth White Yoga Centre
Church Farm House,
Springclose Lane, Cheam
Tel: 020 8644 0309
Fax: 020 8287 5318
▶ Runs Yoga weekends including bed and board. The centre can take up to 40 people at a time; all meals are vegetarian. Courses cater for complete beginners and the more experienced. Both John and Ruth White teach Iyengar Tradition.

School of Complementary Health
38 South Street,
Exeter EX1 1ED
Tel: 01392 410 954
Fax: 01392 5410 954
Email: 101650.60@compuserve.com
Open: Mon-Fri 9am-5pm
▶ Offers comprehensive training in therapeutic skills to those intending to set up in practice or established professionals who wish to integrate complementary expertise into their caring. The school began as a training centre in 1983 and presently occupies a spacious and secluded location in central Exeter. Accommodation includes a large seminar room, lecture studios, and treatment and practice areas. The School incorporates The Café, situated on the ground floor, where fresh menus and relaxed eating are poromoted. For a prospectus, call the number above or write.

School of Homœopathy
Yondercott House,
Uffculme EX15 3DR
Tel: 01873 856 872
Fax: 01873 858 962
Email: sgracie@alternative.demon.co.uk
Web: www.homeopathyschool.com
Open: Mon-Fri 9.30am-5.30pm
▶ Professional training courses around the world. Challenging, stimulating and creative study that will provide a thorough and enjoyable understanding of classical Hahnemannian Homeopathy. Distance learning courses in any country, or 4-year part-time attendance courses in Devon, England and in New York. Practitioner training at the highest standards since 1981. Visit the website or call for details.

School of Meditation
158 Holland Park Avenue,
London W11 4UH
Tel: 020 7603 6116
Fax: 020 7603 6116
Web: www.schoolofmeditation.org
Open: Mon-Fri 9.30am-4pm;
evening events for the public
▶ Run by those who meditate, the school's only paid staff is one member who runs the office. Since the early Sixties, when the school was formed, contact has been maintained with the head of the tradition from which the School's method of meditation comes, and regular guidance and confirmation have been received on the way the School operates and on the practice of meditation. The School is a registered charity and holds regular public meetings at which you can learn about meditation and talk to someone about the method.

School of Natural Health Sciences
Dept 10, 2 Lansdown Row,
Berkeley Square, London W1X 8HL
Tel: 020 7413 957
Fax: 020 7493 4935
Email: trinsnhs@teleline.es
Web: www.members.xoom.com/schatsc
Open: Mon-Fri 9am-5pm
▶ Tutored diploma correspondence study courses in a range of complementary therapies including Acupressure, Herbalism, Aromatherapy, Homeopathy and Reflexology. Also relaxation therapy, sports psychology and stress management. Plus 24 further courses, both tutored and self study. Degree courses in each subject available. Members of the Complimentary Medical Association (CMA).

Sciences & Department of Social Work
University of Salford, Allerton Building,
Frederick Road, Salford M6 6PU
Tel: 0161 295 2426
Fax: 0161 295 2378
Email: enquiries@health-sci.salford.ac.uk
Web: www.salford.ac.uk
Open: Mon-Fri 9am-5pm
▶ Offers a BSc (Hons) in Complementary Medicine and Health Sciences, including modules in Reflexology, stress management and homeopathy (in association with the NW College of Homeopathy). Also, a BSc (Hons) in Counselling Studies and Complementary Medicine.

Shiatsu College of London
Unit 62, Pall Mall Deposit, 126 Barbly Road, London W10 6BL
Tel: 020 8987 0208
Fax: 020 8987 0208
Web: www.shiatsucollege.co.uk
Open: Friday afternoon clinic open to public 0208964 1449
▶ A network of shiatsu schools throughout the UK are co-ordinated through this college which offers a number of courses including introductory weekend courses, a three year practitioner training course and a postgraduate course. A student clinic and graduate support programme are also offered.

South Trafford College
Manchester Road, Timperely,
Altringham WA14 5PQ
Tel: 0161 952 4600
Fax: 0161 952 4672
Open: Mon-Fri 9am-5pm
▶ Reflexology practitioner training course accredited by the Association of Reflexologists. Full and part time Health & Holistic, Sports Therapy courses and a full time, one year Stress Management course. Call for a prospectus.

Stress Management Training Institute
Foxhills, 30 Victoria Avenue,
Shanklin PO37 6LS
Tel: 01983 868 166
Fax: 01983 866 666
Email: admin@smit.org
Web: www.smit.org
Open: Mon-Fri 9am-4pm
▶ Founded in 1972, the Institute is a centre of excellence with external validation providing a range of training in Stress Management, Relaxation,

Massage, Aromatherapy and Applied Cognitive Therapy. Specialists in intensive distance learning packages which include residential block tutorials based at Foxhills. Workshops and seminars can be arranged for business and organisations including on-site training if required. A wide range of self-help materials and resources is available to the public.

Tisserand Institute
23-31 Beaver Lane,
London W6 9AP
Tel: 020 8748 1060
Fax: 020 8748 1364
Open: Tues-Thurs 9am-5pm
▶ Full or part-time aromatherapy Diploma course accredited by the RQA at a purpose-built school in West London offering holistic massage and aromatherpy. Call for further details at head office on 01273 206640

TouchPro Institute of Chair Massage
176 Melrose Avenue,
London NW2 4JY
Tel: 020 8450 3366
Fax: 020 8450 2026
Email: uk@touchpro.org.uk
Web: www.touchpro.org
Open: Mon-Fri 9am-6pm
▶ Training in on-site chair massage following the TPI sequence which incorporates advanced acupressure and massage techniques. This course is open only to people with massage technique qualifications.

UK College for Complementary Health Care Studies
St Charles Hospital,
Exmoor Street, London W10 6DZ
Tel: 0800 783 5130
Fax: 020 8964 1207
Email: info@ukcollege.com
Web: www.ukcollege.com
Open: Mon-Fri 9am-5pm
▶ Offers training for Hypnotherapy, Counselling, Reflexology, Massage and Aromatherapy, leading to BTEC, City and Guilds and Vocational Awards International Awards. Modular designed programmes delivered in partnership with De Montfort University, part-time, from interest-only to practitioner level qualifications. Call for a free prospectus, or to reserve a place on the introductory days and free open sessions.

University of Greenwich School of Health
Mansion Site, Bexley Road,
Eltham, London SE9 2PQ
Tel: 020 8331 8494
Fax: 020 8331 9160
Email: Margaret.Denise.Tiran@gre.ac.uk & info@gre.ac.uk
Web: www.greenwich.ac.uk
Open: Mon-Fri 9am-5pm
▶ The BSc (Hons) Complementary Therapies offers students a choice of three routes: a Generic Route, enabling them to study the broad subject of complementary medicine but not necessarily involving the acquisition of skills and knowledge in a specific therapy; the Aromatherapy Specialism, and the Stress Management Specialism. The students on these latter two routes will be eligible for registration with the Guild of Complementary Practitioners as Aromatherapists or Stress Management practitioners.

University of Westminster
115 New Cavendish Street,
London W1M 8JS
Tel: 020 7911 5000
Fax: 020 7911 5709
Email: cavadmin@wmin.ac.uk regent@wmin.ac.uk
Web: www.wmin.ac.uk
Open: Mon-Fri 9am-5.30pm
▶ The Centre for Community Care and Primary Health is a specialist unit. Its courses and research share a common aim of facilitating an integrated, responsive whole-person approach to health. The University, in collaboration with the London School of Acupuncture and Traditional Chinese Medicine and the London College of Classical Homeopathy, has developed a unique portfolio of BSc Honours degree courses in complementary therapies including Acupuncture and Homeopathy as well as Herbal Medicine, Nutritional Therapy and Chiropractic in collaboration with the McTimoney Chiropractic College.

Whitefriars College
129 Orford Lane,
Warrington WA2 7AR
Tel: 01244 301 246
Fax: 01244 303 133
▶ Offers courses in holistic therapies incorporating home study as well as optional practical training at own purpose built therapy rooms. On completition of a course, you will be automatically entered onto the Guild of Holistic Therapists. Many courses are internationally recognised, and they include acupressure, aromatherpay, herbalism, Reflexology, shiatsu, positive life skills, neuro linguistic programming, allergy testing, and much more.

ORGANISATIONS

Action Against Allergy
PO Box 278, Twickenham TW1 4QQ
Tel: 020 8892 2711
▶ Registered charity providing information to those made chronically ill through different forms of allergy and to those who care for them. Encourages diagnosis and treatment through the national health service and maintains a register of nationwide resources. Co-ordinating an information centre on all aspects of allergy and allergy-related illness and on relevant treatments. Raises funds for vital research into the causes and treatment of allergic illness. Also provides the *Allergy Newsletter*, a referral system, a Talk-Line and advice.

Anthroposophical Medical Association
c/o Park Attwood Clinic,
Trimpley, Bewdley DY12 1RE
Tel: 01299 861 444/01299 861 561
Fax: 01299 861 375
Email: movementoffice@amt.btinternet.com
Open: 24hour helpline
▶ Open to all doctors, pharmacists and medical and pharmaceutical students who have a positive interest in anthrosophical medicine. The AMA is the professional body of doctors practising anthroposophical medicine in the UK. Full membership is open to all practitioners who are registered with the General Medical Council in the UK and who are members of the General Anthroposophical Society. Publishes a list of doctors who have a positive interest in anthroposophical medicine and who are available for consultation by appointment.

Anthroposophical Society in Great Britain
Rudolph Steiner House,
35 Park Road, London NW1 6XT
Tel: 020 7723 4400
Fax: 020 7724 4364
Email: RSH@cix.compulink.co.uk
Web: www.anth.org.uk/rsh
Open: Mon-Fri 10am-6pm
▶ Information on anthroposophic

medicine, doctors and therapies. Some curative eurythmy available. Information on curative homes for disabled adults and children.

Aromatherapy Organisations Council
PO Box 19834, London SE25 6WT
Tel: 020 8251 7912
Fax: 020 8251 7942
Web: www.aromatherapy-uk.org
Open: Mon-Fri 10am-2pm
▶ The UK governing body for Aromatherapy is a democratic organisation representing 12 professional associations, their 115 or so accredited training establishments and their 6,000 therapists. AOC training standards were implemented in January 1994 and are mandatory for all member associations. Common Accreditation procedures are in place for inspecting and accrediting training establishments. National Occupational Standards for Aromatherapy developed over a three-year period were published in June 1998 and agreement has been reached with Middlesex University to develop a BSc Degree in Aromatherapy. The AOC is currently exploring the statutory regulation of title route. A general information booklet and list of Research Sources is available on receipt of an A5 SAE.

Association for Systematic Kinesiology
39 Brown's Road, Surbiton KT5 8ST
Tel: 020 8399 3215
Fax: 020 8390 1010
Email: info@kinesiology.co.uk
Web: www.kinesiology.co.uk
Open: Mon-Fri 8.30am-5pm
▶ Kinesiology is a preventive medicine using muscle testing to analyse functions and malfunctions of body systems and to facilitate investigation of what is happening in the body without intrusion, finding underlying causes. Energy balance is restored to the whole person, mentally, physically, chemically and energetically. Natural healing is enhanced, health and well-being improves. All practitioners undergo a two-year diploma course before graduating. Provides training courses in Kinesiology for lay people and professionals plus listings of practitioners nationwide.

Association for Therapeutic Healers
The Acorn Centre, 57A Railway Approach, East Grinstead RH19 1BT
Tel: 07074 222284
Open: Mon-Fri 9am-5pm
▶ Association for professional healers who combine healing with other therapies. Helps to promote health, well-being and self-wisdom through a broad-based approach. Defines healing as a process in which a person's natural self-healing ability is activated and harmonised by the channelling of universal energy through laying on of hands. Therapeutic healers integrate this with a variety of other therapeutic approaches such as visualisation, Psychotherapy, biofeedback, massage, movement, Shiatsu and soundwork. Member of the Confederation of Healing Organisations.

Association of Child Psychotherapists
120 West Heath Road, Hampstead, London NW3 7TU
Tel: 020 8458 1609
Fax: 020 8458 1482
Email: acp@dial.pipex.com
Open: Mon-Fri 9.30am-3.30pm
▶ Maintains standards within the profession, safeguards the interests of its membership and is the designated authority for the profession. Can refer the public to a child psychotherapist.

Association of Holistic Biodynamic Massage Therapists
20 Oak Drive, Larkfield, Aylesford ME20 6NU
Email: peter@ahbmt.demon.co.uk
▶ Founded in 1992 and a member of the British Therapy Council and the British Complementary Medicine Association. Major aims are: to keep a register of qualified practitioners and maintain high standards of practice in accordance with its Code of Ethics and Complaints Procedure; to provide information to the general public and to other professionals about the nature and benefits of Biodynamic Massage; to update and develop Biodynamic Massage and encourage research. The Association has 75 members, all of whom are qualified Biodynamic Massage practitioners.

Association of Independent Biodynamic Psychotherapists
30 Styles House, The Cut, London SE1 8DF
Tel: 020 7401 3582
Email: u.deniflee@publiconline.co.uk
Open: Mon-Fri 9am-5pm
▶ Offers referral list for people seeking Biodynamic Psychotherapy.

Association of Independent Psychotherapists
8 Victoria Mansions, 135 Holloway Road, London N7 8LZ
Tel: 020 7700 1911
Fax: 020 7281 6219
Email: referrals@aip.org.uk
Web: www.aip.org.uk
Open: Mon-Fri 9am-5pm
(24 hour answerphone)
▶ Founded in 1988 to encourage and support the continuing professional development of its members, to run a training programme in psychodynamic Psychotherapy and to offer a Psychotherapy referral service to the public. The training maintains a creative tension between analytical psychology and psychoanalysis. It is pluralistic and emphasises an historical perspective on analytical theory and practice.

Association of Natural Medicine
19a Collingwood Road, Witham CM8 2DY
Tel: 01376 502 762
Fax: 01376 502 762
Email: association.naturalmedicine@talk21.com
Web: www.anm.org.uk
Open: Mon 10am-1pm; Wed 9.30am-3.30pm
▶ Established in Witham in 1983, this registered charity trains students wanting to practise natural medicine. Tutors run a number of courses in Homeopathy, Aromatherapy, Massage, Acupuncture, Hypnotherapy, Radiology, Diet and Nutrition, Counselling and Kinesiology. Has good links with Anglia University as a learning partner.

Association of Professional Astrologers
1 Cold Springs Court, Penrith CA11 8EX
Tel: 01768 866 529
Fax: 01768 866 529
Email: apa@astrocalc.freeserve.co.uk
Web: www.astrocalc.freeserve.co.uk
Open: Mon-Fri 9am-5pm
▶ Formed in 1989 to meet the growing demand for professional work of the highest standard. Its consultants offer a confidential astrological service which follows the guidelines of the APA code of ethics. The qualifications for professional acceptance together with the above code can be obtained from the APA secretary. The fee may vary according to the type of work required. Astrologers sometimes specialise, necessitating a discussion of your specific needs and their individual fee structures.

Association of Professional Healers
92 Station Road, Bamber Bridge, Preston PR5 6QP
Tel: 01772 316 726
Fax: 01772 316 726
Email: Marjorie@aph98.freeserve.co.uk
Open: Mon-Fri 9am-6pm
▶ Charity founded five years ago, primarily for established, mainstream healers, people of integrity who understand the needs of sick people. A member of the Confederation of Healing Organisations, it seeks to promote healing through good practice and education. Aims and objectives: to accept everyone for healing; to raise monies to promote research into healing; to promote healing and mainstream medicine. For more details, send an SAE.

Association of Qualified Curative Hypnotherapists
10 Balaclava Road, Kings Heath, Birmingham B14 7SG
Tel: 0121 441 1775
Fax: 0121 441 1775

Email: info@aqch.org
Web: www.aqch.org
Open: Mon-Thurs 9am-6pm
(answering machine at other times)
▶ Formed in 1985, this registered charity is devoted to promoting the most specialised use of hypnosis – Curative Hypnotherapy. This advanced form of hypnotherapy aims to provide the permanent alleviation of many problems. All therapists listed in the free nationwide Register have fulfilled strict criteria through interviews and examinations and must adhere to a strict code of ethics/conduct. AQCH motto: 'Find the cause to cure'.

Association of Reflexologists
27 Old Gloucester Street,
London WC1N 3XX
Tel: 0870 5673 320
Fax: 01989 567 676
Web: www.reflexology.org/aor
Open: Mon-Fri 9am-5.30pm
▶ Largest, independent non-profit making Reflexology organisation in the UK, representing over 5,000 members nationwide and over 90 schools and colleges. Sets the standards for reflexologists throughout the country. Reflexologists that have met the demands of this association have the letters MAR after their name. Call for a list of accredited schools and professional practitioners in your area.

Association of Women Psychotherapists
167 Sumatra Road,
London NW6 1PN
Tel: 020 8202 0816
(24 Hour answerphone)
Web: www.awp.org.uk
▶ Highly qualified psycho-analytically trained psychotherapists, who established the Association in 1982, in affiliation to the Women's Therapy Centre. All therapists are registered with the United Kingdom Council for Psychotherapy and/or the British Confederation of Psychotherapists. Considerable clinical experience and work in a wide variety of mental health settings, eg in the NHS, in addition to private practice. Offers a consultation and referral service for women and men, for help with emotional problems such as relationship difficulties, low self-esteem, depression, anxiety/panic, experience of abuse and eating disorders, with special expertise in women's issues. As a first step offers a consultation to enquirers. This is seen as a vital opportunity to talk over particular concerns in confidence, and to explore the various possibilities that would offer the most appropriate help to the individual, couple or family. The outcome of a consultation may be referral to a suitable therapist. Options include individual psycho-analytical Psychotherapy, short-term or focused therappy, counselling, crisis intervention or group therapy. If contacted by phone, a therapist will return your call promptly. Consultations are offered immediately. Sliding scale on payments is available. Therapists are registered with BUPA.

Astrological Association
Unit 168, Lee Valley Techno Park,
Tottenham Hale, London N17 9LN
Tel: 0906 716 003
Fax: 020 8880 4849
Email: astrological.association@zetnet.co.uk
Web: www.astrologer.com/aanet
Open: Mon-Fri 10am-4pm
(24 hour recorded message)
▶ Founded in London on 21st June 1958 at 7.22pm, the AA has been co-ordinating astrological activities in Britain and worldwide for 40 years. Generally considered to be one of the most important and influential astrological organisations in the world, the AA is open to students and professionals at all levels. Has a worldwide membership.

Ayurvedic Medical Association UK
59 Dulverton Road, Selsdon,
South Croydon CR2 8PJ
Tel: 020 8682 3876
Fax: 020 8333 7904
Open: Mon-Fri 10am-7pm
▶ Maintains a register of qualified Ayurvedic Medical Practitioners who have completed at least five years full time training in a University in India or Sri Lanka in Ayurvedic Medicine.

Bates Association For Vision Education
PO Box 25,
Shoreham-by-Sea BN43 62F
Tel: 01273 422 090
Fax: 01273 279 983
Email: bave@sts.clara.net
Web: www.seeine.org
Open: Mon-Fri 9am-5pm
▶ Professional body for vision teachers trained in the tradition of the Bates Method. All members have completed recognised trainings and are fully insured. Can help with a wide range of eyesight-related problems including simple refractive errors (long and short sight), squints and lazy eyes, and many common eye diseases. A full information pack is available for £2 from: BAVE (GG) at the above address.

Bowen Association UK
122 High Street, Earl Shilton,
Leicester LE9 7LQ
Tel: 0700 269 8324
Fax: 01455 851 384
Email: info@bowen-technique.co.uk
Web: www.bowen-technique.co.uk
Open: Mon-Fri 9am-5.30pm
▶ The Bowen Therapeutic Technique involves a gentle yet dynamc system of muscle and connective tissue therapy that is revolutionising health care treatment worldwide. Developed in Australia by Thomas A Bowen (1903-1982) the goal of a Bowen treatment is to restore the body processes for self healing. It uses a series of gently rolling moves over muscles and soft tissue to realign the body, which creates balance and stimulates energy flow. This seems to affect the body's automomic nervous system, creating homeostasis at the cellular level. A Bowen treatment resets the body to heal itself and is useful for anyone from newborn infants to the elderly, the chronically ill and disabled benefit also. Producing a deep sense of relaxation and providing lasting relief from a wide variely of ailments and discomforts, the Bowen Technique is cost and time effective, in many casesonly 1 or 2 treatments are required to resolve problems, though some people may require further sessions in orde r to gain benefits of the therapy. For details of your local qualified, registered practitiner, call the secretary on 01455 841800

Bowen Technique European Register
Homelea, Bow Street,
Langport TA10 9PQ
Tel: 01458 252 599
Email: bowen@bter.freeserve.co.uk
Open: 9am-7pm daily
▶ BTER was formed in October 1998 in order to assure the public of good practice in the Bowen Technique. Establishes and enforces training and qualifications criteria for BTER membership and maintains the BTER-accredited Practiner List which is available to the public. For further information, send an SAE to the above address.

British Acupuncture Council
63 Jeddo Road, London W12 9HQ
Tel: 020 8735 0400
Fax: 020 8735 0404
Email: info@Acupuncture.org.uk
Web: www.acupuncture.org.uk
Open: Mon-Fri 9.30am-5.30pm
(closed 1-2pm)
▶ Formed in 1995 following the amalgamation of five separate Acupuncture associations whose members agreed that a single body should represent and govern its professionally qualified acupuncturists. All its members are fully qualified and have undergone training of at least two years full-time or the part-time equivalent. Training includes Western medical subjects relevant to the practice of Acupuncture. The BAcC register is the largest register of professionally trained acupuncturists in the UK and is the only register that regulates its members through standards of education, codes of practice and disciplinary procedures. Members who practise in the UK are all covered by Medical Malpractice and Public Product Liability Insurance. To obtain free list of local practitioners contct the council.

British Allergy Foundation
Deepdene House, 30 Bellegrove Rd,
Welling DA16 3PY
Tel: 020 8303 8525;
Helpline: 020 8303 8583

Fax: 020 83038792
Email: Allergybaf@compuserve.com
Web: www.allergyfoundation.com
Open: Mon-Fri 9am-5pm
▶ National charity established to increase understanding and awareness of allergy, to help sufferers overcome its effects and to raise funds for allergy-related research projects. Encompasses all types of allergy and provides information, advice and support to sufferers, including details of NHS allergy clinics and the specialists involved. For an information pack on your particular allergy, plus a year's membership, write to the address above, enclosing a cheque for £10.

British Alliance of Healing Associations
40 Cosawes Park House,
Perranarworthal, Truro CR3 /Q5
Tel/Fax: 01872 865 827
Web: working on at present
Open: Mon-Fri 9am-5pm
▶ BAHA was formed in 1977. Today, the Alliance comprises of 25 Associations with a total membership of approximately 3,500 healers. Currently, 'would-be' healers are expected to complete a two-year probationery training period under the guidance of an experienced healer. Member of the Confederation of Healing Organisations

British Association for Counselling
1 Regent Place, Rugby CV21 2PJ
Tel: 01788 578 328
Open: 24hr answer phone or send SAE for information
▶ Produces a directory of counsellors, publishes a leaflet: 'Finding a Counsellor'. For more information, call the number above or send an SAE.

British Association of Applied Chiropractic
The Old Post Office, Cherry Street,
Stratton Audley,
near Bicester OX6 9BA
Tel/Fax: 01869 277 111
Open: Mon-Fri 9am-5pm
▶ Professional regulatory body for McTimoney-Corley (Oxford College of Chiropractic) chiropractors. Aims to further and better the practice of the McTimoney-Corley method of chiropractic and the public's understanding of the method. Also to ensure the maintenance of professional standards in the practice of the McTimoney-Corley method. Call for further information.

British Association of Nutritional Therapists
BCNT, London WC1N 3XX
▶ Maintains a list of practitioners.

British Association of Psychotherapists
37 Mapesbury Road,
London NW2 4HJ
Tel: 020 8452 9823
Fax: 020 8452 5182
Email: mail@bap-psychotherapy.org
Web: www.bap-psychotherapy.org
Open: Mon-Fri 9am-5pm
▶ One of the major professional training bodies in the country for adult (psychoanalytic and Jungian) and child psychotherapists. Professional training to qualification and membership of BAP takes a minimum of four years and the training adheres to rigorous and agreed standards. The organisation, which has members throughout Britain, offers prompt assessment and referral for children, adolescents and adults requiring Psychotherapy. Member of the BCP.

British Astrological & Psychic Society
Robert Denholm House,
Bletchingley Road, Nutfield RH1 4HW
Tel: 07071 780 796
Fax: 01634 323006
Email: baps@tlpplc.com
Web: www.baps.co.uk
Open: Mon-Fri 9am-5pm
▶ Founded in 1976 by Russell Grant, now President Emeritus, the Society exists to provide a means of bringing together those actively working in, or interested in, the many different aspects of esoteric, spiritual and 'New Age' teachings, such as psychic perception, astrology, palmistry, tarot, numerology and healing. The aspect of sharing knowledge across many different disciplines is the quality which has made the society a strong force for the dissemination of esoteric teachings. A core of professionals at the heart of the Society enjoy an excellent reputation for the breadth and quality of their work. In this context, the Society's Consultants and BAPS 'stands' have become a regular and well known feature at many festivals around this country and abroad.

British Autogenic Society
c/o Royal London Homœopathic Hospital, NHS Trust, Great Ormond Street, London WC1N 3HR
Tel: 020 7713 6336
Fax: 020 7713 6336
Web: www.autogenic-therapy.org.uk
Open: Mon-Fri 9am-6pm
▶ Autogenic Therapy (AT) is a self-help therapy which brings about profound relaxation and relief from the negative effects of stress. Following an assessment interview, AT is taught individually or in small groups over 8-10 weeks. Practice at home for a few minutes several times a day during the course is essential. A series of easily learnt mental formula are used allowing the mind and body to become calm.

British Biomagnetic Association
The Williams Clinic,
31 St Marychurch Road,
Torquay TQ1 3JF
Tel/Fax: 01803 293 346
Email: secretary@britishbiomagneticsoc.fsnet.co.uk
Open: 24 hour answerphone
▶ Responsible for training practitioners of Western, complementary and alternative medicine at post-graduate level in Biomagnetic Therapy. It is a practitioner technique, using small dot magnets on the master points of the Acupuncture Eight Extra-Ordinary meridians. Acupuncture without needles, Osteopathy without manipulation.

British Chiropractic Association
Blagrave House, 17 Blagrave Street,
Reading RG1 1QB
Tel: 0118 950 5950
Fax: 0118 958 8946
Email: enquiries@chiropractic-uk.co.uk
Web: www.chiropractic-uk.co.uk
Open: Mon-Fri 9am-5pm
▶ Only chiropractors trained at an accredited college can become members of the BCA, the largest profession in the UK and now representing over 800 UK chiropractors. Before a student is awarded the Diploma in Chiropractic, he or she must complete a postgraduate year on the British Chiropractic Association's Vocational Training Scheme. Members of the BCA together with the Scottish Chiropractic Association, the McTimoney Chiropractic Association and the British Association for Applied Chiropractic worked to achieve legislation through Parliament for Chiropractic.

British Complementary Medicine Association
Kennsington House, 33 Imperial Square, Cheltenham GL50 1QZ
Tel: 01242 519 911
Fax: 01242 227 765
Email: info@bcma.co.uk
Web: www.bcma.co.uk
Open: Mon-Fri 9am-5pm
▶ Association with 75 member organisations representing nearly 30 complementary therapies and 26,000 practitioners. Exists to encourage a diverse range of organisations within the field of alternative medicine and to facilitate collective action. All members must subscribe to a code of conduct. Can refer you on to a range of alternative therapists practising in your area.

British Confederation of Psychotherapists
37 Mapesbury Road,
London NW2 4HJ
Tel: 020 8830 5173
Fax: 020 8452 3684
Email: mail@bcp.org.uk
Web: www.bcp.org.uk
Open: Mon-Fri 9am-5pm
▶ Linking body of training institutions, professional associations and accrediting organisations which have their roots in psychoanalysis and analytical psychology. The purpose of the Confederation is to promote the maintenance of appropriate standards in the selection, training, practice and

Health

the professional conduct of psychoanalytic psychotherapists. Each member society has a Code of Ethics which complies with the Confederation's requirements. The BCP publishes an annual register of psychotherapists which lists practitioners trained in work with adults, children and adolescents. Most of those on the BCP Register have trained first in counselling, social work, psychology or psychiatry. The BCP publishes a brochure called *Finding a Therapist*. It lists referral services and reduced fee schemes run by member societies. The BCP also publishes a brochure, *Psychoanalytic Psychotherapy*, which describes how psychoanalytic pychotherapy works. Both brochures are available free of charge on receipt of an SAE to take size A5.

British Federation of Massage Practitioners
78 Meadow Street, Preston PR1 1TS
Tel/Fax: 01772 881 063
Email: jolanta@jolanta.co.uk
Web: www.jolanta.co.uk
Open: Mon-Fri 9am-5pm
(24 hour answerphone)
▶ A professional organisation for the practitioners of natural therapies. Holds a list of members available to the general public. The BFMP also offers a multi-discipline insurance scheme for practitioners. The office answers many enquiries from the public everyday, particularly in response to press articles on massage and natural therapies.

British Herbal Medicine Association
Sun House, Church Street,
Stroud GL5 1JL
Tel: 01453 751 389
Fax: 01453 751 402
▶ Promotes the use of herbal medicine and campaigns to make herbal treatments more widely available.

British Holistic Medical Association
59 Lansdowne Place, Hove BN3 1FL
Tel/Fax: 01273 725 951
Email: bhma@bhma.org
Web: www.bhma.org
Open: Mon-Fri 9am-5pm

▶ Formed in 1983 by a group of medical doctors and students, the Association is an organisation of professionals and members of the public who care about the future of healthcare and want to adopt a more holistic approach to their own life and work. Healing is about making whole and establishing connections where they have failed or been forgotten. Holistic medicine involves re-integrating psychological and spiritual dimensions into healthcare. The Association's motto, 'physician heal thyself', refers to the potential each of us has for caring, responsiveness and adaptability. We need to keep these qualities alive within ourselves if we are to help others develop them.

British Homœopathic Association
27a Devonshire Street,
London W1N 1RJ
Tel: 020 7935 2163
Web: www.nhsconfed.net/bha
Open: Mon-Fri 9am-5pm
▶ Maintains a register of homeopathic doctors and pharmacies. Affiliated to the Faculty of Homœopathy which runs a postgraduate training course for doctors. Send an A4 SAE (66p worth of stamps) for a list of homeopathic practitioners in your area – and a list of homeopathic vets for your pets!

British Institute for Allergy & Environmental Therapy
Llangwyryfon, Aberystwyth SY23 4EY
Tel: 01974 241 376
Email: don.harrison@virgin.net
Web: www.allergy.org.uk
Open: Mon-Fri 9am-5pm
▶ The Institute responds to requests for information from members of the public and health professionals. It maintains a national register of therapists all of whom offer diagnosis and treatment of allergic conditions.

British Medical Acupuncture Society
Unit 12, Newton House,
Newton Lane, Whitley WA4 4JA
Tel: 01925 730 727
Fax: 01925 730 492
Email: bmasadmin@aol.com

Web: www.medical-acupuncture.co.uk
Open: Mon-Fri 9am-5pm
▶ Society for medically qualified practitioners with an interest in or practising Acupuncture.

British Natural Hygiene Society
3 Harold Grove,
Frinton-on-Sea CO13 9BD
Tel: 01255 672 823
▶ Promotes and publishes information on healthy lifestyles and alternatives to orthodox allopathic medicine for the prevention and treatment of illnesses. Publishes The Hygienist, a quarterly journal in its 41st year. Subscriptions cost £12.50 (UK) per year.

British Reflexology Association
Monks Orchard, Whitbourne,
Worcester WR6 5RB
Tel: 01886 821 207
Fax: 01886 822 017
Email: bra@britreflex.co.uk
Web: www.reflex.co.uk
Open: Mon-Fri 9am-4.30pm
▶ Founded in 1985 to act as a representative body for reflexologists, the Association publishes a yearly Register of Members (price £2.00) and a quarterly newsletter, *Footprints*, to which non-members can subscribe. The association also carries out research projects. The official teaching body of the BRA is the Bayley School of Reflexology which runs regular practitioner training courses in London, regionally (Birmingham, Edinburgh, Leeds, Liverpool) and overseas.

British Society for Allergy, Environmental & Nutritional Medicine
PO Box 7, Knighton LD8 2Wt
Tel: 023 8081 2124
(0906 372 0010 premier line)
Open: 24 hr answerphone
▶ Members are medically qualified doctors. Send an SAE for information.

British Society For Music Therapy
25 Rosslyn Avenue,
East Barnet EN4 8DH
Tel/Fax: 020 8368 8879

Email: denize@bsmt.demon.co.uk
Web: www.bsmt.org.uk
Open: Mon-Fri 9.30am-3.30pm
▶ Registered charity which aims to promote the use and development of music therapy. It holds meetings, workshops and conferences. Publishes a journal, jointly with the Association of Professional Music Therapists, and a bulletin for members. Membership open to all interested in music therapy. Sends an information booklet to all enquiries and gives advise on music therapy as a career. Sells its own publications (conference papers) and books on music therapy.

British Society of Clinical Hypnosis
7 Middleton Avenue, Yorkly S29 0AD
Tel/Fax: 01943 609 036
Email: sec@bsch.org.uk
Web: www.bsch.org.uk
Open: 24 hour answer phone
▶ Society of highly trained and ethical hypnotherapists with extensive practical experience. All members are bound by a strict Code of Conduct and complaints procedure. For details of competent hypnotherapists in your area, call the above number.

British Society of Experimental & Clinical Hypnosis
Derbyshire Royal Infirmary,
Department of Clinical Oncology,
London Road, Derby DE1 2QY
Tel: 01332 766 791
Fax: 01332 776 863
Email:
phyllis@alden-residence.demon.co.uk
Web: www.bsoc.demon.uk
Open: Home number of secretary
▶ Learned society for doctors, dentists and psychologists who use hypnosis in clinical practice or are engaged in academic research. The society only accepts those with professional qualifications. Produces scientific journals.

British Society of Hypnotherapists
37 Orbain Road, London SW6 7JZ
Tel: 020 7385 1166
Fax: 020 7385 1166

▶ The society was founded in 1950 with the primary object of spreading knowledge of hypnotherapy. The society gathers information on hypnotherapy from many sources throughout the world and maintains contact with learned bodies. It disseminates information on hypnosis, its use in therapy and training to the media and the general public.

British Society of Iridologists/The Anglo European School of Iridology
998 Wimborne Road,
Bournemouth BH9 2DE
Tel: 01202 518 078
Email: iridology@iridology.co.uk
Web: www.iridology.co.uk
Open: Mon-Fri 9am-5.30pm
▶ Training faculty at the European School of Iridologists Ltd. The school offers a home study course that has been developed over many years which covers iris colour, constitution, marks, signs and pigments. The AESI is the oldest school in the UK and is a leading authority in Iridology. Aims to provide a series of services for the public, including an official List of Registered Iridologists. This is sent to all requesting the name of their local iridologist. Also aims to offer the public protection from unqualified practitioners.

British Society of Medical & Dental Hypnosis
17 Keppel View Road, Kimberworth,
Rotherham S61 2AR
Tel/Fax: 07000 560 309
Email: nat.office@bsmdh.org
Web: www.bsmdh.org
Open: Answerphone
▶ Formed in 1952, the BSMDH exists to promote the education and training of doctors, dentists and other health professionals in the principals and practice of hypnotherapy and to encourage research relating to hypnosis. It also aims to educate both professionals and the public in the safe use of hypnosis. Accreditation requirements include training courses (14 days or more) spread over three years during which practical experience is gained with hypnosis in a field where they already have professional competence to advise and treat patients. Written submission of case histories is followed by an oral assessment by two examiners.

British Wheel of Yoga
1 Hamilton Place, Boston Road,
Sleaford NG34 7ES
Tel: 01529 306 851
Fax: 01529 303 233
Email: wheelyoga@aol.com
Web: www.wheelyoga@aol.com
Open: Mon-Fri 9am-5pm
▶ Formed in the Sixties and has developed into the Governing Body of Yoga in this country, as recognised by the Sports Councils. Non-profit making charity run by voluntary support. Has a structured part-time teacher training course. Other Yoga organisations can and do apply for the nationally recognised teacher qualification. The Yoga Biomedical Trust is one such group. Yoga is becoming a real force in complementary healthcare and heads the list of classes in many Further Education establishments, as well as private classes which cover: the physical postures; breathing exercises; relaxation, meditation, stress release. Wheel Yoga as taught by British Wheel is the synthesis of the best of Yoga teaching emphasising health and safety.

Cancerlink
11-21 Northdown Street,
London N1 9BN
Tel: 0207 833 2818;
Helpline: 0800 132 905
(open 9.30am-5pm)
Fax: 0207 833 4963
Email: cancerlink@cancerlink.org.uk
Open: Mon-Fri 9am-5pm
▶ National charity providing support and information about cancer to those with cancer, their families, friends and health professionals working with them. Services are free, confidential and designed to meet the needs of people from any community. Information and support are given by phone, post and through a range of publications and audio-visuals. Helplines are staffed by a highly trained team. Also provides training, consultancy and support to individuals and cancer self-help groups.

Central Register of Advanced Hypnotherapists
PO Box 14526, London N4 2WG
Tel: 020 7354 9938
▶ Established in 1991 to make available to the public a register of competent hypnotherapists who have undergone full training with the National School of Hypnosis and Psychotherapy – N-SHAP. CRAH therapists work to a stringent Code of Ethics and Practice with a complaints procedure. CRAH is run by its Governing and Advisory Council, which carries out all necessary duties on a voluntary basis. Explanatory booklet plus full register available by SAE.

Colour Therapy Association
PO Box 309, Camberley, GU15 2LE
Tel/Fax: 01276 682113
Email: cta.co.uk
Open: 24 hour answer phone
▶ Independent organisation run by a committee. The CTA is an active body deeply involved with colour which aims to spread the message about the latest research and innovation in the use of colour therapy. Sets standards and lists practitioners and training establishments/ schools. CTA is a non-profit making organisation, giving access to a cohesive and experienced team. An authoritative information source for anyone interested in finding out more. For information membership, send an SAE to the above address or leave a message.

Complementary Medicine Association
The Meridian, 142a Greenwich High Road, London SE10 8NN
Tel/Fax: 020 8305 9571
Web: www.the-cma.org.uk
Open: Mon-Fri 10am-4pm
▶ Promotes ethical, responsible complementary medicine to the public and medical profession. A referrals scheme helps you find a bona fide practitioner or training college near you. Send two first class stamps and details of your requirement to the CMA and they will get your nearest practitioner/college to send you details. Also runs introductory courses in all forms of complementary medicine. Call for an information pack.

Confederation of Healing Organisations
Suite J, 2nd Floor, The Red & White House, 113 High Street,
Berkampstead HP4 2DJ
Tel: 01442 870 660
Email: cho.healing@virgin.net
Web: drive.to/cho
Open: 24 hour answer phone
▶ Registered charity and national confederation of sixteen independent Healing Associations (also charities), representing over 12,000 insured contact and distant healers – the largest complementary therapy group in the UK. CHO's objective is to establish healing as a standard therapy for the NHS as well as private medicine. CHO says: 'We are proud that the standards demanded of our healers have resulted in more doctors working with us.'

Corporation of Advanced Hypnotherapy
PO Box 70, Southport PR8 3JB
Tel: 01704 576 285
Fax: 01704 576 285
Email: abc@hypnotapes.co.uk
▶ Nationwide register of Advanced Hypnotherapy practitioners, all of whom have received post-graduate training.

Council for Complementary & Alternative Medicine
63 Jeddo Road,
London W12 9HQ
Tel: 0208 735 0632
Open: Answer phone
▶ Officially launched in the House of Commons in 1985, the Council provides a forum for communication and co-operation between professional bodies representing Acupuncture, Herbal Medicine, Homeopathy and Naturopathy. The Council's intention is to promote and maintain the highest standards of training, qualification and treatment in complementary and alternative medicine and to facilitate the dissemination of information relating to it. The Council is deeply concerned with the safety of the public and committed to the principle that all those who practise non-orthodox medicine are ethically controlled and bound by codes of conduct.

Health

Craniosacral Therapy Association of the UK
Monomark House,
27 Old Gloucester Street,
London WC1N 3XX
Tel: 0700 0784 735
Fax: 01883 723 300
Email: craniosacral.co.uk
Web: www.craniosacral.co.uk
Open: 24 hour answerphone service
▶ Established ten years ago, the Association evolved from the need for Craniosacral Therapy graduates to stay in touch in order to further their career and knowledge. Holds a list of over 300 accredited craniosacral therapists. To register with the Association, practitioners must successfully complete a one-year course from an accredited school. The course includes a minimum of 300 hours of tuition and 400 hours project work.

Dr Edward Bach Centre
Mount Vernon, Bakers Lane,
Sotwell, Wallingford OX10 0PZ
Tel: 01491 834 678
Fax: 01491 825 022
Email: bach@bachcentre.com
Web: www.bachcentre.com
Open: Mon-Fri 9.30am-4.30pm
▶ Dr Bach's home and workplace, where the mother tinctures for the Bach Flower Remedies are still made by appointed successors. World centre for education and referral to practitioners registered with the Dr Edward Bach Foundation. Home of the Dr Edward Bach Healing Trust, a registered charity. Offers free help and advice on using remedies and on any aspect of Dr Bach's work.

Environmental Medicine Foundation
Breakspear Hospital,
Lord Alexander House,
Waterhouse Street,
Hemel Hempstead HP1 1 DL
Tel: 01442 261 333
Fax: 01442 266 388
Email: amonro@breakspear.org
Web: www.breakspear.org
Open: Mon-Sat 9am-5pm
▶ Charity which exists to promote environmental medicine. It has the following objectives: to research into illness caused by environmental factors; to benefit sufferers from such illness; and to provide scientific evidence leading to the creation of a healthier environment. Members receive a regular newsletter. Call for a catalogue of EMF publications.

Erasmus Foundation
Moat House, Banyards Green,
Laxfield, Woodbridge IP13 8ER
Tel: 01986 798 682
Fax: 01986 798 041
Email: satiti@breathemail.net
▶ Natural healing and spiritual teaching organisation, offering healing (free of charge), counselling, Reflexology, and Homeopathy. Also run seminars and workshops covering subjects such as self-analysis, self-realisation, meditation, past civilisations, ecology, and other topical subjects such as communication in today's world, and how we see the future of the planet and the work that is required. Publishes a quarterly newsletter. Members of the Confederation of Healing Organisations and the British Complementary Association, and attend meetings of the Parliamentary Group for Alternative and Complementary Medicine.

Federation of Holistic Therapists
3rd Floor, Eastleigh House, Upper Market Street, Eastleigh SO50 9FD
Tel: 023 8048 8900
Fax: 023 8048 8970
Web: www.fhd.org.uk
Open: Mon-Fri 9am-5pm
▶ Offers a free service to members of the public. Can provide names of qualified therapists in beauty, holistic and sports therapies. Call for details.

Feldenkrais Guild UK
PO Box 370, London N10 3XA
Tel: 0700 785 506
Email: 106222:1342@compuserve.com
▶ Non-profit professional organisation of practitioners and teachers of the Feldenkrais method. Only people professionally trained by Dr Feldenkrais, graduated from an accredited professional training programme or a training recognised by the Feldenkrais Guild UK, are eligible to be full members of the Guild or to use the legally registered name: Feldenkrais Method. The method is an educational one, focusing on learning and movement to bring about improved functioning.

Flower And Gem Remedy Fellowship
Laurel Farm Clinic, Northbeach,
Ashton Hill, Corston, Bath BA2 9EY8
Tel: 01225 872663
Fax: 01225 874988
Open: Mon-Fri 8am-5pm by appointment only
▶ Constituted body formed by individuals interested in Flower Essence Therapy and the Professional Training of Therapists. Being a member of FEF entitles you to 10% off all FEF courses and Essences, a quarterly newsletter on what has been happening in the area of Flower Therapy both in the UK and Europe. The FEF is a full member of the BCMA and represents the wishes of its members in Inner Council. It has an active membership in terms of keeping ahead with the possible introductions of standards of training throughout complementary medicine.

Friends of Yoga Society
'Priskey' 5 Weston Crescent,
Old Sawley, Long Eaton,
Nottingham NG10 3BS
Tel: 0115 973 5435
Open: Mon-Fri 9am-5pm
▶ The Western world community of FRYOG is affiliated to the Institute for Complementary Medicine. FRYOG is noted for its comprehensive/holistic approach to Yoga. All work is done on a voluntary basis within the administrative section of the society. This is done by the Hon Vice President, Registrar and Diploma Board Members. The internationally recognised FRYOG Diploma for tutors cannot be commenced until a student has completed at least two years in Yoga with a qualified tutor. A junior Yoga Diploma is also available for youngsters who wish to participate.

General Chiropractic Council
344-354 Gray's Inn Road,
London WC1X 8BP
Tel: 0207 713 5155
Fax: 0207 713 5844
Email: enquiries@gcc-uk.org
Web: www.gcc-uk.org
Open: Mon-Fri 9am-5pm
▶ The General Chiropractic Council is a UK-wide statutory body with regulatory powers, established by the Chiropractors Act 1994. It has four main duties: to protect the public by establishing and operating a scheme of statutory regulation for chiropractors, similar to the schemes for other health professionals such as medical doctors and dentists; to set the standards of chiropractic education, conduct and practice; to ensure the development of the profession of chiropractic, using a model of continuous development improvement in practice; and to promote the profession of chiropractic so that its contribution to the health of the nation is understood and recognised. The GCC register opened on 15 June 1999 and chiropractors have until 14 June 2001 in which to register. After this date the title of chiropractor will be protected and it will be a criminal offence for anyone in the UK to claim to be a chiropractor, whether implicitly or explicitly, if not registered with the GCC.

General Council and Register of Naturopaths
Goswell House, 2 Goswell Road,
Street BA16 0JG
Tel: 01458 840 072
Fax: 01458 840 075
Email: admin@naturopathy.org.uk
Web: www.naturopathy.org.uk
Open: Mon-Fri 9am-6pm;
Sat 9am-1pm
▶ Maintains and publishes a register of suitably qualified naturopathic practitioners. Also enforces a code of professional conduct and monitors educational standards in naturopathic colleges for the protection and benefit of the public.

General Osteopathic Council
Osteopathy House, 176 Tower Bridge Road, London SE1 3LU
Tel: 020 7357 6655
Fax: 020 7357 0011
Email: gosc@osteopathy.org.uk
Web: www.osteopathy.org.uk
Open: Mon-Fri 9am-5.30pm
▶ Osteopathy is the first of the profes-

sions previously outside conventional medical services to achieve statutory recognition. In 1993, the Osteopathic Act was passed to establish a single governing body, the GOsC. The Council has a statutory duty to regulate, develop and promote the profession of Osteopathy. Existing practitioners now have two years to register with the GOsC. After this time, the title 'osteopath' will become protected and it will be illegal for anyone not registered to practise as an osteopath. Subsequent registrants will qualify by gaining a recognised qualification from an accredited school. The GOsC has a duty to safeguard patients by ensuring a high standard of ethical and clinical practice which will be achieved by working in partnership with the profession. Through that partnership, it is hoped that all osteopathic bodies and institutions will develop a wide understanding of the implications of statutory regulation and the duties of the GOsC under the law.

Green Solutions for Biomedical Research
PO Box 18653, London NW3 4DG
Tel/Fax: 020 7813 3670
▶ Directory and database (on the internet) of biomedical research methods which demonstrate global and green principles of sustainability, ecological, ethical, scientific, not alatering, modifying or harming any life forms, gender, race, social class, species or planet.

Guild of Naturopathic Iridologists International
94 Grosvenor Road,
London SW1V 3LF
Tel/Fax: 0207 821 0255
Web: www.gni-international.org
Open: Mon & Wed 10am-6pm;
Thurs & Fri 10am-12pm
▶ Established in 1993, the Guild is the UK umbrella body for Iridology. Has 11 affiliated training courses and the largest register of qualified iridologists. All members have professional insurance and qualifications in at least one therapeutic science. Provides protection and recourse for the public, practitioners and prospective students; post graduate training and support; a strict code of ethics; constitution and management committees. For all interested in the valuable analytical tool of iris analysis.

Guild of Psychotherapists
47 Nelson Square, London SE1 0QA
Tel/Fax: 020 8540 4454
Email: guild@psycho.org.uk
Web: www.psycho.org.uk
Open: By appointment only
▶ Aims to promote the relief of psychological illness or disorder by providing for the public benefit psychoanalytic Psychotherapy and education and training in Psychotherapy. Founded in 1974, it is a registered charity and a member of the UK Council for Psychotherapy. Therapists practice in their own consulting rooms throughout London. On average, fees are £30 per session, although there is provision for those who cannot afford the usual fee.

Healing Foundation
Half Acre House, Upper Battle Field,
Shrewsbury SY4 4AA
Tel/Fax: 01939 210 980
Email: healing@globalnet.co.uk
Open: Mon-Fri 8am-6pm
▶ Nationwide membership and training organisation for healers of every level of experience. Refers healers onto members of the public and health care professionals. Also holds seminars for the public on self-healing techniques and stress management. Member of the Confederation of Healing Organisations.

Holistic Association of Reflexologists
92 Sheering Road,
Old Harlow CM17 0JW
Tel: 01279 429 060
Fax: 01279 445 234
Email: bsr@footreflexology.com
Web: www.footreflexology.com
Open: Mon-Fri 9am-5.30pm
▶ Formed to provide a professional association for the qualified therapist. Member association of the BCMA. Provides a referral register, insurance and a help line for practitioners. Its link with the Michelle Matsuyama International School broadens its international base.

Homœopathic Medical Association
6 Livingstone Road,
Gravesend DA12 5DZ
Tel: 01474 560 336
Fax: 01474 327 431
Email: info@the-hma.org
Web: www.the-hma.org
Open: Mon-Fri 10am-1pm & 2-4pm
▶ Established in 1985, the HMA is a non-profit making recognised body of qualified professional homeopaths. Members must have passed a qualifying examination at a college approved by the Council and/or proved their worthiness to practise the art and science of Homeopathy to the satisfaction of the council. Members are bound by a strict Code of Ethics and Practice and are obliged to carry Professional Indemnity Insurance so that the public may seek treatment with absolute confidence. The Association represents its members with Government and other professional bodies and is affiliated with the Complementary Medical Association.

Homœopathic Trust
15 Clerkenwell Close,
London EC1R 0AA
Tel: 020 7566 7800
Fax: 020 7566 7815
Email: info@trusthomoepathy.org
Web: www.trusthomoepathy.org
Open: Mon-Fri 9am-5pm
▶ The Homeopathic Trust is a registered charity founded in 1948. It aims to advance the teaching, knowledge and practice of Homeopathy to the highest standard, and to promote Homeopathy to healthcare professionals, purchasers of healthcare and the general public. The Trust can provide a list of doctors qualified in Homeopathy on receipt of an SAE. The Trust also publishes information about Homeopathy and a quarterly magazine, *Health and Homœopathy*. The Homeopathic Trust also supports the academic activities of the Faculty of Homœopathy, which was incorporated by an Act of Parliment in 1950. The Faculty regulates the education, training and practice of Homeopathy by doctors, vets and other health care professionals.

Incorporated Society of Registered Naturopaths
328 Harrogate Road,
Moortown LS17 6PE
Tel: 0113 268 5992
Open: Mon-Fri 9am-5pm
▶ Members practise Naturopathy, a therapy which includes wholefood and restricted diets, fasting, hydrotherapy, Massage, manipulation, remedial exercise and relaxation. The Society also offers advice on breast-feeding, pediatric care and counselling on family, occupational and emotional problems. Naturopathy also endorses organic agriculture, natural child-birth and is anti-pollution. The philosophy seeks to understand and rectify basic causes of ill-health rather than prescribe 'remedies'. Members have undergone a minimum four-year full-time training or equivalent. Professional practice is monitored by the Naturopathic Council. Extensive publications list available.

Institute for Complementary Medicine
PO Box 194, London NE16 7 QZ
Tel: 020 7237 5165
Fax: 020 7237 5175
Email: icm@icmmedicine.co.uk
Web: www.icmedicne.co.uk
Open: Mon-Fri 10am-2.30pm
▶ Registered charity which provides information to the public on complementary medicine, a directory of registered, insured and qualified complementary practitioners and details on colleges and schools of complementary medicine. Supports research into complementary medicine and administers the British Register of Complementary Practitioners.

Institute for Optimum Nutrition
Blades Court, Deodar Road,
London SW15 2NU
Tel: 020 8877 9993
Fax: 020 8877 9980
Email: allion@ion.ac.uk
Web: www.info@ion.ac.uk
Open: Mon-Fri 9am-5pm
(possible appointments on Saturday)
▶ Non-profit making organisation which means that all the funds it receives are used to achieve its goal –

Health

to advance the education of the public and health professionals in all matters relating to nutrition. Runs courses starting with the one-day Optimum Nutrition Workshop that puts you straight where health and nutrition are concerned, right up to a three-year Nutrition Consultants Diploma Course. For an information pack please call the above number of contact our website.

Institute of Psychosynthesis
65a Watford Way, Hendon,
London NW4 3AQ
Tel: 020 8202 4525
Fax: 020 8202 6166
Email: institute@psychosynthesis.org
Open: Mon-Fri 9.30am-5.30pm
▶ Established in 1973 with the encouragement and support of Roberto Assagioli, founder of psychosynthesis, to actualise its principles and practice. This is carried out through training professionals, through research, publishing and offering educational, counselling and Psychotherapy services to the general public.

International Association of Clinical Iridologists
Tel: 0207 262 5142
Open: Mon-Fri 9am-5pm
▶ Affiliated to ICM and the Canadian Institute of Iridology. Its approved college is the UK College of Iris Analysis.

International Association of Colour
PO Box 3, Potters Bar EN6 3ET
▶ Non-profit making umbrella organisation promoting the unity of people working in colour. The Association includes other areas of colour work such as psychology, art and design and science and technology. Schools which teach colour healing and are members of the IAC Schools Section are required to incorporate the IAC Core Curriculum into their syllabuses. IAC can also supply details of members to the public on a regional basis.

International Federation of Aromatherapists
Stamford House,
184 Chiswick High Road,
London W4 1TH
Tel: 020 8742 2605
Fax: 020 8742 2606
Web: www.int-fed-aromatherapy.co.uk
Open: Mon-Fri 9am-5pm
▶ Largest established organisation for professional aromatherapists in the world. It was formed in 1985 to act as an independent representative body for the profession of Aromatherapy. A register of all its qualified aromatherapists is available for £2.50 from its Chiswick address. Publishes a quarterly journal which is available by subscription. Also has a list of registered schools who teach the IFA syllabus. Send an SAE to the Chiswick address. All full members are fully insured.

International Federation of Reflexologists
76-78 Edridge Road,
Croydon CR0 1EF
Tel: 020 8667 9458
Fax: 020 8649 9291
Email: ifr44@aol.com
Web: reflexology-ifr.com
Open: Mon-Fri 9.30am-5pm
▶ Formed in the Eighties by a group of like-minded professional reflexologists. These therapists felt that training standards and levels of professional competence were not high enough and that the general public had no way of contacting a therapist whom they could trust to treat them with care and competence. The Federation has grown to be a leader in the field and now has many hundreds of members working all over the world, bound together by a strict code of ethics and practice. As well as keeping a register of professional therapists, the IFR has a list of accredited schools which all teach to a centrally agreed syllabus. All therapists take a separate course in Anatomy and Physiology over and above that of Reflexology.

International Flower Essence Repertoire
The Living Tree, Milland,
near Liphook GU30 7JS
Tel: 01428 741 572
Fax: 01428 741 679
Email: flower@atlas.co.uk
Web: www.ifer.co.uk
Open: Mon-Fri 9am-5.30pm;
Sat 10am-4pm
▶ Primary importer and distributor of flower and other vibrational remedies in the UK, carrying 19 different lines from around the world, including the Australian Bush Flower Essences and over 1,500 other essences. Offers expert advice and counselling with vibrational remedies as well as an efficient mail order service. Workshops conducted throughout the year. Maintains a list of practitioners who work with new flower essences from abroad. Visit the centre and browse amidst the healing energies of flower and gem essences. Mail order available.

International Network of Esoteric Healing
New Rose Cottage, Bushmoor,
Craven Arms SY7 8DW
Tel: 01694 781 295
Fax: 01694 781 466
Web: ww.wineh.org
Open: Mon-Fri 9am-6pm
▶ Formed in 1982, the Network teaches and practises an approach to Spiritual Healing known as 'esoteric healing'. Healers do not claim to heal, but rather to help the individual through their own healings processes, invoking the aid of their soul. Offers a referral list for the general public. All practitioners on the list have completed the INEH training. Call for more information.

International Register of Consultant Herbalists and Homeopaths
32 King Edward Road,
Swansea SA1 4LL
Tel/Fax: 01792 655 886
Email: office@irch.org
Web: www.irch.org
▶ Founded with the aim of ensuring that any one of its members would provide skilled, ethical and professional care and conform to a Code of Ethics. Training is in the form of home study and seminars, followed by clinical and pharmacological experience under the personal supervision of established practitioners. Member of the BHPA/EHPA (Herbal Medicine and Homeopathy) organisations working towards Statutory Self-Regulation (SSR) and a common Register. A register of members or prospectus can be obtained by contacting the registered office, or visiting the website.

International Register of Holistic Therapists
38a Portsmouth Road, Woolston,
Southampton SO19 9AD
Tel: 023 8048 8900
▶ Register of IFHT members, available free to libraries, doctors, health centres, leisure centres, health clubs and the media. Costs £4 (including p&p) to members of the public. Covers a range of holistic therapies from Massage to colour analysis.

International Self-Realisation Healing Association
1 Hamlyn Road, Glastonbury BA6 8HS
Tel: 01458 831 353
Fax: 01458 835 148
Email: Isrha@btinternet.com
Open: Mon-Fri 9am-6pm
▶ Independent international association of healers and Progressive Counsellors and a registered charity. Healers are trained to a high professional standard and are committed to working with love and spirituality. ISRHA practitioners work with all problems and conditions. Healing can help a return to balance and wholeness within and can deepen understanding of the meaning and purpose of life.

Kinesiology Federation
PO Box 83, Sheffield S7 2YN
Tel: 0114 281 4064
Fax: 0114 8817 998
Email: Kinesiology@btinternet.com
▶ Umbrella organisation for several schools of Kinesiology. Offers a choice of different branches of Kinesiology for professional training. For Professional Membership, the minimum required training period is 150 hours training and 200 hours of clinical experience within a period of two to three years. There are six other membership categories and all practising members must be insured and follow the code of conduct and ethics. The method of the KF is one of respect and support for all members while maintaining high standards of professionalism.

McTimoney Chiropractic Association
21 High Street, Eynsham, Oxford OX8 1HE
Tel: 01865 880 974
Fax: 01865 880 975
Email: admin@mctimoney-chiropractic.org
Web: mctimoney-chiropractic.org
Open: Mon-Fri 9am-5pm
▶ The governing body for chiropractors trained at the McTimoney Chiropractic College in Oxford. Formed to protect and support McTimoney chiropractors and uphold and promote the essential principles of Chiropractic as developed by the late John McTimoney. Members are registered annually with the MCA which also governs insurance, membership and ethical and professional conduct. There are currently nearly 400 members throughout the UK.

Metamorphic Association
67 Ritherdon Road, Tooting, London SW17 8QE
Tel: 020 8672 5951
Fax: 020 8672 5951
Email: Metatechone@compuserve.com
Web: www.geocities.com
Open: Mon-Fri 9.30am-5.30pm
▶ Registered charity created in 1979 to help promote Metamorphosis technique by providing instruction to the public generally through classes and workshops, individual tuition and lectures to interested groups. It maintains a register of members who are all practitioners and offers a referral service. It also provides for an exchange of information to members and to the public generally through its journal and various publications. Membership is open to all practitioners with the necessary training and experience.

National Asthma Campaign
Providence House, Providence Place, London N1 0NT
Tel: 020 7226 2260;
Helpline: 0345 010 203
Fax: 020 7704 0740
Web: www.asthma.org.uk
Open: Mon-Fri 8.30am-5.30pm
▶ Independent UK charity working to conquer asthma, in partnership with people with asthma and all who share their concerns, through a combination of research, education and support. More and more of the UK's 3.4 million people with asthma are integrating complementary medicine with orthodox treatment. Publishes a free factsheet on asthma and complementary medicine.

National Council for Hypnotherapy
PO 5779, Berton on Wolds, Loughton LE12 5ZF
Tel: 0800 952 0545
Open: Mon-Fri 9am-5pm (24 hour answerphone)
▶ Holds the largest register of independent hypnotherapists in the UK, and is the founding member of the UK Confederation of Hypnotherapy Organisations (UKCHO). The Council is the only organisation covering hypnotherapy mentioned in the recent British Medical Association report on complementary medicine (ie under its former title, The Hypnotherapy Register and previously administered by the National Council of Psychotherapists). There are established entry criteria, an agreed code of conduct, a complaints and disciplinary procedure and obligatory insurance requirements.

National Federation of Spiritual Healers
Old Manor Farm Studio, Church Street, Sunbury-on-Thames TW16 6RG
Tel: 01932 783 164;
Healer referral service: 0891 616 080 (charged at premium rate)
Fax: 01932 779 648
Email: office@nfsh.org.uk
Web: www.nfsh.org.uk
Open: Mon-Fri 9am-5pm
▶ Founded in 1955, the NFSH is acknowledged as the principal organisation for Spiritual Healing in the UK with over 60 centres and more than 6,000 members. The federation is not associated with any religion but sees the source of healing energy as divine. NFSH offers an extensive educational and training programme, support groups, information and can arrange Distant Healing. NFSH is a member of the Confederation of Healing Organisations.

National Institute of Medical Herbalists
56 Longbrook Street, Exeter EX4 6AH
Tel: 01392 426 022
Fax: 01392 498 963
Email: nimh@ukexeter.freeserve.co.uk
Web: www.btinternet.com/tildanimh
Open: Mon & Fri 10am-5pm; Tues, Wed & Thurs 9.30am-3.30pm
▶ Established in 1864, this is the oldest body of practising medical herbalists in the world. All members have completed a four-year training course and adhere to a strict professional code of ethics. Patients are seen on a private fee basis. Call for more information.

National Register of Hypnotherapists and Psychotherapists
12 Cross Street, Nelson BB9 7EN
Tel: 01282 699 378
Fax: 01282 698 633
Email: nrhp@btconnect.com
Web: www.nrhp.co.uk
Open: Mon-Fri 9am-12.30pm & 1.30pm-5pm
▶ Holds a nationwide database of qualified hypno-psychotherapists and provides a public referral service, free of charge by phone (or send an SAE). Area listings of all therapists are available on the website. All members are bound by a strict Code of Ethics. NRHP is a non-profit making professional body, with members drawn from the national College of Hypnosis and Psychotherapy and equivalent trainings. Provides supervision network, insurance and other professional back-up services for practising hypno-psychotherapists. Member of UK Council for Psychotherapy. Member of European Association of hypno-psychotherapists.

Natural Medicines Society
PO Box 232, East Molsey, KT8 1YF
Tel/Fax: 020 89741 166
Open: Mon-Fri 9am-5pm
▶ Registered charity established in 1985. The only UK consumer body that defends your freedom of choice in medicine. Works to protect and develop the availability of natural medicines and advance the practice and expertise of alternative and complementary medical treatments by promoting education, research and discussion.

New Approaches to Cancer
St Peter's Hospital, Guilford Rd, Chertsey KT16 0PZ
Tel: 01932 879 882
Fax: 01932 874 349
Email: help@anc.org.uk
Web: www.anc.org.uk
Open: Mon-Fri 9am-6pm
▶ National registered charity set up to promote the benefits of holistic and self-help methods of healing for cancer patients. Acts as the nerve centre for a network of local self-help groups, holistic practitioners and clinics throughout the UK. Also has connections with other parts of the world, such as Europe, the USA, Mexico, Australia and so on. Operates a referral system and information service, directing people with cancer to their nearest sources of help.

Northern Ireland Association for the Study of Psycho-Analysis
75 Ballybentragh Road, Muckamore BT41 2HJ
Tel: 01232 648 038
Fax: 01232 491 991
Email: siobhanoconnor@msn.com
▶ Member of the British Confederation of Psychotherapists. Full members of NIASP are accredited by the BCP, including Psychoanalytic Psycho-therapists and Psychoanalysis. It is a training organisation and is actively involved in teaching Psychoanalysis to a wider public, through the MA (Psychoanalytic Studies) at Queen's University and by sponsoring public conferences and seminars.

Pathways Information Service
12 Southcote Road, London N19 5BJ
Tel: 020 7607 7852
Fax: 020 7609 7112
Email: info@pathwaysnetwork.co.uk
Web: www.pathwaysnetwork.co.uk
Open: Mon-Fri 10am-3pm

Health

▶ Founded in 1988, promotes a wide variety of activities in the area of therapy and complementary medicine. Publishes its own bulletin, now in its 54th issue, which is distributed in London and residential centres in the UK, with a northern UK edition now in its 11th issue. Display leaflets at major exhibitions and insert them in their mailings and in support of these activities they provide database, typesetting and printing services.

Pilates Foundation UK Limited

80 Camden Road,
London E17 7NF
Tel: 07071 781 859
Fax: 020 8281 5087
Email: admin@pilatesfoundation.com
Web: www.pilatesfoundation.com
Open: Wed 9am-11am & Fri 9am-5pm

▶ The governing body of the Pilates Method in Great Britain. Its members must have completed a year's training followed by a six-month apprenticeship. All members are bound by its rules and Code of Conduct. For a list of qualified teachers, please send an SAE.

Radionic Association Ltd, The

Baerlein House, Goose Green,
Deddington, Banbury OX15 0SZ
Tel: 01869 338 852
Fax: 01869 338 852
Email: radiionics@association.freeserve.co.uk
Web: www.radionic.co.uk
Open: Mon 9am-5pm;
Tues-Fri 9am-12noon

▶ Radionics is a technique for analysing imbalances in the energy field due to stress, pollution, etc and correcting them by thought-directed approaches, including distant healing. It is equally useful for animals, plants and soils. The Association, which was founded in1943, has two roles. First, it is the professionl society of qualified Radionic Practitioners. Secondly, it is a society of laymen interested in Radionics who wish to keep in touch with the development of the subject. The Association's aims are to protect and to promote the practice of Radionics as an honourable and skilled profession, to foster research into the sciece of Radionics and to provide a clearing house for the collection and dissemination of relevant information. In addition to publishing the *Radionic Journal*, the Association holds an annual weekend conference; publishes various brochures and monographs; supplies books and other publications about Radionics; issues a list of practising members and handles a large volume of requests for information, literature and general advice about Radionics from all over the world. Training is available through the School of Radionics. The RA is a member of the Confederation of Healing Organisations and the BCMA. Associate Membership is open to all with a bona fide interest in Radionics.

Reiki Association

2 Manor Cottages, Stockley Hill,
Peterchurch, Hereford HR2 0SS
Tel: 01981 550 829

▶ Networking organisation which holds a register of its members in many parts of the UK. Membership of the organisations is open to any Reiki practitioner and membership does not imply minimum standards.

Research Council for Complementary Medicine

60 Great Ormond Street,
London WC1N 3JF
Tel: 020 7833 8897
Fax: 020 7278 7412
Email: rccm@gn.apc.org
Web: www.gn.apc.org/rccm
Open: Mon-Fri 9am-6pm

▶ Provides research information to health professionals.

Rolf Institute

23 Highbury Villas, Kingsdown,
Bristol BS2 8BY
Tel: UK contact: Simon Wellby
0117 946 6374
Email: simonrolfing@yahoo.com
Web: www.rolf.org
Open: Mon-Fri 9am-5pm

▶ The Rolf Institute was founded in 1971 to carry on Dr Rolf's work. Its major purposes are to train Rolfers and Rolfing Movement teachers, to carry on research and to provide information to the public. Only individuals trained and certified by the Rolf Institute may use the Rolfing service mark. The Rolf Institute conducts trainings in Rolfing for individuals who have completed the required coursework in anatomy, physiology and Kinesiology, have demonstrated an ability in hands-on work such as Massage or physical therapy, and who have the maturity and sensitivity to work with people using this technique.

SAD Association

PO Box 989, Steyning BN44 3HG
Tel: 01903 814 942
Fax: 01903 879 939

▶ Voluntary organisation and registered charity which informs the public and health professions about SAD and supports and advises sufferers of the illness. It produces a newsletter three times a year and other publications, holds meetings, has a network of contacts, a lightbox hire scheme and raises money for research into SAD. Receives no funding so has to charge for the information and membership.

Saneline

Tel: 0345 678 000
Open: Helpline: 2pm-midnight
365 days a year

▶ Confidential mental health helpline with a database with information about counselling services in your area, including free services.

Shiatsu Society

Suite B, Barber House,
Storeys Bar Road, Fengate,
Peterborough PE1 5YS
Fax: 01733 758 342
Open: Mon-Fri 9am-5pm

▶ Formed in 1981 to facilitate communication within the field of Shiatsu and to inform the public of the benefits of this form of natural healing. Since then, the Society has grown to form a network linking interested individuals, students and teachers and additionally, to fulfil the role of professional association for practitioners of Shiatsu. Member both of the British Complementary Medicine Association and the Institute of Complementary Medicine.

Society for the Promotion of Nutritional Therapy

Email: spnt@compuserve.com &
nutrition.therapy@virgin.net
Web: visitweb.com/spnt

▶ An internet site where you can find more information on nutritional therapy, help campaign for its greater recognition, and communicate with other like-minded people on the bulletin-board.

Society of Homœopaths

4a Artizan Road,
Northampton NN1 4HU
Tel: 01604 621 400
Fax: 01604 622 622
Email: info@homoeopathy-soh.org
Web: www.homoeopathy-soh.org
Open: Mon-Fri 8.30am-5pm

▶ Publishes a register listing qualified and experienced homeopaths who have agreed to abide by the Society's Code of Ethics and Practice. Those listed are issued with a Certificate of Registration and may use the initials RSHom after their names. Also publishes a number of leaflets, a list of recognised homeopathic courses and a recommended booklist. All available free of charge on receipt of an SAE.

Society of Teachers of Alexander Technique

129 Camden Mews,
London NW1 9AH
Tel: 020 7284 3338
Fax: 020 7482 5435
Email: enquiries@stat.co.uk
Web: www.stat.org.uk
Open: Mon-Fri 9am-5pm

▶ Established in 1958, the Society of Teachers of the Alexander Technique (STAT) maintains and monitors standards of training and practice, and provides a directory of members and information to the public. Members have undergone three years full time training to become qualified Alexander teachers and adhere to a published code of professional conduct. Extensive information is available on the website.

Health

Sufi Healing Order of Great Britain
91 Ashfield Street,
Whitechapel, London E1 2HA
Tel: 020 7377 5873
Email: caduceus@oryx.demon.co.uk
Open: Mon-Fri 9am-5pm
▶ Practises distant healing by prayer for anyone who asks to receive healing. The Sufi tradition is an ancient way of developing awareness through meditation and exploration of life's meaning. Associated with music, poetry and spirituality beyond sectarianism, it is called 'the way of heart'. Holds monthly day workshops in London and regular meditation/healing meetings.

Taoist Tai Chi Society of Great Britain
Taoist Tai Chi Centre,
Bounstead Road,
Colchester CO2 0DE
Tel: 01206 576 167
Fax: 01206 572 269
Email: ttcsgb@taoist-tai-chi-gb.org
▶ Registered charity dedicated to making the health-improving qualities of Taoist Tai Chi available to all. Classes are held daily.

The Association of Light Touch Therapists
6 Combermere Road,
St Leonards on Sea TN38 0RR
Tel: 01424 430 001
Fax: 01424 430 001
Email: lighttouch@callnetuk.com
▶ ALTT was formed to promote therapies that can be termed 'light touch' and to speak for the less-known therapies that use touch techniques to re-align the subtle energy fields of the body. These are non-invasive and involve very gentle touch on the body – they do not involve pressure or manipulation but are very powerful in overcoming ailments by releasing pain. They help the body heal itself and restore equilibrium, balancing both the body and the subtle body. ALTT is a professional organisation for qualified practitioners of non-intrusive body energy therapies affiliated to the British Complementary Medicine Association. For details of joining or for a register of practitioners contact the Secretary at the above address.

The Association of Professional Music Therapists
26 Hamlyn Road,
Glastonbury BA6 8HT
Tel: 01458 834 919
Email: apmtoffice@aol.com
Web: www.apmt.org.uk
Open: Mon-Fri 2.30pm-5.30pm
▶ Professional association formed to assist qualified and student music therapists in matters of training, employment, standards of practice and liaison with government bodies. Will provide information to the general public on receipt of an SAE.

Tibet Foundation
10 Bloomsbury Way,
London WC1A 2SH
Tel: 020 7404 2889
Fax: 020 7404 2366
Email: getza@gn.apc.org
Web: www.gn.apc.org/tibetgetza
Open: Mon-Fri 9am-5pm
▶ Registered charity working towards creating more awareness of all aspects of Tibetan culture and the teachings of the Dalai Lama and supporting Tibetans in exile and in Tibet. Programmes include visits by Tibetan doctors to the UK, lectures and events at the London Culture Centre, sponsorship of children, the elderly monks and nuns, health initiatives, medical centres in Tibet, Yak replacement scheme and aid to Tibetan refugee communities.

Transcendental Meditation
Beacon House, 1-3 Willow Walk,
Woodley Park,
Skelmersdale WN8 6SW
Tel: 08705 143 733
Email: tminfo@maharishi.org.uk
Web: www.transcendental-meditation.org.uk
Open: Mon-Fr i 9am-5pm
▶ Transcendental Meditation is a simple technique practised for 20 minutes morning and evening. During TM the mind and body gains a state of deep rest and relaxation. Benefits are cumulative. The mind becomes calmer and more alert, thinking is clearer, and energy increased. Call for a free information pack and details of local TM Centres throughout Britain

United Kingdom Polarity Therapy Association
Monomark House,
27 Old Gloucester Street,
London WC1N 3XX
Tel: 0208 339 9061
▶ The leading professional body for polarity therapy in Great Britain, affiliated to the BCMA. Registered Polarity practitioners are fully trained and work to a code of ethics. This holistic healing system, a blend of Eastern and Western concepts developed by Dr Randolph Stone, uses bodywork, energy exercises, awareness skills and diet to restore an optimum flow of life energy. It helps most physical or stress-related problems.

Women's Nutritional Advisory Service
PO Box 268, Lewes BN7 1QN
Tel: 01273 487 366
Fax: 01273 487 576
Email: wnas@wnas.org.uk
Web: www.wnas.org.uk
Open: Mon-Fri 9am-5.30pm
▶ Offers scientifically based, tailor-made programmes for women (and men where applicable) for PMS, the menopause, IBS, fatigue, weight loss and nutrition. Has clinics in London, Lewes and Hove and offers a phone consulatation service. For more information, send an A5 SAE plus four separate first class stamps.

World Federation of Healing
1 The Oaks, Hexham NE40 2PZ
Tel: 01434 600 911
Fax: 01434 600 911
Email: alexadymond@lineone.net
Web: www.wfh.org.uk
Open: Mon-Fri 9.30am-1pm
▶ Registered charity which aims to unite all practitioners in the healing fields in the recognition of the holistic approach to health. Seeks to offer the knowledge and research of the world from within its membership to help aid the less developed countries and to encourage the use of the complementary therapies, especially where medical aid is limited. Accepts into membership those healers and potential healers for training in the various training centres. Member of the Confederation of Healing Organisations.

Yoga Biomedical Trust
The Yoga Therapy centre at
The Royal London Homœopathic Hospital, 60 Great Ormond Street,
London WC1N 3HR
Tel: 020 7419 7195
Fax: 020 7419 7196
Email: yogabio.med@virgin.net
Web: www.yogatherapy.org
Open: Mon-Fri 9am-6pm
▶ YBT's aim is to advance the study and practice of Therapeutic Yoga to improve the health and well-being of individuals and the public. YBT uses a comprehensive three-pronged approach, which includes: 1) Research – researching the effectiveness of Yoga as an aid to health, and disseminating the results to the medical community; 2) Training – training of Yoga therapists and teachers; 3) Practice – providing Yoga therapy and classes to the public.

Teaching, informing and empowering

Global warming, destruction of the rain forests, pesticide pollution... it is easy to think nothing you can do will make any difference to the environmental ills of the world. But actually we have great power as individuals and with a little concerted effort can bring about major changes. **Liz Sutton** *of the Women's Environmental Network shows us how.*

The Women's Environmental Network (WEN) was started in 1988 by a group of women who wanted to connect women's desire for change with their power as consumers – our history to date is proof that consumer pressure really does make a difference. Our first campaign – persuading manufacturers to reduce chlorine bleaching in nappies and sanitary protection – had lasting impact across the paper products industry. Disposable nappies and sanitary protection (sanpro) are still with us, but at least now their manufacture is less polluting.

Our 'Wrapping is a Rip Off' campaign enabled women across the country to take a stand against unwanted packaging by returning it to their supermarket with a polite message that it was unnecessary. Waste is a huge concern yet, until recently, local authorities – responsible for waste management – had no powers to try to prevent it at source.

WEN spotted this anomaly and initiated the Waste Minimisation Act, which became law in 1998. This gives local authorities those powers. And that means you have more power too: you can press your council to use the Act to introduce measures to cut the amount of waste created by local businesses and households.

Nationally, WEN provides information about ideas such as refill schemes, repairing and refurbishing appliances and valuing the resources we have, and advises local authorities on strategies for achieving 'zero waste'.

WEN's primary aim is to educate, inform and empower women and men who care about the environment. We believe people have the right to information and to be able to make fair choices. We are not exclusive: we recognise that everybody is affected by environmental degradation and that we all live together in society and must work together. But, women around the world are disproportionately affected by environmental degradation.

Some issues specifically affect women. Take, for instance, breast cancer. Campaigns to improve screening and treatment have popular support. Yet, although many women have gut feelings about what may have caused their cancer, primary prevention – research into causal factors and action to prevent cancer before it starts – is low on the national agenda. WEN is working to raise it up the agenda and to ensure women's experience is not sidelined or ignored. Action to reduce the incidence of breast cancer may well help reduce other cancers as well.

Women's energy and concern for their families and the environment drives other work, such as the Real Nappy Project, jointly organised by WEN and the Real Nappy Association. Real Nappy Week each April raises awareness of the environmental impact of disposables and the availability of modern fitted cloth nappies. Did you know, for instance, that eight million nappies are thrown away in the UK every day? Or that disposables leave an ecological footprint two and a half times the size of the footprint left by cloth nappies washed by a laundry service?

Women are growing their own organic food – and strengthening communities – through our *Taste of a Better Future* network of ethnic minority growing groups. Reclaiming urban spaces, they are able to keep alive traditional skills and grow cheap produce and plant varieties that might otherwise be expensive or hard to find.

To do all this, WEN relies on its members and donors, both to provide vital funds to maintain and develop campaigns and to spread the word and take action locally. So, if you want to get involved or just to help us carry on our work, join us! ■

To join WEN or find our more, send a large SAE marked 'gg-membership' to WEN, PO Box 30626, London E1 1TZ or visit the website at www.wen.org.uk

Learning on a human scale

How can we help children grow into confident and responsible adults? How can we create schools and learning experiences which will develop in young people the attitudes, skills and knowledge to shape a fairer and more sustainable world? **Fiona Carnie** *provides some solutions.*

Human Scale Education is a national charity which believes that children's needs are best met and their potential most fully realised in human scale settings. Small classes, small schools and large schools restructured into smaller units help to provide an environment in which children can flourish. Smaller structures allow children to feel secure and develop self confidence. They enable teachers to know their students as individuals and respond to the specific needs (personal and academic) of each. Students can feel part of a community with a sense of ownership of their learning environment. And it is much easier for parents and the wider community to be involved in the education of their children.

There is a growing body of research in the United States which indicates the effectiveness of smaller schools and smaller classes and which is the driving force behind many innovative reforms there. In the UK many different solutions to the problems in our education system are being implemented – numeracy hour, literacy hour, out of school centres, homework clubs, new post-14 arrangements. But these are all add-ons to a crumbling and out-dated system. They do not represent the kind of changes which are needed to make education into a positive experience for the majority of young people.

Human Scale Education wants to see more radical changes which put children at the centre of the learning process. The organisation is encouraging new educational initiatives in this country within mainstream education as well as in the alternative sector. Within mainstream education it supports large schools wishing to find ways of working in smaller units so that children can be treated as individuals. It offers grants to secondary schools for innovative projects which enable them to make education into a more personal experience for their students.

In the alternative sector it supports parents and teachers wishing to set up a small school or learning centre and is pressing for state funding for these schools. Schools such as these receive public funding in a growing number of European countries (Denmark, Holland, Germany, Hungary, Czech Republic to name a few) because their governments are committed to providing a variety of schools within the state system so that parents can choose an education which suits their child.

The UK Government needs to look carefully at what the alternative sector has to offer both in philosophy and practice and consider funding a variety of different forms of education on an experimental basis. ∎

For more information, contact Human Scale Education at 96 Carlingcott, Bath BA2 8AW.
*Tel/fax: **01275 332 516***
*Email: **hse@clara.net***
*Web: **www.hse.org.uk***

IMPACT Being a green parent

- Buy reusable cotton nappies and use a nappy service if the washing overwhelms you. If you must use disposables at any time, such as long distance travelling, use non-gel, non-plastic ones which can be composted.

- Make your own fresh babyfood and children's meals – eliminate packaging waste and save money.

- Breastfeed your baby for as long as you can – at least six months and ideally one to two years.

- Teach your child how to grow food – sprouts and herbs on windowsills or carrots, tomatoes or potatoes in buckets on a balcony or an allotment.

- Clothe your family in chemical-free (ideally organic) natural fibres wherever possible. Also try using natural, untreated bedding to eliminate exposure to formaldehyde, solvents and other chemicals.

- Use public transport wherever possible and/or walk or cycle your child to and from school and shops to reduce car emission pollution, traffic hazards and improve your and your child's health.

Innovative education

The Steiner Waldorf Schools Fellowship represents the 26 autonomous mainstream Steiner Waldorf schools and 56 Kindergartens in the UK and Ireland. There are now over 800 Steiner Waldorf schools worldwide, some 1500 Kindergartens and 60 Teacher Training Institutes in 56 countries. For over 80 years, Waldorf students have been proving themselves to be resourceful and creative individuals, well-rounded and equipped to meet life's challenges. They are world citizens with a strong respect for cultural diversity.

All schools are fully comprehensive, mainstream, non-selective, non-denominational educational charities. They are self-govering learning communities and work together within the Steiner Waldorf Schools Fellowship and international bodies such as the European Council of Steiner Waldorf Schools. Each school implements a Fellowship Code of Practice for administration and management.

Pupils in Waldorf schools benefit from the continuity and personal commitment of their teachers. Through ages 14-18/19 students are supported by the pastoral care of a class guardian and a self-chosen tutor. Such longer term pupil-teacher-parent relationships provide stability and continuity. Contiuous formative assessment rather than internal testing means that school life can be a happy, anxiety-free time for learning with enthusiasm and self-confiedence.

Where traditional culture, community and religious values are questionned, young people seek support in establishing trust, compassion and the inner capability to distinguish between good and evil. In Steiner Waldorf schools, spiritual and human values are consciously addressed by parents, teachers and community in partnership. The teaching approach itself underpins this, inspiring children to respect the world and their fellow human beings and ensuring an education that is inherently ecological.

Steiner Waldorf education represents the essential nature of childhood, enabling each child to develop their strengths in a warm, structured and child-sensitive environment. In the early years, a secure, unhurried setting gives children vital social, linguistic and dexterity skills, sound foundations for emotional and cognitive intelligence. A sense of values, of wonder and enthusiasm can mature from homely activities and creative play through self-motivated inquiry; this maintains intact the qualities essential for lifelong learning. ■

*For more information on the Steiner approach to education, contact the Steiner Waldorf Schools Fellowship on **01342 822 115** or visit the website at*
www.steinerwaldorf.org.uk

CASE STUDY: Looking after baby

Having a baby has always tested the way parents maintain their green lifestyle. Believing there is no green alternative to wrapping their baby in chemically saturated nappies or feeding it chemically enhanced 'substitute' breast milk, many parents are forced to compromise their green ideals as soon as their baby arrives. BORN offers an alternative solution.

Green parenting is not just about putting you baby into cotton nappies or reducing the burden on farming by breastfeeding. Natural, instinctive parenting is by definition green: sleeping with your baby, long-term breastfeeding, cotton nappies, and baby carrying are far greener options;

it's the way four fifths of the world's population operates.

At BORN, where ever possible, we source products made in the UK or Europe. We sell a range of organically produced items, including organic nappies, clothes for babies and toiletries. Many of the products BORN sells are new to the high street – having previously been available only by mail order.

We are also keen to promote other issues that affect the environment. We sell reusable menstrual products because a huge amount of sanitary products are dumped into landfill; there are more women menstruating than there are babies in nappies!

As well as being a place to shop we believe BORN should be a place that parents (and parents-to-be) can come to get information to help them on their journey. Natural, green parenting is easy if you open yourself to being instinctive about the way you care for your child. ■

*Written by Eva Fernandez. BORN is open Mon-Sat 9.30am-5.30pm at 64 Gloucester Road, Bishopston, Bristol BS7 8BH. Tel: **0117 924 5080** or visit the website at **www.first-born.co.uk** for online ordering.*

Family & Community

BABIES & CHILDREN

Birth

Active Birth Centre
25 Bickerton Road, London N19 5JT
Tel: 020 7482 5554
Fax: 020 7267 9683
Email: mil@activebirthcentr.demon.co.uk
Web: www.activebirthcentre.com
Open: Mon-Fri 9.30am-5pm
▶ Offers informative courses for the full range of childbirth options, including yoga for pregnancy and baby massage. Also offers a nationwide portable pool hire service and NHS-approved installed birth pools. Mail order service for books, tapes and videos, its own Aromatherapy range, maternity bras, baby carriers and equipment.

Birthworks Bristol
11 Bartletts Road, Bristol BS3 3PL
Tel: 0117 966 7311
Email: email@s-and-n.fsnet.co.uk
Web: www.naturalbabies.co.uk
▶ The longest established Birthing Pool hire company in the UK, offering national pool hiring services together with regular waterbirth workshops. Prices from £25-£53 per week. Heated models come complete with circulating heater, water maintenance kit and filtration system. These unique pools can also be used as a relaxing spa to relieve tension in the weeks before you give birth. Once baby is born they provide a wonderful opportunity to relax with your new family

Independent Midwives Association
1 The Great Quarry,
Guildford GU1 3XN
Tel: 01483 821 104
(24 hour answerphone)
Web: www.stripe.force9.co.uk/ima
▶ Midwives working in an independent capacity from the NHS. Offers continuity of care and empowers women to make informed choices and decisions at every stage of their care. A large proportion of the Association's bookings are for homebirths and the rest for planned hospital births. Liaises with other health professionals if and when necessary. All visits are generally in women's homes. Looks after clients from booking until four weeks after the birth and are available (or a colleague) at all times.

Natures Gate: Tens Pain Control
PO Box 371, Basingstoke RG24 8GD
Tel: 01256 346 060
Fax: 01256 346 050
Email: naturesgate@virgin.net
Web: www.naturesgate-uk.com
▶ Mail order supplier of Tens, a safe, effective, easy-to-use machine used for drug-free relief of pain. Used for childbirth, arthritis and backpain and many other conditions. Call for free information pack.

Splashdown Water Birth Services
17 Wellington Terrace,
Harrow-on-the-Hill HA1 3EP
Tel: 020 8422 9308
Fax: 020 8422 9308
Web: www.waterbirth.co.uk
(also www.splash-down.com)
▶ Offers waterbirthing services with either NHS or private midwives throughout the UK and birth pools from local outlets or door-to-door delivery from £130 for four weeks hire. Also organises water birth workshops for parents-to-be and English National Board Study Days for midwives. Videos and books available by mail order.

The Association of Radical Midwives
62A Greetby Hill, Ormskirk L39 2DT
Tel: 01695 572 776
Fax: 01695 572 776
Email: arm@midwifery.org.uk
Web: www.midwifery.org.uk
Open: Mon-Fri 9am-5pm
▶ ARM is an umbrella organisation offering information and local support to those having difficulty in getting or giving sympathetic, individualised NHS maternity care. Over 50 local contacts around UK, many holding regular local group meetings. Free information leaflets 'What is a Midwife?' and 'Choices in Childbirth'. Quarterly National meetings. Membership open to midwives, students and non-midwives (includes quarterly journal *Midwifery Matters*). Annual fee £25, (half-price concession to students, unemployed, etc.)

Breastfeeding

Expressions Breastfeeding
CMS House, Basford Lane,
Leekbrook, Leek ST13 7DT
Tel: 01538 386 650
Fax: 01538 399 572
▶ Sells breast pumps and related breast-feeding products through a nationwide mail order service. Also operates a home rental scheme for the Medela Lactina Electric Breastpump which is excellent for short term use, especially if you want to keep up your milk supply if your baby is in special care.

La Leche League (Great Britain)
BN Box 3424, London WC1N 3XX
Tel: 020 7242 1278
Web: www.laleche.org.uk
Open: 24 hour telephone helpline
▶ Voluntary organisation providing breastfeeding help and information, primarily through mother-to-mother support in local groups. All breastfeeding counsellors are trained mothers with breastfeeding experience. A bi-monthly newsletter is available to regular subscribers and health professional subscribers receive other specialist publications. Leaflets, books, tapes and Braille available.

Mothernature
Acorn House, Brixham Avenue,
Cheadle, Hulme SK8 6JG
Tel/Fax: 0161 485 7559
Email: felicity@mothernaturebras.co.uk
Web: www.mothernaturebras.co.uk
Open: Mon-Fri 9am-5pm (Order Line); 24 hour answerphone
▶ A small mail order company offering one of the best ranges of nursing bras available in the UK. Sizes range up to J cup and 48" back and include Royce, Berlei, Bravado and Anita. Also stocks many garments from the Anita Maternity range. Advice on bra sizing is freely available and aims for a delivery time of three days. Aromatherapy blends for pregnancy are also available in the mail order brochure. Call for a brochure.

Baby Food & Milk

**Baby Organix
(Organix Brands)**
FREEPOST BH1336,
Christchurch BH23 1BR
Tel: 0800 393 511
Fax: 01202 479 712
▶ Range of organic baby foods including cereals and jarred products available in most supermarkets and selected health food shops. Call for more information, free copies of recipe cards or weaning guide.

Babynat
SdF Limited, 63 High Street,
London N8 7QB
Tel: 020 8340 0401
Fax: 020 8340 0402
Email: info@organico.co.uk
Web: www.organico.co.uk
▶ A full range of organic baby foods, including the most nutritionally advanced organic follow-on milk and baby food jars which came first in Good Housekeeping Institute tatse test of eight organic brands. The brand guarantees 100% organic ingredients, full ingredient percentage labelling, no fillers, no added sugars in cereals, milk or jars, full control over raw materials, no added flavouring, GM-free and no use of water as an ingredient.

Hipp Organic Baby Foods
Hipp Nutrition UK Ltd, 165 Main Street, New Greenham Park,
Newbury RG19 6HN
Tel: 01635 528 250
Fax: 01635 528 271
▶ Organic baby food range from Germany and available in the UK since 1994 through health food shops, branches of Boots and larger supermarkets. Although Hipp believes breastfeeding to be the best option for babies, it realises that this is not always possible and so produces Organic Follow-On Milk for infants from four months onwards. Hipp solid foods include breakfast cereals and porridge, full meals and desserts and a range of dried products.

Holle Baby Foods
19/20 Stockwood Business Park,
Stockwood, Near Redditch B96 6SX
Tel: 01386 792 622
Fax: 01386 792 623
Email: elysia@ava.cix.co.uk
▶ Holle Baby Milk Powder (suitable from birth) and four Baby Cereals (suitable from three months) including gluten-free rice. All products have been made with food grown to stringent Demeter organic standards using no chemicals, synthetic fertilizers or herbicides. Natural baby toiletries and sunblock are also available.

OSSKA Ltd
204 Church Road, Hove BN3 2DJ
Tel: 01273 730 777; Freephone 0800 328 9818 for stockists
Fax: 01273 440 433
Email: john.deverell@btinternet.com
▶ Britain's first Fresh Organic Baby Food is now available to parents. The range of both savoury and sweet recipes includes flavours such as Lentil Delight and Raisin Porridge. OSSKA is fresh; it is kept refrigerated and contains no added sugars, salts, flavours, fillers, preservatives or colours. It is available in a wide selection of health food stores and delicatessens and is certified by the Soil Association.

Nappies

Bambino Mio
12 Staveley Way,
Brixworth NN6 9EU
Tel: 01604 883 777
Fax: 01604 883 666
Email: enquiries@bambino.co.uk
Web: www.bambino.co.uk
Open: Mon-Fri 8am-5.30pm;
Sat 9.30am-12.30pm
▶ Mail order supplier of 100% pure cotton nappies, velcro-closing outer covers and accessories. Available in a range of sizes and styles to fit every baby from birth to potty. Write or call for a free brochure.

Earthwise Baby
PO Box 1708, Aspley Guise,
Milton Keynes MK17 8YA
Tel: 01908 585 769
Fax: 01908 585 771
Email: sales@earthwisebaby.com
Web: www.earthwisebaby.com
▶ Snap-to-fit, reusable, 100% unbleached, cotton, fitted nappies and accessories. Mail order only, call for a free catalogue.

Eco-Babes
79 Orton Drive, Witchford,
Ely CB6 2JG
Tel: 01353 664 941
Email: cakebread@eco-babes.co.uk
Web: www.eco-babes.co.uk
▶ Supplies a large range of washable nappies and nappy essentials which are available to order online. If you are not sure which nappy is right for your baby, there are newborn and trial kits for hire. Also a wide range of eco-friendly goods for mother and baby, including breast pads, sanitary wear, hemp slings and clothing, toiletries and household goods.

Ethos Baby Care Ltd
64 Alma Road, Clifton,
Bristol BS8 2DJ
Tel: 0117 923 7586
Fax: 0117 923 7354
Email: enquiries@ethosbaby.com
Web: www.ethosbaby.com
Open: Mon-Fri 9am-5.30pm
▶ Mail order company offering a wide range of reusable nappies for the modern family, including shaped, prefolds, and unbleached cottons, all with easy popper or velcro fastenings. Also supplies a large selection of natural baby care products such as creams, soaps, shampoos, massage oils, all made from 100% natural ingredients, plus many soft and wooden toys in a range of classic and new designs. Call for a free brochure.

Nappi Nippas
PO Box 35, Penzance TR18 4YE
Tel: 01736 351 263
Fax: 01736 351 263
Open: 24 hour answering
▶ Nappi Nippas nappy fasteners, for use with terries, are much easier and safer to use than traditional pins. Simply stretch and grip for no-fuss changing. Terries become as easy to use as disposables. Call for order details.

National Association of Nappy Services
St Georges House,
Hill Road,
Birmingham B5 4AN
Tel: 0121 693 4949
▶ Nappy network group connecting parents with local nappy washing services in their area.

Natrababy Cotton Nappies
c/o Bodywise (UK) Ltd,
Bristol BS32 4DX
Tel: 01454 615 500
Fax: 01454 613 805
Email: info@natracare.com
Web: www.natracare.com
▶ Offers cotton, form-fitting, all-in-one nappies. Their unique design and velcro fasteners means that the nappy can be fitted and changed quickly. Pure cotton next to baby's skin and a breathable, leakproof nylon pant on the outside, makes for comfort and reliability without the environmental headache and expense of disposables.

Natural Baby Company
63 Queenstown Road,
London SW8 3RG
Tel: 020 7498 9490
Fax: 0870 054 3757
Email: info@naturalbabycompany.com
Web: www.naturalbabycompany.com
▶ Sells two kinds of eco-friendly disposable nappy by mail order. Moltex is an unbleached disposable with no lotions, perfumes, deodorants or other unnecessary chemicals to come into contact with a baby's skin, and no bleaching agents or processes to harm the environment. These have an absorbent gel and woodpulp core to help keep baby dry. Tushies are gel-free disposables with a cotton and woodpulp padding of high natural absorbency and also no perfumes, lotions or dyes. Both types are fully shaped with adjustable closing tapes for ease of use and comfort. Also sells Tushies hypo-allergenic and alcohol free baby wipes which contain aloe

---

visit **BORN** and discover a **different** approach to parenting
different nappies ★ **different** slings ★ **different** pushchairs
different toys ★ **different** clothing ★ **different** shoes
different books ★ **different** toiletries ★ **different** accessories...
64 Gloucester Road Bishopston Bristol BS7 8BH
telephone: 0117 924 5080 email: born@dial.pipex.com www.first-born.co.uk
Open Monday to Saturday 9.30 - 5.30

vera. Prices compare favourably with other disposables. Call for more information and a free sample nappy.

Nature's Baby
PO Box 2995, London NW2 1DW
Tel: 020 8905 5661
▶ Range of cotton nappies including the unique all-in-one shaped nappy and also a budget two part system. Both include soft, absorbent 100% cotton layers and a waterproof outer layer and need no pins or overpants closing by way of velcro-style fastenings. Call for mail order catalogue.

Perfectly Happy People
31-33 Park Royal Road,
London NW10 7LQ
Tel: 0870 607 0545
Fax: 020 8961 1333
Email: claire@phpbaby.com
Web: www.phpbaby.com
Open: Mon-Fri 9am-6pm
▶ UK distributors of the award-winning brand leader in washable cloth nappies, Kooshies. Available via mail order or through retailers such as Sainsburys, Safeway and Tesco Direct. Call the above number to claim a free catalogue, which lists the whole range of Kooshies reusable nappies and accessories.

Real Nappy Association
PO Box 3704, London SE26 4RX
Tel: 020 8299 4519
Web: www.realnappy.com
▶ The Association now runs the Real Nappy Project together with the Women's Environmental Network. It is the central source of information and advice on all nappy-related issues, for local authorities, health professionals, the media and individuals. It provides practical support including advice on adult incontinence. Quarterly newsletter, local Real Nappy Networks, discounts on nappies. Send a large S.A.E. with two stamps on it to the above address.

Sam-I-Am
4 Sharon Road, London W4 4PD
Tel: 020 8995 9204
Fax: 020 8995 9207
Email: samiam@nappies.net
Web: www.nappies.net
Open: Mon-Fri 9am-5pm
▶ Sam-I-Am cotton nappies were awarded 'Best Buy' by Pregnancy and Birth Magazine. These nappies are easy to use and wash over and over again. Some families have used Sam-I-Am nappies on three children. Sample packs containing one nappy, one waterproof pant and four flushable liners are available for £9.95 including p&p. Call to order. Major credit cards accepted. Visit the website for more information.

Spirit of Nature Ltd
Burrhart House, Cradock Road,
Luton LU4 0JF
Tel: 01582 847 370
Fax: 01582 847 371
Email: oliver@spiritofnature.co.uk
Web: www.spiritofnature.co.uk
Open: Mon-Fri 9am-5.30pm
▶ Washable nappy systems and nursery accessories made from 100% organically grown, unbleached and undyed natural materials. Cotton shaped nappies with velcro fastening, cotton knitted nappies, cotton and silk napy liners, wollen and microfibre overpants that allow the skin to breathe. Moltex eco-disposable nappies with unique unbleached cellulose core, certified free from harmful residues. Voted best disposable nappy by German Oko-Test magazine. Also available: natural clothing collection for adults, babies and toddlers, eco-household products, unbleached cotton sanitary protection products. Call for a free catalogue.

Health

Earth Friendly Baby (Healthquest Ltd)
7 Brampton Road, Kingsbury,
London NW9 9BX
Tel: 020 8206 2066
Fax: 020 8206 2022
Email: info@healthquest.co.uk
Web: www.earthfriendlybaby.com
▶ For parents who demand natural quality, this range of natural baby toiletries is both gentle and smells wonderful. Includes a relaxing lavender cleansing bar, rich chamomile shampoo and bodywash, protective calendula daily care cream and soothing red clover nappy care cream. No synthetic colouring or fragrances, no sodium lauryl sulphate and no testing on animals. Call for stockists or mail order.

Healthpol
62 Hoodcote Gardens,
London N21 2NE
Tel: 020 8360 0386
Fax: 020 8360 0386
Email: echodoro@uk.packardbell.org
Web: www.delacet.com
▶ Sole importer of Delacet, a scalp and hair cleanser. A unique herbal product, it was formulated by a European company in order to eliminate head lice and nits in a single treatment. It contains no harmful pesticides and has not been tested on animals. It is effective, safe and simple to use, wlth 100% natural ingredients (herbs are organically grown) make it suitable for children 12 months and over and all hair types. It has a 'watery' consistency making it particuarly easy for application on Afro hair or dreadlocks (no need to use a nit comb). Available in the UK from independent chemists, health food shops and by mail order from Healthpol. As recommended by *Woman's Own*.

Maristows
57 Manor Fields, Bratton BA13 4ST
Tel: 01380 830 978
Fax: 01380 831 484
Email: maristows@skarab.demon.co.uk
Web: www.maristows.co.uk
Open: 24 hours tele line.
▶ Maristows B12 N12 Headlice Repellent, contains no organophosphates, non-flammable. Winner of Natural Product News Award for Best New Product 1998. Available all Good Health Stores, Superdrug, Tesco, Safeway, Holland & Barrett.

Natrababy Babycare Toiletries
c/o Bodywise (UK) Ltd,
Bristol BS32 4DX
Tel: 01454 615 500
Fax: 01454 613 805
Email: info@natracare.com
Web: www.natracare.com

Family & Community

Toiletries specially formulated using only the finest essential oils and petroleum-free, plant-derived ingredients. Products are also vegan, biodegradable and perfume-free. Very gentle for sensitive skin.

VAN UK National Vaccination Information Centre
178 Mansfield Road,
Nottingham NG1 3HW
Tel: 0115 948 0829
Fax: 0115 844 7066
Email: enquiries@van.org.uk
Web: www.van.org.uk
▶ Provides information on vaccination to help people make informed decisions. Annual subscription to SHOTS newsletter is £7.00 waged and £5.00 unwaged. Please send a large SAE for info. Booklet on all vaccines is £1.80.

Furniture, Clothing & Carriers

Better Baby Sling
60 Sumatra Road, London NW6 1PR
Tel: 020 7433 3727
Fax: 020 7431 9984
Email: info@betterbabysling.freeserve.co.uk
Web: www.betterbabysling.freeserve.co.uk
Open: Mon-Fri 9.30am-6pm;
Sat 9am-12 noon
▶ An over-the-shoulder carrier suitable for single babies and twins, the sling is an incredibly simple and practical way to carry your baby. Manufactured in a range of beautiful cotton fabrics, the sling can be worn in a variety of carrying positions for newborn to 32 pound toddlers. Comes complete with an instructional video demonstrating a range of positions.

BORN
64 Gloucester Road, Bishopston,
Bristol BS7 8BH
Tel: 0117 924 5080
Fax: 0117 924 9040
Email: born@dial.pipex.com
Web: www.first-born.co.uk
▶ One of the first shops to put natural holistic family living on the High Street. BORN offers a huge range of washable nappies and accessories, organic cotton and woollen clothing, reusable menstrual products, slings, books on natural parenting, toys made only from natural materials, organic and natural toiletries and off-road pushchairs. All are chosen for their excellent quality and minimal impact on the environment. A mail order service is also available via the web site.

Bushbaby (Pushchairs & Child Carriers)
Calange Ltd, PO Box 61,
Stockport SK3 0AP
Tel: 0161 474 7097
Fax: 0161 476 2647
▶ Mail order supplier of tough, durable pushchairs and child carriers including all-terrain models. Brightly coloured, waterproof all-in-one suits in 3-6 month and 6-12 month sizes are also available.

Children's Seating Centre
11 Whitcomb Street,
London WC2H 7HA
Tel: 020 7930 8308
Fax: 020 7925 0250
Open: Tues-Fri 10am-5pm;
Sat 10am-2pm
▶ Children's chairs designed to Alexander Technique principles for good posture development.

Eco Clothworks
PO Box 16109, London SE23 3WA
Tel: 020 8299 1619
Fax: 020 8299 6997
▶ Organic 'eco-textile' clothes and bed linen, including range for kids under five years, hemp, silk and organic linen shirt collections.

Firstborn
32 Bloomfield Avenue, Bath BA2 3AB
Tel: 01225 422 586
Email: deborah@dods-steele.demon.co.uk
▶ Supplies Wunderpants hand-knitted outer pants made from pure untreated wool which allows skin to breathe whilst protecting the outer clothes. Available ready-made or in an easy-knit kit. Mail order only, so call for a brochure.

Full Moon Futons
20 Bulmershe Road,
Reading RG1 5RJ
Tel/Fax: 0118 926 5648

▶ Cribs and cot mattresses in 100% pure cotton with unbleached cotton covers (see listing in Chapter Three: Home for adult futons). Call for mail order catalogue.

Green Baby Co Ltd
345 Upper Street, Islington,
London N1 0PD
Tel: 020 7226 4345
Fax: 020 7226 9244
Email: enquiries@greenbabyco.com
Web: www.greenbabyco.com
Open: Mon-Sat 10am-5pm
▶ With a rise in asthma and other allergic complaints amongst children, it is no wonder parents are looking for healthier, less chemically-oriented products for their children. Green Baby offers a comprehensive choice of ecological products that are both kinder for baby and the environment. They also pride themselves on providing advice for parents needing help choosing the right products for their needs. Products include: washable nappies, gel-free disposable nappies, hypoallergenic baby wipes, baby and maternity toiletries, organic cotton and chemical-free clothing and a wide range of nursery furnishings, toys and gifts. All Green Baby's products are available to buy on their secure website. Alternatively, call or a free catalogue or visist the shop.

Huggababy Natural Baby Products
Great House Barn, New Street,
Talgarth, Brecon LD3 0AH
Tel: 01874 711 629
Fax: 01874 711 037
Email: margaret@huggababy.co.uk
Web: www.huggababy.co.uk
Open: Mon-Fri 9am-5pm
▶ Set up in 1994 to manufacture and market the Huggababy Baby Carrier, a side sling for babies from birth to toddler that makes it easy to keep your baby close while you get on with your life. Has developed a small catalogue featuring their own-brand products along with carefully chosen and tested products from other companies, with

Protect him naturally

In our modern world we're surrounded by an ever increasing range of chemicals.

Babies, with their delicate systems and skin, are particularly vulnerable to irritants.

Green Baby offers a wide range of ecological baby products. Using only kind, natural ingredients they protect both your baby and the environment.

Ring **020 7226 4345** for a free copy of Green Baby's catalogue, or visit our website at www.greenbabyco.com

Green Baby, 345 Upper Street, London N1 0PD. Tel: 020 7226 4345
www.greenbabyco.com

an emphasis on top quality natural and practical products for babies, including products made from organic materials. Own-brand products include Huggababy Natural Lambskins, which are machine-washable, undyed, unbleached British lambskins tanned for baby use, and since sheep come in colours other than white, so do the lambskins. Another range is bedding woven in Wales from soft merino wool, including cot blankets and a baby sleeping bag which is free from polyester padding. Other ranges featured are Natural Bedtime, Natural Playtime, Natural Health and Outdoor Adventure and the products include books, baby massage kits and Aromatherapy kits, all-terrain pushchairs, high specification hiking backpacks, wooden toys, natural cot mattresses and nursing bras.

Kids in Comfort
172 Victoria Road, Wargrave,
Reading RG10 8AJ
Tel/Fax: 0118 940 4942
Email: k.lloyd@mcmail.com
Open: School hours
▶ Supplies Sling Easy, a baby sling worn across the chest and available in four sizes (newborns to toddlers). It is made of 100% cotton in several patterns. Also sells dolls slings.

Mountain Buggy
9 Cromwell Road,
Camberley GU15 4HY
Tel/Fax: 01276 502 587
Email: mountainbuggy@compuserve.com
▶ Mail order suppliers of the Mountain Terrain Buggy, tough pushchairs for all-terrain use. Available in single and double models.

Naturally
102 Louden Hill Road, Orchard Park,
Robroyston, Glasgow G33 1GG
Tel: 0141 400 6456
Fax: 0141 400 6455
▶ Mail order company specialising in natural products mainly for babies and young children with some adult natural fibre underwear. Supplies reusable nappies; organic cotton clothing; chemical-free woollen vests that are as soft as silk; handknits such as rainbow jumpers; soft and wooden handmade toys with some organic cotton cuddlies; nursey accessories such as willow cradle, organic sheepskin, and horn teaspoons; natural skincare products including herbal baths and remedies for all the family; books on natural parents; and much more. Many products are bought from ethical manufacturers supporting worldwide initiatives. Fast, efficient and friendly business. Send an A5 SAE (33p) for free catalogue.

Pegasus Pushchairs Ltd
Westbridge, Tavistock PL19 8DE
Tel: 01822 618 077
Email: info@allterrain.co.uk
Web: www.allterrain.co.uk
▶ British Manufacturer of All Terrain Pushchairs for an active lifestyle. The complete family can enjoy the freedom of the great outdoors without being restrained by the limitations of an ordinary pushchair.

Spirit of Nature Ltd
Burrhart House, Cradock Road,
Luton LU4 0JF
Tel: 01582 847 370
Fax: 01582 847 371
Email: oliver@spiritofnature.co.uk
Web: www.spiritofnature.co.uk
Open: Mon-Fri 9am-5.30pm
▶ Family-run business selling comprehensive range of organic clothing and accessories for babies and children from 0-4 years old. Undyed, unbleached underwear, sleepwear and fashion clothing for newborns and children with allergies plus a collection of more colourful fashion clothing that is also kind to the skin. Other products include nappies (unbleached washables and disposables), organic cotton nursing bras and breastpads, organic nursing pillows, bedlinen, lambskins and toys. Also available: natural clothing collection for adults, eco-household products, natural bodycare products. Call for a free catalogue.

Su Su Ma Ma
243 Holcroft Court, Clipstone Street,
London W1P 7DZ
Tel/Fax: 020 7436 6768
Email: carli@easynet.co.uk
Open: Wholesale enquiries 24 hours

▶ One-woman company selling fairly traded children's clothes made from traditionally produced textiles from around the world. Only buys from small businesses which pass its fair trade criteria. Call for a brochure.

Suantrai Slings
16a Ballyman Road,
Bray, Co Wicklow,
Tel: 020 7499 9505
Fax: 020 7499 9505
Email: suantrai@iol.ie
▶ Mail order supplier of slings for carrying babies and toddlers, available in several materials including tie dye, denim, plains and patterns. Slings cost £22.50 (including p&p). Also makes tie-dye childrens and babies clothes, some recycled.

The Healthy House
Cold Harbour, Ruscombe,
Stroud GL6 6DA
Tel: 01453 752 216
Fax: 01453 753 533
Email: info@healthy-house.co.uk
Web: www.healthy-house.co.uk
▶ The Healthy House is a mail order company specialising in products for people with allergies, asthma, skin disorders and environmental illness. Send for a free catalogue which includes untreated cotton bedding, dust mite proof bedding cases, air purifiers, water purifiers, products for electromagnetic pollution, non toxic paints, vacuum cleaners, steam cleaners, masks, light boxes and much more. Offers natural bedding and dust mite proof covers for cots and single beds as well as cotton mittens and gloves for eczema sufferers.

Traidcraft plc
Kingsway North,
Gateshead NE11 0NE
Tel: 0191 491 0591
Fax: 0191 482 2690
Email: comm@traidcraft.co.uk
Web: www.traidcraft.co.uk
▶ Sell a range of fairly traded children's t-shirts, organic pyjamas and bedding. Available by mail order catalogue from 0191 491 1001. Wholesale range now available from hotline 0191 491 3388.

Wilkinet Baby Carrier (Yep Ltd)
Freepost NWW 3643A,
Telford TF1 722
Tel: 0800 1383400/01952 277079
Email: wilkinet@yep.ltd.uk
Web: www.wilkinet.co.uk
Open: Mon-Fri 9am-5pm
▶ Designed by a mother, this baby carrier adapts to the changing needs of you and your baby from tiny 5lb newborn to 30lb toddler. 100% cotton and handcrafted in Wales. Its excellent weight distribution makes it ideal for parents with back problems. More information and fabric samples available upon request.

Toys

Colour Wood
1 New Town Street, Chartham Hatch,
Canterbury CT4 7LT
Tel/Fax: 01227 730 204
▶ Hand-crafted and painted children's wooden toys, furniture and other furnishings (mirrors, trays, picture frames, etc). All products are made of wood from sustainable resources (mostly Finnish birch) and all paints and varnishes are non-toxic. All toys correspond to European Safety Standards. Call for a free colour catalogue.

Community Playthings
Robertsbridge TN32 5DR
Tel: 0800 387 457
Fax: 01580 882 250
Email: sales@bruderhof.com
▶ Large range of quality wooden children's furniture and toys available by mail order produced by an international religious community called the Darvell Bruderhof. Large catalogue available upon request.

Dawson & Son Wooden Toys & Games
Winstanley House, Market Hill,
Saffron Walden CB10 1HQ
Tel: 01799 526 611
Fax: 01799 525 522
Email: toys@dawson-and-son.com
Web: www.dawson-and-son.com
▶ Over 200 wooden toys for children of all ages, all crafted using natural materials from replenishable sources

Family & Community

and non-toxic paints. Many of the toys are educational and assist in children's development in ways which make learning fun. The only limitations on most of the toys are those of the child's own imagination. Call for a free mail order catalogue or visit the online shop.

Escor Toys
Elliott Road, Bournemouth BH11 8JP
Tel: *01202 591 081*
Fax: *01202 570 049*
Email: *escortoys@bournemouth.gov.uk*
▶ Wooden toys made from well-seasoned hardwoods and hand-finished in top quality paint or clear lacquer. Range includes peg and hammer sets, cars, tractors and trains, fairground rides and constructional toys. Mail order. Phone or email for catalogue. Employer of disabled people.

Green Board Game Company
34 Amersham Hill Drive,
High Wycombe HP13 6QY
Tel: *01494 538 999*
Fax: *01494 538 646*
Email: *info@greenboardgames.com*
Web: *www.greenboardgames.com*
▶ Sells award-winning boardgames, card games and CD Roms that are educational, fun to play and produced in an enviromentally conscious way. Bestsellers include Walking with Dinosaurs, Blue Peter Explorer, Alpha Animals and Atlas Adventures. Please call for a free catalogue, or visit the website.

Hill Toy Company
71 Abingdon Road, London W8 6AW
Tel: *020 7937 8797*
Fax: *020 7937 0209*
Email: *hannah.hilltoy@onyxnet.co.uk*
Open: *Mon-Fri 9.30am-5.30pm;*
Sat 10am-5pm
▶ Mail order supplier of wooden toys made from replenishable sources of wood to a high standard of design and quality. Call for a catalogue.

Norfolk Dolls
Wayside Cottage, Thwaite Common,
Erpingham NR11 7QQ
Tel: *01263 761 665*
▶ Handmade dolls carved in wood, finished in beeswax and with soft linen bodies. Portrait dolls and other commissions welcome.

Omshanti Ltd
Lyn House, Wells Road, Hallatrow,
Bristol BS39 6EN
Tel: *01761 453 433*
Fax: *01761 453 976*
Email: *lynhse@globalnet.co.uk*
▶ A board game with a roll-up felt mat across which one throws glide balls – like a cosmic version of Shove Ha'Penny. It is a game requiring relaxed concentration. The calmer you are, the more successful your game! Price £25 (incl p&p).

Soup Dragon
27 Topsfield Parade, Tottenham Lane,
Crouch End, London N8 8PT
Tel: *020 8348 0224*
Fax: *020 8348 9555*
Web: *www.soupdragon.co.uk*
Open: *Mon-Sat 9.30am-6pm*
▶ Traditional wooden toys, games and puzzles all crafted from natural materials. Puppets, rag dolls, rocking horses, doll's houses and more. Unusual children's clothing from 0-9 years. Mail order available.

Stuart Lennie Woodcrafts
Cardova, 44 Bisley Road,
Stroud GL5 1HF
Tel: *01453 750 791*
Open: *Workshop can visited by prior arrangement*
▶ Solid wood dolls houses, Noah's Arks, nativity scenes, dolls furniture, toy farm buildings, stables etc. All materials used sourced from renewable and sustainable reserves – all hardwoods used are British, very often local to the Cotswolds. Awards: Ogle Design Trophy 2000 for best toy for under six years olds, Marjorie Abbatt Award 1998 for Playability, 1996 Best Newcomer to British Toymakers Guild.

Tall Ships Play Frames
Unit 1, Highfield Industrial Estate,
Camelford PL32 9RA
Tel: *01840 212 022*
Fax: *01840 212 022*
Email: *janice@tallships.co.uk*
Web: *www.tallships.co.uk*
▶ Wood and rope outdoor play equipment, including climbing frames, swings, slides, bridges, rope rides, treehouses and much more.

Toys for Children
The Old Foundry, Steam Mills,
Cinderford GL14 3JE
Tel: *01594 824 007*
Open: *Mon-Fri 9am-5.30pm*
▶ Wonderful, simple, wooden toys including native wood building bricks, trucks, trains and the full range of farm yard animals. Call for a catalogue.

Traditional Wooden Toys
The Lodge, Pickhill Hall,
Wrexham LL13 0UG
Tel: *01978 780 787*
Fax: *01978 780 787*
▶ Handmade, hard-wearing, long-lasting, traditional wooden toys made with hard or soft wood.

Traidcraft plc
Kingsway North,
Gateshead NE11 0NE
Tel: *0191 491 0591*
Fax: *0191 482 2690*
Email: *comm@traidcraft.co.uk*
Web: *www.traidcraft.co.uk*
▶ Sells a range of fairly traded, handcrafted children's toys, mostly wooden, musical instruments and footballs. Available by mail order catalogue from 0191 491 1001. Wholesale range now available from hotline 0191 491 3388.

Books

Barefoot Books Ltd
18 Highbury Terrace,
London N5 1UP
Tel: *020 7704 6492*
Fax: *020 7359 5798*
Email: *info@barefoot-books.com*
Web: *www.barefoot-books.com*
▶ Independent children's book publisher with an emphasis on original, high quality, colour picture books from traditional cultures all over the World. Internationally acclaimed for its lively and carefully researched texts and dramatic, full colour artwork, its titles introduce children to the values and traditions of other cultures and are intended to be enjoyed and treasured for life. The list includes Picture Books for ages 1-6, Barefoot Books: picture books for ages 4-adult, Barefoot Collections: anthologies for ages 4-adult, Barefoot Poetry Collections: poetry for ages 4-adult. Available by mail order and through some good bookshops. Call for a catalogue.

Friends of the Earth (FoE)
26-28 Underwood Street,
London N1 7JQ
Tel: *020 7490 1555*
Fax: *020 7490 0881*
Email: *info@foe.co.uk*
Web: *www.foe.co.uk*
▶ Publishes an extensive range of environmental information and books for children. Call on the above number for a catalogue.

Letterbox Library
Unit 2D, Leroy House,
436 Essex Road, London N1 3QP
Tel: *020 7226 1633*
Fax: *020 7226 1768*
▶ Children's book supplier specialising in non-sexist, multi-cultural and green books. A team of reviewers from a wide range of publishers selects the best books from the UK and abroad. Call for a free catalogue.

Words of Discovery
82 Holmfield Road,
Leicester LE2 1SB
Tel: *0116 273 3000*
Fax: *0116 273 3000*
Email: *sales@wordsofdiscovery.com*
Web: *www.wordsofdiscovery.com*
▶ The largest company in the UK to specialise in children's holistic, spiritual and personal growth books, promoting books and resources for children, teenagers, parents and teachers which all have the common aim of nurturing children's personal development. We believe these resources can make a profoundly positive difference to the lives of children and parents by promoting confidence, self-esteem, morals, values, creativity, positive relationships and self-awareness.

Organisations & Advice

For other organisations that can provide information on birth, family planning and maternity services, see section on Birth.

Association for Improvements in the Maternity Services (AIMS)
21 Iver Lane, Iver SL0 9LH
Tel: 01753 652 781
Fax: 01753 654 142
Email: pa.thomas@virginnet.co.uk
Web: www.aims.org.uk
Open: Mon-Fri 9am-5pm
▶ AIMS was founded in 1960. It offers information, support and advice to parents about all aspects of maternity care, including parents' rights, choices available, technological interventions, natural childbirth and complaints procedures. Produces a series of information leaflets and a quarterly journal which contains information about obstetric and midwifery practices, research and accounts of individual experiences. Send an SAE for free information leaflet 'What is AIMS?' and publications list to Publications Secretary, 2 Bacon Lane, Hayling Island, Hants PO11 0DN.

Baby Milk Action
23 St Andrews Street,
Cambridge CB2 3AX
Tel: 01223 464 420
Fax: 01223 464 417
Email: info@babymilkaction.org
Web: www.babymilkaction.org
Open: Mon-Fri 9.30am-6pm
▶ Non-profit organisation which aims to save infant lives and to end the avoidable suffering caused by inappropriate infant feeding by working within a global network to strengthen independent, transparent and effective controls on the marketing of the baby feeding industry worldwide. To achieve this, Baby Milk Action works to end the inappropriate marketing policies and practices of the baby feeding industry and to ensure that mothers and infants worldwide are effectively represented wherever decisions affecting infant feeding are made.

Chernobyl Children's Project
Kinder House, Fitzalan Street,
Glossop SK13 7DL
Tel: 01457 863 534
Fax: 01457 857 169
Email: linda@ccprojectuk.fsnet.co.uk
▶ Charity which brings children from the Chernobyl-affected region of Belarus to the UK for recuperative holidays. Also delivers humanitarian aid to hospitals and children's homes in the region, organises exchanges of medical staff and special needs teachers, helps to facilitate independent living for young disabled people, and is involved in setting up a fostering system to get children with disabilities out of orphanages. Donations welcome, as is anyone interested in fund-raising or in providing accommodation for Russian children during the summer holidays. Call the above number for further info.

Community Hygiene Concern
160 Inderwick Road, London N8 9JT
Tel: 020 8341 7167
Fax: 020 8292 7208
Email: bugbusters2k@yahoo.co.uk
Web: www.chc.org; www.nits.net
Open: Help Line: Mon-Fri 10am-4pm
▶ Non-profit making vountary organisation to protect people and pets from parasites and rekindle enthusiasm for community hygiene. Help with common UK parasites, particularly lice and nits (Help Line 020 8341 7167), threadworms and scabies (Help Line 020 7387 1990). Produce family Bug Buster Kit, recommended by the Department of Health, for detection and treatment of head lice without using pesticides. It is reusable, only one kit per family required.

Fertility UK
Clitherow House, 1 Blythe Mews,
Blythe Road, London W14 0NW
Tel: 020 7371 1341
Fax: 020 7371 4921
Email: jknight@fertilityuk.org
Web: www.fertilityuk.org
▶ Fertility Awareness and natural family planning education which can also be used to plan or avoid pregnancy. Also publishes the book and video Fertility by Dr Elizabeth Clubb and Jane Knight about natural family planning methods (£7.99 plus £1.50 p&p). Call for details of local accredited teacher.

Informed Parent
PO Box 870, Harrow HA3 7UW
Tel: 020 8861 1022
▶ Promotes awareness and understanding about vaccinations to enable parents to make an informed decision about whether to vaccinate or not. Publishes a quarterly newsletter containing a reading list and details of talks on vaccination. Runs a support network for concerned parents wanting to make contact with others and provides guidance in alternative and holistic practitioners.

National Childbirth Trust
Alexandra House, Oldham Terrace,
Acton, London W3 6NH
Tel: 020 8992 8637
Fax: 020 8992 5929
Web: www.nct-online.org
Open: Mon-Fri 9.30am-5pm
▶ Offers information and support in pregnancy, childbirth and early parenthood. Aim to give every parent the chance to make informed, and try to make sure their services, activities and membership are fully accessible to everyone. Activities include antenatal classes and information on maternity issues, breastfeeding and postnatal support including specialist groups for caesareans and miscarriage. 348 branches nationwide. Research incorporates a survey of parents' needs for information and support around pregnancy, birth and early parenting. Campaigning to halt the rising caesarean section rate; to promote breastfeeding – including a publication of 'You CAN do it here!' – a directory of breastfeeding friendly places; to safeguard home birth as an option and for family centre policies. Affiliations include Maternity Alliance, Baby Milk Action, National Children's Bureau, Unicef Baby Friendly Initiative.

Parentibility
PO Box 72, Ruislip HA4 6XU
Tel: 01600 860 186 Fri 10am-4pm;
01785 612 592 Mon 10am-1pm
▶ Group providing peer support for people with disability who are thinking about, or are, parents or grandparents. A newsletter is available as well as an equipment hotline, a professional links register and a contact register for people to meet others with similar disabilities. The helpline is staffed by volunteers with disabilities working from home.

The Natural Nurturing Network
P.O. Box 5622, Wigston LE18 2ZA
Tel: 0116 288 0844
Fax: 0116 257 1897
Email: flykeith@cwcom.net
▶ Shares certain ideas about the nature and needs of people, and aims to put these ideas into practice with regard to ourselves, our children and each other. Convinced that people are born good and social creatures. Committed to nurturing children during their natural stage of dependence with love, respect, and patience, so they may grow up to become responsible, self reliant and fulfilled. The network offers nationwide support, gatherings, regular newsletters and local group activities.

WATch
60 Bridge Street,
Pershore WR10 1AX
Tel: 01386 561 635
Fax: 01386 561 635
Email: watch@clasen.demon.co.uk
Web: www.jbaass.oc.demon.co.uk/watch
▶ National charity promoting parental responsibility with a particular emphasis on the emotional needs of children during their crucial first three years through media, education and health services. Campaigns for pre-school education for 3-5 year olds.

Family & Community 133

EDUCATION

Schools, Kindergartens & Nurseries

Cherrytrees Kindergarten
c/o 16 Milking Stile Lane,
Lancaster LA1 4QB
Tel: 01524 33018
▶ Independent Early Years Centre affiliated to the Steiner Waldorf Schools Fellowship.

Creative Therapies
7 School Road, Sale M33 7XY
Tel: 0161 962 6272
▶ Creative clubs with an holistic approach for children aged 8-13, which take place after school in Sale, Manchester and North Midlands. Individuals can train to run a creative club on a 10 month course over weekends or weekdays.

Kidsunlimited
Kids of Wilmslow Ltd, Westhead,
10 West Street, Alderley Edge SK9 7EG
Tel: 01625 585 222
Fax: 01625 583 444
Email: enquiries@kidsunlimited.co.uk
▶ Award winning company operates day nurseries throughout the UK, in areas including Cambridge, Oxford, London and the North-West. Corporate clients include The Body Shop and Amnesty International. The unique KU philosophy is very much about a pioneering and natural approach to childcare. A progresssive range of activies and expereinces are offered, ensuring that the individual needs of each child are met. The KU curriculum is constantly monitored and amended, consequently obtaining glowing OFSTED reports. Extra curricular activities include Baby Yoga, Baby massage and for mums and dads, parenting classes. A skincare range KU-Chi has been developed and tested extensively in the nurseries and is now available by mail order. Other products are currently under development.

Manchester, Three Cities Initiative
65 Austin Drive, Didsbury,
Manchester M20 6FA
Tel: 0161 445 7661
▶ Initiative registered with the Steiner Waldorf Schools Fellowship.

Merlin Kindergarten
2 Meadow Bank Road,
Sheffield S11 9AH
Tel: 0114 250 8274
▶ Independent Early Years Centre affiliated to the Steiner Waldorf Schools Fellowship.

Merseryside Play Action Council
1-27 Bridport Street, Liverpool L3 5QF
Tel: 0151 708 0468
Fax: 0151 709 0336
▶ A non-profit making charity, which was set up over 40 years ago. Has a 'Scrounge Room' packed with reusable waste materials, and through this, over the years many play schemes have been able to have things they couldn't afford to buy from local shops. To help with running costs, offers printing and photocopying facilities, an art and craft shop and equipment for hire.

Michael House School
The Field, Shipley, Heanor DE75 7JH
Tel: 01773 718 050
Fax: 01773 711 784
Web: www.compulink.co.uk/~waldorf
▶ Member of the Steiner Waldorf Fellowship. Opened in 1934 and accepts children from 4 to 16 years. Pupils are prepared for GCSE examinations in the Upper School. Boarders can be accomodated in the homes of school parents. The school lies in countryside between Ilkeston and Heanor.

Sheffield St School Project
74 Bower Road, Crookes,
Sheffield S10 1ER
Tel: 0114 266 6484
▶ School registered with Steiner Waldorf Schools Fellowship.

Organisations & Resources

Association for Outdoor Learning, The
12 St Andrews Churchyard,
Penrith CA11 7YE
Tel: 01768 891 065
Fax: 01768 891 914
Email: afol@adventure-ed.co.uk
Web: www.adventure-ed.co.uk
Open: Mon-Fri 9am-5pm
▶ A membership organisation and registered charity providing a range of services which include: a specialist bookshop offering discounts; Horizons, the only magazine for outdoor educators, which offers inspiration for training, teaching, events, support, job opportunities and news for the outdoor professional, teacher, leader or instructor; insurance, comprising of a special package for those who lead groups outdoors; a quarterly newsletter; courses and conferences; a website pages; special interest groups; careers information; safety consultants; and regional groups.

Countryside Foundation for Education
Unit 2 Brier Hey Industrial Estate,
Mytolmroyd, Halifax HX7 5PF
Tel: 01422 885 566
Fax: 01422 885 533

Email: barbara-mccluskey@countrysidefoundation.org.uk
Web: www.countrysidefoundation.org.uk
▶ An educational charity that 'brings the countryside into the classroom' by producing educational resources for both primary and secondary schools which help to promote an understanding of the countryside as a living, working environment. Also carries out in-service teacher training courses (INSET) and organises countryside days for schools at country estates nationwide.

Development Education Centre
Gillett Centre, 998 Bristol Road,
Sellyoak, Birmingham B29 6LE
Tel: 0121 472 3255
Fax: 0121 415 2322
▶ Small educational charity working in partnership with teachers to bring a global dimension and development perspective to the cirriculum.

"Beautiful, pure, wild-crafted herbs and environmentally friendly - what else would I use on my children?"
Caron Keating

"As a mother, I am delighted to have discovered the KU-CHI skincare range".
Emma Forbes

● Baby Shampoo & Bath Cleanser
● Nappy Barrier & Moisturising Lotion
● Family Skin Wash
● Nappy Barrier Cream
● Massage Oil
● Tissue Wipes

● pure essential oils
● no petro-chemicals
● lanolin fre
● not animal tested
● contains no nut oils
● infused vegetable oils
● vegetable derived cleansing agents
● packaging p.v.c. free
● natural preservative
● no artificial colour or fragrance

For a pricelist and order form contact:
Kids Unlimited
Westhead, 10 West Street,
Alderley Edge, Cheshire SK9 7EG
t 01625 585222 f 01625 583444
e ku-chi@kidsunlimited.co.uk

KU-CHI™
THE ART OF INFANT MAINTENANCE

Earth Science Teachers Association
Thomas Rotheram College,
Moorgate Road,
Rotherham S60 2BE
Tel: 01709 300 600
Fax: 01709 300 601
Email: dawn.windley@thomroth.ac.uk
▶ Encourages and supports the teaching of earth science at all levels.

Eco-Schools Project
c/o Tidy Britain Group, Elizabeth House, The Pier, Wigan WN3 4EX
Tel: 01942 824 620
Fax: 01942 824 778
▶ European environmental award programme for schools – of interest to teachers, local authorities and LEA advisers – which aims to encourage schools to look at the impact they have on the environment and to put in place measures to reduce that impact. At the heart of Eco-schools is pupil involvement in decision-making regarding action undertaken by the school.

Education Now
113 Arundel Drive, Bramcote Hills, Nottingham NG9 3FQ
Tel: 0115 925 7261
Fax: 0115 925 7261
Web: www.gn.apc.org/educationnow
▶ Non-profit making research, writing and publishing company and a co-operative devoted to developing a more flexible education system to cope with the wide variety of learning styles, forms of intelligence and the needs of a rapidly changing society.

Education Otherwise
PO Box 7420, London N9 9SG
Tel: 0900 1518 303
Email: e_o@netlink.co.uk
▶ Membership organisation which provides support and information for families whose children are being educated outside school. Publishes a regular newsletter and runs a nation-wide network of local groups who meet for social and educational activities.

Educational Heretics Press
113 Arundel Drive,
Bramcote Hills,
Nottingham NG9 3FQ
Tel: 0115 925 7261
Fax: 0115 925 7261
Web: www.gn.apc.org/edheretics
▶ Non-profit making research and publishing company devoted to questioning the dogmas of schooling in particular and education in general with a view to developing the logistics of the next learning system. Call for a catalogue.

Greater Manchester Play Resource Unit (GRUMPY)
GRUMPY House, Vaughan Street, West Gorlton, Manchester M12 5DU
Tel: 0161 223 9730
Fax: 0161 220 9664
Email: resources@grumpy.org.uk
Web: www.grumpy.org.uk
Open: Mon 1-7pm; Tues-Fri 10am-2pm
▶ Waste materials from businesses and industry collected for children's play schemes and art and crafts project. Call for further details.

Home Education Advisory Service
PO Box 98,
Welwyn Garden City AL8 6AN
Tel: 01707 371 854
Fax: 01707 371 854
Email: admin@heas.org.uk
Web: www.heas.org.uk
▶ National charity which provides information, advice and support for home educating families. Subscription is open to families and to others who are interested. HEAS publishes a range of leaflets and the Home Education Handbook and exists to spread the word about home education: it's legal, it's practical and it's your own choice.

Human Scale Education
96 Carlingcott,
Near Bath BA2 8AW
Tel: 01275 332 516
Fax: 01275 332 516
Email: hse@clara.net
▶ National educational charity promoting smaller structures in education, supporting parents and teachers wishing to set up their own school. Also encourages large schools to find ways of working in smaller units so that the needs of each individual can be met. Membership, which includes a newsletter three times a year giving information about human scale initiatives, costs £18 per annum.

Manchester Development Education Project
c/o The Manchester Metropolitan University, 801 Wilmslow Road, Didsbury, Manchester M20 2QR
Tel: 0161 445 2495
Fax: 0161 445 2360
Email: depman@gn.apc.org
Web: www.dept.org.uk/
▶ One of a network of educational centres providing support and information, raising issues and doing research to expand a global perspective. Runs a Resource Centre and Bookshop providing support and advice on all areas of Global Education through in-service training and curriculum support projects and a large number of educational books and other teaching resources.

Manchester Environmental Education Network
c/o The Manchester Metropolitan University, 801 Wilmslow Road, Didsbury, Manchester M20 2QR
Tel: 0161 445 2495
Fax: 0161 445 2360
Email: depman@gn.apc.org
Web: www.dep.org.uk/
▶ As part of the Manchester Development Education Project (see above), MEEN is a forum for people involved in the planning of structured learning experience relating to environmental education. The purpose of this forum is to share ideas, develop the means and deliver the strategies to promote, develop and support education throughout Greater Manchester. Members receive a termly newsletter, The Beehive. Call Anne Strachan for further info.

National Association of Environmental Education
University of Wolverhampton, Walsall Campus, Gorway Road, Walsall WS1 3BD
Tel: 01922 631 200
Fax: 01922 631 200
Open: Mon-Fri 9.30am-3pm
▶ Teachers' organisation promoting environmental education in schools and colleges. It produces a termly journal called Environmental Educational Susainability and a series of practical guides. It holds an annual residential conference at different locations in the UK around Easter. Membership of the NAEE costs £20 per annum and includes copies of the journal.

Steiner Waldorf Schools Fellowship
Kidbrooke Park,
Forest Row RH18 5JA
Tel: 01342 822 115
Fax: 01342 826 004
Email: postmaster@waldorf.compulink.co.uk
▶ Represents the 26 autonomous Rudolf Steiner Waldorf Schools for normal children in the UK and Eire. There are now over 780 schools worldwide, 1500 kindergartens, and 60 teacher training institutions in 50 countries. Key characteristics of the

---

Natural Friends
Britain's best introduction agency for all green-minded singles
FREE BROCHURE
0800 281 933
info@natural-friends.co.uk
www.natural-friends.com
100% non-smokers

education include a careful balance in the artistic, practical and intellectual content of the international Steiner Waldorf curriculum and a co-educational structure for students from three to 19 years. Shared Steiner Waldorf curriculum for all pupils. GSCE and A-level examinations taken without pressure. A broad education based on Steiner's anthroposophical approach to the nature of the human being. Steiner Waldorf education is rapidly gaining in popularity all over the world.

Sunshine Puppets
4 Mallow Street,
Manchester M15 5GD
Tel: 0161 232 7807
Fax: 0161 227 8501
Email: circus@zapparelli.co.uk
Web: www.zappme.com
▶ Performs puppet shows and educational workshops, with support from the Groundwork Trust and Global Action Plan, and which deal with environmental and healthy living issues. The shows are accompanied by workshops, with the children making puppets and writing and performing their own show. The children work in small groups, on a variety of situations dealing with issues raised in the show.

WATCH Trust for Environmental Education
The Kiln, Waterside, Mather Road,
Newark NG24 1WT
Tel: 01636 677 711
Fax: 01636 670 001
Email:
general@wildlife-trusts.cix.co.uk
Open: Mon-Fri 9am-5pm
▶ Section of the Royal Society for Nature Conservation that produces useful educational project packs for kids.

Wildlife Watch
The Wildlife Trusts, The Kiln, Mather Road, Newark NG24 1WT
Tel: 01636 677 711
Fax: 01636 670 001
Email:
watch@wildlife-trusts.cix.co.uk
Open: Mon-Fri 9am-5pm
▶ Wildlife Watch is an environmental action club for kids, producing magazines and posters and supporting a network of groups. Across the UK volunteers involve thousands of children in wildlife and environmental activities, investigations and games. As the junior branch of the Wildlife Trusts, are committed to providing a variety of opportunities for young people to engage in the issues which affect their environment and the wildlife they share it with. In addition to membership resources and groups, projects offer a unique investigative approach to exploring the natural world and our impact upon it. Participation can be through subscription or though the volunteer leader network.

Woodcraft Folk
13 Ritherdon Road,
London SW17 8QE
Tel: 020 8672 6031
Fax: 020 8767 2457
Email:
folk_hov@woodcraft.demon.co.uk
▶ Educational organisation that works with children and young people from six to 20 years old in four age groups. Runs a programme designed to encourage understanding of environmental issues in the context of living in a world where equality, peace and friendship are important. Produces educational resources for environmental work with children. Call for details of local offices.

Worldwide Education Service
Blagrave House, 17 Blagrave Street, Reading RG1 1QA
Tel: 0118 958 9993
Fax: 0118 958 9994
Email: office@weshome.demon.co.uk
▶ Courses for 3-12 year olds, based on the national curriculum, for parents who want to teach their children at home, either in the UK or overseas. Call for a free copy of its booklet and newsletter.

FRIENDS & PARTNERS

Calico
California Road, Mistley CO11 1JE
Tel/Fax: 01206 393 160
Email: info@calico.co.uk
Web: www.calico.co.uk
▶ Members are passionate about vegetarian diet and growing, cooking and eating good, natural food.

Dragonpaths
12 Sanbed Road, St Werburghs,
Bristol BS2 9TX
Tel: 0117 941 1557
Email: annie-dragonpath@virgin.net
▶ Offers alternative ceremonies – marriages, namings, funerals – arranged by an experienced, professional celebrant according to the client's personal preference. From grand old country houses to a quiet woodland glade, Annie Wildwood has performed unique, beautiful ceremonies in a variety of settings. She also runs workshops, makes Imagework tapes and conducts Spirit Path divination.

Friendships
51 Besbury Park, Minchinhampton,
Stroud GL6 9EN
Tel: 01453 731 196
▶ Nationwide agency for people whose interests are in the area of green issues, New Age understanding, alternative therapies, naturalism, conservation, rambling, organic living and peace. Call or write for more details.

Natural Friends
15 Benyon Gardens, Culford,
Bury St Edmunds IP28 6EA
Tel/Fax: 01284 728 315
Email: info@natural-friends.com
Web: www.natural-friends.com
Open: 24 hours
▶ Unique, international introduction agency for environmentally friendly and socially conscious, non-smoking singles. Well-educated members aged from 25 to 65 with a 50:50 ratio of men to women. Founded in 1985 with more than 17,000 satisfied members. Call or email for more information or vist the website.

VMM (Vegetarian Matchmakers)
Concord House, 7 Waterbridge Court, Appleton, Warrington WA4 3BJ
Tel: 01925 601 609
Fax: 01925 860 442
Email: vmm@cybervillage.co.uk
Web: www.cybervillage.co.uk/vmm
▶ Dating and friendship agency specially for vegetarians, vegans and aspiring vegetarians of opposite sexes. Membership for six or twelve months.

VETS & PETS

British Association of Homœopathic Veterinary Surgeons
Tel: 01367 718 115
▶ Association for veterinary surgeons who are interested in Homeopathy. Names and telephone numbers of veterinary surgeons with homoeopathic qualifications are given on the above number. For further information, please send an SAE to the Honorary Secretary, The Alternative Veterinary Medicine Centre, Chinham House, Stanford-in-the-Vale, Oxfordshire SSN7 8NQ. Note when contacting any of these vets that not all of them treat farm animals and horses.

By Natural Selection
66 Mountfield Road,
Wroxall PO38 3BX
Tel/Fax: 01983 852 165
Email: sales@bynaturalselection.com
Web: www.bynaturalselection.com
Open: Mon-Sat 10am-5pm
▶ Offers a range of natural remedies and products for pets, incorporating Homeopathy, Aromatherapy and herbal preparations for a range of common pet ailments. Also stocks food supplements and accessories. Mail order or online from the website. Call for a copy of the free catalogue.

Green Ark Animal Nutrition
Unit 7B, Lineholme Mill, Burnley Road, Todmorden OL14 7DH
Tel/Fax: 01282 606 810
Email: greenark@cwcom.net
Web: www.greenark.mcmail.com
▶ Small family run business, the core products of which are their

unique whole grain and herbal cereal mix for dogs, created from an original 1940's recipe, and a range of herbal supplements to complete the diet and concentrate on problem areas of health. Uses organically grown products wherever possible to create a wholesome food for dogs. Products available by mail order.

Herbaticus
76 Snape Hill Lane,
Dronfield S18 2GP
Tel: 01246 411 949
Fax: 01246 418 482
Email: enquiries@herbaticus.co.uk
Web: www.herbaticus.co.uk
Open: Mon-Fri 9am-5pm
▶ Sells mail order herbal mineral and vitamin nutritional supplements for animals, in particular Wolle's Nature System, a combination system of supplements for everyday and long term well-being and hip, hoof, gum, respiratory and temperament conditions in dogs, horses and cats. Expansion into organic herbs, tinctures and topical application products are planned and the range available will grow throughout the year. Call for free literature or visit the website.

People's Dispensary for Sick Animals
Warwick Road South, Old Trafford,
Manchester M16 0JW
Tel: 0161 881 0222
Fax: 0161 860 5153
Email: manchester.vc@pdsa.org.uk
Web: www.pdsa.org.uk
▶ Offers free treatment for pets belonging to owners on means-tested benefits. Treat small animals with sickness or injury. Deal with 40,000 cases and perform 2,000 operations a year.

People's Dispensary for Sick Animals (Head Office)
Whitechapel Way, Priorslee,
Telford TF2 9PQ
Tel/Fax: 01952 291 035
▶ Since 1917, has offered free treatment for pets belonging to owners on means-tested benefits. Treats small animals with sickness or injury, ie curative treatment. Treats nearly 5,000 pets each day in 4 centres Nationwide. Call 0800 731 2502 for details of your nearest branch. Volunteers and donations always warmly accepted.

Wafcol
Haigh Avenue, Stockport SK4 1NU
Tel: 0161 480 2781
Fax: 0161 474 1896
▶ Vegetarian dog food based on vegetable and cereal protein with added nutrients. Call for details of local stockists.

COMMUNITIES

Townhead Collective
1-19 Townhead Cottages,
Dunford Bridge, Sheffield S36 4TG
Tel: 01226 762 359
Email: pp3mo@aol.com
▶ A community of 30 adults and 8 children living in the Peak District in Yorkshire in 19 houses, with one acre of organic vegetable gardens, and which are currently being renovated by the community using reclaimed and environmental materials. Also acts as a child home education centre. All energy produced on site from the wind and sun. The community is not looking for new members or visitors but is happy to exchange news and advice by phone or email.

NATURAL DEATH

Association of Nature Reserve Burial Grounds
c/o The Natural Death Centre,
20 Heber Road, London NW2 6AA
Tel: 020 8208 2853
Fax: 020 8452 6434
Email: rhino@dial.pipex.com
Web: www.naturaldeath.org.uk
▶ Launched in 1994 by the Natural Death Centre as an attempt at increasing the number of woodland burial grounds nationwide where trees can be planted instead of headstone. Contact them for publications listing burial grounds in your area or advice on setting up your own ground.

Green Undertakings
44 Swain Street, Watchet TA23 0AG
Tel: 01984 632 285
Fax: 01984 633 673
▶ Advice, help and supplies in arranging environmentally friendly funerals and self-help funerals. Call for more information.

Greenfields Coffins
2-6 Lakes Road, Braintree CM7 3SS
Tel: 01376 327 074
Fax: 01376 342 975
▶ Supplies ecologically friendly biodegradable coffins made of corrugated cardboard. Available in a variety of finishes. Fully biodegradable linings. The coffins are accepted by local authorities for use at crematoria, cemetaries and at designated greenfield and woodland burial sites. Delivery to any mainland UK destination within 48 hours. Call for a brochure.

Guild of Soul Midwives
BCM Soul Midwives,
London WC1N 3XX
▶ Voluntary organisation of women and men dedicated to the spiritual empowerment of the dying and the compassionate support of their family and friends. Send an SAE for further details.

Natural Death Centre
20 Heber Road, London NW2 6AA
Tel: 020 8208 2853
Fax: 020 8452 6434
Email: rhino@dial.pipex.com
Web: www.naturaldeath.org.uk
Open: Mon-Fri 9.30am-6.30pm (phone only)
▶ Charitable project supporting people dying at home and their carers and assisting with funeral arrangements. Recently published a new edition of *The Natural Death Handbook* which gives information on organising inexpensive family-organised and environmentally friendly funerals, 120+ woodland burial grounds, cardboard coffins and more.

New Manchester Woodland Cemetery
City Road, Ellenbrook, Worsley,
Manchester M28 1BD
Tel/Fax: 0161 790 1300
Open: Mon-Fri 9am-5pm
▶ Privately-run green burial site (member of the Association of Nature Reserve Burial Grounds) set within 12 acres of rural land on the outskirts of Manchester. Offers traditional and green burials and will accept home-made, cardboard or wicker coffins, or shrouds.

Saddleworth Cemetery
c/o Saddleworth Parish Council,
Civic Hall, Lee Street, Upper Mill,
Oldham OL3 6AE
Tel: 01457 876 665
Fax: 01457 872 929
Email: saddleworth.parish-council@virgin.net
Web: www.saddleworth.net/parishcouncil
▶ Moorland cemetery is a beautiful site overlooking the villages of Saddleworth. Green burials follow the rules and regulations of the Natural Death Centre and include cardboard coffins and wicker baskets in a special, one-depth burial site. There are no headstones but families are allowed to plant indigenous trees or shrubs over graves. Call for more info.

ORGANISATIONS

British Humanist Association
47 Theobolds Road,
London WC1X 8SP
Tel/Fax: 020 7430 0908
Email: robert@humanism.ork.uk
▶ Provides an accredited list of officiants who will tailor a ceremony according to the needs and wishes of a family.

A transport system fit for the future

Steve Hounsham of Transport 2000 suggests how the vision of a country where traffic no longer dominates people's lives can be achieved.

The reality is that traffic is growing by the day, leading to congestion, pollution, safety concerns, health problems, climate change and a reduction in our quality of life. The total distance travelled by all motor vehicles in Britain in 1999 was a staggering 467 billion kilometres, the same as 40 round trips from Earth to the planet Pluto. Meanwhile, if all the cars in Britain were lined up head to tail they would go twice round the world. These figures are scary but things are set to get even worse. Road traffic in Britain is forecast to increase by another 48% by 2026.

Meanwhile public transport in many areas is inadequate and traffic danger prevents many people undertaking everyday journeys by walking and cycling. This is the background against which Transport 2000 aims to make a difference. Since 1973 the national environmental transport body has been working to find solutions to transport problems. It believes we would all benefit from less use of cars and more use of public transport, walking and cycling.

Transport 2000 includes over 30 affiliated organisations, including environmental and transport bodies, representing the transport interests of around 3 million people. Through the European Federation for Transport and the Environment, Transport 2000 exchanges ideas and good practice with similar bodies in 19 other countries. It lobbies national government to set a policy framework that relies less on cars and road-building and more on sustainable transport. It convinces local authorities to take action on traffic, campaigns for change at a local level and contributes towards changing transport habits. Its campaigns are underpinned by research and project work.

Transport 2000 believes the only way to tackle effectively all the problems associated with traffic is to reduce the amount of traffic on our roads. Transport 2000 is calling for a 10% cut in traffic by 2010, with a larger cut in London. This could be achieved by introducing congestion charging and workplace parking, raising vehicle and fuel taxes and providing further incentives for goods to be moved by rail rather than road.

Critical to the success of traffic reduction policies is a dramatic improvement in alternatives to the car, particularly public transport. Most parts of the UK need to see a step change in the quality and quantity of public transport to provide real transport choice. Bus services need to be extended in rural areas and at off-peak times, speeded up through bus priority measures and made more accessible to elderly and disabled passengers. Transport 2000 would like to see all towns with more than 25,000 inhabitants back on the rail network with dedicated bus-rail links for other significant settlements. Light rail, including street-running trams, can provide a transport solution in many cities.

Meanwhile our provision for cycling is shamed by other European countries. We need more cycle routes, lanes through the traffic and secure parking facilities. Pedestrians need to be given greater priority with better pavements and crossings. Both cyclists and pedestrians would benefit from a safer street environment brought about by slowing traffic down. Transport 2000 is calling for 20mph to be the normal speed limit in built-up areas with a limit of 40mph on country lanes. This could halve child road casualties as well as create a better, more pleasant environment for us all. We need to take this one step further on appropriate roads in both urban and rural areas with a national programme of Home Zones and Quiet Lanes where traffic moves very slowly and much greater emphasis is given to walking, cycling and even just passing the time of day.

A recently launched campaign highlights the growing impact of the rapidly expanding aviation industry on people and the environment, involving excessive noise and possibly increased rates of cancer around airports, as well as growing emissions of climate-change gases. Transport 2000 is calling for an environmental charge on air travel, the ending of tax exemptions on aviation fuel and more stringent standards on noise and emissions around airports.

In the longer term our planners need to lay the foundations for more sustainable living. All new developments should be tested for their accessibility by public transport, by bicycle and on foot. Priority should be given to those developments that cut car use or reduce the need to travel. Similarly out-of-town developments should be curbed and greater efforts made to promote local services. ■

*For just £20 a year (£10 for the unwaged and £25 for families) you can become a supporter of Transport 2000. Contact Supporter Services at Transport 2000, The Impact Centre, 12-18 Hoxton Street, London N1 6NG or call **020 7613 0743***

Getting people on their bikes

Sustrans works on practical projects to encourage people to walk and cycle more in order to reduce motor traffic. Helping protect and preserve the environment is a vital goal. Their flagship project, the National Cycle Network, was opened in June 2000 with over 5,000 miles of traffic-free routes through urban centres all over the UK. This project is the start of a network that promises to be a safe and attractive network for cyclists, as well as a new gift for walkers and the disabled. The project's goal is to create 10,000 miles of routes for cyclists and walkers by 2005.

The programme has had many positive results. Historic landmarks are seeing a renewed life and green tourism is delivering income to towns and rural areas. In addition, the Network links local cycling networks all over the country. Sustrans is working to map routes on the National Cycle Network with novice cyclists and families in mind.

Another project, 'Safe Routes to Schools', encourages children to bike and walk to school with improved street designs and calmer traffic. Currently less than 2% of children in the UK cycle to school and Sustrans wants to increase that figure by creating spaces free of traffic that link with the National Cycle Network. A similar project, 'Safe Routes to Stations', is based on the same principle, making train and tube station commutes easier.

The work Sustrans undertakes is crucial to helping to solve the problem of global warming. Sustrans is taking immediate action by implementing programmes to help reduce fossil fuel emissions that continue to damage the air we breathe and the environment as a whole. The creation of cycle and walking routes encourages a more active approach to transportation that helps the environment.

Sustrans has built over 400 miles of traffic-free paths over two decades. For example, the Bristol & Bath Railway Path was the first traffic-free path to be built by volunteers in 1978 and is used today for over 1.7 million journeys a year.

Sustrans estimates that 100 million cycle trips and 40 million walking trips will eventually be taken at the current rate of expansion. Funding for the charity is made possible through a strong backbone of supporters. These donations and monthly contributions have been doubled by a Millennium Commission grant. However the grant runs out at the end of 2001, which means the organisation will be relying more on annual donations from supporters to reach its goal of 10,000 miles by 2005. ∎

*For more information on Sustrans or to make a donation, call **0117 929 0888** or visit the website at **www.sustrans.org.uk***

CASE STUDY: Wise about travel

Travel is a major part of everybody's life, whether you are a child going to school, an employee getting to work or travelling on business, or a family having a day out. However, the way we currently cater for our travel needs is causing the country no ends of problems. Our inefficient and often inconsiderate use of the private car is giving rise to congestion and resulting in accidents on the road network. This in turn is having an impact on the environment in terms of noise and air pollution, and our own quality of life is suffering – the health of the nation's population is deteriorating through lack of exercise.

The National TravelWise Association (NTWA) evolved from pioneering work done by Hertfordshire County Council in 1993 and became firmly established in 1998. It set itself the aims of reducing society's dependence on car use by raising awareness of the effects of car use; changing attitudes towards car use; promoting more sustainable modes of travel, and encouraging a change in travel behaviour. Today, there are over 100 members from local authorities across the country, and this is growing on a weekly basis.

The Association goes about its work in a variety of ways. It runs all-year-round campaigns focused on local, regional and national travel issues and supports the campaigns of other groups and organisations that have an interest in sustainable travel. Its members engage with all the key stakeholders who can make a difference at a local level – working closely with schools and businesses. The Association also encourages networking and has established an excellent electronic communication and support network, at the heart of which is the new NTWA website where members can ask for help on specific problems, place requests for information, or just disseminate best practise. ∎

*For more information, contact the NTWA Secretary, Dr Wyn Hughes, on **01223 717 500***

IMPACT: Using your car less

- Hop on a bus or try a train. It's safer, less polluting and you don't have to park. Compare the true costs of running a car, including purchase and HP, insurance, fuel, tax, repairs and servicing. The true financial cost of a journey is not just the cost of the fuel you use.

- Consider that if you do less than 5,000 miles per year, it may not be worthwhile owning a car at all. Using public transport, taxis, cycling, walking and hiring a car only for weekend may work out cheaper and be better for the environment.

- Cycle more. It's good for you and the environment.

- Walk more. One in three car journeys are under two miles.

- Have your groceries and provisions delivered to your home.

- Consider car sharing.

- Talk to your local council about setting up car hire clubs. Member have access to a local pool of cars.

- Organize a rota for the school run or try walking children to school. Campaign to bring back school buses. Persuade your school to work on safer and car-free routes to school.

If you do need to use the car, remember to:

- Drive gently – careful acceleration uses 60% less fuel than pulling away fast. 50mph uses 30% less fuel than 70mph and produces 40% less CO_2 emissions.

- Don't idle! Only start the engine when you are ready to move off. Preheating modern car engines is unnecessary, wastes fuel and increases emissions. Turn off the engine when stationary for a minute or more.

- Keep your car properly maintained. It should comply with the MoT emissions tests all the time.

- Cut your speed. At 30mph, 45% of pedestrians struck by a car die. At 20mph only 5% are killed.

- Use lead-free petrol. 50% of cars currently run on it but 85% could.

CASE STUDY: Putting your best foot first

Imagine villages, towns and cities where people feel at home. Mothers walk their children to school, friends gossip or chat at pavement cafés, people window-shop or pass by on their way to the station, the cinema or to change their library books. Streets that are pleasant, safe and clean are what the Pedestrians Association believes people deserve.

Very few would disagree but walking is still not high enough on any political agenda. However, attitudes are beginning to change and the Pedestrians Association is at the forefront of a new drive, happy to assist any community in ways that make streets more pleasant.

Through its national campaigns and local activities the Association is aiming to get the UK back on its feet again, working to create the living streets we all deserve. Streets that people on foot can use and enjoy. Streets with wide, clean pavements, good pedestrian crossings and excellent street lighting. Streets free of litter, graffiti and dog dirt, with less pollution, congestion and grime. And streets where people feel safe, day and night.

The Pedestrians Association has a UK-wide network of motivated and informed local volunteers translating national policy changes into a safer and more attractive street environment. Local volunteers empower communities to take action to improve their own environment. They undertake a range of activities, on their own or in partnership with other local organisations. These include residents' associations, disability groups and local groups concerned with crime. They can provide a source of advice and information to the public and local authorities on all aspects of improvements to the public realm, such as how to create a Home Zone, or to get a crossing installed. They represent the national organisation but use their greater local knowledge to give informed comment on local issues. The Association welcomes offers from individuals who want to be a local volunteer in their area. ■

*If you are interested in finding out more about the work of the Pedestrians Association or becoming a local volunteer, call David Early, Development Manager, on **020 7820 1010***

Transport

Transport Information

British Rail
Tel: 0345 484 950 (24 hours)

Metrolink
Queens Road, Manchester
Tel: 0161 205 2000
▶ Since 1992, Metrolink has been transporting people around Greater Manchester in a safe, fast, frequent and environmentally-friendly way. A fleet of 32 electrically-powered trams run both on-street and on traditional railway lines and offer a real alternative to the car. Taking customers to the heart of towns and cities, seven days a week, 364 days a year, from early until late, they are ideal for both business and leisure use.

National Express Coaches
Tel: 0990 808 080

British Rickshaw Network
40 Cowley Road, Oxford OX4 1HZ
Tel: 01865 251 620
Fax: 01865 251 134
▶ Nationwide network which promotes the use of rickshaws in the UK. Offers consultancy services and information to individuals, councils and others through feasibility studies and advice on the implementation of rickshaw projects. The Network can also provide rickshaws for weddings, green fundraising and commercial promotion around the country. Founded the groundbreaking, successful Oxford Rickshaw Company. Call for information pack.

Transport Initiatives

Green Transport Week
c/o Environmental Transport Association, 10 Church Street, Weybridge KT13 8RS
Tel: 01932 828 882
Fax: 01932 829 015
Email: eta@eta.co.uk
Web: www.eta.co.uk
▶ Annual event – in June – with activities and campaigns going on all over the country, including Car Free Day.

Trans Pennine Trail
Barnsely Metropolitan Borough Council, Central Offices,
Kendray Street, Barnsley S70 2TN
Tel: 01226 772 574
Fax: 01226 772 599
Email: transpenninetrail@barnsley.gov.uk
▶ Stretching over 200 miles east-west from Southport to Hornsea, the TPT is a recreational and transport route for walkers, cyclists, horseriders and people using wheel-chairs or pushchairs, offering a means of getting out from urban centres to the countryside without the use of a car. It links major towns and cities of the north including Manchester, Leeds, Barnsley, Doncaster, Sheffield, Chesterfield, York and Hull. Guides to the trail for walkers and cyclists are now available. Call for copies or for further details.

Transport Resource Unit
Gmcvo, St Thomas Centre,
Ardwick Green North,
Manchester M12 6FZ
Tel: 0161 273 7451
Fax: 0161 273 8296
Email: stuart.murray@gmcvo.org.uk
▶ Aims to provide informtion, support, advice and skills which will aid the development and effectiveness of voluntary and community groups concerned with transport and transportation related issues in and across the ten districts of Greater Manchester.

Car Sharing & Clubs

Car Club Kit
PO Box 1237, Coventry CV6 3ZB
Tel: 024 7623 6292
Fax: 024 7623 6291
Email: info@smartmoves.co.uk
Web: www.smartmoves.co.uk
▶ Practical guide to shared car ownership and use for small groups of people who want to share cars in a non-profit making, non-commercial way. The kit explains how car clubs can help reduce the negative impacts of large numbers of cars and encourage drivers to become less car dependent. Information on highly successful European schemes is included.

Community Car Share Network
The Studio, 32 The Calls,
Leeds LS2 7EW
Tel: 0113 234 9299
Fax: 0113 242 3687
Email: office@carshareclubs.co.uk
Web: www.carshareclubs.co.uk
▶ The Community Car Share Network is a 'not for profit' organisation which provides information, support and technical assistance to community groups and Local Authorities interested in developing city car share clubs and rural car sharing schemes. Car share clubs help to reduce car dependency and encourage use of other modes of transport, as well as offering a great way of enjoying the flexibility of owning a car without owning one.

Local Organisations

Healthstart Ltd
1st Floor, Cavern Court,
8 Mathew Street, Liverpool L2 6RE
Tel: 0151 236 1737
Fax: 0151 227 4539
Email: info@health-start.com
Web: www.health-start.com
▶ Events management company specialising in promoting healthier lifestyles across the North West. Organise events and promotions, write literature and press releases and create campaigns on behalf of customers to specifically encourage positive lifestyle change. Major themes are; 'Health Improvement' and 'Green Transport', and past events have included bike rides, walks, corporate evenings and running events.

Transport 2000 (East Lancs)
10 Walton Street, Colne BB8 0EN
Tel: 01282 861 272
Email:
mattg@water-side.fsnet.co.uk
▶ Aims to reduce the environmental, social and economic problems asso-

HEALTH START

Promoting green transport and healthier lifestyles in the North West – from cycle rides to corporate games.

For more information and details of our events
Ring: 0151-236 1737 or
Visit: www.health-start.com

ciated with transport in the area. Working alongside neighbouring local groups, as part of a national campaign, promotes sustainable transport modes including walking, cycling and high quality public transport. Seeks planning policies that do not enourage car or lorry use, support appropriate use of rail and water for freight and address the increasing impacts of aviation. New members are always welcome. Children and young people, women, pensioners, disabled people and those on low incomes are particularly disadvantaged by transport inequality in Lancashire. Argues that poorer households also bear the brunt of the ill health, noise and injuries from road traffic. Supports reallocating spending from expensive roads into green travel plans. The group supports proposals for a Rapid Transit System and initiatives to tackle unsafe driving. Also believes that car share clubs and low speed home zones can begin to address the problems.

North Lancs Transport 2000
26 Williamson Road,
Lancaster LA1 3QA
Tel: *01524 845 448*
Email: *t2000nl@bigfoot.com*
Web: *pages.zoom.co.uk/t2000nl*
▶ Lancaster-based branch involved in; lobbying the council regarding sustainable transport policy, giving transport issues a high media profile, finding out what residents and transport users want, and lobbying transport providers. Some of the important changes they seek are; making the highways safer and more pleasant for pedestrians and cyclists, making train travel a more viable and attractive option for people and goods, making bus travel more reliable and attractive, and increasing opportunities to travel without a car.

North West Transport Activist's Roundtable
St Thomas Centre,
Ardwick Green North, Ardwick,
Manchester M12 6FZ
Tel: *0161 273 7451*
Fax: *0161 273 8296*
Email: *gmcvo@gmcvo.org.uk*

▶ NWTAR is an umbrella group of representatives from environmentally aware organisations in the North West, publishing a newsletter and holding meetings across the region bimonthly. Aims to promote and encourage environmentally sustainable transport solutions, through constructive engagements with regional authorities such as the Regional Development Agency and Government Office North West.

UK Organisations

Environmental Transport Association (ETA Services Ltd)
10 Church Street,
Weybridge KT13 8RS
Tel: *01932 828 882*
Fax: *01932 829 015*
Email: *eta@eta.co.uk*
Web: *www.eta.co.uk*
Open: *Mon-Fri 8am-6pm;*
Sat 9am-4pm
▶ The ethical alternative to the road lobby organisations such as the AA and RAC. It provides breakdown cover as well as travel, house, home, motor and cycle insurance at competitive prices. Where it differs is that profits are used to campaign, lobby and conduct research on behalf of the environment.

Institute of Logistics & Transport, The
11/12 Buckingham Gate,
London SW1E 6LB
Tel: *01536 740100*
Fax: *01536 740101*
Email: *enquiry@iolt.org.uk*
▶ Exists to promote and encourage knowledge of the science and art of transport and to communicate views to government and the community.

National Travelwise Association
Lancashire County Council,
Guild House, Cross Street,
Preston PR1 8RD
Tel: *01772 263 649*
Fax: *01772 262 833*
Email: *howerdb@travelwisenet.com*
▶ Largest green transport campaign in the UK. NTA is a partnership of local authorities and other organisations that aims to promote more sustainable travel and encourage the use of public transport, cycling and walking.

Pedestrians' Association
31-33 Bondway, London SW8 1SJ
Tel: *020 7820 1010*
Fax: *020 7820 8208*
Email: *info@pedestrians.org.uk*
Open: *Mon-Fri 9.30am-5.30pm*
▶ Works to make walking safer, more convenient and easier and also to make it possible for people to leave their car at home when travelling short distances. Protects and promotes the rights and safety of people travelling on foot and provides information and advice to the public, other organisations and the Government. Works with the Government, local authorities and other bodies to promote the benefits of walking as an environmentally friendly, sustainable and healthy form of transport.

Royal Society for the Prevention of Accidents
353 Bristol Road, Edgbaston Park,
Birmingham B5 7ST
Tel: *0121 248 2000*
Fax: *0121 248 2001*
▶ Provides information on a range of transport/accident related topics including the RSPA Bicycle Owner's Handbook, a useful guide for all cyclists.

Sustrans
35 King Street, Bristol BS1 4DZ
Tel: *0117 926 8893*
Fax: *0117 929 4173*
Web: *www.sustrans.org.uk*
▶ UK transport charity which aims to reduce dependency on cars. Its name is short for 'sustainable transport'. Best known for its pioneering work in the design and development of high quality routes for walkers, cyclists and people with disabilities, Sustrans is promoting and co-ordinating the creation of the National Cycle Network. This will provide an 8,000 mile strategic set of routes going through centres of population, serving public transport and linking towns to the countryside. Sustrans has 40,000 supporters and publishes a range of maps, guides and technical advice. Call for more information and details of local groups.

Transport 2000
The Impact Centre,
12-18 Hoxton Street,
London N1 6NG
Tel: *020 7613 0743*
Fax: *020 7613 5200*
▶ Campaigns for a 'coherent and sustainable' national transport policy, which meets transport needs with the least damage to the environment. Works on the full range of transport issues from road tax to road building and traffic congestion, from cycling to public and community transport.

CYCLING

For companies that organise cycling activities, holidays and tours, see Chapter Eight: Travel & Leisure.

Supplies

Bicycle Doctor
68-70 Dickenson Road,
Rusholme, Manchester M14 5HF
Tel: 0161 224 1303
Fax: 0161 257 3102
Email: sales@bikedoc.demon.co.uk
Web: www.bicycledoctor.co.uk
Open: Mon-Fri 10am-6pm; Sat 10am-5.30pm
▶ A co-operative selling all things cycling. Also repairs bikes, and where possible, sells reconditioned used bikes. The North's leading Brompton dealer, also sells Birly folding bikes, Dawes Touring bikes, Trek & Main city and mountain bikes along with recumbents, children's bikes, tandems and trailers. Runs a maintain bike club and once a month organises a more leisurely ride around leafy Cheshire. Details about joining Greater Manchester cycle campaign can also be obtained from the shop.

Bikehouse
177 School Lane, Didsbury,
Manchester M19 1EN
Tel: 0161 443 1235
Fax: 0161 442 5568
Open: Mon-Sat 9am-6pm
▶ Bike shop with a range of bicycles including trailers for children and bikes for the disabled. Also bike accessories and repairs.

Encycleopedia
Open Road Mail Order,
FREEPOST NEA3279,
Beverley HU17 0BR
Tel: 01482 880 399
Email: peter@bcqedit.demon.co.uk
Web: www.encycleopedia.com
▶ Colour annual guide to cycling packed with informative editorial, information on buying classic bikes, portables and city bikes, recumbents, racers, kids' models and innovative rarities, complete with contact numbers for bike manufacturers. Mail order price £12 plus £1.50 p&p. Open Road also publishes a bi-monthly subscription magazine Bicycle (£18 for six issues). Join its National Cycling Club for £29 per annum. Organises residential breaks in the York area and many other cycling activities. Call for a leaflet.

Living Lightly Limited
14 Holly Terrace, Ambrose Street,
Falford, York YO10 4DS
Tel: Freephone 0800 074 332
Email: info@livinglightly.co.uk
Web: www.livinglightly.co.uk
Open: Mail order
▶ Sells a range of quality cycle luggage trailers and luggage carriers at very affordable prices. From the simple child's buggy carrier to the heavy duty 'Bumblebee' cycle trailer their products provide solutions for those who wish to use their bikes as their main means of transport. Catologue is available.

Pashley Hand Built Cycles
Masons Road,
Stratford-upon-Avon CV37 9NL
Tel: 01789 292 263
Fax: 01789 414 201
Email: pashleyworld@pashley.co.uk
Web: www.pashley.co.uk
▶ Hand-built cycles for adults available in a large range of modern and traditional styles, including a recumbent model and a very popular tricycle courier model with a wire basket or two seats. Also has cycles for special needs and commercial use.

Peddlers
46-48 Barbourne Road,
Worcester WR4 9BB
Tel: 01905 24238
▶ Traditional bike shop with a difference – believe in the use of the bicycle as a means of transport. Sell the 'Brompton Folding Bike', as they consider it to be the most practical and useful machine available.

CycleCity Guides
Wallbridge Mill, The Retreat,
Frome BA11 5JU
Tel: 01373 453 533
Fax: 0870 055 8569
Email: info@cyclecityguides.co.uk
Web: www.cyclecityguides.co.uk
▶ Publisher of cycling maps for cities. London West and London North West maps have been produced for the London Cycling Campaign, Glaxo Wellcome and the London Boroughs of Ealing & Hillingdon. The maps are available in bookshops or bikeshops. Also publishes maps for Bristol & Bath, Oxford, Birmingham, Manchester, Glasgow, Tyneside, Rotherham, Bradford, Leeds and Leicester. The maps show more than 500 miles of recommended routes including all official cycle networks.

Sinclair Research Ltd
7 York Central, 70 York Way,
London N1 9AG
Tel: 020 7837 6150 (info); 01933 279 300 (orders)
Fax: 020 7278 3101
Web: www.sinclair-research.co.uk
▶ Manufacturer of small, lightweight motors which give electric power assistance to bicycle pedal power at the flick of a handlebar switch. It consists of a rechargable battery pack which powers a lightweight motor unit over the front wheel. Complete packs cost £100; back-up batteries £30.

Local Organisations

Critical Mass
Manchester
▶ An 'organised coincidence' of cyclists cycling together around the city before departing on their own separate ways home. The group meets at 5pm outside the Central Library on the last Friday of every month. Everyone is welcome.

Cycle Stockport
5 Avon Road, Heald Green,
Stockport SK8 3LS
Tel: 0161 282 0273
Email: derekkelly@aol.com
▶ Group promoting all forms of cycling and campaigning for improved cycling facilities in Stockport. Also organises various events and activities throughout the year and is currently devising leisure cycle routes in the borough. A bi-monthly newsletter updates members on national and local cycling issues and events. Currently meets on the fourth Tuesday of every month at the Kimberley Day Centre, Kimberley Street, Shaw Heath, Stockport.

Cycling Project for the North West
Unit 1, Agecroft Enterprise Park,
Agecroft Road, Pendlebury,
Manchester M27 8WA
Tel: 0161 745 9099
Fax: 0161 745 9088
Email: cpnw@cycling.org.uk
Web: www.cycling.org.uk
▶ Works to promote cycling and the interests of cyclists throughout the north west. Stocks an extensive collection of leaflets and publications on cycle routes in the area. Join the project and help the development of cycling in the region!

Greater Manchester Cycling Campaign
c/o One World Centre,
6 Mount Street, Manchester M2 5NS
Tel: 0161 434 3570
Email: secretary@gmcc.org.uk
Web: www.gmcc.org.uk
▶ Cycling campaign group, regular meetings and on-going campaigns. Quarterly newsletter and website.

UK Organisations

British Cycling Federation
National Cycling Centre,
Stuart Street, Manchester M11 4DQ
Tel: 0161 230 2301
Fax: 0161 231 0591
Email: 10170.2260@compuserve.com
▶ Internationally recognised governing body of cycle sport in the UK with a network of over 1,200 clubs promoting the sport and pastime of cycling with people of all ages. Members receive free third party insurance cover, free legal advice and assistance, a tailored cycling insurance policy and the membership magazine. Call for membership details.

Bycycle Club
158 Market Place,
Chippenham SM15 3HD
Tel: 0870 240 2128
Fax: 0870 240 2128

Transport

Email: bycycleclub@thepartnershipforum.com
Web: www.bycycle.com
▶ Cycling club offering benefits including *Bycycle Magazine*, third-party insurance, many discounts and special offers and much more.

Cycle Aid
9 Starkie Street, Preston PR1 3NA
Tel: Freephone 0800 132 383
Fax: 01772 203 418
Email: injuries@cycle-line.demon.co.uk
Web: www.cycleaid.co.uk
▶ Independent group offering a 24-hour accident, advice and appraisal service for cyclists who have been involved in accidents. The Cycle Aid Assist Scheme helps cyclists pursue claims for damages and, in some cases, can find funds to replace a damaged bike in the immediate term.

Cyclists' Touring Club
Cotterell House, 69 Meadrow, Godalming GU7 3HS
Tel: 01483 417 217
Fax: 01483 426 994
Email: cycling@ctc.org.uk
Web: www.ctc.org.uk
▶ Governing body for recreational and utility cycling. The largest (and oldest – established 1878) association for cyclists in the UK, working to ensure that cycling has a role in the nation's transport policy, thereby helping to promote healthy living and a cleaner environment. Membership costs £25 (adult) and includes a bi-monthly magazine, insurance advice, a legal aid handbook, technical and touring information, events, local groups and mail order.

Festival of Cycling
c/o CTC, Cotterell House, 69 Meadrow, Godalming GU7 3HS
Tel: 01483 417 217
Fax: 01483 426 994
Email: helpdesk@ctc.org.uk
Web: www.ctc.org.uk
▶ Co-ordinated by the Cyclists' Touring Club since 1923, the Festival of Cycling, formerly National Bike Week, is the largest cycling extravaganza in the world. All over the UK, individuals, organisations, businesses, schools, local councils and community groups join the Festival to show that cycling is a fun, healthy and sustainable activity suitable for leisurely weekend jaunts or even that journey to work.

National Cycle Network
c/o Sustrans, 35 King Street, Bristol BS1 4DZ
Tel: 0117 929 0888
Fax: 0117 915 0124
Web: www.sustrans.org.uk
▶ NCN will provide an 8,000 mile strategic set of routes going through centres of population, serving public transport and linking towns to the countryside. Promoted and co-ordinated by Sustrans, the UK transport charity. Call for further information of routes close to you.

WATER TRANSPORT

Inland Waterways Association
PO Box 114, Rickmansworth WD3 1ZY
Tel: 01923 711 114
Fax: 01923 897 000
Email: iwa@waterways.org.uk
Web: waterways.org.uk/index.htm
▶ Formed in 1946 the Association acts as a watchdog, an adviser, a campaigner, an educator and a restorer to the inland waterways network. Regularly lobbies Government, Local Authorities and navigation authorities about matters affecting the waterways and their users. Holds discussions with specific user groups, such as boaters and anglers.

Waterway Recovery Group
35 Sylvester Road, London SE22 9PB
Tel: 020 8693 3266
Email: editor@navvys.demon.co.uk
▶ Subsidiary of Inland Waterways, the WRG is a registered charity carrying out restoration work on inland waterways in the UK.

SUSTAINABLE VEHICLES

Suppliers & Organisations

Alternative Vehicles Technology (AVT)
Blue Lias House, Station Road, Hatch Beauchamp TA3 6SQ
Tel: 01823 480 196
Fax: 01823 481 116
Web: www.avt.uk.com
▶ Founder members of the Electric Car Association, AVT builds electric cars to order and can also convert existing petrol cars to battery electric drives. Also can supply cars and conversions in kit form for DIY completion and is developing a hybrid car for sale. Call for more information.

RoSPA (Royal Society for the Prevention of Accidents)
Edgbaston Park, 353 Bristol Road, Birmingham B5 7ST
Tel: 0121 248 2000
Fax: 0121 248 2001
Email: help@rospa.co.uk
Web: www.rospa.com
▶ Registered charity actively involved in the promotion of safety in all areas of life – at work, in the home, on the roads, in schools and on or near water. Produce a variety of journals, and have published the *Greener Motoring Guide* which includes advice and practical driving tips to make motoring less harmful to the environment.

Car Manufacturers

While the Green Guide continues to support walking, cycling and the use of public transport, the truth is that – for those of us with families or who live in a countryside gradually denuded of public transport services – the car still represents convenience, independence, even freedom. Car manufacturers are starting to take on board environmental concerns. We contacted every major car manufacturer in the UK to find out what they offered the concerned consumers. Those who replied are listed below. We urge car-using readers to begin to question manufacturers and dealers about their environmental policies and to use their consumer power to bring about further changes. And while we applaud these first few steps by manufacturers, they are only tiny steps. More needs to be done, especially in terms of research and development and certainly it must be done more quickly. As some of the largest and most powerful organisations on the planet, car manufacturers must face up the continuing damage they are causing and be aware that educated and discerning consumers will not be fobbed off by greenwash.

Audi
Yeomans Drive, Blakelands, Milton Keynes MK14 5AN
Tel: 01908 601 629
Fax: 01908 601 366
▶ Preservation of resources is seen as crucial for Audi as is the efficient conservation of energy and use of recyclable materials. Audi is committed to a reduction of harmful emissions, fuel consumption and noise. Has been developing electric drive systems since 1988. Recently developed a hybrid vehicle, combining a conventional combustion engine with electric drive. Vehicles have a recycling rate of more than 85%.

Chrysler
Poulton Close, Dover, Kent CT17 0HP
Tel: 01304 220 210
Fax: 01304 225 815
Email: info@chrysler.co.uk
Web: media.chrysler.co.uk
▶ Chrysler's Ecco Jeep is made entirely of aluminium and plastic, making it almost 100% recyclable.

Fiat Auto UK
266 Bath Road, Slough SL1 4HJ
Tel: 01753 511 431
Fax: 01753 516 871
Web: www.fiatgroup.com
▶ The environmental compatibility of Fiat's products and processes are seen as important to the company. Provides environmental training for employees and is currently developing electrically powered vehicles. Since 1960, Fiat has been developing

various prototypes and, in fact, recently built and distributed three electric vehicles for urban use. A prototype hybrid car was recently built. Fiat's aims for recycling rates of 85% by 2002 and 95% by 2010, including 5% in energy recovery. Fiat is a member of associations and organizations concerned with the environment and energy such as the World Business Council for Sustainable Development.

Ford

1/455 Eagle Way,
Brentwood CM13 3BW
Tel: *01227 252 211*
Fax: *01277 251 976*
Email: *fpress.ford@e-mail.com*
Web: *media.ford.com*

▶ Ford analyses the environmental impact of all its vehicles. Design for the Environment training has been established, identifying environmental improvement opportunities. Ford believes that alternative fuel vehicles are part of a long term environmental solution and is also piloting a $2.2 million solar power programme at the Bridgend plant in Wales. The Henry Ford European Conservation Awards raises financial and media support for conservation projects throughout Europe.

Honda

No 4, Power Road, Chiswick,
London W4 5YT
Tel: *020 8747 1400*
Fax: *020 8747 3594*
Web: *www.honda.co.uk*

▶ Has a Clean Air Vehicle project which aims to reduce the level of toxic air pollutants from exhaust fumes; the amount of carbon dioxide by cutting fuel consumption and to address the problem of diminishing fossil fuels by developing research into alternative forms of energy. EV Plus electric cars will soon be available as will a natural gas powered vehicle.

Mazda UK

77 Mount Ephraim, Tunbridge Wells,
Kent TN4 8BS
Tel: *01892 511 877*
Web: *www.mazda.co.uk*

▶ Hybrid vehicles are seen as an alternative that can make use of technology already developed for electric vehicles. Mazda has researched and developed electric vehicles since 1966 and has set up a Recycling Promotion Committee, developing technologies for recycling plastic and rubber components. Mazda are looking at ways to use recycled materials for making new car parts and at cars with a higher percentage of recyclable parts. The company is developing new approaches and technologies to facilitate the efficient removal of reusable parts and to ensure the proper treatment of harmful materials.

Mitsubishi Motors

Watermoor, Cirencester GL7 1LF
Tel: *01285 655 777*
Fax: *01285 658 026*
Email:
d.miles@mitsubushi-cars.co.uk
Web: *www.mitsubishi-cars.co.uk*

▶ In 1993, Mitsubishi Motors set up an Environmental Action Program to address 'green' issues. They have recently introduced enviromentally friendly technology into vehicles with the GDI (gasoline direct injection) petrol engine and the DI-D (direct injection engine) which aim to reduce CO_2 emissions and improve fuel economy. Other 'green' objectives are to develop vehicles which are 90% recyclable and promote the research and development of hybrid, natural gas and other low emission vehicles.

Nissan

Denham Way, Maple Cross,
Rickmansworth WD3 2YS.
Tel: *01923 899999*
Fax: *01923 899 969*

▶ Has been researching and developing different types of alternative fuel vehicles, including ones powered by electricity, compressed natural gas, methanol, solar energy and hydrogen. Nissan is developing a hybrid system that reduces fuel consumption and exhaust emmisons. With other Japanese car manufacturers, Nissan formed the Recycling Promotion Committee in 1990, promoting the effective utilization of natural resources, reducing waste and protecting the environment. In February 1998, it announced its Vehicle Recycling Program. Aims to have a recyclable rate of 90% or higher for all new vehicles from year 2000 onward. Aims to elevate environmental protection awareness among employees with support for volunteer activities such as collecting cans and donating proceeds to afforestation projects.

Toyota

The Quadrangle, Redhill RH1 1PX
Tel: *01737 768 585*
Fax: *01737 789 807*
Web: *www.toyota.co.uk*

▶ Toyota has developed diesel engine catalysts that reduce hydrocarbon and other chemical emissions by more than 50% compared to conventional diesel engines. A hybrid vehicle has been developed, using a continuous variable combination of gasoline and electric power. The company has also developed a fuel cell electric vehicle using methanol to produce hydrogen which reacts with oxygen from the air to create electricity for the motor. Toyota is involved in global activities covering education, the environment, culture and the arts, international exchange and local communities.

Vauxhall

Griffin House, Osborne Road,
Luton LU1 3YT
Tel: *01582 721 122*
Fax: *01582 426 926*
Email: *environmental.affairs@*
vauxhall.co.uk
Web: *www.vauxhall.co.uk*

▶ Vauxhall is developing alternative propulsion and alternative fuel vehicles such as those using electric, hybrid, fuel-cell, liquified petroleum gas and compressed natural gas. Aims to reduce vehicle exhaust emissions and fuel consumption. Looks at emissions, waste and consumption reduction at its facilities and works with industry and governments to develop vehicle recycling. On a national level, Vauxhall is a sponsor of the Young Environmentalist of the Year Award and locally supports many projects including Local Agenda 21 project support in Luton.

Volkswagen UK

Yeomans Drive, Blakelands,
Milton Keynes MK14 5AN
Tel: *01908 601 777*
Web: *www.volkswagen.co.uk*

▶ Volkswagen has a policy of restricting environmental impact and contributing to resolving environmental problems at regional and global level. Researches into and develops ecologically efficient products and processes and 'advanced hybrids'. Involved in the industrial scale production of electric vehicles for the German market and has developed a hybrid propulsion system.

Volvo

Globe Park, Marlow SL7 1YQ
Tel: *01628 477 977*
Fax: *01628 473 644*
Web: *www.volvocars.volvo.co.uk*

▶ Volvo's environmental work is geared towards continual improvement. The environmental impact of all manufacturing is considered. The company is commited to the reduction of fuel consumption.

Punching above its weight

Tourism Concern is a small charity which has taken on the world's biggest industry, Tourism and Travel, in an attempt to persuade it and the public to act in a more fair and sustainable manner.

If you travel or go on holiday, you will be interested in Tourism Concern. Founded in 1989, to monitor the impact of tourism all over the world, Tourism Concern is a UK-based charity, actively campaigning for tourism that is just, sustainable and participatory. Tourism Concern aims to increase people's understanding of socially responsible tourism, and to promote tourism that respects the rights and interests of the people in the host communities visited by tourists.

Tourism is now said to be the biggest industry in the world, affecting the lives of millions of people worldwide. As a result it is very powerful, and at times it seems that nothing can stand in its way. Tourism Concern aims to influence the public as well as challenge this massive industry through its work on human rights issues, such as the displacement of people for tourism development, through its education work and through its efforts to find alternatives, such as fairly traded tourism. Although small in comparison, the organisation punches very much above its weight!

Almost all of us have been tourists at one time or another, or we live in tourism destinations ourselves, and have experienced some of the negative impacts of tourism. With luxurious hotel resorts standing side by side with local shanty towns, it is obvious that the development of tourism brings benefits to some but clearly not to all. Less visible is the failure of tourist developers to give the interests and rights of the indigenous population equal importance to those of their visitors. Local people are often moved out of their homes to make way for a new golf course or safari park. This displacement isn't a simple matter of persuasion, compulsory purchase and compensation, it's often a matter of force. Tourism Concern's Human Rights campaign has done much to raise awareness of these abuses and encourage change.

In Burma (Myanmar), the 5,200 people living among the many ancient pagodas of Pagan, were given two weeks to pack up and leave their homes. Their traditional wooden frame houses, regarded as eye sores, were replaced by highways and strings of modern street lamps. Moved by gunpoint, they now live several miles away in New Pagan, a site of bare, parched earth with little shelter. Few countries match the human rights abuses inflicted upon people by Burma's military junta specifically to develop tourism, such as using slave labour to build roads, airports and hotels. Tourism revenues prop up the brutal regime. Respecting the wishes of Burma's democracy, Tourism Concern has managed to persuade several tour operators to pull out and has mounted campaigns to encourage possible visitors to think twice before going.

There are many other examples of human rights abuses committed in the interests of tourism. The trekking porters in Nepal, who carry extremely heavy loads up steep mountain paths for tourists on trekking holidays is one example. They work without adequate clothing or shoes, and when they fall ill with altitude sickness or lose fingers and toes from frostbite, they are often given little or no medical help by their employers. Nor are they given assistance getting back to their homes. The trekking companies which employ them seem to assume that they are superhuman.

But there are real moves at a local level all over the world towards a new type of tourism that involves and benefits local people. These are community based holidays and Tourism Concern works to support them as much as possible.

If you want to change tourism for the better, become a Tourism Concern supporter, member or donor and help to make its campaigns more effective. Tourism Concern is still a small but dynamic organisation, taking on the world's biggest industry. Your support will help to strengthen it and make sure its voice is heard. ■

To join Tourism Concern, call **020 7753 3330**
or email **info@tourismconcern.org.uk**
or visit **www.tourismconcern.org.uk**

Setting the standard

Green Globe 21 is the global brand for Sustainable Travel & Tourism. Established in 1994 as a result of the Rio Earth Summit, it has the support of major industry and government organisations. Green Globe set the environmental standards for the Travel and Tourism industry and has continuously lifted performance thresholds for sustainable tourism.

When Green Globe was formed it introduced the first worldwide branded system of environmental management for travel and tourism companies. In 1997 it extended the scheme to communities and in 1999 it introduced a branded certification system.

Currently, there are Green Globe 21 companies and communities in more than 100 countries across all continents and the programme is expanding rapidly as a result of the evolution of its products, services and delivery. The company has impressive in-house research capabilities that underpin its product development. CRC Tourism in Australia and Green Global Village, the first sustainable tourism laboratory in the UK, provide Green Globe's research platform and its web development.

The Green Globe Path is the latest product development that was introduced in Spring 2001. It is designed to progressively extend involvement, encourage performance improvement and strengthen the brand for consumer recognition. It not only focuses on corporate and community improvement systems, but also addresses global environmental concerns by giving priority to greenhouse gas reduction. The key elements of the Green Globe Path are:

- low price accessibility to millions of travel companies, communities and suppliers
- it reduces operational costs and increases market appeal
- its standard reflects ISO 14000, Agenda 21 and triple bottom line principles
- it highlights climate change
- it includes social parameters and multi-stakeholder involvement
- it incorporates company actions into community sustainability plans
- guided by an International Advisory Committee
- web delivery ensures efficiency and quality support
- its logo informs consumers of high sustainability goals and achievement. ■

For more information, contact Green Globe at 45 High Street, Royal Tunbridge Wells TN1 1XL.
*Tel: **01892 541 717** Fax: **01892 528 433***
*Email: **info@ greenglobe21.com***
*Web: **www. greenglobe21.com***

IMPACT   Step lightly, travel wisely

When you travel abroad, follow these basic rules.

- Ask your travel agent or tour operator about their ethical and environmental policies. The more these questions are asked, the more they will respond. Tourism Concern publishes a list of questions to ask.
- Save precious resources – don't waste water and energy.
- Support local trade and people by only buying locally-made souvenirs. But avoid souvenirs made from ivory, fur, skins or other wildlife.
- Recognise land rights. Tribal people's ownership of the lands they use and occupy is recognised in international law and should be acknowledged, irrespective of whether the national government applies the law or not. Behave as you would on private property.
- Always ask permission before taking photographs or video recordings of people – even a smile and a gesture will be appreciated.
- Don't give money or sweets to children – it only encourages begging and demeans the child. Instead, make a donation to a recognised project.
- Respect local etiquette. In many countries, loose, light weight clothes are preferable to revealing shorts, skimpy tops and tight-fitting wear.
- Learning something about a country's history and current affairs helps you understand its people's attitudes and idiosyncrasies and may help prevent misunderstandings.
- If you are thinking of going to an unspoilt place, be aware that this could be the first step towards spoiling it.

CASE STUDY: CERT – promoting ecologically sensitive travel

The Centre for Environmentally Responsible Tourism (CERT) was formed in 1994 as an independent, non profit-making and non-political organisation, to support the ideals of a sustainable future for holiday destinations which would ultimately benefit the travel and tourism industry. Each destination has its own unique environment, people, wildlife, history and culture that need to be understood, appreciated and protected.

CERT aims to harness the power of the travel and tourism industry with the consumer, in the promotion of responsible tourism practices, in which the enjoyment of nature and our relationship within the environment are brought together to secure the long-term prosperity of destinations and their peoples. CERT promises to promote ecologically sensitive services through a responsible and concerned attitude towards the environment. It will provide the maximum benefit to local communities and wildlife by operating in an honest, thoughtful and concerned manner towards customs and needs. Through association with the travel industry, it will install and monitor environmental policies at home and abroad.

CERT is unique in its co-operative approach in combining the power of the travel and tourism industry, with consumers and conservationists. The programme is divided into three distinct operational areas: Membership (for Tour Operators, Hotels, Consumers, Corporates, etc); Environmental Auditing; and its Awards. For the scheme to have true credibility, CERT recognises that the involvement of the consumer is essential – it cannot be a trade initiative alone. Customer feedback thus forms the core of the environmental monitoring process and ultimately reflects on award nominations. Involvement of the consumer provides the industry with immediate recognition. There are also excellent marketing and promotional opportunities for those who become members of CERT. ■

For more information, contact the Centre for Environmentally Responsible Tourism at Indaba House, 1 Hydeway, Thundersley SS7 3BE.
*Tel: **01268 752 827** Fax: **01268 759 834***
*Email: **cert.org@virgin.net***
*Web: **www.c-e-r-t.org***

CASE STUDY: Tailor-made tours to tropical destinations

Reef and Rainforest Tours specialises in arranging natural history orientated individual tailor-made tours and escorted group tours to tropical destinations. Established for over a decade, the tours include twelve countries covering much of Latin America, South East Asia and Africa. The company specialises in Madagascar, Belize, Costa Rica and the Galapagos Islands. Activities include wildlife spotting, snorkelling, scuba diving, riding, canoeing, specialised photographic tours and birdwatching holidays.

The company maintains a strong and proven belief that small-scale, natural history-oriented tourism is tourism of the best kind. It benefits areas of outstanding natural beauty and importance in that it offers an incentive to landowners and governments to preserve their wilderness areas intact, instead of logging and converting them to grazing and agriculture. They are able to see that the sustainable long-term rewards of a steady stream of paying visitors far outweigh the unsustainable short-term gains of clear-felling and slash-and-burn, whilst also conserving their irreplaceable natural heritage for the enjoyment of future generations.

Examples include the Rio Bravo Conservation Area in Belize, the Santa Rosa Dry Tropical Forest Reserve in Costa Rica, Berenty Reserve in Madagascar, Manu Biosphere Reserve in Peru, Venezuela's Henri Pittier National Park and Brazil's Pantanal wilderness.

The company uses local guides wherever and whenever possible, benefiting not only the local economy but also its clients, who gain from the unique knowledge the guides possess of their own environments. This has the added advantage of broadly educating the local inhabitants in conservation matters, imbuing them with a pride in the species which share their land, and strengthening the desire of the local communities to protect their natural resources through enthusiastic interaction with visitors. A great many of the company's locations are designated UNESCO World Heritage Sites. ■

For more information, contact Reef and Rainforest Tours at 1 The Plains, Totnes, Devon TQ9 5QQ.
*Tel: **01803 866 965** Fax: **01803 865 916***
*Email: **reefrain@btinternet.com***
*Web: **www.reefrainforest.co.uk***

North West

Tourist Boards and Information Centres

Tourist boards and centres are good starting points if you want to find out what's happening in your area.

Bolton Tourist Information Centre
Victoria Square, Bolton BL1 1RU
Tel: 01204 334 400
Fax: 01204 398 101
Email: touristinfo@bolton.gov.uk

Bury Tourist Information Centre
The Met Arts Centre, Market Street, Bury BL9 0BW
Tel: 0161 253 5111
Fax: 0161 253 5919
Open: Mon-Fri 9.30am-5pm; Sat 10am-4pm
▶ Networked tourist information centre. Providing local and regional information to visitors and tourists. Theatre booking service, accomodation booking. Gifts and free Bury guide available.

Manchester Tourist Information Centre
Town Hall Extension, Lloyd Street, Manchester M60 2LA
Tel: 0161 234 3157/8
Fax: 0161 236 9900
Email: manchester_visitor_centre@notes.manchester.gov.uk
Web: www.manchester.gov.uk/vistorcentre
Open: Mon-Sat 10am-5.30pm; Sun/Bank Hols 11am-4pm
▶ Contact for tourist information and local places to visit.

The North West Tourist Board
Swan House, Swan Meadow Road, Pier, Wigan WN3 5BB
Tel: 01942 821 222
Fax: 01942 820 002
Email: info@nwtb.org.uk
Web: www.visitbritain.com/north-west-england
Open: Mon-Fri 9am-5pm
▶ Partnership between the English Tourist Council, British Tourist Authority, 39 Local Authorities, and 1,000 tourism businesses in the Region. It aims to increase the benefits tourism brings; £1.5 million, and supporting 200,000 jobs and representing 3% of the Region's GDP.

Places to Visit

Alexandra Park
Alexandra Road South/Claremont Road, Moss Side, Manchester
Tel: 0161 881 9014
▶ Hosts the annual Manchester International Caribbean Festival, formerly the Moss Side Carnival and holds Fundays throughout the summer.

Animal World & Butterfly House
Moss Bank Park,
Moss Bank Way, Bolton
Tel: 01204 846 157
▶ Animal World is located in beautifully landscaped gardens with waterfalls, bridges and a duck pond. Free entry for children and adults to take a close look at the collection of goats, agoutis, deer, llamas, alpaca, chipmunks, rabbits, pheasants and exotic birds. The Butterfly House holds a collection of beautiful butterflies and moths from around the world in free flight among tropical plants.

Arley Hall and Gardens
Arley, nr Northwich CW9 6NA
Tel: 01565 777 353
Fax: 01565 777 465
Email: enquiries@arleyestate.zuunet.co.uk
Open: Tues-Sun 11am-4.30pm (Easter to Sept)
▶ Quintessential English garden of great charm and beauty with double herbaceous borders laid out in 1846, bleached lime avenue, two walled gardens and a topiary. The family hall (open on Tuesdays and Sundays) has superb plasterwork ceilings, fine panelling and paintings. There is a gift shop and a Tudor barn restaurant serving home-made meals, snacks and cream teas. Rooms available for private hire, weddings, corporate events and dinners. Special events throughout year. Call for further information.

Bolton Greenwood Group
c/o 82 Crantock Drive,
Heald Green, Cheadle SK8 3HA
Tel: 0161 437 7040
▶ Runs the Bolton Craft Centre in Moses Gate Country Park in Bolton. Traditional woodland crafts and traditional blacksmithing.

Brookdale Park
Droylsden Road, Newton Heath
Tel: 0161 223 1209
▶ 44 acre site well known locally for its wide variety of birds, with some of the less common species represented.

Burrs Country Park
Burrs, Woodhill Road, Bury BL8 1DA
Tel: 0161 764 9649
Fax: 0161 763 7610
▶ Site set in a developing country park next to the River Irwell. Beside Burrs Activity Centre for abseiling, canoeing, climbing and orienteering.

Chorlton Park
Mauldeth Road/Barlow Moor Road, Chorlton-cum-Hardy
Tel: 0161 881 9014
▶ Offers relaxation and active leisure. Hosts the annual Community Unity Festival early in July, summer pleasure fairs, Fundays, an annual bonfire/firework display, plus Easter and summer children's treasure hunts.

Clayton Vale
Bank Street, Clayton
Tel: 0161 223 1209
▶ 114 acre site which forms a picturesque semi-mature woodland with over 250,000 trees and bushes and features a wide range of wild flowers and a variety of fauna. The River Medlock runs through the centre of the Vale. Registered as a site of biological importance, Clayton Vale is ideal for walkers, conservationists and for more informal leisure pursuits. The Vale hosts cycle events, and marked the finish of the first ever 'Race for Life' charity event in Manchester in 1997.

Etherow Country Park Visitor Centre
George Street, Stockport SK5 6JD
Tel: 0161 427 6937
Web: www.stockportmbc.gov.uk
Open: Visitor Centre Weds 11.30am-4.30pm; Sat-Tues 10am-4.30pm; closed Thur & Fri
▶ A beautiful 240 acre country park on the edge of the Pennines and Stockport conurbation. Ancient woodland, lakes and fine views over the Etherow river valley. The visitor centre is open for information on walks, events, wildlife, etc and sells a range of goods and crafts. Fishing, sailing, model boating and café facilities also available. Disabled access to most areas.

Gelderwood Country Park
Ashworth Road, Heywood,
Rochdale OL11 5UP
Tel/Fax: 01706 364 858
Open: April-Oct
▶ Small, quality, family-run park suitable for people who treasure the peace and tranquility of the countryside.

Healey Dell Nature Reserve
Visitor Centre, 34 Dell Road, Shawclough, Rochdale OL12 6BG
Tel: 01706 350 459
Fax: 01706 350 459
▶ Situated between Rochdale and Whitworth, the reserve is open all year round and encompasses a wide diversity of habitat which is reflected in the variety of plants, animals and birds which can be found there. A variety of paths, including a disused railway line provides access for all.

Heaton Park Farm Centre
Prestwich, Manchester M25 2SW
Tel: 0161 773 1085
Fax: 0161 798 0107
Email: heatonpark@ukonline.co.uk
Web: www.manchester.gov.uk/leisure/parks
▶ Heaton Park is the largest municipal park in Europe, consisting of 640 acres. There is something for everyone: visit the Farm Centre, Pets Corner or the Horticultural Centre, take a trip round the lake or relax in the historical atmosphere of Heaton Hall. There is the 18 hole golf course or the easier 18 hole pitch and putt. Orienteering and horse riding also available, along with tennis, football, bowling and basketball. Regular events take place and for details contact the general office.

Travel & Leisure

Hetcher Moss Gardens
Wilmslow Road, Didsbury
Tel: 0161 445 4241
▶ Renowned for their botanical beauty, the gardens contain many antiquated and unusual plants and flowers. The park has retained many of its original features such as the rock and heather gardens, and the orchid houses situated in the Parsonage Gardens adjacent to Fletcher Moss. Together, they form a picturesque, tranquil haven for visitors. The park also provides an excellent setting for the annual summer Park Play Performance.

Heywood Park
Bridgeman Street, Great Lever, Bolton
Tel: 01204 334 165
▶ Town park most suited to children and young people looking for active play. Attractions include Heywood Adventure Playworld, play equipment and indoor play facilities for all ages. Bowling, kickabout and an artificial soccer pitch.

Hollingworth Lake Country Park and Visitor Centre
Rakewood Road,
Littleborough, Rochdale
Tel: 01706 373 421
Fax: 01706 378 753
Web: www. rochdale.gov.uk
▶ Gateway to the South Pennine area, the 118 acre Hollingworth Lake Country Park includes a nature reserve with bird hide, lake trips on the River Alice, rowing boat hire, trails and walks, fishing, outdoor activity water centre for watersports, picnic and play areas and guided walks. Visitor centre has exhibtions, regular events and entertainments, and a café. Wheelchair accessible.

Leverhulme Park
Long Lane, Darcy Lever, Bolton
Tel: 01204 334 074
▶ Open park with tree lined walks leading down to the steeply sloping river valley of Bradshaw Brook. Wide open parkland with paths that connect to the Croal Irwell Valley, and paths and trails leading on as far as Jumbles Country Path to the North and Moses Gate Country Park to the South. Events include Bolton Show every August, as well as fairs, fun days, firework displays, and equestrian events.

Macclesfield Riverside Park Information Centre
Riverside Park, Beechwood Mews,
Macclesfield SK10 2SL
Tel: 01625 511 086
Email: bollin@cheshire.gov.uk
▶ Country park which lies at the start of the Bollin Valley which continues for 23 miles from Macclesfield to Partington at the Manchester Ship Canal. A herd of rare breed cows – Old English Long-horn – graze on the pastures. Events such as bird walks, halloween walks, and games for children are arranged.

Moses Gate Country Park
Hall Lane, Farnworth, Bolton
Tel: 01204 334 343
▶ Offers many recreational opportunities and a wide range of interesting wildlife. Located in Croal Irwell Valley, the park houses Rock Hall Visitor Centre where information, exhibitions and displays can be found. Lakes and wildfowl, as well as extensive woodland, riverside and lakeside walks. Kingfisher trail follows 11 miles throughout the Croal Irwell Valley leading to the North, Jumbles Country Park. Irwell Valley Way and Sculpture Trails lead into Bury and as far as the centre of Salford into Peel Park.

Moss Bank Park
Moss Bank Way, Halliwell, Bolton
Tel: 01205 334 165
▶ Lively town park with an excellent range of facilities for all the family. Animal world, butterfly house, children's play area, minature steam railway, ornamental gardens and Marie Curie Field of Hope every springtime. Events programme featuring fairs, brass band concerts, fun days and more. Café, toilets, sports facilities and car parking.

Park Bridge Heritage Centre
The Stables, Park Bridge, Ashton under Lyne, Tameside OL6 8AQ
Tel: 0161 330 9613
Fax: 0161 343 1834
Open: Wed-Thur 12noon-4pm;
Sat-Sun 11am-4pm
▶ Early industrial settlement, based on an iron rolling mill and forge to provide parts for the cotton spinning trade and other industries. Trace their fascinating history in the carefully restored remains of the buildings, old railway lines and other artefacts.

Prestwich Forest Park
c/o Bury MBC Leisure Services Dept,
Knowsley Street, Bury BL9 0SW
Tel: 0161 253 5269
▶ Offers 200 hectares of land in and around the Irwell Valley for quiet enjoyment of woodland in a particularly built-up part of the Borough of Bury. A pleasant local area to walk or ride around which is big enough to give a countryside feel. Much of the Forest Park is designated a site of biological importance, encompassing a variety of rich habitats.

Queens Park
Chorley New Road, Bolton
Tel: 01204 334 067
▶ Bolton's oldest purpose designed public park, opened in 1866 following the great cotton famine. Attractions include a superb historic town park, lakes and wildfowl, children's play area, riverside walks from Bolton Town Centre, sunken flower garden and dramatic sun terrace overlooking Bolton.

Red Rose Forest
Red Rose Forest Team,
Community Forest Centre,
Dock Office, Trafford Road,
Salford Quays, Manchester M5 2XB
Tel: 0161 872 1660
Fax: 0161 872 1680
Email: team@redroseforest.co.uk
▶ A partnership of the Countryside Agency, the Forestry Commission and six Greater Manchester Authorities. The Forest is an inspiring vision of the future that is already transforming and regenerating a large part of Greater Manchester to create a thriving environment for the 21st Century. The Forest will transform the life of 1.5 million people in the region by bringing in jobs, investment, education opportunities, cleaner air and the most extensive change to the landscape since the Industrial Revolution.

RHS Garden Wisley
Wisley, Woking GU23 6QB
Tel: 01483 224 234
▶ Britain's most famous garden, extending to over 240 acres, contains practical demonstration areas, model gardens with beautiful features such as the alpine meadow, Battleston Hill alive with rhododendrons and azaleas in early summer, immense rock garden and water features. Extensive catering facilities book, gift and plant centre. Adults £5.00, children 6-16 years £2.00.

Rixton Clay Pits Nature Reserve
Moat Lane, Rixton,
Warrington WA3 6ED
Tel: 0161 777 9726
▶ An 80 acre SSSI comprising woodland, scrub, small lakes and meadow areas. The reserve is open access but with few recreational facilities and will appeal most to those interested in the flora and fauna. Visitors are advised to wear appropriate clothing and good walking boots, to stay to foot paths and keep dogs on leads. Rangers conduct a variety of guided walks for the general public, specialist groups and societies. Call for a programme of events.

Smithills Hall Gardens & Country Park
Smithills Dean Road, Smithills, Bolton
Tel: 01204 334 011
▶ 2,000 acres of woodland, farmland and moorland and offers superb views over Bolton and the surrounding area. It also links with other Country Parks, Rivington and Jumbles. Ornamental grounds around the Hall include a parterre garden, terraces, pools and cascade. Extensive network of paths and bridleways leading up onto Winter Hill and the West Pennine Moors. Wonderful views of moorlands and across Greater Manchester and beyond.

Stalybridge Country Park
c/o Parkbridge Heritage Centre,
The Stables, Park Bridge,
Ashton-under-Lyne OL6 8AQ
Tel: 0161 330 9613
Fax: 0161 343 1834

▶ Managed by Tameside Council in partnership with North West Water and lying just over a mile to the north east of Stalybridge, this developing country park centres on Brushes Valley and Carrbrook which lies in the shadow of Buckton Castle, a 12th/13th century stronghold.

The Medlock Balley and Daisy Nook Country Park
John Howarth Countryside Centre,
Daisy Nook Country Park,
Newmarket Road,
Ashton under Lyne OL7 6ER
Tel: *0161 308 3909*
▶ The River Medlock follows an attractive valley between Oldham and Ashton, continuing all the way to the city centre of Manchester. Daisy Nook comprises 85 acres of woodland, riverside meadow, lake and canal, straddling the boundary between Tameside and Oldham.

Werneth Low Country Park
Lower Higham Visitor Centre,
Higham Lane, Hyde,
Tameside SK14 5LR
Tel: *0161 368 6667*
▶ Offers pleasant walks and events for the family all year round. Werneth Low has long been famed for its stunning views of North Wales beyond the Cheshire Plain, the Peak District Valley, hills and moors and the towns of Greater Manchester.

West Dean Gardens
West Dean,
Chichester PO18 0QZ
Tel: *01243 811 301*
Fax: *01243 818 280*
Email: *marketing@westdean.org.uk*
▶ The 35 acres that comprise the Ornamental Grounds of these Gardens are surrounded by the South Downs. There have been gardens here since 1622 and features today include the restored walled kitchen garden with its extensive glasshouses, fruit, cold frames and hot beds and a parkland walk. Adults £4.00, over 60's £3.50, children £2.00. Events held include the Garden Event, Chilli Fiesta, Totally Tomato Show and Apple Day.

City Farms

Acorn Venture Urban Farm
Depot Road, Kirkby,
Liverpool L33 3AR
Tel: *0151 548 1524*
▶ Affilated to the Federation of City Farms and Community Gardens.

Clayton Community Farm
Turner Street, Clayton,
Manchester M11 4TR
Tel: *0161 220 8851*
▶ City farm working extensively with the disabled and the young, offering the opportunity to get close to farm animals, learn about organic farming and gardening or simply to have a picnic in the pleasant farm surroundings. Free to the public. Barbeques and fund-raising events are occasionally organised. Call for details of opening times and events. Affilated to the Federation of City Farms and Community Gardens.

Rice Lane City Farm
Walton Park Cemetary,
Rawcliffe Road, Liverpool L9 1AW
Tel: *0151 530 1066*
▶ Affilated to the Federation of City Farms and Community Gardens.

Tam O'Shanter Urban Farm
Boundary Road,
Birkenhead L43 7PD
Tel: *0151 653 9332*
▶ Affilated to the Federation of City Farms and Community Gardens.

Wythenshawe Community Farm
Ellasmore Cottage, Wythnshaw Park,
Manchester M23 0AB
Tel: *0161 946 0726*
▶ Affilated to the Federation of City Farms and Community Gardens.

Activities

Cecile Elstein (Art as Environment)
25 Spath Road, Didsbury,
Manchester M20 2QT
Tel: *0161 445 1723*
Fax: *0161 445 7680*
▶ Sculptor, printmaker and artist with special interest in designing for or working with the disabled.

Trafford Ecology Park
Lake Road, Trafford Park,
Manchester M17 1TU
Tel: *0161 873 7182*
Fax: *0161 876 0523*
Open: *Mon-Sat 9am-5pm*
▶ Offers a wide range of activities for children, including pond-dipping and Minibeast Hunts (for creepy-crawlies). The 11 acre park has an interesting range of trees and flowers, a small information centre and picnic areas. Open – and free – to the general public. Call to confirm opening times.

Festivals & Fairs

Association of Festival Organisers
PO Box 296, Aylesbury HP19 3TL
Tel: *01296 394 411*
Fax: *01296 392 300*
Email: *afo@mrscasey.co.uk*
Web: *www.mrscasey.co.uk*

Circus Zapparelli
4 Mallow St, Manchester M15 5GD
Tel: *0161 232 7807*
Fax: *0161 227 8501*
Email: *circus@zapparelli.co.uk*
Web: *www.zappme.com*
▶ A group of performers and eco-activist providing a mobile circus school, performers, walkabout acts and face painters, for schools, festivals, street parades and other events.

Festival Eye
BCM 2002, London WC1N 3XX
Tel: *01568 760 492*
Fax: *01568 760 492*
Email: *festivaleye@stones.com*
Web: *www.festivaleye.com*
Open: *Mon-Fri 3.30pm-4.30pm*
▶ Comprehensive list of alternative, fringe and mainstream festivals and camps in Britain. Also includes some European dates.

Festival of Green Cuisine
Penrhos Court, Kington HR5 3LH
Tel: *01544 230 720*
Fax: *01544 230 754*
Email: *martin@penrhos.co.uk*
Web: *www.penrhos.co.uk*
▶ This summer Festival, set in the six acre homestead of award-winning Penrhos Court, is a celebration of plant life and the food it gives us. It is the one festival to visit if you are interested in food and health. There is an organic food market for you to see, taste and buy organic produce; exhibitors who can advise you on anything from ethical finance to insulation and Aromatherapy to waste disposal. Also highly qualified speakers to inspire you on organic gardening, farming, wine, food and health.

Green Futures Festivals
Unit 34 Platt's Eyot,
Hampton TW12 2HF
Tel/Fax: *020 8941 6277*
Email: *info@gfutures.demon.co.uk*
Web: *www.gfutures.demon.co.uk*
Open: *Mon-Fri 9am-5pm*
(visits by appointment only)
▶ Organises green events showcasing renewably-powered stages with performers enjoying both the technology and the spirit of it. Organisers of Glastonbury Green Futures field yearly. Other events/festivals organised on request. All events powered by renewable energy and feature environmental education for children, campaigners, music, dance, speakers, veg/vegan caterers. Supports environmentally active events with consultancy for planning and management, alternative technology power providers, stewarding, security and site crew and ethical trading.

Manchester International Arts
3 Birch Polygon, Manchester M14 5HX
Tel: *0161 224 0020*
Fax: *0161 248 9331*
Email: *mia@streetsahead.org.uk*
Web: *www.streetsahead.org.uk*
▶ Organises the popular Streets Ahead festival and other cultural animation events in urban centres. Events are free, outdoor and pedestrianised occasions. Priortise and encourage use of public transport by attenders.

Manchester International Caribbean Carnival
c/o The Moss Side and Hulme Business Federation Ltd,
1st Floor, 111 Princess Street,
Manchester M14 4RB
Tel/Fax: *0161 226 0486*

Email: busfed@onefreenet.co.net
▶ Supported by the Moss Side and Hulme Business Federation in collaboration with local entertainment, fashion and business associations, artists and promoters. Manchester's annual carnival is one of the city's most lively events. Regular events include music, dance and a procession featuring troupes, floats and colourful costumes. Call for more information.

Mersey River Festival
c/o Healthstart, 1st Floor,
Cavern Court, 8 Matthew Street,
Liverpool L2 6RE
Tel: 0151 236 1737
Fax: 0151 227 4539
Email: info@health-start.com
Web: www.health-start.com
▶ A host of river and land-based events, entertainment and spectacular displays to celebrate the 'marriage between the land and the river.'

Northern Quarter Street Festival
Northern Quarter Association
1st and 2nd Floors,
100-102 High Street,
Northern Quarter,
Manchester M4 1HP
Tel: 0161 834 5143
Fax: 0161 819 1430
Email: sarah.nqa@good.co.uk
Web: www.nqa.org.uk
▶ Annual summer event designed to celebrate and promote the cultural and creative diversity of Manchester's Northern Quarter. The Festival is only one part of the regeneration initiative for the Northern Quarter. Other activities include the public art scheme and Radio Spaces, the Northern Quarter radio station.

Organisations & Advice

Federation of City Farms and Community Gardens
The Green House, Hereford Street,
Bedminster, Bristol BS3 4NA
Tel: 0117 923 1800
Fax: 0117 923 1900
Email: farmgarden@btinternet.com
▶ Federation representing City Farms and Community Gardens around the country. Send an A4 SAE for a list of farms and gardens in your area.

National

Places to Stay

The hotels, guesthouses and B&Bs in this section have been selected for their foods (vegetarian, vegan or organic), ethos and/or green activities.

Abbey Farm Caravan Park
Dark Lane, Ormskirk L40 5TX
Tel/Fax: 01695 572 686
▶ Family run, quality park set in 25 acres of rural countryside. Level mown grass pitches and restaurants within 5 minutes walk.

Amadeus Vegetarian Hotel
115 Franklin Rd, Harrogate HG1 5EN
Tel/Fax: 01423 505 151
Open: All year except Christmas
▶ Small hotel situated close to the centre of this spa town, serving breakfasts. Non-smoking.

Avingormack Guest House
Boat of Garten, PH24 3BT
Tel: 01479 831 614
Email: avin.gormack@ukgateway.net
Web: www.smoothhound.co.uk/hotels/avingormack
▶ A vegetarian guest house with stunning views of the Cairngorm Mountains set in the heart of the Scottish Highlands. Award winning vegetarian and vegan food using organic produce from their own garden. Also runs stop smoking courses from the house and is now on the new Dover to Inverness cycle route. Email or call for more information.

Beech Tree
Yewdale Road, Coniston LA21 8DX
Tel: 01539 441 717
▶ Charming 18th Century former vicarage set in its own attractive gardens 150 yards from the village centre. Providing vegetarian/ vegan bed and breakfast in comfortable accomodation and a smoke free atmosphere. Excellent centre for walking, and exploring the Southern lakes and fells. Brochure on request.

Boswednack Manor
Zennor, St Ives TR26 3DD
Tel: 01736 794 183
Open: Easter to Oct.

▶ Deeply peaceful guesthouse on the wild North coast of Cornwall. Vegetarian B&B (5 double bedrooms) and self-catering cottage on an organic smallholding. Surrounded by superb countryside, history, culture and wildlife. There is a detached meditation room and a large carpeted barn space suitable for group workshops. Full board offered to groups organising retreats or other spiritually orientated holidays. Also offers guided wildlife walks.

Bradwell Mill
West Down, Ilfracombe EX34 8NS
Tel: 01271 863 319
▶ Small holding in North Devon producing natural foodstuffs and running holidays, courses and events. Camps in the scheduled streamside meadow include arts and crafts, healing skills, music beach visits, relaxation and fun and shamanic/ Native American teachings. Small groups can be accommodated in the converted mill. Produces vegetables, apple juice, cider and beef, offers woodland burials and are members of Celtic folk and Ceilidh band 'Through The Mill'.

Capesthorne Hall Caravan Park
Siddington, Macclesfield SK11 9JY
Tel: 01625 861 779
Fax: 01625 861 619
▶ Five acre site situated in the park adjoining Capesthorne Hall, one of Cheshire's premier stately homes. Parkland, lakes, gardens and woodland to explore.

Chestnut House
Crosby Garrett,
Kirkby Stephen CA17 4PR
Tel: 01768 371 230
Email: chestnut@kenconp.net
▶ Traditional cottage B&B offering vegetarian and vegan breakfast with homemade bread and evening meals. Non-smoking en-suite available £19, without £18 and evening meal £11 per night.

Cuddyford
Rew Road, Ashburton TQ13 7EN
Tel: 01364 653 325
Open: All year except Christmas

▶ Family-run vegetarian bed and breakfast in Dartmoor National Park – ideal for exploring the Moor, Dart Valley and the South Devon Coastline. Wholesome cookery with home-baked bread, free range eggs, honey from their own hives, organically grown fruit and vegetables. Special diets are catered for and children are welcome.

Dickwilletts
Toft Road, Knutsford WA16 9EH
Tel: 01565 634 443
Fax: 01565 632 603
Email: willetts@gadrite.freeserve.co.uk
Open: All year
▶ Vegetarian hotel in farm house open Monday to Thursdays to business clientele and tourists. Vegetarian cuisine, no smoking. Single rate £55 including B&B.

Earth Spirit Centre
Dundon, Somerton TA11 6PE
Tel: 01458 272 161
Fax: 01458 273 796
▶ Venue for residential weekends and retreats, located five miles from Glastonbury. Camping available, vegetarian cuisine. Can accommodate up to 35 people. Call for information

Eden Green Vegetarian Guest House
20 Blencathra Street,
Keswick CA12 4HP
Tel: 01768 772 077
Fax: 01768 771 331
Email: 106143.1772@compuserve.com
Web: www.smoothhound.co.uk/hotels/edengrn.html
Open: All year
▶ Vegetarian guesthouse close to Keswick town centre, in the heart of the lake district. B&B in a standard room from £17.

Eller Close
Eller Close House,
Grassmere LA22 9RW
Tel: 015394 35786/ 077887 109 57
Fax: 015394 35786
▶ Self catering cottages on elevated position overlooking the vale of Grassmere. Spectacular views to Silver Howe, Lang Howe and Helm

Travel & Leisure 151

Crag. Many walks from leisurely strolls to more serious fell-walking. Perfect base for exploring the Lake District and North Yorkshire. Peaceful orchard gardens and tranquil lake. The cottages are tastefully furnished with antiques, including a four-poster bed.

Falcon Guest House
29 Falcon Terrace, Whitby YO21 1EH
Tel: 01947 603 507
Open: Year-round
▶ Small vegetarian guesthouse in a quiet location close to Whitby town centre and harbour. B&B with organic breakfast £17 per adult and reductions for children. Tea making facilities in bedrooms, no smoking. Whitby lies between sea and unspoilt moors, latter containing 'heartbeat' country and North Yorkshire moor steam railway. Boasts own authenticity and quaintness, and with its abbey, Captain Cook Musuem, Dracula Musuem, Sutcliffe Photo Gallery, and annual folk festival to name a few.

Firleas Vegetarian & Vegan Guesthouse
8 Colway Close,
Lyme Regis DT7 3BE
Tel: 01297 443 528
Open: All year except Christmas week
▶ Guesthouse, overlooking the sea, offers B&B and evening meals in a very quiet corner of Lyme Regis near cliffs and river walks to the sea and town. Homemade organic bread and home grown organic vegetables when available. Brochure on request.

Fox Hall Vegan B&B
Sedgwick, Kendal LA8 0JP
Tel/Fax: 01539 561 241
Email: Fox.Hall@btinternet.com
▶ Purely vegan guesthouse in converted seventeenth century barn. Evening meal £11.00. Two rooms, none en-suite. No charge for children under five. A self-catering holiday cottage, sleeping four plus a baby, is also available.

Gaunts House
Wimborne BH21 4JQ
Tel: 01202 841 522
Fax: 01202 841 959
Email: gaunt.demon.co.uk
▶ Set in 2,000 acres of Dorset countryside, Gaunts House offers year round retreats, private breaks, events and a programme of events. Call for details of the spring and summer Festivals.

Glenrannoch Vegetarian Guesthouse
Kinloch Rannoch,
near Pitlochry PH16 5QA
Tel: 01882 632 307
Email: margaretlegte@compuserve.com
Open: Feb-Nov
▶ Large Edwardian guesthouse with beautiful views of the Caledonian mountains offering 100% vegetarian (vegan on request) meals, made using homegrown organic produce whenever possible. Non-smoking.

Glenwood Vegetarian & Vegan Guesthouse
134 Lightwood Road,
Buxton SK17 6RW
Tel: 01298 77690
Email: ray.blakey@care4free.net
Open: All year
▶ Situated close to the centre of the Georgian spa town of Buxton, with its famous Opera House, and surrounded by the Peak National Park, Glenwood is exclusively vegetarian and vegan and non-smoking. Offers evening meals, using organic and fairly traded products wherever practicable. Spacious double and family rooms, each with private bathroom. Rates from £21 to £25 per night, including breakfast.

Globe Farm Guest House
Huddersfield Road, Delph,
Oldham OL3 5LU
Tel/Fax: 01457 873 040
Open: All year except Christmas & New Year
▶ Set in the countryside, the Farm is good for backpackers (and business people) and has good walking opportunities. All 14 rooms are en-suite.

Graianfryn Vegetarian Guest House
Penisarwaun, Caernarfon LL55 3NH
Tel: 01286 871 007
Email: info@vegwales.co.uk
Web: www.vegwales.co.uk
▶ Set in spectacular countryside on the edge of Snowdonia and close to Anglesey's sandy beaches, Graianfryn is an ideal centre for touring North Wales or for a walking, climbing or beach holiday, situated just three miles from Llanberis at the foot of Snowdon. Graianfryn, an early Victorian ex-farmhouse, is beautifully furnished and offers luxurious accomodation. The delicious meals are imaginative, created on the premises and exclusively vegetarian, wholefood and organic where possible.

Granville Hotel
124 Kings Road, Brighton BN1 2FA
Tel: 01273 326 302
Fax: 01273 728 294
Email: granville@brighton.co.uk
Open: Mon-Sun
▶ Stay beside the sea in ethical style. Most of the food is produced organically and only environmentally friendly cleaning products are used. Superb rooms, some with four poster beds and a jacuzzi. All the rooms are individually-designed. B&B from £37.50 per person per night. Sea views from £47.50.

Green House
5 Bank View, off Stainbeck Lane,
Chapel Allerton, Leeds LS7 2EX
Tel: 0113 268 1380
Open: All year
▶ Lovely Victorian house with peaceful atmosphere and outstanding decor by artist/designer proprietor. Down a leafy lane, with large garden, its peace and seclusion evoke the country rather than the bustling city two miles away. Green House's relaxing atmosphere is an excellent haven after a busy day.

Greenside Guest House
48 Saint John Street, Keswick-On-Derwent Water CA12 5AG
Tel: 01768 774 491
Open: All Year
▶ Vegetarian B&B from £16 per person. Close to lake and town centre. All bedrooms en-suite with colour TV, fridge, snack making facilities in Georgian house. Call for a brochure.

Grimstone Manor
Yelverton PL20 7QY
Tel: 01822 854 358
Fax: 01822 852 318
Email: enquiries@grimstonemanor.co.uk
Open: Closed January
▶ Set in 27 acres on the edge of Dartmoor, Grimstone Manor offers plentiful vegetarian food, an indoor swimming pool, jacuzzi and sauna. Venue for workshops including Yoga courses, family weeks and Summer solstice retreats for women and more.

Invernia Guest House
10 Kirby Road, Blackpool FY1 6EB
Tel: 01253 621 636
Open: Easter-early Nov
▶ Vegetarian and vegan hotel close to the promenade. Evening meal available. B&B from £12 per night. Non-vegetarians also catered for.

Lakeland Natural Vegetarian Guest House
Low Stack, Queen's Road,
Kendal LA9 4PH
Tel: 01539 733 011
Fax: 01539 733 011
Email: relax@lakelandnatural.co.uk
Web: www.lakelandnatural.co.uk
▶ Comfortable Victorian guesthouse on 3/4 acre premises overlooking Kendal and Fells. Only 5 minute walk from town centre. All rooms are spacious and fully on-suite. Secure parking on-site. Non-smoking. Licensed. Children and dogs welcome.

Lancrigg Vegetarian Country House Hotel
Easedale, Grasmere LA22 9QN
Tel: 01539 435 317
Fax: 01539 350058
Open: All year
▶ Set in 30 acres of private woodland, this hotel offers individually styled rooms, some with four poster beds and whirlpool baths and with vegetarian meals. Costs range from £49-95 per night depending on the room chosen and the season. Also caters for special diets.

Lower Shaw Farm
Old Shaw Lane, Shaw,
Swindon SN5 5PJ
Tel: 01793 771 080
Fax: 01793 771 080
Email: enq@lsfarm.globalnet.co.uk
Web: www.swindonlink.com

▶ Once a dairy, this farm is now a residential centre for weekend and week-long workshops which include crafts, gardening, writing and seasonal celebratory events. Meals are vegetarian and are prepared with mostly organic, homegrown and locally produced ingredients. There are gardens, ponds, poultry, sheep, a campfire circle and play spaces. Write, phone or email for details of programmes.

Making Waves
3 Richmond Place, St Ives TR26 1JN
Tel: 01736 793 895
Email: simon@making-waves.co.uk
Open: March-October
▶ Beautiful eco-renovated Victorian house. Stunning sea views overlooking tropical gardens, small veganic garden and sun terrace. Food is completely animal fee and virtually all organic. 2 minutes walk from harbour, 5 minutes to breathtaking beaches. Local seal and dolphin watching trips available. Children and non-vegans welcome!!

Minton House
Findhorn Bay, Findhorn IV36 3YY
Tel: 01309 690 819
Fax: 01309 691 583
Email: minton@findhorn.org
Web: www.mintonhouse.co.uk
Open: All year
▶ Retreat/workshop centre and guest house accommodation in a beautiful pink mansion on the shores of Findhorn Bay. A place of peace with a unique atmosphere of warmth and healing. The food is vegetarian and the vegetables are mainly organic and locally grown.

Mount Pleasant Farm
Gorran High Lanes,
St Austell PL26 6LR
Tel: 01726 843 918
Email: jlucas@mpfarm.fsnet.co.uk
Open: 25th Mar to 5th Nov
▶ Re-built in the 1970's retaining part of the 18th Century cottage, the farm is in a quiet and peaceful location situated in typical rural Cornish Countryside. The spectacular cliffs and beautiful South Cornish coastline are only one mile away affording easy access to some of the finest beaches in Cornwall. One of the most famous gardens in Cornwall, Heligan is close by. The hosts are both vegetarian and invite visitors to enjoy their organic breakfast, traditional, vegetarian or vegan. Other special diets are catered for with prior notice. Bees and chickens are kept and organic vegetables are grown on their small holding. Approved by the Cornish Tourist Board, with full central heating and parking available. Children are welcome. Yoga weekends, bike hire and alternative therapies are provided. The comfortable accommodation comprises of one double room, one family/twin room both with wash hand basins and one double en-suite room.

Old Post Office Bed and Breakfast
Llanigon, Hay-on-Wye HR3 5QA
Tel: 01497 820 008
Open: All year
▶ Seventeenth century Grade II listed house beautifully restored with beams and oak floorboards. Set in a quiet rural village in the Brecon Beacons National Park, only two miles from the famous book town of Hay-on-Wye. Guests have their own sitting room and superb vegetarian or vegan breakfast. Walks from the doorstop, recommended by the Which Guide. Prices from £17 pppn.

Penrhos Court Hotel and Restaurant
Penrhos, Kington HR5 3LH
Tel: 01544 230 720
Fax: 01544 230 754
Email: martin@penrhos.co.uk
Web: www.penrhos.co.uk
Open: March-Dec
▶ Penrhos Court is a 700-year-old Manor Farm on the border of Herefordshire and Wales. It has been saved from demolition and rebuilt over the last 25 years, and is now devoted to food and health and ecology. The businesses are run for the sake of the buildings, Penrhos Court Hotel and Restaurant and the Penrhos School of Food and Health. There is an annual 'Festival of Green Cuisine' every May featuring organic food and ecology.

Poplar Herb Farm
Burtle, Bridgewater TA7 8NB
Tel: 01278 723 170
Email: richardfish@lineone.net
Open: All year
▶ Organic herb farm and guesthouse offering vegetarian and vegan breakfast and evening meal with organic produce from the farm. Evening meals available. About nine miles from Glastonbury. B&B from £15 per night.

Portman Lodge
Durweston, Blandford DT11 0QA
Tel: 01258 452 168
Fax: 01258 450 456
Open: All year
▶ Classic Regency house set in a seven acre garden in an area of outstanding natural beauty. It is a centre for learning and natural therapies with the aim of providing a warm and friendly open space for people to explore and learn about their inner selves. Healing the body and balancing the mind by gentle means comes first. There are a full range of complementary therapies available. Guests who stay for B&B can book these treatments and may also use their room as a private retreat for total relaxation.

Prospect Cottage B&B
Bank End, Ingleton,
via Carnforth LA6 3HE
Tel: 01524 241 328
Open: All year round
▶ Exclusively vegetarian and provides comfortable but inexpensive accommodation with full cooked vegetarian or vegan breakfast. A picturesque stone cottage situated only a few miles walk from Ingleton's famous Waterfalls Walk, it is close to village shops, cafés and pubs. Breathtaking views from the garden and wonderful walks in all directions. If required, guests can be picked up by previous arrangement from Bentham or Ribblehead stations.

Quiraing Lodge Retreat Centre
Staffin, Isle of Skye IV51 9JS
Tel: 01470 562330
Open: All year except Christmas
▶ Open retreat centre offering both structured retreats and quiet space just to 'be' and to enjoy the beauty of Skye. Wide variety of walks, seaviews, open fires, library and meditation room. All catering is home-cooked and vegetarian.

Ranworth Vegetarian Guesthouse
Church Road, Ravenscar,
Scarborough YO13 0LZ
Tel: 01723 870 366
Open: All year
▶ Victorian stone-built villa overlooking the village cricket field. Has been offering 100% vegetarian/vegan wholefoods for 14 years. Uses many organic ingredients in freshly-prepared meals and caters for any dietary requirements. Vegan, organic wines and beers available, as are organic cordials. Recycles all waste and use own compost for growing salad vegetables and herbs. Furniture is 95% reclaimed pine and is locally bought. Pets and children are especially welcome as there is a large organic garden and playroom.

Mount Pleasant Farm B&B / Retreat
Nr Mevagissey

Enjoy the peace and quiet of the beautiful Cornish countryside, staying at our organic smallholding. The spectacular South Cornish coastline is only one mile away, with some of Cornwall's best beaches. Organic food Vegetarian/Vegan speciality bike hire, alternative therapies, yoga weekends non smoking, central heating, parking, children welcome, comfortable CTB approved
Tel: 01726 843 918
email: jlucas@mpfarm.fsnet.co.uk

Aromatherapy Massage, and summer house for meditation. Situated 600 feet high on the coast close to Robin Hood's Bay.

Seashells Hotel
7 Burlington Road,
Swanage BH19 1LR
Tel: 01929 422 794
▶ Set in the spectacular Purbeck Hills, Seashells is five minutes from the Dorset coastal path and opposite safe, sandy beaches. Offers good walking and delicious vegetarian cuisine.

Shepherd's Purse
95 Church Street, Whitby YO22 4BH
Tel/Fax: 01947 820 228
Open: All year
▶ Guesthouse with vegetarian wholefood restaurant and shop attached. Evening meal available. B&B with double room from £45 per night.

Six Mary's Place
Raeburn Place, Stockbridge,
Edinburgh EH4 1JH
Tel: 0131 332 8965
Fax: 0131 539 7375
Email: sixmarysplace@btinternet.com
Web: www.socialfirms.org.uk/guesthouse
Open: All year except Christmas
▶ Vegetarian guesthouse in the Stockbridge area of Central Edinburgh. Non-smoking. Special & vegan diets catered for.

St Judes
St Ives Road, Cardis Bay,
St Ives TR26 2SF
Tel: 01736 795 255
Open: All year
▶ Vegetarian and vegan guesthouse overlooking St Ives Bay. B&B from £16.75. Self-catering appartment available.

Temple Lodge
51 Queen Caroline Street,
London W6 9QL
Tel: 020 8748 8388
Open: All year
▶ Vegetarian B&B in a listed Georgian house, within easy distance of the river and walks along the tow path, at the same address as The Gate vegetarian restaurant.

The Edgecliffe Hotel
Clarence Gardens, Shanklin,
Isle of Wight PO37 6HA
Tel: 01983 866 199
Fax: 01983 868 841
Email: edgecliffe.hotel@nationwideisp.net
Web: www.wightonline.co.uk/edgecliffehotel
▶ Victorian style property in a fantastic location for enjoying the best of Shanklin and the Isle of Wight. All guest rooms, from singles to family rooms, four posters, doubles and twins. All en-suite, comfortable and tastefully decorated. Overlooking the colourful secluded garden, the dining room offers a choice for both breakfast and dinner, with traditional and special diets catered for. One minute to cliff path. Winter offer valid Oct to Dec 2000 (excluding Christmas to New-Year); valid for two people in a twin or double room, midweek or weekend break, two nights b&b including car ferry for only £109 per couple. Up to two extra nights for just £19 per person extra. Evening meal available for only £8.95 per head. Contact by telephone, fax or email for reservations, more details, or a brochure.

The Old Court House
Trefin, Near St Davids,
Haverfordwest SA62 5AX
Tel: 01438 837 095
▶ An exclusively vegetarian guesthouse situated on the stunning North Pembrokeshire Coast. Relax and unwind in the 200 year-old cosy cottage with ensuite accomodtion and an open fire. The manager Lynne is a Cordon Vert cook and uses local produce to produce delicious vegetarian and vegan food each day. Trefin is an ideal base to walk the coastal path, visit sandy beaches, off-shore islands and the city of St Davids. Lynne also runs vegetarian cookery courses and demonstrations.

The Rossan
Auchencairn, Castle Douglas DG7 1QR
Tel: 01556 640 269
Fax: 01556 640 278
Email: bardsley@rossan.freeserve.co.uk
Open: All year round

▶ Delightful B&B in nineteenth Century Victorian ex-Manse situated close to excellent walking and bird watching areas and with two sandy beaches close by. Evening meals are optional and special diets are a forte; the owner caters for vegetarians and vegans and those with special medical diets, as well as providing wholefoods, organically grown fruit and veg (whenever possible), free range eggs and home-baked bread using organic flour. Meat-eaters catered for too, using local beef, lamb, wild boar and fish. Three family rooms (none ensuite). Can take a maximum of six guests at a time including children, so call first. B&B costs £15 per night; dinner, bed and breakfast £25.

The West Usk Lighthouse
Lighthouse Road, St Brides,
Wentloog, Newport NP10 8SF
Tel: 01633 810 126/01633 815 860
Fax: 01633 815 582
Email: lighthouse@tesco.net
Web: www.smoothhound.co.uk/hotels/westusk.html
▶ Built in 1921, the Lighthouse is a Grade II listed building and offers a great B&B in kingsize and four-poster beds. All rooms are ensuite. A superb break with a difference. Enjoy the panoramic views from the Lantern room and relax in a flotation tank. Other therapies are also available at the Lighthouse including Aromatherapy, Reflexology, Reiki and more. You can sit by a log fire, go birdwatching or wander along the reedy dykes, looking for the plants that botanists find of particular interest. B&B rate for two people is £80 per night.

Tregynon Country Farmhouse Hotel
Gwaun Valley,
Near Fishguard SA65 9TU
Tel: 01239 820 531
Fax: 01239 820 808
Email: tregynon@online-holidays.net
Web: www.online-holidays.net/tregynon
▶ Escape to Wales' 16th Century award-winning Country Farmhouse Hotel in the foothills of Preseli mountains in Pembrokesire Coast National Park. Magnificent views, ancient forest, abundant wildlife, mountain and coastal walks. Renowned cuisine with wholefood and vegetarian also a speciality. Licensed, with log fires in Winter. AA Rosette and Wales Tourist Board 3 Star Country Hotel.

Tremeifion Vegetarian Hotel
Soar Road,
Talsarnau LL47 6UH
Tel: 01766 770 491
Fax: 01766 771 272
Email: tremeifion@mcmail.com
Web: www.tremeifion.mcmail.com
Open: All Year
▶ Small vegetarian hotel with spectacular views over the river estuary towards Portmeiron. Close to Harlech Beach. Relaxing and friendly environment, excellent home-cooked vegetarian and vegan cuisine. Organic food used from the garden when possible, organic vegetarian wine list with no smoking throughout.

Trericket Mill Vegetarian Guesthouse, Bunkhouse & Camping
Erwood, Builth Wells LD2 3TQ
Tel: 01982 560 312
Fax: 01982 560 768
Email: mail@trericket.co.uk
Web: www.trericket.co.uk
Open: All year (except Christmas)
▶ Offers a range of accommodation to appeal to the environmentally aware, with camping in a cider orchard, cosy bunkrooms sleeping up to four and en-suite B&B rooms. All catering is vegetarian using wholefood, organic, free-range and fair trade produce wherever possible. Designated site of special scientific interest in the upper Wye valley. Good stop-over on the Wye Valley Walk and Sustrans Cycle Route 8.

Wild Pear Centre
King Street,
Combe Martin EX34 0AG
Tel/Fax: 01271 883 086
▶ Residential workshop and holistic holiday venue on the Exmoor coast of North Devon. Founded in 1994, the centre hosts a variety of different workshops such as yoga, meditation, bodywork, voicework, movement, dance and personal growth as well as

providing an unusual setting for groups and extended families seeking to holiday together. Offers a group room measuring 37 ft by 18ft, a communal hall of 37ft by 33ft, two kitchens, four bathrooms, six separate bedrooms and ample dormitory accommodation. Groups of up to 25 or so can be accommodated. Self-catering, £12 pp, whole vegetarian full board £28 pp, B&B (Wild Pear's version 'Futon and Muesli'!) also available £12 per night. The centre does not have grounds of its own but is five minutes walk away from the beach and immediately adjacent to six miles of unspoilt coastline and moorland owned by the National Trust.

Wildlife Hotel
39 Woodfield Road, South Shore,
Blackpool FY1 6AX
Tel: 01253 346 143
Open: All year
▶ Totally vegetarian and vegan hotel near the sea and other major Blackpool attractions. B&B from £16 per night. Non-smoking. Mostly organic. All rooms en-suite with TV.

Willows Vegetarian Guest House
19 Tolsta Chaolais,
Isle of Lewis HS2 9DW
Tel: 01851 621 321
▶ Small, family-run guesthouse in lochside croft within easy reach of the Callanish Stones, sandy beaches and wildlife. Vegetarian and vegan meals. STB three stars commended.

Woodcote Hotel
The Saltings, Lelant, St Ives TR26 3DL
Tel: 01736 753 147
Open: Mar-Oct
▶ The oldest vegetarian hotel in the UK, established in the Twenties. Situated in its own grounds overlooking the estuary and bird sanctuary. Serves home-cooked vegetarian and vegan food made using local produce whenever possible.

Yeo Cottage
Sandwell Lane, Totnes TQ9 7LJ
Tel: 01803 868 157
Open: All year
▶ Thatched cottage in Devon Countryside between the moors and the sea offering retreat for peace, relaxation, healing, tarot and meditation. B&B at £16 per night and evening meal by arrangement.

Yewfield Vegetarian Guesthouse
Hawkshead Hill,
Ambleside LA22 0PR
Tel: 015394 36765
Fax: 015394 36096
Email:
derek.yewfield@btinternet.com
Web: www.yewsfield.co.uk
Open: Feb-mid Nov
▶ Quiet and peaceful retreat in 30 acres of glorious gardens and grounds with splendid walks throughout the Lake District. Grounds include organic vegetable gardens, orchards and a herb patio. The house is non-smoking.

Activities

Bicycle Beano Cycle Tours
Erwood, Builth Wells LD2 3PQ
Tel: 01982 560 471
Email: mail@bicycle-beano.co.uk
Web: www.bicycle-beano.co.uk
Open: April-Sept
▶ Cycling holidays exploring idyllic lanes of Wales and Welsh Borders of England. Delicious vegetarian cuisine (lunchtime meat options available). Guided on-road bicycle tours in the Brecon Beacons, Pembrokeshire Coast, and Snowdonia National Parks. Lively friendly groups, all abilities welcome, three-seven days, April to September. Venues include a watermill, country house and an old priory by the sea. Prices includes accommodation, breakfast, dinner, and afternoon tea, detailed maps and written instructions, a mechanic on-hand and full back-up.

Centre for Alternative Technology (CAT)
Machynlleth SY20 9AZ
Tel: 01654 702 400
Fax: 01654 702 782
Email: steven.jones@cat.org.uk
Web: www.cat.org.uk
▶ In the heart of beautiful Snowdonia, this unique visitor attraction is guaranteed to entertain, inform and fascinate all the members of the family. Lifted up by 'the water-balanced' cliff railway with its breathtaking views visitors arrive at the seven acre display gardens, crammed with exhibitions displays and information. The Centre is concerned with presenting solutions to environmental problems, rather than the doom and gloom view, and takes a positive and uplifting approach, demonstrating all kinds of environmental technologies in an interesting and informative way. Whether you want learn all about the environment, how to save energy and money in your home or just enjoy the gardens, shops and restaurant it will be an experience to treasure and remember. CAT began as an experimental, sustainable community over 25 years ago. Since 1974 it has evolved into Mid Wales' most unique and popular visitor attraction. In the main holiday periods runs special events for children, with drama, interactive fun and a presentation on their unique 'Gaiascope' – a giant television kaleidoscope. Other activities at the Centre include publishing, residential courses, day visits for schools and colleges, as well as an extensive mail order service, an award winning website and a free information service.

Green & Away
PO Box 40, Malvern WR14 1YS
▶ Arranger of indoor and outdoor conferences and events for organisations working or social and environmental renewal. Occupies an organic site near Gloucester for serveral weeks each summer to host a range of inspiring events and meetings. For information on the wide-ranging programme, send an SAE to the above address.

Hill House Retreats: Centre for Wholistic Living
Hill House, Llansteffan,
Carmarthen SA33 5JG
Tel/Fax: 01267 241 999
Email: jane@hillhouseretreats.com
Web: www.hillhouseretreats.com
Open: All year
▶ Ecologically restored superbly situated country house overlooking castle, church and bay and coastal village conservation area. Healing diets (special diets catered for): vegan, vegetarian, wholefood, organic and fair traded foods; spring water. One acre organic garden to heal mind, body & spirit. Large workshop/meditation space. Wide variety of workshops and activities: guided walks, cycle and kayak hire, retreats including working retreats.

The Old Court House Walking Holidays
Trefin, Near St Davids,
Haverfordwest SA62 5AX
Tel: 01348 837 095
▶ Enjoy walking the Pembrokeshire Coastal Path. Offers self-guided walking packages all year round, with drop-offs and pick-ups available. Distances to suit all abilities with expert advice and local knowledge, with maps and guides, packed lunches and advice on equipment and clothing. Call for more details.

Vegetarian Vacations – The Veggie Tours Directory
Erwood, Builth Wells LD2 3PQ
Tel: 01982 560 471
Email: bicycle@beano.kc3.co.uk
Web: www.kc3.co.uk/~bicycle/veggie/index.html
▶ A directory of tours, holidays and courses offering vegetarian or vegan food.

Wild and Free Travel
6 Old Bridge Court, Forres IV36 1ZR
Tel: 01309 671 736
Email: wild.dolphin@virginnet.com
Web: www.dolphinswims.co.uk
▶ Dolphin swim holidays and nature tours. Swim with a wild and free friendly dolphin in the Red Sea. Superb location, friendly people. Peaceful and healing. Children welcome.

Woodland Skills Centre
Greenwood Courses,
The Church Hall, Llanafan,
Builth Wells LD2 3PN
Tel/Fax: 01597 860 469
Web: www.greenwoodworking.co.uk
▶ Arts and crafts holidays in this centre in the woods of mid-Wales. Learn a range of skills from chair and coracle-making to forging and tool-making. Call for a brochure.

Organisations & Advice

Caravan Club
East Grinstead House, East Grinstead RH19 1UA
Tel: 01342 326944
Fax: 01342 410258
Web: www.caravanclub.co.uk
▶ The premier organisation for caravanners, motor caravanners, and trailer tenters with over 200 caravan sites in the UK.

Continental Drifts
Hilton Grove, Hatherley, London E17 4QP
Tel: 020 8509 3353
Fax: 020 8509 9531
Email: christofu@continentaldrifts.co.uk
Web: www.continentaldrifts.co.uk
Open: All year
▶ Represents an exciting range of circus, cabaret, nightclub and walkabout performers and musical arts. The group is widely involved with fringe events and the festival scene.

Distinctly Different
Masons Lane, Bradford-on-Avon BA15 1QN
Tel/Fax: 01225 866 648
▶ Accommodation guide with recycling at its heart, listing places to stay which have been 'recycled' in some way, ranging from converted brothels to defrocked churches. A high proportion of vegetarian options. For a copy of the latest booklet send a cheque for £3, payable to P Roberts, to the above address.

Farms for City Children
Nethercott House, Iddesleigh, Winkleigh EX19 8BG
Tel: 01837 810 573
Fax: 01837 810 866
Email: ffcc.nethercott-house@freeserve.co.uk
Open: School term-time
▶ Exists to give urban children from all over the country the opportunity to live and work on one of three organic farms for a week.

Federation of City Farms and Community Gardens
The Green House, Hereford Street, Bedminster, Bristol BS3 4NA
Tel: 0117 923 1800
Fax: 0117 923 1900
▶ Association representing City and Community Farms around the country. Call for a list of farms in your local area.

Green Flag Park Awards
ILAM House, Lower Basildon, Reading RG8 9NE
Tel: 01491 874 800
Fax: 01491 874 801
Email: info@ilam.co.uk
▶ The Green Flag Park Awards recognise and encourage high standards of environmental protection and enhancement, community use, landscape design and maintenance, safety, cleanliness and accessibility in public parks. A joint project of the Pesticides Trust, the Institute of Leisure and Amenity Management, The Chartered Institution of Water and Enviromental Management and English Nature, the Awards have been funded by the DETR. In 1997, seven parks and in 1998, 16 parks received awards.

Green Wood Trust
Station Road, Coalbrookdale, Telford TF8 7DR
Tel/Fax: 01952 432 769
Email: sue.challis@greenwoodtrust.demon.co.uk
▶ Registered charity which aims to promote the sustainable management of nature broad-leafed woodland through teaching traditional skills. A wide range of Green Woodworking weekend or week-long courses from Reading the Landscape and Cider Making to chair making or constructing a yurt, held in the Shropshire country side. Accommodation available in timber-framed tents. Call for details and booking form.

Head for the Hills
Garth, Builth LD4 4AT
Tel: 01494 794 060
Fax: 01494 776 066
Open: Mon-Fri 9am-5pm
▶ Walking holidays in Wales and England across a range of landscapes and terrains. The luggage and camp equipment is carried ahead so walkers 'travel light' and all meals are vegetarian food.

Long Distance Walkers Association
c/o Bank House, Wrotham, Sevenoaks TN15 7AE
Tel: 01732 883705
Email: tom@bankhouse.f9.co.uk
Web: www.ldwa.org.uk
▶ Aims to further the interest of those who enjoy long distance walking. Over 40 groups nationwide. Inhouse journal thrice yearly listing local group walks and challenge walks.

Neal's Yard Agency for Personal Development
BCM Neal's Yard, London WC1N 3XX
Tel/Fax: 0870 444 2702
Email: info@nealsyardagency.com
Web: www.nealsyardagency.com
Open: Mon-Fri 11am-6pm
▶ Provides information on 'inner and outer' journeys, giving advice on a range of holistic and healthy weekends and holidays in Britain, the Mediterranean and Asia. Keep informed and up-to-date on holidays, retreats and personal development workshops via the free Events Guide. Call or email to receive it four times a year.

Ramblers Association
1-5 Wandsworth Road, London SW8 2XX
Tel: 020 7339 8500
Fax: 020 7339 8501
Email: ramblers@london.ramblers.org.uk
Web: www.ramblers.org.uk
Open: All year
▶ Promotes rambling throughout the British countryside and campaigns to protect public rights of way and access to open country. Individual membership costs £18 and includes subscription to the colour magazine, Rambling Today.

Willing Workers on Organic Farms (WWOOF) UK and International
PO Box 2675, Lewes BN7 1RB
Email: fran@wwoof.org
Web: www.wwoof.org
▶ Worldwide organisation offering first hand experience of living and working on organic farms and smallholdings. In return for working, you will receive meals, accommodation and the opportunity to learn about environmentally friendly systems. Midweek, longterm and overseas stays are available. Send SAE to above address for further details.

Youth Hostels Association
Trevelyan, 8 St Stephens Hill, St Albans AL1 2DY
Tel: 01727 855 215
Fax: 01727 844 126
Web: www.yha.org.uk
▶ Offers an unrivalled network of 230 Youth Hostels providing affordable accomodation in a variety of often historic buildings. Locations include city centres, coastal, countryside and National Parks. Although security and standards at all Youth Hostels are paramount, value for money is also a primary concern. Facilities include; full board, educational packages, animation packages, classrooms and conference equipment, sole occupancy and local attraction discounts. Call 0870 870 8808 for more specific information.

ABROAD

Travel Agents

Key Travel
3rd Floor Royal Buildings,
2 Mosley Street, Manchester M2 3AN
Tel: 0161 8198900
Fax: 0161 8393893
▶ Specialist travel agents offering a range of specially-negotiated flight-only airfares to all destinations world-wide. Over 15 years experience of serving the conscientious and ethical traveller.

North South Travel (NST)
Moulsham Mill Centre, Parkway,
Chelmsford CM2 7PX
Tel: 01245 608 291
Fax: 01245 608 291
Email: brenda@nstravel.demon.co.uk
Open: Mon-Fri 9am-6pm
▶ Travel agency offering discounted fares to destinations worldwide, together with full travel agency back-up. Profits are channelled to grass-roots projects (especially ones that benefit disadvantaged sectors of the community or that contribute to the promotion of sustainable tourism) in Africa, Asia and Latin America through the NST Development Trust.

Holidays

Beau Champ
24610 Montpeyroux,
Tel: 01248 602 300 (UK)
Fax: (33) 557 40 65 65 (FR)
Email: johncant@in-net.inba.fr
Web: www.phdcc.com/bc
▶ Permaculture centre set in 20 acres of meadows and woodland in the Dordogne, SW France, formed in 1991 by a group of friends aiming for an ecologically sound lifestyle. During the summer, visitors are welcome to join an 'experience week' – a low cost holiday with a specific focus such as self-build, greenwood construction, perma-pottery, mosaics, cycling, etc.

Bike Tours Ltd
Victoria Works, Lambridge Mews,
Larkhall, Bath BA1 6QE
Tel: 01225 310 859
Fax: 01225 480 132
Email: mail@biketours.co.uk
Open: Mon-Fri 9am-5pm
▶ Long-established company running bike tours in the UK, Bordeaux to Barcelona, Prague to Venice, Holland, Vienna to Prague, Brittany to Bordeaux, Ravenn to Rome and San Francisco to Los Angeles. Travel by ferry or Eurostar. Tours range from laid-back pottering to challenging excursions. Participants cycle independently. Full back-up service and luggage carried.

Cortijo Romero
Little Grove, Grove Lane,
Chesham HP5 3QQ
Tel: 01494 782 720
Fax: 01494 776 066
Email: bookings@cortijo-romero.co.uk
Web: www.cortijo-romero.co.uk
▶ Year-round alternative holidays in the Alpujarra region of Southern Spain. Offers a different holiday each week with courses varying from yoga, Tai Chi, dance, meditation and more, with plenty of free time. Set in an 800-year-old olive grove amongst the mountains, gardens and a pool. Write or call for a brochure.

Earthwatch
57 Woodstock Road, Oxford OX2 6HJ
Tel: 01865 318 838
Fax: 01865 311 383
Email: info@uk.earthwatch.org
Web: www.earthwatch.org
Open: Mon-Fri 9am-5pm
▶ An international science and education charity which recruits paying volunteers to help research scientists in fields from archaeology to zoology on 140 research projects in over 50 countires around the year. Some 3,400 volunteers aged 17 or over are welcome, and most do not need technical skills to participate.

Hotel Mocking Bird Hill
P.O. Box 354, Port Antonio
Tel: 876 993 7267
Fax: 876 993 7133
Email: mockbird@cwjamaica.com
Web: www.hotelmockingbirdhill.com
▶ Hotel Mocking Bird Hill seduces with its tranquil luxury and hospitality. Panoramic mountain and ocean vistas from this close-to-the-beach hilltop retreat nested in lush, tropical gardens. An intimate hideaway providing comfortable, warm hospitality, gracious atmosphere and friendly service. An environmental and socially friendly philosophy complements the setting.The restaurant delights with creative cuisine including vegetarian selections.

Huzur Vadisi
The Old Mill, Water Street,
Aberaeron SA6 0DG
Tel: 01545 570 742
Fax: 01545 570 742
Open: Mon-Fri 9am-6pm
▶ Alternative holidays in SW Turkey on a peaceful farmstead in a mountain valley close to the Mediterranean coast – virgin forests, mountain walks, spectacular coastline. Swimming pool. Creative and holistic courses on offer. Also provides old mill short holidays in Wales. Call for a brochure.

Natural Heights
15 Northbourne Road,
London SW4 7DR
Tel/Fax: 020 8675 7878
Email: naturalheights@dial.pipex.com
Web: www.travelmatters.co.uk/natural heights
Open: Mon-Fri 9.30am-5.30pm
▶ Small holiday company offering accommodation in the conservation area of Portugals South West Algarve. Guided walking, mountain biking, horseriding arranged locally. Costs ranging from £300-£400 per person including flights, accommodation.

Naturally Morocco Ltd
Hill House, LLansteffan SA33 5JG
Tel/Fax: 01267 241 999
Email: info@moroccoecotours.com
Web: www.bigfoot.com/-jane.bayley
Open: 8am-10pm
▶ Ecotourism project based in a well equipped house in the ancient walled town of Taroudant. Access to mountains, oases and the sea. Wonderful Moroccan staff provide an experience of culture and environment: a range of interests including wildlife, trekking, cooking and crafts catered for. Vegetarian food a speciality. Spacious house offers many facilities including library, roof terraces with excellent views, apartments or rooms to hire for individuals or groups.

Reef & Rainforest Tours Ltd
No 1, The Plains, Totnes TQ9 5DR
Tel: 01803 866 965
Fax: 01803 865 916
Email: reefrain@binternet.com
Open: Mon-Fri 9am-6pm
▶ Small-scale, natural history tours to Costa Rica, Madagascar, Ecuador, Peru, Indonesia, Honduras. and more. Eco-friendly lodges and local guides are used wherever possible. Activities include riding, canoeing, wildlife spotting, snorkelling, scuba diving and nature walking. Also offers the opportunity to join aid conservation-based research projects in Belize and Costa Rica. Tailored-made itineraries and school educational trips for A-level and university students.

Skyros Holistic Holidys
92 Prince of Wales Road,
London NW5 3NE
Tel: 020 7267 4424
Fax: 020 7284 3063
Email: skyros@easynet.co.uk
Web: www.skyros.com
Open: Mon-Fri 9.30am-6pm
▶ The Greek island of Skyros from May to October is home to two unique holiday communities, offering sun, sea, spectacular scenery, good food and company and a choice of over 200 courses facilitated by a staff team of 90. Call for a brochure and details of winter activities.

Teaching & Projects Abroad
Gerrard House,
Rustington BN16 1AW
Tel: 01903 859 911
Fax: 01903 785 779
Email: info@teaching-abroad.co.uk
Web: www.teaching-abroad.co.uk
▶ With Teaching & Projects Abroad you can enjoy adventurous foreign travel with a chance to do a worth-while job. You can teach conversational English or gain experience in medicine, conservation, journalism, business, and much more. No teaching qualifications or local languages are needed. All degree disciplines welcomed. Volunteers are

needed in China, Ghana, India, Mexico, Nepal, Peru, Russia, Thailand, Togo and Ukraine.

VegiVentures
Castle Cottage,
Castle Acre PE32 2AJ
Tel: 01760 755 888
Fax: 01760 755 888
▶ Provides small groups of people with vegetarian and vegan food on a range of holidays from weekends in Wales (at the Centre for Alternative Technology) or the Four Winds Centre in Surrey to a week in the Lake District or longer breaks in Peru, Bali and Crete.

West Crete Holidays
c/o Footloose Adventure Travel, 105 Leeds Road, Ilkley LS29 8EG
Tel: 01943 604 030
Fax: 01943 604 070
▶ Self-growth and good health are the themes for its special interest holidays and healings set in beautiful west Crete close to the sea. Workshops include Reiki, Massage, Shiatsu, Alexander Technique, Yoga, art and dance, and much more. Call for a brochure.

Wildwings
International House, Bank Road, Bristol BS15 8LX
Tel: 0117 984 8040
Fax: 0117 961 0200
Email: wildinfo@wildwings.co.uk
Web: www.wildwings.co.uk
Open: Mon-Fri 9am-5.30pm
▶ Whale and dolphin watching holidays all over the world, led by experienced biologists. They take care to put the welfare of the animals first, and this is reflected in how they conduct the tours and in their choice of professional and sympathetic boat operators. They also offer a range of birdwatching tours under the name Wildwings.

Organisations & Advice

Campaign for the Advancement of Responsive Travel
70 Dry Hill Park Road, Tonbridge TN10 3BX
Tel/Fax: 01732 352 757
Email: rmillman@dial.pipex.com

▶ Personal consultancy offering advice to travellers who are concerned for better cross-cultural understanding. CART focuses on preliminary planning, group processes and dynamics, social and cultural considerations and gathering information. Founder Member of Tourism Concern.

Centre for Environmentally Responsible Tourism
Indaba House, 1 Hydeway, Thundersly SS7 3BE
Tel: 01268 795 772
Fax: 01268 759 834
Email: certdesk@aol.com
Open: 24 hours
▶ Positive initiative which seeks to encourage good environmental practice within the travel industry by working with tour operators and communicating the industries' commitment to their customers and the public at large.

Green Globe
20 Grosvenor Place,
London SW1X 7TT
Email: info@greenglobe.org
Web: www.greenglobe.org
▶ Environmental management programme for Travel & Tourism Companies and tourism destinations. Its membership, in over 100 countries and from all sectors including hotels, airlines and travel agents, is dedicated to improving environmental practices and increasing awareness within the industry. Look out for the Green Globe logo when you travel but remember that this is a trade organisation and that Green Globe cannot give out free environmental information to the general public or other non-members. Contact instead the website for up-to-date information including a membership list.

Proyecto Ambiental Tenerife
55 Monmouth Street,
London WC2H 9DG
Tel: 020 7240 6604
Fax: 020 7240 5795
Email: edb@huron.ac.uk
Web: www.interbook.net/personal/dolphinsea
▶ Provides information on a variety of local, community-based eco-tourism opportunities such as whale and dolphin watching, Spanish language courses (Cuba and Tenerife), scuba diving, walking trips, etc. All activities promoted put your money directly into the local community and are environmentally sensitive. Conservation projects can also be joined by tourists and volunteers on a paying basis, including whale and dolphin studies and solar energy, community development and organic urban gardening in Cuba.

Sustainable Travel and Tourism
14 Greville Street, London EC1N 8SB
Tel: 020 7871 0123
Fax: 020 7871 0111
Email: sclout@sustravel.com
Web: www.sustravel.com
▶ Online information and news and resources showing best practice on sustainable and environmentally sensitive travel and tourism. Highlighting destinations and resorts that care about their environment and tips on being a good guest when on holiday.

Tourism Concern
Stapleton House,
277-281 Holloway Road,
London N7 8HN
Tel: 020 7753 3330
Fax: 020 7753 3331
Email: info@tourismconcern.org.uk
Web: www.tourismconcern.org.uk
Open: Mon-Fri 10am-5pm
▶ Campaign group focusing on the impacts of tourism, particularly in developing countries, and aiming to promote greater understanding of the impact on host communities and their environments. Recently launched an on-line directory of community-based holidays which lists commercial tour operators, non-profit NGOs and communities who run their own tours: the key factors are whether a project benefits the local community. Their Himalayan Tourist Code lists environmental do's and don'ts for mountain travellers.

World Travel & Tourism Council
1-2 Queen Victoria Terrace,
Sovereign Court, London E1W 3HA
Tel/Fax: 0870 727 9882
Email: enquiries@wttc.org
Web: www.wttc.org
▶ Global Business Leaders Forum for Travel & Tourism. Members are Chief Executives from all sectors of the industry, including accomodation, catering, entertainment, recreation, transportation and other travel-related services. Its central goal is to work with governements to realise the full economic impact of the world's largest generator of wealth and jobs – Travel & Tourism. Representative offices worldwide. WTTC's Strategic Priorities identify the potential for Travel & Tourism to generate some 5.4 million new jobs or 252 million jobs by 2010 across the world economy, with new public/private sector cooperation.

Promoting socially responsible investment

The UK Social Investment Forum (UKSIF) aims to promote and encourage the development of socially responsible investment throughout the UK. **Penny Shepherd**, *the UKSIF's Executive Director, describes its work.*

Socially responsible investment or ethical investment integrates investors' financial objectives with social, ethical and environmental issues such as social justice, economic development, peace and a healthy environment. It includes ethical screening of investments on positive and negative criteria, shareholder activism and company dialogue, economically targeted private investment to create jobs and social capital in disadvantaged communities and environmental investment in projects like renewable energy and organic farms.

Our members and affiliates include about fifty financial institutions together with financial advisers, consultants, researchers, non-governmental and community based organisations and some private individuals. We are deliberately a 'broad church' – involving both specialist and mainstream organisations rather than only those which regard themselves as 'ethical' or value-based. We believe that this allows us to have the greatest impact on the financial services available to individuals and organisations.

As well as providing information to our members, government, the press, other organisations and members of the public, we offer networking support to our members and seek to encourage a public policy and legal framework that enables the use of socially responsible investment. We provide the secretariat for the All-Party Parliamentary Group on Socially Responsible Investment in the UK parliament.

UKSIF has supported the introduction of the government's pensions disclosure regulation which, since July 2000, requires occupational pension funds to disclose the degree to which, if any, they take account of social, environmental and ethical considerations in their investment strategies.

In October 2000, we published a report 'Response of UK Pension Funds to the SRI Disclosure Regulation' which analysed the initial statements of social, ethical and environmental considerations made by the UK's largest pension funds and by local authority pension funds. Pension funds responding to our survey represented 302 billion pounds in assets and 6.4 million pension fund members. We found that 59% of them, representing 78% of the total assets, sought to incorporate socially responsible investment into their investment strategies – either by direct engagement with the companies in which they held shares or by request to their fund managers to consider, at a minimum, the impact of social and environmental issues on future financial performance. The challenge now is for fund managers to demonstrate how they are responding to this demand. In 2001, we will be monitoring access to socially responsible investment via the new Stakeholder Pensions.

We also initiated and supported the Social Investment Taskforce that was chaired by venture capitalist Sir Ronald Cohen of Apax Partners & Co. In October 2000, it made recommendations to the Chancellor of the Exchequer on how to increase private sector investment available to small businesses and social and community enterprises in disadvantaged communities. HM Treasury had observer status on the Taskforce. The Social Investment Taskforce recommended:

- A Community Investment Tax Credit to encourage investment in community development financial institutions

- Community Development Venture Funds financed by a matched funding partnership between Government on the one hand and the venture capital industry, entrepreneurs, institutional investors and banks on the other.

- Disclosure of individual bank lending activities in under-invested communities

- Greater latitude and encouragement for charitable trusts and foundations to invest in community development initiatives

- Other support for Community Development Financial Institutions, including Community Development Banks, Community Loan Funds, Micro-loan Funds and Community Development Venture Funds.

The government has welcomed the report and UKSIF is now supporting the implementation of its recommendations.

Our web site provides answers to commonly asked questions, a comprehensive database of our members and affiliates with links to their web sites, and a library of information.

If you are considering investing significant sums ethically, we recommend consulting an Independent Financial Adviser with expertise in socially responsible investment. Our online database includes details of Independent Financial Advisers who are committed to working together to advance socially responsible investment. These are drawn from adviser firms who are UKSIF members together with individual advisers who are members of the Ethical Investment Association, a professional association for independent financial advisers specialising in socially responsible investment that we work closely with. ■

For further information, visit the UK Social Investment Forum, website at **www.uksif.org** *or email* **info@uksif.org** *UK Social Investment Forum, Holywell Centre, 1 Phipp Street, London EC2A 4PS. Tel:* **020 7749 4880** *Fax:* **020 7749 4881**

CASE STUDY: Inspiring business

Business in the Environment (BiE) inspires companies to make sustainable development an essential part of business excellence. BiE is the business-led campaign for environmental responsibility of Business in the Community and its leadership and advisory teams promote the key role of sustainable development as a strategic competitive issue for business. BiE's business-to-business approach helps to get attention in corporate boardrooms and demonstrates to companies that working towards sustainable development makes business sense through three key areas.

State of the world – vital signs

- natural resources – it is estimated that half the earth's forests are gone – 16 million hectares disappear each year (World Resources Institute).
- Water consumption – over the past 50 years, water use has tripled to 4,200 cubic km.
- Emissions – over the past 50 years, carbon dioxide emissions have more than quadrupled to 7.0 billion tonnes a year – mainly as a result of fossil fuel-based industrialised processes.
- Waste – on average 9 tonnes raw materials are used to make 1 tonne of product.

The Business Case

- Corporate reputation – 86% of UK adults consider the environment to be a 'very or extremely important' part of corporate responsibility (MORI, 1999).
- Innovation – designing products, processes and services with reduced environmental impact stimulates innovation throughout the supply chain.
- People – companies with good environmental management should find it easier to recruit, train, develop, motivate and retain higher calibre employees.
- The environmental technology market is worth $200 billion and is expected to grow upto $600 billion.

The Financial Case

Practical trials show that companies can reduce their annual energy and waste costs by 10% without capital investment – a saving of £2.6 billion a year by businesses in the UK alone.

- Profitability – case studies suggest that profitability could be doubled through improved resource productivity (Report to the Club of Rome 1998).
- Investment potential – environmental issues have an impact on the cost of capital for businesses of all types and sizes – from environmental risk to regulation on producer responsibility and waste. Therefore environmental issues affect the value of a company over the longer term.
- Environmental management and performance is increasingly regarded as an indicator of the quality of management in general – the more traditional business disciplines by which City analysts assess the investment potential of companies.

For more information, contact Business in the Environment at 137 Shepherdess Walk, London N1 7RQ. Tel: **0870 600 2482** *Email:* **bie@bitc.org.uk** *Web:* **www.business-in-environment.org.uk**

Sustainable solutions are just a phone call away

At the start of the new millennium, there is a real and pressing need for business to balance the demands of progress with the impacts it creates on society and the environment. The NCBS provides a route for business to address this need.

Understanding this delicate balancing act is the main purpose of The National Centre for Business & Sustainability (NCBS). Since it was set up in 1995, originally as The National Centre for Business & Ecology, the Centre has been busy advising private and public sector clients on a wide variety of sustainability issues – from applied environmental advice and services, to social accountability and auditing. Inspired and set up by The Co-operative Bank, the NCBS advocates environmentally and socially sustainable solutions to a range of businesses and organisations. The Centre represents a unique partnership between The Co-operative Bank and the four universities of Greater Manchester (UMIST, Manchester, Salford and Manchester Metropolitan), drawing on the ecological and ethical policies of The Bank, and the technical expertise from across the four universities and the wider scientific community.

The NCBS is a not-for-profit organisation and receives funding from a range of sources including direct private sector contracts, European funds, landfill tax credit monies, and support from the Co-operative Bank. Expertise is supplied primarily from the Centre's highly trained staff. Additional technical support can be secured from the 2,500 academic partners in the four Universities as well as a number of associates based outside the university sector.

In the short period since its inception, the NCBS has built up a respected reputation in both the academic and business communities, local government and the non-government organisation sector. Some of the Centres achievements to date include:

- being the first organisation to produce a social audit of a local authority best value programmes

- being the first organisation to gain approved status to offer the Institute of Social and Ethical Accounting's (ISEA) Social Auditors course

- being one of the country's leading providers of sustainable strategies using The Natural Step, a tool promoted by Forum for the Future

- providing co-ordination and technical advice for a unique food retailer/plastic manufacturer liaison group dedicated to improving the understanding of the social and environmental performance of PVC and chaired by Jonathan Porritt

- the provision of numerous environmental solutions reports, including better ways of treating landfill leachates, reducing the environmental impacts of pesticides, and recycling fluorescent tubes and food product collation trays.

NCBS customers have included Asda Group plc, Biffa Waste Services plc, Carillion, CIS, The Co-operative Bank, CWS, Manchester Airport plc, Tarmac Quarry Products, Tesco Stores Ltd, AstraZeneca, Trafford Park Business Forum, Aldi Stores, Stagecoach, AMEC, United Villages Partnership, Waitrose Ltd, Watford MBC, Norsk Hydro, UK Waste, Mercury Recycling, EVC, Yorkshire Water.

The business outlook for the NCBS may serve as a barometer for the way the sustainability agenda is being accepted and taken up by business. The interest in social responsibility (both training and management strategies) has grown markedly over recent months. This is due in part to the trailblazer companies (such as United Utilities and The Co-operative Bank) that have reported on their performance in this area.

It is also due to the rash of performance and reporting standards that have been released recently. These include SA 8000 (on employee conditions at supplier's premises), the UN Compact (on environmental employment performance), AA1000 (a process standard on the management of social and ethical performance), and GRI (a standard on environmental and social reporting).

These, and many other special issue yardsticks, are making organisations in both the public and private sector re-evaluate the way they are doing business. The continuing success of the NCBS will be a good indication that these important issues are here to stay. ■

---

*For further information on The National Centre for Business & Sustainability, contact: Erik Bichard, Director on **0161 295 5276** or visit the website at **www.thencbs.co.uk***

Ethical investment – why bother?

*Financial expert **Robin Currie** provides an introduction to the world of ethical and sustainable investment.*

Do you remember Seattle? The World Trade Organisation was meeting in the home town of Boeing and Microsoft and was besieged by furious protestors from across the USA and the rest of the world. The meeting was to mark a further stage in the WTO's agenda of the continued liberalisation of international trade. Depending on your point of view, this can be read as a way of opening up inefficient feudal economies to healthy competition, or of crushing local communities with the monstrous resources of international capital.

Either way, the effect is to stifle emerging Third World economies, while liberté, fraternité and egalité are subordinated to the requirements of the multinationals. For many years, the World Trade Organisation has portrayed itself as an association founded on mutuality, where decisions were made by consensus following full participation. This is patently untrue, and much of the disharmony in Seattle, and subsequently in Geneva and London, reflects a general sense of unhappiness at the self-interest, bullying and coercion of the large countries.

'And what', you may be asking 'has this to do with me?' Sadly, if you are an investor, everything. And if you have savings or life insurance or a mortgage or a pension or stocks and shares – then you are an investor.

Let's take pensions as an example. Until now, institutional pension fund managers have had a legal requirement to invest in companies that make as much money as possible, irrespective of ethical, social or environmental costs. And because people are living longer and retiring earlier but not starting their pension funds until later, the returns that need to be generated have to be much greater. This puts pressure on the companies to produce high dividends as their main business focus, rather than allowing them to concentrate on sustainable growth that will produce a decent yield as a by-product. The more money we put aside to support us in later life, the greater grows the power of the pension funds. These are now the largest single investors in the City of London, and are amongst the most powerful forces in Western capitalism.

So the squeeze is on. We, the public, need more money, so the pension fund has to make more profit, so the companies in which they invest have to be produce greater dividends by whatever means, so the organisations that represent those companies set out to tip the balance of business in their favour.

And is there a way out? Amazingly, yes. It's called ethical investment, and it's the fastest growing sector of the stockmarket. Ethical or Socially Responsible Investment (SRI) is the name given to financial strategies which aim to make your money work in line with your values. This includes screening out companies with a negative bias (eg armaments, tobacco, environmental degradation, factory farming, poor employee relations, etc) and emphasising those which are actively committed to fairness, equality and sustainable development.

The results have been staggering. Since being established in Britain in 1984, ethical investment has become the fastest growing area of the stockmarket, attracting more than £1.5 billion of investment. There are now more than two dozen different ethically-screened investment funds in the UK, each with a slightly different series of criteria.

What is even more heartening is the amount of muscle these funds now wield. SRI funds were behind a recent resolution at BP Amoco's Annual General Meeting. This sought to divert funds allocated to oil exploration into solar power and research into renewable energy sources. The resolution failed, but the board was shaken by the level of support, and is increasing its support for sustainable energy.

Unlike more conventional investment funds, SRIs are willing to enter a dialogue with the companies whose shares they hold and seek to promote social, ethical and environmental issues as well as profitability. While a conventional fund wouldn't dream of selling shares in a profitable company because of a deterioration in its environmental record, this is exactly what SRI funds have threatened to do, and have done. The result has been salutary. An increasing number of companies have started paying attention to the effects of their policies on their workers, the societies in which they operate, the countries in which they have influence and the geosphere in which we all live.

No-one but a financial masochist would invest in something that they thought was going to lose money. Nevertheless, it comes as a surprise even to ethical specialists how profitable SRIs are. Excluding companies whose sole motivation is 'profit at any price' positively enhances fund performance.

Just for example, NPI's Pension Global Care fund has an annual growth rate of 24.7%pa over the last five years, and is ranked 6th out of 132 funds in its sector. Its sister fund, the Pension Global Care Managed fund, has been first in sector over three years! I suggest you read that bit again. These are two of the most stringent ethical funds around, and they're knocking spots off the opposition.

SRI funds also decrease the chances of future legal action of the type that have been the bane of the tobacco and asbestos industries in recent years. Proper ethical investment produces a coherent and dynamic portfolio of well-balanced, profitable companies which put back into the world at least as much as they take out.

Products

Increasing concern for the fate of the environment coupled with excellent returns have led to the development of a large number of financial instruments. Ethical funds can now be accessed by virtually any financial product with an investment element – these include:

- Individual Savings Accounts (ISAs)
- personal, executive and company pension plans
- unit and investment trusts
- life insurance policies
- critical illness protection policies
- mortgage repayment plans.

In addition, ethical screening is available for private client portfolios, school fees plans and Inheritance Tax schemes.

From reading this, it would be easy to get the impression that simply buying an ethical financial product will make you huge amounts of money while solving the world's problems. The truth is rarely so simple. Financial planning involves a serious commitment to making the best choices available towards the financial future of the client. This is not a light matter, and should be dealt with in consultation with a specialist independent financial advisor. ■

To talk to Robin Currie, call on **01727 833441** *or email at* **Robin@newmoney.demon.co.uk**

All figures from Money Management, *May 2000.*

IMPACT Make your office or workplace more sustainable

- Minimise office waste by the reduction, reuse and recycling of materials.
- Collect paper and toner cartridges for recycling.
- Use double-sided copying where possible.
- Re-use envelopes.
- Re-use paper for scrap pads and draft documents and avoid the use of fax header sheets.
- Control the level of junk mail you receive by returning unwanted items to sender.

- Buy recycled paper and remanufactured toner cartridges.
- Repair and refurbish furniture and equipment rather than always buying new.
- Use eco-friendly cleaning materials.
- Try using recycled stationery products or products made from recyclable materials.
- Fit low energy light bulbs and switch off lights in rooms not in use.
- Don't leave computers and machinery on overnight.
- Cycle or walk to work.

- Promote the use of public transport and car-share schemes for work colleagues.
- Ensure efficient journey planning for deliveries and collection and use fuel efficient and low emission vehicles.

BUSINESS & OFFICE

Advice

Bio-wise
PO Box 83, Didcot,
Oxfordshire OX11 OBR
Tel: 0800 432 100
Fax: 01235 432 997
Email: biowise.help@aeat.co.uk
Web: www.dti.gov.uk/biowise
▶ UK Government Programme funded by the Department of Trade and Industry. Offers free, independent advice about biotechnology and seeks to encourage a wide range of UK industry sectors to use biotechnology to enhance their competitiveness and to further develop the UK biotechnology supplier base. Further information available; either call the freephone number, or access the website.

Bury Business Environment Association
Link House,
35 Walmersley Road,
Bury BL9 5AE
Tel: 0161 763 4185
Fax: 0161 761 3090
▶ Exists to assist companies, both industrial and commercial, to improve their environmental performance. Gives advice on energy, waste and recycling, pollution, legislation and air and water emissions. The Association is a key supporter of the Bury Environmental Forum. Call the above number for more info.

Business and Ecology Demonstration Project
c/o National Centre for Business Ecology (NCBE), The Peel Building,
University of Salford,
Manchester M5 4WT
Tel: 0161 295 5276
▶ Project developed by the National Centre for Business Ecology (see separate listing) with a view to helping small businesses in the Greater Manchester area to find environmental solutions to problems.

Business & Environment Practitioner Series
c/o Earthscan, Freepost 1, 120 Pentonville Road, London N1 9BR
Tel: 020 7278 0433
Fax: 020 7278 1142
Email: earthsales@earthinfo.co.uk
▶ Series of reports published by Earthscan (see listing in Chapter Eleven: Media) on environmental information for businesses. Aimed at busy managers, each report presents relevant information and practical guidance in a concise and accessible manner. Titles include *The Link Between Company and Environmental and Financial Performance*, *Business and Environment Accountability*, *The Eco-Management and Audit Scheme*, and *The Environment and the Planning System*. Call for a catalogue.

Environmental Business Communications Ltd
The Environment Business Centre,
BHC, Aston Science Park,
Birmingham B7 4BJ
Tel: 0121 693 8338
Fax: 0121 693 8448
Email: ebc@dircon.co.uk
Web: www.envirobiz.co.uk
Open: Mon-Fri 9am-5pm
▶ The UK's foremost communications organisation operating in and specialising across the environmental business sector since 1991. The company's expertise is based on its team's extensive and wide-ranging public and private sector experience running businesses and operating public relations, advertising, exhibition and conference design and staging for government, central and local, and its agencies as well as for charitable bodies and commercial clients both in the UK and abroad.

Environmental Technology Best Practice Programme
Environmental & Energy Helpline
B156, Harwell OX11 0RA
Tel: 0800 585 794
(Environment & Energy Helpline)
Fax: 01235 463 804
Email: ebbppnhelp@a80.co.uk
Web: www.ebsu.com/html/helplines.html
▶ Jointly funded by the Department of Trade and Industry and the Department of Environment, Transport and the Regions, this programme works to help UK companies become more competitive and profitable while also reducing environmental impact by encouraging waste minimisation and clean technology. Runs the free Environment & Energy Helpline on 0800 585 794.

National Centre for Business and Sustainability
The Peel Building,
University of Salford,
Manchester M5 4WT
Tel: 0161 295 5276
Fax: 0161 295 5041
Email: thencbs@thencbs.co.uk
Web: www.thencbs.co.uk
▶ There is a real and pressing need for business to balance the demands of progress with the impacts it creates on society and the environment. Understanding this delicate equation is the main purpose of the the NCBS. Since it was set up in 1995, originally as the National Centre for Business & Ecology, the NCBS has been busy advising private and public sector clients on a wide variety of sustainability issues – from applied environmental advice and services, to social accountability and auditing. Inspired and set up by The Co-operative Bank, the NCBS advocates environmentally and socially sustainable solutions to a range of businesses and organisations. The Centre represents a unique partnership between The Co-operative Bank and the four universities of Greater Manchester, drawing on the ecological and ethical policies of the Bank and the technical expertise from the universities and the wider academic community.

Regional Development Agencies
Tel: 020 7890 3000
(public enquiry unit)
▶ Business-led bodies for each of the eight regions of England. Launched on April 1st 1999, the RDAs are lead bodies at the regional level for co-ordinating inward investment, raising peoeple's skills, improving competitiveness of business and social and physical regeneration. Each will develop and implement a regional economic strategy and have an important role in advising Government.

Sustainable Solutions for Business
PO Box 2739,
Bradford-on-Avon BA15 1XH
Tel: 0794 125 1155
Email: sussol.fb@virgin.net
▶ Specialist consultancy dealing in business strategy, policy, markets and organisation. Practical advice on the sustainable growth of companies and improved business performance. Call for a free, no obligation exploratory meeting.

Tameside Business Environment Association
Room 3.71, Council Offices,
Wellington Road,
Ashton-Under-Lyne OL6 6DL
Tel: 0161 342 2885
Fax: 0161 342 2273
Email:
andy.brunt@mail.tameside.gov.uk
Web: www.tbea.org.uk
▶ Publicly-funded business support organisation which specialises in the provision of free guidance and support to smaller companies in the Tameside area. TBEA's mission is to enable local companies to save money whilst improving their environmental performance, and a range of high quality services are available to companies to help them achieve this, for example, in reducing waste and improving energy efficiency. A 24 hour helpline is available (0161 342 2885) and a dedicated website packed with useful tips. Free site visits help companies with specific issues.

Office Recycling

If you have old toner cartridges, computers or paper, a contractor will collect and recycle them. Cartridges can also be refilled and used again. See Chapter Four: Energy & Recycling for more recycling services.

Business & Finance 165

Cartridge Family, The
The Rural Business Centre,
Winterborne Whitechurch,
Blandford Forum DT11 9AW
Tel: 01258 880 050; 0870 789 2001
(national access telephone)
Fax: 01258 881 448; 0800 980 9238
(free fax enquiry)
Email: euros@nildram.co.uk
Web: www.thecartridgefamily.com
▶ Approved Greenman Dealer, UK re-manufacturer of laser and inkjet toner cartridges that are recycled and guaranteed to European Quality Standard ISO 9002, not 'just' refilled. To ensure sufficient supplies of empties and to discourage landfill, offers cash back on all empties, sending unwanted or damaged units to approved waste carriers for dismantling and material recycling. Regional collection points sought. Free bulk collection of empties. Also sells most OEM brands.

Greenman-Sykom Group
Longmead Business Centre, Felstead Road, Epsom KT19 9UP
Tel: 01372 748 550
Fax: 01372 748 540
Email: information@sykom.com
▶ National supplier of computer consumables offering access to brand toner and ink jet cartridges, manufactured in factories from new and previously used parts. Also offers a nationwide toner and inkjet collection and recycling programme. Free of charge collection over 10 units.

Recycle-IT!
c/o SKF (UK) Ltd, Sundon Park Road, Luton LU3 3BL
Tel: 01582 492 436
Fax: 01582 597 778
Email: recycle_it@cix.co.uk
Open: Mon-Fri 8.30am-5pm
▶ Nationwide free collection service for redundant computer equipment from companies which are refurbished and sold to charities, voluntary organisations, schools, and disabled people at low cost.

Products

Conservatree Print & Design
36b Church Street, Caversham,
Reading RG4 8AU
Tel: 0118 947 9120
Fax: 0118 946 3959
Email: sales@conservatree.co.uk
Web: www.conservatree.co.uk
Open: Mon-Fri 9am-5.30pm
▶ Graphic designers and printers of recycled stationery, business stationery, letterhead business cards, compliment slips, flyers, newsletters, brochures, re-use envelope labels.

Green Stationery Company
Studio 1, 114 Walcot Street,
Bath BA1 5BG
Tel: 01225 480 556
Fax: 01225 481 211
Email: jay@greenstat.co.uk
Web: www.greenstat.co.uk
Open: Mon-Fri 9am-5pm
▶ Complete green office supplier, stocking recycled laser, inkjet, copier and fax papers, labels, envelopes, pads, files and desk accessories. Recycles and re-manufactures laser and inkjet printer cartridges and holds a full range of original machine consumables. Offers mail order service and a commercial division that supplies businesses at discount rates. Call for a catalogue.

John Hanson/CHT
Malthouse, Mill Lane, Lyme Regis
Tel: 01297 443 082
Web: treefree.co.uk
Open: office hours or leave message
▶ Supplier of treefree, hemp content, long-life paper which is an entirely woodless, watermarked paper made only from indigenous plant fibres – ideally the unbleached wastes of true hemp, corn straws or flax. Aims to help save the world's forests and their peoples. Universally suitable for writing and printing papers. Send three second class stamps for samples, prices and publications.

Paperback Ltd
Unit 2, Bow Triangle Business Centre, Eleanor Street,
London E3 4NP
Tel: 020 8980 5580
Fax: 020 8980 2399
▶ Supplier of recycled papers and environmentally friendly office products. Call for samples and a free catalogue.

Steve & Susan Hammett
Gate Farm, Fen End,
Kenilworth CV8 1NW
Tel: 01676 533 832
Email: hammett@compuserve.com
Web: www.recycled-paper.co.uk
▶ Mail order supplier of 100% recycled stationery. Specialist designers and printers of recycled paper, offering individually designed business, personal stationery, leaflets, newsletters, etc. Call for a free catalogue or send three first class stamps for sample swatches.

Services

APEM Ltd
Enterprise House, Manchester Science Park, Lloyd Street North, Manchester M15 6SE
Tel: 0161 226 2922
Fax: 0161 226 0753
Email: apem@apemltd.co.uk
Web: www.apemltd.co.uk
Open: Mon-Fri 8.30am-5.30pm
▶ A specialist aquatic science consultancy providing an integrated approach to environmental management in freshwater, estuarine and marine environments. Its scientists are recognised experts in their individual fields, covering virtually evry aspect of aquatic science. Has a reputation for providing a high quality and innovative service.

Arup Environmental
St James Building, Oxford Street,
Manchester M1 6FQ
Tel: 0161 228 2331
Fax: 0161 236 1057
Email: olenka.brain@arup.com
Web: www.arup.com
▶ One of the largest and most respected environmental consultancies in the UK, serving a broad client base from local offices around the country. Offers a variety of environmental consulting disciplines, including EIA and environmental auditing, waste management, air and water quality modelling, contaminated land assessment and landscape architecture.

Recycle IT!

c/o SKF (UK) Ltd, Sundon Park Road, Luton LU3 3BL
Tel: 01582 492 436
Fax: 01582 597 778
Email: recycle_IT@cix.co.uk

Nationwide free collection service of old computer equipment from offices, for resale to charities, schools, voluntary organisations or churches on tight budgets.

PRINTER • FAX • PHOTOCOPIER
ORIGINAL & RECYCLED LASER & INKJET CARTRIDGES WITH FREE DELIVERY

The Cartridge Family

euros@nildram.co.uk   EMAIL
0800 328 6680   FREEFAX
0870 789 2001   TELE-SALES
CASH BACK ON EMPTIES
FOR PURCHASE DISCOUNT OR FUND RAISING

Business & Finance

Babtie Group, Allott and Lomax Ltd
Fairbairn House, Ashton Lane, Sale, Manchester M33 6WP
Tel: 0161 962 1214
Fax: 0161 905 5855
Email: jwhitton@allott.co.uk
Web: www.allott.co.uk
▶ Environmental services include due diligence, contaminated land, waste management, risk assessment and environmental impact assesment.

Brian Milligan Associates
57 Wensley Road, Salford M7 3GJ
Tel: 0161 792 2269
Fax: 0161 792 2269
Email: brian@brian-milligan.co.uk
Web: www.brian-milligan.co.uk
▶ Consultancy service to industry, assisting in the identification, measurement and control of risks to health in the workplace (eg noise, dust, fumes, chemicals). Also monitors levels of pollutants generated to the environment by industrial processes.

Bullen Consultants
38 Woodside Business Park, Birkenhead CH41 1EL
Tel: 0151 647 2312
Fax: 0151 647 4742
Email: birkenhead@bullen.co.uk
Web: www.bullen.co.uk
▶ Multi-disciplinary science, management and engineering consultancy offering specialist services including; environmental impact assessment, environmental management systems, environmental appraisal, sustainability analysis, landscape and archaeological services, and ecological habitat creation.

Casella Science and Environment Ltd
Yorkshire House, Chapel Street, Liverpool L3 9AG
Tel: 0151 255 1115
Fax: 0151 258 1511
Email: liverpool.consultancy@cafella.co.uk
Web: www.cafella.co.uk
▶ Rapidly expanding environmental company. The instrumentation division manufactures specialised equipment to monitor pollutants like asbestos, dust, noise, toxic metals etc. The consultancy division deals with asbestos project management, land remediation, waste management, air quality, risk and impact assessment, ecology and architectural landscaping. Their services are used by industry, local and central government, quasi-govenrment organisations (such as health services) and other professional service providers (such as lawyers and accountants).

David Markham Associates
1 Deva Close, Poyton, Stockport SK12 1HH
Tel: 01625 876226
Fax: 01625 876226
Email: dmacoustics@netscapeonline.co.uk
Open: Mon-Fri 9am-6pm
▶ Acoustic consultancy specialising in environmental and industrial noise control, building and architectural acoustics, mineral extraction, planning appliactions, and public enquiries. Noise and vibration surveys, assessments, design, recommendations and specifications are the different methods employed. Member of the Institute of Acoustics (MIOA), Institute of Safety and Health (MIOSH), and the Society of Environmental Engineers (MSEE).

Deaft Design
44 Park Hill Grove, Cornholme, Todmorden OL14 8PF
Fax: 01706 812 190
Email: deaftdesign@zen.co.uk
▶ Illustration and design service from an artist with over 18 years of experience in the alternative and mainstream sectors, specialising in education, environmental, social and disability issues – and humour! Send off for a 'doggie-bag' of samples to put you in the picture.

Ecotropic
Parracombe, Chapel Lane, Forest Row, East Sussex RH18 5BU
Tel: 01342 824 622
Fax: 01342 824 949
▶ Private consultancy specialising in organic and biodynamic farm projects in developing countries.

Eleventh Hour
The Rural Business Centre, Winterborne Whitechurch, Blandford Forum DT11 9AW
Tel: 01258 880 050; 0870 789 2001 (national access telephone)
Fax: 01258 881 448; 0800 980 9398 (free fax enquiry)
Email: marketing@eleventhhour.nildram.co.uk
Web: www.eleventhhour.nildram.co.uk
▶ Creative agency with a professional and economical approach for environmentally biased products or services. Projects may consist of more than one marketing discipline: corporate identity & strategy, design for print, direct mail, sales promotions, press and public relations, media advertising, the internet & wired marketing, creative copy writing for a brochure, leaflet or advertisement headline, to an on going requirement (eg newsletter or sales promotional literature) etc.

Environmental Field Work Ltd
Barn Countryside Centre, Philips Park, Whitefield, Manchester M45 7QJ
Tel: 0161 796 9557
Fax: 0161 796 8846
Open: Mon-Fri 9am-5pm
▶ Workers' co-operative, supported by The Prince's Youth Business Trust, providing countryside management services to local authorities and other landowners. Undertakes woodland management, tree/hedge planting, footpath works, fencing, hedging, dry stone walling, habitat management and management plans. References and grants advice available. Call for further info.

Environmental Policy Consultants
45 Weymouth Street, London W1N 3LD
Tel: 020 7935 1675
Fax: 020 7486 3455
Email: adrian.eic@mcmail.com
▶ Specialist environmental lobbying and PR consultancy assisting businesses to meet and profit from environmental policy challenges. Operates in London and Brussels and offers a range of services including policy analysis, strategic advice, lobbying and PR. For £195 per year, businesses can sign up to their EC Environmental Policy Monitor which updates on new policy measures and existing legislative proposals.

Environmental Resources Management
26 Office Village, Exchange Quay, Manchester M5 3EQ
Tel: 0161 958 8800
Fax: 0161 958 8888
Web: www.erm.com
▶ ERM has a well established reputation as one of the world's largest providers of environmental management and technical consulting services. Believes that if economic development is to be sustainable, it must be responsible. Has 25 years' experience working with clients in both the private and public sectors to help them address environmental concerns and challenges within their organisation. Services go far beyond traditional consulting work. Using an integration framework, as opposed to selling a set of technical services, looks at each client's unique needs – both financial and technical – to design innovative solutions that incorporate environmental concerns into business management, economic, technological and social issues. Is qualified to provide advice and assistance at all phases of a company's evolution. Whether it's helping to obtain permits, devising solutions to reduce hazardous waste or finding ways to reduce liabilities prior to an M&A, ERM consultants can help make the most of a business while building a consistent environmental agenda.

Fichtner Consulting Engineers
Frederick House, 8 Acorn Business Park, Heaton Lane, Stockport SK4 1AS
Tel: 0161 476 0032
Fax: 0161 474 0618
Email: sales@fichtner.co.uk
Web: www.fichtner.co.uk
▶ Independent environmental and energy consultants, with 75 years of

Business & Finance

experience in providing practical, cost-effective solutions to complex problems. Manage every aspect of a project from initial assessment to final installation, including technical and economic feasibility, IPPC applications, planning, design and project management.

First Effluent Ltd
42a High Street,
Sutton Coldfield B72 1UJ
Tel: *0121 355 2907*
Fax: *0121 355 6134*
Email: *firsteff@globalnet.co.uk*
▶ Offers a design and advisory service for water supply and waste-water treatment in industry. Since 1977, installations have been completed world-wide, using both old-established and more modern technologies. Call for brochure and reference lists.

FSC Environment Training
Preston Montford,
Montford Bridge,
Shrewsbury SY4 1HW
Tel: *01743 852 170*
Fax: *01743 852 101*
Open: *Year round*
▶ Offers environmental management systems (EMAS, ISO14001) training and implementation. Also Local Authority Agenda 21, sustainability, community involvement training, energy efficiency, waste minimisation training and implementation. Provides advice on cuntryside survey protocols, National Vegetation Classification, Freshwater monitoring, Biological Monitoring, Working Party Scores training. Foreign exchanges for various Central and Eastern European & Asian business/industrial sectors, study tours and eco-tourism to many parts of the world.

Geoffrey Collett Associates (UK) Ltd
Babington Lodge, 128 Green Lane,
Derby DE1 1RY
Tel: *01332 362 411*
Fax: *013322 290 855*
Email: *gcaderby@btinternet.com*
Open: *Mon-Fri 8.30am-5.30pm*
▶ Consulting civil, structural and highway engineers, undertaking work for private and public clients in the appraisal and design of structures and facilities.

GIBB Environmental
GIBB House, London Road,
Reading RG6 1BL
Tel: *0118 963 5000*
Fax: *0118 949 1056*
Email: *droberts@gibb.co.uk*
Web: *www.gibbltd.com*
▶ A leading environmental consultancy operating throughout the UK and internationally, assisting clients in the public and private sector to achieve excellence in environmental management and sustainability in all of their operations. With a permanent staff of over 2,000 scientists and engineers, GIBB offers expert advice on all aspects of pollution prevention and control, assessment and remediation of land contamination, environmental impact assessment, environmental risk management, waste management, corporate environmental and social responsibility.

Green Land Reclamation Ltd
1 Furze Platt Road,
Maidenhead SL6 7ND
Tel: *01628 778 077*
Fax: *01628 634 340*
Email: *greenland2.glr@dial.piper.com*
▶ Small independent consultancy working in the fields of energy and environment. Undertakes research and project development in the recovery of energy from biomass and wastes. Particularly active in the development of European Standards for Solid Biofuels and Solid Recovered Fuels (manufactured from post-consumer wastes).

Green Pastures Public Relations
7-1-7 Cameron House, White Cross,
Lancaster LA1 4XQ
Tel: *01524 36401*
Fax: *01524 388 411*
Email: *grpast2000@aol.com*
▶ A small, friendly ethical concern formed in 1999 by Francis and Judith Allison. They hold professional and academic qualifications and are dedicated to green issues. Their marketing services include: health writing/editing/advertisement-advertorial copywriting, all forms of company literature, editing, mailshots, liaison with health editors and healthfood trade.

Groundwork National Office
85-87 Cornwall Street,
Birmingham B3 3BY
Tel: *0121 236 8565*
Fax: *0121 236 7356*
Email: *info@groundwork.org.uk*
Web: *www.groundwork.org.uk*
▶ Leading environmental regeneration charity putting the theory behind sustainable development into practice. Works with local people, local authorities and businesses to bring about economic and social regeneration by improving the local environment. Environmental Business Services teams (EBS) work with businesses to help them identify, manage and minimise their impacts on the environment. Services offered range from initial environemtal 'healthchecks' through to consultancy and training in the minimisation of waste, energy and raw materials, to implementation of ISO 14001 and EMAS environmental management systems.

Industrial Relations Services
Lincoln House,
296-302 High Holborn,
London WC1V 7JH
Tel: *020 7420 3500*
Fax: *020 7420 3520*
Email: *conferences@irseclipse.co.uk*
Web: *www.irseclipse.co.uk*
Open: *Mon-Fri 9am-5pm*
▶ Runs over 100 events per year, offering independent expert guidance and advice to professionals working in the fields of employment law, personnel, occupational health and safety, remuneration, pensions and IT. All the conferences and courses are based on the company's original research, as published in journals and reports. The website gives up-to-date information on the conferences and courses available.

Manchester Area Resource Centre (MARC) Ltd
28 Edge Street, Manchester M4 1HN
Tel: *0161 839 0839*
Open: *Tues, Thurs, Fri 10am-4.30pm*
▶ Runs courses on word processing, graphic design, the internet and other computer-related subjects and sells green office stationery.

Matan International Group
Royal Liver Building,
Pier Head, Liverpool L3 1JH
Tel: *0151 236 0200*
Fax: *0151 236 2488*
Email: *enquiries@matan.co.uk*
Web: *www.matan.co.uk*
▶ Provide environmental consultancy services independently, or as part of a professional team. Scope of work includes; derelict & contaminated land investigation & development, landfill gas survey & gas migration control & monitoring, environmental impact assessment & hazard assessment, environmental auditing & review, waste & energy management, public inquiry and more.

Mott MacDonald
Spring Bank House,
33 Stamford Street, Altringcham,
Manchester WA14 1ES
Tel: *0161 927 7445*
Fax: *0161 926 8670*
Email: *manchester@mottmac.com*
Web: *www.mottmac.com*
▶ A multi-disciplinary environmental and engineering consultancy, based in the UK, with global experience in 130 countries and a staff of over 4,000 people. Services include: contaminated land; water pollution; ecology; landscape; impact assessment; auditing; air quality; and solid waste engineering.

Naturesave Policies Limited
58 Fore Street,
Totnes TQ9 5RU
Tel: *01803 864 390*
Fax: *01803 864 441*
Email: *mail@naturesave.co.uk*
Web: *www.naturesave.co.uk*
Open: *Mon-Fri 9.15am-5.15pm*
▶ Seeks to use the insurance industry as a vehicle for the greater adoption of sustainable development. Sells household building and contents insurance and annual travel insurance, where 10% of all the premiums are deposited in a fund (The Naturesave Trust) to benefit specific environmental and conservationist

projects which support sustainable development. Also sells commercial combined insurance polices for businesses and voluntary organisations which includes a free Environmental Performance Review which includes an audit to show businesses how to become more environmentally aware in their trading practices.

NIFES Consulting Group
NIFES House, Sinderland Road, Broadheath, Altrincham WA14 5HQ
Tel: 0161 928 5791
Fax: 0161 926 8718
▶ Independent consultancy offering environmental services to clients in the public, industrial and commercial sectors. NIFES understanding of the interactions between plant and processes, energy efficiency, environmental protection and safety offer a unique perspective incorporating legal compliance, operating effectiveness and risk management.

NNC Ltd
Booths Hall, Chelford Road, Knutsford WA16 8QZ
Tel: 01565 633 800
Fax: 01565 633 659
Email: dave.robotham@nnc.co.uk
Web: www.nnc.co.uk
▶ Multi-disciplinary environmental consultancy providing services to major organisations, SME's, national and local government bodies. With the experience of over 900 technical staff and one of the largest laboratories in the UK, NNC has knowledge and expertise in all areas of the environmental consultancy business. Main areas of work include environmental auditing, IPPC authorisation, contaminated land and EMS.

OHS Ltd
23 Manchester Science Park, Lloyd Street North, Manchester M15 4FN
Tel: 0161 227 9757
Fax: 0161 232 9660
▶ Safety and environmental consultancy. Work includes asbestos identification and management, occupational hygiene, health & safety, contaminated land, and environmental management systems.

Ove Arup & Partners
Whitefriars House, 25 Friars Lane, Nottingham NG1 6DB
▶ Independent consulting engineers with expertise in environmental planning and assessment; Air quality; contaminated land and waste disposal; Ecology; Landscape architecture; sustainable development and building solutions; embodied energy and environmental management. Delivers global expertise and local knowledge through 70 countries world wide.

Philip Dunbavin Acoustics
Vincent House, 212 Manchester Road, Warrington WA1 3BD
Tel: 01925 418188
Fax: 01925 577 116
Email: philipdunbavin@pdaltd.com
Web: www.pdaltd.com
▶ Independent acoustic consultancy, providing expert analysis, advice and design in all areas of acoustics, noise and vibration. Provide a comprehensive service, including analysis, initial design work, problem solving and troubleshooting. Scope of work includes occupational noise, environmental noise, architectural acoustics, legal work and project management.

Portfolio
58a High Street, Heathfield TN21 8JB
Tel: 01435 866 215
Fax: 01435 866 216
Email: lynport@dircon.co.uk
Open: 24 hours (ansaphone & email)
▶ Provides skilled and experienced facilitators who enable and empower groups of individuals, or teams in small, medium and large organisations, to achieve their maximum potential. By releasing their creative powers, staff are freed to enjoy their work, to think outside the box, and so achieve their optimum performance. Previous clients include British Airways, Canon and Shell.

RPS Consultants
21 Bridge Road, Woolston, Warrington WA1 4AT
Tel: 01925 831 000
Fax: 01925 831 231

Email: rpswa@rpsplc.co.uk
Web: www.rpsplc.co.uk
▶ Europe's largest independent environmental consultancy, providing expert advice on the environment, safety and resource conservation. The four main areas are: Risk Management for safety and environmental liability matters; Monitoring and laboratories for environmental emissions, occupational hygiene and water resource management; Planning for environmental assessment, agricultural, urban and transport planning; and Consultancy for architecture, landscape design, land remediation, utilities design and plant safety.

RPS Laboratories
Unit 12, Waters Edge Business Park, Modwen Road, Salford MS 3EZ
Tel: 0161 872 2443
Fax: 0161 877 3959
Email: rpsma@rpsplc.co.uk
Web: www.rpsplc.co.uk
▶ Europe's largest independent environmental consultancy, providing expert advice on the environment, safety and resource conservation. The four main areas are: Risk Management for safety and environmental liability matters; Monitoring and laboratories for environmental emissions, occupational hygiene and water resource management; Planning for environmental assessment, agricultural, urban and transport planning; and Consultancy for architecture, landscape design, land remediation, utilities design and plant safety.

RSK Environment Ltd
Spring Lodge, 172 Chester Road, Helsby WA6 0AR
Email: sswivic@rsk.co.uk
Web: www.rsk.co.uk
▶ Multi-disciplinary environmental consultancy providing services to industry and governent. Specialises in environmental impact assessment of major projects; air quality modelling and air emissions studies; data management using GIs; environmental training; and auditing.

Sustainability
49-53 Kensington High Street, London W8 5ED
Tel: 020 7937 9996
Fax: 020 7937 7447
Email: info@sustainability.co.uk
Web: www.sustainability.co.uk
▶ Registered environmental audit practice. Award-winning strategic management consultancy and think tank. Founded in 1987, they are the longest-established international consultancy dedicated to promoting the business case for sustainable development.

The Organic Food Consultancy
59 Thames Road, Chiswick, London, W4 3PR
Tel: 020 8994 2130
Fax: 020 8994 2130
Email: maxted-frost@declare.com
▶ Offers trade services, PR and consultancy

URBED
41 Old Birley Street, Hulme, Manchester M15 5RF
Tel: 0161 226 5078
Fax: 0161 226 7307
Email: urbed@urbed.co.uk
Web: www.urbed.co.uk
▶ Not-for-profit urban and economic regeneration consultants, URBED combines a solid research base with practical consultancy and training. Focuses on town centre revitalisation, sustainable urban neighbourhoods, voluntary sector management and urban policy and project research. Information and advice given to the public and voluntary groups. Also supports the Sustainable Urban Neighbourhood Initiative (SUN), a network of organisations and individuals interested in sustainable urban development. A regular SUN newsletter is distributed free of charge.

Work For Change Ltd
Unit 25, 41 Old Birley Street, Hulme, Manchester M15 5RF
Tel: 0161 232 1588
Fax: 0161 232 1582
Email: build-for-change@urbed.co.uk

Business & Finance

▶ The country's only managed workspace run by its tenants. Every member business is of an ethical or cultural nature creating an environment flavoured with the spirit of co-operation and mutual support. Including offices, shops, recording studio, café and a small theatre, the workspace is situated in a mixed-use building, shared with Homes for Change housing co-operative, which was constructed in 1996 to the highest environmental standards.

Organisations

Business in the Environment
44 Baker Street, London W1M 1DH
Tel: 020 7224 1600
Fax: 020 7486 1700
Email: bie@bitc.org.uk
Web: www.business-in-environment.org.uk
▶ Seeks to inspire business to achieve corporate social responsibility by making continuous progress towards environmentally sustainable development an essential part of business excellence. Supports companies' progress towards understanding and applying the principles of sustainable development. Publishes the UK Environmental Business Club Directory – available on the website.

Country Landowners Association
16 Belgrave Square,
London SW1X 8PQ
Tel: 020 7235 0511
Fax: 020 7235 4696
Email: mail@cla.org.uk
Web: www.cla.org.uk
▶ Membership organisation and lobby group representing 50,000 rural businesses in England and Wales. Membership benefits include free monthly magazine, legal, tax, land-use, diversification and economic advice and a free ticket to annual CLA Game Fair. A network of regional offices serves members, with support from London-based head office. Current campaigns include Let's Rout Ragwart, tackling the spread of weeds poisonous to livestock. For up to date information, press releases and membership details, see the website.

Environmental Industries Commision
45 Weymouth Street,
London W1N 3LD
Tel: 020 7935 1675
Fax: 020 7486 3455
Email: eic@mcmail.com
▶ EIC's mission is to promote the international competitiveness of the UK's environmental technology and services industry. EIC works to win support for favourable a legislative and fiscal framework and advocates to UK and EU Government practical, cost-effective policies which will promote the UK's environmental technology and service industry. Policy platforms call for effective enforcement of existing legislation, enactment of progressive regulation and introduction of economic instruments, boosting British exports by supporting export initiatives to assist companies in the growing work market for environmental technology and services, and promoting innovation and technology transfer by providing links with the UK's research organisations. Promotes standards when needed to enhance the industry's competitiveness.

Institute of Ecology and Enviromental Management
45 Southgate Street,
Winchester SO23 9EH
Tel: 01962 868 626
Fax: 01962 868 625
Email: enquiries@ieem.demon.co.uk
Web: www.ieem.org.uk
Open: Mon-Fri 9am-5.30pm
▶ Inaugurated in 1991, the IEEM is the largest professional body in the UK representing ecologists and environmental managers. It aims to raise the profile of the profession, establish, maintain and enhance professional standards and to promote an ethos of environmental care within the profession and to clients and employers of members. Organises a varied programme of training workshops, two annual symposia and a quarterly bulletin, Ecology and Environmental Management in Practice.

New Academy of Business
17-19 Clare Street, Bristol BS1 1XA
Tel: 0117 925 2006
Fax: 0117 925 2007
Email: info@new-academy.ac.uk
Web: www.new-academy.ac.uk
Open: Mon-Fri 9am-5pm
▶ An independent business school whose purpose is to change the way business works, through education, learning and action. Its vision is to play a part in building a future which is just and enterprising, working with entrepreneurs, educators, managers, policymakers and agents of change to produce educational activities and resources. These include: an MSc in Responsibility and Business Practice which is run with the University and is a ground-breaking, part-time, two year course; issue-specific initiatives focusing on human rights, partnerships and gender issues; research, working with international organisations on applied research projects; MBA teaching, working with universities to develop specialist modules for integration within existing MBA programmes; the Innovation Network, a forum for managers from leading edge companies; and in-company education, which involves tailored events for individual corporations which enable them to use leading-edge practice to explore strategic and operational issues to take action as corporate citizens.

Project Partners
Ayton House, Roberts End,
Hanley Swan, Worcester WR8 0DL
Tel: 01684 310 346
Fax: 01684 311 370
Email: projectpartners@compuserve.com
▶ Helps develop and manage projects for conservation and environmental organisations.

UK Social Investment Forum
Holywell Centre, 1 Phipp Street,
London EC2A 4Ps
Tel: 020 7749 4880
Fax: 020 7749 4881
Email: info@uksif.org
Web: www.uksif.org
▶ Promotes socially responsible investment. With 240 members, including national and community-based organisations and individuals involved in ethical, environmental and socially-directed investment. Members receive access to information, networking, seminars and conferences. Send a 45p A4 SAE for membership directory and information. Provides a secretariat for the All-Party Parliamentary Group on Social Investment.

New Money
Email: info@newmoney.co.uk
Web: www.newmoney.co.uk
▶ A free online magazine which addresses the areas of money, alternative belief systems and ways of bridging the gap between capitalism and the 'new age'. Written by Robin Currie, an independent financial advisor, specialising in ethical investment, and focuses on this area to some extent. Other topics include reconciling spirituality with financial success, green issues and the author's personal enthusiasms. Free factsheets available plus links to other sites.

ETHICAL INVESTMENT

Advice

Barchester Green Investment
45-49 Catherine Street,
Salisbury SP1 2DH
Tel: 01722 331 241
Fax: 01722 414 191
Email: info@barchestergreen.co.uk
Web: www.barchestergreen.co.uk
Open: Mon-Fri 9am-5pm
▶ Founded in 1985, Barchester Green is the UK's longest established green IFA with a national network of advisers. A one-to-one service at home or workplace is offered over the whole of mainland Britain. Pensions, ISAs, life assurances, unit trusts and investments from a range of ethical providers. Committed and professional service for personal, corporate and third sector organisations. Call for the free newsletter, Barchester Chronicle.

David Walters Financial Services
Horseshoe Cottage, Brownbread Street, Ashburnham TN33 9NX
Tel: 01424 893 113
Fax: 01424 893 443
Email: davidwalters2@compuserve.com
▶ Independent financial advisors specialising in ethical investments and providing a full range of services including insurance and pensions. Ethical investment advice is provided by David Walters who is a vegetarian and a member of Animal Aid and the Vegetarian Society.

Ethical Consumer Research Association
Unit 21, 41 Old Birley Street,
Manchester M15 5RF
Tel: 0161 226 2929
Fax: 0161 226 6277
Email: ethicon@mcr1.poptel.org.uk
Web: www.ethicalconsumer.org
Open: Mon-Fri 11am-6pm
▶ Research group specialising in invetsigations into companies' ethical records. Offers online access to a database of over 25,000 companies detailing environmental, animal welfare and human rights abuses. Also provides a consultancy service which can give essential company information for ethical investors and fundraisers, plus background information for campaigning organisations. Ideal for charities, NGOs, ethical investments or LA21 groups. Contact for an information pack.

Ethical Financial Ltd
Regus House, Malthouse Avenue,
Cardiff Gate, Cardiff CF23 8RU
Tel: 029 2026 3622
Fax: 029 2026 3729
Email: ethical@ethical-financial.co.uk
Web: www.ethical-financial.co.uk
Open: Mon-Fri 9am-5pm
▶ One of the largest independent financial advisers in the UK specialising in socially responsible investment. Founded by the current chairman Brian Spence in 1989, Ethical Financial Ltd has in the region of 20 franchised offices covering all parts of the UK and Eire. Assists individuals, charities and businesses with all financial concerns.

Ethical Investment Co-operative Ltd
Vincent House, 15 Victoria Road,
Darlington DL1 5SF
Tel: 01325 267 228
Fax: 01325 267 200
Email: greeninvest@gn.apc.org
The Ethical Investment Co-operative is a group of independent financial advisers around the UK who are all committed to the socially responsible use of money. It is now possible to sort out a wide variety of personal financial arrangements in an ethical or socially responsible way. Savings, investments, pensions, life asssurance and even mortgages can be set up or rearranged to support positive activities such as the increased use of renewable energy or the development of more organic food production. Money can also be steered away from investment in activities, which many people would rather avoid, such as nuclear power, animal experimentation or the production of armaments. Initial discussions or meetings are held without obligation, and subsequent advice can be given on a fee or commission basis.

Ethical Investment Consultancy, The
St. Walburges Centre,
Walburges Gardens, Preston PR2 2QJ
Tel: 01772 733 338
Email: invest@profitwithprinciple.co.uk
Web: www.profitwithprinciple.co.uk
▶ Independent Financial Advisers specialising in SRI.

Ethical Investment Research Service
80-84 Bondway, London SW8 1SF
Tel: 020 7840 5700
Fax: 020 7735 5323
Email: ethics@eiris.org
Web: www.eiris.org
▶ Charity, which aims to promote a wider understanding of ethical investment and corporate responsibility. Its subsidiary, EIRIS Services, undertakes research for clients and provides commercial services. Research and associated services are designed to help instituitional and individual clients develop and implement ethical invesment portfolios. Publications include a bi-monthly newsletter, The Ethical Investor, and Choosing an Ethical Fund – a guide for financial advisors to help them advise their clients on ethical investment products. For an information pack, including a free copy of The Ethical Investor, and a list of financial advisers who specialise in ethical investment, call the Order Line on 0845 606 0324.

Ethical Investment Services
610 Friargate, Preston PR1 2XS
Tel: 01539 823 041
Fax: 01539 825 041
Email: office@ethicalservices.co.uk
Web: www.ethicalservices.co.uk
▶ Set up to promote ethical investment and provide a one-stop shop for a complete range of ethical financial services. Operates on a local basis, unlike most other ethical advisors, and offers services including ethically managed stockbroking, unbiased advice on pensions and ISAs and a guide to ethical funds and discounts on investments. Also provides regular updates, discounts and ethical screening on existing investments. Call for more information, application form or full information pack.

GAEIA (Global & Ethical Investment Advice)
Investment House, 425 Wilmslow Road, Manchester M20 4AF
Tel: 0161 434 4681
Fax: 0161 445 8421
Email: brigid@gaeia.co.uk
Web: www.gaeia.co.uk
Open: Mon-Fri 9.30am-5.30pm
▶ A firm of independent financial advisers specialising in ethical investment, as well as environmental and socially responsible investments. If you are looking for pensions, lump-sum investments, regular savings or general financial advice, GAEIA can help you.

Kingswood Consultants
FREEPOST, Kingswood House,
29 North Street, Bicester OX26 6NB
Tel: 01869 252 545
Fax: 01869 240 759
Email: advice@kingswoodconsultants.com
▶ Ethical investment advisers offering life assurance, pension, savings and mortgage services. Member of the World Development Movement and founder Member of the UK Social Investment Forum.

Robinson Sterling
277 Ilford Lane, Ilford IG1 2SD
Tel: 020 8478 4008
Fax: 020 8514 5222
Email: post@robinsonsterling.com
▶ Established IFA practice providing a friendly, personal and comprehensive service. Specialist areas include pensions, investments, protection, savings and mortgages. Gives ethical investment advice on the client's request.

Shared Interest
25 Collingwood Street,
Newcastle-upon-Tyne NE1 1JE
Tel: 0191 233 9100
Fax: 0191 233 9110
Email: post@shared-interest.com
Web: www.shared-interest.com

▶ Cooperative lending society with 8500 members/investors in the UK. Lends money on fair terms to enable Third World Producer groups involved in fair trade to buy raw materials and pay for labour before goods are shipped. Members can invest a minimum of £100 and maximum of £20,000. A modest rate of interest is paid to investors.

Banking

Co-operative Bank
PO Box 101, 1 Balloon Street,
Manchester M60 4EP
Tel: 0161 832 3456
Fax: 0161 829 4475
Web: www.co-operativebank.co.uk
▶ The only high street bank that takes an ethical and green stance on which companies it will and will not do business with. Offers armchair banking from 6am-midnight seven days a week, access to LINK cash machines and a national network of outlets.

Ecology Building Society
Freepost, 18 Station Road,
Cross Hills,
Near Keighley BD20 5BR
Tel: 0845 674 5566
Fax: 01535 636 166
Email: info@ecology.co.uk
Web: www.ecology.co.uk
▶ Uses the money deposited by savers to grant mortgages on the renovation of derelict properties (recycling them), building new energy and resource efficient homes, organic farms, housing associations, charities and other beneficial projects. In this way, savers know that their money is being put to positive use. A range of accounts are offered, for individuals, charities and other organisations. The Society is a mutual organisation and a member of the UK Social Investment Forum

Triodos Bank
Brunel House,
11 The Promenade,
Clifton, Bristol BS8 3NN
Tel: 0117 973 9339
Fax: 0117 973 9303
Email: mail@triodos.co.uk
Web: www.triodos.co.uk
Open: Mon-Fri 9am-4.30pm
▶ One of Europe's leading social and environmental banks, lending money only to projects and enterprises which create social and environmental value. Offers an extensive range of competitive savings services, some of them highly innovative such as the Organic Savers Account recently launched with The Soil Association which targets investments for enterprises working in the organic sector. Newsletters and a project list show where the bank is lending. Call or email for further information.

Investment

Abbey Life Investment Services
Abbey Life Centre,
100 Holdenhurst Road,
Bournemouth BH8 8AL
Tel: 01202 292 373
Fax: 01202 292 403
▶ Ethical investment fund with a minimum £1,000 initial lump sum. Looks to invest in healthcare, environmental protection, education and family leisure. Avoids armaments, alcohol and pornography as well as many others. Launched in September of 1987.

Aberdeen Ethical Unit Trust
Trust Managers,
One Bow Churchyard,
Cheapside, London EC4M 9HH
Tel: 020 7463 6000
Fax: 020 7463 6507
▶ Objective is to provide capital growth over long term by investing internationally in companies which meet the ethical criteris determined by the managers and the investment advisers from time to time. Companies invested in benefit the community, avoid significant involvement in armaments, gambling or other activities with an adverse effect on health, the

---

So you think you are financing a healthy environment

Well, That depends on your Investments!

For a Free Guide to Ethical Investment please call, or return the section below

Alan Seward
FINANCIAL SERVICES
Telephone: 01225 448832
19 Gay Street Bath
BA1 2PD

email: alan.seward@alanseward.co.uk
jill.beavis@alanseward.co.uk

Please detach and return to: Alan Seward Financial Services 19 Gay Street Bath

Name :
Address :

Postcode :
Telephone No: _____ Work: _____
Please tick box to exclude further mailings ☐

Taking a holistic approach

Holden Meehan

Good financial planning ensures that you have enough money to meet your day-to-day needs, that you can provide for your family and that you can look forward to a financially secure future.

At Holden Meehan, we firmly believe in a holistic approach to your objectives as well as your ethical values. As the UK's leading independent financial advisers specialising in ethical and environmental investments, we understand the broader picture.

We were voted second in the Best IFA category in the year 2000 Guardian/Observer/ Money Observer reader poll.

For an informal discussion about your finances, telephone one of the numbers below.

London office
Holden Meehan IFA Ltd
New Penderel House, 283-287 High Holborn, London WC1V 7HP
Telephone 0207 692 1700
Fax 0207 692 1701

Bristol office
Holden Meehan IFA Ltd
Clifton Heights, Triangle West,
Clifton, Bristol BS8 1EJ
Telephone 0117 925 2874
Fax 0117 929 1535

Email hm@holden-meehan.co.uk
Web www.holden-meehan.co.uk

Holden Meehan IFA Ltd is regulated by the Personal Investment Authority

Business & Finance

environment or human dignity. Lump sum of £500 or £50 per month. Launched in September of 1992.

Albert E Sharp Ethical Unit Trust
105/108 Old Broad Street,
London EC2N 1ET
Tel: 020 7638 7275
Fax: 020 7638 7270
▶ Ethical Unit Trust with initial minimum lump sum investment of £1,000. Focuses on medium sized companies with very wide spread of investment across all types of companies, although some sectors are excluded, such as pharmaceuticals. Dialogue with investors is encouraged.

Allchurches Amity Fund
Beaufort House, Brunswick Road,
Gloucester GL1 1JZ
Tel: 01452 305 958
Fax: 01452 311 690
▶ Ethical Unit Trust with minimum lump sum investment of £500 or monthly savings scheme of £50. Involves investors when changing ethical policies. Healthcare, home safety and housing are postives in the Fund. Avoids alcohol, tobacco, gambling, pornography as well as many other sectors. Contacts companies before adding or dropping one from the fund for ethical reasons.

AXA Sun Life Investment Management
107 Cheapside, London EC2V 6DU
Tel: 020 7645 1000
Fax: 020 7457 2363
▶ Ethical Unit Trust with a minimum £4,000 initial lump sum or £50 per month. investors are invited to contact AXA Sun Life directly about general views in relation to specific criteria.

CIS Environ Trust
PO Box 105, Manchester M4 8BB
Tel: 0161 837 5060
Fax: 0161 837 5070
▶ Ethical Unit Trust with minimum lump sum investment of £500. Monthly savings scheme available. Positive criteria principally relate to environment and human health and safety and avoid tobacco and tobacco related products and the generation of nuclear power. Launched in May of 1990.

Clerical Medical Evergreen Trust
Clerical Medical Unit Trust Managers, Narrow Plain,
Bristol BS2 0JH
Tel: 01179 290 290
Fax: 0345 772 234
▶ Investment fund applying negative selection criteria based on arms, oppressive regimes, animal tests, meat and tobacco production and positive green criteria. Charges at 6% as an initial charge and 1.5% as an annual charge from there onwards. Minimum investment of £500 lump sum or £40 a month. Launched in February of 1990.

Credit Suisse Fellowship Fund
Beaufort House,
15 St Botolph Street,
London EC3A 7JJ
Tel: 020 7426 2929
Fax: 020 7426 2959

Ethical Funds Guide 2000

Isas, peps, pensions & unit trusts. Our guide compares all the ethical options in an unbiased way.

Visit www.ethicalservices.co.uk

If you want **advice** we have a **network** of nationwide associates who can advise you on a personal basis. To arrange a consultation or to be sent a free copy of the guide contact Ethical Investment Services Ltd.
FREEPOST NWW6682, 61a Friargate, Preston, PR1 3XS.
Email: greenguide@ethicalservices.co.uk

24 HOUR FREEPHONE 0800 018 8557
Ethical Investment Services Ltd. is regulated by the Personal Investment Authority for Investment Business

▶ Ethical Unit Trust with lump sum investment of £1,000. Monthly savings scheme available. Ethical criteria includes avoiding weaponry, alcohol, tobacco, gambling and banned pesticides as well as others. Fund includes numerous smaller companies with a large degree of diversification. Launched in July of 1986.

Equitable Ethical Trust
City Place house,
55 Basinghall Street,
London EC2V 5DR
Tel: 020 7606 6611
Fax: 020 7796 4824
▶ Ethical Unit Trust with lump sum investment of £500. Monthly savings scheme available. Seeks investment in pollution control, environmental protection, alternative energy and healthcare services. Seeks to avoid alcohol, armaments, gambling as well as many other sectors. Launched in January of 1994.

Framlington Health Fund
155 Bishopgate,
London EC2M 3FT
Tel: 0845 777 111
Fax: 020 7330 6638
Email: contact@framlington.co.uk
Web: www.framlington.co.uk
Open: Mon-Fri 9am-5.30pm
▶ Ethical Unit Trust with lump sum investment of £500. Monthly savings scheme available. Focus is on pharmaceutical and biotechnology companies, many of which are US. Launched in April of 1987.

Friends Provident Unit Trust Managers Ltd
72-122 Castle Street,
Salisbury SP1 3SH
Tel: 01722 715 834
▶ Ethical investment is about investing wisely without abusing the world's natural resources or exploiting its people and wildlife. This concept is referred to by Friends Provident as Stewardship. It seeks to invest in companies which make a positive contribution to society and avoid those which harm the world, its people or its wildlife. Longest running ethical funds with more money than any other ethical fund. Ethical funds range from UK only to International inclusion. Engage in shareholder activism.

Hanson Environment Fund
The Kiln, Waterside,
Mather Road,
Newark NG24 1WT
Tel: 01636 670 000
Fax: 01636 670 001
Email: grants@rsnc.cix.co.uk
▶ One of the UK's largest environmental funds set up under the landfill tax credit scheme. The Fund is managed by the Royal Society for Nature Conservation.

Henderson Ethical Fund
3 Finsbury Avenue,
London EC2M 2PA
Tel: 0345 832 832
Fax: 020 7410 4492
▶ Ethical Unit Trust with minimum lump sum investment of £1,000. Monthly savings scheme available. Pariculary well developed criteria on corporate operations in the developing world. Launched in February of 1995.

Jupiter Ecology Fund
Knightsbridge House,
197 Knightsbridge,
London SW7 1RB
Tel: 020 7412 0703
Fax: 020 7581 3857
▶ Ethical Unit Trust with lump sum minimum investment of £1,000. Very 'green' fund with emphsas on supporting companies which are leaders in environmental improvement or have best environmental records in their sector. Avoids environmentally destructive companies, polluters, alcohol, tobacco, gambling, pornography, nuclear power as well as others. Launched in April of 1988.

Jupiter International Green Investment Trust
Knightsbridge House,
197 Knightsbridge,
London SW7 1RB
Tel: 020 7412 0703
Fax: 020 7581 3857
▶ Ethical Unit Trust with lump sum investment of £1,000. Monthly savings scheme available. Launched in December of 1989. Management of the fund by 'green' managers.

National Provident Institution (NPI)

National Provident House,
55 Calverley Road,
Tunbridge Wells TN1 2CE
Tel: 01892 515 151
Email: info@npi.co.uk
Web: www.npi.co.uk/globalcare

▶ Aims to be the world's leading specialist in Socially Responsible Investment (SRI). Their funds are managed on the premise that the sustainable development agenda will be one of the key drives of industry and commerce in the next century. Believes that by combining social and environmental analysis with more traditional stock selection processes that it will be able to identify those companies which will make a positive contribution to society. In turn, this positive contribution will manifest itself in superior returns for its investors. Provide two ethical investment funds, The NPI Global Care Income Fund launched in July of 1995 and The NPI Global Care Fund launched in August of 1991, the latter focusing on international equity growth.

Scottish Equitable Ethical Trust

Edinburgh Park, Edinburgh EH12 9SE
Tel: 0131 549 3120
Fax: 0131 549 4264

▶ Ethical Unit Trust with lump sum investment of £500. Monthly savings scheme available. Criteria focuses more on avoidance of certain type of companies, especially in regards to animal welfare. Launched in April of 1989.

Skandia Ethical Managed Fund

PO Box 37, Skandia House, Portland Terrace, Southampton SO14 7AY
Tel: 01703 334 411
Fax: 01703 726 637

▶ Ethical Unit Trust with lump sum investment of £1,000. Monthly savings scheme available. Launched in March of 1992 and serves as a 'fund of funds', investing in other manager's unit trusts. Today, still invests in other ethical and green trusts as well as directly in equities. Managed by Jupiter.

Sovereign Ethical Fund

Tringham house, Wessex Fields,
Deansleigh Road,
Bournemouth BH7 7DT
Tel: 01202 435 000
Fax: 01202 421 988

▶ Ethical Unit Trust with lump sum investment of £1,000. Monthly savings scheme available. Avoids weaponry, nuclear processing, animal testing as well as many others. Seeks good employers, community involvement and environment improvement. Launched in May of 1989.

Standard Life UK Ethical Fund

30 Lothian Road,
Edinburgh EH1 2DH
Tel: 0131 245 8276
Fax: 0131 245 8282

▶ Ethical Unit Trust with lump sum investment of £1,000. Monthly savings scheme available. Excludes companies that contravene the specified ethical criteria. Launched in February of 1998.

TSB Environmental Investor Fund

Charlton Place, Andover SP10 1RE
Tel: 01264 345 678
Fax: 01264 346 794

▶ Ethical Unit Trust with lump sum investment of £500. Monthly savings scheme available. More focus on environment than ethics particularly in forestry, ozone, recycling, acid rain and energy conservation in proper context as well as many other sectors. Launched in June of 1989.

Wind Fund

c/o Triodos Bank, 11 Promenade,
Clifton, Bristol BS8 3NN
Tel: 0117 973 9339
Fax: 0117 973 9303
Email: mail@windfund.co.uk
Web: www.windfund.co.uk

▶ Recognise energy investment fund managed by Triodos Bank which owns a hydro-electric plant in Scotland and a wind farm in Cumbria on behalf of its 1700 shareholders.

NEW ECONOMICS

New economics looks at the way we create wealth and what we mean by wealth. It puts people at the centre of economic thinking and argues for a just, humane, sustainable and culturally appropriate economic system – based squarely on people's needs and environmental concerns. It finds new, equitable ways of solving old problems and embraces fair trade, green consumers, ethical investment, community banks, LETS, social auditing, community entrepreneurs and much more.

Local Groups

Creative Living LETS

c/o Creative Living Centre,
Bury New Road, Prestwich,
Manchester M25 3BL
Tel: 0161 772 3524
Fax: 0161 772 3797
Open: Mon-Fri 10am-4pm

▶ See The Creative Living Centre in Chapter 5: Health. Additional program regarding exchange without currency for goods and services.

CVS Exchange (Voluntary Organisations LETS)

Bury CVS, 6 Tenterden Street,
Bury BL9 OEG
Tel: 0161 764 2161
Fax: 0161 761 5881
Email: info@burycvs.demon.co.uk

▶ Advice and support for local groups within the borough on issues such as funding and training.

Greater Manchester LETS

Box 300, Frontline Books, 255 Wilmslow Road, Rusholme M14 5LW
Tel: 0161 224 5309
Email: lets@mlets.fsnet.co.uk

▶ LETS is a system in which members exchange goods and services without using 'real' money. Instead, people use a local currency called 'Bobbins' to pay for goods and services offered by other members. Things on offer include second-hand items for 'sale' or loan, health and healing services, babysitting, DIY, tuition and much more. Open for anybody to join, including individuals and small businesses.

Organisations

Campaign for Interest-Free Money

Global Café, 15 Golden Square,
London W1P 3AG
Tel: 020 7328 3701

▶ Campaign group advocating tools for exchange that are free from debts and interest. It has submitted a petition to the European Parliament and regularly informs media, politicians and like-minded organisations on 'Greening the Money Supply'.

Forum for Stable Currencies

21a Goldhurst Terrace,
London NW6 3HB
Tel: 020 7328 3701
Email: sabine@globalnet.co.uk
Web: intraforum.com/money

▶ A voluntary initiative of parliamentarians and concerned citizens advocating economic democracy through freedom from debt. Regular meetings at the House of Lords and tapping into a wide network of related groups; bank victims, LETS, commercial barter, ethical investment banking.

ICOF Group (Industrial Common Ownership Finance Ltd)

115 Hamstead Road, Handsworth,
Birmingham B20 2BT
Tel: 0121 523 6886
Fax: 0121 554 7117
Email: icof@icof.co.uk
Web: www.icof.co.uk

▶ ICOF's provides loans to employee owned co-operatives and to social enterprises. The money available to lend is raised by ethical share issue to the general public. Investing in ICOF is by way of shares in ICOF Community Capital. Shares can be bought in amounts from £250 to £20,000. Dividends are paid where possible in line with inflation. It must be stressed that this is an ethical investment since greater returns can be obtained elsewhere. In order to borrow from ICOF, you must be either a genuine worker owned co-operative or a social enterprise. Both of these are organisations which have explicit social objectives and whilst

Business & Finance

they must be viable businesses, they are not for private profit. Amounts can be borrowed from £5,000 to £50,000 in terms from two months to two years.

LETSlink UK
Quinnell Centre, 2 Kent Street,
Portsmouth PO1 3BS
Tel: *023 9273 0639*
Fax: *023 9273 0629*
Email:
newslink@letslink.demon.co.uk
Web: *www.letslink.demon.co.uk*
▶ National Body for Local Exchange Trading Schemes (LETS). LETS provide a way for communities to overcome cashflow problems by creating a local currency. It works very much like conventional money, except that there is no interest or fixed overdraft limit and it stays in the community. The systems are voluntary, not-for-profit groups run and managed by mutual agreement between members. Produces a directory of goods and services offered or used by members. To a business, LETS is good marketing as well as a source of interest-free funding. It is taxable, VATable and deductable.

New Economics Foundation
Cinnamon House, 6/8 Cole Street,
London SE1 4YH
Tel: *020 7407 7447*
Fax: *020 7407 6473*
Email: *info@neweconomics.org*
Web: *www.neweconomics.org*
▶ Working towards putting people and the environment at the centre of economic thinking. Produces the monthly newspaper – *News from the New Economy* – which acts as a guide to ideas and practice in the field. Currently working in the areas of community finance, corporate accountability, the global economy, local regeneration, community participation and alternative currencies.

Radical Routes Network
c/o Cornerstone Resource Centre,
16 Sholebroke Avenue,
Leeds LS7 3HB
Tel: *0113 262 9365*
Email: *cornerstone@gn.apc.org*
Web: *www.radicalroutes.org.uk*

▶ National co-operative network which helps fund new member co-operatives (in housing, trading, farming, etc) run by people who are often unemployed or homeless and who would otherwise find it hard to raise the finance. Contact the Ethical Investment Office (28 Hanstead Road, Hockley, Birmingham B19 1DB, 0121 551 1132) if you are interested in secure ethical investment (£50 upwards) or would like fo find out more about setting up or joining a co-operative.

Rebuilding Society Network
Tel: *0121 551 7770*
Email: *rsn@gn.apc.org*
▶ Group attempting to introduce the idea of microcredit into Europe. Microcredit refers to the loan of small sums of money to individuals for new projects and business enterprises, and has been used successfully in developing countries.

Law of the land

There's a law to deal with every type of protester – and a way round most of them, says **Michael Schwarz**

The bad news

Over the years, an incredible range of laws have accrued to deal with protesters. Take, for example, 'breaches of the peace'. Powers to deal with anti-social behaviour, disturbing 'the Queen's peace', stem, in part, from case-law going back to the tenth century and a statute passed in 1361, the Justice of Peace Act. Despite its age, High Court judges have observed in recent years that 'a comprehensive definition of the term 'breach of the peace' has very rarely been formulated and that 'the conduct in question does not itself have to be disorderly or a breach of the criminal law. It is sufficient if its natural consequence would... be to provoke others to violence, and so some actual danger to the peace is established'. That means that the more short-fused the person against whom a campaigner protests, the more likely it is that the latter, not the former, will feel the weight of the State.

And what is the State's power? Police can detain a protester, anywhere, for as long as it takes for the perceived danger of a breach of the peace to pass. The protester can, in addition, be taken to the Magistrates Court where, he or she can 'agree' to be 'bound over to be of good behaviour'. If the protester refuses, he or she will be sent to prison. Some laws are tailor-made for particular campaigners. 'Aggravated trespass' was expressly passed to deal with hunt saboteurs. It soon, however, became fashionable to prosecute anti-roads protesters with the same offence, or, when a formal eviction was taking place, with obstructing sheriffs and bailiffs in the execution of their duty.

More conventional campaigners can always fall to the old favourites – eg the offence of obstruction of the highway, used against those handing out leaflets or picketing. Larger demonstrations attract police powers to ban or impose conditions on assemblies and processions. When the old powers started to look tired, they were spiced up by the 1994 Criminal Justice and Public Order Act.

Some laws crop up in unexpected places. The Protection from Harassment Act 1997, supposed to deal with stalkers, was very quickly used against the Hillgrove Farm animal rights protesters. Similarly, the offence of intentionally causing harassment, alarm or distress was conceived in 1986 to deal with racist behaviour, but, soon, any reference to racism was taken out and it is now used regularly against protesters. Environmental protesters at Jesmond Dene and at the M65 were the guinea pigs for the offence of 'watching and besetting' under the Trade Union and Labour Relations (Consolidation) Act 1992.

And, lest we forget, there is also the civil law. SLAPPs (Strategic Litigation Against Public Participation) are a US import, employed by private business and government departments alike to suppress campaigns and debate by bringing intimidatory litigation against key individuals in a popular movement. Thus, protesters against Twyford Down were sued by the Department of Transport for compensation totalling £3,500,000 for trespass and interference with business.

The good news

But, to different degrees, these proceedings have all backfired, either in legal or in PR terms. Rather than quell campaigns and suppress issues, they have brought them to the attention of the public. And the protester can use the law pro-actively. One of the ingredients of aggravated trespass is that the defendant must have interfered with a 'lawful activity'. Hunt sabs have been acquitted because the hunt went on land without consent. Similarly, roads protesters have been able to argue that breaches of environmental standards and health and safety regulations tainted the 'victim's' record.

Recently, the Director of Public Prosecutions, the top prosecutor, intervened to drop charges against protesters who had torn up a test site of GM maize. They were charged with criminal damage but their defence was that they had a 'lawful excuse'. The threat of GMs to the neighbouring organic farmer, wildlife, humans and environment led them to believe that these interests were 'in immediate need of protection' and that 'the means of protection adopted... were reasonable having regard to all the circumstances'. Anyway, 'it is immaterial whether a belief is justified or not if it is honestly held' (section 5 of the the Criminal Damage Act 1971).

And, of course, there is the European Convention on Human Rights, which guarantees freedom of expression and freedom of assembly. The Human Rights Act, passed in 1998, will allow us to rely on the Convention in UK litigation early in the new millennium. It has already had an effect – reducing the scope of the breach of peace powers and the police's power to limit processions. But we should not be too optimistic. The Human Rights Act will do nothing to change the make up of judges: it will just allow campaigners to argue their corner using phrases like 'the right to...'. ∎

---

*Michael Schwarz is a Partner at Bindman & Partners Solicitors. For help or legal advice, call on **020 7833 4433***

Rivitalising the countryside

Over the past few years farming and rural industries have stumbled from one crisis to another, leaving those living in and dependent upon the countryside for their livelihoods under growing strain. With a brief to protect and enhance our countryside, the Countryside Agency has plans to revive rural England.

The aims of the Countryside Agency are: to conserve and enhance England's countryside; to spread social and economic opportunity for the people who live there; to help everyone, wherever they live and whatever their background, to enjoy the countryside and share in this priceless national asset.

It pursues these aims by influencing those whose decisions affect the countryside, through its expertise and its research and by spreading good practice by showing what works. But the Agency also takes the lead directly, implementing specific work programmes. Some of these programmes are described.

1. Rural Assurance – influencing the quality of rural life

Most policies and actions of government and others are developed with the majority in mind but the goal is to increase awareness of the rural dimension so that policies reflect the particular needs of rural businesses and people, and so deliver a better quality countryside.

2. Countryside Capital – making the most of the natural asset

A thriving countryside has a broad economic base. The goal is to influence market forces through the 'Eat the View' programme and promote rural tourism projects, and to influence subsidy reform so that profitable rural enterprises, especially farming and forestry, can enhance the qualities of the countryside.

3. Market Towns – revitalising rural service centres for the wider countryside

Over the last 50 years many of the traditional functions of market towns have changed and many are now in urgent need of revitalisation. The goal is to bring a new lease of life to market towns so that they provide convenient access to the services that surrounding rural communities depend on, such as retail and professional services, training and jobs, and leisure and cultural opportunities

4. Vital Villages – equipping communities to shape their futures

England's villages, while outwardly prosperous, face enormous challenges, including poor access to services, lack of local jobs and affordable housing, and inadequate public transport. Many are the domain of the wealthy and commuters, hiding pockets of social exclusion. The goal is to achieve socially and economically active rural communities, addressing their own priorities and well equipped to shape their own futures

5. Wider Welcome – opening up more of the countryside for more people, from all backgrounds, to enjoy

Access to the countryside has become increasingly popular – bringing income and jobs to rural areas, but in some parts of the country people still can't rely on a well maintained and signed network of usable paths. The goal is to establish more areas for visitors to the countryside, particularly on foot, horse or cycle.

6. Countryside on your doorstep – creating attractive, accessible greenspaces close to home

The countryside in and around towns and cities is often poorly managed. Regeneration of these areas will ensure good quality access to greenspaces for city dwellers, reducing stress and promoting a sense of well being. The goal is that everyone should be able to enjoy attractive, accessible greenspaces near to where they live.

7. Finest Countryside – securing the quality of our best landscapes

Even the finest landscapes, such as National Parks and Areas of Outstanding Natural Beauty (AONBs), are subject to change. These areas need special management so that conservation and enjoyment go hand in hand. The goal is to designate two new National Parks in the New Forest and the South Downs and to secure first class management in all of England's finest countryside.

8. Local Heritage Initiative – helping people to care for their landscapes, landmarks and traditions

The diversity and detail of local landmarks and traditions give richness and distinctiveness to our landscapes and have great significance to local people. The goal, with the support of the Heritage Lottery Fund and the Nationwide Building Society, is to provide small grants to local communities to conserve and enhance their local heritage and promote wider understanding and enjoyment of it, at the same time strengthening those communities. ∎

---

*To find out more about the work of the Countryside Agency, and for information about the countryside, visit the website at **www.countryside.gov.uk***

IMPACT: Get campaigning

Letters

- Make your complaint in writing to the relevant Council Department or Public Body, so you have an official reply on record.

- Seek the support of your councillor or MP in writing so your letter can be included by them when taking the matter up with officials. One MP said that, for every letter he/she receives on an issue, 10 other people are presumed to feel the same.

Community Voice

- Circulate a community questionnaire to those who may be similarly affected.

- Petitions allow those sympathetic to the campaign to lend their support.

- Letters are better, but postcards to elected representatives do highlight the issue.

- Poster campaigns gives the issue visibility and gets across the campaign with a simple message.

- Public meetings are good for obliging council representatives to explain themselves to the local community.

- Local referenda help to crystallise community opinion.

Lobbying

- Lobbying councillors or MPs is the most useful, yet under-used form of seeking to influence decision takers and to recruit support.

- Mass lobbies of council meetings should be used sparingly since a good turnout is required to make it effective.

- Forming a delegation to speak at council meeting can be very powerful; any community group can request the right to put their case directly to a council meeting.

- Get others behind you. Environmental groups with an interest in your issue might well support you.

Media

- Write letters to the local newspaper's letters page. It's the easiest, most effective way of getting your message across.

- Photocall for the local press. National papers will want to take their own. A good photograph can make a big impact and get the issue across without lots of text.

- Get your concerns coverage through phone-ins on local/national radio. Do not overlook national radio – it loves case studies which help provide a focus for current issues.

- Keep the press informed by providing regular press releases about what is happening in the campaign. A report back from lobbying your representative or commenting on a letter received from an MP can be used as a new element.

- Write a feature article for local press. Drop the editor a line with an outline of what you want to say.

From Protecting our environment: a citizen's guide to campaigning and environmental rights *(£4.95 pbk, Friends of the Earth Scotland). For copies, call FOE on* **020 7490 1555**

CASE STUDY: A far-reaching brief

Established in 1995, the Environment Agency aims to create a healthy, rich and diverse environment in England and Wales, for present and future generations. For many people the only time they hear about the Agency is when flooding is front-page news. However, the Agency's responsibilities go far beyond developing flood defences and issuing flood warnings. They include everything from integrated pollution control, radioactive and non-radioactive waste management, contaminated land, water quality, water resources, fisheries, conservation and recreation, environmental planning and development control. The Agency also advises the Government on implementing environmental objectives and targets and provides technical support for international negotiation.

Many environmental challenges remain as we enter the 21st century. The Agency is committed to creating a healthier environment, rich in wildlife and natural diversity that people will care for and can use and enjoy. Enhancing the environment for wildlife is also high on the Agency's agenda. It is working to improve the quality of habitats to sustainable levels for the benefit of all species and recent times we have seen vast improvements in the health of many native species. The Agency is also helping to manage, prevent and overcome issues relating to climate change. ■

For more information call the Environment Agency on **01454 624 400**.

LOCAL GOVERNMENT

LA 21 Councils

Allerdale Borough Council
Allerdale House,
Workington CA14 3YJ
Tel: 01900 326 333
Fax: 01900 326 346
Email: t.rourke@allerdale.gov.uk
Web: www.allerdale.gov.uk
Open: Mon-Fri 9am-5pm
▶ Currently preparing an LA21 strategy, linking much of what it does with Local Authority thinking and processes and encompassing all aspects of the environment, housing, transport and recycling. For more information visit the website.

Bolsover District Council
Sherwood Lodge, Bolsover,
Chesterfield S44 6NF
Tel: 01246 240 000
Fax: 01246 242 424
Web: www.bolsover.gov.uk
Open: Mon-Fri 9am-5pm
▶ Is currently working on a new environmental policy which incorporates Local Agenda 21 issues such as housing, public health and transport.

Bolton Metropolitan Borough Council
The Environment Team,
Milton House, Wellington Street,
Bolton BL3 5DG
Tel: 01204 336 659
Fax: 01204 363 257
Email: p.cathery.bolton.gov.uk
Web: www.bolton.gov.uk
Open: Mon-Fri 9am-5pm
▶ One of the first to be published nationally, Bolton's LA21 is the community's own action programme to make its environment cleaner, greener, healthier and more prosperous. The Environment Forum has the task of taking the LA21 forward. It is a voluntary partnership of organisations (including Bolton MBC) and individuals, seeking to identify the future for Bolton through five subject working groups (economy and work, energy, waste and pollution, built and natural environment, and transport). Projects to date include an established youth forum, EMAS scheme, schools energy saving seminars, waste directory, green commuting and sustainability indicators. Contact Peter Cathery for more info.

Bury Metropolitan Council
Department of Planning &
Development, Town Hall,
Knowsley Street, Bury BL9 0SW
Tel: 0161 253 6020
Fax: 0161 253 5105
Email: t.jones@bury co.uk
Web: www.bury.gov.uk
Open: Mon-Fri 9am-5pm
▶ The Council's Local Agenda 21 Strategy sets out a vision to create a greener, brighter, healthier, better Bury. It consists of four documents which include a Council Charter for Sustainable Development, an Internal Environmental Audit, the first State of the Environment Report for Bury and the Strategy document itself. The LA21 Strategy contains 200 Action Plans based on 14 topic areas and 54 key objectives, all to be implemented in the next 5 years. For more information, contact Tim Jones, Policy Development Officer on the above number.

Calderdale Metropolitan Borough Council
Northgate House, Northgate,
Halifax HX1 1UN
Tel: 01422 332 250
Fax: 01422 392 399
Web: www.calderdale.gov.uk
Open: Mon-Fri 9am-5pm
▶ Call Stephen Bhowmick for further information.

Carlisle City Council
Environmetal Services Department,
Civic Centre, Carlisle CA3 8QG
Tel: 01228 817 000
Fax: 01228 817 346
Email: mikeg@carlisle-city.gov.uk
Open: Mon-Fri 9.30am-5pm
▶ The team is woking to complete the formalised plan at the moment. It encompasses 12 themes under the environmental protection bracket, including recycling, energy efficiency and transport, in order to promote a more sustainable, greener and cleaner environment.

City of Bradford Metropolitan District Council
Central House, Forster Square,
Bradford BD1 1DH
Tel: 01274 751000
Fax: 01274 390076
Web: www.bradford.gov.uk
Open: Mon-Fri 9am-5pm
▶ Does not have a formal plan in place. Call the council for general information

City of Manchester Council
Environment and Development,
PO Box 463, Town Hall,
Manchester M60 3NY
Tel: 0161 234 4579
Fax: 0161 234 4679
Web: www.manchester.gov.uk
Open: Mon-Fri 9am-5pm
▶ Co-ordinates a Local Agenda 21 strategy for the city and supports a full range of recycling facilities. The Council is currently experimenting with the kerbside collection of segregated household waste and supplies subsidised home composters to residents. New recycling service will commence in July 2000 in the north of the city and aims to reach 20,000 households within 2 years. Works in partnership with Red Rose Forest and the Forestry Commission on the regional Millennium Woodland initiative, one of the aims is to plant 10,000 trees on a former landfill site. Also co-ordinates a centre for environmental issues called Manchester ERIC (see Chapter 12). ERIC is based at the Central Library and is open to the public during library opening hours.

Derbyshire County Council
County Hall, Matlock DE4 3AG
Tel: 01629 580 000
Fax: 01629 580 482
Web: www.derbyshire.gov.uk
Open: Mon-Fri 9am-5.30pm
▶ The council is currently in the process of formulating its LA 21 strategy. Call the above number for further information or use the website.

Kirklees Metropolitan Borough Council
Environment Unit,
23 Estates Building, Railway Street,
Huddersfield HD1 2JY
Tel: 01484 223 568
Fax: 01484 223 576
Email: environmentunit@kirkleesmc.gov.uk
Web: www.kirklees.gov.co.uk
Open: Mon-Fri 9.30am-5.30pm
▶ The LA21 agenda department is currently evolving a sustainable development plan including issues such as energy efficiency, transport and environmental management and improvement.

Knowsley Metropolitan Borough Council
Department of Plannng &
Development, PO Box 26,
Municipal Buildings,
Archway Road, Huyton L39 3FB
Tel: 0151 489 2278
Fax: 0151 431 1977
Web: www.knowsley.co.uk
Open: Mon-Fri 9am-5pm
▶ The council is currently updating its LA21 strategy dealing with aspects of environmental management, including transport, recycling and noise pollution. Call for further details.

Lake District National Park Authority
Murley Moss, Oxenholme Road,
Kendal LA9 7RL
Tel: 01539 740 555
Fax: 01539 740 822
Email: hq@lake-district.gov.uk
Web: www.lake-district.gov.uk
▶ The protection and conservation of what is widely regarded as the finest upland scenery in England is the main responsibility of this Authority, which has a fundamental influence on a wide range of policies and activities. The Authority was established by Parliament in 1951 to protect the area's outstanding beauty and promote its quiet enjoyment by the public. As a local authority, it also takes into account the needs of the 42,000 people who live inside the National Park boundary. The Authority is a local government body with two purposes: to conserve and enhance the natural beauty, wildlife and cultural heritage of the National Park; and to promote opportunities for the understanding and enjoyment of the special qualities of the National Park by

the public. In pursuing these opportunities the Authority also seeks to foster the economic and social well-being of local communities within the National Park.

Lancashire County Council
Guild House, Cross Street, Preston
Tel: 01772 264 185
Fax: 01772 263 423
Email: w.horse@lancshire.gov.uk
Web: www.lancs.gov.uk
Open: Mon-Fri 9am-5pm
▶ The Council is working very closely with the community and small business to provide a sustainanable agenda for the environment.

Liverpool City Council
Department of Planning, Milleniuim House, 2nd Floor, Victoria Street, Liverpool L16 JF
Tel: 0151 225 4915
Fax: 0151 233 4290
Email: steve.lindfield@liverpool.gov.uk
Web: www.liverpool.gov.uk
Open: Mon-Fri 9am-5pm
▶ Working to develop a series of projects which link to sustainable development and Local Agend 21. Within the council, work on the development of eco-clubs, environmental management and audit schemes and green communting strategies is presently taking place. External bodies from private, community, voluntary and other public sector bodies are also providing support and action.

Oldham Metropolitan Borough Council
3rd Floor, Metropolitan House, Hobson Street, Oldham OL1 1QD
Tel: 0161 911 4475
Fax: 0161 911 4162
Email: ppr.stratpol.oldham.gov.uk
Web: www.oldham.gov.uk
Open: Mon-Fri 9am-5pm
▶ Has been working together with the Oldham Borough Environment Forum to produce a truly participative Oldham Agenda 21 Plan, which reflects the views and aspirations of local people. The Council and Forum are now working to implement the Plan.

Rochdale Metropolitan BoroughCouncil
Environmental Health, Telegraph House, Ballie Street, Rochdale L16 1JF
Tel: 01706 647 474
Fax: 01706 864 184
Email: andyswaby@rochdale.gov.uk
Web: www.rochdale.gov.uk
Open: Mon-Fri 9am-5pm
▶ Is developing an LA21 strategy, building on long-standing policies to protect environmental assets and overcome problems. Committed to sustainable development as a key to policies for economic and community regeneration.

Rossendale County Council
Town Hall, Engineering and Planning Department, Bucklylee, Buckylee Lane, Backup OL13 0AR
Tel: 01706 217 777
Fax: 01706 871 618
Web: www.rossendale.gov.uk
Open: Mon-Fri 9am-5pm
▶ Provides environmental services, advice and information for business and individuals on a broad spectrum of environment issues. Currently preparing a LA21 strategy document in association with Rossendale Groundwork and the Rossendale Partnership, involving the community as a whole and will outline work for the next 12 months. Contact Rossendale Groundwork on 01706 211 421.

Rotherham Metropolitan Borough Council
Department of Environment, Elm Bank, 77 Alma Road, Rotherham S60 2BU
Tel: 01709 382 121
Fax: 01709 882 183
Web: www.rotherham.gov.uk
Open: Mon-Fri 9am-5pm
▶ Currently working on transport, recycling and community issues for a cleaner, better environment.

Salford City Metropolitan Council
Forward Planning, Development Services Directorate, Civic Centre, Chorely Road, Swinton, Salford M27 5BW
Tel: 0161 794 4711
Fax: 0161 794 4000
Email: forward.plan@gov.uk
Web: www.salford.gov.uk
Open: Mon-Fri 9am-5pm
▶ Call Nick Lowther for details of Salford's LA21 initiatives and projects.

Sefton Metropolitan Borough Council
Environmental Protection Department, 3rd Floor, Balliol House, Bootle L20 3AH
Tel: 0151 934 4023
Fax: 0151 934 4276
Email: r.stronge@sefton.co.uk
Web: www.sefton.gov.uk
Open: Mon-Fri 9am-5pm
▶ Is currently facilitating the production of a LA21 strategy which will be an action plan for local progress towards sustainable development, highlighting actions and activities that everyone can do to help improve the quality of their local environment.

South Lakeland District Council
South Lakeland House, Department of Planning & Deveolpment, Lowther Street, Kendal LA 9 4UQ
Tel: 01539 733 333
Fax: 01539 740 300
Email: p.ridgeway@southlakeland.gov.uk
Web: www.southlakeland.gov.uk
Open: Mon-Fri 9am-5pm
▶ The LA21 strategy is concerned with conservation and environmental planning issues, including aspects of greenfield protection and planning, transport, education and raising public awareness about a sustainable and workable lifestyle which works both for and with the environment.

St Helens Metropolitan Borough Council
Environmental Protection Department, CSMU, 5th Floor, Wesley House, Corporation Street, St Helens WA10 1HF
Tel: 01744 456 470
Open: Mon-Fri 9am-5.15pm
▶ Currently working on the LA21 issues, focusing on improving local quality of life without damaging the global environment. It will draw on ideas and themes discussed at public gatherings held in March. A project to identify how community groups can best be supported to help each other is under way. The aim is to use the findings to bid for funds to support for further development of the St Helens Community Action Network (CAN). A booklet called St. Helens@PlanetEarth – To Boldly Go is available. Call for further information.

Staffordshire County Council
Development Services Department, Riverway, Stafford ST16 3TJ
Tel: 01785 223 121
Fax: 01785 211 279
Web: www.staffordshire.gov.co.uk
▶ The Council decided to approach LA21 by sampling opinions and working with a cross section of people. Membership of the four Specialist Working Groups, formed in 1993, was voluntary and open to anyone with an interest. Members were asked to submit a list of concerns they felt LA21 should address and worked towards identifying solution to these issues. Appropriate agencies responsible for action were also identified and attempts made to define indicators and targets for each action. The Staffordshire Environment Forum prepared three documents as part of LA21 for submission to the United Nations: an Interim report, an action programme and the first report. Call for further information and to find out how you can participate.

Stockport Metropolitan Borough Council
Local Agenda Department, Town Hall, Stockport SK1 3XX
Tel: 0161 474 4214
Fax: 0161 474 4586
Email: agenda.21@stockport.gov.uk
Web: www.stockport.gov.uk
Open: Mon-Fri 9am-5pm
▶ Currently preparing Stockport's LA21 strategy in partnership with local people, businesses, schools and organisations. Areas for action include nature, waste, sustainable communities, energy and education and raising awareness. Call the Sustainability Team on the above number to find out more or to get involved.

Tameside Metropolitan Borough Council
Department of Environmental Services, Council Offices, Wellington Road, Ashton-under-Lyne OL6 6DL
Tel: 0161 342 3102
Fax: 0161 342 3111
Email: planning.specialprojects@mail.tameside.gov.uk
Web: www.tameside.gov.uk
Open: Mon-Fri 9am-4pm
▶ Published a Charter for Sustainable Development in 1996 and has spent the two years on public consultation exercises with businesses, voluntary organisations, environmental groups, community groups and trade unions. The Council published a final LA21 Action Plan at the end of 1998. Topics include education, health, poverty, transport, pollution, built environment and energy.

Trafford Metropolitan Borough Council
Chief Executive's Office, Special Projects Unit, PO Box 10, Trafford Town Hall, Talbot Road, Stretford, Manchester M32 0YZ
Tel: 0161 912 4037
Fax: 0161 912 4184
Email: mick.rearden.trafford.gov.uk
Web: www.trafford.gov.uk
Open: Mon-Fri 9am-5pm
▶ Has taken an incremental approach to LA21, building on long-standing policies to protect its environmental assests and overcome problems. The Council is committed to sustainable development as a key part of policies for economic and community regeneration of the Borough. In May 1998 a group of Councillors were appointed to develop policy on health and LA21 and will produce, with the wider community, the Borough's LA21 Strategy.

Wakefield Metropolitan Borough Council
Department of Environmental Health Services, 49 King Street, Wakefield WF1 2SY
Tel: 01924 306 906
Fax: 01924 305 965
Email: g.butler@wakefield.gov.uk
Web: www.wakefield.gov.uk
Open: Mon-Fri 9am-5pm

▶ The Council is ensuring issues concerning waste management, transport and pollution are included in the Local Agenda plan.

Wigan Metropolitan Borough Council
Borough Planning Department, Civic Buildings, New Market Street, Wigan WN1 1RP
Tel: 01942 404 376
Fax: 01942 404 222
Email: la21@wiganmbc.gov.uk
Web: www.wiganmbc.gov.uk/pub/agenda21
Open: Mon-Fri 9am-5pm
▶ Five cross-sectoral LA21 Topic Groups have been established, covering natural and built environment, energy, housing, transport, poverty, equity, employment, health, pollution, waste minimisation and young people's issues. An LA21 elected members sub-committee, an LA21 officer working group and an LA21 website are already established. Green Council vehicles are being piloted and an over-arching Forum is planned along with recycling initiatives, transport strategies, a clean-up campaign and a parish map project.

Wirral Metropolitan Borough Council
Environmental & Housing Department, Westminster House, Hamilton Street, Birkenhead, Wirral CH4 5FN
Tel: 0151 638 7070
Fax: 0151 666 1343
Web: www.wirral.gov.uk
Open: Mon-Fri 9am-5pm
▶ The Council is working in conjunction with volunteers and private businesses to enhance the environment in the area. The Local Aenda 21 strategy has been put together to incude all aspects of transport, waste planning and management and energy efficiency.

Organisations

Centre for Environmental Initiatives (CEI), The
The Old School House, Mill Lane, Carlshalton SM5 2JY
Tel: 020 8770 6611
Fax: 020 8647 0719

Email: info@thecei.org.uk
Web: www.thecei.org.uk
▶ Small charity specialising in LA21 sustainable development and community-based environmental initiatives.

Institute for Local Government
J G Smith Building, University of Birmingham, Edgbaston, Birmingham B15 2TT
Tel: 0121 414 4966
Fax: 0121 414 4989
Email: a.c.coulson@bham.ac.uk
▶ Offers research and consultancy on matters connected with local government, not least in connection with the environment. Holds seminars on how local government councillors and officers can best promote sustainability. Works mainly with councils, government departments and agencies.

Manchester LA21 Forum
c/o Voluntary Action Manchester (VAM), Fourways House, Hilton Street, Manchester M1 2EJ
Tel: 0161 236 3206
Fax: 0161 228 0464
▶ Interim and informal first point of contact for LA21 during Manchester LA21's period of reorganisation.

National Association of Local Councils
109 Great Russell Street, London WC1B 3LD
Tel: 020 7637 1865
Fax: 020 7436 7451
Email: nalc@nalc.gov.uk
Web: www.nalc.gov.uk
Open: Mon-Fri 9am-5pm
▶ The national voice for around 10,000 parish, town and community councils in England and Wales. The Association gives advice and guidance to member councils on financial, legal, employment, policy and media matters and takes an enthusiastic role in protecting and advancing the rights and interests of member councils in parliament and other national bodies.

Nuclear Free Local Authorities Secretariat
Environment and Development, PO Box 463, Manchester City Council, Manchester M60 3NY

Tel: 0161 234 3244
Fax: 0161 234 3379
Email: nfznsc@gn.apc.org
Web: www.gn.apc.org/nfznsc
Open: Mon-Fri 9am-4pm
▶ On behalf of those local authorities which have declared their opposition to some or all current proposed practices within the nuclear weapon and fuel cycle and in the context of local authority powers, NFLAS considers and recommends action which could be taken by such authorities acting together or otherwise to support: the safe phasing out of nuclear power in the UK in the shortest practicable time; the removal of hazards posed by the transportation and disposal of spent fuel and nuclear waste; and the promotion of positive alternatives to nuclear power and employment in an expanded non-nuclear sector. NFLAS monitors development and advises member authorities accordingly to promote these objectives.

Government & Organisations

NATIONAL GOVERNMENT

Countryside Agency (Head Office)
John Dower House, Crescent Place, Cheltenham GL50 3RA
Tel: 01242 521 381
Fax: 01242 584 270
Email: info@countryside.gov.uk
Web: www.countryside.gov.uk
▶ Advisors to the Government on aspects of the countryside. Instigated the Millenium Greens initiative with funding of a £10 million Lottery Grant from the Millenium Commission. Over 250 local communities are involved in this initiative creating green spaces right across Engalnd. Millenium Greens will be areas of open space, to be enjoyed permanently by the local community and looked after by a newly established Charitable Trust.

Countryside Agency (North West)
7th Floor Bridgewater House, 58 Whitworth Street, Manchester M1 6LT
Tel: 0161 237 1061
Fax: 0161 237 1062
Web: www.countryside.gov.uk
▶ Regional office of Government agency helping and advising with a broad range of initiatives designed to encourage the protection, enjoyment and use of the countryside. Call for more information.

Countryside Agency – Regional Office
Haweswater Road, Penrith CA11 7EH
Tel: 01768 865 752
Fax: 01768 890 414
▶ Regional office of Government agency helping and advising with a broad range of initiatives designed to encourage the protection, enjoyment and use of the countryside. Call for more information.

English Nature
Northminster House, Peterborough PE1 1UA
Tel: 01733 455 000
Email: enquiries@english-nature.org.uk
Web: www.english-nature.co.uk
▶ Government agency that champions the conservation of wildlife and natural features throughout England. Responsible for designating National nature reserves and notifying Sites of Special Scientific Interest.

Environment Agency – Head Office
Rio House, Waterside Drive, Aztec West, Almondsbury, Bristol BS32 4UD
Tel: 01454 624 400
Fax: 01454 624 409
▶ The Environment Agency for England and Wales was created by merging the National Rivers Authority, HM Inspectorate of Pollution, the Waste Regulation Authorities and several smaller government units and acts as a combined regulator of land, air and water. It regulates a large number of business and services including over 2,000 industrial processes with the greatest polluting potential, in addition to advising on environmental policy and strategy.

Environment Agency – Central Area Office
Lutra House, Dodd Way, Walton Summit, Bamber Bridge, Preston PR5 8BX
Tel: 01772 339 882
Fax: 01772 627 730
▶ Regional office of the Environment Agency.

Environment Agency – North Area Office
Ghyll Mount, Gillian Way, Penrith 40 Business Park, Penrith CA11 9BP
Tel: 01768 866 666
Fax: 01768 865 606
▶ Regional office of the Environment Agency.

Environment Agency – North West
Regional Headquarters, Richard Fairclough House, Knutsford Road, Warrington WA4 1HG
Tel: 01925 653 999; General Enquiries: 0645 333 111
Fax: 01925 634 840
Email: enquiries@environment-agency.gov.uk
Web: www.environment-agency.gov.uk
▶ Regional office of the Environment Agency.

Environment Agency – South Area Office
Appleton House, 430 Birchwood Boulevard, Birchwood, Warrington WA3 7WD
Tel: 01925 840 000
Fax: 01925 852 260
▶ Regional office of the Environment Agency.

Global Wildlife Division
Department of the Environment, Transport and the Regions (DETR), Tollgate House, Houlton Street, Bristol BS2 9DJ
Tel: 0117 987 8503
Fax: 0117 987 8373
Email: cites_ukma@detr.gov.uk
Web: www.ukcites.gov.uk
▶ Responsible for implementing the convention on international trade in endangered species (CITES) in the UK. CITES is an international agreement wherby more than 150 nation states protect endangered species of plants and animals by restricting and monitoring international trade in them.

Going for Green & Tidy Britain (National Office for England)
Premier House, 3rd Floor, 12-13 Hatton Garden, London EC1N 8AN
Tel: 020 7831 4484
Fax: 020 7430 2859
Email: london@tidybritain.org.uk
Web: www.tidybritain.org.uk
▶ Government agency that campaigns for litter education and environmental improvement. Publishes a newsletter plus information packs on the effect of litter on the environment.

Ministry of Agriculture Fisheries and Food (MAFF)
Nobel House, 17 Smith Square, London SW1P 3JR
Tel: 0645 335 577
Web: www.maff.gov.uk
▶ Aims to ensure that consumers benefit from competitively priced food, produced to high standards of safety, environmental care and animal welfare and from a sustainable, efficient food chain; contributing to the well-being of rural and coastal communities. Essentially, MAFF's job is to help improve the economic performance of these industries, especially in the expanding markets of Europe and the wider world. At the same time, it has to protect our health and conserve our natural environment.

United Nations Environment and Development UK (UNED-UK)
3 Whitehall Court, London SW1A 2EL
Tel: 020 7930 2931
Fax: 020 7930 5893
Email: unadmcr1.poptel.uk
Web: www.onewild.org/oned~
▶ National commitee for UNEP and Focal Point for UNDP, focuses on the follow-up to the Rio Summit. Its main work is in preparation for Earth Summit III in 2002. Organises multi-stakeholder Round Tables on education, oceans, agriculture, forests, transport, tourism. Co-ordinates UK NGO involvement in training in the UN process, women, social development, sustainable development and human settlements.

CAMPAIGNS & ORGANISATIONS

Animal Welfare

Animal Aid
The Old Chapel, Bradford Street, Tonbridge TN9 1AW
Tel: 01732 364 546
Fax: 01732 366 533
Email: info@animalaid.org.uk
Web: www.animalaid.org.uk
▶ High profile group that runs a wide range of campaigns on living without cruelty. Produces a quarterly magazine called *Outrage* for members and supporters, plus an ethical mail order catalogue with toiletries, campaign materials, vegan, organic wine, vegan footwear, t-shirts etc. Also has a youth group for under 18s. Call for more info.

Animal Defenders
261 Goldhawk Road, London W12 9PE
Tel: 020 8846 9777
Fax: 020 8846 9712
Email: navs@cygnet.co.uk
Web: www.cygnet.co.uk/navs
▶ International animal welfare and conservation organisation working to suppress cruelty, alleviate suffering and to conserve and protect animals and their environment. As the leading campaigners against animal circuses, the group undertook an 18 month study into the use (and abuse) of circus animals, published in Feb 1998. This resulted in the conviction for cruelty of circus animal trainer Mary Chipperfield. The group also campaigns for other animals and conservation issues.

Animal Rights Coalition
PO Box 339, Wolverhampton WV10 7BZ
Tel: 01902 711 935
Email: james@arcnews.co.uk
Web: www.arcnews.co.uk
▶ Promotes grass roots animal rights campaigning by networking local animal rights groups and campaigners. ARC organises national animal rights meetings every other month. All are welcome. Produces a magazine called *ARC News* aimed at grass roots campaigning, available on subscription £7 per annum.

Bleakholt Animal Sanctuary
Rochdale Road, Edenfield, Ramsbottom BL0 0RX
Tel: 01706 822 577
Fax: 01706 822 812
Open: Mon-Fri 10am-4pm
▶ Takes in distressed or abandoned animals including dogs, cats, sheep, cows, pigs, old working horses and Blackpool donkeys. Adoption scheme helps with the rehousing of many animals. A shop on the premises sells secondhand bric-a-brac, and all profits go to the animals. Donations welcome.

Born Free Foundation
3 Grove House, Foundry Lane, Horsham RH13 5PL
Tel: 01403 240 170
Fax: 01403 327 838
Email: wildlife@bornfree.org.uk
Web: www.bornfree.org.uk
▶ Dynamic and high profile international wildlife charity, founded by actors Virginia McKenna and Bill Travers following their starring roles in the classic film *Born Free*. Runs seven projects devoted to animal welfare and conservation: Zoo Check, Elefriends, Big Cat Project, Wolf Project, Primate Project, Orca Project and UK Wildlife project. Born Free believes wildlife belongs in the wild and works to alleviate suffering and investigate cruelty.

British Beekeepers Association
National Bee Centre, NAC, Stoneleigh Park, Coventry CV8 2LG
Tel: 02476 696 679
Fax: 02476 690 682
Email: bbka@demon.co.uk
▶ Educational charity promoting beekeeping.

BUAV (British Union for the Abolition of Vivisection)
16a Crane Grove, London N7 8NN
Tel: 020 7700 4888
Fax: 020 7700 0196
Email: info.@buav.org
▶ Founded in 1898, the BUAV is the world's leading anti-vivisection campaigning organisation. Dedicated to using all peaceful means possible to end animal experiments. Through high profile media activities, celebrity support and quality educational material, it succeeds in spreading its campaign message to as wide and diverse an audience as possible. Work with Parliamentarians, corporate relationships, hardhitting undercover investigations, political lobbying and legal expertise means that the BUAV is at the forefront of the campaign to consign vivisection to the history books. Their 'Parliamentary Bulletin' is received quarterly by MP's, MEP's, SMP's, Members of the Welsh Assembly and Peers, together with up-to-date briefings and scientific reports on a range of issues. Current campaigns include: ending the use of dogs in research; addressing the international trade in primates for research; and opposing the genetic engineering and patenting of animals.

Care for the Wild International
1 Ashfolds, Horsham Road, Rusper RH12 4QX
Tel: 01293 871 596
Fax: 01293 871 022
Email: info@careforthewild.org.uk
Web: www.careforthewild.com
Open: Mon-Fri 8am-5pm
▶ Effective international wildlife charity dedicated to protecting wild animals from cruelty and exploitation. In the UK, it funds rescue centres and animal protection groups, helping a wide range of wildlife. Overseas help includes funding projects in Africa and Asia and supporting work to protect tigers, elephants, gorillas and other animals and their habitats.

Compassion in World Farming (CIWF)
Charles House, 5A Charles Street, Petersfield GU32 3EH
Tel: 01730 264 208
Fax: 01730 260 791
Email: compassion@ciwf.co.uk
Web: www.ciwf.co.uk
▶ The UK's leading group campaigning for improved welfare for farm animals and the abolition of factory farming. Also campaigns against live animal exports.

Donkey Sanctuary
Sidmouth, Devon EX10 0NU
Tel: 01395 578222
Fax: 01395 579266
Email: thedonkeysanctuary@compuserve.com
Open: From 9am until dusk every day of the year
▶ Care and welfare of donkeys and mules both in the UK and abroad.

Dr Hadwen Trust For Humane Research
84a Tilehouse Street, Hitchin SG5 2DY
Tel: 01462 436 819
Fax: 01462 436 844
Email: info@drhadwentrust.org.uk
Web: www.drhadwentrust.org.uk
Open: Mon-Fri 9am-5.30pm
▶ The Dr Hadwen Trust is funding non-animal research into major human health problems such as cancer, heart disease and meningitis. Our research projects could save thousands of animals from suffering in laboratories, and make a vital contribution to the battle against these dreadful diseases. Committed to saving lives tomorrow without taking life today.

EarthKind
Town Quay, Poole BH15 1HJ
Tel: 01202 682 344
Fax: 01202 682 366
Email: info@earthkind.org.uk
Web: www.earthkind.org.uk
Open: Tues-Sun 10am-4pm
▶ One of the UK's oldest animal welfare and environmental charities, founded in 1955. In 1994 launched the Ocean Defenders Project, converting an ex-whaling vessel, built in 1912, to become the world's first marine wildlife rescue ship, a floating casualty unit for marine animals. Over the past five years has carried out an active programme of humane and environmental education, marine conservation and marine wildlife rescue. Earthkind's volunteer crew of marine wildlife paramedics has responded to some of the worst oil wildlife disasters in the world.

Farm Animal Welfare Council
1a Page Street, London SW1P 4PQ
Tel: 020 7904 6534
Fax: 020 7904 6533
Email: p.a.mcdonald@aw.maff.gov.uk

▶ Independent advisory body, whose terms of refernce are to keep under review the welfare of farm animals on agricultural land, at market in transit and at place of slaughter; and to advise agricultural ministers of any legislation or other changes that may be necessary.

Friends of Animals League
Foal Farm, Jail Lane,
Biggin Hill TN16 3AX
Tel: 01959 572 386
Fax: 01959 572 386
Open: Wed-Mon 2pm-5pm
(including Sundays and Bank Holidays)
▶ A registered charity aiming to take in as many sick, distressed and unwanted animals as possible and then to restore them to health and happiness and to place them in good, vetted homes. No healthy animal is ever destroyed so if no home can be found, the animal remains for the rest of its life at FOAL.

Fund for the Replacement of Animals in Medical Experiments
Russell & Burch House,
96-98 North Sherwood Street,
Nottingham NG1 4EE
Tel: 0115 958 4740
Fax: 0115 950 3570
Email: frame@frame-uk.demon.co.uk
Web: www.frame-uk.demon.co.uk
▶ Charity founded in 1969, which aims to eliminate the need for live animal experiments and put an end to the suffering inflicted upon millions of laboratory anaimals. Researches, develops and promotes practical alternative techniques that can be used to replace live animals in biomedical research. It maintains an informed and balanced viewpoint from where it can advise politicians on the legislation controlling animal experiments, work with scientists in industry and academia to find effective ways of reducing the need for animal experiments and provide authoritative information for scientists, journalists, students, schoolchildren and members of the public.

Greenmount Wild Bird Hospital
Kirklees Valley, Garside Hey Road,
of Brandlesholme Road, Bury BL8 4LT
Tel: 01204 884 086
▶ Situated in a 2 acre wooded valley, 10 miles north of Manchester, the sole purpose of this hospital is to care for wounded and sick wild birds brought to the hospital by the public. Birds and rehabilitated and released once they are fully recovered. Those that are permanently incapacitated are safely housed elsewhere. Staffed entirely by volunteers and funded by membership and donations.

Hillside Animal Sanctuary
Hill Top Farm, Hall Lane,
Frettinham, Norwich NR12 7LT
Tel: 01603 891 227
Fax: 01603 891 458
▶ One of the UK's leading farm animal sanctuaries, Hillside was founded in 1995 and provides sanctuary to around 700 rescued animals and birds. As well as offering a safe, permanent home to individual rescued animals, Hillside also campaigns against factory farming. Hillside recently rescued a heifer, named Liberty, who escaped from an abattoir in Devon minutes before she was due to be slaughtered. The media interest that this generated allowed Hillside to draw people's attention to the 100 animals a second in the UK who are less fortunate than Liberty, and are slaughtered for meat. Several of Hillside's animals are available for 'adoption' by the general public – for a small sum each year, to help feed and care for the animals, you receive photos and information about your adopted animal. To adopt an animal or to receive regular newsletters, write or phone. The sanctuary is open to visitors every Sunday, until the end of October, from 1-5pm; also Bank Holiday Mondays, and Mondays in July and August, 1-5pm

Humane Slaughter Association
The Old School, Brewhouse Hill,
Wheathampstead, St Albans AL4 8AN
Tel: 01582 831919
Fax: 01582 831 414
Email: info@hsa.org.uk

▶ Millions of animals and birds are slaughtered every day across the world. The HSA is the only registered charity to specialise in the welfare of these livestock in markets, during livestock and at slaughter. It takes a practical approach to animal welfare, providing constructive advice, educational videos, publications and practical training for all those involved in livestock handling and slaughter. Please become a member and support the HSA.

Hunt Saboteurs Association
PO Box 2786, Brighton BN2 2AX
Tel: 01273 622 827
Email: info@huntsabs.org.uk
Web: www.huntsabs.org.uk
▶ Campaign group aiming to end hunting animals for sport through non-violent, direct action. Members of the HSA have been saving the lives of hunted animals for over 35 years. The HSA aims to help wild animals directly in the very place where they are hounded and harassed for 'sport' – the hunting field itself! The HSA works against all sports involving the future of wildlife – that includes the hunting of foxes, hare, deer and mink, hare coursing, badger baiting, game shooting and angling. Call for details of local groups.

International Fund for Animal Welfare
Warren Court, Park Road,
Crowborough TN6 2GA
Tel: 01892 601 900
Fax: 01892 601 913
Web: www.ifaw.org
▶ One of the largest animal protection and conservation organisations. Worldwide campaigns against all abuse of animals and their environment.

Lord Dowding Fund for Humane Research
261 Goldhawk Road, London W1Z 9PE
Tel: 020 8846 9777
Fax: 020 8846 9712
Email: havs@cygnet.co.uk
Web: www.cygnet.co.uk/navs

Hillside Animal Sanctuary
Hall Lane Frettenham
Norwich NR12 7LT

Hill Top Farm, Hall Lane, Frettinham,
Norwich NR12 7LT
Tel: 01603 891 227
Fax: 01603 891 458
The sanctuary is open to visitors every Sunday,
until the end of October,
from 1-5pm;
also Bank Holiday Mondays,
and Mondays in July and
August, 1-5pm.

▶ Supports, sponsors and promotes humane methods of scientific and medical research for testing products and curing disease. Working to replace animal testing, the LDF's activities embrace educational, scientific and medical research. To date, it has awarded grants worth more than £750,000 in areas such as breast cancer, Parkinsons disease, cataracts and cot-death.

Movement for Compassionate Living
Burrow Farm, Highampton, Beaworthy EX21 5JQ
Tel: 01409 231 264
▶ Promotes a health giving vegan lifestyle dependent largely on local production. It advocates the phasing-out of livestock farming and giving the land released to trees that can meet nearly all human needs, reverse global warming and restore and maintain environmental health. Produce low-priced quarterly journals, booklets and leaflets. It runs stalls and meetings and answers queries.

National Anti-Vivisection Society
261 Goldhawk Road, London W12 9PE
Tel: 020 8846 9777
Fax: 020 8846 9712
Email: navs@cygnet.co.uk
Web: www.cygnet.co.uk/navs
▶ The premier anti-vivisection campaign group, exposing the futility and cruelty of animal experiments. Undertakes in-depth investigations, scientific reports, films and publicity campaigns to educate Parliament and public of the dangers of relying upon animal research.

National Canine Defence League
17 Wakley Street, London EC1 7RQ
Tel: 020 7837 0006
Fax: 020 7833 2701
Web: www.ncdl.org.uk
▶ National group working for the protection of dogs through a network of care centres and education and welfare campaigns. Never destroys a healthy dog.

Naturewatch
122 Bath Road, Cheltenham GL53 7JX
Tel: 01242 252 871
Fax: 01242 253 569
Email: info@naturewatch.org
Web: www.naturewatch.org
▶ A not-for-profit animal welfare campaigning organisation, aiming to promote the prevention of cruelty to animals and to conduct and support the publication of information concerning animals in furtherance of their welfare. Main campaigning areas are animal experimentation and live export. Produces a *Compassionate Shopping Guide*, a cruelty-free toiletries range and a newsletter for more active supporters. The charitable & educational arm, Naturewatch Foundation, is working in Eastern Europe to improve animal welfare standards.

Respect for Animals
PO Box 6500, Nottingham NG4 3GB
Tel: 0115 952 5440
Fax: 0115 956 0753
Email: respect.for.animal@dial.pipex.com
Web: www.respectforanimals.org
▶ Non-governmental organisation (formerly LYNX) dedicated solely to campaigning against the cruel and unnecessary international fur trade. By using peaceful consumer campaigns it has virtually destroyed the UK fur trade, but the sad fact is that worldwide one animal dies every second for 'fashion'. Relies solely on public donation. Annual subscription costs £15, and you will receive regular newsletters and updates.

Royal Society for the Prevention of Cruelty Against Animals (RSPCA)
Causeway, Horsham RH12 1HG
Tel: 01403 264 181;
Cruelty Line: 08705 555 999
Fax: 01403 241 048
Web: www.rspca.org.uk
▶ National organisation that deals with cruelty against and neglect of animals. Runs a Cruelty Line for reporting incidents of cruelty in the UK.

RSPCA Oldham Animal Centre
21a Rhodes Bank, Oldham OL1 1UA
Tel: 0161 624 4725
Fax: 0161 284 6032
Open: All days except Wed 11am-4pm
▶ Centre for re-homing unwanted, but unfortunately not stray, animals only. The centre is fairly small – 18 kennels and 20 cat pens – so phone before bringing in an unwanted pet. Volunteers and donations are always very welcome.

The British Horse Society
Stoneleigh Deer Park, Kenilworth CV8 2XZ
Tel: 0870 1202 244
Fax: 0192 6707 800
Email: pr@bhs.org.uk
Web: www.bhs.org.uk/ www.britishhorse.com
Open: Mon-Thur 9am-5pm; Fri 9am-3pm
▶ The Society is an equine welfare charity funded largely by its membership of 55,000 and is concerned with training and education on all aspects of horse care and riding. It runs the professional qualifications for the equine industry and also concerns itself with access and rights of way as they affect the horse and rider, and with the safety of riders, particularly when riding on the road. It advises and liaises with government, both in the UK and in Europe, on legislation as it affects the horse. BHS Bookshop offers wide selection of equestrian books and videos, as well as gifts.

The Humane Research Trust
Brook House, 29 Bramhall Lane South, Bramhall, Stockport SK7 2DN
Tel: 0161 439 8041
Fax: 0161 439 3713
Email: members@humane.freeserve.co.uk
Web: www.btinternet.com/~shawweb/hrt
Open: Mon-Fri 9am-4.30pm
▶ Registered charity funding medical research into human illnesses without the use of live animals or animal tissue. The Trust is a non-confrontational organisation working with scientists funding a range of research throughout the UK hospitals and universities. Current projects funded include cancer (including cervical and ovarian), diabetes and neurodegenerative diseases.

Uncaged Campaigns
14 Ridgeway Road, Sheffield S12 2SS
Tel: 0114 253 0020
Fax: 0114 265 4070
Email: uncaged.anti-viv@dial.pipex.com
Web: www.uncaged.co.uk
▶ Anti-vivisection organisation. Current campaigns include a boycott of Procter and Gamble and the Pigs Might Fly! campaign against xenotransplantation (use of animal organs in human transplant operations). Vegan and cruelty-free merchandise by mail order.

Viva!
12 Queen Square, Brighton BN1 3FD
Tel: 01273 777 688
Fax: 01273 776 755
Email: info@viva.org.uk
Web: www.viva.org.uk
Open: Mon-Fri 9.30am-6pm
▶ Vegetarian and animal charity which regularly launches hard-hitting, issue-based campaigns to end factory farming. Offers plenty of information about vegetarian and vegan diets including health, animals, the environment and the developing world. Includes a special youth section and a schools information service.

World Society for Protection of Animals
89 Albert Embankment, London SE1 7TP
Tel: 020 7793 0540
Fax: 020 7793 0208
Email: wspa@wspa.org.uk
Web: www.wspa.org.uk
▶ Works in co-operation with over 350 member organisations in 70 countries to promote animals welfare and conservation. Aims to promote humane education programmes to encourage respect for animals and responsible stewardship, and laws and enforcement stuctures to provide legal protection for animals. A registered charity with consultative status at the United Nations and Council of Europe.

Government & Organisations

Animal Conservation

Amateur Entomologists' Society
P.O. Box 8774, London SW7 5ZG
Email: aes@theaes.org
Web: www.theaes.org
▶ Promotes the education and conservation of insects, particularly among the younger generations. Members receive newsletters bi-monthly and can attend annual events at the Natural History Museum and Kempton Park. The Society's insect fair is the largest in Europe and is held on the 1st Sat of October.

Barn Owl Trust
Waterleat, Ashburton TQ13 7HU
Tel: 01364 653 026
Fax: 01364 654 392
Email: info@barnowltrust.org.uk
Web: www.barnowltrust.org.uk
▶ National barn owl charity carrying out conservation, education, information, provision and research. You can become a friend, adopt an owl and buy from range of goods. Publishes a twice-yearly newsletter. Send large SAE for free barn owl information.

British Arachnological Society
2 Egypt Wood Cottages, Egypt Lane, Farnham Common SL2 3LE
Email: helen.read@btinternet.com
▶ The aim of the society is to promote the study of arachnids other than mites, in Britain and throughout the world. Membership is open to all interested in arachnology. Activities include spider identification courses, ecological surveys, workshops, lectures and field meetings. The society publishes a bulletin (including scientific papers) three times a year and also a newsletter which is a forum for exchange of information. A library of around 11,000 reprints and books is housed in Liverpool and it also has a slide library.

British Divers Marine Life Rescue
39 Ingram Road, Gillingham ME7 1SB
Tel/Fax: 01634 281 680
Email: mark@bdmlr.org.uk
Web: www.bdmlr.org.uk
▶ BDMLR works all around the UK in the field of marine wildlife rescue with rescue vessels, whale re-floatation equipment and over 500 trained and insured medics. It is the UK's largest marine wildlife rescue group with regular newsletters and training courses. Membership is open to all and costs £15.

British Hedgehog Preservation Society
Knowbury House, Knowbury, Ludlow SY8 3LQ
Tel: 01584 890 287
Email: bhps@dhustone.fsbusiness.co.uk
Open: Mon-Fri 9am-5pm
▶ The Society was formed in 1982 and its aims are: to make the public aware of hedgehogs and to give advice on their care, particularly when injured, sick, orphaned, treated cruelly or in any other danger. Also to encourage the younger generation to value and respect natural wildlife and, by supplying information and giving lectures, to foster their interest in hedgehogs; to fund serious research into the behavioural habits of hedgehogs and to ascertain the best methods of assisting their survival. The Society has already contributed £12,500 towards the research of Dr Pat Morris, of the Department of Biology, London University, an acknowledged expert on hedgehogs. Has also helped to support other research projects, including donations to St. Tiggywinkles and other Hedgehog Carers throughout the UK. However, more money is still needed to continue this essential work.

British Tarantula Society
81 Phillimore Place, Radlett, Hertfordshire, WD7 8NJ
Tel: 01923 856 071
▶ Conservation, protection and education regarding captive tarantulas.

British Trust for Ornithology; National Centre for Ornithology
The Nunnery, Thetford, Norfolk IP24 2PU
Tel: 01842 750 050
Fax: 01842 750 030
Web: www.bto.org
▶ The BTO promotes and encourages the wider understanding, appreciation and conservation of birds through scientific studies using the combined skill and enthusiasm of its members, other bird watchers and staff.

Dian Fossey Gorilla Fund
110 Gloucester Avenue, London NW1 8HX
Tel: 020 7483 2681
Fax: 020 7722 0928
Email: dfgfeurope@aol.com
Web: www.dianfossey.org
▶ The last 650 mountain gorillas in the World exist only in the rainforests of war-torn Central Africa. Through anti-poaching work, veterinary support and community-based conservation, the Dian Fossey Gorilla Fund is helping to ensure a better future for both the wildlife and the people.

Environmental Investigation Agency
69-85 Old Street, London EC1V 9HX
Tel: 020 7490 7040
Fax: 020 7490 0436
Email: info@eia-international.org
Web: www.pair.com/eia/
▶ Dubbed the 'Eco-Detectives' by the press, the EIA is an international, independent organisation committed to investigating and exposing environmental crime. EIA works undercover and presents documented information exposing the illegal trade in wildlife to government authorities and the media, with the aim of securing improved enforcement measures.

Froglife
Mansion House, 27/28 Market Place, Halesworth IP19 8AY
Tel: 01986 873 733
Fax: 01986 874 744
Email: info@froglife.org.uk
▶ Non-profit making charitable organisation that works to conserve and promote native species of amphibians and reptiles throughout Great Britain. Increase public awareness and education by providing and running national projects such as Toads on Roads, the Frog Mortality Project and the London Garden Pond Project. A new initiative launched for 2000 is the Froglife Friendship Scheme which aims to provide financial support for Froglife's activities. Also work to identify conservation priorities with respect to habitat creation, restoration and safeguarding sites against development, and supports amphibian and reptile conservation groups in Britain, who provide knowledge and practical assistance to carry out local conservation work.

National Federation of Badger Groups
2 Cloisters Business Centre, 8 Battersea Park Road, London SW8 4BG
Tel: 020 7498 3220
Fax: 020 7627 4212
Email: elaine.king@ndirect.co.uk
Web: www.geocities.com/rainforest/canopy/2626
▶ Umbrella organisation for over 80 local voluntary badger groups in the UK. Promotes the conservation, protection and welfare of badgers, their setts and their habitat. Deals with all issues relating to badgers, offers information and advice and has a membership facility.

Orangutan Foundation
7 Kent Terrace, London NW1 4RP
Tel: 020 7724 2912
Fax: 020 7706 2613
Email: info@orangutan.org.uk
Web: www.orangutan.org.uk
▶ Only registered charity in the UK devoted to saving orangutans in the wild and their rainforest habitat. Orangutans are in danger of extinction because their sole habitat, tropical rainforest, is being destroyed by the marked increase in illegal logging and the conversion of land to agriculture. Through conservation, education and research, the Foundation aims to promote awareness of the plight of these highly endangered animals.

People's Trust for Endangered Species
15 Cloisters House, 8 Battersea Park Road, London SW8 4BG
Tel: 020 7498 4533
Fax: 020 7498 4459

Email: enquiries@ptes.org
Web: www.ptes.org
Open: Mon-Fri 9am-5pm
▶ Founded in 1977 with the aim of helping to ensure a future for many species of endangered creatures worldwide. To achieve these aims, the Trust: provides funding for specific research projects and commissions research on key conservation issues; manages and supports conservation field projects involving volunteers; purchases and manages reserves for wildlife; organises a programme of educational events and visits; organises conferences and symposia on conservation issues. The work of the trust is funded largely through donations of individual supporters. Although working in partnership with a range of other organisations, the trust is an independent charity, and seeks to promote best practice in wildlife conservation. Recent projects include work with red squirrels, lions, Ethiopian wolves and pine martens.

Royal Society for the Protection of Birds (RSPB)
UK Headquarters, The Lodge,
Sandy SG19 2DL
Tel: 01767 680 551
▶ Europe's largest wildlife conservation charity with more than a million members. Campigns for the conservation of wild birds and the environment. Currently seeking better legal protection for wildlife sites, working to reserve the declines in farmland birds and addressing transport and climate change issues. Creates a safe haven for wildlife on its 158 nature reserves which attract over a million visitors a year. Network of local groups for adults and young people brings the environment to life through meetings, events and projects.

South Lancashire Bat Group
15 Lakeland Crescent, Bury BL9 9SF
Tel: 0161 797 4745
Email: slbg@cwcom.net
▶ Affiliated to the national Bat Conservation Trust, the group aims to promote the conservation and better understanding of bats and to offer advice to those who have bats roosting in their houses. Call for more information on the group's bat walks.

TRAFFIC International
219c Huntingdon Road,
Cambridge CB3 0DL
Tel: 01223 277 427
Fax: 01223 277 237
Email: traffic@trafficint.org
Web: www.traffic.org
Open: Mon-Fri 9am-5pm
▶ Conservation organisation which aims to conserve wild flora and fauna worldwide. Works mainly with non-governmental organisations and governments.

Whale & Dolphin Conservation Society
Alexander House, James Street West,
Bath BA1 2BT
Tel: 01225 334 511
Fax: 01225 480 097
Email: info@wdcs.org
Web: www.wdcs.org
▶ Charity dedicated to the conservation and protection of all whales, dolphins and porpoises by campaigning on whaling, captivity and relevant environmental issues, funding over 50 projects worldwide and by working closely with local communities to preserve their wildlife. Offers a whale and dolphin adoption scheme.

Wood Cottage Wildlife Sanctuary
Alkrington Woods,
Middleton M24 1WE
Tel: 0161 654 8278
Fax: 0161 654 8278
▶ Family-run sanctuary specialising in birds of prey. Liaises with other sanctuaries and returns birds to the wild if at all possible. Provides talks and demonstrations in schools and residential care homes.

WWF-UK
Panda House, Weyside Park,
Godalming GU7 1XR
Tel: 01483 426 444
Fax: 01483 426 409
Email: info@wwf-uk.org
Web: www.wwf-uk.org
Open: Mon-Fri 9am-5pm
▶ WWF, the global environment network, is the world's largest and most respected independent conservation organisation, with a global network of some 27 national organisations. WWF works to conserve endangered species, protect endangered spaces, address global threats to nature by seeking long-term solutions with people in government and industry, education and civil society. Publishes *WWF News* (quarterly magazine).

Natural Environment

Association of Professional Foresters of Great Britain
7-9 West Street,
Belford NE70 7QA
Tel: 01668 213 937
Fax: 01668 213 555
Email: jane@apfs.demon.co.uk
Web: www.apf.org.uk
▶ Established in 1960 for all those who derive their livelihoods from forestry, it endeavours to promote and contribute to the future of employment in the many aspects of the home-based industry. Information via quarterly news, annual conference, exhibitions, diary and much more. Information and contacts supplied to general public, eg careers, contractors for tree work. All enquiries welcomed.

Bollin Valley Project
County Offices,
Chapel Lane,
Wilmslow SK9 1PU
Tel: 01625 534 791
Fax: 01625 534 790
Email: bollin@cheshire.gov.uk
▶ Countryside management organisation principally looking after the Bollin Valley. The partnership has a wide range of activities including: voluntary and community work; educational and special needs works; country park and picnic site management; grassland and woodland management; and stream care. There are 14 full time staff, 27 registered volunteers and another 50 informal volunteers – and a herd of longhorn cattle! For more info on projects, publications and volunteering, call the above number.

Government & Organisations

Bolton Wildlife Project
125 Blackburn Road,
Bolton BL1 8HF
Tel: 01204 361 847
Fax: 01204 397 800
Web: www.bwp.org.uk
Open: Mon-Fri 9am-5pm
▶ Regional office for conservation within Greater Manchester. Specialises in providing advice in habitat creation and management within urban areas as well as organising school and community projects. Manages five nature reserves in the region.

British Trust for Conservation Volunteers (BTCV North West)
6 Oakham Court, Avenham Lane,
Preston PR1 3XP
Tel: 01772 204 647
Fax: 01772 257 106
Email: lancashire@btcv.org.uk
Web: www.btcv.org.uk
Open: Mon-Fri 9am-5pm
▶ Regional office for the country's largest charity devoted to practical conservation work. Operated by directing an enthusiastic volunteer labour force towards improving the local environment. Activities include hedgelaying, pond renovation, footpath construction, woodland management, to name but a few. Weekend and week-long Natural Break working holidays and a training course programme available. Free transport and training on all projects which are run by experienced leaders. Call for details of local projects.

British Trust for Conservation Volunteers (BTCV South Manchester)
24 Seymour Grove, Old Trafford,
Manchester M16 0LH
Tel: 0161 872 7640
Fax: 0161 877 8059
Web: www.btcv.org.uk
Open: Mon-Fri 9am-5pm
▶ Manchester office for the country's largest charity devoted to practical conservation work. BTCV organise conservation projects in and around Greater Manchester providing opportunities for volunteers to participate. Activities include hedge laying, pond renovation, footpath construction, woodland management and more. Week-end and week-long working holidays and a traing course programme available on request. Free transport and training on all projects which are run by experienced leaders. Call for details of local projects.

BTCV
36 St Mary's Street,
Wallingford OX10 0EU
Tel: 01491 821 600
Fax: 01491 839 646
Email: information@btcv.org.uk
Web: www.btcv.org
Open: Mon-Fri 9am-5pm
▶ BTCV is the UK's largest practical conservation charity and each year helps around 13,000 people to take practical action to improve the environment. A network of over 150 local offices in the UK organises a wide range of environmental projects and training. BTCV organises around 500 conservation holidays a year both in the UK and worldwide. From turtle monitoring in Thailand and footpath repair work in Iceland, to dry stone walling in Cumbria and hedge laying in Sussex, there is something to suit all tastes. Members of the public can support BTCV either through volunteering or through an annual subscription. In return they will receive the BTCV magazine *Conserver* and will have access to special offers and services.

CEI Associates Ltd
Progress Centre,
Charlton Place, Ardwick Green,
Manchester M12 6HS
Tel: 0161 274 4911
Fax: 0161 274 4911
Email: cei@cei-associates.org
▶ Concerned with the wise management, development, public understanding and enjoyment of places with natural and historic significance. Its prime activities are consultancy and training in the field of interpretation and visitor management. Main clients are national and regional non-departmental public bodies concerned with the historical and natural environment, local authorities, national parks and NGOs (including wildlife trusts).

Cheshire Wildlife Trust
Grebe House, Reaseheath,
Nantwich CW5 6DG
Tel: 01270 610 180
Fax: 01270 610 430
Email: cheshirewt@cix.co.uk
▶ The trust works to promote and protect wildlife, involve the community in environmental initiatives and offer advice, education and training. Organises community recycling and food growing projects and practical conservation and habitat management with volunteers, trainees and schools. Undertakes ecological survey work, monitors planning applications that affect wildlife and offers access to data information on environmental issues and education.

Coastnet
School of Conservation Sciences,
Bournemouth University,
Talbot Campus, Poole BH12 5BB
Tel: 01202 595 178
Fax: 01202 595 255
Email: coastnet@bournemouth.ac.uk
▶ Networking and membership organisation for those interested in coastal management. Organises training events and seminars on issues relevant to coastal interest groups. Publishes a coastal directory of contacts in the UK and a quarterly bulletin for members.

Conservation Foundation, The
1 Kensington Gore,
London SW7 2AR
Tel: 020 7591 3111
Fax: 020 7591 3110
Email: conservef@gn.apc.org
Web: www.conservationfoundation.co.uk
▶ Charity initiating and managing conservation projects around the world. Launched in 1982, the Foundation creates and manages a wide range of programmes and initiatives covering all environmental interests including award schemes, special events, publications and information services. Current projects include the Henry Ford European Conservation Awards and Grants, Parish Plumps, Wessex Watermarks, the David Bellamy Conservation Awards for Holiday Parks, and the Native Elm Programme.

Council for National Parks
246 Lavender Hill, London SW11 1LJ
Tel: 020 7924 4077
Fax: 020 7924 5761
Email: info@cnp.org.uk
Web: www.cnp.org.uk
▶ National charity working to protect and enhance the National Parks of England and Wales, and areas that meet National Park status and promote understanding and quiet enjoyment for the benefit off all.

Council for the Protection of Rural England (CPRE)
Warwick House,
25 Buckingham Palace Road,
London SW1V 0PP
Tel: 020 7976 6433
Fax: 020 7976 6373
Email: cpre@gn.apc.org
Web: www.greenchannel.com/cpre
▶ National charity which helps people to protect their local countryside where there is threat to enhance it where there is opportunity and to keep it beautiful, productive and enjoyable for everyone.

Council for the Protection of Rural England (CPRE) Cheshire
Victoria Building,
Lewin Street, CW10 9AT
Tel: 01606 835 046
Fax: 01606 835 046
Email: cpre@cheshirem.freeserve.co.uk
Open: Mon-Fri 9am-5pm
▶ CPRE county branch, covering the whole of the historic county of Cheshire. As a county branch, CPRE Middlewich seeks to influence planning and development of local authorities and private developers in a similar direction (see below for CPRE Head Office for the North West listing).

Council for the Protection of Rural England (CPRE) North West
Derby Wing, Worden Hall,
Worden Park, Leyland PR5 2DJ
Tel: 01524 845 617
Fax: 0870 284 6649
Email: cprenw@clara.net

▶ Head Office for the North West of the CPRE, a registered charity concerned with the protection of the rural environment. Campaigns inside and outside Parliament in the cause of rural conservation. CPRE County branches seek to influence the planning and development of local authorities and private developers.

Countryside Trust
John Dower House, Crescent Place, Cheltenham GL50 3RA
Tel: 01242 533 338
Fax: 01242 584270
Email:
rachel.chitty@countryside.gov.uk
▶ Small charity, willing to distribute grants of up to £5,000 for fundraising events where the money raised will help towards costs of enhancing the English countryside, encouraging landscape enhancement through community action.

Cumbria Wildlife Trust
Brockhole, Windermere LA23 1LJ
Tel: 015394 48280
Fax: 015394 48281
Email: cumbriawt@cix.co.uk
▶ The trust works to promote and protect wildlife, involve the community in environmental initiatives and offer advice, education and training. Organises community recycling and food growing projects and practical conservation and habitat management with volunteers, trainees and schools. Undertakes ecological survey work, monitors planning applications that affect wildlife and offers access to data information on environmental issues and education.

Earth Love Fund
9 Standingford House, Cave Street, Oxford OX4 1BA
Tel: 01865 200 208
Email: earthlove@gn.apc.org
Web: www.earthlovefund.com
▶ Earth Love Fund raises funds and awareness to support environmental conservation projects in tropical rainforests and endangered forests worldwide. Through this work, ELF also helps to empower and support indigenous communities, aiding their sustainable development and traditional ways of life. Founded by three individuals from the music industry in 1989, ELF has raised funds through the arts for over 120 projects worldwide, in 1996 winning a UN Global 500 Award for its outstanding practical achievements in the protection and improvement of the environment. ELF runs the Artists for the Environment programme, a nationwide awareness-raising scheme under which groups are awarded small start-up grants for arts events inspired by the relationship between people and forests. Details of how to take part in AFTE 2001 are available from the above address; the deadline for project applications is December.

English Nature
Ormond House,
26-27 Boswell Street,
London WC2 3JZ
Tel: 01733 455 101 (Head Office)
Fax: 020 7404 3369
Email:
enquiries@english-nature.org.uk
Web: www.english-nature.org.uk
▶ The government's advisor on nature conservation in England, responsible for the management of over 180 Nature Reserves and a number of Sites of Special Scientific Interest in the UK.

English Nature (North West)
Pier House, Wallgate,
Wigan WN3 4AL
Tel: 01942 820 342
Fax: 01942 820 364
Email:
northwest@english-nature.org.uk
Open: Mon-Fri 9am-5pm
▶ The North West team of English Nature is working with local people, local authorities, landowners and other organisations to incorporate nature conservation into their activities and provides help, advice and financial support to landowners and managers for managing and enhancing important sites. Also provides advice on protected species in the countryside. Believes that enhancing biodiversity and promoting its value for the future of the North West and the quality of life is essential. Call for more information and a list of publications.

Forests Forever
4th Floor, Clareville House, 26/27 Oxendon Street, London SW1Y 4EL
Tel: 020 7839 1891
Fax: 020 7839 659494
Email:
gbruford@forestsforever.org.uk
Web: www.forestsforever.org.uk
▶ Represents the environmetal views of timber and wood using industries in the UK on issues affecting trading. Aim to secure timber's future as an environmentally desirable building and manufacturing material, and help promote members and their trade.

Friends of the Earth (FoE)
26-28 Underwood Street,
London N1 7JQ
Tel: 020 7490 1555
Fax: 020 7490 0881
Email: info@foe.co.uk
Web: www.foe.co.uk
Open: Mon-Fri 9am-6pm
▶ One of the UK's leading environmental charities, researching, publishing and providing information on a wide range of local, national and international issues. Actively campaigns on environmental issues including pollution and waste, genetically modified food, energy, transport and habitats. FOE receives over 90% of its income from individual donations. Call for information or a free list of publications.

Friends of the Earth (Manchester)
6 Mount Street, Manchester M2 5NS
Tel: 0161 834 8221
Fax: 0161 834 8187
Email: info@mcrfoe.dabsol.co.uk
▶ Local FoE group campaigning on a wide range of local and national environmental issues including waste, transport, wildlife conservation, global warming and energy. For further info or details of membership, publications and meetings, call the above number.

Friends of the Earth – North West
60 Duke Street, Liverpool L1 SAA
Tel: 0151 707 4328
Fax: 0151 707 4329
▶ Local branch of the national charity.

Green Cross UK
Millennium House,
Kingston University, 21 Eden Street, Kingston-upon-Thames KT1 1BL
Tel: 020 8547 8274
Fax: 020 8547 7789
Email: greencross@kingston.ac.uk
Web: www.bluekey.co.uk/gcuk
▶ Founded by Mikhail Gorbachev in 1993, building on the 1992 Earth Summit in Rio de Janeiro and Agenda 21, Green Cross' mission is to help create a sustainable future by cultivating harmonious relationships bewteen humans and the environment. Focuses on the integration of environmental considerations into disaster prevention, preparedness and response through its Environmental Response Network. Call for further information and information on future conferences.

Greenpeace
Canonbury Villas,
London N1 2PN
Tel: 020 7865 8100
Fax: 020 7865 8200
Email: info@uk.greenpeace.org
Web: www.greenpeace.org.uk
▶ International, independent, environmental pressure group acting against abuse to the natural world. Current campaigns include: climate change, renewable energy, genetic engineering and threats to marine wildlife. Runs a network of local campaigning groups. Call to join.

Greenpeace (Manchester)
c/o One World Centre,
6 Mount Street,
Manchester M2 5NS
Tel: 0161 494 2163
Email:
gpeace@mcrgroups.fsnet.co.uk
Web: www.greenpeace.org.uk
▶ Local campaign and fundraising group working to further the aims of Greenpeace UK. Current campaigns include genetic engineering, climate change and the promotion of renewable energy sources. Operates as several groups throughout Greater Manchester; Manchester, Eccles/ Salford, Stockport and Oldham, each group holding their own regular meetings. Call for further details.

Government & Organisations

Industry Nature Conservation Association
1 Belasis Court, Belasis Hall Technology Park, Billingham TS23 4AZ
Tel: 01642 370319
Fax: 01642 370288
Email: plover@inca.uk.com
▶ Organisation with a broad membership including industry, local authorities, regulators and conservation bodies. Works with industry to promote the management of industrial land for nature conservation and to help balance industrial development needs with conservation.

Lancashire Wildlife Trust
125 Blackburn Road, Bolton BL1 8HF
Tel: 01204 361 847
Fax: 01204 397 800
Email: lancswtbolton@cix.co.uk
▶ The Trust works to promote and protect wildlife, involve the community in environmental initiatives, offering advice, education and training. Organises community recycling, food growing projects, practical conservation and habitat management with volunteers, trainees and schools. Undertakes ecological survey work, monitors planning applications that affect wildlife and offers access to data information on environmental issues and education.

Learning Through Landscapes
3rd Floor, Southside Offices, The Law Courts, Winchester SO23 9DL
Tel: 01962 846258
Fax: 01962 869099
Email: schoolgrounds-uk@ltl.org.uk
Web: www.ltl.org.uk
▶ National charity helping schools improve their grounds for the benefit of children. Research has demonstrated that school grounds across the UK are significantly undervalued as a resource and for having a profound influence on pupils' attitude and behaviour. LTL helps by: providing info and advice on all aspects of school grounds, organising training events, carrying out research into best practice, lobbying at a local and national government level, and promoting campaigns and special events linked to school grounds.

Marine Conservation Society
9 Gloucester Road, Ross-on-Wye HR9 5BU
Tel: 01989 566 017
Fax: 01989 567 815
Email: mcsuk@mcsmail.com
Web: www.mcsuk.
▶ The only UK charity devoted solely to protecting the marine environment for wildlife and for the appreciation of future generations. Recently launched the 'Adopt a Beach Project' (for more information on this call 01989 762 064). Local group meets regularly. Non-members welcome.

Mersey Basin Trust
28th Floor Sunley Tower, Manchester M1 4BT
Tel: 0161 228 6924
Fax: 0161 228 3391
Email: trust@merseybasin.org.uk
Web: www.merseybasin.org.uk
Open: Mon-Fri 9am-5pm
▶ Sustainable development initiative launched in 1985 with aims to improve water quality so that all streams and rivers can support fish, to stimulate economic regeneration alongside water courses, and to encourage all those living and working in the Mersey Basin area to value and cherish their watercourses. Free membership to organisations, schools and groups in the area, stretching from Pendle to Crew and Nantwich, and from Wirral to High Peak. Membership includes information, advice, education resources, funding and newsletter. Call for more information.

National Society for Clean Air and Environmental Protection
44 Grand Parade, Brighton BN2 2QA
Tel: 01273 878 770
Fax: 01273 606 626
Email: admin@nsca.org.uk & info@nsca.org.uk
Web: www.nsca.org.uk
▶ Non-governmental, non-political organisation and charity. Aims to secure environmental improvement by promoting clean air through the reduction of air, water and land pollution.

National Urban Forestry Unit
The Science Park, Stafford Road, Wolverhampton WV10 9RT
Tel: 01902 828 600
Fax: 01902 828 700
Email: info@nufu.org.uk
Web: www.nufu.org.uk
▶ Established in 1995, the National Urban Forestry Unit is a charitable company with central government backing to promote and demonstrate best practice in urban and community forestry. It encourages planting of more new woodland in towns and better care of existing urban trees. The NUFU works in partnership with a range of national and regional organisations in the UK and is involved in a wide variety of activities, including training, advisory work, practical demonstration projects, conferences and publications.

North Western Naturalists' Union
c/o School of Biological Sciences, 3-614 Stopford Building, University of Manchester, Manchester M13 9PL
▶ A federation of local natural history students and individual members whose objectives are to promote and further an interest in natural history in the North West of England.

Pesticide Action Network UK
Eurolink Centre, 49 Effra Road, London SW2 1BZ
Tel: 020 7274 8895
Fax: 020 7274 9084
Email: admin@pan-uk.org
Web: www.pan-uk.org
▶ Promotes healthy food, agriculture and a sustainable, safe environment to provide food and meet public health needs without dependence on toxic chemicals. Works for the elimination of pesticide hazards and promotes policies and practices which minimise the exposure of people and communities to pesticides. Works nationally and internationally. Runs an online Pesticide Information Service which includes Press Releases and campaign info. If you wish to sign up you can do so from their home page.

Powerful Information
21 Church Street, Loughton, Milton Keynes MK5 8AS
Tel: 01908 666275
Fax: 01908 666275
Email: powerinfo@gn.apc.org
Web: www.gn.apc.org/powerful-information
▶ Independent, non-profit group supporting local initiatives concerned with environmental conservation and sustainable development in low and middle-income countries, notably in Eastern Europe and West Africa. Work almost exclusively with community-based NGOs (Non-Governmental Organisations) and key institutions involved in environmental protection, education, research or regulation. Aim to complement local knowledge and expertise, and increase the effectiveness with which essential information and know-how is accessed, disseminated and applied.

Rainforest Foundation
Suite A5, City Cloisters, 188-196 Old Street, London EC1V 9FR
Tel: 020 7251 6345
Fax: 020 7251 4969
Email: rainforestuk@gn.apc.org
Web: www.rainforestfoundationuk.org
▶ Supporters of projects working with indigenous communities of the tropical rainforests to protect their environment and human rights. Current projects in Venezuela, Cameroon, Guyana, Peru and Madagascar.

Save Our World
14 Richborne Terrace, Lambeth, London SW8 1AU
Tel: 020 7640 0492
Fax: 020 7793 9212
Email: s-our-w@cwcan.net
Web: www.save-our-world.org
▶ Exists to help protect and sustain the natural world by increasing awareness and caring, and inspiring and empowering people to change attitudes, habits and lifestyles, personally, locally, nationally, globally and spiritually – aims are achieved through campaigning, lobbying, networking, organising 'Save our World Festivals' in local areas, inviting to anyone around the

world to do likewise in his/her own area on the same date at midsummer (in the Northern Hemisphere).

Scientific Exploration Society
Expedition Base, Motcombe,
Shaftsbury, Dorset SP7 9PB
Tel: 01747 854 898
Fax: 01747 851 351
Email: base@ses-explore.org
Web: www.ses-explore.org
Open: Mon-Fri 9am-5pm
▶ The Scientific Exploration Society is a leading organisation in the field of scientific exploration and endeavour. The society organises expeditions for all ages which usually run for 2-4 weeks in remote regions of the world. Teams of 10-15 people tackle a variety of tasks which include scientific research, medical aid, conservation, environmental and community work. For more details of how to join an expedition please contact Melissa Dice at the above address or email.

Soundwood
c/o Flora & Fauna International,
Great Eastern House, Tenison Road,
Cambridge CB1 2DT
Tel: 01223 571 000
Fax: 01223 461 481
Email: info@fauna/flora.org
▶ Campaign group concerned with the use of threatened timber species in musical instruments. Works in co-operation with the music business and encourages the use of certified, sustainable timbers that are produced in partnership with local communities. Free annual leaflet available as well as *The Good Bulb Guide* and *The Soundwood Guide To The Guitar* (£3 including p&p).

Tree Aid
28 Hobbs Lane, Bristol BS1 5ED
Tel: 0117 934 9442
Fax: 0117 934 9592
Email: treeaid@compuserve.com
▶ Do you value trees for their beauty? In the UK we have that luxury but, in Africa, trees mean life for millions of families. Rapid deforestation deprives them of survival items like fuelwood for cooking and heating; wood for building homes; fruits, nuts and berries for food and berries for food and medicines. Loss of trees leads to soil erosion, thus threatening food supplies. You can help by joining Tree Aid to fight against environmental degradation and poverty.

Tree Council, The
51 Catherine Place,
London SW1E 6DY
Tel: 020 7828 9928
Fax: 020 7828 9060
Web: www.treecouncil.org.uk
▶ Aims to improve the environment in town and country by promoting the planting and conservation of trees and woods throughout the UK; to disseminate knowledge about trees and their management; to act as a forum for organisations concerned with trees; to identify national problems; and to provide initiatives for co-operation.

Wilderness Trust
The Oast House, Hankham,
Pevensey BN24 5AP
Tel: 01323 461 730
Fax: 01323 761 913
Email: chris@wilderness-trust.org
Web: www.wilderness-trust.org
Open: Mon-Fri 9am-5pm
▶ The Trust is a membership organisation of friends who share the same objectives and conservation ideas and welcomes new members at all times. Helps organise and introduce members to programmes of minimum impact, wilderness experience journeys. These are currently arranged in South Africa at the Wilderness Leadership School but there are limited opportunities available elsewhere. Supports campaigns to prevent wilderness areas that are threatened by insensitive or uncaring development being destroyed and aims to remain the benchmark for high ethical standards in the use of wilderness areas and conservation. Links with youth development and conservation organisation are being strengthened continuously.

Wildfowl & Wetlands Trust – Head Office
Slimbridge Wildfowl & Wetlands
Centre, Slimbridge GL2 7BT
Tel: 01453 890 333
Fax: 01453 890 827
Email: communications@wwt.org.uk
Web: www.wwt.org.uk
Open: Mon-Fri 9.30am-5.30pm
(4.30pm in Winter)
▶ Registered UK wildlife conservation charity in the UK with over 80,000 members. Aims to successfully promote the conservation of wetlands and their biodiversity, which are vitally important for the maintenance and quality of life. Focuses on wetland birds, waterfowl and their habitats, specifically by undertaking and encouraging direct conservation action on behalf of threatened wetland birds worldwide. Also operates visitor centres. The nine centres provide safe refuge for wetland birds and house outstanding bird collections for education and to convince the public of the importance of wetland biodiversity. Membership contributes directly to the conservation work currently being undertaken, and members receive free access to WWT centres and a quarterly magazine. Volunteers warmly welcomed.

Wildfowl & Wetlands Trust – WWT Martin Mere
Burscough,
Ormskirk L40 0TA
Tel: 01704 895 181
Email: communications@wwt.org.uk
▶ Regional office of the national charity – see separate listing.

Wildlife and Countryside Link
89 Albert Embankment,
London SE1 7TP
Tel: 020 7820 8600
Fax: 020 7820 8620
Email: enquiry@wcl.org.uk
Web: www.wcl.org.uk
▶ Wildlife and Countryside Link (WCL) is a coalition of the UK's major non-governmental organisations concerned with the protection and conservation of wildlife and the countryside. WCL acts as a forum to allow its members to develop their views on national and international issues affecting wildlife and the countryside, and to work together to influence UK policy. WCL is not a representative body and does not issue statements on its own behalf.

Wildlife Trust for Lancashire, Manchester and North Merseyside
Cuerden Park Wildlife Centre,
Shady Lane, Bamber Bridge,
Preston PR5 6AU
Tel: 01772 324 129
Fax: 01772 628 849
Email: rwebb@lancswt.cix.co.uk
Web: www.wildlifetrust.org.uk/lancashire
▶ Cares for 34 Nature Reserves, covering over 2,000 acres – woodlands, meadows, uplands and wetlands. Campaigns for wildlife and the environment – helping to protect threatened places and rare species. Encourages people to enjoy the natural world with walks, talks and events, both in town and country. Works with schools and community groups to support local action for the environment. Promotes ways for volunteers to help with practical projects and local activities throughout the region.

Wildlife Trusts – UK Operations Centre
The Kiln, Waterside,
Mather Road, Newark NG24 1WT
Tel: 01636 677 711
Fax: 01522 511 616
Email: general@wildlife-trusts.cix.co.uk
Web: www.wildlifetrusts.org.uk
Open: Mon-Fri 9am-5pm
▶ Network of local wildlife charities and groups concerned with all aspects of wildlife conservation which alerts the public and government to threats to wildlife and cares for nearly two thousand nature reserves. Call for membership details and a list of reserves.

Woodland Trust
Autumn Park,
Grantham NG31 6LL
Tel: 01476 581 111;
Freephone 0800 026 9650
Fax: 01476 590 808
▶ The UK's leading charity dedicated solely to the protection of our native woodland heritage. Creates more new native woodland than anyone else in the UK.

Government & Organisations

Built Environment

Association for Industrial Archeology
School of Archaeology,
University Road, Leicester University,
Leicester LE1 7RH
Tel: 0116 252 5337
Fax: 0116 252 5005
Email: aia@le.ac.uk
Web:
www.industrial-archaeology.org.uk
▶ Promotes the study, preservation and presentation of Britain's industrial past, bringing together people who research, record, preserve and present the variety of industrial heritage. The AIA is a valuable forum for amateur groups and professional bodies working in the field. Produces a bi-annual publication and quarterly newsletter, as well as holding an annual conference, field trips and awards.

Association of Building Engineers
Lutyens House,
Billing Brook Road, Weston Favell,
Northampton NN3 8NW
Tel: 01604 404 121
Fax: 01204 784 220
Email:
building.engineers@abe.org.uk
Web: www.abe.org.uk
▶ Professional body for those specialising in the technology of building. Founded in 1925, they provide the prime qualification of Building Engineer, a title that exactly reflects the professional expertise of members and is more readily understood in the EU and beyond than the title 'building surveyor'. Members in the UK and overseas. It is free from constitutional restraints, independent and recognised nationally and internationally for its qualification by both private and public sectors and the construction industry.

Association of Gardens Trusts
70 Cowcross Street,
London EC1M 6EJ
Tel: 020 7251 2610
Fax: 020 7251 2610
Email: gardenstrusts@btinternet.com
Web: www.gardenstrusts.co.uk
Open: Tues 10.30am-5.30pm

▶ National organisation representing the rapidly-growing County Gardens Trusts, which are actively engaged in researching, documenting and caring for the heritage of designed landscapes. Its aims are to provide support for the Trusts and to promote a proper understanding of the importance of parks and gardens at a local and national level. To these ends, the AGT fosters liaison between member Trusts, encouraging the sharing of information, resources, training and experience and organising seminars, visits, meetings and publications. Also communicates with local and national government, and other relevant agencies, to encourage appropriate historic landscape conservation and restoration strategies.

Aviation Environment Federation
5 High Timber Street,
London EC4V 3NS
Tel: 020 7329 8159
Fax: 020 7329 8160
Email: info@aef.org.uk
Web: www.aef.org.uk
Open: Mon-Fri 9am-5pm
▶ The only organisation in the UK concerned principally with environmental effects of air travel and airports.

British Association of Landscape Industries
Landscape House, Stoneleigh Park,
Near Kenilworth CV8 2LG
Tel: 02476 690 333
Fax: 02476 670 077
Email: admin.assistant@bali.co.uk
▶ National body representing Landscape Contractors in the UK. Founder member of the Joint Council for Landscape Industries which liaises with the Government on behalf of the Landscape Industry. Aims to improve and maintain the standing of the landscape industry through the strength of corporate representation. To foster greater awareness among professional bodies, public authorities and the public, by improved promotion of the industry.

British Plastics Federation
6 Bath Place, Rivington Street,
London EC2A 3JE

Tel: 020 7457 5000
Fax: 020 7457 5045
Email: bpf@bpf.co.uk
Web: www.bpf.co.uk
▶ The BPF is the principal trade association responsible for the UK plastics industry.

Centre for Alternative Technology (CAT)
Machynlleth SY20 9AZ
Tel: 01654 702 400
Fax: 01654 702 782
Email: steven.jones@cat.org.uk
Web: www.cat.org.uk
▶ Concerned with the search for globally sustainable technologies and ways of life. CAT aims to inspire people to use resources wisely and live in harmony with nature. The display and education centre, researcher and information provider offer practical ideas and information on environmentally sound technologies. An eight acre visitor centre has working displays of wind, water and solar power, low energy building, organic growing and natural sewage systems. Also offers residential courses, facilities for school groups, a 'green' shop and mail order service, free information and a professional consultancy service. Also runs the Alternative Technology Association which publishes *Clean Slate* magazine, a practical journal of sustainable living.

Churches Conservation Trust
89 Fleet Street, London EC4Y 1DH
Tel: 020 7936 2285
Fax: 020 7936 2284
▶ Charity set up in 1969 by Parliament and the Church of England to care for churches of historical, architectural or archaeological importance which are no longer needed for regular worship. The Trust currently cares for over 320 churches in England, and warmly welcomes visitors to them. Contact for further information about the work of the Trust and for churches in your area.

Civic Trust
17 Carlton House Terrace,
London SW1Y 5AW
Tel: 020 7930 0914
Fax: 020 7321 0180

Email: pired@civictrust.org.uk
Web: www.civictrust.org.uk
▶ Charity aiming to create, enhance and sustain the quality of the urban environment. The library is open to visitors by appointment.

Council for British Archaeology
Bowes Morrell House,
111 Walmgate, York YO1 9WA
Tel: 01904 671 417
Fax: 01904 671 384
Email: info@britarch.ac.uk
Web: www.britarch.ac.uk
▶ The CBA is an educational charity which works to promote the study and safeguarding of Britain's historic environment, to provide a forum for archaeological opinion, and to improve public interest in, and knowledge of, Britain's past. Founded in 1944, CBA is: the key independent voice promoting conservation of the whole historic environment; the principal non-governmental organisation for involving young people in archaeology; the foremost independent advocate for life-long learning in archaeology; the main promoter of voluntary involvement in archaeology; the leading provider of digital and other information services for archaeology; the key publisher and disseminator of information to a variety of audiences; a membership-based organisation serving a growing number of individuals and organisations; and the statutory consultee for proposals affecting listed buildings in England and Wales. CBA publishes a bi-monthly magazine *British Archaeology*, sent free to all members and available on subscription.

English Heritage
PO Box 569, Swindon SN2 2GZ
Tel: 01793 414 910
Fax: 01793 414 926
Web: www.english-heritage.org.uk
▶ English Heritage are the government's advisors on listed buildings and the historic environment. Membership entitles visits to many historic properties free of charge and also free or reduced entry to hundreds of events and summer concerts. Also reduced or free admission

to its sister organisation in Scotland, Wales and the Isle of Man. English Heritage also has a remit for the listing of buildings, for archaeology, educational services and publishes a range of books and technical leaflets, and also provides grant aid for historic buildings. A quarterly magazine *Heritage Today* is sent to members.

English Partnerships
16-18 Old Queen Street,
London SW1H 9HP
Tel: 020 7976 3231
▶ Established by the Leasehold Reform, Housing and Urban Development Act 1993 and launched in 1993, English Partnerships (EP) focuses on the 'promotion of the regeneration of areas through the reclamation, development or redevelopment of land and buildings.' Since its launch, EP has helped create or safeguard an estimated 90,000 jobs and reclaimed almost 6,000 hectares of derelict land.

Heritage Education Trust
Boughton Trust, Kettering, NN14 1BJ
Tel: 01536 515 731
Fax: 01536 417 255
Web: www.heritageontheweb.co.uk/HET
▶ Promoting and recognising quality education concerning historic properties through the Sandford Award for Heritage Education. Since 1982, the Trust has recognised and promoted the excellence of educational services offered in historic houses, castles, gardens, museums and galleries, through the granting of Sandford Awards. Any historic property, artefact and historic landscape is eligible. The Award should be regarded as an independently judged quality assured assessment of heritage education in historic properties, and is recognised by the Historic Houses Association and the National Trust.

Heritage Railway Association
7 Robert Close, Potters Bar EN6 2DX
Tel: 01707 643 568
Fax: 01707 643 568
Web: ukhrail.uel.ac.uk
▶ The Heritage Railway Association represents the interests of heritage/tourist railways, railway museums, railway centres and railway preservation societies throughout the UK. HRA negotiates with government and other official bodies and provides a wide range of services including advice on technical and legal subjects. It produces various publications and holds meetings and seminars on relevant topics. It also undertakes various marketing and publicity projects to promote members' activities including the production of the *Steam Guide*. The guide can be obtained by sending an SAE to the address above.

Landlife
National Wildflower Centre,
Court Hey Park, Liverpool L16 3NA
Tel: 0151 737 1819
Fax: 0151 737 1820
Email: info@landlife.org.uk
Web: www.landlife.org.uk
Open: Mon-Fri 9am-5pm
▶ Charity taking action for a better environment by creating new opportunities for wildlife and encouraging people to enjoy them. Specialises in growing and providing seeds and plants of native origin and known provenance to the trade and public through its trading arm Landlife Wildflowers. Call for catalogue. Developing the National Wildflower Centre on the outskirts of Liverpool, opening in Autumn 2000. Publishes a regular newsletter and also offers a consultancy service.

Landmark Trust
Shottesbrooke, Maidenhead SL6 3SW
Tel: 01628 825 920
Fax: 01628 825 417
Web: www.landmarktrust.co.uk
▶ Independent preservation charity that rescues and restores architecturally and historic buildings at risk, giving them a future and renewed life by letting them for self-catering holidays. Full details of all 170 Landmark Trust buildings are available in the *Landmark Handbook*, price £9.50 inc p&p. Order over the telephone on 01628 825 925 or online. The Trust also manages Lundy, an island 11 miles off the North Devon coast famous for its wildlife and natural beauty (www.lundyisland.co.uk). In May 2000 the Landmark Appeal was launched which aims to raise £10 million over the next 2 years to rescue significant historic buildings in distress.

Landscape Institute, The
6-8 Barnard Mews,
London SW11 1QU
Tel: 020 7350 5200
Fax: 020 7350 5201
Email: mail@l-i.org.uk
Web: www.l-i.org.uk
▶ Chartered professional body for landscape architects in the UK, comprising landscape designers, planners, managers and scientists. Landscape architects work on all types of external space, large and small, urban and rural, and make a vital contribution to developing the modern environment in towns, cities and the countryside. Founded in 1929, the Institue sets out to promote the highest standards of education and professional service in the application of the arts and sciences of landscape architecture. Currently has 4400 members working in both the private and public sectors, on all types of external space. The professional journal, *Landscape Design*, is published monthly.

Manchester Wildlife
c/o 82 Crantock Drive,
Heald Green, Cheadle SK8 3HA
Tel: 0161 437 7040
▶ Urban wildlife group working to protect wildlife and habitats. The group has been involved in the monitoring of planning applications to help reduce the negative impact of development on wildlife, surveying open spaces to assess wildlife and in creating new wildlife sites. The group is involved in the LA21 process in Greater Manchester and is a good source of education and information.

Millennium Greens National Project Team
Countryside Agency,
1st Floor Vincent House, Tindal Bridge, 92-93 Edward Street, Birmingham B1 2RA
Tel: 0121 233 9399
Fax: 0121 233 9286
Web: www.countryside.gov.uk
▶ The Countryside Agency (see separate listing) has received funding from the Millennium Commission to go towards giving 250 communities in England their own open, green public space, known as a Millennium Green, by the year 2000. Closed for new applications but contact the above address for any other info.

National Trust, The
36 Queen Anne's Gate,
London SW1H 9AS
Tel: 020 7222 9251
Fax: 020 7222 5097
Email: enquiries@ntrust.org.uk
Web: www.nationaltrust.org.uk
Open: Mon-Fri 9.30am-5.30pm
▶ One of the Europe's leading conservation charities, supported by 2.5 million subscribing members and 35,000 volunteers. With over 250 beautiful and historic places to visit throughout England, Wales and Northern Ireland, plus outstanding countryside and coastline in its care, there is likely to be a National Trust property near you to enjoy.

National Trust – North West Office
The Hollens, Grassmere, LA22 9QZ
Tel: 015394 35599
Fax: 015394 35353
Web: www.nationaltrust.org.uk
▶ Regional office of the National Trust.

Rescue, The British Archaeological Trust
15a Bull Plain, Hertford SG14 1DX
Tel: 01992 553377
Fax: 01992 553377
Email: rescue@rescue-archaeology
Web: www.rescue-archaeology.freeserve.co.uk
▶ Independent body and registered charity which promotes archaeology in Britain, specifically aiming to raise public awareness and to encourage better funding and legislation to preserve or record threatened archaeological sites. Run by a comitee elected from the open membership. 'Rescue News' is published thrice yearly; other occasional publications

Government & Organisations

relate to the practice of archaeology. Meetings and conferences on topical subjects are also organised.

Room, the National Council for Housing and Planning
14 Old Street, London EC1V 9BH
Tel: 020 7251 2363
Fax: 020 7608 2830
▶ Registered educational charity working for better housing, planning and regeneration. It is unique in having member organisations from across the spectrum of housing, planning and regeneration who are in a position to introduce and manage change for the better, such as local government, housing associations and other Registered Social Landlords, partnership agencies and builders, specialist consultants, and academics, and in encompassing both practitioners and politicians and, increasingly, community groups. It has a strong regional base, with 12 regions in England and Wales, each having its own programme of events, and a sister organisation in Scotland. It puts forward a well-considered and nonpartisan view on issues at national, regional and local levels, through campaigning and lobbying; undertaking research; publishing reports; running conferences and seminars; publishing its own bi-monthly journal *Axis*; speaking at events; and running an awards scheme.

Sale and Altrincham Conservation Volunteers
Flat 9, 180/2 Withington Road,
Whalley Range,
Manchester M16 8WA
Tel: 0161 860 6910
▶ Meet regularly on Sundays for a variety of voluntary conservation tasks in roughly a 10 mile radius of Sale and Altrincham. Work includes fencing, tree-planting and sometimes thinning, making and repairing of footpaths and steps, clearing and improving ponds for wildlife as well as traditional rural skills such as coppicing and hedge-laying. There is no members fee although voluntary donations are welcome. Full instruction, tools, insurance and transport to work site are provided.

Society for the Protection of Ancient Buildings
37 Spital Square, London E1 6DY
Tel: 020 7377 1644
Fax: 020 7247 5296
Email: info@spab.org.uk
Web: www.spab.org.uk
Open: Mon-Fri 9am-5.30pm
▶ William Morris founded the SPAB in 1877 to protect ancient buildings from modern zeal. Today it runs courses on the repair of old buildings, ranging from one day to nine months, that cater for the needs of homeowners, professionals and craftsmen. Over 1,000 architects, surveyors, builders and homeowners use its telephone technical advice line with questions about building repairs every year. Publishes pamphlets on subjects such as building with lime and supplies other specialist books. Members receive a magazine and a list of historic buildings that are for sale and in need of repair.

Community & Society

Action with Communities in Rural England (ACRE)
Somerford Court, Somerford Road,
Cirencester GL7 1TA
Tel: 01285 653 477
Fax: 01285 654 537
Email: acre@acre.org.uk
Web: www.acreciro.demon.co.uk
▶ National charity facilitating the development of thriving, diverse and sustainable communities throughout rural England.

ActionAid
Chataway House, Leach Road,
Chard TA20 1FR
Tel: 01460 238 000
Fax: 01460 67191
Email: mail@actionaid.org.uk
▶ Works with children, families and communities to help them alleviate their poverty, provide access to their basic rights and needs to secure lasting improvements in the quality of their lives. ActionAid is non-sectarian and non-political and currently works in 30 countries through Africa, Asia, Latin America and the Caribbean. Call, write or email if you would like to sponsor a child or community projects overseas, to make a donation or campaign for change.

'Are You Doing Your Bit?'
77 Kingsway, London WC2B 6ST
Tel: 0345 868 686
Fax: 020 7242 4202
Email: aydyb@fishburn-hedges.co.uk
Web: www.doingyourbit.co.uk or www.useitagain.org.uk
Open: Mon-Fri 9am-5.30pm
▶ The Government's major publicity campaign helping individuals to protect the environment in their day-to-day lives. It offers advice and information on simple ways to 'Do Your Bit' for the environment in everyday situations – for example, at home, whilst travelling and when shopping – which can also help save you money and improve your health.

Blake Shield B.N.A. Trust
P O Box 5681, Rushden NN10 8ZF
Tel: 01933 314 672
Fax: 01933 314 672
▶ The Blake Shield competition is open to young people between the ages of 7 and 18. There are 3 sections. The Ward Cup 7-11 is open to groups of children with an adult team leader for a natural history/conservation project.

Botanical Society of the British Isles
c/o Department of Botany, Natural History Museum, Cromwell Road, London SW7 5BD
Tel: 020 7942 5002
▶ Learned society of professional and amateur botanists dedicated to the study and conservation of the British and Irish vascular plant and charophyte flora.

British Association for the Advancement of Science
23 Savile Row, London W1S 2EZ
Tel: 0207 973 3078
Fax: 0207 973 3051
Email: sallie.robins@britassoc.org.uk
Web: www.britassoc.org.uk
▶ A scientific society that exists to promote understanding of science, engineering and technology as well as contributing to economic, cultural and social life. You can join the BA and be actively involved in many activities nationwide. Organises National Science Week, and the BA Festival of Science – a week long festival with over 400 top level speakers from all the sciences. Also runs a dynamic nationwide programme of science activities for young people, publishes *Science & Public Affairs* and runs forums for public debate of key scientific issues alongside many other programmes for individuals of all backgrounds, abilities and ages.

British Glass Manufacturers Confederation
Northumberland Road,
Sheffield S10 2UA
Tel: 0114 268 6201
Fax: 0114 268 1073
Email: recycling@britglass.co.uk
Web: www.britglass.co.uk
▶ Confederation for all sectors of the UK glass industry, representing it in dealings with governments, both in the UK and Europe. Provides information and advice on glass recycling, collates bottle bank statistics. Provides educational material, including Key Stage I and II approved CD rom with website and teachers notes.

British Water
1 Queen Annes Gate,
London SW1H 9BT
Tel: 020 7957 4554
Fax: 020 7957 4565
Email: info@britishwater.co.uk
Web: www.britishwater.org
▶ Trade association for the water and wastewater industry.

Campaign Against Depleted Uranium
c/o GM & DCND, One World Centre,
6 Mount Street, Manchester M2 5NS
Tel: 0161 834 8176
Fax: 0161 834 8187
Email: gmdcnd@gn.apc.org
Web: www.cadu.org.uk
Open: Mon-Fri 10am-4pm
▶ Campaign for a ban on depleted uranium weaponry. Works with European and international organisations and produces a briefing pack, leaflets and quarterly newsletter. Has an exhibition available to loan.

Campaign Against the Arms Trade (CAAT)
St Marks Church, Tetlow Lane,
Cheetham Hill, Manchester M8 9HF
Tel: 0161 740 8600
Fax: 0161 740 4181
Email: families@surfaid.org
▶ Broad coalition of groups and individuals committed to following basic objectives of an end to the international arms trade and the UK's role in it as one of the world's leading arms exporters and the conversion of military industry to civil production. Runs a number of campaigns including the International Anti-Arms Trade Week and the Clean Investment Campaign which looks at the military investments of public bodies. Call for more information and details of local activities.

Campaign for Nuclear Disarmament (CND)
162 Holloway Road, London N7 8DQ
Tel: 020 7700 2393
Fax: 020 7700 2357
Email: enquiries@cnduk.org
Web: www.cnduk.org/cnd
Open: Mon-Fri 10am-6pm
▶ High profile and well-known group campaigning to rid the world of nuclear weapons and other weapons of mass destruction and to create genuine security for future generations. Works through lobbying, research, education and direct action to expose nuclear escalation, accidents and pollution and pressures countries towards a global ban on nuclear weapons, technology and fissile materials. Members are encouraged to get involved in lobbying, direct action, media work and in the democratic decision-making structures of CND.

Centre for Human Ecology
12 Roseneath Terrace,
Edinburgh EH9 1JB
Tel: 0131 624 1972
Fax: 0131 624 1973
Email: info@che.ac.uk
Web: www.che.ac.uk
▶ Independent 'green' think-tank and action network, CHE is a charity working for social and ecological justice. A unique organisation, working with community groups on one hand, and in academia on the other – and everywhere in between! CHE is an independent research institute, publishes a newsletter, and runs a MSc course in Human Ecology. The CHE is a leading catalyst and advocate for ecological thinking in Scotland and beyond.

Chartered Institution of Water and Enviromental Management
15 John Street, London WC1N 2EB
Tel: 020 7831 3110
Fax: 020 7405 4967
Email: admin@ciwem.org.uk
Web: www.ciwem.com
▶ A multi-disciplinary professional and examining body for environmentalists, engineers, scientists and other qualified professionals engaged in environmental management and stewardship.

Christian Ecology Link
20 Carlton Road, Harrogate HG2 8DD
Tel: 01423 871 616
Email: info@christian-ecology.org.uk
Web: www.christian-ecology.org.uk
Open: Mon-Fri 7.30am-9pm
▶ A network of Christian people and churches dedicated to 'greening the church' from within. Resources include: an information service for individuals, churches, schools and theological colleges; a journal 'Green Christians', published thrice yearly, free to members; a free newsletter 'Churchlink' for churches and other bodies; topic leaflets, worship suggestions, environmental audit guidelines, etc; and conferences on topical issues. CEL is a national charity open to all denominations. New members are always welcome.

Civic Trust
Gostings Buil, 32-36 Hanover Street,
Liverpool L1 4LN
Tel: 0151 709 1969
Fax: 709 2022
▶ Environmental Action Fund Grants administration.

Clothes Code Campaign
Tel: Clothes Line: 01865 312 456
▶ Promotes codes of conduct for garment workers worldwide. Call the Clothes Line or your local Oxfam office for more information.

Common Ground
PO Box 25309, London NW5 1ZA
Tel: 020 7267 2144
Fax: 020 7267 2144
▶ Emphasises the value of our everyday surroundings and the positive investment people can make in their own localities. Forges links between the arts and the conservation of nature and our cultural landscapes, town and country. Offers ideas, information and inspiration through publications, exhibitions and projects such as field days, parish maps and the campaign for Local Distinctiveness and Confluence.

Conscience – The Peace Tax Campaign
601 Holloway Road,
London N19 4DJ
Tel: 020 7561 1061
Fax: 020 7281 6508
Email: info@conscienceonline.org.uk
Web: www.conscienceonline.org.uk
▶ Campaigns for the legal right for those who are ethically opposed to war to have the military part of their taxes (currently 10%) spent on peace-building initiatives.

Corporate Watch
16b Cherwell Street,
Oxford OX4 2BG
Tel: 01865 791 391
Email: mail@corporatewatch.org
Web: www.corporatewatch.org
▶ Campaign group aiming to end corporate dominance. Provides information to empower those seeking to challenge big business on social, ethical or environmental issues. Undertakes research, publishes Corporate Watch magazine, networks information and hosts conferences and workshops.

Council for Posterity
20 Heber Road, London NW2 6AA
Tel: 020 8208 2853
Fax: 020 8452 6434
Email: rhino@dialpipex.com
Web: www.globalideasbank.org
▶ Launched in 1990, the core group includes Professor Scorer, Brian Aldiss, Lord Young of Dartington, Doris Lessing and Anita Roddick. Aims to: provide legal representation for the interests of future generations; stimulate the development of the Declarationsof the Rights of Posterity; to involve young people through a £1,000 Adopt-a-Planet competition; and to present awards for the best published articles or books about future generations. The Council says that 'Posterity offers you an altruistic aim independent of age, sex, family, creed or nationality; that is, a life with added meaning.'

Countryside Education Trust
Out of Town Centre, Palace Lane,
Beaulieu, Brockenhurst SO42 7YG
Tel: 01590 612 401
Fax: 01590 612 405
Email: mail@cet.org.uk
Open: Mon-Fri 9am-5pm
▶ A registered charity that provides environmental education to all groups – day visits for school groups Key Stages 1-4, A-level and beyond; residential visits for 32-40 pupils plus staff; a wide range of courses and lectures on environmental subjects; holiday activities for children; public farm open days two Sundays per month for all the family. Application is being made for Eco-Centre status. New courses on sustainability and citizenship are being developed.

Earth First!
PO Box 1TA,
Newcastle-upon-Tyne NE99 1TA
Tel: 0797 4791841
Email: actionupdate@gn.apc.org
▶ Contact for details of direct action campaigns.

Ecology Research Group
Science Department,
Canterbury Christ Church College,
North Holmes Road,
Canturbury CT1 1QU
Tel: 01227 767700
Fax: 01227 470442
Email: gbd1@cant.ac.uk
Web: www.cant.ac.uk/depts/acad/science/resweb/scdepres.htm
▶ Undertakes academic research, consultancy and applied research. It comprises a flexible group of postgraduate and postdoctorate biologists with interests in a wide variety of aca-

Government & Organisations

demic disciplines. Welcomes applicants who wish to employ its expertise or to use the Group as a platform for research proposals for funding. Areas of interest are currently water pollution, land reclamation, biological control and raptor research.

Eden Fellowship
c/o 59 Chapel Road,
Ramsgate CT11 0BS
Tel: 01843 589 010
▶ Offers support to Christians who may feel isolated because of their veganism. While supportive to all Christians, the Fellowship itself embraces the Roman Catholic faith and works to promote non-violence, peace and justice issues in the church. They are particularly drawn to Franciscan Spirituality and look to live Christ-centred, vegan lifestyles, with a simplicity befitting disciples of St Francis.

Empty Homes Agency
195-197 Victoria Street,
London SW1E 5NE
Tel: 020 7828 6288
Fax: 020 7828 7006
Email: eha@globalnet.co.uk
Web: www.emptyhomes.com
Open: Mon-Fri 9am-5pm
▶ Launched in 1992, the agency is dedicated to tackling the problem of the 772,300 empty homes in England. EHA gives guidance and assistance on how to start to tackle empty homes and supports community groups, local authorities and others concerned with the problem. The project provides information, contacts and training. Whether your concern is urban dereliction, homelessness or the loss of green fields to new homes, contact the project for further details or visit the website. Community Action on Empty Homes if funded by the National Lottery Charities Board.

Enough Anti-Consumerism Campaign
One World Centre, 6 Mount Street,
Manchester M2 5NS
Tel: 0161 226 6668
Fax: 0161 226 6277 (FAO: enough)
Web: www.enviroweb.org/
enviroissues/enough/
▶ Campaigns against over-consumption. Draws attention to its links with global poverty, environmental destruction, consumerism and its effects on the environment, poor people in the Third World and on contentment and quality of life. Organises and co-ordinates an International No Shop Day in the UK.

Ethical Consumer Research Association
Unit 21, 41 Old Birley Street,
Manchester M15 5RF
Tel: 0161 226 2929
Fax: 0161 226 6277
Email: ethicon@mcr1.poptel.org.uk
Web: www.ethicalconsumer.org
Open: Mon-Fri 11am-6pm
▶ Voluntary organisation which exists to promote universal human rights, environmental sustainability and animal welfare by encouraging a better understanding of the ability of ethical purchasing to address these issues. Publishes the excellent *Ethical Consumer Magazine* which features specialist reports on different products and services such as banks and building societies, carpets and floorcoverings. Call for more information and subscription rates.

Farm and Food Society
4 Willifield Way, London NW11 7XT
Tel: 020 8455 0634
▶ Voluntary group established in 1966 working towards humane, wholesome and fair farming. Part of organic movement dedicated to lifting farming out of its present decline. Publishes lively and informative *Farm and Food News*, covering biotechnology, farm animal welfare, food matters, book reviews etc. Widely consulted on farming and related matters. AGM in London always includes Members' Forum. Any member eligible for election to Commitee.

Farming and Wildlife Advisory Group
National Agricultural Centre,
Stoneleigh, Kenilworth CV8 2RX
Tel: 024 7669 6699
Fax: 024 7669 6760
Email: info@fwag.org.uk
Web: www.fwag.org.uk
▶ Offers on-farm advice to farmers and landowners on the integration of commercial agriculture with the retention and creation of wildlife habitats.

Federation of City Farms and Community Gardens
The Green House, Hereford Street,
Bedminster, Bristol BS3 4NA
Tel: 0117 923 1800
Fax: 0117 923 1900
Email: admin@farmgarden.org.uk
Web: www.farmgarden.org
▶ Promotes and supports sustainable regeneration through community-managed farming and gardening. Each city farm is unique, varying in size, services and facilities offered to the public for recreation and education. To find out more about local City Farms in your area and their activities, send an SAE for a free list of UK City farms (see also the individual city farm listings in Chapter Eight: Travel & Leisure).

Findhorn Foundation Community
Cluny Hill College, Forres,
Moray IV36 0RD
Tel: 01309 673 655
Web: www.findhorn.org
▶ Centre of spiritual service in co-creation with nature, encompassing education and community. Charitable educational trust based at a well-known community in the north of Scotland, working to bring increased recognition of spirit to thousands of visitors from all over the world. Part of an international network of communities and community ventures with links in education, the arts, the spiritual growth movement and environmental organisations.

Free Form Arts Trust
57 Dalston Lane, London E8 2NG
Tel: 020 7249 3394
Fax: 020 7249 8499
Email: contact@freeform.org.uk
Web: www.freeform.org.uk
▶ A non-profit-making arts practice, which pioneers arts projects for urban regeneration to benefit artists, communities and the environment. Delivers art strategies for Local Authorities and developers, provides mentoring for artists in public arts projects and commissions approximately 50 artists annually.

Garden History Society
70 Cowcross Street,
London EC1M 6EJ
Tel: 020 7608 2409
Fax: 020 7490 2974
Email: gardenhistorysociety@
compuserve.com
Web: www.gardenhistorysociety.org
▶ Founded in 1965 to promote the study of the history of gardening, landscape gardening and horticulture in all its aspects. Promotes the protection and conservation of historic parks, gardens and designed landscapes and advises on their restoration.

Genetics Forum, The
94 White Lion Street,
London N1 9PF
Tel: 020 7837 9229
Fax: 020 7837 1141
Email: geneticsforum@gn.apc.org
Web: www.geneticsforum.org.uk
Open: Tues-Thurs 11am-4pm
▶ Founded in 1989, the Forum is the UK's only public interest group exclusively devoted to policy development, campaigns and publications on genetic engineering from a social, ethical and environmental perspective.

Genetix Snowball
6 Mount Street,
Manchester M2 5NS
Tel: 0161 834 0295
Fax: 0161 834 8187
Email: genetixsnowball@onet.co.uk
▶ Campaigns against genetic engineering and the introduction of genetically-modified crops in the UK's farming system.

GeneWatch UK
The Mill House, Manchester Road,
Tideswell, Buxton SK17 8ln
Tel: 01298 871 898
Fax: 01298 872 531
Email: mail@genewatch.org
Web: www.genewatch.org
▶ An independent organisation working to promote environmental, ethical, social, human health and animal welfare considerations in decision making about genetic engineering and other genetic technologies. Believes

that public participation is crucial for robust and effective decision making and that this can only take place in the context of openness, where debate is well informed and proper weight is attached to public concerns and aspirations for the future.

Geological Society
Burlington House, London W1J 0BG
Tel: 020 7434 9944
Fax: 020 7439 8975
Email: enquiries@geolsoc.org.uk
Web: www.geolsoc.org.uk
▶ UK National body for Geoscience and Geoscientists. International membership of over 9,000 and publishes a wide range of prestigious journals and other publications.

Global Action Plan
8 Fulwood Place, London WC1V 6HG
Tel: 020 7405 5633
Fax: 020 7831 6244
Email: all@gapuk.demon.co.uk
Web: www.globalactionplan.org.uk
▶ Independent charity whose aim is to help improve the quality of life now and for generations to come. Has helped thousands of people throughout the country to take practical environmental action. Individuals can take Action at Home, schools can take Action at School, and businesses can undertake Action at Work or Environmental Champions. These programmes promote realistic, positive and pragmatic actions. Believes small individual changes make a big collective difference.

Global Ideas Bank
20 Heber Road, London NW2 6AA
Tel: 020 8208 2853
Fax: 020 8452 6434
Email: rhino@dial.pipex.com
Web: www.globalideasbank.org
▶ A charitable green think tank and international suggestions box for the most imaginative ideas and projects, with money awards, from around the world, in every sphere from relationships to ecology to jobs to health.

Going For Green
Elizabeth House, The Pier,
Wigan WN3 4EX
Tel: 01942 612 621
Fax: 01942 824 778

Email: gfg@dircon.co.uk
Web: www.gfg.iclnet.co.uk
▶ Going for Green is the biggest environmental campaign ever to be aimed at the British public. Its Green Code aims to do for environmental behaviour what other public awareness campaigns have done, for instance, drink-drive, anti-smoking and seatbelt issues. Supported by government and private sector, Going for Green's slogan, 'by doing your bit', is the focus of the campaign. The message is that one person cannot make much difference to the environment, but if everyone carries out many small actions together, it can make a big difference.

Going for Green & Tidy Britain North West
Elizabeth House, The Pier,
Wigan WN3 4EX
Tel: 01942 612 600
Fax: 01942 612 601
Email: enquiriesnw@tidybritain.org.uk
Web: www.tidybritain.org.uk
▶ Regional office of national group which campaigns, educates, enforces and takes action against litter and waste.

Greater Manchester and District Campaign for Nuclear Disarmament (CND)
One World Centre, 6 Mount Street, Manchester M2 5NS
Tel: 0161 834 8301
Fax: 0161 834 8187
Email: gmdcnd@gn.apc.org
Open: Mon-Fri 10am-4pm
▶ Connected to the national, high-profile and well-known group campaigning against the spread of nuclear weapons. This is an active local group that, amongst other activities, has set up an emailing list for the exchange of networking news and views on nuclear campaigns.

Greater Manchester Coalition of Disabled People
Carisbrooke, Wenlock Way,
Gorton, Manchester M12 5FL
Tel: 0161 273 5155
Fax: 0161 273 4164
Email: gmcdp@globalnet.co.uk

▶ An organisation of disabled people, controlled and staffed by disabled people, promoting the integration of the disabled into society at all levels. Publishes an information bulletin and quarterly magazine. The Disability Action Training (DAT) project provides disability equality training to various groups. Two projects work specifically with young disabled people.

Green Alliance
40 Buckingham Palace Road,
London SW1W 0RE
Tel: 020 7233 7433
Fax: 020 7233 9033
Email: ga@green-alliance.demon.co.uk
Web: www.green-alliance.demon.co.uk
▶ Independent charity promoting sustainable development by ensuring that the environment is at the heart of decision-making. Works with senior people in government, parliament, business and the environmental movement to encourage new ideas, dialogue and constructive solutions. Aims to influence politics and policy, so that environment is more central by convincing, and working with, government and the environmental community. Work may be part of planned agenda, or reactive.

Groundwork Blackburn
Bob Watts Building,
Nova Scotia Wharf, Bolton Road,
Blackburn BB2 3GE
Tel: 01254 265 163
Fax: 01254 692 835
▶ Local charity with a very wide range of activities which seeks to bring about sustainable improvements to the local environment through partnerships and contributes to economic and social regeneration.

Groundwork Creswell
96 Creswell Road, Clowne S43 4NA
Tel: 01246 570 977
Fax: 01246 813 200
▶ Local charity with a very wide range of activities which seeks to bring about sustainable improvements to the local environment through partnerships and contributes to economic and social regeneration.

Groundwork East Lancashire
Curate Street (Off Town Hall Square),
Great Harwood BB6 7EL
Tel: 01254 877 877
Fax: 01254 887 788
▶ Local charity with a very wide range of activities which seeks to bring about sustainable improvements to the local environment through partnerships and contributes to economic and social regeneration.

Groundwork Liverpool
1st Floor, Hamilton House, Pall Mall,
Liverpool L3 6AL
Tel: 0151 255 2615/6
Fax: 0151 236 1668
▶ Local charity with a very wide range of activities which seeks to bring about sustainable improvements to the local environment through partnerships and contributes to economic and social regeneration.

Groundwork Macclesfield & Vale Royal
The Adelphi Mill Gate Lodge,
Grimshaw Lane, Bollington,
Macclesfield SK10 5JB
Tel: 01625 572 681
Fax: 01625 574 160
▶ Local charity with a very wide range of activities which seeks to bring about sustainable improvements to the local environment through partnerships and contributes to economic and social regeneration.

Groundwork Manchester
Phoenix House, 61 Spear Street,
Manchester M1 1DF
Tel: 0161 237 5656
Fax: 0161 237 3939
▶ Local charity with a very wide range of activities which seeks to bring about sustainable improvements to the local environment through partnerships and contributes to economic and social regeneration.

Groundwork National Office
85-7 Cornwall Street,
Birmingham B3 3BY
Tel: 0121 236 8565
Fax: 0121 236 7356
▶ Aims to bring about sustainable improvements through partnerships, to the local environment and to contribute to economic and social regen-

Government & Organisations

eration. Its range of services includes: physical environmental improvements to derelict land, community building grounds, recreation sites, housing estates, school grounds and industrial estates; improving countryside access for all; undertaking environmental campaigns; recycling projects; environmental art; Princes Trust Volunteers; energy advice for schools and households; training for schools, long term unemployed community groups; environmental business services, educational buisness links; environmental and health – basically any activities under Local Agenda 21.

Groundwork Rochdale, Oldham & Tameside
Groundwork Environment Centre,
Shaw Road, Higginshaw,
Oldham OL1 4AW
Tel: 0161 624 1444
Fax: 0161 624 1555
Open: Mon-Fri 9am-5pm
▶ Local charity with a very wide range of activities which seeks to bring about sustainable improvements to the local environment through partnerships and contributes to economic and social regeneration.

Groundwork Rossendale
New Hall Hey Road, Rawtenstall,
Rossendale BB4 6HR
Tel: 01706 211 421
Fax: 01706 210 770
▶ Local charity with a very wide range of activities which seeks to bring about sustainable improvements to the local environment through partnerships and contributes to economic and social regeneration.

Groundwork Salford & Trafford
Trafford Ecology Park,
Lake Road, Trafford Park,
Manchester M17 1TU
Tel: 0161 873 7182
Fax: 0161 876 0523
▶ Local charity with a very wide range of activities which seeks to bring about sustainable improvements to the local environment through partnerships and contributes to economic and social regeneration.

Groundwork St Helens, Knowsley & Sefton
19-27 Shaw Street,
St Helens WA10 1DF
Tel: 01744 739 396
Fax: 01744 24081
▶ Local charity with a very wide range of activities which seeks to bring about sustainable improvements to the local environment through partnerships and contributes to economic and social regeneration.

Groundwork Tameside
Cheetham's Mill, 4th Floor,
Park Street, off Acres Lane,
Stalybridge SK15 2BT
Tel: 0161 303 1336
Fax: 0161 303 0985
▶ Local charity with a very wide range of activities which seeks to bring about sustainable improvements to the local environment through partnerships and contributes to economic and social regeneration.

Groundwork West Cumbria
Crowgarth House, 48 High Street,
Cleator Moor CA25 5AA
Tel: 01946 813 677
Fax: 01946 813 059
▶ Local charity with a very wide range of activities which seeks to bring about sustainable improvements to the local environment through partnerships and contributes to economic and social regeneration.

Groundwork Wigan & Chorley
74-80 Hall Gate, Wigan WN1 1HP
Tel: 01942 821 444
Fax: 01942 820 347
▶ Local charity with a very wide range of activities which seeks to bring about sustainable improvements to the local environment through partnerships and contributes to economic and social regeneration.

Groundwork Wirral
7 Royal Standard Way, Expressway Business Park, New Chester Road,
Birkenhead CH42 1NB
Tel: 0151 644 4700
Fax: 0151 644 4701
▶ Local charity with a very wide range of activities which seeks to bring about sustainable improvements to the local environment through partnerships and contributes to economic and social regeneration

HDRA – the organic organisation
Ryton Organic Gardens,
Coventry CV8 3LG
Tel: 024 7630 3517
Fax: 024 7663 9229
Email: enquiry@hdra.org.uk
Web: www.hdra.org.uk
Open: Mon-Fri 9am-5pm
▶ HDRA is Europe's largest organic organisation. Based at Ryton Organic Gardens in Warwickshire, HDRA also runs Yalding Organic Gardens in Kent and an organic walled garden at Audley End in Essex. All three gardens are open to visitors and have shops and restaurants. At Ryton there are also conference facilities. HDRA members enjoy an organic gardening telephone advice line, a quarterly magazine, free entry to many gardens plus other benefits. HDRA runs the Heritage Seed Library which saves rare and endangered varieties of vegetables. There is also an organic gardening catalogue, organic garden and landscape design consultancy, a wide range of books, various schools projects and a network of local groups.

Homes For Change Housing Co-operative
Unit 25, 41 Old Birley Street,
Hulme, Manchester M15 5RF
Tel: 0161 232 9801
Fax: 0161 232 1582
▶ The largest new build housing co-operative in the country, designed by its residents to create a genuinely sustainable building incorporating special glass, super-insulation, turf roofs and recycled materials, including toilets. The courtyard block is designed to maximise flora and fauna while providing safe play space for the growing number of children in the block.

Humanist Movement
124 Northmoor Road,
Manchester M12 5RS
Tel: 0161 224 0749
Fax: 0161 257 3686
Email: stevenknight@compuserve.com
Web: www.humanism.org
▶ Social movement which aims for profound changes to the structures of both society and the current system of values. Holding the human being as the 'central value and main concern', the Humanist Movement is involved in neighbourhood projects, helping to build real communities and improve the quality of life; in international campaigns, co-ordinating human rights campaigns; new economics, aiming to help stop the growing gap between rich and poor; and study groups and commissions on specific issues.

Institute for Social Inventions
20 Heber Road, London NW2 6AA
Tel: 020 8208 2853
Fax: 020 8452 6434
Email: rhino@dial.pipex.com
Web: www.globalideasbank.org
▶ Aims to promote socially innovative ideas and projects such as new social services, new laws, electoral systems, organisations and ways for people to relate to each other. Encourages public participation in problem solving and runs the Global Ideas Bank on the internet with a £1,000 annual prize for the best idea (deadline June 1st). Publishes an annual book-length journal *The Book of Ideas*, costing £15 which includes membership for one year.

Institute of Biology
20-22 Queensbury Place,
London SW7 2DZ
Tel: 020 7581 8333
Fax: 020 7823 9409
Email: info@iob.org
Web: www.iob.org
Open: Mon-Fri 9am-5pm
▶ The Institute of Biology is the 'voice of British Biology', with 76 affiliated societies and 17,000 members representing the entire range of bioscience. This enables the IOB to respond quickly and authoritatively to policy-making bodies and the Government on science issues. The Institute's mission is to promote biology and the biological sciences, to foster the public understanding of the life sciences in generally, to serve the needs of its

members, to enhance the status of the biology profession as a whole to government and other bodies. Local branches organise activities and events. Career publications are available for students and teachers. The Biologist and Journal of Biological education are its publications. The web site provides a forum for discussion and news of the life sciences.

International Foundation for Alternative Trade
30 Murdock Road, Bicester OX6 7RF
Tel: 01869 249 819
Fax: 01865 246 381
Email: cwills@ifat.org.net
Web: www.ifat.org
▶ IFAT is a global network of fair trade organisations which work to improve the livelihood and wellbeing of disadvantaged people in developing countries, and to change the unfair structure of international trade.

International Society for Ecology & Culture
Foxhole, Dartington TQ9 6EB
Tel: 01803 868 650
Fax: 01803 868 651
Email: isecuk@gn.apc.org
Web: www.isec.org.uk
▶ Promotes discussion of the impacts of conventional development models and economic globalisation, whilst supporting policies and local strategies for ecological restoration. Produces books, videos and other materials, some translated into nearly 30 languages. Its Resistance and Renewal programme provides community groups with educational material and advice.

ITDG
The Schumacher Centre for Technology and Development, Bourton Hall, Bourton-on-Dunsmore, Rugby CV23 9QZ
Tel: 01788 661 100
Fax: 01788 661 101
Email: carolr@itdg.org.uk
Web: www.oneworld.org/itdg
▶ ITDG is a charity which specialises in helping people to use technology for practical answers to poverty. It works in four continents to promote sustainable technology with local communities. This is technology which draws on people's experience, and feeds it; which recognises their potential, and releases it; which respects their environment, and nurtures it; and which builds on their past, to sustain the future. Its subsidiary ITDG Publishing produces books and journals on appropriate technology for development.

Labour Behind the Label
The Centre for Employment Research, Room 126,
MMU Humanities Building,
St Augustines, Lower Chatham Street,
Manchester M15 6LL
Tel: 0161 247 1760
Fax: 0161 247 6333
▶ Network of UK organisations concerned about working conditions in the international garment industry. Co-ordinated by Women Working Worldwide. Membership is open to organisations (£50 per annum for national, £20 for local); individuals join for free. Members receive regular bulletins and news updates and member organisations are mentioned on publicity material.

Land is Ours, The
16B Cherwell Street,
Oxford OX4 1BG
Tel/Fax: 01865 722 016
Email: office@tlio.demon.co.uk
Web: www.oneworld.org/tlio/networking
Open: Tues & Thurs 12noon-5pm
▶ Campaigns peacefully for access to land, its resources and the decision making process affecting them, for everyone, irrespective of race, age and gender. Current campaigns include 'Rural Futures' and 'Legacy of Colonialism', and 'The Right to Roam', as well as advice and information on land related issues. Contact to subscribe to newsletter (£3) or for information about other publications and merchandise.

Lifestyle Movement, The
34 Quebec Road, Ilford IG1 4TT
Tel: 020 8554 2553
▶ Network of people who believe that global consumerism is destroying the Earth and causing desperate hardship to millions of people in the Third World. The group exists to inform, encourage and support people who choose a simpler lifestyle. Write for further information or to join the movement.

Manchester Amnesty Group
c/o 51 Thornton Road, Rusholme,
Manchester M14 7NU
Tel: 0161 248 7968
▶ Local group for Amnesty, the world-wide human rights movement working for the release of prisoners of conscience, fair trials for political prisoners and an end to torture, extra-judicial executions, 'disappearances' and the death penalty.

Manchester Civic Society
PO Box 436, Manchester M60 2AJ
Tel: 0161 343 7100
Email: carolyn.blain@compuserve.com
▶ Aims to foster civic pride and to give a voice to members' concerns. Produces a newsletter and administers an awards scheme.

Manchester Community Information Network
MANCAT, Moston Campus, Room A6, Ashley Lane, Manchester M9 4WU
Tel: 0161 203 4422
Fax: 0161 203 4422
Email: Linda@mcin.poptel.org.uk
Web: www.magictouch.org.uk/mcin
▶ Registered charity which works collaboratively with all agencies in the community to promote access to information and to ensure that disadvantaged people are not left behind in the information society. Provides information to the public through an internet gateway website (as above) and free access public information systems. The site offers details of job vacancies, training courses, where to get advice, community organisations, health and leisure services. Users can also send email messages to information providers such as Manchester Citizens Advice Bureaux. A public information kiosk is available in Manchester's Central Library in the General Readers section and other locations across the City. For further details, send an SAE to the above address.

Manchester Earth First!
Dept.29, 255 Wilmslow Road,
Manchester M14 5LW
Tel: 0161 226 6814
Email: mancef@nematode.freeserve.co.uk
Web: www.snet.co.uk/ef/
▶ Publishes the monthly Loombreaker (loombreaker@nematode.freeserve.co.uk) for campaigning news from around Manchester. To get involved in Manchester, come along to the Riotous Assembly, 1st Tuesday of each month at 7.30pm, Yard Theatre, 41 Old Birley Street, Hulme. Earth First! is not a cohesive group or campaign, but a convenient banner for people who share similar principles to work under. The general principles behind the name are a non-hierarchical organisation and the use of direct action to confront, stop and eventually reverse the forces that are responsible for the destruction of the earth and its inhabitants. Nationally, to get in touch with your nearest EF! group, or to subscribe (£5+) to the EF! Action Update, contact EF!AU, PO Box 1TA, Newcastle-upon-Tyne NE99 1TA, Tel: 0797 4791841, email: actionupdate@gn.apc.org.

Manchester Schumacher Lectures
Farway, Wilderswood, Horwich,
Bolton BL6 7ET
Tel: 01204 697 411
Fax: 01204 697 411
Email: chris.lyons@zen.co.uk
▶ Local Schumacher group holding regular meetings and lectures at the Friends Meeting House, 6 Mount Street, Manchester. Call for details of forthcoming events.

McLibel Support Campaign/ London Greenpeace
5 Caledonian Road,
London N1 9DX
Tel: 020 7713 1269
Fax: 020 7713 1269
Email: lgp@envirolink.org
Web: www.mcspotlight.org
▶ Open anarchist, ecological group supporting a wide range of radical, social and environmental issues, networking with other activists and initiatives. Emerged victorious from a

Government & Organisations

huge legal and public battle with the McDonald's Corporation over libel allegations against two campaigners charged with distribution of anti-McDonald's leaflets.

Merseyside Environmental Trust
c/o Dep of Civic Design,
University of Liverpool,
PO Box 147, Liverpool L69 3BX
Tel: *0151 794 3137*
Fax: *0151 794 2766*
Open: *Mon-Wed 9am-1pm*
▶ MET is an awareness raising organisation covering the whole of Merseyside. It organises public meetings and events, produces a quarterly newsletter *METMAIL*, and administers a yearly grants scheme under the title of 'Merseyside Environmental Week'.

National Federation of Women's Institutes
104 New Kings Road,
London SW6 4LY
Tel: *020 7371 9300*
Fax: *020 7736 3652*
Email: *pa@nfwi.org.uk*
Web: *www.womens-institute.org.uk*
Open: *Mon-Fri 9am-5pm*
▶ The NFWI is the largest national charity for women with 250,000 members and 8,000 local Women's Institutes. It plays a unique role in enabling women to turn their concerns into campaigns; in particular, supporting a five year moratorium on GM food. It has a long standing commitment to sustainable development and Agenda 21.

National Playing Fields Association
25 Ovington Square,
London SW3 1LQ
Tel: *020 7584 6445*
Fax: *020 7581 2402*
Email: *npfa@npfa.co.uk*
▶ Protecting playing fields throughout the UK is the NPFA's prime purpose. It safeguards land in several ways and campaigns for statutory and other protection for recreational land, advising on all matters to do with the play, sport and recreation environment, from floodlighting and muddy goal mouths to play equipment and dog fouling. Most recent projects include multisport rebound walls 'urban village halls' managed locally, and a learning programme, called 'Midnight Basketball'.

Naturesave Trust
58 Fore Street,
Totnes TQ9 5RU
Tel: *01803 864 390*
Fax: *01803 864 441*
Email: *mail@naturesave.co.uk*
Web: *www.naturesave.co.uk*
Open: *Mon-Fri 9.15am-5.15pm*
▶ The purpose of the Trust is to benefit specific environmental and conservationist projects which support sustainable development. Is keen to support those projects with a long term benefit which deal proactively with the root of a particular problem as opposed to merely reacting to the effects. The projects considered must be from environmental and conservationist groups and organisations who seek funding for specific projects and not the general administrative costs of their respective organisations.

Oldham Development Agency for Community Action
Unit 12 Manchester Chambers,
Oldham OL1 1PL
Tel: *0161 633 6222*
Fax: *0161 628 5803*
Email: *information@odaca.fsnet.co.uk*
Web: *www.odaca.freeserve.co.uk*
Open: *Mon-Fri 9am-5pm*
▶ ODACA provides support to voluntary and community groups in Oldham. It offers help with funding, training, information, volunteering opportunities, translating, community ecomonic development and has computer and print shop facilities. It produces a quarterly newsletter.

One World Week
National Office, PO Box 2555,
Reading RG1 4XW
Tel: *0118 939 4933*
Fax: *0118 939 4936*
Email: *oneworldweek@gn.apc.org*
Web:
www.gn.apc.org/oneworldweek
▶ Join others with a concern for justice, peace and respect for the earth in taking a stand. The One World Week offices can provide action materials, backup and support if you are thinking of organising a local celebration as well as local contacts and a list of events planned in your area.

Organic Targets Bill Campaign
c/o Sustain: The Alliance for Better Food & Farming, 94 White Lion Street, London N1 9PF
Tel: *020 7837 1228*
Fax: *020 837 1141*
Email:
orgsnictargetsbill@sustainweb.org
Web: *www.sustainweb.org*
▶ The Bill aims to encourage the Government to: develop a strategy for the organic farmin sector; ensure that 30% of agricultural land in England and Wales is organic by 2010; ensure that 20% of the food that is marketed in England and Wales is organic by 2010; to make organic food more affordable to all sectors of society. People can get involved in the campaign by lobbying their MPs, distributing 'Aim for Organic' postcards, getting involved in days of action or encouraging local organisations to sign up to the campaign.

Permaculture Association
BCM Permaculture Association,
London WC1N 3XX
Tel: *07041 390 170*
Fax: *07041 390 170*
Email: *office@permaculture.org.uk*
Web: *www.permaculture.org.uk*
Open: *Mon-Fri 9am-5pm*
▶ Supports people and projects through training, networking and research and shares skills and designs sustainable solutions for local communities. Endeavours to be accessible to everyone in Britain and to play an active part in the developing culture of positive change. Permaculture is an ethical and ecological design system that is being applied across the world, transforming schools, businesses, farms, homes and neighbourhoods. Call for more information and to join. Provides course listings, project and group listings and finds information to help with sustainability activities.

Permaculture Manchester
11 Hunmanby Avenue, Hulme,
Manchester M15 5FF
Tel: *0161 227 8750*
Email:
permaculture@redbricks.org.uk
Web:
www.redbricks.org.uk/permaculture
▶ Aims to apply permaculture principles, to integrate new and existing projects in Manchester into a cohesive model for urban sustainability. This is acheived through: supplying specific services which support local projects; the development of knowledge and skills; and development of community infrastructure. Projects include local food and land management initiatives, LETS, education, ICT and research.

Population Concern
Studio 325, Highgate Studios,
53-79 Highgate Road,
London NW5 1TL
Tel: *020 7241 8500*
Fax: *020 7267 6788*
Email:
info@populationconcern.org.uk
Web: *www.populationconcern.org.uk*
▶ Aims to raise funds for population and development programmes around the world and to raise awareness about the nature, size and complexity of world population especially as it affects the social and economic development of mankind. Recognised by the United Nations Population Fund (UNFPA).

Red Rose Forest
Red Rose Forest Team,
Community Forest Centre,
Dock Office, Trafford Road, Quays,
Salford M5 2XB
Tel: *0161 872 1660*
Fax: *0161 872 1680*
Email: *team@redroseforest.co.uk*
▶ A partnership of the Countryside Agency, the Forestry Commission and six Greater Manchester Authorities. The Forest is an inspiring vision of the future that is already transforming and regenerating a large part of Greater Manchester to create a thriving environment for the 21st Century. The Forest will transform the life of 1.5 million people in the region by bringing in jobs, investment, educa-

tion opportunities, cleaner air and the most extensive change to the landscape since the Industrial Revolution.

Soil Association
Bristol House, 40-56 Victoria Street, Bristol BS1 4BY
Tel: 0117 929 0661
Fax: 0117 925 2504
Email: info@soilassociation.org
Web: www.soilassociation.org
▶ The UK's leading organisation working to promote the benefits of organic food, farming and sustainable forestry to human health, animal welfare and the environment. Its symbol can be found on numerous food products as a sign of quality and high standards. Organic is a term defined by law and all organic food production and processing is governed by a strict set of rules. The main campaign is currently the promotion of organic farming as a means to increase the level of wildlife in the countryside: this follows the publication of the Biodiversity Report in May 2000. The Soil Association is a membership organisation with more than 14,000 members, with benefits including the quarterly magazine, *Living Earth*. Books and guides on a wide variety of organic subjects can be purchased through a mail order service and the website has a comprehensive library with information on all aspects of organic food and farming.

Surfers Against Sewage
Unit 2 Workshops, Weal Kitty, St Agnes TR5 0RD
Tel: 01872 553 001
Fax: 01872 552 615
Email: info@sas.org.uk
▶ Nationwide campaign group calling for sewage to be fully treated before discharge, for the liquid and sludge components to be regarded as a resource, for complete cessation of marine dumping of toxic waste and for finding better ways of dealing with viruses and bacteria.

Survival International
11-15 Emerald Street, London WC1N 3QL
Tel: 020 7242 1441
Fax: 020 7242 1771
Email: info@survival-international.org
Web: www.survival.org.uk
Open: Mon-fri 10am-6pm
▶ Worldwide organisation which supports tribal peoples, stands for their right to decide their own future and helps them protect their lives, lands and human rights. Current campaigns range from Sarawak to Siberia and Kenya to Canada. Members are encouraged to join regular letter-writing campaigns.

The Low Pay Unit
27-29 Amwell Street, London EC1R 1TL
Tel: 020 7713 7616
Fax: 020 7713 7581
Email: publications@lowpayunit.org.uk
Open: Mon-Fri 9.30am-5.30pm
▶ An independent organisation established in 1974, the Low Pay Unit is the leading research, advice and campaigning body on the causes and effects of low pay in the UK. The Unit maintains its authoritative position through extensive research, tracking government policy and action, as well as working with local authorities, MPs, MEPs, trade unions, the voluntary sector, employees and employers to tackle low pay, poor terms and conditions of employment and social exclusion.

Tidy Britain Group
Elizabeth House, The Pier, Wigan WN3 4EX
Tel: 01942 824 620
Fax: 01942 824 778
Email: enquiries@tidybritain.org.uk
Web: www.tidybritain.org.uk
Open: Mon-Fri 9am-5pm
▶ Independent charity campaigning for the improvement of local environments. It has a specific brief as the national anti-litter organisation.

Traidcraft Exchange
Kingsway North, Gateshead NE11 0NE
Tel: 0191 491 0591
Fax: 0191 482 2690
Email: fionat@traidcraft.co.uk
Web: www.traidcraft.co.uk
▶ Leading international development organisation working to fight poverty through fair trade. It does this by sup-

porting business in the developing world, raising awareness amongst consumers in the UK and promoting ethical business practice.

Trees of Time & Place
PO Box 94, Aldershot GU12 4GJ
Tel: 0345 078 139
Email: kate.m.lowmdes@exxon.sprint.com
▶ National initiative which encourages people to collect seeds from a favourite tree, sow them and grow a personal tree, to celebrate the new millennium. Runs an education action phase called Growing with Trees involving schools and youth groups throughout the UK. The campaign is backed by a unique partnership of over 70 organisations, including most of the country's leading envrironmental and community organisations.

UK Centre for Economic And Environnmental Development (UK CEED)
Suite 1, Priestgart House, Priestgart, Peterborough PE1 1JN
Tel: 01733 311 644
Fax: 01733 312 782
Email: jselwyn@ukceed.org
Web: www.ukceed.org
▶ UK CEED is an independent foundation providing sustainable development solutions for government, industry, non-governmental organisations and individuals. The centre specialises in: early identification of emerging issues; innovative research and project work; independent policy advice and guidance; public engagement and partnership building; dynamic training and education programmes. Publishes *Inland, Costal and Estuarint Waters* (ICE) magazine, a bi-monthly magazine targeted at water environment professionals. Navigate with Nature is an initiative aimed at promoting environmentally responsible boating. Call for further information on the above or for details of other projects in sectors such as tourism, sustainable business and communications, recreation, radioactive waste, transport and consensus building.

UKOWLA
Town Hall, Chesterfield S40 1LP
Tel: 01246 345 236
Fax: 01246 345 252
▶ Formed in 1985 for people in the UK interested in community linking with partners in the Southern hemisphere. It is a voluntary organisation supported by contributions from its own members. Works on behalf of link groups all over the UK. Members have contacts with many parts of the world including Africa, Latin America, Asia and the Caribbean.

Vale Royal Environment Network
The Council House, Church Road, Northwich CW9 5PD
Tel: 01606 41224
Fax: 01606 350616
Email: vren@care4free.net
Web: www.vren.care4free.net
▶ Network linking over 70 active environmental groups in the mid-Cheshire area, offering support to community groups who want to get involved in any type of environmental work. Existing projects include Painting by Numbers, which gets all sections of the community to pledge action in their own lives to improve the local environment, and Green Schools Network which provides resources and information to schools and youth groups on environmental issues. Setting up a local food project which will encourage organic growing and local purchasing.

VIRSA Educational Trust
Little Keep, Bridport Road, Dorchester DT1 1SQ
Tel: 01305 259 383
Fax: 01305 259 384
Email: virsa@ruralnet.org.uk
Web: www.virsa.org
▶ VIRSA (Village Retail Services Association) Educational Trust is a registered charity established to assist small rural communities in England and Wales to retain or re-instate their retail services. Deals mainly with general stores and post offices. Has been instrumental in saving or starting many shops and worked with over 200 communities last year. For further information or if your village needs help call or visit the website.

Government & Organisations

Voluntary Action Manchester
Fourways House, 57 Hilton Street, Manchester M1 2EJ
Tel: 0161 236 3206
Fax: 0161 228 0464
Email: vam@pop3.poptel.org.uk
Web: www.poptel.org.uk/vam
▶ Offers advice, information and support to voluntary and community groups in the city of Manchester. Outreach and in-house support available. Call for further info.

Voluntary Sector North West
St Thomas Centre, Ardwick Green North, Manchester M12 6FZ
Tel: 0161 273 7451
Fax: 0161 273 8296
Email: vsnw@vsnw.org.uk
Open: Mon-Fri 9am-5pm
▶ Set up in 1994 to help develop a coherent and organised voluntary sector voice in the north west, VSNW promotes the contribution of voluntary organisations and community groups in securing the well being of people and the regeneration of local communities in the region. Membership includes child care organisations, environmental campaigns, voluntary youth bodies, carers and self-help associations and many others.

War on Want
37-39 Great Guildford Street, London SE1 0ES
Tel: 020 7620 1111
Fax: 020 7261 9291
Email: rcartridge@waronwant.org
Web: www.waronwant.org
▶ The campaign against world poverty. Founded by Harold Wilson and the labour movement, it funds progressive organisations around the world and campaigns in the UK on issues such as debt. Currently campaigning for a tax on currency speculation (Tobin Tax). Free booklets and magazines available.

Women Working Worldwide
Centre for Employment Research, Room 126, MMU Humanities Building, Rosamond Street West, Manchester M15 6LL
Tel: 0161 247 1760
Fax: 0161 247 6333
Email: women-ww@mcr1.poptel.org.uk
▶ Manchester-based group working with a global network of women worker organisations. The aim is to develop strategies for supporting the rights of women workers in a globalised economy. WWW also co-ordinates the Labour Behind the Label network (see separate listing) which campaigns for the improvement of conditions in the international garment industry. Both individuals and organisations are welcome to join the network.

Women's Environmental Network (WEN)
PO BOX 30626, London E1 1TZ
Tel: 020 7481 9004
Fax: 020 7481 9144
Email: wenuk@gn.apc.org
Web: www.gn.apc.org/wen
▶ WEN campaigns on environmental issues from a women's perspective. Provides information on positive alternatives for a more sustainable lifestyle. Current camapigns include waste prevention, genetics, health and the environment and local food growing project. Membership organisations with quarterly newsletter.

World Development Movement
25 Beehive Place, London SW9 7QR
Tel: 020 7737 6215
Fax: 020 7274 8232
Email: wdm@wdm.org.uk
Web: www.wdm.org.uk
▶ Runs high profile campaigns to change the policies of governments, and multinational corporations in wealthy countries and the unaccountable international instituitons that they control. WDM works with campaigning groups in the Third World, supporting their fight against the injustice of poverty. Its goal is to create the conditions that will enable the world's poorest people to achieve equitable and sustainable development.

World Voices
21 Lonsdale Road, London NW6 6RA
Tel: 020 7372 7117
Fax: 020 7928 3233
Email: uk@worldvoices.org
Web: www.worldvoices.org
▶ A network of students, activists, academics, artists and business executives from around the world – exploring and demonstrating alternatives and solutions to replace unsustainable forms of progress, wealth and power. Organises imaginative conferences and events and also publishes books.

Young People's Trust for the Environment and Nature Conservation
8 Leapole Road, Guildford GU6 7BW
Tel: 01483 539 600
Fax: 01483 301 992§
Email: info@yptenc.org.uk
Web: www.yptenc.org.uk
Open: Mon-Fri 9am-5pm
▶ The Young People's Trust for the Environment is a charity which aims to encourage young people's understanding of the environment and the need for sustainability. The Trust's services include a free information service for schools and individual young people, free school talks, environmental discovery courses for school groups. Schools may register as a group member of the Trust and receive a free termly bulletin *Conservation Education*, which covers a variety of environmental topics related to the national curriculum. Details of the Trust's services can be found on the website.

Political Parties

Green Party
1a Waterlow Road, London N19 5NJ
Tel: 020 7272 4474
Fax: 020 7272 6653
Email: office@greenparty.org.uk
Web: www.greenparty.org.uk
▶ The political wing of the green movement campaigning on behalf of social justice and the environment, successfully so on issues of conservation and road traffic reduction. Stands candidates at local, national and European levels and is gaining increasing representation under proportional representation. Also has Green representation in the House of Lords.

Green Party (Manchester)
21 Parry Road, Longsight, Manchester M12 5QD
Tel: 0161 225 4863
Fax: 0870 160 4862
▶ Political party whose aims are to help develop a socially just and ecologically sustainable society by contesting elections at all levels and other campaigning, from Runway 2 to local community campaigns. Call for further info about meetings, campaigns, publications and membership.

SERA – (Socialist Environment and Resources Association)
11 Goodwin Street, London N4 3HQ
Tel: 020 7263 7389
Fax: 020 7263 7424
Email: seraoffice@aol.com
▶ An independent environment group, affiliated to the Labour Party, whose membership includes 103 MPs and 6 Cabinet Ministers. They believe that social and environmental concerns must be addressed together and works to integrate green thinking into Labour policies. Campaigns by organising events, such as conferences and seminars, and publishes a regular magazine and briefings campaign. Has a number of working groups at national and local levels.

Legal Support

Andrew Fitzpatrick Solicitor
349 Claremont Road, Rusholme, Manchester M14 7NB
Tel: 0161 248 9799
Fax: 0161 248 5785
▶ Activist-friendly lawyers. Contact David Lees.

Bindman & Partners
275 Gray's Inn Road, London WC1X 8QF
Tel: 020 7833 4433
Fax: 020 7837 9792
▶ Small group of solicitors specialising in civil liberties and the rights of the individual. The firm regularly handles environmental direct action cases and is instructed by campaigning and pressure groups. With the assistance of the Environment Law Foundation, the practice is developing an in-house green policy.

Government & Organisations

Environmental Law Foundation
Suite 309, 16 Baldwins Gardens, Hatton Square, London EC1N 7RJ
Tel: 020 7404 1030
Fax: 020 7404 1032
Email: info@elf-net.org
Web: www.greenchannel.com/elf
Open: Mon-Fri 10am-5pm
▶ National charity linking communities and individuals with the legal and technical expertise to help prevent damage to the environment. Its network of members include specialists providing information and advice on how the law can be used to resolve environmental problems, ranging from air and water pollution to the loss of open spaces and habitats. Provides public access to local sources of expertise to defend and improve the quality of life, a referral service with a free initial consultation and further work at reduced costs where possible.

Richard Buxton Environmental Lawyers
40 Clarendon Street, Cambridge CB1 1JX
Tel: 01223 328 933
Fax: 01233 301 308
Email: law@richardbuxton.co.uk
Web: www.richardbuxton.co.uk
▶ Environmental lawyer specialising in water resources, nature conservation, environmental assessment, noise, public law/judicial review. Provides advice on policy, litigation and disputes.

UK Environmental Law Association
Honeycroft House, Pangbourne Road, Upper Basildon
Tel: 01491 671 631
▶ Association formed in response to the growing need for a common professional forum in environmental law. Aims to advance the education of the public in all matters relating to the development, teaching, application and practice of environmental law. Current members of the association come from a wide range of interests including private practice, industry, the public sector and academia.

Campaign Support

Community Matters
8/9 Upper Street, Islington, London N1 0PQ
Tel: 020 7226 0189
Fax: 020 7354 9570
Email: communitymatters@communitymatters.org.uk
Open: Mon-Fri 9am-5pm
▶ Aims to listen to, support and guide community organisations and promote and represent them at national level with a vision for healthy, sustainable communities. It provides information and advice, training consultancy services, local network development publications and a community buildings licensing scheme (PPL). Services are provided to members and non-members (with membership benefits).

Directory of Social Change
24 Stephenson Way, London NW1 2DP
Tel: 020 7209 4422
Fax: 020 7209 4130
Email: info@dsc.org.uk
Web: www.dsc.org.uk
Open: Mon-Fri 9am-5pm
▶ Aims to help voluntary and community organisations become more effective. A leading provider of information and training for the voluntary and community sector, the charity was founded in 1975 and is based in London and Liverpool. Publishes books and runs the largest programme of training courses, seminars and conferences in the UK, covering fundraising, management, charity and employment law, charity finance marketing, lobbying and other topics. Organises the largest charity fair in the UK every Spring at the Business Design Centre in Islington.

Greater Manchester Centre for Voluntary Organisation
St Thomas Centre, Ardwick Green North, Manchester M12 6FZ
Tel: 0161 273 7451
Fax: 0161 273 8296
Email: gmcvo@gmcvo.org.uk
Web: www.gmcvo.org.uk
▶ Exists to promote a thriving, effective and influential voluntary sector concerned with addressing social injustice. Promotes countrywide and regional initiatives involving voluntary organisations by providing training, consultancy, information, advice and practical support to groups working with the most disadvantaged sections of the community. Publishes the Information Bulletin ten times a year which covers a wide range of issues and topics of interest to voluntary and community groups in Greater Manchester including news of local and national groups and and campaigns, details of Government legislation and social and economic policy developments affecting the voluntary sector, information on sources of funding and a diary of meetings, training courses and other events.

Manchester Area Resource Centre (MARC) Ltd
28 Edge Street, Manchester M4 1HN
Tel: 0161 839 0839
Fax: 0161 839 0840
Email: marc@mcr1.poptel.org.uk
Open: Tues, Thurs, Fri 10am-4.30pm
▶ Resource centre for charities, individuals and community groups offering computers, scanners, printers, photocopiers, a graphics library, electric finishing equipment and more. As well as being a good place to find free leaflets and newsletters on campaigns and groups active in the city, the centre also runs courses on word processing, graphic design, the internet and other computer-related subjects.

Small World Productions
1b Waterlow Road, London N19 5NJ
Tel: 020 7272 1394
Fax: 020 7263 5975
Web: www.smallworldtv.co.uk
▶ Small company providing media support for campaigns working for environmental and social justice. Aims to get campaigners' own footage onto TV news. Also make films for charities and documentaries for broadcast.

Still Pictures
199 Shooters Hill Road, Blackheath, London SE3 8UL
Tel: 020 8858 8307
Fax: 020 8858 2049
Email: info@stillpictures.com
Web: www.stillpictures.com
▶ Photo-library providing photo images illustrating issues concerning the environment, Third World, wildlife and nature for the media and the Green Movement. Charities are charged at a special discount rate.

Undercurrents
16b Cherwell Street, Oxford OX4 1BG
Tel: 01865 203 662
Fax: 01865 243 562
Email: underc@gn.apc.org
Web: www.undercurrents.org
▶ Provides video training to activists to bring about real change for social and environmental justice. Has alternative news videos (1-10) available about varied direct action campaigns. Get in touch with them if you use a video and want to join the Camcorder Action Network. Offers training to campaigns who want to set up or improve their own website and internet broadcasts every Tuesday 9pm-2am.

Publishing for a future

If the pen is mightier than the sword then the increasing number of books, magazines and journals currently being published about sustainable development and environmental issues means there might be hope for a more eco-friendly future. Earthscan is one of the more established publishers and here **Nim Morthy** *outlines their approach*

'**Sustainable development**' is a term that is becoming increasingly prevalent in so many areas of our lives. But what does it in fact mean and why is it seen as so important? The catastrophic effects of global warming; the immense social and economic problems faced by people in the developing world; the environmental and social impacts of modern business; the irreversible losses of the planet's unique biodiversity due to human activity; the threat of globalisation to local communities. These are just a few examples of the issues to which the concept of sustainable development must be applied.

Earthscan is widely recognized as the UK's leading publisher of books on the entire spectrum of issues relating to sustainable development. Our publishing aim is to increase understanding and awareness of these critical issues and their implications at all levels, from the local to the global; working with leading academics, researchers and writers enables us to influence opinion and policy in ways that promote development sensitive to the needs of the planet as well as the needs of future generations. Our readership is varied, including policy makers, environmental professionals, business people, academics and increasingly, general readers who share the need to be informed on these crucial topics.

Earthscan's publishing can be divided into four, generalised categories:

1. Environmental policy, economics and law – this is concerned with the technical, managerial dimension of sustainable development. It encompasses international agreements such as The Kyoto Protocol on climate change and regional environmental legislation, as well as discussions surrounding the economic arguments supporting sustainable development. This is a vital issue for successful sustainable development as we can only genuinely make progress if international agreements are in place to facilitate it.

2. Ecology, conservation and natural resource management – this looks at human interaction with the natural world and concerns methods to combat biodiversity loss and threats to endangered species. It also covers management of the world's water resources to ensure that the needs of the world's population are met equitably.

3. Sustainable business – this looks at the social, environmental and ethical responsibilities of business. Environmentally, the use of raw materials by business must be accounted for along with the impact of manufacturing processes and the recycling of wastes. Socially and ethically legislation is increasingly used to persuade companies to consider the local and global impact of their practices; similarly, consumers have never been more aware of their power to make corporations more accountable for their actions.

4. Social and community development – from the genetic modification of food to the economic decline of communities, these issues are at the forefront of current debates. Many of our books take a relatively local look at urban life and argue for the importance of more sustainable communities with viable transport networks, poverty reduction and the minimisation of public health hazards. Others consider larger scale issues relating to international development, famine and disaster, and the working of the aid industry including the political and financial institutions that (mis)manage it.

The future can bring only an increase in concern for sustainable development: demonstrations against the genetic modification of food; the campaign to declare a moratorium on debt repayment; the backlash against multinational companies that exploit workers, and consumers, in the developing world; these are all tangible examples of people reacting to the effects of unsustainable development. Earthscan, in over a decade of publishing, has provided and continues to provide balanced yet committed coverage of all these issues, informing the debates and setting agendas.

As our readers make clear to us, it's time that governments, policy makers and businesses, the de facto decision makers of the world, begin to take account of these trends, and accept the reality of the ideas behind the agenda of sustainable development. ■

For more information about their range of publications, contact Earthscan Publication Ltd at 120 Pentonville Road, London N1 9JN. Tel: ***020 7278 0433*** *Fax:* ***020 7278 1142*** *Web:* ***www.earthscan.co.uk***

Harnessing the power of the Internet

If you have ever considered getting online or are concerned about some of the giant media companies that provide Internet services, GreenNet has the solution.

GreenNet is a not for profit Internet Service Provider, dedicated to supporting individuals and organisations working for peace, the environment, human rights and social justice. Set up in 1986, GreenNet began to collaborate and exchange information with similar ISPs in countries around the world, helping to found the Association for Progressive Communications (APC) (at www.apc.org) in 1991. The APC is a global computer network, with about 25 member networks, all working for individual activists and NGOs worldwide.

GreenNet is an active member of the NGO community and works alongside other organisations, groups and individuals involved in communications, advocacy, civil liberties and politics to:

- greatly increase perception amongst both the public and politicians of the potential of the Internet for increasing democracy
- defend and expand the space and opportunities for social campaigning work on the Internet against the threats that are emerging from growing commercialisation, restrictive regulation and censorship
- provide training, resources and tools for civil society organisations to safely and productively use the Internet to campaign on social justice issues.

Current GreenNet projects builds forth from these areas and include:

The Civil Society Internet Rights Project (CSIR)

A GreenNet sponsored initiative aimed at increasing awareness of the Internet as a vitally important area for the development of civil society, presenting opportunities for dialogue, debate, participation and action that do not exist elsewhere. However, while the Internet's full capacity to extend these opportunities still remains largely untapped, it is already being increasingly threatened by commercialisation, government regulation and censorship. As the major world network for organisations and individuals using the Internet for social campaigning purposes, the APC has been made increasingly aware of these threats and the need to counter them. The CSIR Project has arisen out of confronting some concrete problems affecting other member networks. It is designed to provide knowledge, resources and tools to defend and promote the Internet as an accessible and secure global communications medium for civil society. Further details about this campaign can be found at www.gn.apc.org/action/csir/index.html

Women's ICT training

The GreenNet Educational Trust (GET), the charitable arm of GreenNet, has received funding from the European Social Fund (ESF) to begin a training centre in the use of Information and communication technologies (ICTs). The core focus of the project is women and employees of small NGOs who are experiencing barriers to access and training. The project will run for two years from March 2001 to March 2003. This project is being developed with the support of the APC WNSP (Women's Networking Support Programme) which works to promote gender aware Internet design, implementation and use. Further information can be found at www.apcwomen.org

As a leading ethical collective ISP, GreenNet provides services aimed specifically at a user community of activists and NGOs, members of civil society and other campaigning organisations. Services include: connection to the Internet and email; web services and design; consultancy; e-commerce; global roaming and training, all supported extensively and in person by an expert team.

Recently, in the December/January issue of Ethical Consumer, GreenNet was voted as a 'best buy' in a study of the 10 largest UK ISPs and 2 alternative ISPs (GreenNet and Poptel). ISPs were evaluated on issues such as: environmental reporting, pollution, workers' rights, and irresponsible marketing. GreenNet scored the top rating in all categories, 'show(ing) real understanding of the need to engage in environmental issues.' ■

*Information on all of GreenNet's services and activities can be found on their website at www.gn.apc.org or by emailing Joanne Doyle for further information at **coord@gn.apc.org***

*GreenNet can also be contacted at 74-77 White Lion Street, London, N1 9PF. Tel: **0845 055 4011** local call rate or **020 7713 1941** Fax: **020 7837 4632***

Taking a fresh approach to the news

Alan Massam *of the Environmental Communicators' Organisation suggests that there is a different way to interpret and report on events.*

Established in 1972 after the first UN Conference on the Human Environment in Stockholm, the Environmental Communicators' Organisation (ECO) is a small, low energy and radical group, staffed by volunteers. The group's aim is to bring a green interpretation of significant news events to the attention of professional journalists and broadcasters.

In 1972 leading scientists expressed warnings about the growth of human population and the potential breakdown of the planet's ecosystems if rampant consumption was not curbed. Many words have been said and printed subsequently to endorse this, but very little has actually happened to reverse the trend. In fact the conclusions of the Earth Summit in Rio in 1992 were very similar to those of Stockholm 20 years earlier.

The ECO group believes that much of this is due to the bias of the media towards optimism so that consumption will proceed upwards, the frame of mind being that negative papers do not sell. However, the ECO Journalists, as they are also known, assert that radical changes in human behaviour will not be achieved by a pessimistic approach and work to draw attention to positive developments.

An example of misleading media coverage is the BSE crisis which was still concentrating on the effect of beef exports when it had become clear that a potential very devastating and horrible disease had been released into the human food chain. Similar doubts in the angle of this type of media coverage can be seen with the more recent foot and mouth epidemic.

The same applies to global warming which could have very serious effect in this island when our coastal nuclear power stations begin to face flood threats, but these factors are never discussed. Global warming may turn out to be the biggest disaster in human history but when will the media recognise these threats?

An example of ECO's complacency is the press's response to the meeting of the UN's Intergovernmental Panel on Climate Change in Shanghai in January 2001. This body not only announced that the 'human factor' was now perceived to be a major contributory factor to global warming, but that increased temperatures could provoke flooding which would 'endanger millions of people in low-lying areas.' However, the news received very modest coverage compared to the political dramas in the UK.

ECO works to help publicise environmental issues such as: tropical rain forest destruction; the extinction of species; severe pollution of habitat; global warming; human population growth; depletion of finite natural resources and Third World debt.

The relevance of such issues to individuals remain unappreciated by many despite the millions of words written annually about the environment.

The group publishes an occasional newsletter dealing with key environmental topics like energy policy, transport policy, land access. ECO believes their publications 'often make the apparently illogical behaviour of politicians easier to understand.' They also draw attention whenever possible to positive developments in environmental issues, for example the publication of Agenda 21 which arose from the Earth Summit in Rio in 1992. Additionally, ECO offers PR support to selected green pressure groups

As ECO writes: 'Trying to get the media to take biological problems seriously is an uphill struggle, partly due to the concern of proprietors to avoid upsetting the applecart and reducing profits. All 'Greens' must work much harder to achieve a sustainable lifestyle and a secure future for our children and grandchildren.' ■

For more information, contact Alan Massam at 8 Hooks Cross, Watton-at-Stone, Hertford SG143RY.
*Tel: **01920 830527** Fax: **01920 830538***
*Email: **alanmassam@compuserve.com***

BOOKSHOPS & BOOKS BY MAIL ORDER

Barefoot Books Ltd
18 Highbury Terrace,
London N5 1UP
Tel: 020 7704 6492
Fax: 020 7359 5798
Email: info@barefoot-books.com
Web: www.barefoot-books.com
▶ Independent children's book publisher with an emphasis on original, high quality, colour picture books from traditional cultures all over the World. Internationally acclaimed for its lively and carefully researched texts and dramatic, full colour artwork, Barefoot's titles introduce children to the values and traditions of other cultures and are intended to be enjoyed and treasured for life. The list includes picture books for ages 1-6, picture books for ages 4-adult. Barefoot Collections include anthologies for ages 4-adult. Also available Barefoot Poetry Collections: poetry for ages 4-adult. Available by mail order and through some good bookshops. Call for a catalogue.

Centre for Alternative Technology Mail Order
Mail Order Department,
Centre for Alternative Technology,
Machynlleth SY20 9AZ
Tel: 01654 702 400
Fax: 01654 702 782
Email: steven.jones@cat.org.uk
Web: www.cat.org.uk
▶ The UK's most successful green mail order catalogue has a good selection of books on alternative health therapies and green and environmental issues.

Cygnus Book Club
Bwlch Agored, Carregsawdde,
Llangadog SA19 9DB
Tel: 01550 777 1701
Fax: 01550 777 569
Email: enquiries@cygnus-books.co.uk
Web: www.cygnus-books.co.uk
▶ Provides a friendly and supportive service for buying books on transformation, healing arts, spirituality, wisdom, complementary healthcare and sustainable ways of living. A free monthly magazine allows readers the freedom to buy books at considerably reduced prices and the wealth of experience gained by the club can be shared by consulting the complete list of titles on the website.

Frontline Books
1 Newton Street,
Manchester M1 1HW
Tel: 0161 249 0202
Fax: 0161 236 1101
Email: frontline-books@mcr1.poptel.org.uk
Web: www.poptel.org.uk/BookFinder
Open: Mon-Sat 10am-6pm;
Sun 1-5pm
▶ Manchester's leading radical bookshop, selling green and environmental politics books, newspapers and magazines as well as audios and videos, badges and cards. Campaign groups can make use of the shop's large noticeboard, leaflet rack, box number service, photocopiers, fax machine and computer facilities. The shop also has a 'DIY corner' with easy chairs and tables for customers to browse and for groups to hold meetings.

Greenspirit Books & Schumacher Book Service
14 Beckford Close,
Warminster BA12 9LW
Tel: 01985 215 679
Email: alan@csbooks.karoo.co.uk
Web: www.greenspirit.org.uk
▶ Assembles and offers a wide range of resources – books, videos and audiotapes – by mail order and website. A free, annotated catalogue is produced twice a year, touching on most areas of green interest, including aspects of ecology, 'new' science and cosmology, green economics and enlightened business, green spirituality, creation spirituality, art and creativity, spiritual traditions, aspects of psychology and children's books. Also offers a request service and fast supply of US titles.

Growing Needs Bookshop
11 Market Place,
Glastonbury BA6 9HH
Tel: 01458 833 466
Fax: 01458 834 040
Email: growingneeds@line1.net
Open: Mon-Sat 9am-5pm;
Sun 10.30am-5pm
▶ Supplies a wide range of titles from New Age subjects and alternative therapies to environmental issues and permaculture to parenting. Call for mail order service

Intermediate Technology Bookshop
103-105 Southampton Row,
London WC1B 4HH
Tel: 020 7436 9761
Fax: 020 7436 2013
Email: itpubs@gitpubs.org.uk
Web: www.oneworld.org/itdg/publications.html
Open: Mon-Fri 9.30am-6pm;
Sat 11am-6pm
▶ Europe's leading specialist bookshop on international development. Stocks books on all aspects of development from agriculture to small business development, economics, anthropology and technology. Customers range from World Bank economists to VSO volunteers, anthropologists to water engineers. Part of Intermediate Technology (IT), the organisation founded by EF Schumacher, author of *Small is Beautiful*. IT's overall aim is to build the technical skills of poor people in developing countries, enabling them to improve the quality of their lives and the lives of future generations. Worldwide mail order book service available.

Maya Books
PO Box 379, Twickenham TW1 2SU
Tel: 020 8287 7964
Fax: 020 8287 9068
Email: sales@mayabooks.ndirect.co.uk
Web: www.mayabooks.co.uk
▶ Mail order book company with titles covering subjects ranging from general environmental issues, politics, alternative technology, renewable energy, organic gardening and farming, ecological building, water purification, waste management, etc. An internet site and a resources page is kept up-to-date with information, new titles and a newsgroup list is provided for related subjects.

Mind, Body & Spirit Bookclub
PO Box 199, Swindon SN3 4PX
▶ Bookclub with a wide range of publications on positive health, happy relationships, inner peace, inner potential and much more. Members receive a free magazine approximately every ten weeks, offering them the best and latest books on every aspect of personal growth, health and wellbeing. There is a guaranteed discount on recommended retail prices. Write to the above address for more information on becoming a member.

Natural History & Environment Mail Order Bookshop
2-3 Wills Road,
Totnes TQ9 5XN
Tel: 01803 865 913
Fax: 01803 865 280
Email: nhbs@nhbs.co.uk
Web: www.nhbs.com
Open: Mon-Fri 9am-5pm
▶ Provides a very large, wide ranging list of titles including academic and general interest books on animals, birds, plants and environment, conservation and development issues.

New Aeon Books
110 Tib Street, Manchester M4 1LR
Tel: 0161 839 9293
Fax: 0161 834 4493
Email: bookshop@newaeonbooks.demon.co.uk
Web: www.neweonbooks.demon.co.uk
Open: Mon-Sat 10am-6.30pm;
Sun 12noon-4.30pm
▶ Specialist mind, body and spirit bookshop with a good range of books on pagan matters, the Celtic tradition, shamanism and much more. Call for a customised catalogue.

Now! Books Direct
8 The Arena, Mollison Avenue,
Enfield EN3 7NJ
Tel: 020 8443 5333
Fax: 020 8804 0044
Email: now@airlift.co.uk
Web: nowbooks.co.uk

▶ Mail order and online source specialising in books and audios dedicated to postive change. From Personal Growth, Health & Wellness, and Alternative Healing to Tai Chi and Buddhism, provides products that heal the body, illuminate the mind and enrich the human spirit. View 1,000's of new, classic, and best-selling titles on the website or call for colour catalogues.

Nutri Centre Bookshop
73 Duke Street, London W1N 3HE
Tel: 020 7323 2382
Fax: 020 7636 0276
Email: enq@nutricentre.com
Web: www.nutricentre.co.uk
Open: Mon-Fri 9am-7pm;
Sat 10am-5pm

▶ A well-stocked bookshop and library with access to over 7,000 natural health and holistic living titles, attached to an equally well-stocked natural health product shop (see separate listing). Gentle music and free tea and coffee lead to a chilled out atmosphere perfect for browsing the extensive shelves. For those who can't make it to the shop, a mail order service is offered which promises next day delivery.

Rudolf Steiner Bookshop
35 Park Road, London NW1 6XT
Tel: 020 7724 7699
Fax: 020 7724 4364
Email: rsh@cix.compulink.co.uk
Open: Tues 10.30am-2pm & 3-6pm;
Wed-Fri 10.30am-6pm;
Sat 10.30am-2pm & 3-5pm

▶ Specialist bookshop for the works of Rudolf Steiner and related authors. Topics include Anthroposophy, Steiner-Waldorf Education, Goethean Science, Biodynamic Gardening and Agriculture, Social Sciences, Arts and children's books. Weleda and Hauschka products also available. Call for mail order service.

Soil Association Books and Publications
Bristol House,
40-56 Victoria Street,
Bristol BS1 6BY
Tel: 0117 929 0661
Fax: 0117 925 2504
Email: info@soilassociation.org
Web: www.soilassociation.org

▶ Books available on nutrition and alternative health from the UK's leading group working to promote the benefits of organic food, farming and sustainable forestry.

Tao of Books, The
Station Warehouse, Station Road,
Pulham Market IP21 4XF
Tel: 01379 676 000

▶ Mail order company selling a large number of alternative publications, mostly with a mind, body, spirit focus ranging from books on chakra energies to the pocket *Karma Sutra*, and from Feng Shui to juicing. Call for a free mail order catalogue.

PUBLICATIONS

Food & Drink

Agra Europe (London) Ltd.
80 Calverley Road,
Tunbridge Wells TN1 2UN
Tel: 01892 533 813/511 807
Fax: 01892 527 758/544 895
Email: marketing@agra-europe.com
Web: www.agra-food-news.com

▶ Publishers of *World Organic News*, a global report for the organic food industry. Reports on marketing initiatives and interesting new product lines aimed at both children and adults.

Animal Free Shopper
c/o Vegan Society, 7 Battle Road, St Leonard's-on-Sea TN37 7AA
Tel: 01424 427 393
Fax: 01424 717 064
Email: info@vegansociety.com
Web: www.vegansociety.com

▶ Comprehensive, pocket-sized book listing products suitable for vegans from supermarkets and mainstream shops. An updated edition has recently been published.

BBC Vegetarian Good Food Magazine
AG175 BBC Worldwide,
80 Wood Lane, London W12 0TT
Tel: 020 8576 3767
Fax: 020 8576 3825
Email: veg.good.food@bbc.co.uk
Open: Mon-Fri 9.30am-5.30pm

▶ Designed to advise, support and inspire anyone who wants to cut meat and fish out of their diet and their lifestyles, whether totally or partially. Every issue proves that, as well as the health benefits of being veggie, it has never been easier, tastier or more normal to enjoy a meat-free diet. It is available from newsagents at £1.85. Call for more information.

Country Smallholding Magazine
Station Road, Newport,
Saffron Walden CB11 3PL
Tel: 01799 540 922
Email: info@countrysmallholding.com
Web: www.countrysmallholding.com

▶ The UK's smallholding magazine for small farmers, poultry keepers and organic gardeners. Also smallholding books and videos shop on-line.

FLAG (Food Labelling Agenda) Newsletter
PO Box 25303, London NW5 1WY
Tel: 020 7428 9577
Fax: 020 7428 9577

▶ Regular newsletter from the the Food Labelling Agenda packed with news updates on the various food labelling campaigns active today. FLAG has thousands of supporters ranging from food organisations to individuals, united in their concern about the poor quality of food labelling in the UK. Send an SAE for FLAG leaflet which has information on how to get on to its mailing list in order to receive its newsletter.

Food Magazine
94 White Lion Street, London N1 9PF
Tel: 020 7837 2250
Fax: 020 7837 1141
Email: foodcomm@compuserve.com

Why Not Write a Book?

Find out more about our requirement for new authors on complementary therapy and related subjects by writing to the address below. We will send you further information and a copy of our Authors' Guide. Editorial advice and guidance is available for new and inexperienced writers. (No subsidy is required from authors.)

GUILD HUNT PUBLISHING

The Senior Editor
Guild Hunt Publishing
10a Westbourne Place
Hove, BN3 4GN
(Quote ref GG)

▶ An independent, not-for-profit magazine that has campaigned for safer, healthier food in the UK since 1988. *The Food Magazine* provides unbiased, accurate research on a wide range of issues including genetically modified foods, additives, pesticides, food labelling and animal welfare. Call for a free sample copy, publications list and membership details.

GenEthic News
FREEPOST (LON 6013),
PO Box 6313, London N16 0DY
▶ Bi-monthly newsletter on the ethical and environmental issues raised by genetic engineering.

Jewish Vegetarian Magazine
855 Finchley Road, Golders Green, London NW11 8LX
Tel: *020 8455 0692*
Fax: *020 8455 1465*
Email: *ijvs@yahoo.com*
Open: *Mon-Fri 10am-4pm*
▶ Quarterly magazine sent out to members all over the world (see Chapter One: Food & Drink for details on the Jewish Vegetarian Society).

Pure Modern Lifestyle
271 Upper Street, London N1 2UQ
Tel: *020 7354 2709*
Fax: *020 7226 1311*
Email: *info@greenguide.co.uk*
Web: *www.greenguideonline.com*
▶ Covers the whole range of natural lifestyle issues with interviews, reviews, news, features and product & taste tests. Topics include organic and natural food and drink, eating out, health, beauty, travel, kids, parenting, the home, finance, plus much more. Every issue has great competitions, celebrity interviews and plenty of reader offers and give aways. Subscription costs £35.40 for 12 issues. The best and most comprehensive magazine available for peple who want more from life, naturally.

Organic Living Magazine
9 North Park Road,
Harrogate HG1 5PD
Tel: *01423 705 052*
Fax: *01423 705 051*
Email: *info@organicliving.co.uk*
Web: *www.organicliving.co.uk*

▶ Concentrates on food, drink and health. Call or visit the website for subscription details.

Real Food News
123 Mercers Road, London N19 4PY
Tel: *020 7281 6977*
Email: *kjb@realfoodnews.com*
Web: *www.realfoodnews.com*
▶ Features, interviews, information, listings and special offers for people who care about the food they eat. A newsletter aiming to give people access to great food from traditional producers in Britain. Each newsletter has something to interest, entertain and help the reader find good ingredients to make food that satisfying to cook and eat. Food that's healthy for everyone – and which really tastes good. By subscription only at £34 for 11 issues.

Health Food Business Magazine
Target Publishing, The Old Dairy, Hudsons Farm, Fieldgate lane, Ugley Green CM22 6HJ
Tel: *01279 816 300*
Fax: *01279 816 496*
Email: *carlota@targetpublishing.com*
▶ Published monthly and dedicated to offering the latest information and advice to all matters relating to alternative health, natural food products and the business of retailing. HFB is an essential tool for all health food retailers seeking to grow market share and grasp the opportunities in an expanding marketplace.

Vegetarian
Parkdale, Dunham Road, Altringham WA14 4QG
Tel: *0161 928 0793*
Fax: *0161 926 9182*
▶ Magazine of the Vegetarian Society which promotes vegetarianism as a way of life that respects animals, protects the environment and provides a safer, healthier diet.

Vegetarian Times
4 High Ridge Park,
Stamford CT 06905, USA
Fax: *00 203 322 1966*
▶ American monthly vegetarian magazine now widely available in newsagents in the UK. It has a similar format to other veggie publications in the market with short features and lots of recipes, though it tends more to the health products and supplements side of the field than similar British publications.

VOHAN News International Magazine
58 High Lane, Chorlton, Manchester M21 9DZ
Tel/Fax: *0161 860 4869*
Email: *vohan@net-work.co.uk*
Web: *www.veganvillage.co.uk.*
▶ Published by VOHAN every three to four months, this magazine covers both research in and current news on horticulture and agriculture. A sample copy is available for £2.

The Home

Green Building Press
Nant-y-Gareg, Saron, Llandysul SA44 5EJ
Tel/Fax: *01559 370 908*
Email: *keith@aecb.net*
▶ Publishes the directory *Greener Building* for the Association for Environmentally Conscious Building (see separate listing), its quarterly journal *Building for a Future* and the *Real Green Building Book* annually.

Manchester Fairtrade Guide
c/o Manchester Oxfam (North West) Campaigns Office, 7th Floor, Graeme House, Wilbraham Road, Manchester M21 9AS
Tel: *0161 861 9731*
Fax: *0161 862 9146*
Email: *mancanp@oxfam.org.uk*
▶ Free directory of fair trade stockist in the Manchester area. Originally published in April 1997. Includes information about the Fairtrade Foundation, the fair trade marque and fairly traded products currently on the market. Distributed through local Oxfam shops (see Chapter Two: Clothing & Cosmetics), fair trade stockists and from the address above.

Organic Gardening Magazine
PO Box 29, Minehead TA24 2YY
Tel/Fax: *01984 641 212*
Open: *Mon-Fri 9am-5pm*
▶ Britain's only monthly magazine exclusively for the organic gardener. Provides expert hands-on advice on every aspect of the garden – absolutely chemical free. As a special introductory offer: send an A4 40p SAE for a free sample copy as part of 12 issues for the price of 10 subscription at £22.50. Keep the sample copy whatever you decide and, if you subscribe, the next issue is also free.

Salvo News
18 Ford Village, Berwick-upon-Tweed TD15 2QG
Tel: *01890 820 333*
Fax: *01890 820 499*
Email: *salvo@salvo.co.uk*
Web: *www.salvo.co.uk*
Open: *Mon-Fri 9am-6pm*
▶ Publishes information on architectural antiques, garden ornaments and reclaimed building materials. Directories are available for England, Scotland, Wales, Ireland, France and Belgium. *Salvo News* is published fortnightly and covers environmental and conservation issues, eco-building and news on auctions, exhibitions and architectural theft alerts. Also campaigns for the greater use of reclaimed materials in new build projects and for the dismantling of buildings rather than demolition, enabling materials to be saved and reused.

Self Build
The Well House, High Street, Burton-on-Trent DE14 1JQ
Tel: *01283 742 950*
Fax: *01283 742 957*
Email: *ww@wellhouse.easynet.co.uk*
▶ Monthly magazine covering all issues relating to designing and building your own home. Practical information, contacts and services. Includes regular Helpfile sections that together comprise a comprehensive guide to self-build.

Warmer Bulletin
1st Floor, The British School, Otley Street, Skipton RD23 1P
Tel: *01756 709 800*
Fax: *01756 709 801*
Email: *info@residua.com*
Web: *www.residua.com*
▶ A journal for sustainable waste management.

Health

Caduceus Journal
38 Russell Terrace,
Leamington Spa CV31 1HE
Tel: 01926 451 897
Fax: 01926 885 565
Email: caduceus@oryx.demon.co.uk
▶ For the past 12 years, *Caduceus Journal* has established a reputation internationally for its unique coverage of healing: healing as transformation, embracing the individual, community and planet, and promoting the interconnection between spiritual, ecological, psychological and creative perspectives. *Caduceus* honours real knowledge and experience. The full set (42) of back issues is available for £99, offering a valuable reference resource.

Cahoots
PO Box 12, Levenshulme PDO,
Manchester M19 2EW
Tel: 0161 225 2410
Fax: 0161 225 2410
Email: cahoots@nildram.co.uk
▶ Launched in 1982, *Cahoots* is the North West's regional quarterly guide to alternatives. The 60 page magazine includes a directory of around 250 alternative practitioners and voluntary work charities active in the region, an extensive events and courses calendar, and book and workshop reviews. Recent features, all written by local therapists, have covered the healing power of laughter, ley lines, dowsing, Feng Shui, psychodrama and drama therapy, Homeopathy and much more. Each issue costs £2.50. Annual subscription £12.99 including p&p.

Clinical Acupuncture and Oriental Studies
Tel: 01462 488 900
(sales, subscriptions & enquiries only)
Fax: 01642 483 011
Email: journals@harcourtbrace.com
▶ First international peer-reviewed Acupuncture journal which aims to provide an authoritative and international source of clinical and professional information for the global community. Focuses on the clinical practice and issues of Acupuncture and Oriental medicine.

Fusion Magazine
177 Ditchling Road,
Brighton BN1 6GB
▶ The magazine of The Practice Place centre in Crete which offers courses and workshops on Astanga Yoga amongst other alternative body, breath and movement orientated practices. It takes a particular focus on yoga but also includes features and information on a wide range of other practices from Alexander Technique to Pilates, salsa to swimming, and Tai Chi and other martial arts to diving.

International Journal of Aromatherapy
PO Box 746, Hove BN3 2BD
Tel: 01462 488 900
(subscriptions & enquiries)
Email: journals@harcourtbrace.com
▶ Leading journal for Aromatherapy professionals. Covers the pursuit of health and well-being, whether mental, emotional or physical through Aromatherapy treatment. Contains excellent peer-reviewed articles in subjects ranging from the use of natural, aromatic plant oils and essential oils to Massage and Touch Therapy. Aimed at practitioners from full-time aromatherapists to massage therapists to nurses and physical therapists. Subscription costs £25 per year for individuals.

Journal of Alternative & Complementary Medicine
The Green Library, 9 Rickett Street,
London SW6 1RU
Tel: 020 7385 0012
Fax: 020 7385 4566
▶ Published monthly and available by subscription, the *Journal* contains news, letters and features on a variety of subjects in alternative and complementary health. The Green Library also publishes and sells books on alternative and complementary therapies, diet, nutrition and Mind Body Spirit.

Kindred Spirit
Foxhole, Dartington, Totnes TQ9 6EB
Tel: 01803 866 686
Fax: 01803 866 591
Email: kindredspirit.co.uk
Web: www.kindredspirit.co.uk
▶ The UK's leading guide for Mind, Body and Spirit for over a decade. This glossy quarterly contains news and features. Recent issues included articles on a defence of herbal medicine, food additives, eco-fashion and ethical clothing, wisdom of tribal elders from around the world and much more.

Positive Health
Positive Health Publications Ltd,
51 Queen Square, Bristol BS1 4LH
Tel: 0117 983 8851
Fax: 0117 908 0097
Email: sandra@positivehealth.com
& mike@positivehealth.com
Web: www.positivehealth.com
Open: Mon-Fri 9.30am-5.30pm
▶ The UK's definitive magazine in complementary medicine with authoritative features written by experts in their field, covering all therapies including Acupuncture, Aromatherapy, Asthma, Bodywork, herbal and Chinese Medicine, Massage, Nutrition, Reflexology and Yoga. Published monthly in full colour, *Positive Health* is available from quality newsagents and health food stores. Call for subscription details and visit the website.

PROOF! What Works in Alternative Medicine
Satellite House, 2 Salisbury Road,
London SW19 4EZ
Tel: 020 8944 9555
Fax: 020 8944 9888
Email: wddty@zoo.co.uk
Web: www.wddty.co.uk
▶ A quarterly magazine which provides the latest scientific evidence of how alternative treatments and therapies can be successful in treating many illnesses and conditions. Also consumer-tests leading brands of vitamins, supplements and other health products and tells you which ones live up to their claims and which are a waste of money.

What Doctors Don't Tell You
Satellite House, 2 Salisbury Road,
London SW19 4EZ
Tel: 020 8944 9555
Fax: 020 8944 9888
Email: wddty@zoo.co.uk
Web: www.wddty.co.uk
▶ Published every month for the past eleven years, *WDDTY* is a newsletter which lifts the lid on modern medicine and tells you in plain language what's really working, what isn't and what may harm you. The aim is to give the reader the power to make informed choices about the best treatments for you and your family, and to help you prevent illness by avoiding things in your home and environment that can cause you damage.

Family & Community

AQUILA Magazine
22 Eversfield Road,
Eastbourne BN21 2AS
Tel: 01323 431 313
Fax: 01323 731 136
Email: aquila@pavillion.co.uk
Web: www.aquila.co.uk/aquila
Open: Mon-Fri 9am-5.30pm
▶ A monthly magazine for children aged 8-13 who enjoy challenges. Aims to help children to reason, to encourage them to create and to promote a caring attitude towards others and their environment. Available on subscription from the above address.

LIBED – For the Liberation of Learning
Phoenix House, 157 Wells Road,
Bristol BS4 2BU
Email: editors @ libed.demon.co.uk
Web: www.libed.demon.co.uk
▶ For over 25 years, LIBED has been actively promoting freedom in education by publishing books, pamphlets and magazines and organising meetings, conferences and other events. It examines positive alternatives to the present system of education and how it can be changed. For a free sample of LIBED magazine, send a large SAE to the above address.

Namaste (inc Wholelife News)
Namaste Publishing House,
PO Box 127, Shrewsbury SY3 7WS
Tel: 01743 341 303
Fax: 01743 244 421
Email: namastepublishing-uk@virgin.net
Open: Mon-Fri 9am-6pm
▶ Provides a forum for those who wish to share deeper knowledge and

Media

understanding of what is happening to the planet.

Natural Parent Magazine
Satellite House, 2 Salisbury Road,
London SW19 4EZ
Tel: 020 8944 9555
Fax: 020 8944 9888
Email: wddty@zoo.co.uk
Web: www.wddty.co.uk
▶ Bi-monthly magazine of holistic family living for parents who think a little more deeply about how best to raise their children. Regular features on health, education, dilemmas, your child's spiritual and emotional development, organic living, etc.

Radical Motherhood
60 Osbaldeston Road,
London N16 7DR
Tel: 020 8806 6462
Email: radma@dircon.co.uk
Web: www.radma,dircon.co.uk
▶ Definitely not a 'Mother and Baby' sort of magazine! An alternative journal for parents full of features on a range of topics. Back issues cover vaccination, homebirth, mothering and marijuana, alternatives to state education and regular homoeopathic advice. Some features are particularly directed at those living in the Hackney area, but it's still worth subscribing if you live elsewhere.

UK Express
Subscriptions, SGI-UK, Taplow Court, near Maidenhead SL6 0ER
Fax: 01628 591 238
▶ Monthly publication of SGI-UK, part of the Soka Gakkai International, the worldwide lay organisation of Nichiren Daishonin's Buddhism which is devoted to the creation of value through peace, education and culture. Recent features included: Making Dreams Come True, the Basics of Buddhism and What is True Consideration.

Transport

A to B Magazine
19 West Park, Castle Cary BA7 7DB
Tel: 01963 351 649
Fax: 01963 351 649
Email: post@a2bmagazine.demon.co.uk
Web: www.a2bmagazine.demon.co.uk
▶ Bi-monthly magazine promoting environmentally-friendly forms of transport and specialising in electric and folding bikes. Subscription: £10 per annum.

Bike Culture Quarterly
Open Road Mail Order, FREEPOST NEA3279, Beverley HU17 0BR
Tel: 01482 880 399
Fax: 01482 880 399
Email: openroad@nite-direct.demon.co.uk
Web: www.bikeculture.com
▶ Much praised, advertising-free, quarterly magazine which provides a colourful, informative international forum for all to do with cycling from design and technology to inventions and ideas and campaign issues. Call for subscription details.

Bycycle Magazine
Open Road Mail Order, FREEPOST NEA3279, Beverley HU17 0BR
Tel: 01904 654 654
Fax: 01904 654 684
Web: www.bycycle.com
▶ Bi-monthly magazine for the intelligent cyclist, cycling as transport but no racing or mountain bikes.

Business & Finance

The Environment Post
58 Kingley Close, Wickford SS12 0EN
Tel: 01268 450 024
Fax: 01268 451 111
Email: info@environmentpost.co.uk
Web: www.environmentpost.co.uk
▶ Has been published fortnightly for the past six years. It contains an excellent selection of reports, legislation, env contracts and lots of job opportunities.

Government & Organisations

Animal Contacts Directory
c/o Veggies@ The Rainbow Centre,
180 Mansfield Road,
Nottingham NG1 3HW
Tel: 0115 958 5666
Email: veggies@innotts.co.uk
Web: www.innotts.co.uk/~rainbow/veggies/acdirect.htm
▶ Compiled by Veggies Catering Campaign, the Animal Contacts Directory is comprehensive and has a publicly available up-to-date database, with over 4,000 contacts in the UK and 70 other countries. As well as listing local and national animal rights and welfare campaigns, the directory has many related contacts covering environmental issues and human rights.

Corporate Watch
16b Cherwell St,
Oxford OX4 2BG
Tel: 01865 791 391
Email: mail@corporatewatch.org
Web: www.corporatewatch.org
▶ Campaign group aiming to end corporate dominance. Provides information to empower those seeking to challenge big business on social, ethical or environmental issues. Undertakes research, publishes the Corporate Watch magazine, networks information and hosts conferences and workshops.

Ecologist, The
PO Box 357, Sittingbourne ME9 8UL
Tel: 01795 414 963
Fax: 020 7351 3617
Email: theecologist@galleon.co.uk
Web: www.theecologist.org
Open: Mon-Fri 9am-5.30pm
▶ Founded in 1970, and read in 150 countries, The Ecologist has now been expanded and redesigned, with new writers, new sections and full colour throughout. Economic growth; science; environmental destruction; politics; globalisation; technology; health and big business – are all subjected every month to the scrutiny of our expert writers, commentators and a unique style of investigative journalism. The Ecologist is essential reading for those prepared to rethink basic assumptions. 10 issues per annum.

Environmental Health News
Chadwick Court, 15 Hatfields,
London SE1 8DJ
Tel: 020 7827 9928
Fax: 020 7827 5883
Email: enh&ehj@chgl.com
Web: www.cieh.org.uk
▶ Weekly news magazine for members of the Chartered Institute of Environmental Health (free for members). Also publishes a monthly Environmental Health Journal.

Ethical Consumer Magazine
ECRA Publishing Ltd, Unit 21,
41 Old Birley Street, Hulme,
Manchester M15 5RF
Tel: 0161 226 2929
Fax: 0161 226 6277
Email: ethicon@mcr1.poptel.org.uk
Web: www.ethicalconsumer.org
▶ Bi-monthly, Which? style, ethical consumers' magazine produced by an independent workers co-operative. It rates the companies behind the brand names on a range of ethical and social criteria, assesses the environmental impact of products and advises as to environmental best-buys. Also provides news of the latest ethical and green products, campaigns and boycotts.

Green Futures
Unit 55, 50-56 Wharf Road,
London N1 7SF
Tel: 020 7608 2332
Fax: 020 7608 2333
▶ Leading source of information and debate on how the UK can move towards a sustainable future. Each issue includes lively briefings on the latest news in environmental solutions, along with in-depth features, profiles and opinion pieces. Covers a wide range of issues including energy, transport, eco-taxes, LETs, recycling, rethinking.

Green World
49 York Road,
Aldershot GU11 3JQ
Tel: 01252 330 506
Fax: 01252 330 506
Email: greenworld@btinternet.com
Web: www.greenparty.org.uk/greenworld
▶ Quarterly magazine sponsored by the Green Party containing a good mix of articles, interviews, campaign updates, reviews and letters concerning a range of issues: green politics, economics, animal rights, human rights, the arms trade, transport, energy, globalisation and more.

Local Environment

Centre for Local Environmental
Policies and Strategies,
School of Urban Development and
Policy, South Bank University,
London SW8 2JZ
Tel: 020 7815 7326
Fax: 020 7815 7330
Email: evansb@vax.sbu.ac.uk
▶ International journal focusing on local environmental and sustainability politics and action. Articles cover LA21, recycling, sustainability and local authorities and local housing policy.

Networking Newsletter Project

6 Mount Street,
Manchester M2 5NS
Tel: 0161 226 9321
Fax: 0161 834 8187
Email: networking.newsletter@dial.pipex.com
Web: dialspace.dial.pipex.com/town/terrace/gdn22/NNP
▶ Regular bi-monthly newsletter packed full of local campaign news, the region's most comprehensive campaign events diary, and listings of all campaigning groups in and around Manchester. Subscriptions £6 (individuals), £10 (voluntary bodies without staff), £25 (voluntary bodies with staff), £60 (statutory bodies and ethical businesses).

New Internationalist

Tower House, Lathkill Street,
Market Harborough LE16 9EF
Tel: 01858 439 616
Fax: 01858 434 958
Email: newint@subscription.co.uk
Web: www.newint.org
Open: Mon-Fri 9.30am-5.30pm
▶ The *New Internationalist Magazine* is a unique window on the world. It exists as a voice for those who are forgotten or ignored by the mass media and is one of the world's best sources of alternative news and views. Each month, it will feed your mind with carefully researched facts, spreads, charts, photos and beautifully written articles. Each issue it has a main theme which covers anything from Fair Trade to Torture or Climate Change to Cuba. It's an ideal and succinct introduction to essential subjects. There are also lots of short snappy sections to get you hooked: fact file – bare essentials and basic necessities such as clean water or oil; mixed media – books, films, music and website reviews; world beaters – a monthly meander around the morals of the rich and famous; country profiles; readers' letters; and current news and snippets from the world's media. Cover price is £2.50 with 11 issues per year (Jan/Feb is a bumper issue). 12 month sub £24.85 (UK), Rest of World (£29.85).

Positive News

The Six Bells, Church Street,
Bishop's Castle SY9 5AA
Tel: 01588 640 022
Fax: 01588 640 033
Email: positive.news@btinternet.com
Web: www.oneworld.org/positive_news
▶ Free newspaper that is as positive as its name! Created to report and expand on the activities and solutions that are successful within nations and communities and to make them more widely available, *Positive News* chooses to be a counterbalance in the media in order to promote hope rather than despair.

Prosperity: Freedom from Debt Slavery

268 Bath Street,
Glasgow G2 4JR
Tel: 0141 332 2214
Fax: 0141 353 6900
Email: admcc@admcc.freeserve.co.uk
Web: www.prosperityuk.com
▶ *Prosperity* is a monthly newsletter dedicated to generating grass-roots demand for the government, not the banking system, to create a supply of money debt-free, and to spend it, not lend it, into society on the basis of proven need. Designed as an activists tool which can be used to educate, convince and mobilise, it develops the principles, aims, arguments and rebuttals for this progressive alternative. Subscription: £10 donation for 12 issues, payable to Prosperity.

Red Pepper

1b Waterlow Road, London N19 5NJ
Tel: 020 7281 7024
Fax: 020 7263 9345
▶ A red-green monthly magazine that provides an arena for intelligent political debate. Also takes an international and feminist approach.

Resurgence

Ford House, Hartland,
Bideford EX39 6EE
Tel: 01237 441 293
Fax: 01237 441 203
Email: subs.resurge@virgin.net
Web: www.resurgence.org
▶ Beautifully produced, deeply inspirational bi-monthly magazine at the cutting edge of radical thinking, advocating the use of ethics and spiritual values in science, politics, economics and technology. Inspired by figures such as Mahatma Gandhi, E F Schumacher and Rachel Carson, Resurgence believes that 'small is beautiful'. Content includes biodiversity, human scale education, renewable energy, economic equity and ecology. It carries a large book review section and regular arts pieces. 6 issues annually. Subscriptions: £23.50 UK, £35 overseas (airmail); £28 overseas (surface).

Schnews

c/o On the Fiddle, PO Box 2600,
Brighton BN2 2DX
Tel: 01273 685 913
Fax: 01273 685 913
Email: schnews@brighton.co.uk
Web: www.schnews.org.uk
▶ The 'national newsletter of the protest movement', according to *The Guardian*. Packed with info for action, covering issues such as British Petroleum, road protests, anti-arms movement and much more. Call for info on getting *Schnews* free by email. Otherwise, send as many first class stamps as issues you want to receive or pay a £15 pa subscription. Has a regularly updated party and protest listings on the website.

Squall

PO Box 8959, London N19 5HW
Email: mail@squall.co.uk
Web: www.squall.co.uk
▶ A multimedia forum for radical quality journalism, photography and culture including direct action, environment, genetics, human rights, frontline community initiatives and street culture. It presents accessibly investigative articles and photographic galleries on its regularly updated web service and via its monthly *SQUALL DL* magazine. Also publishes a yearbook in collaboration with direct action news hounds *Schnews* as well as operating a mobile café, photographic exhibition, conscious cinema and sound system at live events. Entirely run by volunteers, with all profits ploughed back into the projects. Subs for *SQUALL DL* are £10 for 12 issues. Cheques payable to SQUALL. The encyclopedic yearbook, *SchQUALL*, is out now and available for £8 (includes P&P).

PUBLISHERS

Animus Ltd
2 Onslow Gardens, London E18 1NE
Tel: 01929 422 727
▶ Vegetarian cooking books available by mail order, including *Meals for All Seasons* and *Light Meals and Snacks*. Send an SAE or order by phone.

Berrydales
Berrydale House, 5 Lawn Road, London NW3 2XS
Tel: 020 7722 2866
Fax: 020 7722 7685
▶ Publishes books on health, food allergies and special diets.

Booklist
78 Castlewood Drive, Eltham, London SE9 1NG
Tel: 020 8856 7717
▶ Supplier of a range of health and healing, mind and body, and natural therapy publications. Call for a mail order catalogue.

CABI Publishing
CAB International, Nosworthy Way, Wallingford OX10 8DE
Tel: 01491 832 111
Fax: 01491 829 198
Email: cabi@cabi.org
Web: www.cabi.org
▶ Dynamic and expanding division of CAB International, a not for profit international organisation dedicated to improving human welfare worldwide through the dissemination, application and generation of scientific knowledge in support of sustainable development. One of the world's foremost publishers of databases, books and journals in agriculture, forestry, veterinary science and related disciplines, and is at the forefront of many of today's development in electronic publishing.

C W Daniel Company Ltd
1 Church Path, Saffron Walden CB10 1JP
Tel: 01799 526 216
Fax: 01799 513 462
Email: cwdaniel@dial.pipex.com
Web: www.cwdaniel.com
▶ Independent book publisher of more than 200 books on alternative healing and the metaphysical since 1903

Directory of Social Change
24 Stephenson Way, London NW1 2DP
Tel: 020 7209 4422
Fax: 020 7209 4130
Email: info@dsc.org.uk
Web: www.dsc.org.co.uk
▶ Publisher of books for the voluntary sector including titles on charity management and fundraising.

Earthscan
120 Pentonville Road, London N1 9JN
Tel: 020 7278 0433
Fax: 020 7837 1816
Email: aluck@kogan-page.co.uk
Web: www.earthscan.co.uk
Open: Mon-Fri 9.30am-5.30pm
▶ The leading UK publisher in the environmental field, specialising in environmental and sustainable development issues and their implications at all levels, from the local to the global. With a worldwide distribution and a wide-ranging readership including general readers, academics, professionals, business people and policy makers, Earthscan aims to influence opinion and policy in ways that promote responsible behaviour towards the environment.

Eco-Logic Books
10-12 Picton Street, Bristol BS6 5QA
Tel: 0117 942 0165
Fax: 0117 942 0164
Email: books@eco-logic.demon.co.uk
▶ Publisher of books that provide practical solutions to environmental problems, LETS and Agenda 21 issues. Call for mail order details.

Element Books Ltd
The Old School House, The Courtyard, Bell Street, Shaftesbury SP7 8BP
Tel: 01747 851 448
Fax: 01747 855 721
▶ Publishes books on a wide range of subjects including alternative health and much more.

Environment Council
212 High Holborn, London WC1V 7BF
Tel: 020 7632 2626
Fax: 020 7242 1180
Email: info@envcouncil.org.uk
Web: www.the-environment-council.org.uk
Open: Mon-Fri 9am-5pm
▶ Produces a range of directories and publications.

Environmental Data Services (ENDS)
Finsbury Business Centre, 40 Bowling Green Lane, London EC1R 0NE
Tel: 020 7278 4745
Fax: 020 7415 0106
Web: www.ends.co.uk
▶ Environmental information journal targeted at the environment sector. Information also available over the internet.

Floris Books
15 Harrison Gardens, Edinburgh EH11 1SH
Tel: 0131 337 2372
Fax: 0131 346 7516
Email: floris@floris.demon.co.uk
Open: Mon-Fri 9am-5.30pm
▶ Publishes books with a holistic world view, including parenting, self-development, health and a range of illustrated children's picture and story books, as well as resource books for parents on how to creatively celebrate festivals and engage young children in craft activities. Call for catalogue.

Gaia Books Ltd
66 Charlotte Street, London W1P 1LR
Tel: 020 7323 4010
Fax: 020 7323 0435
Email: gaiabook@star.co.uk
▶ Produces beautiful, colourful books on green issues and alternative and complementary medicine.

GMC Publications
166 High Street, Lewes BN7 1XU
Tel: 01273 477 374
Fax: 01273 478 606
▶ Publishers and distributors of a wide range of practical books and videos on crafts and similar subjects, including woodcarving, woodturning, green woodworking using handtools, seat weaving, upholstery, gardening, needlecrafts, miniatures, pyrography and much more. Also publishers magazines on similar subjects, such as exotic gardening, furniture making and outdoor photography. Complete catalogue available free of charge.

Green Books
Foxhole, Dartington, Totnes TQ9 6EB
Tel: 01803 863 260
Fax: 01803 863 843
Email: paul@greenbooks.co.uk
Web: www.greenbooks.co.uk
▶ Over the past 10 years, Green Books has built up an impressive list of new and backlist titles on a range of green issues, including renewable energy and ecological building, organic gardening and wholefoods, politics, new economics and community, traditional cultures and spirituality and eco-philosophy. Acts as the UK distributors for Chelsea Green Publishing Co, the leading US publishers in the field of sustainable living. Call for a free catalogue.

Green Guide Publishing Ltd
271 Upper Street, London N1 2UQ
Tel: 020 7354 2709
Fax: 020 7226 1311
Email: info@greenguide.co.uk
Web: www.greenguide.co.uk
▶ Publisher of the Green Guides, directories of eco-friendly goods and services. There are nine editions of the Green Guide – London, The North West, The North East, The South West, Scotland, Wales, The East, The South, and The Midlands, all available in their areas at WH Smith, Waterstones, other bookstores and health and wholefood shops. Alternatively, each can be purchased from the publishers online or from the above address for £9.99 plus £1.50 postage and packaging. For more info, call the number above or send us an email.

Green Tourism and Heritage Guide
97 Heaton Street, Standish, Wigan WN6 0DA
Tel: 01257 423333
Fax: 01257 424444
▶ Annual publication promoting green issues concerning tourism and heritage.

Harcourt Publishers Ltd
32 Jamestown Road,
London NW1 7BY
Tel: 020 7424 4259
Fax: 020 7424 4515
Email: fiona_macnab@harcourt.com
Web: www.churchillmed.com/
journals.html
Open: Mon-Fri 9am-5pm
▶ Owns some of the world's most prestigious publishing imprints which distinguish quality products for the educational, scientific, technical, medical, professional and trade markets worldwide. Under the imprints of Churchill Mosby and WB Saunders, it publishes books aimed specifically at the different areas of the complementary therapies market. Call for further information and a catalogue.

Hawthorn Press
Hawthorn House, 1 Lansdown Lane,
Stroud GL5 1BJ
Tel: 01453 757 040
Fax: 01453 751 138
Email: info@hawthornpress.com
Web: www.hawthornpress.com
▶ Publishers of books on: conflict and peace building; crafts, festivals and family activities; holistic parenting; Rudolf Steiner/Waldorf education; social ecology and renewal; spiritual psychology and anthroposophy; women's and men's development and early years.

Homeopathy Supply Company
Fairview, 4 Nelson Road,
Sheringham NR26 8BU
Tel: 01263 824 683
Fax: 01263 821 507
Email: homsup@paston.co.uk
▶ Mail order company supplying general and specialists books on Homeopathy as well as a wide range of products for the practicising homeopath. Homeopathic remedy posters are also available. Call for a catalogue.

Iron Bridge Film and Television
45 Muswell Road, London N102BS
Tel: 020 8444 9574
Fax: 020 8365 3664
Email: auriemoore@compuserve.com
▶ Produce award-winning complementary health videos regarding asthma, allergies, intolerance and weight. Videos also help viewer find appropriate therapist and therapy right for them. Credit cards accepted.

Jon Carpenter Publishing
Alder House, Market Street,
Charlbury OX7 3PH
Tel: 01608 811 969
Fax: 01608 811 969
Email: joncarpenterpublishing@
compuserve.com
▶ Publishes and distributes books on green politics and economics, sustainability, animal rights, health, education, non-violence, development studies, ethical investment, personal and community development, the built environment, medidation, child-rearing, vegetarianism and more. Call for a free catalogue.

Newleaf
Gill & Macmillan Publishers,
Hulme Avenue, Park West Ireland
Tel: (+353)1 500 9500
Fax: (+353)1 500 9599
Web: www.gillmacmillan.ie
▶ Newleaf is the imprint for an expanding range of Mind, Body and Spiritbooks. The reputation of the list has been established by authoritative books which help transform the way people think, widening their horizons and empowering them to grow with a deeper understanding of their whole self. Subjects cover health and healing, complementary medicine, popular psychology and lifestyle.

Permanent Publications & Permaculture Magazine
The Sustainability Centre,
Hyden House Limited, East Meon,
Petersfield GU32 1HR
Tel: 01730 823 311
Fax: 01730 823 322
Email: hello@permaculture.co.uk
Web: www.permaculture.co.uk
▶ Publishes *Permaculture Magazine – Ecological Solutions for Everyday Living*. Provides information on permaculture for the cool temperate climate and a networking service for the international permaculture community. Also publishes the *Earth Repair* catalogue containing over 350 selected books, journals and videos about all aspects of sustainable living. Send £1 in stamps for a free sample *Permaculture Magazine* and catalogue.

Piatkus Books
5 Windmill Street, London W1P 1HF
Tel: 020 7631 0710
Fax: 020 7436 7137
Email: info@piatkus.co.uk
Web: www.piatkus.co.uk
▶ An independent publishing house specialising in books on health, mind, body and spirit and personal development.

Prion Books Limited
Imperial Works, Perren Street,
London NW5 3ED
Tel: 020 7482 4248
Fax: 020 7482 4203
Email: paulaw@ftech.co.uk
Web: www.prionbooks.com
▶ Publishes books on alternative health, psychology, martial arts, nutrition and more.

Rider Books
Random House UK Limited,
20 Vauxhall Bridge Road,
London SW1V 2SA
Tel: 020 7840 8400
Fax: 020 7233 7398
Web: www.randomhouse.co.uk
▶ An imprint of Ebury Press, a division of Random House Group Ltd, Rider publishes a wide alternative range. Subjects include Buddhism, Feng Shui, Health and Healing, Philosophy and Religion, Psychology and Self-Help, Spirituality, Tarot and Divination.

Rudolf Steiner Press
51 Queen Caroline Street,
London W6 9QL
Tel: 020 8563 2759
Fax: 020 8748 5451
Email: office@rudolfsteinerpress.com
Web: www.rudolfsteinerpress.com
▶ Publisher of titles concerned with the principles of Rudolf Steiner.

Sage Publications
6 Bonhill Street, London EC2A 4PU
Tel: 020 7374 0645
Fax: 020 7374 8741
▶ Books available on health, counselling, Psychotherapy, social work, social policy, education, linguistics, psychology, psychiatry, environmental studies and development.

Schumacher UK
Create Environment Centre,
Smeaton Road, Bristol BS1 6XN
Tel: 0117 903 1081
Fax: 0117 903 1081
Email: schumacher@gn.apc.org
Web: www.one world.org/
schumacherscoc
Open: Tues-Thurs 9am-5pm
▶ The Society was formed in 1977 to build on the legacy of EF Schumacher, the author of *Small is Beautiful*. It works to promote good economic practice, ecological and spiritual values and human scale sustainable development through its annual lectures and seminars in Bristol, Liverpool, Manchester and London. It presents an annual Schumacher award to an unsung hero of the UK environmental movement and publishes *Schumacher Briefings* on environmental issues for policy makers and provides a Schumacher Book Service on related subjects. There are Schumacher Societies in the UK, US, Germany and Ireland. Schumaker UK is part of the Schumaker Circle which includes the Soil Association, New Economics Foundation, Intermediate Technology, the Schumacher College, Green Books and *Resurgance Magazine*.

Sustainability
49-53 Kensington High Street,
London W8 5ED
Tel: 020 7937 9996
Fax: 020 7937 7447
Email: info@sustainability.co.uk
Web: www.sustainability.co.uk
▶ Publish a range of publications which look at the relationship of businesses with their environment and society.

Thorsons
Harper Collins,
77-85 Fulham Palace Road,
London W6 8JB
Tel: 020 8741 7070
Fax: 020 8307 4440
▶ Part of the Harper Collins publishing house, Thorsons produces books

on a wide variety of subjects including Health, Positive Thinking, Complementary Therapies, Astrology, Feng Shui, Healing and Meditation.

Trotman & Co Ltd
2 The Green, Richmond TW9 1PL
Tel: 020 8486 1150
Fax: 020 8486 1161
Email: tom@trotman.co.uk
Web: www.trotmanpublishing.co.uk
▶ UK's leading independent careers publisher. With books and CD-ROM products targeted to the needs of a variety of age groups, ranging from school students to postgraduate and beyond, Trotman & Co have a deserved reputation for providing insightful independent careers guidance on how to progress across the full spectrum of industries.

Vermilion
Random House UK Limited,
20 Vauxhall Bridge Road,
London SW1V 2SA
Tel: 020 7840 8435
Fax: 020 7828 6081
▶ Imprint of Ebury Press, a division of Random House UK Ltd, Vermilion publishes books on a variety of subjects including: Diet and Fitness; Eating for Health; Having a Baby; Parenting; Positive Thinking; Relationships; Natural Therapies and Health.

World Music Network UK
Unit 6, 88 Clapham Park Road,
London SW4 7BX
Tel: 020 7498 5252
Fax: 020 7498 5353
Email: post@worldmusic.net
Web: www.worldmusic.net
▶ Produce a series of music CDs, introductions to the music of different parts of the world, in association with Rough Guides, as well as fund raising World Music compilations with Oxfam, Amnesty and other development and human rights organisations.

Worldly Goods
10-12 Picton Street, Bristol BS6 5QA
Tel: 0117 942 0165
Fax: 0117 942 0164
Email: books@eco-logic.demon.co.uk
▶ Trade distributor for Friends of the Earth, Common Ground, London Ecology Unit, The Environment Council and many others. It is also the main UK importer of permaculture books. As well as distributing to shops, it also serves environmental centres, LETS groups, local and special interest groups.

INTERNET

Epsilon Press Ltd
Longdene House,
Longdene Road, Haslemere
Tel: 01428 656 159
Fax: 01428 641 723
Email: paulw@western-pr.demon.co.uk
Web: www.epsilon-ltd.co.uk
▶ Provides downloadable information on business and environment issues, for example, *Green Management Gurus* and *Towards Sustainable Publishing*.

GreenNet
74-77 White Lion Street,
London N1 9PF
Tel: 020 7713 1941
Fax: 020 7837 5551
Email: coord@gn.apc.org
Web: www.gn.apc.org
▶ Established in 1986, GreenNet is a not-for-profit organisation dedicated to support and promote groups and individuals working for peace, human rights and the environment through the use of information and communication technologies (ICTs). A one-stop resource for the provision of email, connection to the internet, website hosting and design; developed specifically to support small to medium organisations. Also offers training in basic internet skills and web design, training and maintenance.

Health and Fitness Arcade
57 Brantwood Way,
Bromley BR5 3WA
Tel: 01689 837 350
Fax: 01689 837 660
Email: health@oaktree.co.uk
Web: www.health.oaktree.co.uk
▶ An internet resource for a healthy and happy lifestyle, check out their pages and subscribe to their free newsletter.

WWW Design Plus
57 Brantwood Way, Bromley, St Paul's Cray BR5 3WA
Tel: 01689 877 350
Fax: 01689 837 660
Email: info@crystalspirit.com
Web: www.crystalspirit.com/wdp
Open: 8am-8pm
▶ Designs fast loading and elegant websites for alternative small and medium sized companies. Call for free quote.

ORGANISATIONS

Emergency Exit Arts
PO Box 570, Greenwich,
London SE10 0EE
Tel: 020 8853 4809
Fax: 020 8858 2025
Email: info@eea.org.uk
Web: www.eea.org.uk
▶ Leading celebratory arts company in the UK. Its work encompasses a variety of forms. Provides firework displays, which can include sculptural bonfires with various additional elements such as Son et Lumiere, soundtrack and community involvement through lantern processions. Also created the Bollywood Brass Band, the only Indian Wedding Brass Band in the UK. See the website for further information and an opportunity to subscribe to its monthly email newsletter.

Environmental Communicators' Organisation (ECO Journalists)
8 Hooks Cross, Watton-at-Stone,
Hertford SG14 3RY
Tel: 01920 830 527
Fax: 01480 830 538
▶ Set up after the first UN Conference on the Human Environment in 1972, this group aims to bring a green interpretation of significant events to the attention of professional journalists and broadcasters. Publishes an occasional newsletter dealing with key environmental topics like energy policy, transport policy, land access, global warming, etc. Also offers PR support to selected green pressure groups.

INK
170 Portobello Road,
London W11 2EB
Tel: 020 7221 8137
Email: ink@pro-net.co.uk
Web: www.ink.uk.com
Open: Tues-Fri by appointment
▶ Umbrella organisation for most of the alternative press and is a business rather than a political organisation. Currently organising distribution and subscriptions initiatives. Longer term, INK is hoping to help publishers with the business side of their operations and create economies of scale. At April 1999, there were 35 members including The Ecologist, New Internationalist, Red Pepper, Ethical Consumer and Resurgence.

Mailing Preference Service
FREEPOST 22, London W1E 7EZ
Tel: 020 7766 4410
▶ Free service offered to the public that allows you to have your name removed from, or added to, most mailing lists in the country. Just write with your details and requirements to the above address. Call also for more information on the Fax Preference Service which can help prevent junk faxes.

Chosing a sustainable career

When Allan Shepherd, author of The Sustainable Careers Handbook, *left university ten years ago, a careers advisor told him to take up accountancy. Ten years after rejecting the idea out of hand he might be changing his mind.*

Ten years ago a rumour went round my university campus that anyone visiting the careers advisor not knowing what to do with their life would come away with an armful of brochures about accountancy. Luckily I knew I wanted to be a professional environmentalist – even if I didn't know how I was going to become one. I could visit him without fear, or so I thought 'Ever considered being an accountant in the environmental movement?' He said it with such earnest sincerity I couldn't help but laugh out loud. I laughed so much I had to leave his office – never to return.

Which is a shame, because by now I could have been like B&Q's Head of Sustainability Dr Alan Knight OBE – saving millions of pounds' worth of waste, improving working conditions for people in the third world and earning £60,000 a year for doing it. 'My remit,' he told me, 'is to ensure that B&Q is at the cutting edge of social, ethical and environmental issues, and of course maximise commercial benefit.'

Alan Knight is one of a new breed of professional environmentalists whose vision of sustainability lies firmly in the ledger. They help their companies make massive cost savings by shaving waste from the manufacturing, distribution and sales processes, and in doing so add value to their products by giving them an environmental respectability their rivals don't have.

It's what the World Resources Institute (WRI) calls 'four clear reasons for adopting sustainability as a goal:

- preserving the right to operate by meeting the demands of society
- reducing cost and liability by making processes cleaner, more efficient, and community-friendly
- enhancing customer loyalty and market position by taking stewardship for the product throughout its life cycle
- accelerating revenue growth in new markets for environmentally and socially preferable businesses, products and services.'

(Taken from The Next Bottom Line: Making Sustainable Development Tangible)

Prompted by media and consumer interest, B&Q started an environmental programme in 1990. The board of directors were convinced that sustainability was becoming a business issue and set about creating a programme which they hoped would add value to their own products, save money and help the environment. Alan Knight was appointed to do the job.

Ten years on the results are quite amazing. Not only have B&Q cut waste and saved energy in their stores, they have introduced better working conditions for employees in developing countries, where many of the products are sourced, and have introduced a green agenda for all their products. Even their own environmental reporting seems transparent: B&Q acknowledge that they are not a sustainable company but a company working towards sustainability.

Alan Knight's philosophy is straightforward. 'Environmental concerns arise because we don't appreciate enough that we live in one neighbourhood – the planet. I work to ensure that B&Q is being a better trading neighbour. Sustainability can be defined as improving our quality of life in a way which helps our local and global neighbours improve theirs, without compromising the ability of future generations to do the same.'

His vision is concerned with the mundane detail of everyday household items – toilet seats for example. B&Q toilet seats were once individually packaged in polystyrene trays. The trays were removed; the company saved £100,000. The savings to the environment were pretty keen, too, as polystyrene can pose problems in both its manufacture and disposal. It may be environmentalism by numbers but it works. His approach has won Alan Knight an OBE for services to ▶

▶ business and the environment. 'I chose this role because it allows me to challenge the paradigm that environment is anti-business. It's not – in fact, done well, it is good business. In my work, I'm in a position to inspire people with power – buyers, non-governmental organisations and our supply chains – to recognise the importance of social and environmental issues. I enjoy everything about my job – it's interesting, worthwhile and fun'.

If many companies are a little slow to adopt points one, three and four of the WRI's charter, the benefits of point two are obvious. Waste reduction cuts costs, increases profitability, lowers prices and raises market share. For most companies 'doing your bit' is a profitable experience. Take Rank Xerox for example.

In 1996 Rank Xerox won the European Better Environment Award for industry for its policy of recovering and reusing photocopiers. Using its existing network of customers and distribution centres, it collected old machines and sent them to three asset management centres for disassembly and rebuilding.

Some parts of the machine go back into new models and others are remanufactured into new products. Today the three centres employ 400 people and the company has so far saved about £50 million on purchasing of virgin raw materials. Non-reusable plastic panels are sold for recycling – another net revenue earner. In addition 7,200 tonnes of material has been saved from the landfill, a further saving to the company.

Although I didn't know it at the time, the UK government has been promoting such cost savings since 1989, through its highly successful Energy Efficiency and Environment Technology Best Practice Programme; for every £1 of government expenditure, UK manufacturing industry has saved £80.

Helen Carver is the programme's marketing manager. She helps UK companies to cost-effectively reduce their raw material, water and energy consumption. 'I do this by taking examples of good practice and promoting them to the rest of the industry; companies see how energy conservation has benefited others and how it can benefit them. I talk to influential people such as trade associations, local business groups and governments'.

Her brief absorbs many industries – volatile organic chemical, metal finishing, printing, ceramic. glass, mineral and paper – and many different companies – from small, independent dry cleaners to the ICI's of this world. Like Alan Knight she finds the task of saving money for companies and helping the environment at the same time very rewarding. 'This is especially so when you see that a company has made a big saving through implementing a low cost measure (waste minimisation action). This gives you a good feeling'.

Although Helen Carver works exclusively with businesses, the private sector isn't alone in playing the numbers game. Local authorities are also turning on their calculators to find solutions to environmental problems; cost saving analysis is proving a useful model to link health savings with good environmental practice.

Under the Home Energy Conservation Act, local authorities have a duty to reduce energy consumption by 15%. Although this may mean spending money on a programme of home improvements to housing stock, including damp-proofing, insulation and more efficient heating, it can often lead to savings in the provision of health care. Why? Because the home improvements treat the root cause of the problem – poor living conditions and fuel poverty.

It's what Jamie Saunders calls 'integrating a concern for the future with social, economic and environmental considerations, to bring about lasting changes in the long term quality of life'. Jamie Saunders is the City of Bradford Metropolitan District Council's sustainability co-ordinator. 'My work allows me to work on the inside of an organisation and within the mainstream to support the integration of sustainable thinking and practice'.

In practice this means making sure sustainability is part of the budgetary planning process across the whole council; Jamie Saunders has always tried to avoid the niche. 'It means I can encourage the bridge-building and joint working required to implement people-focused solutions to the challenges of today and the future'.

OK, so I was wrong all those years ago. Environmental accountancy really does make sense. Maybe numbers can save the world. To paraphrase Reggie Perrin's boss, I wouldn't have got to where I am today if it wasn't for irony. And where am I today – ten years after walking out of my careers interview? I work in accountancy. No, only kidding. I actually work in sales and marketing – an occupation which concerns itself with income flows, returns and earning/spend ratios. I, too, am a numbers man. ■

The Sustainable Careers Handbook *is written by Allan Shepherd and Fiona Rowe for CAT Publications. It is available from CAT Mailorder for £10.00 + £1.75 p+p.*
Tel: **01654 705959**
or visit **www.cat.org.uk/shopping**

Information & Education   217

Hunting down the facts

The British Library Environmental Information Service offers a number of information services to the environmental community, whether industry, the public sector, consultants, students and concerned citizens. Currently services include:

A free enquiry point

For immediate answers to quick questions such as names and addresses of environmental organisations, suppliers and specialists or checks on literature on environmental issues held by the British Library. Ring, fax or email. The Library is open from 9.30am to 5.00pm, Monday to Friday.

Training

Its training programme introduces environmental workers, information professionals and business people to the widely scattered range of electronic and printed information sources which serve the environment and sustainability. Two seminars are currently available: *Environmental Information on the Internet* and *Sources of Environmental Information*. Each seminar lasts for one day at the British Library's central London location and is run several times a year.

Research Service

The Library's experienced online searchers access several hundred commercial databases and can provide fast and cost-effective solutions to information problems. Some examples of typical searches include: *Environmental baseline data for Azerbaijan*; *Photodegradation of pesticides in soil*; *Treatments for sewage sludge*. It will discuss the search solution with you, work to agreed costs and delivery times and arrange for the supply of original documents.

Longer term, in-depth projects are welcomed. Previous projects have included running training workshops for the United Nations Environment Programme, editing the *Environmental Management & Policy Bulletin* for the British Council in China, and managing the DETR transport information centre. ■

The Environmental Information Service can be contacted at The British Library, 96 Euston Road, London NW1 2DB.
*Tel: **020 7412 7955** Fax: **020 7412 7954***
*Email: **eis@bl.uk***

www.greenguideonline.com

Your Internet gateway to the world of natural, organic and sustainable information and services.

Over the past few months Green Guide Online has been relaunched with new services and an easier to use interface and search facility. This is part of a continuous process of development which will see more news and editorial available online as well as the creation of one of the best shopping sites for natural and organic goods and services.

The website started life as a simple shop window for the Green Guides. Then we added a searchable database based on the structure of the Guides and began building up the number of entries. As the market for organic and natural goods has grown alongside the development of sustainable industries and business practices, so our database has grown. From less than 1,000 listings three years ago, Green Guide Online has grown to a database of over 12,000 entries. This number is set to increase again over the coming months.

Already, the databse is the most comprehensive of its kind available to the public in the UK. The next step will see the addition of overseas listings, especially those from Europe, USA and Australia. The aim is for Green Guide Online to become a truly global source of information and inspiration. To make the search facility even easier, we have added a quick search, based upon key words, to the advanced search.

Alongside this we have begun adding editorial from a wide variety of sources, including our magazine, *Pure Modern Lifestyle*. And we are developing our news service in order to provide daily updated news. We have also just added over 1500 products, including items for clothing, the home and the garden, to our shopping site and are set to increase the range of products to include food and drink in the near future. This means that whatever you are looking for, it will be even easier to find on Green Guide Online. ■

To register for the weekly newsletter, visit Green Guide Online at
www.greenguideonline.com

The search facility is free to use and the database of goods, services and businesses is continuously updated. New editorial and news items are posted on a daily basis.

ENVIRONMENT CENTRES

North West

Community Regeneration
Giants Basin, Potato Wharf, Castlefield, Manchester M3 4LA
Tel: 0161 834 6309
Fax: 0161 834 9909
▶ The Visions Centre, managed by Visions Community Design, aims to provide inspiration, advice, resources and specialist architectural aid to groups and individuals who wish to undertake a community led regeneration project. The centre is open to all and facilities include a community projects exhibition, education service, library and café.

MERCi (Manchester Environmental Resource Centre Initiative)
22a Beswick Street, Ancoats, Manchester M4 7HS
Tel: 0161 273 1736
Email: merci@gn.apc.org
Open: Mon-Fri 8.30am-4.30pm
▶ MERCi has established a Centre for Sustainable Development to act as a focus for debate and action around issues of sustainability. The Centre incorporates voluntary and community groups, green buisnesses, a conference and meeting space and an interactive exhibition about Manchester's urban environment. Also plans to incorporate an organic café and accomodation. The building itself is an example of green design using reclaimed materials and has renewable energy, water conservation measures and compost toilets.

Middle Wood Trust
Middle Wood, Roeburndale West, Lancaster LA2 8QX
Tel: 01524 222 214
Email: middlewood@lancaster.ac.uk
Web: www.marketsite.co.uk/middlewd/index.htm
Open: By appointment only
▶ Environmental sustainability centre which runs regular courses on green issues from woodland crafts and permaculture to eco-villages. On site, there is a forest garden, compost toilets, wind power system, and a camping barn, study centre and yurts for hire. Special courses can be arranged to suit the needs of visiting groups. Community and volunteer meetings on Wednesday afternoons and for a week each month.

Wyreside Ecology Centre
River Road, Thornton, Cleveland FY5 5LR
Tel: 01253 857 890
Open: Apr-Oct 10.30am-4.30pm; Nov-Mar 11am-3pm
▶ Tourist and countryside information centre and open access park. Also visitor centre for the Wyre Estuary Country Park offering a wide range of publications on the history of the area and countryside issues, and some souvenirs.

Rest of UK

Centre for Alternative Technology (CAT)
Machynlleth SY20 9AZ
Tel: 01654 702 400
Fax: 01654 702 782
Email: steven.jones@cat.org.uk
Web: www.cat.org.uk
▶ Concerned with the search for globally sustainable technologies and ways of life, CAT aims to inspire people to use resources wisely and live in harmony with nature. Its display and education centre offers practical ideas and information on environmentally sound technologies. The eight acre visitor centre has working displays of wind, water and solar power, low energy building, organic growing and natural sewage systems. Also offers residential courses, facilities for school groups, a 'green' shop and mail order service, free information and a professional consultancy service. Also runs the Alternative Technology Association which publishes *Clean Slate* magazine, a practical journal of sustainable living.

Earth Centre
Denaby Main, Doncaster DN12 4EA
Tel: 01709 322 090
Fax: 01709 512 010
Email: info@earthcentre.org.uk
Web: www.earthcentre.org.uk
Open: Call for details
▶ A fun, educational centre where the fascinating subject of sustainability comes to life. Set within a breathtaking ecology park are indoor and outdoor hands-on exhibitions surrounded by sustainable garden displays, extensive family adventure playgrounds, an organic café and a range of shops. Tailor-made activities and tours can be arranged along with educational packages for all ages. Opening in Spring 2001 are accommodation and conference facilities for all ages. Call for further information and for booking details.

Penrhos Organic Conference Centre
Penrhos Court, Kington HR5 3LH
Tel: 01544 230 720
Fax: 01544 230 754
Web: www.penrhos.co.uk
▶ Penrhos Court is a 700-year-old Manor Farm on the border of Herefordshire and Wales. It has been saved from demolition and rebuilt over the last 25 years, and is now devoted to food, health and ecology. The businesses are run for the sake of the buildings. There is an annual 'Festival of Green Cuisine' every May featuring organic food and ecology.

INFORMATION SERVICES

The groups listed in this section specialise in providing information on environmental issues. Also take a look in Chapter 10: Government & Organisations – many of the groups listed will supply information on request.

North West

Atmospheric Research and Information Centre (ARIC)
Manchester Metropolitan University, Chester Street, Manchester M1 5GD
Tel: 0161 247 1592
Fax: 0161 247 6332
Email: aric@mmu.ac.uk
Web: www.doc.mmu.ac.uk/aric/arichome.html
▶ National, multi-disciplinary centre for public information on air quality, acid rain, climate change and sustainable development. The primary objective of the information programme is the dissemination of information without advocacy to enable individuals to make their own informed decisions about atmospheric issues. Information is provided for all ages from primary to postgraduate level and is available in a wide variety of formats.

Environment Resource and Information Centre (ERIC)
Technical Library (1st Floor), Central Library, St Peters Square, Manchester M2 5PD
Tel: 0161 234 1987
Fax: 0161 234 4679
Email: technic@libraries.manchester.gov.uk
Open: Mon-Thur 10am-8pm; Fri-Sat 10am-5pm
▶ Information resource area situated within the Central Library devoted to environmental issues. Facilities include internet access, publications, journals, videos, CD ROM and online air quality data. Subject areas include air quality, water, business and the environment, sustainable development, LA21 and transport. Drop in any time during Central Library opening hours.

Information & Education

Manchester Environmental Education Network (MEEN)
c/o The Manchester Metropolitan University, 801 Wilmslow Road, Didsbury, Manchester M20 2QR
Tel: 0161 445 2495
▶ Forum for people involved in the planning of structured learning experience relating to environmental education. The purpose of this forum is to share ideas, develop the means and deliver the strategies to promote, develop and support education throughout Greater Manchester. Members receive a termly newsletter, *The Beehive*.

One World Centre
6 Mount Street (basement of the Friends' Meeting House), Manchester M2 5NS
Tel: 0161 834 8221
Fax: 0161 834 8187
▶ Accommodates a wide range of campaign organisations including Manchester Friends of the Earth, Genetix Snowball, CND, Campaign Against the Arms Trade, The Greater Manchester Landmines Initiative and MERCi (see separate listings for details). Many other groups use the centre as a postal address. There are many leaflets available and a small secondhand bookshop on the premises.

Rest of UK

Animal Contacts Directory
c/o Veggies@ The Rainbow Centre, 180 Mansfield Road, Nottingham NG1 3HW
Tel: 0115 958 5666
Fax: 0115 958 5666
Email: veggies@innotts.co.uk
Web: www.innotts.co.uk/~rainbow/veggies/acdirect.htm
▶ Compiled by Veggies Catering Campaign, the *Animal Contacts Directory* is comprehensive and has an up-to-date database publicly available, with over 4,000 contacts in the UK and 70 other countries. As well as listing local and national animal rights and welfare campaigns, the directory has many related contacts covering environmental issues and human rights.

Arboricultural Association
Ampfield House, Ampfield, Nr Romsey, Hampshire SO51 9PA
Tel: 01794 368 717
Fax: 01794 368 978
Email: treehouse@dial.pipex.com
Open: Mon-Fri 9am-5.30pm
▶ The objective of the Association is to advance the science of Arboriculture for public benefit. This is achieved by promoting a series of publications on trees and their care, holding workshops, seminars and conferences on tree related subjects. Classes of membership exist for both professional arboriculturalists and enthusiastic amateurs. Members receive a quarterly newsletter and a quarterly journal.

Biotechnology Means Business
Chemical and Biotechnological Division, DTI, 151 Buckingham Palace Road, London SW1W 9SF
Tel: 0800 432 100
▶ Provides information on biotechnological developments in textile applications.

British Library, The
96 Euston Road, London NW1 2DB
Tel: 020 7412 7473
Fax: 020 7412 7947
Email: stb-marketing@bl.uk
Web: www.bl.uk
▶ As the national library of the United Kingdom, has an unrivalled collection of books, journals, patents, report literature, manuscripts, maps, printed music and sound recordings, and an ever growing range of electronic information sources covering all subject areas and in all known written languages. Its free and priced information services provide invaluable support for all research – business, industrial, academic, and medical – via its rapid and flexible delivery services.

British Library Environmental Information Service (EIS)
96 Euston Road, London NW1 2DB
Tel: 020 7412 7955
Fax: 020 7412 7954
Email: eis@bl.uk
Web: www.bl.uk/services/stb/eis
Open: Enquiry Line: Mon-Fri 9.30am-5pm
▶ The British Library's EIS can help you find environmental information, whether it be data, news or contacts. In addition to publishing a wide range of environmental titles, the library runs a quick enquiry line and a STM Search Research Service which accesses a wide range of online databases and CD-ROM information. There are also training courses relating to environmental information and its use.

CEH Windermere
Ferry House, Ambleside LA22 0LP
Tel: 015394 42468
Fax: 015394 46914
Email: adp@ceh.ac.uk
Web: www.ife.ac.uk
Open: Mon-Fri 8.30am-5pm
▶ A laboratory conducting research and developing integrated theory for the science of fresh and estuarine waters, including investigations of the genetic, physiological and behavioural mechanisms by which organisms interact with their environment. It also collects, validates and manages relevant environmental data and acts as an international resource of expertise and information.

Climatic Research Unit
University of East Anglia, Norwich NR4 7TJ
Tel: 01603 592994
Fax: 01603 507784
Web: www.cru.uea.ac.uk
▶ One of the world's leading centres specialising in climatology and climate change.

Council for Environmental Education (CEE)
94 London Street, Reading RG1 4SJ
Tel: 0118 950 2550
Fax: 0118 959 1950
Email: enquiries@cee.org.uk
Web: www.cee.org.uk
▶ Membership organisation and charity representing over 80 national organisations working in all sectors of education to provide a national focus for sustainable development and environmental education in England. A range of membership services and publications are available as well as policy development and good practice advice. Prior appointment is necessary for visitors to the information centre and library.

ENDS (Environmental Data Services)
Finsbury Business Centre, 40 Bowling Green Lane, London EC1R 0NE
Tel: 020 7814 5300
Fax: 020 7415 0106
Email: post@ends.co.uk
Web: www.ends.co.uk
▶ Independent publisher which has served environmental professionals since 1978. Publishes reliable information and analysis of developments shaping the business climate. The company has a diverse product portfolio to meet the needs of environmental managers, consultants, policy makers, regulators, lawyers, campaigners and lobbyists.

Environment Council
212 High Holborn, London WC1V 7BF
Tel: 020 7632 2626
Fax: 020 7242 1180
Email: info@envcouncil.org.uk
Web: www.the-environment-council.org.uk
Open: Mon-Fri 9am-5pm
▶ The Council, through its independent charitable status, enables business and industry, non-governmental organisations, academia, local and national government, the community and individuals to find sustainable solutions that work. Through the comprehensive programme of events and training, membership schemes, dissemination of supportive literature and stakeholder dialogue, the Council raises awareness of contemporary issues, providing practical solutions and the tools to make a difference.

Environmental Arts Theatre Company
6 New Street, Edinburgh EH8 8DW
Tel: 0131 558 9889
Fax: 0131 558 9889
Email: environmental.arts@virgin.net
Open: Mon-Fri 10am-5.30pm
▶ Established in 1991 by Malcolm Le Maistre formerly of The Incredible

String Band, the company aims to educate, particularly young people, about the environment. More than a producing theatre company, it goes into schools and communities and works with groups on creative projects about the environment. Call the office or send an email for further information. Patron is David Bellamy.

Environmental Change Institute
5 South Parks Road,
Oxford OX1 3TB
Tel: 01865 281 180
Fax: 01865 281 181
Email: jo.hunter@eci.ox.ac.uk
Web: www.eci.ox.ac.uk
▶ The Environmental Change Institute (ECI) is Oxford University's centre for research and teaching on the environment and sustainability. Within the context of its interdisciplinary approach and links to other University departments, the ECI is formally a Research Unit of the School of Geography and represented through the Faculty of Anthropology and Geography. The ECI was established to organise and promote collaborative interdisciplinary research on the nature, causes and impacts of environmental change and to contribute to management strategies for coping with future environmental change. The breadth of research topics covered by the ECI encompasses four strands of sustainability: lifestyle, natural resource, industrial and ecosystems. With links to over 50 other departments and centres the ECI is the hub of environmental activity in the University. It co-ordinates and promotes environmental work across the University through an initiative known as Oxford Environment. Oxford Environment maintains a regularly updated information service on Oxford's termly seminars having an environmental relevance.

Environmental Information Service
PO Box 197, Cawston,
Norwich NR10 4BH
Tel: 01603 871 048
▶ Keeps a database on environmental organisations – a useful place to contact if you are having problems tracking down any particular organisation.

Fertiliser Manufacturers Association
Greenhill House, Thorpe Wood,
Peterborough PE3 6GF
Tel: 01733 331 303
Fax: 01733 332 909
Email: enquire@fma.co.uk
Web: www.fma.co.uk
▶ The role of the FMA is to provide: response to issues of importance; representation to governments; co-operation with other organisations to achieve joint aims; interpretation and advice on fertiliser regulations; advice on health and safety matters; fertiliser storage, handling and transportation; technical guidance notes and advice; promoting codes of good fertiliser practice and pollution prevention; educational material on nutrient management; and UK statistics on fertiliser consumption.

Foundation for International Enviromental Law and Development (FIELD)
c/o SOAS, University of London,
46-47 Russell Square,
London WC1B 4JP
Tel: 020 7637 7950
Fax: 020 7637 7951
Email: field@field.org.uk
Web: www.field.org.uk
Open: Mon-Fri 9am-5pm
▶ Aims to contribute to the progressive development of international law for the protection of the environment and the attainment of sustainable development. Promotes the development of the law through research; dissemination of the law; teaching, training and publishing; application of the law through the provision of advice and assistance. Currently runs three programmes: Climate change; biodiversity; and trade. Publishes a newsletter three times a year.

Friends of the Earth (FoE)
26-28 Underwood Street,
London N1 7JQ
Tel: 020 7490 1555
Fax: 020 7490 0881
Email: info@foe.co.uk
Web: www.foe.co.uk
▶ One of the UK's leading environmental charities, researching, publishing and providing information on a wide range of local, national and international issues. Call for information or a free list of publications.

Green Solutions for Biomedical Research
PO Box 18653,
London NW3 4DG
Tel: 020 7813 3670
Fax: 020 7813 3670
Email: info@greensolutions.demon.co.uk
Web: www.greensolutions.demon.co.uk
▶ Directory and database (on the internet) of biomedical research methods which demonstrate global and green principles of sustainability and which are ecological, ethical and scientific without altering, modifying or harming any life forms, gender, race, social class, species or planet.

Green Guide Online
Email: info@greenguide.co.uk
Web: www.greenguideonline.com
▶ The UK's most extensive and comprehensive directory of eco-friendly, natural and sustainable goods and services. Thousands of listings available to search online free of charge. Updated regularly, the site contains news, ecommerce and editorial plus regular competitions.

Groundwork National Office
85-87 Cornwall Street,
Birmingham B3 3BY
Tel: 0121 236 8565
Fax: 0121 236 7356
Email: info@groundwork.org.uk
Web: www.groundwork.org.uk
▶ Leading environmental regeneration charity putting the theory behind sustainable development into practice. Works with local people, local authorities and businesses to bring about economic and social regeneration by improving the local environment. Activities and programmes join together the themes of people, places and prosperity and range from landscaping former coal tips to cross-community youth projects in Northern Ireland. Education programmes aim to introduce children to their social and economic environment by examining their physical surroundings. Individual projects raise awareness of environmental issues and help children develop workskills and lifeskills through practical action both in school and in the wider community. Projects are carefully designed to link closely with the National Curriculum and offer teachers a practical and rewarding way of exploring issues of citizenship and sustainable development.

Living Earth International
4 Great James Street,
London WC1N 3DA
Tel: 020 7242 3816
Fax: 020 7242 3817
Email: livearth@gn.apc.org
Web: www.gn.apc.org/LivingEarth
▶ Non-profit making organisation that specialises in environmental

---

www.greenguideonline.com

SHOPPING for clothes, furnishings, household items, food books and magazines **NEWS** updated daily **COMPETITIONS** new prizes every month and great giveaways **1,000**s of products & services

The easiest and most comprehesive online source of organic, natural and ethical goods and services – everything you need for a planet-friendly lifestyle

Information & Education

education. Promotes public awareness of, and community participation in, wider environmental management plans. Also co-ordinates development programmes between government, NGO and business and education sectors, gives training in project development, management and evaluation. Call for details of publication list.

Mineralogical Society
41 Queens Gate, London SW7 5HR
Tel: 020 7584 7516
Email: info@minersoc.org
Web: www.minersoc.org
▶ The Society, instituted in 1876, has the general object of advancing the knowledge of the science of mineralogy and its application to other subjects including crystallography, geochemistry, petrology, environmental science and economic geology. The Society publishes three journals: *Mineralogical Magazine*, *Clay Minerals* and *Mineralogical Abstracts*.

National Centre for Business and Sustainability
The Peel Building,
University of Salford,
Manchester M5 4WT
Tel: 0161 295 5276
Fax: 0161 295 5041
Email: thencbs@thencbs.co.uk
Web: www.thencbs.co.uk
▶ There is a real and pressing need for business to balance the demands of progress with the impacts it creates on society and the environment. Understanding this delicate equation is the main purpose of the NCBS. Since it was set up in 1995, originally as the National Centre for Business & Ecology, the NCBS has been busy advising private and public sector clients on a wide variety of sustainability issues – from applied environmental advice and services, to social accountability and auditing. Inspired and set up by The Co-operative Bank, the NCBS advocates environmentally and socially sustainable solutions to a range of businesses and organisations. The Centre represents a unique partnership between The Co-operative Bank and the four universities of Greater Manchester, drawing on the ecological and ethical policies of the Bank and the technical expertise from the universities and the wider academic community.

Natural History Museum
Cromwell Road,
London SW7 5BD
Tel: 020 7942 5000
Fax: 020 7942 5536
Web: www.nhm.ac.uk
Open: Mon-Fri 10am-5.50pm;
Sun 11am-5.50pm
▶ The world's finest museum of nature, the Natural History Museum is home to a wide range of exhibitions certain to appeal to visitors of all ages. It also offers a wide selection of adult education courses and special field study tours. The Museum's aim is to provide an enjoyable experience of the natural sciences, offering expert tuition to those who share a common enthusiasm, however varied their knowledge and prior experience. Tours include studying buildings, birds and flowers, volcanoes, geology and much more around the world.

Nutri Centre, The
7 Park Crescent,
London W1N 3HE
Tel: 020 7436 5122
Fax: 020 7436 5171
Email: enq@nutricentre.com
Web: www.nutricentre.com
Open: Mon-Fri 9am-7pm;
Sat 10am-5pm
▶ The Centre is located on the lower ground floor of the world renowned Hale Clinic. Opened by Prince Charles in 1988, the Clinic has become one of Europe's leading centres for complementary medicine, housing some of the UK's most eminent practitioners, Europe's leading natural medicines dispensary and an extensive library and bookshop covering the whole range of complementary medicine. The dispensary is the UK's leading supplier of nutritional products, from those found in health food shops and practitioner products to exclusive lines and even the occasional batch made up for specific requirements. There are over 22,000 products on offer. The Centre goes to great lengths to source and research new products becoming available. The Complementary Medicine Education Resource Centre incorporates a book shop and library with a range of books and journals on health and nutrition and a wider range of topics for the mind, body and soul. Requests for books not in stock are welcome and hard-to-find US titles will be tracked down.

Open University Energy and Environment Research Unit
Open University, Walton Hall,
Milton Keynes MK7 6AA
Tel: 01908 653 335
Fax: 01908 653 744
▶ Set up in 1986 to co-ordinate research on sustainable energy technology and to support the development of environmentally sound approaches to the generation and use of energy. It is staffed by members of the Faculty of Technology and is currently directed by Dr David Elliott. Runs a course on Renewable Energy within the Open University's undergraduate programme and supports a range of post-graduate research work.

Oxford Centre for the Enviroment, Ethics and Society
Mansfield College,
Oxford University,
Oxford OX1 3TF
Tel: 01865 270 886
Fax: 01865 270 886
Email:
ocees@mansfield.oxford.ac.uk
Web: users.ox.ac.uk/~ocees
▶ Carries out research and education in order to influence environmental attitudes, political processes, policies and practices towards more sustainable ways of living. It does this by addressing the underlying philosophical, ethical, economic, social, political and legal issues across cultures and academic disciplines.

Oxford Forestry Institute
Department of Plant Sciences,
Oxford University, South Parks Road,
Oxford OX1 3RB
Tel: 01865 275 000
Fax: 01865 275 074
Email: jeff.burley@plants.ox.ac.uk
Web: www.plants.ox.ac.uk/ofi
▶ The OFI is Oxford University's main resource for education, training, research, information and advisory services related to forests and forestry. Its main research fields include: ecology and silviculture; forest genetics and tree improvement; forest biodiversity and plant systematics; forest biotechnology; and forest policy and management. It offers doctoral, MSc and undergraduate education programmes. Its library is the world's library of deposit for forestry and related literature and, together with CABI, the OFI offers an information and dcument delivery service. It publishes an *Annual Report*, Tropical Forestry Papers and OFI Occasional Papers.

Royal Geographical Society (with the Institue of British Geographers)
1 Kensington Gore,
London SW7 2AR
Tel: 020 7591 3000
Fax: 020 7591 3059
Email: press@rgs.org
Web: www.rgs.org
▶ The RGS-IBG is the professional body for Geography. One of its aims is to stimulate the awareness and enjoyment of Geography at all levels, for all people, both in the UK and around the world. The Society supports over 20 research groups; promotes Geography within the National Curriculum; produces scholarly publications; provides training in scientific field techniques; assists personal development in young people through expeditions; presents a popular national lecture series; and provides advice and information through its large map collection, library, and picture library.

UK Ecolabelling Competent Body
c/o DETR, Floor 6, D12 Ashdown House, 123 Victoria Street,
London SW1E 6DE
Tel: 020 7944 3167
Fax: 020 7944 6559

Information & Education

Email:
consumer_products@detr.gov.uk
Web: www.environment.detr.gov.uk/ecolabel/index.htm
▶ The EU Ecolabelling Scheme was set up to encourage manufacturers to produce products that do the least harm to the environment. In the UK, the ecolabels are awarded by the Department of the Environment, Transport and the Regions (DETR). Criteria for the label have been agreed for many products already (eg paint, washing machines, light bulbs, detergents and washing powder) and others are in preparation.

World Animal Net (WAN)
UK 24 Barleyfields,
Didcot OX11 0BJ
Tel: 01235 210 775
Fax: 01235 210 775
Email: worldanimalnet@yahoo.com
Web: www.worldanimalnet.org
▶ Global information network for animal protection organisations and the largest animal advocacy network in the world, with over 1,000 affiliated societies. Animal protection organisations working to improve the status and welfare of animals through legal means can apply for affiliation in writing – there is no affiliation fee. Services include a huge website, the WAN Directory, which lists around 10,000 groups and email newsgroups.

COURSES & COLLEGES

The education centres listed offer a good range of environmental courses. For other and more specialised courses – for example, a course in sustainable design – consult Courses or Organisations in the relevant chapters.

North West

Broomfield College
Derbyshire College of Agriculture & Horticulture, Morley,
Derby DE7 6DN
Tel: 01332 836 600
Fax: 01332 836 601
Email: enquiries@broomfield.ac.uk
▶ Courses in organic farming and horticulture at National Certificate Level, BTEC First Diploma and module options on full-time courses. Also offers day, evening and weekend courses on organic gardening.

Community Exchange
Room 14, The John Owens Building,
c/o The University of Manchester,
Oxford Road M13 9PL
Tel: 0161 275 2038
Fax: 0161 275 7145
Email: community.exchange@man.ac.uk
Web: www.commex.man.ac.uk/comex
▶ Charitable organisation which aims to provide students with subject-related projects and work experience and, at the same time, to support local community organisations such as Manchester Environmental Resource Centre. Call for full listings of projects available.

Horticultural Correspondence College
Little Notton Farmhouse,
16 Notton, Lacock,
Chippenham SN15 2NF
Tel: 0800 378 918 (24 hrs)
Fax: 01249 730326
Email: hc.college@btinternet.com
Web: www.btinternet.com/~hc.college
▶ Correspondence courses in horticultural topics including organic gardening (Soil Association-approved), conservation, herbs and floristry. The timetable for study is entirely flexible to suit the varying needs of students.

Stockport College of Further and Higher Education
Department of Complementary Therapies, Hairdressing and Floristry, Wellington Road South,
Stockport SK1 3UQ
Tel: 0161 958 3191
Fax: 0161 480 6636
Email: stockcoll@c.s.stockport.ac.uk
Open: Mon-Fri 9am-9pm
▶ The Department of Complementary Therapies, Hairdressing and Floristry offers a wide variety of full time and part time courses in Beauty Therapy and Holistic Therapies. The department offers Edexcel Higher Diploma in Health and Holistic Therapies. Also runs Holistic Therapy and Stress Management courses and many short courses, including Indian Head Massage, Aromatherapy, Reflexology, Body Massage and Reiki.

Wythenshawe Community Farm
Delamores Cottage,
Wythenshawe Park,
Wythenshawe Road,
Manchester M22 0AB
Tel: 0161 946 0726
▶ This 5 acre NFCF farm runs regular training courses on general farm care and animal husbandry. Works closely with those with special needs and children. Aims to promote city farming and organic farming techniques. Call for further information on courses and opening times.

Rest of UK

Beau Champ
24610 Montpeyroux,
France
Tel: 01248 602 300 (UK)
Fax: (33) 557 40 65 65 (FR)
Email: johncant@in-net.inba.fr
Web: www.phdcc.com/bc
▶ Permaculture centre in the Dordogne, SW France, offering permaculture courses (see Chapter Eight: Travel & Leisure for detailed listing).

THE GREEN WOOD TRUST

Green wood courses for beginners or experts

A year-long programme of one day to one week courses in every aspect of traditional greenwood making and sustainable woodland management, from chair bodging and pole lathe turning to hedgelaying and coppicing, making a coracle or longbow, charcoal or a willow basket, a hazel hurdle, cleftwood gate or yurt.

Our tutors are some of the best green wood craftspeople from all over Britain, the food is good, the shropshire woodland setting beautiful, the company warm and friendly.

Green Heartwood Oak landscape furniture from sustainable woodlands

Durable, vandal-proof and naturally atractive, our solid oak benches, bollards, picnic tables, and fingerposts sell well to schools, canalsides and local councils – plus memorial seats and commissions. Hurdles, besoms and other greenwood crafts.

The Green Wood Trust is a registered national charity which supports the development of native broadleaved woodland through teaching sustainable management and greenwood craft skills. Volunteers welcome.

Book or order Tel/Fax 01952 432769 Station Road Coalbrookdale, Nr Telford, Shropshire TF8 7DR

Carmarthenshire College of Technology and Art (CCTA)
Pibwrlwyd SA31 2NH
Tel: *01554 748 264*
Fax: *01287 221 730*
Email: *steffen.davis@ccta.ac.uk*
▶ Courses in organic production (BTEC First Diploma), organic techniques in commercial fruit and veg growing (NVQ Levels 1 & 2) and various shorter courses on other organic subjects.

Centre for Sustainable Design
Faculty of Design,
The Surrey Institute of Art & Design,
Falkner Road, Farnham GU9 7DS
Tel: *01252 892 772*
Fax: *01252 892 747*
Email: *mcharter@surrart.ac.uk*
Web: *www.cfsd.org.uk*
▶ Britain's first major centre of sustainable design aiming to balance environmental, social and economic needs, through training, workshops and seminars, electronic conferences, consultancy and publications. A full or part-time MA in Sustainable Design and a range of courses for environmental managers, designers and academics are offered.

Environment Training Network
c/o BTCV Enterprises, Red House,
Hill Lane, Great Barr,
Birmingham BL3 6LZ
Tel: *0121 358 2155*
Fax: *0121 358 2194*
Email: *ENTP@dial.pipex.com*
▶ Offers short courses designed for people working on environmental issues and activities. Courses are run in various parts of the country, all easy to get to by train or car. Many are sponsored by the Countryside Commission, giving half price places for people working (paid, voluntary or trainees) with voluntary organisations in the environment sector and for local authority staff in relevant positions. Call for full programme details.

Greenwood Trust
Station Road, Coalbrookdale,
Telford TF3 7DR
Tel: *01952 432 769*
Fax: *01952 432 769*
Email: *SueChall@aol.com*
▶ Leading organisation which aims to promote the sustainability of native managed woodland through teaching traditional crafts using small diameter green (unseasoned) wood. Produces greenwood benches, finger posts, etc. Varied programme of courses from pole lathe turning and basket-making to chair bodging, for beginners or experienced craftspeople. Accommodation available in attractive woodland site. Also courses in coppicing, charcoal-burning and management of small woodlands. Sells green heartwood oak benches, picnic tables, bollards, fingerposts, hurdles, besoms, etc.

International Summer Courses
Centre for Continuing Education,
The University of Edinburgh,
11 Buccleuch Place,
Edinburgh EH8 9LW
Tel: *0131 650 4400*
Fax: *0131 662 6097*
Email: *CCE@ed.ac.uk*
Web: *www.cce.ed.ac.uk/summer*
▶ International Summer Courses of one to four weeks in length for adults during July and August. Students of all ages and backgrounds from all over the world take part and are offered university accommodation, academic credit and a lively social programme. The exciting range of courses includes environmental studies, nature conservation, archaeology, architecture, history, Gaelic studies, drama, philosophy, film and much more. Call for further details and a prospectus.

Lantra
Lantra House, National Agricultural Centre, Kenilworth CV8 2LG
Tel: *0845 7078 007*
Fax: *024 7669 6732*
Email: *nto@lantra.co.uk*
Web: *www.lantra.co.uk*
▶ Organisation offering modern apprenticeships in environmental conservation to young people, covering the whole land-based sector. Visit the website for more details.

Middlesex University
School of Social Science,
Queensway, Enfield EN3 4SF
Tel: *020 8362 5000*
Fax: *020 8362 6957*
Email: *s.bleasdale@mdx.ac.uk & admissions@mdx.ac.uk*
Web: *www.mdx.ac.uk*
▶ Offers a range of undergraduate and post-graduate programmes in the areas of Environment & Development Studies. Most courses offer work experience/study overseas. Specialises in environmental management, aboriculture, rural development and tourism. Regional interests in Africa, Middle East and Latin America, environmental hazards, development policy and project management.

School of Oriental and African Studies
University of London,
Thornhaugh Street, Russell Square,
London WC1H OXG
Tel: *020 7691 3309*
Fax: *020 7692 3362*
Web: *www.soas.ac.uk*
▶ The world's largest centre for alll aspects of the study of Asia, Africa and the Middle East including development, the environment, tourism, anthropology, politics, law, international relations and religions. Choose from over 400 undergraduate or 70 postgraduate programmes. It is also possible to study over 40 non-European languages either as part of a degree or in evening classes or summer schools. Regular exhibitions of Asian/African art are held at the School's Brunei Gallery (free entry).

Schumacher College
The Old Postern, Dartington,
Totnes TQ9 6EA
Tel: *01803 865 934*
Fax: *01803 866 899*
Email: *schumcoll@gn.apc.org*
Web:
www.gn.apc.org/schumachercollege
Open: *By appointment only*
▶ An international centre for ecological studies welcoming participants from all over the world. Courses are residential and run for between one and three weeks. The course programme explores ecological approaches that value holistic rather than reductionist perspectives. Teachers for 2000/1 include: Vandana Shiva, Jonathon Porritt, Wendell Berry, Mae-Wan Ho, Wofgang Sachs, James Hillman and Ernest Callenbach. Also runs a one-year MSc in Holistic Science accredited by the University of Plymouth, and a new series of one week Business and Sustainability courses. For full details of these courses, a comprehensive course programme and prospectus, call or visit the website.

Index

21st Century Health	70	Animal Defenders	182	Association of Electricity		Baby Organix (Organix Brands)	126
60-40 Vegetarian Café Bar	37	Animal Free Shopper	207	Producers	84	Babynat	126
		Animal Rights Coalition	182	Association of Festival		Baldwin's Health Food Centre	19
A		Animal World & Butterfly House	148	Organisers	150	Bambino Mio	127
A to B Magazine	210	Animus Ltd	212	Association of Gardens Trusts	191	Bank House Farm	27
AAA Greenthings	18	Annemarie Börlind	52	Association of Holistic Biodynamic Massage Therapists	112	Barchester Green Investment	170
Abbey Farm Caravan Park	151	Anthroposophical Medical Association	111	Association of Independent Biodynamic Psychotherapists	112	Barefoot Books Ltd	131, 206
Abbey Life Investment Services	171	Anthroposophical Society in Great Britain	111	Association of Independent Psychotherapists	112	Barn Owl Trust	185
Abbots Vegetable and Herb Garden	18	APEM Ltd	165	Association of Natural Medicine	112	Barry M Cosmetics Ltd	53
Aberdeen Ethical Unit Trust	171	Appleseeds	23	Association of Nature Reserve Burial Grounds	136	Bates Association For Vision Education	113
Absolute Aromas	95	Applied Rural Alternatives	40	Association of Professional Astrologers	112	Bayley School of Reflexology	104
Academy of On-Site Massage	103	Aquasaver Ltd	71	Association of Professional Foresters of Great Britain	186	Baywind Energy Co-op	83
Acanthus Lowe Rae Architects	61	AQUILA Magazine	209	Association of Professional Healers	112	BBC Vegetarian Good Food Magazine	207
Acorn Venture Urban Farm	150	Arboricultural Association	219	Association of Qualified Curative Hypnotherapists	112	Bear Café	37
ACRE Recycling	88	Architectural Salvage Register	67	Association of Reflexologists	113	Beau Champ	157, 222
Action Against Allergy	111	'Are You Doing Your Bit?'	193	Association of Self Builders	63	Beauty Without Cruelty	53
Action for Sustainable Rural Communities (ASRC)	63	Arley Hall and Gardens	148	Association of Women Psychotherapists	113	Beech Tree	151
Action with Communities in Rural England (ACRE)	193	Aromatherapy Associates Training	104	Astrological Association	113	Bennett Natural Products	95
ActionAid	193	Aromatherapy Associates	95	Atlantic Energy	81	Benrené Health International	50, 70
Active Birth Centre	126	Aromatherapy Centre	100	Atlow Mill Centre	100	Berrydales	212
AES Ltd	83	Aromatherapy Organisations Council	112	Atmospheric Research and Information Centre (ARIC)	218	Best Care Products Ltd	95
Agra Europe (London) Ltd.	207	Arup Environmental	165	Audi	143	Better Baby Sling	129
Agralan Ltd	74	Ascent	52	AURO Organic Paint Supplies Ltd	65	Bewley's Tea & Coffee	29
Albert E Sharp Ethical Unit Trust	172	Asda Stores Ltd	28	Authentic Bread Company, The	31	Bicycle Beano Cycle Tours	155
Alexandra Park	148	Ashburton Centre, The	40	Automotive Comsortium on Recycling & Disposal	88	Bicycle Doctor	142
Allchurches Amity Fund	172	Ashfield Organic Farm	23	Aveda Cosmetics Ltd	53	Big Oz Industries Ltd	29
Allerdale Borough Council	178	Aspall	31	Aviation Environment Federation	191	Bike Culture Quarterly	210
Allergyfree Direct Ltd	19	Association for Environment Conscious Building (AECB)	63	Avingormack Guest House	151	Bike Tours Ltd	157
Aloe Care – Grace Cosmetics	52	Association for Improvements in the Maternity Services (AIMS)	132	AXA Sun Life Investment Management	172	Bikehouse	142
Aloe Care – Pro-Ma International	99	Association for Industrial Archeology	191	Ayurvedic Medical Association UK	113	Billington Food Group	31
Alpha Health & Beauty	94	Association for Outdoor Learning, The	133			Bindman & Partners	201
Alternative Therapies	103	Association for Systematic Kinesiology	112	**B**		Bio-D Company Ltd	53, 70
Alternative Vehicles Technology (AVT)	143	Association for the Conservation of Energy	81	B.K. Heather Reflexology Practitioner Course	104	Biodanza UK/Rolando Toro School of Biodanza	104
Aluminium Packaging Recycling Organisation (ALUPRO)	88	Association for Therapeutic Healers	112	Babtie Group, Allott and Lomax Ltd	166	Biodesign	83
Amadeus Vegetarian Hotel	151	Association of Building Engineers	191	Baby Milk Action	132	Biodynamic Agricultural Association (BDAA)	40
Amano	48	Association of Child Psychotherapists	112			Bioflow	95
Amateur Entomologists' Society	185					Bioforce (UK) Ltd	99
Amazon Nails	61					biOrganic Hair Therapy	53
Andrew Fitzpatrick Solicitor	201					BioSave	81
Angelgate Foundation	103					Biotechnology Means Business	219
Animal Aid	182					Bio-wise	164
Animal Contacts Directory	210, 219					Birthworks Bristol	126
						Bishopston Trading Company	48
						Blackmores Ltd	53

Index

Blacksmith's Arms	37	British Association for Counselling	114	British Library, The	219	Brookdale Park	148
Blackwall Ltd	73			British Medical Acupuncture Society	115	Broomfield College	222
Blake Shield B.N.A. Trust	193	British Association for the Advancement of Science	193	British Natural Hygiene Society	115	Broughton Pastures Organic Wine	21
Bleakholt Animal Sanctuary	182	British Association of Applied Chiropractic	114	British Oil Spill Control Association	89	Brown Forman Wines International	21
Body Health Products	23, 94						
Body Shop, The	52	British Association of Fair Trade Shops (BAFTS)	42	British Plastics Federation	191	Bruce Copen Laboratories	95
Body Shops	52			British Rail	140	BTCV	187
Bodywise (UK) Ltd	56	British Association of Homœopathic Veterinary Surgeons	135	British Recovered Paper Association	89	BTTG	51
Bodywise Natural Health Centre	100					BUAV (British Union for the Abolition of Vivisection)	182
Bollards Ltd	62	British Association of Landscape Industries	191	British Reflexology Association	115		
Bollin Valley Project	186			British Rickshaw Network	140	Buckingham Nurseries and Garden Centre	73
Bolsover District Council	86, 178	British Association of Nutritional Therapists	114	British School of Complementary Therapies	104		
Bolton Clinic of Traditional Acupuncture	100					Build For Change Ltd	61
		British Association of Psychotherapists	114	British School of Homeopathy	104	Building Advisory Service & Information Network	63
Bolton Greenwood Group	148			British School of Reflex Zone Therapy (RZT) of The Feet	104		
Bolton Metropolitan Borough Council	86, 178	British Astrological & Psychic Society	114			Bullen Consultants	166
				British School of Reflexology	104	Burrs Country Park	148
Bolton Therapy Centre	100	British Autogenic Society	114	British Society for Allergy, Environmental & Nutritional Medicine	115	Burton Manor College	105
Bolton Tourist Information Centre	148	British Beekeepers Association	182			Bury Business Environment Association	164
Bolton Wildlife Project	187	British Biomagnetic Association	114				
Booja Booja Company, The	31	British Chiropractic Association	114	British Society For Music Therapy	115	Bury Complementary Health Centre	100
Booklist	212	British College of Naturopathy and Osteopathy	104				
Booths Supermarkets	28			British Society of Clinical Hypnosis	115	Bury Metropolitan Borough Council	86
Born Free Foundation	182	British Complementary Medicine Association	114				
BORN	129			British Society of Experimental & Clinical Hypnosis	115	Bury Metropolitan Council	178
Bosch	68	British Confederation of Psychotherapists	114			Bury Nutrition Centre	23
Boswednack Manor	151			British Society of Hypnotherapists	115	Bury Tourist Information Centre	148
Botanical Society of the British Isles	193	British Cycling Federation	142				
		British Divers Marine Life Rescue	185	British Society of Iridologists/ The Anglo European School of Iridology	116	Bushbaby (Pushchairs & Child Carriers)	129
Bowen Association UK	113						
Bowen Technique (Courses)	104	British Federation of Massage Practitioners	115			Business & Environment Practitioner Series	164
Bowen Technique European Register	113			British Society of Medical & Dental Hypnosis	116		
		British Glass Manufacturers Confederation	193			Business and Ecology Demonstration Project	164
BPB Recycling UK	88			British Straw Bale Building Association	63		
Bradwell Mill	151	British Glass Manufacturers Confederation	88			Business in the Environment	169
Brahma Kumaris World Spiritual University	102			British Tarantula Society	185	By Natural Selection	135
		British Hedgehog Preservation Society	185	British Trust for Conservation Volunteers (BTCV North West)	187	Bycycle Club	142
Bramley and Gage	21					Bycycle Magazine	210
Brewhurst Health Food Supplies Ltd	31	British Herbal Medicine Association	115			Bytes Twice	88
				British Trust for Conservation Volunteers (BTCV South Manchester)	187	**C**	
Brian Milligan Associates	166	British Holistic Medical Association	115				
Brilliant Bread Company, The	29					C W Daniel Company Ltd	212
Bristol Cancer Help Centre	100	British Homœopathic Association	115	British Trust for Ornithology; National Centre for Ornithology	185	CABI Publishing	212
British Acupuncture Council	113					Cachumba Café	37
British Allergy Foundation	113	British Humanist Association	136	British Water	193	Caduceus Journal	209
British Alliance of Healing Associations	114	British Institute for Allergy & Environmental Therapy	115	British Wheel of Yoga	116	Café Lusid	37
				British Wind Energy Association	85	Café Pop	37
British Arachnological Society	185	British Institute of Homœopathy	104	Brogdale Horticultural Trust	75	Café Vienna	37
		British Library Environmental Information Service (EIS)	219	Brogdale Orchards Ltd	73	Cafédirect Ltd	31

Index

Cahoots	209	Centre for Sustainable Construction	63
Calderdale Metropolitan Borough Council	178	Centre for Sustainable Design	223
Calico	135	Charles MacWatt Handmade Boots & Shoes	51
Cameo Essential Oils	53	Chartered Institution of Water and Enviromental Management	194
Campaign Against Depleted Uranium	193	Chase Organics Ltd	74
Campaign Against the Arms Trade (CAAT)	194	Chernobyl Children's Project	132
Campaign for Interest-Free Money	173	Cherrytrees Kindergarten	133
Campaign for Nuclear Disarmament (CND)	194	Cheshire Recycling	88
		Cheshire Wildlife Trust	187
Campaign for the Advancement of Responsive Travel	158	Chester Fair Trading	23
		Chestnut House	151
Can Makers Information Service	89	Children's Seating Centre	129
Cancerlink	116	Chiltern Seeds	73
Candle Makers Supplies	69	China Traditional Therapy Clinic	100
Canon Frome Court	102	Chirali Old Remedies	99
Capesthorne Hall Caravan Park	151	Choice Organics	29
Car Club Kit	140	Chorlton Park	148
Caravan Club	156	Chorlton Wholefoods	18, 23
Care for the Wild International	182	Chris & Kate Quartermaine	101
Carlisle City Council	86, 178	Christian Ecology Link	194
Carmarthenshire College of Technology and Art (CCTA)	223	Chrysler	143
		Church Farm Organics	23
Cartridge Family, The	165	Churches Conservation Trust	191
Casella Science and Environment Ltd	166	Circus Zapparelli	150
		CIS Environ Trust	172
Cecile Elstein (Art as Environment)	150	City of Bradford Metropolitan District Council	178
Cedar Health Ltd	29	City of Manchester Council	178
CEH Windermere	219	City of Salford Metropolitan Council	86
CEI Associates Ltd	187	Civic Trust	191, 194
Central Register of Advanced Hypnotherapists	116	Clayton Community Farm	150
Central School of Reflexology	105	Clayton Vale	148
Centre for Advanced Reflexology	100	Cleanworld UK	88
		Clearly Natural	53
Centre for Alternative Technology (CAT)	85, 155, 191, 218	Clearspring Ltd	32
		Clearwell Caves	66
Centre for Alternative Technology Mail Order	206	Clerical Medical Evergreen Trust	172
Centre for Environmental Initiatives (CEI), The	180	Climatic Research Unit	219
		Clinical Acupuncture and Oriental Studies	209
Centre for Environmentally Responsible Tourism	158	Clipper Teas Ltd	32
Centre for Human Ecology	194	Clothes Code Campaign	194
Centre for Organic Husbandry and Agroecology	41	Coastnet	187
College of Cranio-Sacral Therapy	105	Continental Drifts	156
College of Healing	105	Cool Temperate	73
College of Homeopathy	105	Co-operative Bank	171
College of Integrated Chinese Medicine	105	Co-operative Stores	28
		Cordon Vert Cookery School	40
College of Natural Nutrition	105	Cornerhouse	37
College of Natural Therapy	105	Corporate Watch	194, 210
College of Naturopathic and Complementary Medicine	105	Corporation of Advanced Hypnotherapy	116
		Cortijo Romero	157
College of Osteopaths Educational Trust	105	Cosmetics To Go	53
		Council for British Archaeology	191
College of Psychic Studies	105	Council for Complementary & Alternative Medicine	116
Colne Farmer's Market	27		
Colour Therapy Association	116	Council for Energy Efficiency Development	81
Colour Wood	130		
Combined Colleges of Homœopathy	106	Council for Environmental Education (CEE)	219
Comfort Chair Company	66	Council for National Parks	187
Common Ground	194	Council for Posterity	194
Community Car Share Network	140	Council for the Protection of Rural England (CPRE) Cheshire	187
Community Exchange	222		
Community Hygiene Concern	132	Council for the Protection of Rural England (CPRE) North West	187
Community Matters	202		
Community Playthings	130	Council for the Protection of Rural England (CPRE)	187
Community Recycling Network (CRN)	89	Country Bumpkin	23
Community Regeneration Ltd	61, 218	Country Landowners Association	169
Community Technical Aid Centre	63	Country Living	23
Compassion in World Farming (CIWF)	182	Country Smallholding Magazine	207
Complementary Medicine Association	116	Country World	94
		Countryside Agency – Regional Office	181
Complete Remedy	94		
Confederation of Healing Organisations	116	Countryside Agency (Head Office)	181
Conker Shoe Co	51	Countryside Agency (North West)	181
Conscience – The Peace Tax Campaign	194	Countryside Education Trust	194
Conscious Earthwear	48	Countryside Foundation for Education	133
Conservation Foundation, The	187		
Conservatree Print & Design	165	Countryside Trust	188
Construction Industry Enviromental Forum	64	County Loos	69
		Craniosacral Therapy Association of the UK	117
Construction Industry Research & Information Association (CIRIA)	64		
		Craniosacral Therapy Trust	106
Constructive Individuals	61	Crazy Jack	29
Contact Centre	42	Creative Living Centre	101
		Creative Living LETS	173

Index

Creative Therapies	133	Downs & Variava	61	Eden District Council	86	Environment Agency – North Area Office	181
Creda	69	Dr Edward Bach Centre	117	Eden Fellowship	195	Environment Agency – North West	181
Credit Suisse Fellowship Fund	172	Dr Hadwen Trust For Humane Research	182	Eden Green Vegetarian Guest House	151	Environment Agency – South Area Office	181
Creightons Naturally Plc	53	Dragonpaths	135	Education Now	134	Environment Conscious Design Group	65
Critical Mass	142	Duchy Originals	32	Education Otherwise	134	Environment Council	212, 219
Crone's	21	Dunsley Heat Ltd	81	Educational Heretics Press	134	Environment Resource and Information Centre (ERIC)	218
Crucial Trading Ltd	62	Duttons Health Foods	24	Edwin Tucker and Sons Ltd	73	Environment Training Network	223
Cuddyford	151	DWI (Drinking Water Inspectorate)	72	Egg Café, The	37	Environmental Arts Theatre Company	219
Culligan International UK Ltd	71	**E**		Element Books Ltd	212	Environmental Business Communications Ltd	164
Culpeper Herbalists	52	Earth	37	Eleventh Hour	166	Environmental Change Institute	220
Cumbria Wildlife Trust	188	Earth Centre	218	Eller Close	151	Environmental Communicators' Organisation (ECO Journalists)	214
CVS Exchange (Voluntary Organisations LETS)	173	Earth First!	194	Elm Farm Research Centre	41	Environmental Construction Products Ltd	62
Cycle Aid	143	Earth Friendly Baby (Healthquest Ltd)	128	Elysia Natural Skin Care	54	Environmental Data Services (ENDS)	212
Cycle Stockport	142	Earth Friendly Supplies Ltd	70	EMERGE Recycling	88	Environmental Field Work Ltd	166
CycleCity Guides	142	Earth Love Fund	188	Emergency Exit Arts	214	Environmental Health News	210
Cycling Project for the North West	142	Earth Science Teachers Association	134	Empty Homes Agency	195	Environmental Industries Commision	169
Cyclists' Touring Club	143	Earth Spirit Centre	151	Encycleopedia	142	Environmental Information Service	220
Cygnus Book Club	206	EarthKind	182	ENDS (Environmental Data Services)	219	Environmental Investigation Agency	185
D		Earthly Goods	71	Energetix	95	Environmental Law Foundation	202
Daniel Field – Organic and Mineral Hairdressing	53	Earthscan	212	Energy and Environmental Programme	82	Environmental Medicine Foundation	117
David Markham Associates	166	Earthwatch	157	Energy Club	82	Environmental Policy Consultants	166
David Walters Financial Services	170	Earthwise Baby	56, 127	Energy Conservation & Solar	82	Environmental Resources Management	166
Dawson & Son Wooden Toys & Games	130	Earthworks Trading	74	Energy Efficiency Advice Centres	82	Environmental Technology Best Practice Programme	164
Dead Sea Magik	54	East West College of Herbalism	106	Energy Efficiency Best Practice Programme	82	Environmental Transport Association (ETA Services Ltd)	141
Deaft Design	166	Eastbrook Farm Organic Meats	20	Energy from Waste Association	85	Ephytem	99
Demeter Wholefoods	23	Eastern Group Plc	83	Energy Saving Trust	82	Epsilon Press Ltd	214
Deodorant Stone (UK) Ltd, The	54	Eco Clothworks	48, 129	Energy Services Ltd	81	Equal Exchange Trading Ltd	32
Derby & Laurel Co Ltd	88	Eco Solutions	66	Energy Solutions	85	Equitable Ethical Trust	172
Derbyshire County Council	178	Eco-Babes	127	Energyways	81	Erasmus Foundation	117
Design Advice Scheme	81	Eco-Co Products	71	English Gardening School, The	75	Erevna	96
Detoxify Naturally	101	Ecofemme UK	56	English Heritage	191	Escential Botanicals Ltd	55
Development Education Centre	133	Eco-Logic Books	212	English Hurdle	74		
Devon School of Shiatsu	106	Ecological Design Association	64	English Nature	181, 188		
Dian Fossey Gorilla Fund	185	Ecologist, The	210	English Nature (North West)	188		
Diana Drummond Ltd	54	Ecology Building Society	171	English Partnerships	192		
Dickwilletts	151	Ecology Research Group	194	Enough Anti-Consumerism Campaign	195		
Directory of Social Change	202, 212	Ecomerchant	62	Entrust	89		
Disos Pure Wine	21	ECOS Organic Paints	66	Envest	63		
Distinctly Different	156	Eco-Schools Project	134	Environet 2000	89		
Dolma	54	Ecotechnica	85	Environment Agency – Central Area Office	181		
Donkey Sanctuary	182	Ecotricity	83	Environment Agency – Head Office	181		
Dove's Farm Foods	32	Ecotropic	166				
Down to Earth	71	Ecover UK Ltd	71				
		Eco-Zone Ltd	32				

Index

Escor Toys	131	Fertiliser Manufacturers		Fresh Food Company	19	Genetics Forum, The	195
Essential Organics	96	Association	220	fresh network	44	Genetix Snowball	195
Essential Trading Co-operative	30	Fertility UK	132	Fresh Water Filter Company	72	GeneWatch UK	195
Etherow Country Park		Festival Eye	150	Friends of Animals League	183	Geoffrey Collett Associates	
Visitor Centre	148	Festival of Cycling	143	Friends of the Earth		(UK) Ltd	167
Ethical Consumer Magazine	210	Festival of Green Cuisine	150	(FoE)	131, 188, 220	Geological Society	196
Ethical Consumer Research		Fiat Auto UK	143	Friends of the Earth –		George Skoulikas Ltd	32
Association	170, 195	Fichtner Consulting Engineers	166	North West	188	Gestalt Centre	106
Ethical Financial Ltd	170	Filsol Solar Ltd	81	Friends of the Earth		Get Real Organic Foods	32
Ethical Investment Consultancy,		Findhorn Foundation Community	195	(Manchester)	188	GIBB Environmental	167
The	170	Fir Tree Farm Food		Friends of Yoga Society	117	Glenrannoch Vegetarian	
Ethical Investment		Processing Ltd	32	Friends Provident Unit Trust		Guesthouse	152
Co-operative Ltd	170	Fired Earth Shop	68	Managers Ltd	172	Glenwood Vegetarian & Vegan	
Ethical Investment		Fired Earth	67	Friendships	135	Guesthouse	152
Research Service	170	Firleas Vegetarian & Vegan		Frog & Bucket Comedy Club	37	Global Action Plan	196
Ethical Investment Services	170	Guesthouse	152	Froglife	185	Global Ideas Bank	196
Ethical Wares	51	First Effluent Ltd	167	Frontline Books	206	Global Wildlife Division	181
Ethos Baby Care Ltd	127	First Quality Foods	32	FSC Environment Training	167	Globe Farm Guest House	152
European Ayur Veda	101	Firstborn	129	Full Moon Futons	67, 129	Glossop Whole Food Co-Op Ltd	24
European College of		Fit As A Fiddle	24	Full of Beans	24	Gluten Free Foods Ltd	33
Bowen Studies	106	FLAG (Food Labelling Agenda)		Full Spectrum Lighting Ltd	70	GM Free	42
European Shiatsu School	106	Newsletter	207	Fund for the Replacement of		GMC Publications	212
European Wind Energy		Floris Books	212	Animals in Medical		Going for Green & Tidy Britain	
Association (EWEA)	85	Flower And Gem Remedy		Experiments	183	(National Office for England)	181
Everfresh Natural Foods	32	Fellowship	117	Furniture Recycling Network	67	Going for Green & Tidy Britain	
Expressions Breastfeeding	126	Flower Essence Fellowship	106	Fusion Magazine	209	North West	196
		Food and Farming Education		FZ Organic Food	32	Going For Green	196
F		Service	43			Good Health	24
		Food Commission	43	**G**		Good Life, The	37
Faculty of Homœopathy	106	Food Ethics Council	43			Goodlife Foods Ltd	33
Fairtrade Foundation	42	Food Magazine	207	G and G Vitamins	99	Gordon's Fine Foods	33
Faith in Nature	55	Food Parcel, The	37	GAEIA (Global & Ethical		Graiafryn Vegetarian	
Falcon Guest House	152	Foodlife	18	Investment Advice)	170	Guest House	152
Farm and Food Society	195	Ford	144	Gaggenau	69	Graig Farm Organics	20
Farm Animal Welfare Council	182	Forest Stewardship Council (FSC)	65	Gaia Books Ltd	212	Grand Illusions	67
Farmhouse Kitchens	24	Forests Forever	188	Gala Coffee & Tea Ltd	32	Granose Foods	33
Farming and Wildlife		Forever Living Products (UK) Ltd	99	Gale & Snowden	61	Granville Hotel	152
Advisory Group	195	Forever Living Products	96	Garden History Society	195	Grapevine Organics	21
Farms for City Children	156	Forum for Stable Currencies	173	Gaunts House	152	Great Bear Trading Co Ltd	24, 37, 94
Farrow & Humphreys Ltd	55	Foundation for Emotional		Gaylord's Indian Restaurant	37	Greater Manchester and District	
Fauna & Flora International	75	Therapy	106	Gazelle Wind Turbines Ltd	85	Campaign for Nuclear	
Federation of City Farms		Foundation for International		Gelderwood Country Park	148	Disarmament (CND)	196
and Community Gardens		Enviromental Law and		General Chiropractic Council	117	Greater Manchester Centre for	
	43, 151, 156, 195	Development (FIELD)	220	General Council and Register		Voluntary Organisation	202
Federation of Holistic Therapists	117	Fox Hall Vegan B&B	152	of Naturopaths	117	Greater Manchester Coalition of	
Feldenkrais Guild UK	117	Fragrant Pharmacy	94	General Nutrition Centre	94	Disabled People	196
Feng Shui Network		Framlington Health Fund	172	General Osteopathic Council	117	Greater Manchester Cycling	
International	65, 106	Free Form Arts Trust	195	GenEthic News	208	Campaign	142
Feng Shui Society	65	Freeplay Energy Ltd	83	Genetic Engineering Network	42	Greater Manchester LETS	173
Fertile Fibre	73			Genetic Food Alert	42		

Index

Greater Manchester Play Resource Unit (GRUMPY)	134	Greenmount Wild Bird Hospital	183
Green & Away	155	GreenNet	214
Green & Black's	33	Greenpeace	188
Green Alliance	196	Greenpeace (Manchester)	188
Green Ark Animal Nutrition	135	Greens Restaurant	38
Green Baby Co Ltd	129	Greenside Guest House	152
Green Board Game Company	131	Greenspirit Books & Schumacher Book Service	206
Green Books	212	GREENTIE	82
Green Building Press	208	Greenwood Trust	223
Green Cross UK	188	Grimstone Manor	152
Green Cuisine Limited	40	Groundwork Blackburn	196
Green Fish Café	37	Groundwork Creswell	196
Green Flag Park Awards	156	Groundwork East Lancashire	196
Green Futures Festivals	150	Groundwork Liverpool	196
Green Futures	210	Groundwork Macclesfield & Vale Royal	196
Green Gardeners	75	Groundwork Manchester	196
Green Globe	158	Groundwork National Office	167, 196, 220
Green Gourmet	19	Groundwork Rochdale, Oldham & Tameside	197
Green Guide Online	220	Groundwork Rossendale	197
Green Guide Publishing Ltd	212	Groundwork Salford & Trafford	197
Green House	152	Groundwork St Helens, Knowsley & Sefton	197
Green Land Reclamation Ltd	167	Groundwork Tameside	197
Green Paints	66	Groundwork West Cumbria	197
Green Party	201	Groundwork Wigan & Chorley	197
Green Party (Manchester)	201	Groundwork Wirral	197
Green Pastures Public Relations	167	Growing Needs Bookshop	206
Green People Company	55, 96	Growing with Nature	18
Green Shoes	51	Guild of Naturopathic Iridologists International	118
Green Shop, The	70	Guild of Psychotherapists	118
Green Solutions for Biomedical Research	118, 220	Guild of Soul Midwives	136
Green Stationery Company	165		
Green Things	55	**H**	
Green Tourism and Heritage Guide	212	H Weston & Sons Ltd	22
Green Transport Week	140	Hahnemann College of Homeopathy	107
Green Undertakings	136	Hakawerk Neutralseife	71
Green Ways Environmental Care	74	Half Moon Wholefoods	24
Green Wood Trust	156	Halzephron Herb Farm	19, 96
Green World	210	Hamacas Mexicanas: The Mexican Hammock Co	68
Greenbank Restaurant	38	Hampstead Tea & Coffee Company Ltd	33
Greenfibres Eco Goods & Garments	48	Hanson Environment Fund	172
Greenfields Coffins	136		
Greenhouse, The	38		
Greenman-Sykom Group	165		
GreenMarque Art and Landscape	61		

Harcourt Publishers Ltd	213	Holden's Herbal Health	96
Hardy Plant Society	75	Holistic Association of Reflexologists	118
Harvest Forestry	63	Holistic Health Consultancy and College	107
Hawthorn Press	213	Holland & Barrett	25
Hazel Grove Nutrition Centre	24, 94	Holle Baby Foods	127
HDRA – the organic organisation	75, 197	Hollingworth Lake Country Park and Visitor Centre	149
Head for the Hills	156	Home Education Advisory Service	134
Healey Dell Nature Reserve	148	Home Energy Efficiency Scheme	82
Healing Foundation	118	Home Farm Deliveries	18
Healing Tao Centre and Zen School of Shiatsu	107	Homeopathy Supply Company	213
Health & Vegetarian Store	24	Homes For Change Housing Co-operative	197
Health and Diet Company Ltd	99	Homœopathic Medical Association	118
Health and Fitness Arcade	214	Homœopathic Trust	118
Health Food Business Magazine	208	Honda	144
Health Food Centre	24	Honesty Cosmetics	55
Health Rack	24, 94	Honeysuckle Health Foods	25
Healthpol	128	Horticultural Correspondence College	222
Healthstart Ltd	140	Hotel Mocking Bird Hill	157
Healthy Herbs	25, 94	Hotpoint	69
Heath & Heather	33	House of Hemp	49
Heaton Park Farm Centre	148	Howbarrow Organic Farm	18
Helios Homœopathic Pharmacy	96	Huggababy Natural Baby Products	129
Hemp Collective Ltd	19, 70	Human Scale Education	134
Hemp Collective, The	48	Humane Slaughter Association	183
Hemp Food Corporation, The	33	Humanist Movement	197
Hemp Pot, The	55	Humus Wyse Ltd	73
Hemp Trading Company, The	48	Hunt Saboteurs Association	183
Hemp Union Foods	20	Huzur Vadisi	157
Hemp Union	48	Hygeia College of Colour Therapy	107
Hempseed Organics	20		
Henderson Ethical Fund	172	**I**	
Herb Society	75	IBIS International Corporation	96
Herbaticus	136	Iceland Frozen Foods Plc	69
Heritage Education Trust	192	ICOF Group (Industrial Common Ownership Finance Ltd)	173
Heritage Railway Association	192	IFOAM (International Federation of Organic Agricultural Movements)	41
Herm College	107		
Heswall Holistic Centre	101		
Hetcher Moss Gardens	149		
Heywood Park	149		
High Street Wholefoods	25		
Highland Organic Foods	19		
Hill House Retreats: Centre for Wholistic Living	155		
Hill Toy Company	131	Incorporated Society of Registered Naturopaths	118
Hillside Animal Sanctuary	183		
Hipp Organic Baby Foods	126		

Subject Index

Independent Dental Practice	101
Independent Midwives Association	126
Indian Champissage Head Massage Course	107
Industrial Relations Services	167
Industry Council for Electronic and Electrical Equipment Recycling	89
Industry Nature Conservation Association	189
Infinity Foods Co-operative Ltd	30
Informed Parent	132
INK	214
Inland Waterways Association	143
Institute for Complementary Medicine	118
Institute for Local Government	180
Institute for Optimum Nutrition	118
Institute for Social Inventions	197
Institute of Biology	197
Institute of Ecology and Enviromental Management	169
Institute of Energy, The	82
Institute of Horticulture	76
Institute of Logistics & Transport, The	141
Institute of Psychosynthesis	107, 119
Institute of Traditional Herbal Medicine and Aromatherapy	107
Institute of Wastes Management	89
Intermediate Technology Bookshop	206
International Association of Clinical Iridologists	119
International Association of Colour	119
International Federation of Aromatherapists	119
International Federation of Reflexologists	119
International Flower Essence Repertoire	119
International Foundation for Alternative Trade	198
International Fund for Animal Welfare	183
International Institute for Energy Conservation (IIEC)	82
International Journal of Aromatherapy	209
International Kinesiology College	107
International Network of Esoteric Healing	119
International Register of Consultant Herbalists and Homeopaths	119
International Register of Holistic Therapists	119
International Self-Realisation Healing Association	119
International Society for Ecology & Culture	198
International Society for the Prevention of Water Pollution	72
International Summer Courses	223
Invernia Guest House	152
Iron Bridge Film and Television	213
ITDG	198

J

J P Textiles	49
J Sainsbury plc	28
Jack in a Bottle	33
James White Apple Juices	33
Jamesfield Organic Meats	20
Jason Griffiths Furniture	67
Jeans Health Foods	25
Jewish Vegetarian Magazine	208
Jewish Vegetarian Society	42
Ji Chun Chinese Medical Centre	101
Jigsaw Pantry, The	38
Jim's Caff	38
John Hanson/CHT	165
Jon Carpenter Publishing	213
Journal of Alternative & Complementary Medicine	209
Jupiter Ecology Fund	172
Jupiter International Green Investment Trust	172
Just Sharing	25

K

Kan Foods	25
Katherine Hamnett Ltd.	49
Key Travel	157
Keysolar Systems	83
Kids in Comfort	130
Kidsunlimited	133
Kindred Spirit	209
Kinesiology Federation	119
Kinetic Enterprises Ltd	55
Kingswood Consultants	170
Kirklees Metropolitan Borough Council	86, 178
Klober Limited UK	63
Knowsley Metropolitan Borough Council	86, 178
Knutsford Farmers Market	27
Komodo	49
Korean Red Ginseng Company Ltd	99
La Leche League (Great Britain)	126
Labour Behind the Label	198
Lake District National Park Authority	178
Lakeland Natural Vegetarian Guest House	152
Lakeland Pedlar Wholefood Café & Bicycle Centre, The	38
Lancashire County Council	86, 179
Lancashire Wildlife Trust	189
Lancrigg Vegetarian Country House Hotel	152
Land Heritage	41
Land is Ours, The	198
Landlife	192
Landmark Trust	192
Landscape Institute, The	192
Lantra	223
Latitude Imports	68
Lawrence T Bridgeman Ltd	68
LEAF – Linking Environment And Farming	44
Learning Through Landscapes	189
LETSlink UK	174
Letterbox Library	131
Leverhulme Park	149
LIBED – For the Liberation of Learning	209
Liebherr	69
Lifestyle Movement, The	198
Limited Resources	18
Linda Harness School of Holistic Massage	107
Little Green Shop	71
Little Salkeld Watermill	20
Liverpool City Council	86, 179
Liverpool John Moores University, School of Pharmacy and Chemistry	108
Liverpool World Shop	49
Living Earth International	220
Living Lightly Limited	142
Lizzy Induni Traditional Paints	66
Local Environment	211
Lodge Farm	27
London College of Massage	108
London College of Traditional Acupuncture & Oriental Medicine	108
London Herb & Spice	34
London School of Eclectic Therapies Ltd	108
Long Distance Walkers Association	156
Longwood Farm	20
Lord Dowding Fund for Humane Research	183
Loseley Chilled Products Ltd	34
Lower Shaw Farm	152
Lye Cross Farm	34

M

Macclesfield Riverside Park Information Centre	149
Made to Last	51
Mailing Preference Service	214
Making Waves	153
Manchester Amnesty Group	198
Manchester Area Resource Centre (MARC) Ltd	167, 202
Manchester Buddhist Centre	101
Manchester City Council	86
Manchester Civic Society	198
Manchester Community Information Network	198
Manchester Cushion Company, The	97
Manchester Development Education Project	134
Manchester Earth First!	198
Manchester Environmental Education Network (MEEN)	134, 219
Manchester Fairtrade Guide	208
Manchester Homeopathic Clinic	101
Manchester International Arts	150

Subject Index

Manchester International Caribbean Carnival	150	Metrolink	140	National Association of Local Councils	180	Natural Choice Therapy Centre	101
Manchester LA21 Forum	180	Michael House School	133	National Association of Nappy Services	127	Natural Choice	25
Manchester School of Massage	108	Middle Piccadilly Natural Healing Centre	102	National Asthma Campaign	120	Natural Collection	49, 56, 68, 71
Manchester Schumacher Lectures	198	Middle Wood Trust	218	National Canine Defence League	184	Natural Cookery School, The	40
Manchester Tourist Information Centre	148	Middlesex University	223	National Centre for Business and Sustainability	164, 221	Natural Death Centre	136
Manchester Vegan Information	42	Midlands Electricity Board (National Power)	84	National Childbirth Trust	132	Natural Delivery	25
Manchester Wildlife	192	Miele	69	National College of Hypnosis and Psychotherapy	108	Natural Energy Systems	83
Manchester, Three Cities Initiative	133	Millennium Greens National Project Team	192	National Council for Hypnotherapy	120	Natural Flooring Company	62
Manweb (Scottish Power)	84	Mind, Body & Spirit Bookclub	206	National Cycle Network	143	Natural Friends	135
Marine Conservation Society	189	Mineralogical Society	221	National Energy Services	82	Natural Health Care	97
Maristows	128	Miniscoff	34	National Express Coaches	140	Natural Health Clinic, The	101
Markets	27	Ministry of Agriculture Fisheries and Food (MAFF)	181	National Farmers' Union	44	Natural Health Network	101
Marks & Spencer	28	Minton House	103, 153	National Federation of Badger Groups	185	Natural Health Remedies	97
Marple Health	25	Misty's Vegetarian Café	38, 39	National Federation of Spiritual Healers	120	Natural Heights	157
Martin Pitt Eggs	34	Mitsubishi Motors	144	National Federation of Women's Institutes	199	Natural History & Environment Mail Order Bookshop	206
Matan International Group	167	Monkton Wyld Court	101	National Institute of Medical Herbalists	120	Natural History Museum	221
Materia Aromatica	97	Montagne Jeunesse	55	National Playing Fields Association	199	Natural Medicines Society	120
MAVMC Ltd	101	Mornflake Oats Ltd/Morning Foods Ltd	34	National Provident Institution (NPI)	173	Natural Parent Magazine	210
Mawson's	25	Moses Gate Country Park	149	National Pure Water Association	72	Natural Selection	49
Maxim Marketing	55	Moss Bank Park	149	National Recycling Forum	89	Natural Therapeutic Research Trust	109
Maya Books	206	Mossley Fine and Organic Foods	25	National Register of Hypnotherapists and Psychotherapists	120	Naturally Morocco Ltd	157
Mazda UK	144	Motherhemp Ltd	49	National School of Hypnosis and Psychotherapy	108	Naturally Nova Scotia	99
McLibel Support Campaign/ London Greenpeace	198	Mothernature	126	National Society for Clean Air and Environmental Protection	189	Naturally	130
McTimoney Chiropractic Association	120	Mott MacDonald	167	National Society of Allotment & Leisure Gardeners Ltd	76	Nature Maid Company	66
McTimoney Chiropractic College (Oxford) Limited	108	Mount Pleasant Farm	153	National Travelwise Association	141	Nature's Alternative	56
Meadowland Meats	20	Mountain Buggy	130	National Trust, The	192	Nature's Baby	128
Meadows Aromatherapy	97	Movement for Compassionate Living	184	National Trust – North West Office	192	Nature's Own	30
Meat Matters	20	Mr Collier's Emporium	70	National Urban Forestry Unit	189	Nature's Plus UK	99
MERCi (Manchester Environmental Resource Centre Initiative)	218	Mrs Moon's	34	National Vegetarian Week	42	Nature's Treasures Ltd	55
Merewood Joinery	62	Muncaster Water Mill	34	Nationwide Food Survey	42	Nature's Way	34
Meridian Foods Ltd	34	MVM Starpoint	81	Natrababy Babycare Toiletries	128	Natures Best	25
Merlin Kindergarten	133	**N**		Natrababy Cotton Nappies	127	Natures Cocoons	97
Merseyside Play Action Council	133	Nad's Natural Hair Removal Gel	55	Natural Baby Company	127	Natures Gate: Tens Pain Control	126
Mersey Basin Trust	189	Namaste (inc Wholelife News)	209			Natures Grace	25
Mersey River Festival	151	Nantwich Farmers Market	27			Natures Remedies	94
Merseyside Environmental Trust	199	Napiers Herbalists	94			Naturesave Policies Limited	167
Metamorphic Association	120	Nappi Nippas	127			Naturesave Trust	199
Metanoia Institute – Counselling and Psychotherapy	108	National Anti-Vivisection Society	184			Naturewatch	184
		National Association of Environmental Education	134			Neal's Yard Agency for Personal Development	156
		National Association of Farmers Markets	44			Neal's Yard Dairy	19
						Neal's Yard Remedies Mail Order	55
						Neal's Yard Remedies	38, 94
						Neff	69
						Network Health	55
						Networking Newsletter Project	211

Index

New Academy of Business	169	Old Post Office Bed and Breakfast	153	Osteopathic Information Service	109	Phytobotanica	98
New Aeon Books	206			Out of this World	28	Phytofoods	20
New Approaches to Cancer	120	Oldham Development Agency for Community Action	199	Outside In (Cambridge) Ltd	97	Piatkus Books	213
New Economics Foundation	174			Ove Arup & Partners	168	Pilates Foundation UK Limited	121
New Internationalist	211	Oldham Metropolitan Borough Council	86, 179	Oxfam Fairtrade Company	70	PJ Onions	34
New Manchester Woodland Cemetery	136	Omshanti Ltd	131	Oxfam Head Office	50	Plamil Foods Ltd	35
		On The Eighth Day	25, 38, 39	Oxfam Shops	50, 51	Planit Earth	71
New Money	169	One Village	68	Oxford Centre for the Enviroment, Ethics and Society	221	Plants for a Future	76
Newleaf	213	One World Centre	219			Plaskett Nutritional Medicine College	109
NHR Organic Oils	97	One World Week	199	Oxford College of Chiropractic	109		
NIFES Consulting Group	168	Open University Energy and Environment Research Unit	221	Oxford Forestry Institute	221	Poplar Herb Farm	153
Nirvana Natural	55			**P**		Population Concern	199
Nissan	144	Oralgum	97			Portfolio	168
NNC Ltd	168	Orangutan Foundation	185	Paperback Ltd	165	Portman Lodge	153
Nordex Foods UK Ltd	30	Organa	73	Papeterie	70	Positive Health	209
Norfolk Dolls	131	Organic Advisory Service	41	Parentibility	132	Positive News	211
Norford Health Foods	95	Organic Botanics	56	Park Attwood Clinic	102	Postcode Plants Database	73
North Lancs Transport 2000	141	Organic Direct	18	Park Bridge Heritage Centre	149	Potions & Possibilities	56
North Manchester Vegetarian Information Centre	42	Organic Farmers and Growers Ltd	40	Party Organic	39	Powerful Information	189
				Pashley Hand Built Cycles	142	PowerGen	84
North South Travel (NST)	157	Organic Food Company, The	30	Patagonia Café	38	Practice, The	103
North West Complementary Therapy Centre	101	Organic Food Federation	41	Patagonia	49	Practitioners School of Reflexology	109
				Pathways Information Service	120		
North West Transport Activist's Roundtable	141	Organic Gardening Catalogue	74	Pearson Waste Paper Services	88	Premier Training and Development Ltd	109
		Organic Gardening Magazine	208	Peddlers	142		
North West Veggie Guide	42	Organic Herb Trading Company	19	Pedestrians' Association	141	Prestwich Forest Park	149
North Western Naturalists' Union	189	Organic Livestock Marketing Co-operative	41	Pegasus Pushchairs Ltd	130	Prion Books Limited	213
Northern Acupuncture & Osteopath Medical Centre	102			Pen y Coed Construction	61	Project Partners	169
		Organic Living Association	41	Pendlewood	67	Prontapanel Ltd	62
Northern College of Acupuncture	109	Organic Living Magazine	208	Penrhos Court Hotel and Restaurant	153	PROOF! What Works in Alternative Medicine	209
Northern Electric	84	Organic Meat	27				
Northern Ireland Association for the Study of Psycho-Analysis	120	Organic Pudding Company, The	19	Penrhos Organic Conference Centre	218	Prospect Cottage B&B	153
		Organic Shop, The	18			Prosperity: Freedom from Debt Slavery	211
Northern Quarter Street Festival	151	Organic Spirits Company Ltd, The	22	People's Dispensary for Sick Animals (Head Office)	136		
Now! Books Direct	206	Organic Targets Bill Campaign	199			Provamel	35
Npower	84	Organic Warehouse Ltd	30	People's Dispensary for Sick Animals	136	Proven Engineering	83
Nuclear Free Local Authorities Secretariat	180	Organic Way, The	18			Proyecto Ambiental Tenerife	158
		Organic Wine Company	22	People's Trust for Endangered Species	185	Pulp & Paper Information Centre	89
Nutcombe Farm	103	Organic-Haldane Foods	34				
Nutri Centre Bookshop	207	Organico	30	Peppers by Post	20	Punjab Tandoori Indian Restaurant	38
Nutri Centre, The	97, 221	OrganicOxygen.com	19	Perfectly Happy People	128		
Nutshell Natural Paints	66	Organicwool Company	49	Permaculture Association	199	Pure H2O Company	72
O		Organix Healthfoods	26	Permaculture Manchester	199	Pure Modern Lifestyle	208
				Permanent Publications & Permaculture Magazine	213	Pure Organic Foods Ltd	21, 35
Oakcroft Organic Gardens	25	Oriental Therapy International	109			Pure Wine Company, The	22
Oasis Training and Trading	49	Original Organics Ltd	74	Pertwood Organic Cereal Co	34	Queens Park	149
OHS Ltd	168	Osho Leela	103	Pesticide Action Network UK	189	Queenswood Natural Foods	26
Old Court House, The	40	OSMO	66	Philip Dunbavin Acoustics	168	Quest Organic Clothing	49
Old Plawhatch Farm	34	OSSKA Ltd	127	Phyto Pharmaceuticals	97	Quiet Revolution	35

Index

Quince and Medlar Fine Food Vegetarian Restaurant	38	Rider Books	213
Quiraing Lodge Retreat Centre	103, 153	Ridgway's Fairtrade Teas	30
		Rishton Waste Paper	88
		Rixton Clay Pits Nature Reserve	149

R

Rachel's Organic Dairy	35
Radical Motherhood	210
Radical Routes Network	174
Radionic Association Ltd, The	121
Rainbow Bridge Studio	110
Rainbow Wholefoods	30
Raindrain Ltd	75
Rainforest Foundation	189
Ramblers Association	156
Ramsons	37
Ranworth Vegetarian Guesthouse	153
Ravensbourne Wine Company	22
Ray Cornmell Organic Foods	26
Real Food News	208
Real Nappy Association	128
Really Healthy Company Ltd	98
Rebuilding Society Network	174
Recycle-IT!	165
Red Pepper	211
Red Rose Forest	149, 199
Red Triangle Café	39
Reef & Rainforest Tours Ltd	157
Regional Development Agencies	164
Reiki Association	121
Reiki Experience	110
Releat Foods	35
RENUE (Renewable Energy in the Urban Environment)	85
Rescue, The British Archaeological Trust	192
Research Council for Complementary Medicine	121
Residual Ltd	89
Respect for Animals	184
Resurgence	211
Retreat Association	103
Retreat Company, The	103
RE-VIV	49
RHS Garden Wisley	149
Rice Lane City Farm	150
Richard Buxton Environmental Lawyers	202

Robinson Sterling	170
Rochdale Metropolitan Borough Council	86
Rochdale Metropolitan BoroughCouncil	179
Rocks Organic Cordials	35
Rocombe Farm Fresh Ice Cream Ltd	35
Rolf Institute	121
ROM UK	50
Room, the National Council for Housing and Planning	193
Rose Blanc Rouge	23
Rosewood Flooring	62
RoSPA (Royal Society for the Prevention of Accidents)	143
Rossendale Borough Council	86
Rossendale County Council	179
Rossendale Natural Health Clinic	102
Rotherham Metropolitan Borough Council	87, 179
Rowan School of Healing and Personal Development	110
Rowan Tree, The	39
Royal Geographical Society (with the Institue of British Geographers)	221
Royal Horticultural Society	76
Royal Institute of British Architects (RIBA) Bookshop	65
Royal Society for the Prevention of Accidents	141
Royal Society for the Prevention of Cruelty Against Animals (RSPCA)	184
Royal Society for the Protection of Birds (RSPB)	186
RPS Consultants	168
RPS Laboratories	168
RSK Environment Ltd	168
RSPCA Oldham Animal Centre	184
Rudolf Steiner Bookshop	207
Rudolf Steiner Press	213
Rush Matters	68
Ruth White Yoga Centre	110

S

S.A.D. Lightbox Co Ltd	99
SAD Association	121
Saddleworth Cemetery	136
Safeway	28
Sage Publications	213
Sale and Altrincham Conservation Volunteers	193
Salford City Metropolitan Council	179
Salvo News	208
Sam-I-Am	128
Saneline	121
Save Our World	189
Saxonbury Wood	21
Scan-Sit Ltd	67
Scarletts Plant Care	75
Schmidt Natural Clothing	50
Schnews	211
School of Complementary Health	110
School of Homœopathy	110
School of Meditation	110
School of Natural Health Sciences	110
School of Oriental and African Studies	223
Schumacher College	223
Schumacher UK	213
Sciences & Department of Social Work	110
Scientific Exploration Society	190
Scope	50
Scottish Equitable Ethical Trust	173
Scottish Power	84
Seagreens Ltd	35
Seashells Hotel	154
Sedlescombe Vineyard	23
Seeboard plc	84
Seeds of Change	35
Sefton Metropolitan Borough Council	87, 179
Self Build	208
Senior & Carmichael	67
SERA – (Socialist Environment and Resources Association)	201
Shanghai Acupuncture & Herbal Medicine Clinic	102

Shanghai Acupuncture Clinic	102
Shared Earth	52, 68
Shared Interest	170
Sheffield St School Project	133
Shelters Unlimited	61
Shepherd's Purse	154
Shepherdboy Ltd	35
Shiatsu College of London	110
Shiatsu Society	121
Shizhen Clinic of Acupuncture & Chinese Herbs	102
Siemens	69
Simmers of Edinburgh Ltd	35
Simply Organic Food Co	19
Simply Soaps	56
Sinclair Research Ltd	142
Sino-European Clinics	102
Six Mary's Place	154
Skandia Ethical Managed Fund	173
Skyros Holistic Holidys	157
Small World Productions	202
Smile Plastics Ltd	68
Smithills Hall Gardens & Country Park	149
Smurfit Recycling	88
Society for the Promotion of Nutritional Therapy	121
Society for the Protection of Ancient Buildings	193
Society of Homœopaths	121
Society of Teachers of Alexander Technique	121
Soil Association	41, 200
Soil Association – Liverpool Organic Gardeners	41
Soil Association – Staffordshire Group	41
Soil Association – Treowweard Organic Conservation Land Army	41
Soil Association – West Yorkshire & Kirklees Group	41
Soil Association – Wirral Organic Group	41
Soil Association Books and Publications	207
Solar Century	85
Solar Energy Society	85

Index

Solar Housing Design & Build	81
Solar Sense	83
Solgar Vitamins	99
Somerfield Stores Ltd	28
Somerset Organics	21
Soundwood	190
Soup Dragon	131
South Derbyshire District Council	87
South Lakeland District Council	87, 179
South Lancashire Bat Group	186
South Trafford College	110
Southern Electric	84
Sovereign Ethical Fund	173
Soya Health Foods Ltd	35
Spice Direct	98
Spirit of Nature Ltd	50, 56, 71, 128, 130
Splashdown Water Birth Services	126
Squall	211
St Annes Wine Stores	26
St Helens Metropolitan Borough Council	87, 179
St Judes	154
St. Peter's Brewery Company Ltd	23
Staffordshire County Council	179
Staffordshire Moorlands District Council	87
Stalybridge Country Park	149
Stalybridge Health & Food Store	26, 95
Stamp Collection, The	36
Standard Life UK Ethical Fund	173
Stargazer Products	56
Steiner Waldorf Schools Fellowship	134
Steve & Susan Hammett	165
Stewart Distribution	56
Still Pictures	202
Stockport College of Further and Higher Education	222
Stockport Metropolitan Borough Council	87, 179
Stockton-on-Tees Borough Council	87
Straw Bale Building Association for Wales, Ireland, Scotland and England	65
Stress Management Training Institute	110
StressBusters UK	102
Stuart Lennie Woodcrafts	131
Su Su Ma Ma	130
Suantrai Slings	130
Suffolk Herbs	74
Sufi Healing Order of Great Britain	122
Sundance Wholefoods	26
SunDog (Renewable Energy & Environmental Services)	83
Sunflower Wholefoods	18
Sunshine Puppets	135
Super Globe	71
Super Natural Ltd	73
Surfers Against Sewage	200
Survival International	200
Sussex High Weald Dairy Products	36
Sustain: The alliance for better food and farming	44
Sustainability	168, 213
Sustainable Solutions for Business	164
Sustainable Travel and Tourism	158
Sustrans	141
Swedish Window Company	62
Swinton Health Foods	26

T

Take It From Here Limited	19
Tall Ships Play Frames	131
Tam O'Shanter Urban Farm	150
Tameside Business Environment Association	164
Tameside Metropolitan Borough Council	87, 180
Tao of Books, The	207
Taoist Tai Chi Society of Great Britain	122
Taste Connection	26
Taylors of Harrogate	36
Teaching & Projects Abroad	157
Temple Lodge	154
Terre De Semences	74
Tesco Stores Ltd	28
Textile Environmental Network	52
Textile Recycling	51
Texture	68
Thames Organic Produce	30
The Aromatherapy Centre	95
The Association of Light Touch Therapists	122
The Association of Professional Music Therapists	122
The Association of Radical Midwives	126
The British Horse Society	184
The Edgecliffe Hotel	154
The Environment Post	210
The Good Food Shop	26
The Granary	26, 27
The Greenhouse	27
The Health Shop	95
The Healthy House	68, 72, 130
The Healthy Option	95
The Humane Research Trust	184
The Laughing Lentil	27
The Low Pay Unit	200
The Medicine Shop and Clinic	95
The Medlock Balley and Daisy Nook Country Park	150
The Natural Home Shop	68
The Natural Nurturing Network	132
The North West Tourist Board	148
The Old Court House Walking Holidays	155
The Old Court House	154
The Organic Food Consultancy	168
The Picturehouse	61
The Rossan	154
The West Usk Lighthouse	154
Think Natural Ltd	98
Thorsons	213
Tibet Foundation	122
Tidy Britain Group	200
Timber Intent	63
Tisserand Institute	111
TopQualiTea	36
TouchPro Institute of Chair Massage	111
Tourism Concern	158
Town & Country Planning Association	65
Townhead Collective	136
Toyota	144
Toys for Children	131
Traditional Acupuncture Clinic	102
Traditional Wooden Toys	131
TRAFFIC International	186
Trafford Ecology Park	150
Trafford Metropolitan Borough Council	87, 180
Traidcraft Exchange	42, 200
Traidcraft plc	36, 50, 68, 130, 131
Traider Pete	70
Trans Pennine Trail	140
Transcendental Meditation	122
Transport 2000	141
Transport 2000 (East Lancs)	140
Transport Resource Unit	140
Tree Aid	190
Tree Council, The	190
Trees of Time & Place	200
Tregynon Country Farmhouse Hotel	154
Tremeifion Vegetarian Hotel	154
Trericket Mill Vegetarian Guesthouse, Bunkhouse & Camping	154
Treske Ltd	67
Trigonos Centre	103
Triodos Bank	171
Tropical Wholefoods	30
Trotman & Co Ltd	214
TSB Environmental Investor Fund	173
Tucano	50
Tumble Home Furniture	67
Twinings Speciality Teas	36

U

UK Centre for Economic And Environnmental Development (UK CEED)	200
UK College for Complementary Health Care Studies	111
UK Ecolabelling Competent Body	221
UK Environmental Law Association	202
UK Express	210
UK Social Investment Forum	169
UK Waste Paper Ltd	88

Index

UKOWLA	200	VOHAN News International Magazine	208	Wigan Metropolitan Borough Council	87, 180	Work For Change Ltd	168
Uncaged Campaigns	184	Volkswagen UK	144	Wiggly Wigglers	73, 88	World Animal Net (WAN)	222
Undercurrents	202	Voluntary Action Manchester	201	Wild and Free Travel	155	World Development Movement	201
Unicorn Grocery	27	Voluntary Sector North West	201	Wild Carrot	27	World Federation of Healing	122
United Kingdom Polarity Therapy Association	122	Volvo	144	Wild Pear Centre	154	World Music Network UK	214
United Kingdom Register of Organic Food Standards (UKROFS)	42	**W**		Wilderness Trust	190	World Society for Protection of Animals	184
		Wafcol	136	Wildfowl & Wetlands Trust – Head Office	190	World Travel & Tourism Council	158
United Nations Environment and Development UK (UNED-UK)	181	Waiting Room Vegetarian Restaurant, The	39	Wildfowl & Wetlands Trust – WWT Martin Mere	190	World Voices	201
		Waitrose	28	Wildlife and Countryside Link	190	Worldly Goods	214
University of Greenwich School of Health	111	Wakefield Metropolitan Borough Council	180	Wildlife Hotel	155	Worldwide Education Service	135
University of Westminster	111	Walker Paper Recycling Ltd	88	Wildlife Trust for Lancashire, Manchester and North Merseyside	190	WWF-UK	186
URBED	168	Walter Segal Self Build Trust	65			WWW Design Plus	214
UVO(UK) Limited	72	War on Want	201	Wildlife Trusts – UK Operations Centre	190	Wybunbury Acupuncture Clinic	102
		Warmer Bulletin	208			Wyreside Ecology Centre	218
V		Warrington Acupuncture Clinic	102	Wildlife Watch	135	Wythenshawe Community Farm	150, 222
Vale Royal Environment Network	200	Waste Management Information Bureau	90	Wildwings	158		
				Wildwood Designs	67	**Y**	
VAN UK National Vaccination Information Centre	129	Wastepaper Services	88	Wilkinet Baby Carrier (Yep Ltd)	130	Yellow Brick Café Catering	40
		Wastewatch	90	Willey Winkle	70	Yellow Brick Café	39
Vauxhall	144	WATCH Trust for Environmental Education	135	Willing Workers on Organic Farms (WWOOF) UK and International	156	Yeo Cottage	155
Vegan Organic Network (VOHAN)	42					Yerba Mate	31
Vegan Society	43	WATch	132			Yewfield Vegetarian Guesthouse	155
Veganline	51	Water UK	72	Willows Vegetarian Guest House	155	Yoga Biomedical Trust	122
Vegetarian & Vegan Bodybuilding	98	Watermill Restaurant, The	39	Wimtec Environmental Ltd	61	Yoga for Health Foundation	103
		Waterside Wholefoods	39	Wind Fund	173	Yoga Mats Express	98
Vegetarian & Vegan	42	Waterway Recovery Group	143	Windmill Wholefoods	27	Yorkshire Electricity Group	84
Vegetarian Charity	43	Wavegen	83	Wirral Metropolitan Borough Council	88, 180	Young People's Trust for the Environment and Nature Conservation	201
Vegetarian Express	36	Weleda (UK) Ltd	56				
Vegetarian Shoes	51	Wellbeing	98	Withington Healthfoods	27	Your Body Limited	56
Vegetarian Society UK Ltd	43	Werneth Low Country Park	150	Women Working Worldwide	201	Youth Hostels Association	156
Vegetarian Times	208	Wesley Community Café	39	Women's Environmental Network (WEN)	201	Yunnan Tuocha	100
Vegetarian Vacations – The Veggie Tours Directory	155	Wesley Community Project	67			Zanussi	69
		West Crete Holidays	158	Women's Farm & Garden Association	76	Zedz Foods	18
Vegetarian	208	West Dean Gardens	150			Zeffirellis	39
Vegfam	43	Westcountry Organics Ltd	21	Women's Nutritional Advisory Service	122		
VegiVentures	158	Whale & Dolphin Conservation Society	186				
Vermilion	214			Wood Cottage Wildlife Sanctuary	186		
Village Bakery	36	Whale Tail, The	39	Woodcote Hotel	155		
Village Health Food Store	27	What Doctors Don't Tell You	209	Woodcraft Folk	135		
Vinceremos Organic Wines	23	Whitefriars College	111	Woodland Skills Centre	155		
Vintage Roots	23	Whole Earth Foods Ltd	36	Woodland Trust	190		
VIRSA Educational Trust	200	Wholebake Ltd	30	Woodspirits	56		
Vitabiotics Ltd	99	Wholistic Research Company	98	Woody's Vegetarian Restaurant	39		
Viva!	184	WI Country Markets Ltd.	27	Woollibacks	50		
VMM (Vegetarian Matchmakers)	135			Words of Discovery	131		

Categories & Sections

Chapter 1: Food & Drink

Organic Home Delivery	**18**
Organic & Wholefoods	18
North West	18
National	18
Other Foods	19
Meat & Fish	20
Organic Alcohol	21
Shops	**23**
Wholefood, Organic & Fair Trade	23
Organic Meat	27
Markets	27
Supermarkets	28
Wholesalers & Distributors	**29**
Brands & Manufacturers	**31**
Restaurants & Cafés	**37**
Organic	37
Vegetarian	37
Catering Services	**39**
Cookery Courses	**40**
Organisations	**40**
Organic	40
Non-GMOs	42
Fair Trade	42
Vegetarian & Vegan	42
General	43

Chapter 2: Clothing & Cosmetics

Clothing	**48**
Natural & Recycled	48
Charity & Secondhand	50
Footwear	51
Textile Recycling	51
Organisations	51
Cosmetics & Toiletries	**52**
Shops	52
Mail Order & Manufacturers	52
Sanitary Protection	**56**

Chapter 3: Home & Garden

Building & Design	**61**
Architects, Designers & Builders	61
Flooring	62
Windows & Joinery	62
Materials	62
Organisations	63
Furniture & Decoration	**65**
Paints	65

New Furniture	66
Salvage & Secondhand	67
Furnishings	67
Fridges, Freezers & Washing Machines	68
Miscellaneous Suppliers	69
Cleaning & Laundry	**70**
Products	70
Water	**71**
Filters	71
Organisations	72
Gardening	**73**
Nurseries & Garden Centres	73
Composting & Growing Mediums	73
Plants & Seeds	73
Supplies	74
Organisations & Services	75

Chapter 4: Energy & Recycling

Energy Efficiency	**81**
Products	81
Services	81
Advice & Organisations	81
Renewable Energy	**83**
Suppliers	83
Utilities	83
Organisations	84
Recycling	**86**
Councils	86
Services	88
Organisations	88

Chapter 5: Health

Products	**94**
Shops	94
Mail Order	95
Manufacturers	99
Centres	**100**
Retreats	**102**
Courses & Colleges	**103**
Organisations	**111**

Chapter 6: Family & Children

Babies & Children	**126**
Birth	126
Breastfeeding	126
Baby Food & Milk	126
Nappies	127
Health	128
Furniture, Clothing & Carriers	129

Toys	130
Books	131
Organisations & Advice	131
Education	**133**
Schools, Kindergartens & Nurseries	133
Organisations & Resources	133
Friends & Partners	**135**
Vets & Pets	**135**
Communities	**136**
Natural Death	**136**
Organisations	136

Chapter 7: Transport

Transport	**140**
Transport Information	140
Transport Initiatives	140
Car Sharing & Clubs	140
Local Organisations	140
UK Organisations	141
Cycling	**142**
Supplies	142
Local Organisations	142
UK Organisations	142
Water Transport	**143**
Sustainable Vehicles	**143**
Suppliers & Organisations	143
Car Manufacturers	143

Chapter 8: Travel & Leisure

North West	**148**
Tourist Boards and Information Centres	148
Places to Visit	148
City Farms	150
Activities	150
Festivals & Fairs	150
Organisations & Advice	151
National	**151**
Places to Stay	151
Activities	155
Abroad	**157**
Travel Agents	157
Holidays	157
Organisations & Advice	158

Chapter 9: Business & Finance

Business & Office	**164**
Advice	164
Products	165
Services	165

Organisations	169
Ethical Investment	**170**
Advice	170
Banking	171
Investment	171
New Economics	**173**
Local Groups	173
Organisations	173

Chapter 10: Government & Organisations

Local Government	**178**
LA 21 Councils	178
Organisations	180
National Government	**181**
Campaigns & Organisations	**182**
Animal Welfare	182
Animal Conservation	185
Natural Environment	186
Built Environment	191
Community & Society	193
Political Parties	201
Legal Support	201
Campaign Support	202

Chapter 11: Media

Bookshops & Books by Mail Order	**206**
Publications	**207**
Food & Drink	207
The Home	208
Health	209
Family & Community	209
Transport	210
Business & Finance	210
Government & Organisations	210
Publishers	**212**
Internet	**214**
Organisations	**214**

Chapter 12: Information & Education

Environment Centres	**218**
North West	218
Rest of UK	218
Information Services	**218**
North West	218
Rest of UK	218
Courses & Colleges	**222**
North West	222
Rest of UK	222

Advertisers

Introduction

Pure Modern Lifestyle	2
Nads	4
Organico	4
CAT	4
Green Guide Online	7
Pertwood Organic Cereal Co Ltd	7
Healthpol	7
Traidcraft plc	8
The Ethical Investment Co-operative Ltd	10
West of England Aloe Vera Centre	10
Empty Homes Agency	10
Energetix	10
Pen Y Coed	10
Graig Farm Organics	12
Green Stationery Company	12
Highland Organic Foods	12
Park Attwood Clinic	12
Stewart Distribution	12
Swedish Windows	12

Chapter 1: Food & Drink

Foodlife	18
Baldwin's Health Food Centre	19
Little Watermill	20
Meat Matters	21
Crone's	21
Vintage Roots	22
Vinceremos Organic Wines	22
Great Bear Trading Co Ltd	24
Taste Connection	26
Unicorn Grocery	27
Crazy Jack	29
Infinity Foods Co-operative Ltd	30
Authentic Bread	31
NVS Limited	33
Village Bakery	36
Red Triangle Café	38
Misty's Vegetarian Café	38
fresh network	43

Chapter 2: Clothing & Cosmetics

Greenfibres	48

Hemp Union	48
Spirit of Nature Ltd	50
Scope	51
Beauty Without Cruelty Charity	53
Clearly Natural	54

Chapter 3: Home & Garden

Ecomerchant	62
Ecology Building Society	64
Ecological Design Association	64
Auro	65
ECOS	66
Full Moon Futons	67
Willey Winkle	70
Aqua Ball	71
Pure H2O	72
Raindrain Ltd	74
HDRA – the organic organisation	75

Chapter 4: Energy & Recycling

Oldham Metropolitan Borough Council	87
Acre Recycling	88

Chapter 5: Health

Napiers Herbalists	94
IBIS International Corporation	96
Wholistic Research Company	98
Northern College of Acupuncture	109

Chapter 6: Family & Children

BORN	127
Maristows	128
Spirit of Nature	128
Green Baby	129
Kids Unlimited	133
Natural Friends	134

Chapter 7: Transport

Healthstart Ltd	140

Chapter 8: Travel & Leisure

Mount Pleasant Farm	153

Chapter 9: Business & Finance

Cartridge Family	165
Recycle IT	165
Holden Meehan IFA Ltd	171
Alan Seward	171
Ethical Investment Services Ltd	172

Chapter 10: Government & Organisations

British Trust for Conservation Volunteers (BTCV) North West	186
Hillside Animal Sanctuary	183

Chapter 11: Media

Guild Hunt Publishing	207

Chapter 12: Information & Education

Green Wood Trust	222

If you'd like to be listed…

We constantly update the nine editions of the Green Guide.
To propose a listing or to amend an existing one, fill out the form and fax on 020 7226 1311 or post to: Green Guide Publishing Ltd, FREEPOST LON1132, PO Box 17568, London N1 2BR

Details

Organisation _____
Address _____
_____
_____
Borough _____
Town/City _____
County _____
Postcode _____
Telephone _____
Fax _____
Email _____
URL _____
Contact _____
Job Title _____
Opening Times _____

Green Guide edition

☐ All editions
☐ London ☐ The North East ☐ Wales
☐ The South West ☐ The North West ☐ Scotland
☐ The East ☐ The Midlands ☐ The South

Chapter

Please indicate which chapter you would like your entry to appear in. Where multiple entries are required, we reserve the right to omit some entries or print abridged versions.

☐ 1 Food & Drink ☐ 7 Transport
☐ 2 Clothing & Cosmetics ☐ 8 Travel & Leisure
☐ 3 The Home ☐ 9 Business & Finance
☐ 4 Energy & Recycling ☐ 10 Politics & Campaigning
☐ 5 Health ☐ 11 Media
☐ 6 Family & Community ☐ 12 Information & Education

Listing text (maximum 75 words)

Please write something particular to your organisation, such as house specialities, current campaigns, etc. We reserve the right to edit this text and we will not print third party endorsements without accompanying proof.

_____
_____
_____
_____
_____
_____
_____
_____

Tell us more about you...

Please complete the response form with as much detail as possible and send to us using our Freepost address overleaf. Reply by 31st December, 2000 and The Day Chocolate Company will send you a 45g bar of Divine chocolate

The Day Chocolate Company produces Divine, delivering delicious chocolate to the hearts and mouths of every chocolate lover in the country! Being fairly traded, Divine guarantees a fair price and long term trading contract to the farmers in Ghana who produce the cocoa. The Day Chocolate Company has created a unique partnership and represents an important step forward for fair trade. Kuapa Kokoo, the farmers growing the cocoa for Divine, are also shareholders in the company, which means they have a direct share of the profits and take part in the decision-making process about how Divine is produced and sold. Two representatives from Kuapa Kokoo sit on The Day Chocolate Company's board and one board meeting is held in Ghana every year. Divine contains real cocoa butter, rather than vegetable fat, with real vanilla and a high percentage of cocoa solids and is also certified GM free. Available in almost all supermarkets, Divine can also be found in whole food and fair trade shops.

1. Who are you?

Name: _____

Address: _____

_____

_____ Postcode: _____

☐ Male ☐ Female Age: _____

Job/profession: _____

Marital status: _____

How many children do you have? _____

Is the place you live:

☐ Owned by you ☐ Rented
☐ Other _____

Salary/wage: ☐ <£12K ☐ £12-25K ☐ >£25K

What mode(s) of transport do you own?

☐ Car ☐ Bicycle ☐ None
☐ Other _____

What mode(s) of transport do you use frequently?

☐ Public transport ☐ Car ☐ Bicycle ☐ Foot
☐ Other _____

Are you Vegetarian? ☐ Yes ☐ No

Are you Vegan? ☐ Yes ☐ No

How often do you recycle?

☐ Always ☐ Frequently ☐ Sometimes ☐ Never

How often do you buy organic produce?

☐ Always ☐ Frequently ☐ Sometimes ☐ Never

What magazines/journals do you read?

_____

_____

_____

_____

How often do you use alternative therapies?

☐ Always ☐ Frequently ☐ Sometimes ☐ Never

2. What do you think of the Green Guide?

Where did you purchase the Guide?

_____

_____

How did you hear about it?

_____

_____

How many people read your copy?

☐ 1 ☐ 2-5 ☐ 6-10 ☐ 10+

How useful do you find it?

☐ Very ☐ Moderately ☐ Not at all

Which chapters did you use the most?

_____

_____

Which chapters did you use the least?

_____

_____

Reader's questionnaire

How satisfactory did you find the design and layout?

☐ Very ☐ Moderately ☐ Not at all

How easy is it to use?

☐ Very ☐ Moderately ☐ Not at all

Did you find the editorial useful?

☐ Very ☐ Moderately ☐ Not at all

Did you find the editorial interesting?

☐ Very ☐ Moderately ☐ Not at all

What else would you like to see included?

_____
_____
_____
_____

Would you be interested in a monthly magazine, concentrating on consumer features and lifestyle?

☐ Yes ☐ No

Would you subscribe to the Guide?

☐ Yes ☐ No

Would you be interested in distributing or selling the Guide?

☐ Yes ☐ No

3. Attitudes towards green consumerism

How influenced are you by a company's ethical stance?

☐ Very ☐ Moderately ☐ Not at all

How important is the origin/provenance of a product's ingredients/constituents?

☐ Very ☐ Moderately ☐ Not at all

How prepared are you to pay a premium for organic/ fairly traded goods?

☐ Very ☐ Moderately ☐ Not at all

How aware are you of sustainability issues when you make a purchase?

☐ Very ☐ Moderately ☐ Not at all

How easy do you find it to shop organically?

☐ Very ☐ Moderately ☐ Not at all

How important is convenience?

☐ Very ☐ Moderately ☐ Not at all

What importance do you attach to packaging/marketing?

☐ Very ☐ Moderately ☐ Not at all

Are you influenced by advertising?

☐ Very ☐ Moderately ☐ Not at all

How often do you purchase via mail order?

☐ Always ☐ Frequently ☐ Sometimes ☐ Never

How green do you think you are?

☐ Very ☐ Moderately ☐ Not at all

4. Attitude towards environmentalism

Where does your main environmental concern lie?

☐ Personal ☐ Local ☐ National ☐ International

How important do you rate environmental issues?

☐ Very ☐ Moderately ☐ Not at all

How active are you politically?

☐ Very ☐ Moderately ☐ Not at all

How important is a political party's stance on green issues?

☐ Very ☐ Moderately ☐ Not at all

What do you consider to be the biggest single threat to your well-being?

_____
_____

What do you consider to be the biggest single threat to the planet's well-being?

_____
_____

Are you prepared to pay more tax to deal with environmental issues?

_____
_____

And finally, please tell us where you normally shop for organic, fair trade, health & whole foods.

_____
_____

☐ Please tick this box if you do not wish to receive future mailings from Green Guide Publishing Ltd

☐ Please tick this box if you do not wish to receive future mailings from other ethical organisations

Send in your completed survey to:

Green Guide Publishing Ltd,
FREEPOST LON1132,
PO Box 17568,
London N1 2BR